Language and Globalization

Series Editors: **Sue Wright**, University of Portsmouth, UK and **Helen Kelly-Holmes**, University of Limerick, Ireland.

In the context of current political and social developments, where the national group is not so clearly defined and delineated, the state language not so clearly dominant in every domain, and cross-border flows and transfers affect more than a small elite, new patterns of language use will develop. The series aims to provide a framework for reporting on and analysing the linguistic outcomes of globalization and localization.

Titles include

David Block
MULTILINGUAL IDENTITIES IN A GLOBAL CITY
London Stories

Diarmait Mac Giolla Chríost
LANGUAGE AND THE CITY

Julian Edge (*editor*)
(RE)LOCATING TESOL IN AN AGE OF EMPIRE

Roxy Harris
NEW ETHNICITIES AND LANGUAGE USE

Clare Mar-Molinero and Patrick Stevenson (*editors*)
LANGUAGE IDEOLOGIES, POLICIES AND PRACTICES
Language and the Future of Europe

Clare Mar-Molinero and Miranda Stewart (*editors*)
GLOBALIZATION AND LANGUAGE IN THE SPANISH-SPEAKING WORLD
Macro and Micro Perspectives

Ulrike Hanna Meinhof and Dariusz Galasinski
THE LANGUAGE OF BELONGING

Leigh Oakes and Jane Warren
LANGUAGE, CITIZENSHIP AND IDENTITY IN QUEBEC

Colin Williams
LINGUISTIC MINORITIES IN DEMOCRATIC CONTEXT

Forthcoming titles

John Edwards
CHALLENGES IN THE SOCIAL LIFE OF LANGUAGE

Alexandra Galasinska and Michael Krzyzanowski (*editors*)
DISCOURSES OF TRANSFORMATION IN CENTRAL AND EASTERN EUROPE

Jane Jackson
INTERCULTURALITY IN STUDY AT HOME AND ABROAD

Language and Globalization
Series Standing Order ISBN 1–4039–9731–4
(*outside North America only*)

You can receive future titles in this series as they are published by placing a standing order. Please contact your bookseller or, in case of difficulty, write to us at the address below with your name and address, the title of the series and the ISBN quoted above.

Customer Services Department, Macmillan Distribution Ltd, Houndmills, Basingstoke, Hampshire RG21 6XS, England

Linguistic Minorities in Democratic Context

Colin H. Williams

Cardiff University

First published 2008 by
PALGRAVE MACMILLAN
Houndmills, Basingstoke, Hampshire RG21 6XS and
175 Fifth Avenue, New York, N.Y. 10010
Companies and representatives throughout the world

PALGRAVE MACMILLAN is the global academic imprint of the Palgrave Macmillan division of St. Martin's Press, LLC and of Palgrave Macmillan Ltd. Macmillan® is a registered trademark in the United States, United Kingdom and other countries. Palgrave is a registered trademark in the European Union and other countries.

ISBN-13: 978–1–4039–8721–1 hardback
ISBN-10: 1–4039–8721–1 hardback

This book is printed on paper suitable for recycling and made from fully managed and sustained forest sources. Logging, pulping and manufacturing processes are expected to conform to the environmental regulations of the country of origin.

A catalogue record for this book is available from the British Library.

A catalog record for this book is available from the Library of Congress.

10   9   8   7   6   5   4   3   2   1
17   16   15   14   13   12   11   10   09   08

Printed and bound in Great Britain by
CPI Antony Rowe, Chippenham and Eastbourne

For Maite

Contents

List of Tables and Figures

Tables

Figures

Acknowledgements

The book was started while I was a Visiting Fellow at Jesus College and Mansfield College, Oxford University. I value the support given by Thomas Charles Edwards and Anthony Lemon. Their subsequent encouragement in involving me within the Oxford network of scholars has provided fresh horizons for my interests. I also wish to thank Judith and David Marquand, former Principal of Mansfield, who offered me the use of their very convivial home in Headington while I worked in Oxford. Closer to home I wish to express my appreciation to colleagues within the School of Welsh, Cardiff University.

Various friends commented on the chapters, including Linda Cardinal, Charles Castonguay, Rob Dunbar, Michael Keating, Alasdair MacLeòid, Wilson MacLeod, Steve May and Sven Tägil. Charles Whebell offered valuable advice on the historical aspects of the Canadian material. They have all helped me enormously, but, of course, I am entirely responsible for the shortcomings that remain.

My involvement with the ESRC Devolution and Constitutional Change Research Programme has enriched my understanding of contemporary British politics. I wish to thank the Programme Director, Charlie Jeffery, for providing excellent opportunities to discuss the themes raised in this volume with distinguished colleagues.

Certain aspects of the legislative dimension of language rights were informed by my co-direction of the "From Act to Action Project" together with Siv Sandberg, Abo Academy and Peadar Ó Flaharta, Dublin City University. The project was sponsored by the EU through the European Bureau for Lesser Used Languages and the Mercator network. Access to data, interviews and financial support for the project were readily forthcoming from the Svenska Kulturfonden, Foras na Gaeilge and the Welsh Language Board, all of whom I thank for their encouragement and support. As a member of the Welsh Language Board during the period within which this book was written, I have gained valuable insights as to how language policy is determined both within the UK and beyond. I thank colleagues within the Board, especially Meirion Prys Jones and Prys Davies, for their professional co-operation and friendship. Under the aegis of the WLB, I have been officially welcomed as a guest by a number of European, Canadian and Japanese government agencies. I also wish to thank all the politicians, senior civil servants, judges and constitutional lawyers on three continents who granted me interviews and shared material with me.

Three sections of the book have been adapted from previously published essays, whose content has been extensively modified and developed to improve the coherence of the central argument. The details of the original publications are as follows:

"Nationalism in a Democratic Context" in J. Agnew, K. Mitchell and G. Toal (eds.), *A Companion to Political Geography*, Blackwell, 2003, pp. 356–77; and "Nationalism and its derivatives", in R. Hudson and A. M. Williams (eds.), *Divided Europe*, Sage, 1999, pp. 79–106, helped provide the structure of Chapter 2.

"Language Policy and Planning Issues in Multicultural Societies", in P. Larrivée, (ed) *Linguistic Conflict and Language Laws*, Palgrave, 2003, pp. 1–56 forms the basis of Chapter 4.

"Recognition and National Justice for Québec: A Canadian Conundrum", in S. Fenton and S. May (eds.), Ethnonational Identities, Palgrave, 2002, pp. 21–47 is revisited and expanded upon in Chapter 9.

Several of the maps were drawn by two outstanding cartographer friends, Jane Williams and Patricia Connor Reid whom I thank for their skill and flair. I am grateful to a much respected friend at Cardiff University, Professor J. Loughlin, for his gracious assistance in adapting the insights gained from the 'Regional and Local Democracy in the European Union' project and for his permission to reproduce Tables 2.1 and 2. 2. The author and publisher are grateful to the original publishers for permission to reproduce this previously published material.

Every effort has been made to secure permission to use copyright items. In the event that any copyright holder has been inadvertently overlooked, the publisher will make amends at the earliest opportunity.

I would also like to express my sincere thanks for the support, encouragement and constructive comments received from Professor Sue Wright, the Series Editor and Jill Lake, the Linguistics Editor at Palgrave.

Colin H. Williams
Cardiff
March 2007

1
Democratic Inclusion for the One and the Many

In the late nineteenth century members of most European national groups assumed that one day their languages and cultures would be nourished within an international political system which appeared to be reconfiguring itself as a result of the rise of the nation-state and the dissolution of the old imperial order. By the mid-twentieth century such hopes seemed impossible because they were inconceivable. At the beginning of the twenty first century similar aspirations now seem partly realisable in a continent which is reshaping itself to contend with forces which challenge so many of the rules and patterns of our interaction as citizens.

During the 1980s I struggled with the issue of how long oppressed minorities could gain recognition in this all too crowded world. How could beleaguered groups be given the space and the freedom to impress their desires and ambitions on seemingly uncaring and hostile hegemonic states.[1] How could selected groups be made more free and begin to participate as permanent entities within increasingly multicultural polities. The fruits of my enquiries were presented in *Called Unto Liberty* published in 1994. In the years since I have been pre-occupied with the challenge of the next phase; namely, how do some minority groups, on achieving various degrees of recognition and indeed real political power, exercise such responsibilities both in terms of their policy formulation and in their dealings with other centres of authority within their respective states? Gaining some degree of liberty and autonomy is a major advance for historically oppressed peoples such as the Basques, the Catalans, the Québécois and the Welsh, where various forms of nationalism have been so persistent and strident. Coping with such responsibility is quite a different challenge, for now both the justification for, and implementation of, differentiated language policy has to grapple with the consequences of being the one among the many. Consequently this book offers an interpretation of how such gains and responsibilities impact on language policy in relation to democratic theory and practice. Its aim is both to celebrate such gains and to offer cautionary remarks about how relatively fragile is the position of linguistic minorities within plurinational democracies.

Dealing judiciously with the exercise of power on gaining a measure of political autonomy throws up quite new challenges, most of which the regional or national authorities seem singularly ill equipped to tackle. Indeed it seems that either by neglect or conscious design, some of the hard-won gains for language minorities are being threatened or reversed. More troubling is that in parts of the EU there is alarming evidence that some newly established regional authorities are practicing the very same discriminatory policies against non-nationals or disaffected groups that they endured for so long. Paraphrasing Gutman (2001) we could say that collective self-determination as a human right does not carry with it the authority to oppress other minorities.

> Whenever collective self-determination is confused with national sovereignty in an unqualified sense, it increases the risk of other rights violations; indeed, it sometimes supports other rights violations. Human rights violations cannot be justified-or even condoned or excused-in the name of nationalism; human rights violations render nationalistic states "subject to criticism, sanction, and, as a final resort, intervention."
>
> (Guttman, 2001, pp. xv–xvi)

My interpretation values the contribution of debates on diversity and citizenship to the study of language politics. The introduction focuses on how minorities struggle to make their case in a majoritarian, multilingual context. It discusses the normative turn in the study of language politics and sociolinguistics looking more specifically at the contributions of legal and political theory. It also seeks to address the weakness of the new normative turn especially its lack of attention to issues such as group participation and the development of bottom-up approach to language planning and policy-making.

I set out to write this book in the belief that the role of "responsible" language minorities in the so-called developed world could be better understood by conceiving of them as active agents of change within a pluralist democratic framework. Too often, I believe, minorities such as the Basque, Catalans, Québécois and Welsh have been portrayed as dependent supplicants who cannot escape their historical condition as beleaguered victims of the state development process. They are characterised as unwilling victims of an arrested nation-building process or as peripheral players in the growth of successful states. Clearly the incorporation of minorities is a significant thread in the development of modern states in Western Europe and in North America. But the interesting question is to what extent such minorities can now play a more active role in determining their own future. My field work allows me to answer in the affirmative but my political antenna warn that there are still far too many forces which will seek to return them to their historically subordinate position.

In seeking to study developments in language politics, such as innovations in democratic theorising, language planning and policy-making, I am conscious that there exist excellent accounts of contemporary democratic theory, such as Held (2006) and of policy making, legislation and human rights, such as Grin (2003), Kymlicka (2001), May (2001) and Wright (2004). However, none of these treatments provide a systematic account of the structural changes which have occurred within selected case studies. My essays seek to illustrate a new social ontology already at work in parts of Europe and Northern America.[2] What is needed is a further elaboration of the potentialities and pitfalls of this new way of looking at sociolinguistic reality so that the gains made hitherto do not become taken for granted or lost in the mire of inter-agency and inter-governmental negotiations.

At root there is a concern for the quality of life experienced by peoples who were long held to be "the other", the outsiders, the marginal within the burgeoning western states. By comparison with the Roma in Europe, or with dispossessed and landless peasants in war-torn central Africa, the plight of the Basques, Celts and Québécois might appear to be a minor concern for democratic inclusion. For surely Celts have risen to prominence in all the spheres of influence of the British Empire and French Canadians have long enjoyed a portion of their share in confederation. While this is true, no one could deny that Irish speakers in Northern Ireland or Catalans and Basques under Franco were not systematically discriminated against and have only relatively recently enjoyed recognition and a measure of co-equality. Thus I maintain that historically the dominant tendency has been to treat such minorities as "the other" and to dismiss their demands as illegitimate or irrelevant to the state project.

Yet I am also conscious that the binary dialectic of identity and difference, of other and oneness, can also be subject to false interpretations and misleading analogies. As Bracken (2001) citing Gunton (1993) observes, there is a

> tendency in contemporary thought theoretically to acknowledge the primacy of the other and yet in practice to reduce the other to the hegemony of the same under a new guise, if only to bring order out of chaos in dealing with masses of individuals. Hence, only if one has thought through the necessary dialectical relationships between otherness and sameness and realized that neither is basically intelligible without the other, can one offer a principled reason to maintain the genuine otherness of the other, quite apart from the pressure to reduce the other to the same all over again in the name of some alleged value or goal.
>
> (Bracken, 2001, p. 79)[3]

On what basis could such a principled reason be sustained?

One candidate is self-determination, another is full democratic participation. But the two principles are not necessarily mutually supportive. Underlying all the chapters is the conviction that the process by which minorities negotiate their relationship with the host state and the world beyond matters, and that it should respect certain principles. It ill behoves any minority which purports to adhere to liberal democratic values if its gains are made at the expense of the very principles of inclusive democracy that it seeks to espouse. Thus the prime test of these principles is that democratic norms should be respected at all stages and by all participants. Non-democratic methods, for example, using violence as a tactic, may bring short term gains, but are likely to render such gains susceptible and vulnerable in future deliberations. The second is that the decision-making process which leads to collective choices based on group aims should be open both to citizen participation and to investigative or regulatory scrutiny. Only under such conditions can minority leaders command respect as the authoritative spokespersons of their people and distinct social groupings. The third is that mutual respect for both minority and majority positions be maintained throughout the relationship between constituent members of the polity. The fourth is the recognition that because fundamental values are often subverted or manipulated for political ends, such differences as are institutionally entrenched are always entitled to respect. They should be guaranteed by a regime of liberty, as free as possible from intimidation and reprisal.

However, constructing such a regime, which is both consistent and responsive to the demands of a multi-ethnic constituency, is both hard to develop and to maintain. The main reason is that the value systems from which such regimes emerge are subject to constant challenge and revision as the human condition itself is re-evaluated and made to fit the vagaries of the political situation. In his biography of Isaiah Berlin, Michael Ignatieff reminds us of the centrality of the human ideal itself to our political deliberations and value construction.

> The conflict of values – liberty versus equality; justice versus mercy; tolerance versus order; liberty versus social justice; resistance versus prudence – was intrinsic to human life.
>
> (Ignatieff, 1998, p. 285)

Given that human life seems to be increasingly threatened, not only by the foreign policies of legitimate states, the incursion of so-called terrorists and the environmental degradation which resource exploitation and incursive capitalism engenders, but also by social malaise and the rupture of established social norms, it is imperative that liberty itself is defended more vigorously.[4] But the defence of a separate identity is a troubling notion to apply in majority – minority relations, for so often minorities have learned at their cost not to be counted, nor to be categorised, to be separated out, to be fully recognised, for fear of something worse! For many national minorities in Central and Eastern Europe in the recent past, and for most minorities in Western Europe historically, to consciously stand apart from the mainstream was to invite ridicule, discrimination and at worse genocide. The decision whether or not to search for official recognition and then routine identification in the affairs of state was literally a matter of security, of life and death itself for many people. There are far too many cases, both in Europe and Africa, of official roles and registers being used to identify, then imprison, relocate and ultimately kill ethnic minority members.

In any pluralist liberal democracy, issues of moral pluralism, liberal freedom and their mutual entailment will become the core refractors by which policy disagreements will be judged. When one adds to this the demands which separate language rights impose on a democracy, it becomes doubly difficult at times to separate out what are the fundamental policy differences and what are the strategic considerations being adopted for linguistic group advancement. Nevertheless Berlin grasped an essential point which I want to advance, namely that

> pluralism entailed liberalism – that is, if human beings disagreed about ultimate ends, the political system that best enabled them to adjudicate these conflicts was one which privileged their liberty, for only conditions of liberty could enable them to make compromises between values necessary to maintain a free social life.
>
> (Ignatieff, 1998, p. 286)

It is at this point that several uncomfortable facts reveal themselves. In an attempt to maintain a free social life within multicultural societies, competing minorities appeal to the same universal human rights conventions, make legitimate claims on the resources of their respective states and, if sufficiently disaffected, adopt a separatist stance. I recognise that not all such claims are necessarily legitimate as there is always some potential for over-reach or "power grabs" in the name of the disaffected minority. The hardest task for a responsive state, faced with these competing claims, is to adopt a consistent line, to apply inclusive citizenship criteria to the weak as well as to the strong, to the recent immigrant language groups as well as to the regional and minority languages within their borders. Policy implementation should follow recognition, but it rarely does. Having said this, the multilingual landscape of many European countries has changed out of all recognition in the past forty years or so. In consequence, far from becoming less salient, as many social scientists used to argue, social cleavages based on language or ethnic criteria, have gained in significance.

Within the broad canvas painted by "pluralists" and "assimilationists" we may discern a smouldering debate on diversity and citizenship in relation to language politics. Each side appeals to recent innovations in democratic theorising, language planning and policy-making, but their conclusions both for individual states and for linguistic diversity both within Europe and North America are strongly divergent. I want to advance this debate by examining how minorities struggle to make their case in a majoritarian, multilingual context. Two areas are pressing: the first is the normative turn in the study of language politics and sociolinguistics which seeks to incorporate recent advances in legal and political theory. The second is an examination of the weakness of the new normative turn, especially its lack of attention to issues such as group participation and the development of a bottom-up approach to language planning and policy-making. An over-reliance on language rights, new legislation and the equalities agenda, although quite understandable, can reduce the need to consult with and consider the community, in the framing of policy. Community has become a difficult term to operationalise as it is claimed that it masks more that it reveals. I do not share this view, although I readily admit that forces such as globalisation and European integration demand a reconceptualisation of community and a re-evaluation of its salience within certain contexts. This is particularly so in terms of political and legal applications, as Held has observed

> The modern theory of the sovereign democratic state, liberal and radical, presupposes the idea of a community which rightly governs itself and determines its own future. This idea is challenged fundamentally by the nature of the pattern of global interconnections and the issues that have to be confronted by the nation state ... The meaning of democracy, and of the model of democratic autonomy in particular, has to be rethought in relation to a series of overlapping local, regional and global structures and processes. Accordingly, questions are raised about the fate of the idea of the political community and about the appropriate locus for the articulation of the democratic good.
>
> (Held, 2006, p. 304)

The rise of regional-level government within Europe has opened up the question as to which is the most appropriate level for the articulation of the democratic good. Regional level government has promised much in the past generation and is normally justified in terms of improving the economic performance of a sub-unit or of improving the administrative efficiency of the state by transferring select functions closer to the point of service delivery. But how has regional level government impacted upon language rights and group equality issues?

A useful frame of analysis whereby one can evaluate the nature of language policy issues has been sketched out by Schmidt (1998). He offers four generalisations. First, linguistic diversity is the norm and not the exception among contemporary states. Second, language policy conflict is becoming increasingly common and is more often than not a reflection of deeper tensions between ethno-linguistic groups over their relative power positions within the political community. Third, such political conflict is conditioned by the ideological dominance of two primary public values: *equality* and *nationalism*.[5] Fourth, language policy approaches employed by states to resolve conflict may be categorised into four fairly self-evident types – domination/exclusion; assimilation; pluralism; and linguistic confederation.[6]

The ideology of historical redress

Many threatened communities have adopted the dominant ideologies of the day to resist incorporation, mobilise alternative political parties and mount a rearguard action in defence of communal interests. Typically, the literature on language, nationalism and communal defence takes for granted the fundamental question of how we make sense of such issues within the ambit of such powerful forces as environmentalism and globalisation. Just as we have been reminded of the salience of time and space, so we need to be reminded of the relevance of the human-nature balance. So much of what passes as detailed social policy actually operates within an environment that is so dynamic and unpredictable that it renders the logical and organised policy initiatives redundant. Context is, if not quite all, then certainly vital and as a professional geographer, I am conscious that all too often policy makers take far too little account of the operative conditions within which policies are implemented.

Thus I am convinced that the ways in which we promote language policy or seek to reverse language shift should take more account of the main tenets of ecological thought and practice (Williams, 1991b). If we step back from the details of language policy we may consider how the interpretation of the human-nature relationship has influenced our current modes of thought in a more profound way than is often realised. In previous work I have sought to interpret this issue by reference to four distinct human-nature positions derived from Judaic, Graeco-Roman, Christian, Modern and other views of nature. The positions are respectively that: nature is neutral and without purpose; nature is a divine creation in the service of man and devoted to the Glory of God; nature as a divine creation is good for its own sake; nature has a meaning and a purpose, and a reflective man must ascertain that purpose and accommodate it (Williams, 1991, 1999). Current manifestations of ecological thought can be traced to each of these separate positions, but they are most commonly associated with the fourth position whereby powerful ideas, such as the GAIA thesis and the "deep green" concern with earth survival and co-existence, are connected to earlier traditions of humanistic thought.[7] What is undoubtedly new about environmentalism is its global concern and sense of urgency. What is new about globalisation is its resistance to planned change and limited choices. Putting the two together makes for a dynamic cocktail with unanticipated consequences.

Each of these forces, namely environmentalism, globalisation and auto-nomist nationalism have impacted on the sovereign state in a different way. Together they demand a reconsideration of the manner in which we interpret and justify the international regime especially in terms of seeking historical redress and social justice. Let me first address nation-alism and environmentalism as both ideologies focus on the state as the central agency of "structured oppression" and the principal upholder of the military-industrial complex. A comprehensive summary of the dif-fering rationales is provided in Galtung's (1986) representation of the opposing characteristics of establishment and ecological values and move-ments. This is summarised in Table 1.1. The dominant characteristic

Table 1.1 Schematic representation of opposing characteristics of establishment and ecological values movements (Galtung, 1986)

A Survey of Green Policies

	Mainstream characteristics	**Green policies, movements**
Economic basis	1. Exploitation of *external proletariat*	Cooperative enterprises, movements: labour buyer/seller difference abolished, customers directly involved
	2. Exploitation of *external sector* relations liberation movements	Co-existence with the Third World: only equitable exchange
	3. Exploitation of *nature*	Ecological balance Person-Nature: building diversity, symbiosis; complete or partial vegetarianism
	4. Exploitation of *self*	More labour- and creativity-intensity: decreasing productivity in some fields; alternative technologies
Military basis	1. Dependency on *foreign trade*	Self-reliance: self sufficiency in food, health, energy and defence
	2. Dependency on *formal sector*, BCI-complex	Local self-reliance, decreasing urbanization, intermediate technology: defensive defence policies with less destructive technology, also non-military non-violent defence
	3. *Offensive* defence policies, very destructive defence technology	
	4. *Alignment with super powers*	Non-alignment, even neutralism de-coupling from superpowers

Structural basis	1. *Bureaucracy*, state (plan) strong and centralized	Recentralization of local level: building federations of local units
	2. *Corporation*, capital (market) strong and centralized	Building informal, green economy: – production of self-consumption – production of non-monetary exchange – production of local cycles
	3. *Intelligentsia*, research strong and centralized	High level non-formal, education: building own forms of understanding Feminist movements, justice/equality and for new culture and structure; movements of the young and the old; movements for racial/ethnic equality
	4. MAMU factor; BCI peopled by middle aged males with university education (and dominant race/ethnic group)	
Bourgeois ways of life	1. *Non-manual work*, eliminating heavy, dirty, dangerous work	Keeping the gains when healthy, mixing manual and non-manual
	2. *Material Comfort* dampening fluctuations of nature	Keeping the gains when healthy, living closer to nature
	3. *Privatism*, withdrawal into family and peer groups	Communal life in bigger units, collective production/consumption
	4. *Security*, the probability that this will last	Keeping security when healthy, making lifestyle less predictable
Chemical circus way of life	1. Alcohol, tranquilisers drugs	*Moderation*, experiments with non-addictive, life-enhancing things
	2. Tobacco, sugar, salt, tea/coffee	*Moderation*, enhancing the body's capacity for joy, e.g. through sex
	3. Chemically treated food, *panem*, natural fibres removed	Bio-organic cultivation, health food, balanced food, *moderation*
	4. *Circenses*, TV, sport, spectatorism	Generating own entertainment, *moderate* exercise, particularly as manual work, walking, bicycling

Source: Galtung (1986) reproduced in Williams (1999), p. 108.

of mainstream, that is, conventional, economic and political systems in the West, is exploitation. The chief characteristic of ecological systems is co-dependence. Government and top-down planning characterises the former, governance and bottom-up creativity is said to characterise the latter.

Environmentalism

Quite often linguistic minorities refashion their nineteenth century nation-alist ambitions and insert the same long-term quest for freedom within a contemporary eco-linguistic ideology. In so doing they emphasise the local, the unique and the sustainable characteristics of their condition and seek to make common cause with other interest groups so as to justify their claim for increased autonomy. Table 1.1 is a useful summary of the ideological paradigms within which many of the leaders of linguistic minorities lodge their appeals.

It is evident that many ethno-linguistic movements share several of the characteristics which Galtung (1986) describes as being attributable to green policies. Thus, for example, many nationalists' movements in post-war Europe have adopted a non-violent form of resistance to the incursions of central state agencies. Many adopt a strong communal form of defence and resistance, and advocate as much autonomy and self-reliance as it is pos-sible to sustain, as we shall see in Chapter Two. Still others have made a common cause with anti-nuclear campaigners and opposed the bi-polar divi-sion of international society during the Cold War and now condemn the hegemonic position of the USA within the current system. Clearly not all such movements have opposed the principles of advocating a just war. Nor have they been slow to condemn the break down of law and order within international society. But as representatives of predominantly small nations, they argue that they share little involvement, and hence responsibility, for the manner in which the international political system was constructed. There is, of course, a limit to such abrogation of consent and participation, for under differing guises the political leaders of, for example, Wales, men such as the British Prime Minister David Lloyd George, were among the prime architects of the post-Versailles political system in Europe. He would have conceived of himself as being a Liberal Welsh Nationalist, able to sym-pathise with the plight of small Baltic and Central European nations and as a defender of the interests of the British Empire as one of the dominant superpowers.

Globalisation

Turning to globalisation, Loughlin and Williams (2007) argue that there is no doubt that the world-economy has changed profoundly in recent decades. But they challenge the claim made by Cerny (1995), Held (1999), Habermas (2001) and Beck (2000) that a specifically new kind of global-isation emerged at the beginning of the 1980s. Rather they point to the interpretation of influential authors such as Hirst and Thompson (1996), who assert that a form of globalisation has been with us since the end of the 19th century, when capitalism first had a truly global reach. Earlier writers, following Wallerstein's (1974, 1979) influential world-system theory, such as Knox and Agnew (1989), Williams (1986) and Taylor (1985), have examined the implications of globalisation for the dynamics of the world economy and global–local relations and have confirmed that the nation-state has survived by transforming itself in the recent period. Garrett and Lange (1991) have argued that despite claims that the nation-state was no longer the most important arena of social and party mobilisation, the "partisan-ideological" thesis, that is, the continuing importance of Left-Right party competition within national political systems, still held up. Furthermore, the claim that accelerated European integration leads to a new kind of European governance system, as put forward by Gary Marks *et al.* (1996), Beate Kohler-Koch (1999) or Wallace and Wallace (2000), is countered by liberal inter-governmentalists, such as Andrew Moravcsik (1993) or Alan Milward (2000), who assert that this allegedly new system is scarcely more than a strong international regime which has modified but little the role of national governments and actors within national states.

Others who point to a new role for regions in a post-national and post-sovereign Europe such as Michael Keating (1998) or John Loughlin (2000, 2001) are countered by Patrick Le Galès and Christian Lequesne (1998) who deny that the region has any great significance and hold up instead the city as the key political unit of territorial politics. In broader terms, post-modernist authors such as Jean Baudrillard (1990) who point with approval to what they claim is the fragmentation both of epistemological and ontological dimensions of society are countered by Alain Touraine's critique of modernity (1992) or Peter Wagner's sociology of modernity (1994), who, while both accepting some of the post-modernist diagnosis, seek to rescue and update the concept of modernity itself.

David Held has done more than most to tease out the essence of such debates in his excellent treatments of globalisation and models of democracy (Held, 1999, 2006). Table 1.2 presents his view of three tendencies in respect of globalisation and it is interesting to note that each of the trajectories offers a different perspective on the capacity of the nation-state to adapt to change.

McGrew (1997) offers a different perspective by emphasising the role of the people in restructuring the state's response to globalisation. Quite different processes of democratisation are occasioned by adopting one or other forms of global and state governance as is evident in Table 1.3. Throughout this volume I will examine these processes in relation to the opportunities afforded to long beleaguered minorities by the restructuring of the political order. I will be arguing that participatory and deliberative democracy commend themselves to the creation of more inclusive and responsive sub-state political systems. However, I will also be demonstrating how frustrating and difficult it is to sustain such systems and how, almost inevitably, long established political structures and cultures conduce to the re-assertion of majoritarian liberal democratic practices.

Table 1.2 Conceptualizing globalization: Three tendencies

	Hyperglobalists	Sceptics	Transformationalists
What's new?	A global age	Trading blocs, weaker geogovernance than in earlier periods	Historically unprecedented levels of global interconnectedness
Dominant features	Global capitalism, global governance, global civil society	World less interdependent than in 1980s	'Thick' (intensive and extensive) globalization
Power of national governments	Declining or eroding	Reinforced or enhanced	Reconstituted, restructured
Driving forces of globalization	Capitalism and technology	States and markets	Combined forces of modernity
Pattern of stratification	Erosion of old hierarchies	Increased marginalization of South	New architecture of world order
Dominant motif	McDonalds, Madonna, etc.	National interest	Transformation of political community
Conceptualization of globalisation	As a reordering of the framework of human action	As internationalization and regionalization	As the reordering of interregional relations and action at a distance
Historical trajectory	Global civilization	Regional blocs/clash of civilizations	Indeterminate global integration and fragmentation
Summary argument	The end of the nation-state	Internationalization depends on state acquiescence and support	Globalization transforming state power and world politics

Source: Held *et al.*, 1999, p. 10.

Table 1.3 Civilizing and democratizing contemporary globalization: A summary of three political projects

	Liberal-internationalism	Radical republicanism	Cosmopolitan democracy
Who should govern?	The people through governments, accountable international organizations and international regimes	The people through governing communities	The people through communities, associations, states, international organizations, all subject to cosmopolitan democratic law
Form of global governance?	*Polyarchy* – pluralistic fragmented system, sharing of sovereignty	*Demarchy* – functional democratic governance devoid of national sovereignty	*Heterarchy* – divided authority system subject to cosmopolitan democratic law
Key agents/ instruments, processes of democratization	Accelerating interdependence, self-interest of key agencies of power in creating more democratic/cooperative forms of global governance	New social movements impending global, ecological, security and economic crises	Constitutional and institutional reconstruction, intensification of globalization and regionalization, new social movements, possible global crises
Traditions of democratic thought	Liberal democratic theory – pluralism and protective democracy-reformism	Direct democracy, participatory democracy, civic republicanism, socialist democracy	Liberal democratic theory, pluralism and developmental democracy, participatory democracy, civic republicanism
Ethic of global governance	"Common rights and shared responsibilities"	"Humane governance"	"Democratic autonomy"
Mode of political Transformation	*Reform* of global governance	*Alternative structures* of global governance	*Reconstruction* of global governance

Source: Adapted from McGrew, 1997, p. 254.

The structure of the volume

The first four chapters of the volume establish the theoretical and conceptual underpinnings of the argument while the remaining chapters seeks to illustrate the dynamics of the shift from dependency to a considerable degree of local autonomy on the part of selected groups. Chapter Two examines the transition from claims and rights conceived within a primarily nineteenth century nationalist vision of international politics, to the more fluid twenty-first century conception of inclusive democratic pluralism. Today the relevance of nationalism and the salience of the nation-state are being questioned and challenged as inappropriate constructs for a post-sovereign era. But these continue to be significant influences on the construction of modern politics.

The broadly similar political imperatives and economic impulses which underscored English or Spanish nation-building processes also characterised Irish, Welsh or Catalan ambitions. That they did not achieve their aims in the same fashion can be put down to military conquest, a form of ethnic cleansing, resettlement of the dominant population in the conquered territory and political and legal absorption into the hegemonic state and its majoritarian culture. Over time elements within the pliant aristocracy, then successive layers of the stratified society were integrated into the burgeoning class system of the ruling power, which busied itself in establishing a largely monolingual, territorial bureaucratic state.[8] Under such colonial pressures the remarkable feature is not that the Irish, Welsh and other languages began to wilt and yield, but that they lasted so long and remain a distinctive element of European diversity.

The competitive nature of classical nationalism and its derivatives are too well known to bear repetition here. What is examined is the way in which the elite groups of selected regions in Western Europe have questioned the nature of the state and how the uses and abuses of nationalism in Eastern Europe have lead to many disastrous excursions into social exclusion and ultimately genocide. Much of nationalism's force and power depends upon the political structure and socio-economic context within which its appeals and demands are made. The very broad geo-political determinants of this context were sketched out for Europe prior to the Second World War by Orridge and Williams (1982). We now need to reconfigure how these early insights and frames of reference help us to interpret, and possibly anticipate, ethno-linguistic cleavages and fault lines within the system.

Yet too often both advocates of nationalist perspectives and scholars working in the field adduce an inherently benign motivation to the nationalist cause. In some cases what starts out as a historical manifestation of the call to liberty can transform itself into an oppressive, discriminatory and at times, exclusionary political movement, especially when it achieves real power to govern in society. Thus nationalism's unwitting, and often strident, contribution to national economic development, social exclusion, and globalisation can twist the pristine claims of liberal democracy to its own cause. Despite claims to always being inclusive, conciliatory and above all equal in its treatment of its constituent citizens, dominant nationalist policies can appear exactly the opposite to the "other" the disposed or the historically dominant group which now finds itself the target of the politics of revenge. Historical redress need not necessarily be just in its treatment of all groups. Take for example, peacetime reprisals and the occupation of Palestinian lands by Israel or the treatment of Russians in the Baltic States at the first flush of independence in the early nineties.

There is a convention to treat certain manifestations of nationalism as ethnic or primordial and others as essentially civic. But even this division leads to over-simplification of what is at best a highly complex phenomenon. Smith (1991) has identified a wide range of purposes for nationalism from that of forming nations and nation states, to the consciousness of belonging to a nation, or having a national identity as well as the active movements designed to achieve the goals attributed to the nation. More recently a great deal of attention has focussed on moving on from Gellner's concern with linking nationalism with broad historical forces such as the development of the vernacular or of print capitalism. Moore (2001) has assessed the various normative arguments which are made for the recognition of national identities and asserts that it is a mistake to dismiss national identities on the grounds that they are "socially constructed". Of especial concern for my argument is the realisation that these identities are not easy to deconstruct for they

> help to explain in broad historical terms why people have divided themselves into different groups, and they also identify the very real advantages in terms of life chances, of being a majority group in the state, and the almost inescapable logic, in the modern context, of identifying oneself in this way (p. 10).

When there is a freedom to choose, to switch identity from a minority to a majority position, then the reinforcing logic of self-advancement kicks in and it becomes almost impossible, if not illogical, to insist on being the "one" among the many. Yet some theorists have sought to provide a justification for this stance as we shall see below, and as Moore recognises, thus Charles Taylor, for example,

> has argued that the inextricable interdependence of nationalism with modern notions of popular will and popular sovereignty suggest that, once we understand the modern context of nationalist consciousness, we will have a strong appreciation of the prominence of nationalism and the centrality of national forms of identity (p. 11).

Following Mann (2005), we may distinguish between two other versions of "we, the people" as the legitimizing factor of political modernity and democracy, namely the *stratified* and *organic* people. "If the people is conceived of as diverse and stratified, then the state's main role is to mediate and conciliate among competing interest groups. This will tend to compromise differences, not try to eliminate or cleanse them. The stratified people came to dominate the Northwest of Europe." Here liberal democracy triumphed in an increasingly class-conscious and stratified set of societies. By contrast "if the people is conceived as organic, as one and indivisible, as ethnic, then its purity is maintained by the suppression of the deviant minorities, and this may lead to cleansing. In Europe this danger began to loom more across its central and eastern regions" (Mann, 2005, p. 55).

Given this division in the broad canvass on which the nationalist inheritance operates, the key questions posed in this chapter concern how the processes summarised under "globalisation" and "deterritorialisation" affect the maintenance of regional identities and the transformation of corresponding regional spaces? The argument suggests that we are not yet at the dawn of a "Europe of the Regions" despite a campaign which has lasted for well over a generation. But the emergence of new regional actors, including sub-state responsible governments, has a profound influence both on the territorial state-nation and on the European super-structural agencies. I have chosen to examine these in terms of the abiding tensions between the maintenance of the nation-state project and newer ideas regarding social inclusion, multi-culturalism and the challenges posed by overcoming gender and race discrimination.

Chapter Three addresses how nationalist and ethno-linguistic movements have sought to re-configure their appeal in the light of globalisation, regionalisation and state adaptation. Who counts as "we, the people"? How are questions of political affiliation based on either ethnic or civic attachments related to broader conceptions of class-based or stratified, democratic representation? Nationalism claims to speak for all co-nationals, but nationalist policies so very often reveal a darker side of exclusionary discrimination, especially against representatives of a former hegemonic power as with the Russians in the Baltic or newer arrivals as with Turks in Germany or Maghrebian Arabs in France. But such ideologies are not set in stone, for even here, as Derderian's study reveals, it is possible for an inclusive nationalism to be nurtured and radicalised from within. He has demonstrated that despite the difficulties of participation and recognition, ethnic minorities in France are actively involved in the democratisation of memory. "In keeping with a long French tradition of revolutionary change ushered in by marginalised groups, ethnic minorities are helping to reinvent the nation making it broader, more inclusive and truer to its original ideals" (Derderian's, 2004, p. 180). This is precisely the transformation which I believe can strain and ultimately strengthen liberal democracy.

However, the challenges posed by the new regionalism, ethnic minority adjustment, European integration and globalisation all complicate the conventional liberal democratic ideology of honouring the rights of individuals and of side stepping the collective rights of specific groups. Throughout the volume the politics of equal respect in multi-cultural societies will figure prominently. This is germane as several of the more astute regional governments, such as the Generalitat de Catalonia and the Wales Assembly Government, are recasting their principal language policies in terms of the social inclusion of migrant and immigrant populations, most of whom feel by-passed by recent gains made in establishing a bilingual, if not necessarily a bicultural, regime. There is an acute need to study the trajectories of regional minority and immigrant languages in tandem, especially where they threaten to run counter to each other or can be exploited for political gain as being counter-productive to the national project as in contemporary Catalonia.

Yet, as Mann (2005) observes, the conventional justification of civil democracy, namely that they first and foremost protect individual human rights, does not square with how such democracies were formed as the "rights and regulations of groups have actually been more central for liberal democracy. The institutionalisation of interest group struggle, especially of class struggle, has ensured toleration and restraint of cleansing by generating a stratified, not an organic, people" (Mann, 2005, p. 55).[9]

Whatever system is in place it is essential not to conflate the terms nation and state. I favour Wilbur Zelinsky's view that the basic distinction lies in the level and direction of the flow of grace and power.

> While the nation may be a freemasonry of brothers and sisters, a more or less democratic confederacy, conjoined through blood, soil, "the mystic chord of memory", or some other web of cultural sentiments, the state floats far above the reach or understanding of the common herd, stern and austere through nurturing; majesty rather than fraternity; compulsion replacing mutuality. An immigrant who is willing and able to endure the red tape can eventually become a citizen of almost any state; to become a full-fledged member of another nation is a much more trying, sometimes impossible feat.
>
> (Zelinsky, 1988, p. 9)

Chapter Four is concerned with the structures of state-civil society relations and explains its relevance for the study of language politics. It applies the earlier general discussion on equal recognition in liberal democracies to the specific field of language policy and planning. The chapter contrasts the bold, noble and honourable aspirations of many language planning agencies with the stark reality of applied state or colonial policy. This cuts to the professional heart of the argument as so often language policy has been used less as an instrument for the empowerment of disaffected citizens and more as an instrument of coercion and exclusion in European practice. A more acute application of this dualism has arisen when language planning has been used as an instrument of development and I offer some thoughts on the African and Asian experience. Despite their obvious social histories the themes of language policy, choice and planning alternatives are not dissimilar between Africa and Europe. Both have grappled with arguments over the choice of language of government and public administration in state and regional affairs; fears of complex forms of language dependency and especially the linguistic hegemony of English; the relatively limited strategic policy deliberations in fields such as curriculum development, Higher Education training methods, the absorption of immigrants, the development of IT and the rapid dissemination of interactive communication systems. It is remarkable to note that the World Bank or NATO may have a greater influence on certain language choices than do specialist government language policy agencies. The chapter then focuses on the conditions of possibility for linguistic minorities to see their languages achieve a greater representation in the key domains of education, public administration and the economy. The chapter concludes with a brief introduction to the case studies which occupy the remainder of the volume.

Chapter Five investigates the broad issue as to how well (or not) minority languages' concerns are integrated within the larger EU determination of language policy. It asks hard-hitting questions as to how language policy is arrived at and what implications this may have for the social inclusion and exclusion of diverse citizens. Then in an interesting twist it seeks to suggest ways in which innovative methodologies and Geographic Information Systems can assist official government agencies in realising the language choice of citizens in receiving public services delivery in Euskadi, Catalonia and Wales. It then concerns itself with the broader perspective as to how both indigenous (RM) and so-called "immigrant language" (IM) groups represent themselves as worthy participants, rather than supplicants, in the promotion of a multi-cultural EU. Finally the chapter reports on current developments to mainstream minority language aspirations within a revised EU language policy framework.

Chapter Six examines the debate in Britain, Ireland and Canada surrounding the attempt by autochthonous language groups to achieve a degree of "official" status. I say "official" guardedly as in most cases the British-inspired code of legal and public practice in these countries has tended to shun the recognition of official languages and the ceding of group rights. However, there have been strong pressures to grant certain Celtic languages a measure of official recognition and the French experience in Canada is invaluable as an example of how such a transition from supplicant to empowered participant came about. By focussing on the discourse of struggle, representation and responsibility it is possible to chart the progress of reversing language shift as one illustration of a larger equal rights agenda in seeking improved social justice.

The chapter also provides examples of the management of "new" actors within the governance of language policies and discusses how these new developments are contributing to our understanding of policy-making in the area of language politics, especially within the devolved territories. The key problematic which is tackled is how devolution, governance and democracy are being transformed with respect to the rights and expectations of "minority language speakers". Having examined the broad parameters of a changing socio-political context, the remaining chapters in the volume provide detailed illustrations of the forging and implementation of language policy in different contexts.

Chapter Seven deals with the quite distinct experiences of language revival, recognition and regulation in Scotland, Northern Ireland and Ireland. Despite the difficulties associated with reversing language shift in these Celtic contexts these are also exciting times to be involved with language policy and the equality agenda. Fresh initiatives abound as a result of the devolution process. In Scotland, the passage of a Gaelic Language Act in 2005 which came into effect in 2006 and the establishment of a statutory *Bòrd na Gàidhlig* have inaugurated a new era of formal language planning. In Northern Ireland, the St Andrew's Agreement of October 2006, which triggered a return to participatory democracy, also acknowledged the groundswell of support for an Irish Language Act. The Agreement included a commitment to introduce legislation on the Irish language and we wait to see how close such legislation will be to POBAL's clear draft proposals for such an Act (POBAL, 2006a). In Ireland, the Official Languages Act (2003) together with the establishment of a Language Commissioner has strengthened government resolve to make Irish a more pertinent language of work, justice and commercial life. We are under no illusion that regulatory and promotional initiatives can provide a substitute for a vibrant socio-linguistic speech community. However, one does need both opportunity and support to maintain a threatened language. Thus after years of hostility, neglect and disparagement of the role of Celtic languages within these isles, there does at last appear to be a concerted attempt to restitute them by granting a degree of official status and some state support in maintaining their presence within the fabric of society.

Chapter Eight focuses on Wales. Here a more strident language policy has been adopted as witnessed by the interpretation and application of the Welsh Language Act of 1993. Wales represents a distinct case in that language policy is determined largely by an agency of the state which operates at arm's length from the daily pressures of national government. Having established itself as an innovative and effective agency during the period from 1993 to 2007, the future of the Welsh Language Board is now under review. This chapter illustrates how successive changes in the British/Welsh political context have impacted on the role of para-governmental institutions and have delivered an unusual, if pragmatic, solution to questions concerning the promotion of a minority language and the development of a bilingual society.

Devolution has been the turning point in the language struggle for it has enabled the governance of the language to be undertaken by politicians and their associated civil servants who are at least broadly sympathetic to the construction of a bilingual society. Nevertheless key questions remain, among which are: How is language policy determined? Which agencies undertake language planning and consider strategic language policy issues? What is the relationship between central, national and local government and such para-public agencies? How has this evolved over the past twenty years? What is the current situation? How is this likely to change and with what effect both in terms of increasing the effectiveness of language policy and in integrating/mainstreaming language considerations into all aspects of governance in Wales?

Chapter Nine discusses recent developments in the area of language planning and policy-making, with reference to the Québécois and Canadian experience. Seven issues are pertinent to this analysis. The fundamental question is upon what criteria is identity in both Canada and Quebec based, ethnic or territorial? Second I discuss the development of federal and provincial language strategies together with their implications for the demolinguistic balance of power and citizenship. Third I rehearse several of the difficulties inherent in any federation with a colonial history, namely how to establish an autonomous legal, political and identity-construction process which Canada has sought to do through constitutional repatriation. Fourth I address the abiding structural tension and cleavage of the Canadian-Québécois relationship as evidenced in the Meech Lake episode and the 1992 referendum. This leads me to question to what extent this relationship is based upon irreconcilable nationalisms which place such great strains on symmetrical federalism and lead to demands for partition, and a more stable form of asymmetrical federalism. Finally I examine the contemporary reforms of the language planning regimes in Canada and Québec.

The final chapter deals with several unresolved issues and discusses the difficulties which language minorities have in advancing their claims for recognition and participation within increasingly multi-level and multi-cultural states. The interpretation relates these developments to the normative debates and to the new EU-wide structure of political opportunities and highlights the limits of language politics. It then moves on to consider three distinct spheres which are in need of development; first, data collection and the provision of appropriate evidence with which to formulate language policies; second, language legislation in relation to other forms of legislation and social justice issues; third, the management of language diversity within the EU. To an extent that is not widely appreciated, the role of official data collection on language-related issues is crucial to the implementation of bi- and multilingual services. Two opposing trends appear to be at work. The first is the harmonisation of data collection as regards the social, linguistic and other characteristics of the resident population throughout the EU. This trend undoubtedly aids comparative analysis, but it can also present an over-simplified portrait of Europe's multilingual citizenry. The second trend is that new spaces for action together with new opportunities have been created by ever increasing co-operation at the European level. The paradox of Europeanisation, as perhaps is also true of globalisation, is that as the EU becomes more integrated so power becomes more diffuse. At one level this makes it harder to guarantee minimum standards of political responsibility, public service and democratic engagement. But it also allows for more innovative forms of local distinctiveness and this in turn enables the better placed linguistic minorities to establish their own networks within the EU and seek to influence mainstream policy. The chapter advances advancing several strands of a strategy by which this may be realised and offers a commentary on the medium-term difficulties which minorities will face in an increasingly harmonised and bureaucratised EU.

The chapter ends with a consideration of the limits to freedom and develops the main messages contained within the volume. The first is that reforms of the nation-state and enhanced democratic engagement can empower linguistic minorities without this necessarily leading to constitutional fragmentation, high levels of sustained violence and separatist victories. The second is the need to underscore the importance of political theory, public policy debates, institutional analysis and comparative politics in the study of language policy. Too often language policy is discussed by linguists and sociolinguists in terms of input only, by that I mean the often very sound ideas related to corpus and status planning which are advanced without much regard for the political context in which they will be discussed, debated and implemented. Minority language policy is not *sui generis*. It is an extension of public policy, albeit with a heightened emotional attachment in most cases. That is why issues of representation and citizenship empowerment are related to the formulation of language policy but must cope with the real structural difficulties in harmonising language policy with other aspects of public policy. A central theme of this volume is that educational reforms and language policies developed by and for minorities are less effective than they might be, because they are often divorced from considerations related to the infra-structure and socio-economic environment which determines the nature of language choice in multicultural democracies. In short, undue attention has been paid to the tripartite foundation upon which reversing language shift rests, namely the family, the community and the education system. These are the crucial elements, I readily admit; but they are insufficient unless due attention is also paid to the formal political and public context within which they operate and to the increasingly dynamic private, informal social networks and interest groups which vitiate or deny the relevance of certain languages in key domains.

In summary, this book argues for more holisitic interpretations of language policy and planning for minorities. I contend that interpretations which simultaneously analyse both the formal and informal influences will yield far more realistic accounts of the challenges which minorities face. But above all, such minorities need democratic legitimacy to carry forward their ambitions. Consequently I believe that we now need to devote some of our energies to debating the relationship between the individual and the collective, the one and the many. This is because we need proposals which are firmly grounded, and not liable to be dismissed as the special pleading of a marginal sub-group, but the reasoned deliberations of fully respected citizens, who while sharing a common European home, want at least one room in the home to reflect their existence.

Notes

1. This concern with language, space and the freedom to be derives from two sources. More generally it reflects my bilingual education and professional training in Geography and Politics and subsequent attempts to promote both geolinguistic analysis and relatively pragmatic real-world solutions as a strategist with the Welsh Language Board over many years. But it also reflects something more personal and accidental. During the early eighties, while I was Fulbright Professor of Geography at Pennsylvania State University, my colleague Peter Gould, on attending my lectures, concluded that I was a "natural Heideggerian". He invited me to attend a weekly seminar on Heidegger taught by Prof. Joseph Kockelmans. There I discovered, in the words of Timothy Clark, that "Heidegger's concern is not the surface phenomena of language, the communication within the already opened space, but with the way language makes possible that space itself, its attitudes, attunements – the sort of world disclosed there ... he would awaken in the tired terminology of philosophical and critical thought the realization that language is at its basis an art-world, a poesis. It is a mode of disclosure, not a mode of re-presentation" (Clark, 2002, p. 74).
2. Bracken provides a useful definition of social ontology which he describes as "a metaphysical vision of reality in which societies or structured fields of activity are the conventional units of reality (the equivalent of 'substances' in classical metaphysics). Within this metaphysical vision", to be sure, actual entities are the ultimate constituents of these societies or structured fields of activity. But inasmuch as actual entities by definition so rapidly come and go societies or structured fields of activity are viewed as 'building blocks' or enduring constituents of reality (both physical and spiritual)" (Bracken, 2001, pp. 220–1).
3. Bracken's concern is to develop the presupposition of the metaphysics of intersubjectivity. Language is an especially vital element of this process for, as he explains, individuals are infinitely different from one another. "Yet paradoxically, from moment to moment, they are in vital contact with one another, in effect, they bridge that infinite difference, through various forms of communication" (p. 79).
4. Speaking of Berlin, "Liberty ought to have a certain priority – without some modicum of it, he said, 'there is no choice and therefore no possibility of remaining

human as we understand the world' – but even liberty might have to be curtailed in the interests of social justice" (Hardy, 1990, p. 12 quoted in Ignatieff, 1998, p. 285).

5. Thus Schmidt writes "the rhetoric of virtually all language policy conflicts centres around the role of the state in resolving disputed interpretations of the impact of language 'competition' on a) the relative degree of 'equality' between ethnolinguistic groups and b) 'national unity' " (Schmidt, 1998, p. 39).

6. In Europe and North America political units with the least diversity are often the result of aggressive linguistic assimilation in the past. For an alternative framework by which one can evaluate the overriding state aims and strategies, see the work of Kallen discussed in Chapter Three below.

7. Intellectual revisionism suggests that what passes for contemporary environmental thought can be traced back to earlier epochs in the long inter-relationship between human speculation and natural conditions.

8. One of the factors that is conventionally highlighted to explain the relative strength of Catalan is the fact that it was never abandoned by the urban bourgeoisie – clearly not so with the Celtic languages.

9. Mann also notes that "liberal democracies *have* committed massive cleansing, sometimes amounting to genocide – but in colonial contexts, where large social groups were defined as lying outside of the stratified people" (Mann, 2005, p. 55).

2
The Nationalist Inheritance in a Globalising World

Over the past thirty years or so rapid changes in the political landscape of Europe, together with the unravelling of globalisation have challenged our established notions of political community, citizenship and crucially national identity. Many argue that the nation-state no longer reflects the apogee of responsible government. This is because the ideas and political desires associated with a nationalist world view reflect processes that are the logical outcome of nineteenth century aspirations. It is further argued that nationalism, its handmaiden, is increasingly anachronistic and has lost much of its salience within an international political and legal order which is responsive to the post-sovereign realities of multinational organisations, transnational agencies and global communication.

Yet so many of our central ideas relating to human freedom, individual liberty and collective responsibility were fashioned in a pre-democratic order and pre-modern era. It is only within the modern nation-state project that such ideas have become truly popular and absorbed into our political conscious-ness as a matter of rights and expectations. True there are very many variants as to how such conceptions should be implemented, and some groups and individuals feel that their fundamental rights are being ignored or trampled upon by the state. Just as there is a structural tension between the indi-vidual and the collective so there is a structural tension between the national and the global. Within national level politics there remains a further ten-sion between the established nation-states and the unfulfilled nations. Both have been animated, at various times, by the same nationalist impulses, in that sense they parallel each other, even if their ambitions have been moul-ded within quite different political epochs. In consequence nationalism has had a profound effect, not only on the establishment of the international political order, but also on influencing our current conceptions of political culture and the interface of domestic and foreign affairs. The nation, how-ever defined, has not withered away and its people are the ultimate refer-ence group in whose name major political reforms and large scale economic projects, declarations of war and individual sacrifices are made. Admittedly more and more commentators are arguing that the attempts by unfulfilled or aspiring nations to accelerate their own nation-building processes are destined to disappoint. That is debatable, what is beyond doubt is the significance of the nationalist inheritance in a globalising world to so many of the themes treated in this volume.

Nationalist movements are often enigmatic in their aims and legitimacy, because they can oscillate between *individualist* conceptions of democratic nationalism and those that are more *communitarian* in orientation. That is, whether a democracy is in essence the free expression of the rights of individual citizens, regardless of putative socio-cultural origins or whether it is an expression of the existence of "communities", which may, in certain respects over-ride individual interests as "individual" autonomy is sublimated to "communitarian" autonomy (Agnew, 1987; Lapidoth, 1997).

This dualism has implications for conceptions of citizenship, group membership, participation, and social inclusion or exclusion. Many nationalist movements espouse philosophies of inclusion or group membership which, if they were to be couched in terms of race rather than national culture, would be deemed abhorrent to liberal democrats. And yet, questions such as, "Who may be represented by nationalist parties?" and "For whom do nationalist speak?" are fundamental elements of the contemporary battle of ideas and political affiliation in many plural polities. Clearly, despite its often exclusionary and reactive framings, the language of nationalism is a widely acceptable discourse among democratic states in Europe and beyond.

For some, this is a matter of the underlying meaning rather than the specific language which is used in reproducing nationalist ideology. For others it goes even deeper, for it problematises the very legitimacy or otherwise of nationalist mobilisation in what are increasingly multicultural democracies. Successful ideologies have to find ways of linking together several layers of consciousness, so that they can challenge hegemonic rule (Eagleton, 1991). Williams (1977) has reminded us that every social formation is an admixture of "dominant", "residual" and "emergent" forms of consciousness and no hegemony can thus be absolute. Elements of this tension between individual and group consciousness are also at the heart of the epistemological, methodological and normative debates within contemporary social sciences (Frazer, 1996; MacIntyre, 1984) and underlie the difficulties of finding an appropriate institutional expression of nationalism in practice.[1]

The literature on nationalism is voluminous.[2] I want to set nationalist ideas within a context which is more sympathetic to geographical and ecological insights for at root this volume is a long essay in holistic interpretation. Historians and social scientists have dominated the field, and although geographers have made a significant contribution, few have analysed the democratic context of nationalism or the internal dynamics of nationalist movements, whether in terms of conflicting aims, ideological/strategic disputes or support base.[3] Most geographical analysis has focused on comparing the electoral fortunes of nationalist movements within various voting systems (Johnston and Taylor, 1989).[4] A second emphasis has been on nationalism and uneven development, the notion of imagined communities, the iconographic representation of nationalist symbols in the landscape,[5] conflict analysis and the use of violence by minority nationalist movements.[6] Some of the outstanding examples of geographical analyses of majoritarian nationalisms include Zelinsky (1988), who offers a penetrating account of the American experience. Additionally, Kaiser (1994) and Smith (1996a,b; Smith *et al.*, 1998) disentangle the Russian and Soviet experience and Jisi Wang (1994) and Zhao (1997, 2000) offer cogent perspectives on nationalism in China, focusing on nativism, anti-traditionalism, and pragmatism.

In this chapter, my focus will be an analysis of the scope for nationalist movements within the context of the contemporary European political system. I believe this system has yet to come to terms with the nation-state nexus, based as it is on differing principles of membership and inclusion.[7] Here I argue that for liberal nationalism to succeed in any measure, current European conceptions of the nation and of nationalism must grapple more effectively with the implications of three simultaneous processes: globalisation, regionalisation and state adaptation (see also Jönsson *et al.*, 2000). And although I agree in the main with scholars such as Wright (2004) that globalisation has profoundly changed the nature of nationalist expression in a post-nationalist world, nevertheless I argue that one should not underestimate the purchase of nationalist ideology today.[8] In many ways this analysis complements Wright's sophisticated interpretation by illustrating one of her central tenets in relation to her observation that

> the new nexus of power and association that accompany globalization and the new awareness of rights and recalibration of identities that come with the demands for minority recognition, both of which appear to be undermining nation statism and affecting language attitudes and behaviour and both of which entail rethinking language policy.
>
> (Wright, 2004, p. 98)

The European context

The main challenge in contemporary European politics is how best to represent the interests of local, regional, state and supra-state authorities within an effective system which commands mutual respect. Nationalist and separatist movements have traditionally sought increased autonomy, and ultimately of course, complete independence as free and equal members of the international system.[9] Given the interdependent and multi-level character of governance we may ask whether the pristine ideals of autonomy, autarchy and self-determination are less realisable now than in the past? If so, what can liberal nationalism still hope to achieve within an integrated quasi-federal Europe? Experts doubt that there will soon be a federal Europe resembling present-day federal states or a Europe of the Regions where nation-states will have disappeared. But they are certain that there will be a regionalised Europe where decentralised and regionalised states will be at an advantage (Loughlin, 1996b). If so, what scope is there for various realisations of nationalism within a democratic system?[10]

Throughout the nineteenth century the coupling of "nation" with "state" led to the development of *nationalism* as an ideology, and the rise of nation-alist political movements.[11] History shows us that nationalism remained a powerful, if highly negative, political force when linked to imperialism, fas-cism and Nazism, rather than to the creation of liberal democracy[12] (Clark, 1996; De Grand, 2000; Dülffer, 1996; Dunnage, 2002; Evans, 2005; Gregor, 2000; Morgan, P., 2004; Smith, 1997). It is also evident that the great kudos which was attached to some nationalist revolutions has become general-ised to most nationalist movements. Their vicarious power to overthrow the great empires needs to be re-assessed. Ferguson has warned that "as for nationalism, it is something of a myth that this is what brought down the old empires of Western Europe. Far more lethal to their longevity were the costs of fighting rival empires – empires that were still more contemptuous of the principle of self-determination" (Ferguson, 2005, p. xiii).

Nationalism owes much to the emergence of the nation-state ideal even if the latter has been contested throughout its existence – most recently by globalisation, and more specifically in our case, by European (EU) integra-tion. What has not been examined systematically are the consequences of this transformation from the point of view of democratic practice, especially at the *sub*-state level, the locus of nationalist angst and mobilisation.

A contemporary approach argues that new forms of governance have direct consequences for the regional and local levels which are becoming increasingly important alongside and implicated within the national and supranational levels.[13] In fact, they may be even more important as the locus of the exercise of power shifts away from national governments represent-ing the territorial state, both upwards to European and other transnational types of organisation, and also downwards to nations, regions and local authorities.[14] The privileging of the territorial state, especially in the literat-ure on international political economy, has been criticised by geographers, most effectively in Agnew and Corbridge's *Mastering Space* (1995). In similar vein Jönsson *et al.* (2000) argue that theories which privilege the state at the expense of other organisational forms are of limited value in understanding the dynamism of change. Their magisterial study of the role of evolving net-works in the organisation of European space points towards the possibility of governance without government as the operational norm for the super-structural level. And as this supra-national dimension has largely escaped control of any kind, this makes it all the more imperative to strengthen regional and local levels and design new institutional forms of expression.[15] Given the greater emphasis on regionalisation as the EU developed it might have been anticipated that nationalist movements would have declined in salience. The old nation-state system, however, will not simply disappear. It has adapted itself as the "negotiating state", capable of dealing both with "globalisation" and "fragmentation".[16]

Yet nationalist movements continue to thrive and have adopted a variety of forms of resistance to the incursions of the central state and its agencies. The most violent expressions, as in Northern Ireland, Corsica and the Basque Country, have dominated both media headlines and academic analysis alike (Cox *et al.*, 2000). To the conventional practice of constitutional electioneering, as happens in Catalonia or Scotland, we may add yet other expressions of resistance such as in Christian pacifism or widespread conscientious objection, which have been used by nationalists as instruments of opposition to warfare in the name of imperial defence and the subjugation (genocide) of minority peoples. There has also been an acute sense of divine destiny in the mobilisation of minority cultures, whether in Catholic Catalonia and Euskadi (Conversi, 1997), Ireland (Goldring, 1993) or Nonconformist Wales (Llywelyn, 1999). Equally revealing has been the concern with the localism and community defence, with self-reliance and with nonalignment, in order to distance supporters from the hegemony of the superpowers and strong states. Both environmental and minority autonomist rights movements seek to place the individual within a wider communal framework, stressing inter-dependence and a shared destiny. Feelings of belonging, of shared responsibility and of rootedness all figure prominently, in contrast to the possessive individualism championed by the post-Fordist culture with its stress on mobility, individual advancement and a regime of flexible accumulation.

Several structural characteristics re-appear in most nationalist struggles. These consistently involve a fear of loss of identity, exploitation of the cultural and physical resources of the nation, resistance to external intervention and control, reinterpretation of the nation's plight in terms of the leaderships' mission-destiny view of their own transcendent existence, the ultimate securing of freedom in a world of free and equal nations (Williams, 1994). Nationalist iconography has raised a triad of political truths – sovereignty, autarchy and cultural integrity. This Chalcedonian-informed interpenetration of place, nation and individual has been described as a "complex, multi-layered phenomena, each involving relationships: of place with time, time with place, and each individual with the transgenerational community of which he or she is a member. The integration of Chalcedonian concepts permits us to describe a relationship in which there is unity, but no merging, and in which the boundaries between metaphysical and psychological dimensions of place and of nation can be allowed their own autonomies without confusion of linguistic registers, or a false transference of ontic realities from one plane to another" (Llywelyn, 1999, p. 74).

I believe that such transgenerational concepts of the nation, defined as a community of communities, are essential to the understanding of European minority nationalism which is detailed below in terms of several structural features.

1. Nationalists insist on the defence of their unique homeland and of the protection of their valued environment. Nationalism almost always has a specific piece of territory to which it must relate as a response to a particular set of circumstances reflecting the classic element of place-centred politics described in Agnew (1989), MacLaughlin (1986), Mar-Molinero (1994) and Williams (1982). It is not an autonomous force. It is evident that resistance, struggle and the politics of collective defence over land and territory dominate the relationship between a minority movement and its incursive, hegemonic state power. More recently, ecologists have taken up this concern with valued environments and in some cases caused common alliance with nationalists to protect threatened spaces.[17] This seems set to become a major issue of the century where conflict over the control of space and resources will quicken our awareness of the commonality of defensive movements, even if their ideological rationale remains distinctly separate.

2. Nationalists also insist on the defence and promotion of their culture and identity, whose diacritical markers are usually a distinct language, religious affiliation, separate social existence and historical experience. Nationalist movements often attach the utmost symbolic significance to the preservation of a separate identity. It does not follow that the majority of its target constituents share such markers as a common language, or religious persuasion. Indeed one of the inherent paradoxes of nationalism is that by searching for a distinct cultural infra-structure to differentiate itself from state-wide political parties or powerful neighbours within the polity, nationalist rhetoric often serves to alienate the very people in whose name the claim to liberty and equality is being made.[18]

3. Resistance to trends which integrate the national territory into the core state apparatus is a significant feature of nationalism. Dismissed as anti-progressive or recidivist, nationalists have faced difficulties in constructing an economic argument to counter the economies of scale justification for state integration. The increasing scale and complexity of political units renders anathema any conscious return to small nations as the basic building block of the international political system. It is argued that the "liberation" of the Baltic States and of the constituent parts of the former Yugoslavia can not offer an exemplar to

Scotland, Euskadi and Québec, for they were born out of civil war and the threat of physical force in the wake of imperial dissolution. But this reasoning undervalues the historical integrity of territorial identities, as found in for example, Slovenia and Croatia, which have an authenticity and integrity pre-dating modern conceptions of the nation-state.[19]

4. Nationalists deny the claim that many putative nations are not economically viable in an increasingly globalised system. They would stress that the Basque Country, Quebec and the like have been systematically exploited and underdeveloped as "internal colonies" (Hechter, 1975). Persistent structural discrimination can only be halted and reversed once the goals of political sovereignty and economic autarchy have been achieved. On realising their plight, the masses will do what all other colonial victims do – rise up and evict their oppressors in the name of national liberation. It matters less that nationalism *per se* offers little that is prescriptive for the post-independence economic recovery; for they believe that the advent of independence itself creates a new social reality, where truth, prosperity and development can be constructed largely from within the nation, rather than being denied from without. Scotland and Wales manifest this, for since May 1999, they have a Parliament and National Assembly, occasioning a concomitant increase in national confidence and ambitions to play a more active role within the international system.

5. A more persistent tendency is for local communities to resist population transfer and demographic changes which adversely affect the majoritarian position of co-nationals. Thus, resistance to outsiders, immigrants, settlers and colonisers as agents of the hegemonic state and its associated culture is as widespread in rural Macedonia and Wales as it is in urban Euskadi. It is manifested in agonising fears over the survival of a threatened language where each child born to the foreigner and the death of each native speaker is logged in a mythical but pervasive national register and the balance of probability against the survival of Welsh or Euskerra weighed anxiously new every morning.

6. Fear of loss of dominance and influence is expressed through cultural attrition and campaigns to save local communities, sacred sites and valued land from rapacious developers, whether they be private companies or government departments conducting legally-binding state business. Several campaigns in Wales opposing the drowning of valleys to create reservoirs ("Cofia Tryweryn"/Remember Tryweryn), the compulsory purchase of farmland for military training purposes, such as the "Tân yn Llŷn" episode at Rhandirmwyn, or campaigns aimed at overturning deleterious second home/tourist development practices, such as "Nid yw Cymru ar Werth" (Wales is not for sale) have been mirrored in Brittany at Plogouf and in Scotland, in relation to opposition to the continued existence of nuclear installations and defence establishments.

These and many other examples demonstrate how the socio-economic infrastructure is transformed to suit external interests. Often dangerous and obnoxious industries such as nuclear power plants, oil terminals and defence establishments, are situated within the minority's territory, who are relatively powerless to stop such exploitation of their land and social fabric. Equally the minority's resources are expropriated, be they natural such as water, a wild and rugged landscape, or human, a well-educated but relatively poorly-paid labour force exploited in the service sector with its seasonal and tourist-dependant characteristics. All of this induces a dependency situation, which is reactive rather than purposive, defensive rather than self-confident, outer-directed, rather than inner-directed.

7. In selected circumstances this perception of being exploited and subdued leads to open conflict and sustained violence as in the Basque Country, Northern Ireland and Corsica (Loughlin and Letamenida, 2000). Attempts to defuse such violence through various stages of regional autonomy, power sharing and state re-structuring do not appear to be wholly successful. Once a culture of violence is established, it tends to have an internal dynamic, self-energising and sustaining, undeterred by piece-meal reform.

8. With the rise of print capitalism and mass communication came the possibility of constructing alternative versions of historical reality (Williams, 1988b). Minority nationalist intelligentsias sought to influence group learning by stressing those aspects of history which explain inequalities in the light of significant acts of oppression. Reconstructed historical discourses contend with orthodox interpretations of popular history and state development. When centralising elites seek to suppress alternative discourses, as Franco sought to ban the political use of Basque because it told the story of the vanquished, then a fresh round of conflict is unleashed. Centralists oppose formal education in the minority's mother tongue precisely because they fear their inability to control the messages circulated through the minority languages.[20]

9. An insistence on the immorality and political illegitimacy of the *status quo* provides a political rationale for the emergence of nationalist movements. "The desire of nations" is to be a fully accepted nation among other nations, and in political terms this necessitates the attainment either of sovereignty or a great deal of devolved autonomy within the international system.

10. Minority nationalists seek evidence which serves to redefine their situation in the light of reforms, concessions, political accommodation and gains for the beleaguered minority within the dominant system. In Western Europe, the nationalist appeal of the 1960s was couched on the basis of a universal trend towards de-colonisation. What was good enough for Nigeria or Niger was good enough for Scotland and

Brittany. In the 1970s it was as a reaction to the overloading of governmental structures in Westminster or Paris, so that developed government became good government, conferring the twin blessings of participatory democracy and enhanced efficiency in government services. In the 1980s it was an appeal to localism, to valued environments, to the appeal of place over placelessness and anomie. In the 1990s, it was an appeal to reconstruct a Europe of the nations, to overthrow the state-centric and hegemonic nineteenth century state system and to return to Europe's organic, constituent nations. Unperturbed by the difficulties in squaring the reality of a multicultural Europe within a national-istic order, nationalists sought to by-pass their state cores, London, Madrid or Paris and allow Edinburgh, Barcelona or Rennes to entreat directly with the Brussels-Strasbourg axis in an increasingly federal Europe.[21]

11. Finally appeals by national minorities to the international community against the sovereign state can have unpredictable consequences. One has to do with institutionalising the right to self-determination in domestic constitutions. Moore (2001, p. 220) has warned that "since the central government is supposed to operate in the interests of the state as a whole state, and of all its citizens in the state viewed collectively, it is difficult to conceive of the central government, or organs of the central government, as impartial arbiters, designing fair rules of the game."[22] But Moore's most telling point as regards the institutionalisation of self-determination within international law, as opposed to domestic constitutions, is the fact that often the "problem of the existing state's neutrality is raised even more acutely ... when the central government is the main agent of their persecution" (p. 220).

Nationalist mobilisation within the various state forms

Orridge and Williams (1982) have demonstrated how the triggering factor of nationalist mobilisation is related to the structural pre-condition of the state system. We now need to relate such features to the contemporary context of West European democracy, that is, the variety of ways in which it is *understood*, *expressed* and *practised* in different countries as summarised by Loughlin and Peters (1997) in Table 2.1.[23] Each of these state traditions has given rise to distinct political and administrative cultures, forms of state organisation and kinds of state-society relationships. Yet within each of these "families", there exist distinct *national* traditions.[24] Different state traditions also express sub-national political systems in distinct ways. The two extremes are the Napoleonic tradition, as in France, which allows little variation across its national territory and the Anglo-Saxon tradition which tolerates wide variations, as in the United Kingdom.

Table 2.1 State traditions

Feature	Tradition			
	Anglo-Saxon	**Germanic**	**French**	**Scandinavian**
Is there a legal basis for the state?	No	Yes	Yes	Yes
State–society relations	Pluralistic	Organicist	Antagonistic	Organicist
Form of political organization	Union state/limited federalist	Integral/ organic federalist	Jacobin, "one and indivisible"	Decentralized unitary
Basis of policy style	Incrementalist, "muddling through"	Legal corporatist	Legal technocratic	Consensual
Form of decentralization	"State power" (US), devolution/local government (UK)	Cooperative federalism	Regionalized unitary state	Strong local autonomy
Dominant approach to discipline of public administration	Political science/sociology	Public law	Public law	Public law (Sweden), organization theory (Norway)
Countries	UK, US, Canada (not Quebec), Ireland	Germany, Austria, Netherlands, Spain (post-1978), Belgium (post-1988)	France, Italy, Spain (pre-1978), Portugal, Quebec, Greece, Belgium (pre-1988)	Sweden, Norway, Denmark, Finland

Source: Loughlin and Peters (1997).

Nationalism in the Context of Regional and Local Democracy

Loughlin *et al.*'s (1999) study of "Regional and Local Democracy in the EU" illustrates the functioning of democracy at sub-state levels through a variety of central-local relations and differing electoral systems (Table 2.2).[25]

In the UK, three different electoral systems are in operation, the "first-past-the-post" or plurality system at the state level; the single transferable vote (STV) system of proportional representation in Northern Ireland; and the "additional-member" system for the Scottish Parliament and the Welsh National Assembly alongside the "first-past-the-post" system. In federal and regionalised states such as Germany, Belgium, Italy and Spain, there may

Table 2.2 Central–local relations in EU member states

Type of state	State	Political region[a]	Administrative /planning regions[b]	Right of regions to participate in national policy-making	Right of regions to conclude foreign treaties[c]	Political/legislative control over sub-regional authorities[c]
Federal	Austria	Länder (10)		Yes	Yes (but limited)	Yes (not absolute)
	Belgium	Communities[d] (3)		Yes	Yes (but limited)	No
		Regions (3)			Yes (but limited)	Yes (not absolute)
	Germany	Länder (16)		Yes	Yes (but limited)	Yes (not absolute)
Regionalized unitary	Italy[e]	Regioni[g] (20)		Consultative	No	
	France	Régions[h] (21)		Consultative	No	No
	Spain	Comunidades autonomas (17)		No		Yes
	United Kingdom[f]	Scottish Parliament Welsh National Assembly Northern Ireland Assembly	English standard regions	No with regard to English regions; still unclear with regard to Scotland, Wales, and Northern Ireland	No at present, but may evolve	Yes in Scotland and Northern Ireland; no in Wales (so far)
Decentralized unitary	Denmark	Faroe Islands	Groups of Amter	No	No	No
	Finland	Aaland Islands	Counties have a regional planning function	No	No (but has a seat in the Nordic Council)	Yes

Netherlands	Rijnmond Region[i]	Landsdelen Regional administrative bodies (13)	consultative	No	No
Sweden			No	No	No
Greece		Regional Development regions	No	No	No
Ireland		Regional authorities (8)	No	No	No
Luxembourg			No	No	No
Portugal	Island regions[j]	Potential planning regions			

(Centralized unitary)

Source: Reproduced with permission from Loughlin (1999), p. 16.

a This refers to regions and nations (as in Scotland, Wales, Catalonia, the Basque Country and Galicia) with a directly elected assembly to which a regional executive is accountable.

b This refers to regions without a directly elected assembly, which exists primarily for administrative/planning purposes.

c There is a sharp distinction between the federal and non-federal states in this regard; however, the majority of non-federal states may engage in international activities with the approval of, and under the control of, the national governments.

d The Flemish linguistic community and the Flanders economic region have decided to form one body; the French-speaking community and the Walloon region remain separate.

e Italy is currently undergoing a process of political reform that involves the transformation of the old state into a new kind of state with some federal features. However, although the position of the regions will be strengthened, this will not be a federal state such as Germany or Belgium.

f The United Kingdom was, until the referendums in Scotland and Wales in September 1997, a highly centralized "Union" state. However, the positive outcome of the referendums means that there will be a Scottish Parliament and a Welsh National Assembly by 1999. A referendum in 1998 on a Greater London Authority with an elected mayor was also successful, and this is seen as a precursor to possible regional assemblies in England. The successful outcome of the Northern Ireland peace process means there will be a Northern Ireland Assembly as well as other new institutions linking together the different nations and peoples of the islands.

g In Italy there are seventeen "ordinary" regions and five regions with a special statute because of their linguistic or geographical peculiarities: Sicily, Sardinia, Trentino-Alto Adige (South Tyrol, large German-speaking population), Val d'Aosta and Friuli-Venezia Giulia.

h There are twenty-one regions on mainland France. However, to this one must add Corsica and the overseas departments and territories (the DOM and TOM). Since 1991 Corsica has a special statute and is officially a *Collectivité territoriale* rather than a region. The TOM too have special statutes, and one of them, in May 1998 New Caledonia was permitted to accede to independence within a period of twenty years.

i In 1991 it was decided to set up a new metropolitan region with an elected government in the Rotterdam area to replace the *Gemeente* of Rotterdam and the Province of South Holland. However, this was rejected by a referendum held in Rotterdam.

j Portugal, while making provision in its Constitution for regionalization, has so far only granted autonomy to the island groups of the Azores and Madeira. The mainland remains highly centralized.

be different party systems at the sub-national level with the existence of regionally based parties, such as the Bavarian *Christlich Sozial Union* (CSU, Christian Social Union), the Catalan *Convergencia i Unío* (CiU, Convergence and Union), and the Basque *Partido Nacionalista Vasco* (PNV, Basque Nationalist Party). Such regionally based parties may also play a role at the national level. In the United Kingdom, there has always been a different party system in Northern Ireland, where, until recently, the British parties did not organise (in recent years, the Conservative Party has permitted a Northern Irish branch). With devolution, the tendency to develop regionalised political cultures and party systems in Scotland and Wales will intensify making nationalists' issues more significant. In Scotland, future political cleavage will concern the political expression and relationship of the Scottish nation to various options, concerning the *status quo*, independence within Europe, or a federal United Kingdom. In Wales there is no sense of "settled nationhood" and even less of a civil society, and the cleavage is between those who support and oppose devolution. In Northern Ireland, even if the Good Friday settlement seems to have bade "A Farewell to Arms" for the time being, there remains the fundamental dispute between unionists and nationalists as to the interpretation of the Agreement and the manner in which devolution will be implemented following its restitution in the Spring of 2007 (Cox *et al.*, 2000).

Similar regionalisation and differentiation of political systems elsewhere is reinforced by the development of regional or sub-national branches of national parties, as for example, the Catalan and Basque sections of the Spanish Socialist Party or the Scottish Conservatives who favour devolution more than their English counterparts do, or the Welsh Labour Party which has adopted much of the symbolism of a national (at times, nationalist) party. In some cases the regional system may develop in an autonomous manner, as in the Iberian experience (Conversi, 1997; Mar-Molinero and Smith, 1996; Moreno, 1995). In others, the regional and local are completely dominated by the centralist national parties as in Ireland and France and, even in the decentralised United Kingdom, the central organs of the Labour Party have difficulty in letting go of control over the parties in the periphery.[26]

Europeanisation, nationalism and the "new" regionalism

A second set of relationships concerns the emergence of the EU at the superstructural level and the refashioning of nationalist movements as inclusive regionalist parties. The relaunch of Europe in the 1980s, with the 1992 Single European Market project, is often interpreted as a response by national governments and business elites to the perceived threat of a global economy dominated by the United States and to a lesser extent, Japan (Ó Loughlin, 1993; Ó Tuathail, 1993; Williams, 1993a). However, it was also the result of intense lobbying by governmental actors and other elites who wished to strengthen federal elements of an integrated Europe (Loughlin, 1996b; Pinder, 1995) and promote the notion of a "Europe of the Regions"[27]. The deepening of integration through the 1987 Single European Act and the revision of the EC treaties at Maastricht and Amsterdam has created a new administrative and legal environment for local and regional authorities. This European system of governance that has both state-like and federal-type characteristics, creates challenges and opportunities for regional and local authorities.

In this changed context, new forms of nationalism and regionalism have emerged as part of a "modernising" project strengthening regional and structural action policy and the reinforcement of the principles of subsidiarity and partnership (Keating, 1998). However, this does not amount to the establishment of a "Europe of the Regions" because it is unclear as to *which* regions would form the constituent parts, and state governments still remain the dominant actors. Regional representation through the Committee of the Regions or via DG XVI of the European Commission or the European Parliament still remains weak. What is new is the sense of a "Europe *with* the Regions"; in that sub-national authorities have more opportunities to interact at a European scale through the Assembly of European Regions and the Conference of Peripheral Maritime Regions (Hooghe and Marks, 1996). The influence of the Committee of the Regions is set to grow (Loughlin and Seiler, 1999) and with it a greater transparency and accountability, for as Loughlin comments it is ironic that despite the success of the EU in incorporating former dictatorial regimes,[28] the Union has itself failed to develop into a fully democratic system. A major criticism levelled by nationalists and others is its serious "democratic deficit". The challenge is to strengthen democratic institutions within the member states and to encourage trends such as the European Parliament's participation in the decision-making processes of the Council of Ministers, thereby increasing democratic control at the European level.[29] The resultant overlapping and nested systems of governance involving European, national, regional and local actors, in new networks may either be viewed as providing an especial focus for nationalist programmes, for they bring the national region back into the picture of governance, or they may be seen as an undermining nationalist rhetoric for they threaten to present its message of group exclusivity as fundamentally undemocratic.

Globalisation and European integration

An additional development compounding the logic of nationalist ideology is the imperfect and developing process known as globalisation. Together with European integration it changes the context within which civil society is mediated, posing a challenge to the conventional territorial relationships and simultaneously opening up new forms of inter-regional interaction. Ethno-linguistic minorities, the most prominent advocates of nationalist ideas, have reacted to these twin impulses by searching for European-wide economies of scale in broadcasting, information networking, education and public administration and establishing their own European alliances and networks to influence EU decision-making bodies. They believe that by appealing to the superstructrual organisations for legitimacy and equality of group rights, they will force both the state and the EU to recognise their claims for varying degrees of political/social autonomy within clearly identifiable territorial/social domains.

These trends must be set against the European policies which strengthen majority language regimes within a refashioned network of nodal sites (Jönsson *et al.*, 2000). But the wider question of the relative standing of official languages makes political representatives wary of further complicating administrative politics by addressing the needs of the many millions of citizens who have a mother tongue which is not the main official language of the state which they inhabit. The most recent expansion of the EU in 2007 has increased the difficulties in translating multi-cultural communication and guaranteeing access to information and hence power for all groups. The real geolinguistic challenge is to safeguard the interests of all the non-state language groups, especially those most threatened with imminent extinction. A critical aspect of constructing these safeguards is access to knowledge. Thus we need to ask and act upon the answers to questions such as who controls access to information *within the mother tongue, home and working languages of* European minorities? Are such languages destined to occupy a more dependant role because of superstructrual changes favouring dominant groups or will they achieve relative socio-cultural autonomy by adopting elements of mass technology to suit their particular needs?

Additional issues concern the adaptation of lesser-used language speakers to the opportunities afforded by changes in global-local networks, the growth of specialised economic segments or services and of information networks which are accessed by language-related skills. Accessibility to or denial of these opportunities is the virtual expression of real power in society which must be taken on board in any discussion of the changing geography of regional economic development and cultural representation. Advanced regions, such as the "Four Motors" group of Baden-Württemberg, Catalonia, Lombardy and Rhône-Alpes have become even stronger while weaker regions such as those in southern Italy and Spain or in Greece or in parts of the United Kingdom have become weaker. Some previously peripheral countries such as Ireland and Portugal and parts of Spain have managed to use the new developments to achieve economic performances that are quite spectacular.[30] What is clear is that the old conceptualisation of centres and peripheries no longer hold, and that spatial and territorial concepts need to be radically reformulated in the search for new representational spaces (Williams, 1997a).

Regional-level challenges to globalisation have to cope with the fact that current approaches to public action are more sympathetic to competition and markets than to solidarity and equalisation among territories. A down-grading of regional development priorities results in the issues being seen in purely economic or financial terms, rather than in a wider sense as social, political and cultural development. Economic actors thus become crucial in conceptions of new forms of governance, which has less real purchase in addressing issues of fragmentation and social exclusion.

Technological developments and the deterretorialisation of society and space

European-level institutions are also reacting to trends such as telematic networking and global communication systems which have reinforced the dominance of English and promoted a Pan-European, Trans-Atlantic melange of culture, values and entertainment. Other international languages, such as French, German and Spanish, are re-negotiating their positions within the educational, legal and commercial domains of an enlarged Europe. English was strengthened initially by the admission of Nordic members and then subsequently by Eastern European members to the European Union, but there is no agreement as to whether other major languages are necessarily weakened by enlargement. Neither do we know how existing lesser-used language organisations will fare given the recent enlargement of the EU with its effect on the management of ethno-linguistic and regional issues.[31]

An abiding concern is that autochthonous language groups, such as the Basques, Bretons, Irish and Welsh will be further marginalised in an increasingly complex and competitive social order (Williams, 2000c) and this is a central theme in this volume. Their main hope lies in establishing regional bilingualism as the dominant pattern and working to increase bilingual practices in domains such as education, public administration and the law which offer encouragement of a more equitable future. Yet even in the midst of success some groups are experiencing the ambiguous effects of mass technology as they experience the erosion of their traditional strength in heartland areas and key cities whilst simultaneously harnessing the potential of mass communication and electronic networking in education, broadcasting and leisure service provision. In Central and Eastern Europe, comparable, but poorer ethno-linguistic groups, face a more difficult future in seeking to reproduce their culture and identity, and this is likely to reinvigorate nationalist tendencies (Kuzio, 2000, 2001; Landsbergis, 2000). If territorial loss and relative economic decline continue for these more vulnerable groups straddling major cultural fault lines, then it is likely that border tensions will spill over between members of the European Union and neighbouring states. Currently we have little detailed foreknowledge of how such trends will impact on the "opening up the frontiers of Europe". But it is inevitable following the accession of Romania and Bulgaria that Turkey's application to join the EU will test the ability of the EU edifice to sustain expansion, and beyond the institutional apparatus, it will call into question the geo-strategic and military role of the EU and NATO in its involvement with both the Middle East and the Russian borderlands. The limited evidence we have to date cannot predict what role intractable ethnic conflicts will play in triggering major regional clashes and how the security architecture of Europe will react to such conflagrations.

A related source of difficulty will be the differential access to innovative regional impulses, information space and power networks that groups enjoy. The extension of international super-grids depends heavily on state investment and capacity-building and if such investment does not reach minority areas they are effectively disenfranchised from competing for the consequent research and development and high-tech industries which depend on access to the grid.[32] Thus we need to investigate what effect globalisation will have on the regional-local infra-structure upon which European ethnic minority groups depend? First, core-periphery differentials are maintained because surplus regional capital is re-invested elsewhere. The established transfer of manufacturing from peripheral locations in Western Europe to Eastern European, Asian or Central American state, mirrors today similar changes in, for example, the textile industry of North-West Europe in the mid-nineteenth century. Thus Galicia, Wales and Brittany find it difficult to sustain vibrant ethno-linguistic communities in the face of out-migration, relative deprivation, and regional infra-structure decline. Secondly, there is the overcoming of temporal and spatial discontinuities in "real time" communication and economic transactions which are increasingly independent of the limitations of specific locations (Brunn and Leinbach, 1991; Castells, 1997). Thirdly, globalisation processes have a simultaneity of *both* increased uniformity and increased diversity, giving birth to alternative identities, practices and preferences which have little if anything to do with conceptions of the nation. Nowhere is this more evident than in the cultural infra-structure of world cities, suffused as they are with multicultural choices and exotic consumption, quite distinct from most of the state's remaining territory. In such a milieu, emerging or re-born linguistic identities are nurtured and expressed. So, also, are their opponents, who wish to impose a pristine cultural order on dissenting ethnic activists, resulting in tension, hostility and racial/ethnic violence. Fourthly, superficial global homogenisation deserves especial scrutiny because the spread of English in particular contributes to the link between globalisation and post-modernity. Many European minorities, despite being bi-or trilingual, face extreme pressures as a result of superstructrual changes and are threatened by a double marginalisation from both the state language and its associated rationalities and by the spread of English as an instrument of global hegemony. Fifthly, there is the counter current of increased religious and/or ethnic identification and confrontation, within and across national frontiers often in violent and emotional forms (Mlinar, 1992; Williams, 1993b).

Globalisation also influences cultural patterns and modes of thought, because as a constant interactive process it is always seeking to break down the particular, the unique and the traditional so as to reconstruct them as a local response to a general set of systematic stimuli. This is the threat of the *deterritorialisation of society and space*. The collapse of both space and time demands a fresh appreciation of global interdependence for we have been quick to characterise the advantages which accrue to well-placed groups and regions. We have been less careful to scrutinise the impact such transitions might have on minorities and the disadvantaged. Some of the changes wrought by globalisation include the denial of human rights; the attack on religious beliefs in an increasingly secular social order; a quickening of the process of deterritorialisation and its obligation to redefine spatial relationships; a shift in the old certainties of global strategic relationships; a change in the nature of the state and its legitimising philosophy of national self-interest enshrined in the sovereignty of the citizen; the direction of world development and our common hopes and fears as we face a succession of global environmental crises.

As with modernisation in past times, globalisation is an ideological programme of thought and action, for it is not merely an account of how the world is changing, but also a *prescription* of how it *should* change. As yet we do not have complete global economic change; rather, we have increased macro-regional functional integration in Western Europe, North America and increasingly, in parts of South and East Asia, especially China. But the cumulative impact of these trading blocs is to establish a new regime whereby barriers to capital, trade and influence are reduced and the race for resources, uniform product standards, manufacturing and technology transfer is increased. Social and cultural change are deeply implicated in this world vision, and we have enough evidence to recognise that some groups and regions will be advantaged, and others marginalised as globalisation is entrenched (Cerny, 1999). However, globalisation is neither an inevitable nor an uncontested process. Fragmentation and dissolution so often follow periods of aggrandisement. We need more information before practical measures can be designed to specify how minorities may cope with these new challenges. We also need data on how the recent strengthening of the European Union influences the impact of these diverse processes on selected regions?

One final element stressed by nationalists and regionalists is the democratic involvement of those who live in a region or locality. This is particularly the case with regard to contested issues such as the environment, urban policy, spatial planning, or tourism (Judge *et al.*, 1995). The answer to this problem may lie in devising new forms of institutional design more appropriate to a system of governance than a system of government. It may be that the latter, based on hierarchy, routine and slow responses, needs to be complemented by a system that is more flexible, horizontal and open and that can respond to the ever-increasing challenges of a turbulent environment. This is the thrust of the volume with its discussion of new forms of governance, deliberative and cosmopolitan democracy and the politics of mutual respect.

Conclusion

The key questions posed in this chapter concern how the processes summarised under "globalisation" and "deterritorialisation" affect the maintenance of regional identities and the transformation of corresponding regional spaces? We are not yet at the dawn of a "Europe of the Regions" despite a campaign which has lasted for well over a generation. But we daily witness the emergence of new regional actors whose cumulative impact on the territorial state-nation will be profound (Keating and Loughlin, 1997). Tension and conflict between all the processes at different levels will be inevitable; such is the nature of our competitive system. But I also detect a strong yearning for mutual understanding, rapprochement and partnership which may yet prevail if the appropriate supportive political and economic infra-structures can be constructed. Chauvinistic nationalism will not entertain constructive partnerships and democrats are right to be alarmed by its growth in Europe. But liberal, communitarian nationalism may yet prove an effective anchor for some who appear to have lost control and purchase in a system dominated by ever-increasing currents of globalisation and systemic integration.

Notes

1. Epistemologically, as Loughlin (1999) argues, the debate concerns the manner in which our minds grasp reality, either analytically or synthetically, or at least which of these two aspects is dominant. Methodologically, the debate is between "methodological individualism", which usually takes the form of rational choice approaches, and approaches that are more structuralist, culturalist or institutionalist. Normatively, in terms of public policy, the question is whether democratic practice can be based on the notion that the individual citizen is a member of a collectivity or whether he/she should be seen as a consumerist, rational individual making choices with regard to the use of public services. If the latter model is adopted, "public" services are increasingly redefined in a more "privatised" fashion.
2. Fascinating accounts may be found in Anderson (2000), Guibernau and Hutchinson (2001), Hutchinson and Smith (1994), McCrone (1998) and Smith (2000). For an excellent overview of geographic perspectives see Kaiser (1999).
3. As illustration see Agnew (1987), Paddison (1993), Williams (1988b, 1999).
4. Johnston *et al.* (1990).
5. e.g. Johnson (1995).

6. Blaut (1987).
7. The two notions of nation as *demos* and nation as *ethnos* are closely related. In France membership of the French nation obliged individuals to assimilate to French culture and language. In Germany, cultural nationhood found its expression in a democratic system or nation as demos – consolidated only in the second half of the twentieth century. However, in all countries and nationalist movements there is a tension between these two aspects of nationhood and this is one of the reasons for the difficulties many contemporary states and nationalist movements have in defining the meanings of nationality and citizenship (Alter 1994; Loughlin, 2001; Loughlin and Williams, 2007).
8. This is especially true given the recent better showing of nationalist parties within the various constituent elements of both the UK and Spain.
9. In multi-ethnic polities ethnic separatism often derives from an acute concern over the erosion of a group's identity and resource base. Separatists, such as ETA, assert that ethnic discrimination can only be halted through the transformation of their territory to form a sovereign state co-equal with all other states. Regionalists assert that one need not go so far as to break up the state but insist that its internal affairs should reflect its plural character. In tandem, both regionalists and separatists pose fresh challenges to the territorially-fixed nature of monopolistic sovereign space.
10. In analysing the nature of those trends which conduce to a regionalised Europe we need to differentiate between *regionalisation*, identified as the regional application of state policy and *regionalism*, defined as the attempt to optimise the interests of a region's population through the manipulation of the political process. In this essay the inter-relationship of globalisation and localism, holistic and ecological ideas, and reformed conceptions of space occasioned by telematic revolutions will figure strongly as we seek to advance our understanding of the role of nationalism in European politics.
11. On typologies of nationalism see Breuilly (1982), Orridge and Williams (1982), Smith (1981, 1982), and for a political geographic overview see Williams (1994), pp. 1–53 and Taylor (1993), pp. 191–228.
12. For a series of insightful geographic essays on the rebirth of the nationalities question in Europe, see van Amersfoort and Knippenberg (1991).
13. This new approach is represented in the work of scholars such as Jönsson *et al.* (2000), and the research of the ECPR "Territorial Politics and Regionalism" group (see Keating and Louhglin, 1997; Loughlin, 2001; Keating, 2004).
14. Democracy is also about citizens holding decision-makers accountable for their activities and this is becoming increasingly difficult given this shift in power.
15. Thus it is almost certain that expressions of nationalism, rather than wither away under the pressures emanating from a stronger EU, will in fact re-vivify themselves, most often perhaps in conjunction with other regional or environmentally-based political movements.
16. Jönsson *et al.* (2000) have used the network metaphor to capture the essence of the three simultaneous processes of globalisation, regionalisation and state adaptation. They warn against repeating the three most common mistakes when speculating about the future: "the first is to assume that the future will be entirely different from the past; the second is to believe that it will be just the same; and the third, and most serious, mistake is not to think about it at all" (p. 189).
17. Nationalism and environmentalism represent themselves as also holistic in thought and deed. The universal desideratum is the ideal nation-state in an international community of free and equal states. Its local manifestation may be at

any one of the varying stages in a continuum from full statehood through to a non-state nation in the making, but whatever its exact position it is always possible to relate the local to the global blueprint and back again. So it is with environmentalism. The unique character of the local environment is only given purchase by the general context of the global milieu. but it is given its urgency by the near-cataclysmic refraction of fundamental global issues viz. the green house effect, the destruction of the tropical rain forest, the degradation of soil and sustenance, the disappearance of species and habitat. Intrinsic to this coupling of the immediate and local to the evolutionary and global is a sense of shared involvement and responsibility, summed up as "Our common future". For an excellent account of such movements see Galtung (1986).

18. However, most minority nationalisms justify their existence by a claim to separateness, usually on the basis of a unique cultural heritage.

19. Klemencic and Klemencic (1997) offer a systematic, cartographic analysis of the historical identification of the north-eastern Adriatic peoples with key locations and illustrate just how rooted are conceptions of land, language and nationhood in the European imagination.

20. How often in Europe have we heard the charge that minority schools are the breeding ground for a new generation of dissenting nationalists? And throughout Western Europe and North America we have new demands for centrally controlled educational curricula rather than tolerate regional variations which may, in part, perpetuate group divisions and sectarian animosities.

21. It is a moot point, however, and one which demands considerable restructuring, to appreciate how such small nations will fare better when faced with a plethora of competing claims in Europe, than in seeking redress of their grievances within the existing state structure. Similarly in Québec, as the movement towards greater autonomy gathers apace, critics argue that increased cultural erosion will accompany independence because the Québécois state will not have the federal system to protect it in its dealings with foreign powers and agencies.

22. Thus serious questions are raised regarding the capacity of the state to render impartial judgements on this issue. Moore also draws attention to the parallel situation of indigenous peoples vis à vis their land claims against forcible occupation and loss of entitlement to traditional land rights.

23. The United Kingdom and the Scandinavian countries passed directly to liberal democracy, without major revolutionary upheavals or reversals. Most other states – France, Germany, Italy, and Spain to name just a few of the large states – alternated between democratic and non-democratic forms of regime before finally settling down in the democratic family. Finland has also progressed smoothly to liberal democracy, although it did experience a civil war in the 1920s.

24. There is also a limited number of distinct state forms such as federal and unitary states capable of further differentiation (Loughlin, 1996a). Thus there exist different types of federations such as "dual federalism", where the different levels of the federation operate independently of each other, as in Belgium or the United States, and "co-operative federalism", where the levels operate in close conjunction with each other, as in Germany (Hix, 1998). However, "unitary" states are also differentiated. First, the United Kingdom has been described as a "union" rather than a unitary state given that its formation occurred through a series of Acts of Union, with Wales Scotland and Ireland respectively (Urwin, 1982). Among the rest, there are a variety of central-local relationships giving rise to distinct models of unitary state: centralised unitary, decentralised unitary, regionalised unitary (Loughlin, 1996b). There thus emerges a complex picture

of the variety of the expression of democracy at the national and subnational levels within the member states of the European Union as illustrated in Table 2.1. All of these state forms, operating within state traditions, would claim to be "nation-states" but, clearly, this general concept has been interpreted in a variety of ways. The importance of state traditions for the understanding and expression of nationalism lies in the ways in which the institutions of liberal democracy and the practices of policy-making have developed.

25. The different ways of electing political parties affects the probability as to whether or not nationalist movements will be represented within the electoral system. In some cases, the regional and local political systems replicate the national, in others it is different. The key question, which few have addressed, is whether nationalist movements are more or less successful if they adopt a form of electoral strategy which mimics that of state-centric parties. A second key question is whether or not the electoral system allows a form of proportional representation, a reform which certainly improved the representation of Scottish and Welsh nationalist members within the devolved bodies of Scotland and Wales.

26. A further point made in Loughlin *et al.*'s (1999) study with regard to changing local patterns of governance is that there is in western and central Europe a tradition of local self-government and autonomy that predates the emergence of the nation-state. Cases in point are the cities of the Hanseatic League or the Italian city states such as Florence and Venice. Although these communes were not fully democratic being ruled by local oligarchies, nevertheless, the tradition of communalism may be regarded as a forerunner of local democracy. Without accepting the thesis of a neo-medievalism (because of the very "modern" or "post-modern nature of these developments) it is clear that one of the consequences of the changing nature of the nation-state and the loosening of central-local bonds is that this tradition is reasserting itself today.

27. This notion originally referred to a federal Europe in which the constituent units would be not the nation-states, but the regions (at least those that possessed a strong identity such as Corsica, Brittany, Flanders, Wales, Scotland, etc.). Clearly, such a federal Europe is highly unlikely today, as nation-states will remain the key levels of government within the Union. Nevertheless, the term is valuable as an indicator of the new importance of regions in the new Europe.

28. Countries such as Spain, Portugal and Greece which became members not long after having experienced non-democratic systems found that membership helped them to consolidate their democratic systems. A similar argument is used in favour of Turkey's accession.

29. The British government has suggested that a new body representing the national parliaments might be created to oversee the activities of the Commission.

30. Ireland is the most spectacular of all and is sometimes referred to as the "Celtic Tiger" by analogy with the Asian tigers.

31. The most significant development was the establishment of the European Bureau for Lesser Used Languages in 1984. Located initially in Dublin but then central-ised in Brussels, this small but effective organisation has sought to co-ordinate and nurture inter-linguistic experience and transfer good practice from one group to another (O'Riagain, 1989; Williams, 1993b). Other initiatives involve the Con-ference on Local and Regional Authorities of Europe with its Charter on European Regional and Minority Languages (Council of Europe, 1992). Politically the most important reinvigorated actor is the Council for Security and Cooperation in Europe (CSCE) which has increased its involvement in minority group rights since 1989. Although still evolving as the re-constituted Organisation for Security and

Cooperation in Europe (OSCE) it has detailed the rights and obligations of both minorities and host governments throughout Europe and has put into practice several of the key ideas advanced by specialist and minority rights agencies alike (Minority Rights Group, 1991; Williams, 1993a).

32. Universities in Wales offer an excellent example of this dependence, for while the UK government has extended the super-grid to Cardif, so that Cardiff University benefits in terms of scientific, engineering, medical and other research areas, all other universities in Wales are effectively cut off from the latest mass developments as they do not have access to the infra-structure.

3
The Democratic Impulse and Social Justice

Introduction

An inherent ambiguity lies at the heart of the debate on the social and cultural future of Europe. Both individuals and a multitude of ethnocultural groups increasingly interact within decentralised and diverse frameworks, while the political system which guarantees such autonomy is becoming evermore centralised within the supra-national structures of an expanding EU and its associated organisations. The traditional method of reducing ethnocultural diversity by closing or redrawing borders no longer applies, as the geography of bounded space gives way – at least in theory – to a geography of communication flows, and a new strategy for mutual coexistence demands the deterritorialisation of identity. The sad truth for many in Europe today, however, is that the direction and speed of this transition is precisely the point at issue. Although the most satisfactory method of ensuring cultural autonomy is to allow individuals to determine group membership for themselves, this dilutes the geographical concentration of ethnic groups and renders many of them vulnerable within a multicultural framework: ambiguity, tension and conflict are the inevitable consequences (Lijphart, 1995).

At the Treaty of Versailles in 1919, European statesmen proclaimed that they had satisfied most of the outstanding claims for national self-determination by redrawing the political geographical boundaries so as to make nation and state congruent, as far as that was feasible (Figure 3.1). National minorities and ethnic nationalism were now likely to give way to the growing class and interest group politics as the dominant pattern of post-war reconstruction. A new normative international system had been established, and despite the dynamics of revolutionary idealism in Russia from 1917 onwards, an uneasy balance between internationalism and nationalism ensued for much of the crisis-ridden twentieth century. Also for much of the period, the influence of revolutionary and socialist thought, first in Europe and later in Latin America, branded political programmes

48

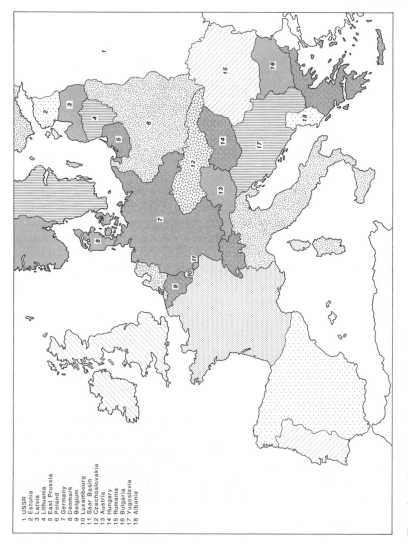

1 USSR
2 Estonia
3 Latvia
4 Lithuania
5 East Prussia
6 Poland
7 Germany
8 Denmark
9 Belgium
10 Luxembourg
11 Saar Basin
12 Czechoslovakia
13 Austria
14 Hungary
15 Rumania
16 Bulgaria
17 Yugoslavia
18 Albania

Figure 3.1 European nation states in 1921

in defence of the nation, and of national minorities, as regressive. Lenin's reformulation of internationalism offered both a new framework for action and the seductive appeal of global impulses having revolutionary local effects. According to Halliday "the result was that in many of the anti-colonial revolutions of the latter half of the twentieth century the core elements of the Marxist perspective were reproduced, in altered or indeed wholly distinct theoretical and political contexts" (1999, p. 88). Lenin's reformulation of an international perspective based on imperialism,

> was to provide a new basis for any international conceptualisation of revolutionary struggle: the unity of the oppressed peoples was given not so much by the workings of a world market, or by the property-less and hence nation-less character of the oppressed, but by the unity of the structure of the oppression, namely imperialism, and the separate but convergent revolts of the Third World peoples against it.
>
> (Halliday, 1999, p. 88)

In contrast to the appeals of Che Guevara, Régis Debray, or Ho Chi Minh, those of an earlier generation of nationalists such as Sabino Arana, Enric Prat de la Riba and Saunders Lewis, appeared not only decidedly Catholic and Conservative, but wholly counter-productive if the aim was to rid the oppressed nations of the double shackles of foreign occupation and imperialism.

But against all expectation, the question of suppressed nations, and that of the rights of national minorities, did not fade away. Indeed it might be argued that the greater struggle between revolutionary communism and liberal democracy, which was played out under the shadow, first of Fascism and then of the Cold War, masked a continued preoccupation with the political programme of the unsatisfied nationalities ignored by the Versailles Treaty makers.

In addressing the contradictory and spatially complex nature of this increasingly multicultural system the chapter focuses on language and, to a lesser extent, religion, as components of a European identity that offer a pro-found insight into the range of possibilities which the contemporary world allows. At one open and receptive pole of a European spectrum are the key players of international politics and commerce, together with their advisors, civil servants, lobbyists and journalists, each of whom brings into play a diverse range of language skills, whether active or passive, and a different set of assumptions as to the appropriate role of cross-cultural communic-ative competence. Close behind, occupying a rather more independent and fluid position, are the educated youth of Europe, whose command of "European Pigeon English" or some other "Language of Wider Communica-tion" allows them access to international culture, sport, entertainment and education. Occupying the centre of the spectrum is the post-1945 generation whose knowledge of two or more languages may be rather limited, but who nevertheless espouse a healthy attitude to European-wide culture, cuisine, films, travel and personal contact. Towards the other end of the spectrum are different types of relatively deprived groups. One is the monolingual majority of long-established nation-states, who may conceive of themselves as participants in European integration, but at a more prosaic level than that of their children. Finally, we have a number of social groups, many of them minorities, who by virtue of their exclusion from decision-making and wealth-creation potential are denied full access to participatory democracy and social progress. The chapter will examine the ways in which language identification and religious affiliation influence access to mainstream European development. In so doing, it addresses the central question as to how we might construct a European identity, which is based upon the recognition of cultural diversity as a key element of social and political life.

Historically, language and religion have often been treated as the critical markers of a distinct cultural identity, a useful shorthand in which to describe a complex reality. Such close correspondence can no longer be entertained, for linguistic identification and religious affiliations are increasingly divorced from each other. As discussed in the previous chapter, the cultural inheritance of a Catholic, Latin civilisation gradually gave way in post-medieval Europe to a system of nation-states. Conflict was inherent in the political, cultural and economic processes, which underpinned the emergence of the territorial bureaucratic nation-state as the prime locus of political activity. This was particularly so in terms of language and religion, where both the past abrogation of rights and the continued refusal of states to grant social demands, promoted ethnic conflict and fragmentation.

Why is a common language so often seen as essential to "nation-building" or state development? If conflict is such a predictable outcome, why not opt for linguistic and cultural pluralism as a dominant ideology? The answer is surely that language is power which enables dominant elites to confer privilege, deny opportunity, construct a new social order and radically modify an inherited past which is not conducive to the pursuit of hegemonic aims. Language choice is thus a battleground for contending discourses, ideologies and interpretations of the multi-ethnic experience.

The argument advanced in this chapter is that it is both advisable, and feasible, to construct a political framework in Europe, which acknowledges the positive virtues of cultural pluralism on the basis of equality as a necessary prerequisite for democracy and freedom of action in an increasingly multicultural world order. This raises issues concerned with the distribution of power in society and the encouragement of democratic participation by previously beleaguered interest groups. A *sine qua non* of their recognition is mutual respect and structures of freedom, which guarantee the conditions for cultural reproduction. As the former Yugoslavia graphically illustrates, and as the reconstruction in Bosnia and Kosova periodically pricks our conscience, open conflict and warfare is too pressing a reality for many beleaguered groups. They also serve to remind us that current periods of peace and tolerance can revert to periodic episodes of resistance and struggle, for such is the fragility of empires of loathing.

The construction of Europe-wide institutions has to deal with the diversity and tensions resulting from an international political system designed to suit the vagaries of nineteenth- and early twentieth-century statecraft, and the ensuing lack of congruence between multicultural citizenries and the sense of order prescribed by national conceptions of the modern state (Williams, 1989b). Although there are indications that the neo-liberal conception of the unitary state, based upon representative democracy, is yielding to the logic of the enabling state with its focus on participatory democracy, this transition is either illusionary or faltering in many parts of Europe. The management of cultural diversity as a permanent feature of the international social order is among the most taxing of political issues facing modern Europe.

Religion, language and diversity: The socio-cultural renegotiation of Europe

The foundation of any modern democracy lies in the ability of citizens to derive maximum security and satisfaction from their contribution to the common wealth of society. Historically, several societies allowed for instrumental pluralism as a societal norm because a broad measure of freedom from state interference provided the necessary breathing space for the peaceful co-existence of citizens. Habermas (1996) argues that such space permitted citizens of widely diverging cultural identities to be simultaneously members of, and strangers in, their own country. The historical reproduction of dissenting cultures was, in part, a function of relatively weak economic-structural assimilation, often compounded by geographical distancing from the cores of the emerging nation-states. Their maintenance today in the face of much stronger pressures for inclusion is all the more difficult. Increased secularisation in the West and the enforced totalitarian conformity that described Central and Eastern Europe prior to 1989, have greatly damaged the primacy of Catholicism, Protestantism and Orthodoxy. When we add the catastrophic effects of the Holocaust on Jewish community life, then it is little wonder that organised religion is a markedly less salient part of mainstream society. The only exceptions which appear to have witnessed real growth are the faiths of non-European migrants and their descendants, such as Sikhs and Hindus in Great Britain, together with Islamic believers throughout much of Europe (Gerholm and Lithman, 1990) and a plethora of evangelical variants of fundamentalist Protestantism. However, although organised Christian religion may have declined absolutely, ample evidence exists to suggest that much of the habit of obedience to their religion displayed by earlier generations was culturally determined, and not the outcome of an individual conviction to join a particular religious community. Thus, despite the absolute decline in the number of adherents, religious faith will continue to contribute to European social life and its diversity and not just as the tabloid banner headline where Catholic is pitched against Protestant in Northern Ireland, or where members of the Muslim nation within Bosnia-Herzegovina are set against their Orthodox and Catholic neighbours (Zametica, 1992).

Turning to language, if it is accepted that a lack of congruence exists between the formal political system and the cultural inheritance of its constituent citizens, this is rendered even more complex by the friction that exists between attempts to maintain linguistic diversity and the increasing linguistic standardisation apparent throughout the world. This contradiction is important because tensions related to religion and language often serve as mobilising factors for conflict within which other grievances are then pursued. At the global scale, it is estimated that some 6170 living languages – exclusive of dialects – are contained within the 185 or so sovereign states (a number that rises to around 200 if dependencies and semi-autonomous polities are included) (Mackey, 1991). Less than 100 of these *c.* 6000 languages are "official", since 120 states have adopted English, French, Spanish or Arabic as their official language, while some 50 states have their own indigenous official language (15 per cent have two or more). If a further 45 regional languages are added, it remains the case that only about 1.5 per cent of the world's total spoken languages are formally recognised. The situation is even more polarised in that only one per cent of the world's languages are used by more than half a million speakers and only 10 per cent by more than 100,000. Hundreds of languages have no adolescent speakers at all and thus we are continuously losing parts of our global linguistic diversity (Williams, 1995b).

If it is also accepted that most minority ethnic-linguistic groups are relatively underdeveloped economically and politically, it is clear that questions of language, culture and identity are not merely supplementary to the more routine socio-economic concerns of development. Rather, they may constitute the very essence of a subordinated group's relationship with the state in whose name the dominant group exercises power and control. It is not surprising that any threat to the immediate territory of a subordinated group is interpreted as a challenge to culture and group survival. Place and territory are critical in the process of control and development and their appropriation by external agencies has a long history in Europe, related to the extension of state hegemony and projects of state-building and nation-formation, processes which are all essentially contestations over space.

The incorporation of ethnically differentiated territories was a necessary precursor to the creation of the territorial-bureaucratic state that came to dominate the political geography of Europe between the eighteenth and twentieth centuries. European state development was often over-centralised around national capital cores, without any corresponding attention to the interests of "minorities", except, of course the need to subject them to political and strategic integration. This has led, as for example in Spain and France, to charges of core discrimination, peripheral marginalisation and the denial of group rights and cultural reproduction. For some this is a necessary product of global development, but should state formation involve the denial of local and regional distinctiveness? Must we perforce sacrifice cultural autonomy – at whatever scale – to promote the hegemony of particular political-economic structures? Multicultural societies necessitate choices but, given the competitive nature of cultures in contact, these options also promote conflicts and tensions, one person's choice being another's denial of opportunity.

In Western Europe, the twin processes of nation-building and state integration engaged language and religion as agencies of political unification. Thus since medieval times, religious competition, for example, was regulated by a layered system of legal securities. This involved the principle of coexistence in religiously mixed imperial cities and the realisation of the *cuius regio eius religio*, following the uneasy agreement between Catholics and Protestants which ensued from the Religious Peace of Augsburg in 1555. The law gave rights to overlords to determine the faith of their territories and not to the subjects, who were theoretically free to emigrate. The principle was hailed as the most important element of the rise of the secular territorial state, one that together with the *ius reformandi* (which was also tied to territorial privileges) formed the legal-geographical basis for the structural transition from Holy Roman Empire to Enlightenment state system. Nevertheless, most dissenting remnants in the secular territorial states, whether Catholic or Protestant, did not survive intact. They could survive "only under cover, in isolation, and for short periods of time. Stringent control made it impossible to establish parties which did not conform to the official creed. Persecution and expulsion followed immediately upon discovery" (Klein, 1978, p. 57).

State sovereignty was given primacy within the international system following the 1648 Peace of Westphalia settlement which ended the Thirty Years War. All other rules that subsequently developed into a system of international law are based on the authority of the state to govern its own internal affairs without let or hindrance from outside bodies. The axiomatic claim that a system based on respecting state sovereignty is necessary to maintain order and stability went unchallenged until the turn of the twentieth century.

Moore (2001) argues that the minimalist rules vision of international law implicit in the Westphalian system has increasingly been challenged by a more solidarist conception of international law, which has gained purchase in the twentieth century. This perspective is characterised by an emphasis on substantive norms and values to govern international security, rather than mere coexistence. Moore demonstrates how increased intervention by external agencies, whether the UN or NATO, was not solely motivated by the self-interest of the most powerful states. In Somalia, Bosnia, Rwanda, Haiti, Kurdistan, Kosovo, East Timor and other places, there was an element of preventing a humanitarian disaster or reducing the scale of ethnic conflict. Such desires outweighed the respect for the territorial inviolability and state sovereignty of the places concerned. Contemporary Iraq, sadly, does not rest so comfortably within the same moral compass, for the "empire of ignorance" which invaded it cannot also claim to be purveyors of democracy abroad. Consider the Economist's view quoted in Alterman and Green (2004, pp. 329–30):

> Imperialism and democracy are at odds with each other. The one implies hierarchy and subordination, the other equality and freedom of choice. People nowadays are not willing to bow down before an emperor, even a benevolent one, in order to be democratised. They will protest, and the ensuing pain will be felt by the imperial power as well as by its subjects.
>
> For Americans, the pain will not be just a matter of budget deficits and body bags; it will also be a blow to the very heart of what makes them American – their constitutional belief in freedom. Freedom is in their blood; it is integral to their sense of themselves. It binds them together as nothing else does, neither ethnicity, nor religion, nor language. And it is rooted in hostility to imperialism – the imperial rule of George III. Americans know that empires lack democratic legitimacy. Indeed, they once had a tea party to prove it.

The realist-nationalist impulses which dominated the Bush administration (Kagan, 2003) may be pushing Europe and America further apart and realists may scoff at the idealist vision of contemporary Europe so often portrayed in the grand rhetoric of EU Presidential pronouncements. Yet there is a sense in which America judged at a very early stage in its constitutional development that an abiding European malaise, namely state religion, should not be allowed to damage its national unity.

Thus both America and Europe have demonstrated that state-enforced linguistic and educational policies can create a common nationality in time. However, both continents have demonstrated, in quite different ways, that religious adherence is less amenable to state intervention. In Europe despite centuries of legally enforced religious observance, frequently at the point of the sword, sometimes the cross, star or crescent, religious antagonism remains. Nowhere is this more evident than in East Central Europe which has long been characterised by its religious plurality. As Davies (1996, p. 504) observes, in a world of "growing religious intolerance, Poland-Lithuania occupied a place apart. A vast territory ... it contained a mosaic of the Catholic, Orthodox, Judaic, and Muslim faiths even before Lutheranism claimed the cities of Polish Prussia or Calvinism a sizeable section of the nobility." Magosci (1993, p. 48) emphasises the region's pivotal role within European religious history when he states that:

> it was at the center of the dividing line between the Catholic and the Orthodox worlds; it experienced the first serious challenges to the unity within these two Christian worlds (Bogomilism in religiously mixed Bosnia during the thirteenth and fourteenth centuries and Hussitism in Catholic Bohemia-Moravia in the fifteenth century); and virtually its entire southern half had by the sixteenth century come under the rule of the Ottomans, who implanted the Muslim faith throughout their expanded domain. With such a tradition of religious pluralism, it is not surprising that the lands of East Central Europe, in particular its northern "non-Ottoman" half, proved to be fertile ground for the spread of the Protestant Reformation.

This in turn led to the promotion of Protestant values at home and abroad. The imperial mission, both Catholic and Protestant, had a powerful substratum of exporting faith as well as goods and services. Contemporary Africa and Asia not only demonstrate the pervasive spread of English and Spanish, but also contribute to the global networks of communication through their participation in science, technology, entertainment and the service sector using both autochthonous and European languages. This dual linguistic trend sometimes leads to a convergence which is well reported and has given rise, for example, to the notion of English in India being considered an "indigenous" language.

However, a parallel trend that has received less attention is

> the almost simultaneous reconfiguration of the religious geography of the world. Religions which were formerly the preserve of the subject peoples of colonial rule – Hinduism, Buddhism and Islam – now have large and growing constituencies in the Western world, and not simply as a result of migration flows. Conversely, Christianity, which in 1900 appeared to be primarily a religion of the very same Western nations that controlled the colonial system, has propagated itself in the former colonial territories and diversified to the extent that it is now in numerical terms more a religion of the South and East than of the North and West, regions in which it is generally in decline.
>
> (Stanley, 2003, p. 1)

The role of the churches and mission societies in propagating the verities of God, Queen and Country in the imperial heyday of Victorian England is very well documented. What is less well understood is the contribution of the churches and mission societies to the democratic impulse of decolonisation and the end of empire. Here a fundamental tension existed between the universality intrinsic to Christian theology and the appeal of anti-colonial nationalism with its insistence on national self-determination, which so often included alongside the establishment of a national army and legal system, a national church.

"Yet orthodox Christianity, which supplied, whether willingly or unwillingly, much of the moral vocabulary and rhetoric undergirding the civilizing mission of empire is seen, strangely, to be irrelevant to its end" (Stanley, 2003, p. 2).

However, I am convinced that the experience of the dissolution of empires, the rise of independent states in Africa and Asia and the increased consciousness of occupying a single, finite planet earth, has quickened the desire for democratic participation and social justice on the part of autochthonous minorities, the main focus of this volume.

Our present conception of the rights of subjects and citizens has evolved such that the principle of freedom from state direction or oppression in religious or linguistic matters has given way to a demand for freedom to be represented on the basis of equality within society as the determining essence of the participative state. Nowhere are these rights so fiercely conjoined and attacked than in the question of ethno-linguistic identities in the modern state. The new politics of recognition in Europe belatedly represents an attempt to compensate for the earlier systematic exclusion of many minority groups from the decision-making structures of society. This is not to deny such earlier attempts to specify the rights and obligations of minority cultures but these prerogatives were often granted on the assumption that no permanent change would result to the state from such reforms. It was understood that the clarification of the nature and meaning of minority rights would not overly interfere with mainstream political business and economic development. However, the current transition from representative democracy to participatory democracy, at least within parts of Europe, requires the decoupling of the state majority from its hegemonic position. As Habermas (1996, p. 289) argues:

> Hidden behind such a facade of cultural homogeneity, there would at best appear the oppressive maintenance of a hegemonic majority culture. If, however, different cultural, ethnic and religious subcultures are to co-exist and interact on equal terms within the same political community, the majority culture must give up its historical prerogative to define the official terms of that *generalized* political culture, which is to be shared by all citizens, regardless of where they come from and how they live. The majority culture must be decoupled from a political culture all can be expected to join.

The nature of civil rights: Inclusion versus exclusion

Thus those who are constructing the new Europe must search for a binding substitute for state nationalism. Geographically fixed identities, based upon real or putative representations of cultural homogeneity, have to yield to more fluid, heterogeneous forms of social interaction. Our conceptions of human rights are now being formulated in an increasingly comprehensive manner to include elements which earlier theorists would have considered to have lain outside the proper remit of the citizen-state relationship (Close, 1995). This relationship is central to my analysis, since democracy avers that citizens are entitled to certain minimum rights, chiefly those of participation in – and protection by – the state. The changing nature of the state, however, both as ideology and practice, has encouraged a more pluralist view of its responsibilities.

The conventional view, characteristic of many Western societies until the early post-World War II period, held that the state should not discriminate against – or be in favour of – particular sub-groups, however these might be defined. This view – the individual rights approach – is often justified by majoritarian principles of equality of all before the law, and is implemen-ted through policies of equal opportunity for socio-economic advancement based upon merit and application. In reality, however, in most multi-faith societies, the state persistently discriminated, by law, against religious and other minorities, be they Jews, Catholics, Protestants or Romany. However, the admittedly patchy improvement in the treatment of minorities, and the resultant constructive dialogue between representatives of interest groups and governmental agencies at all levels in the political hierarchy, bodes well for the medium term future enactment of minority rights.

An alternative view, the group rights approach, has found increasing favour of late, for it recognises that there are permanent entities within society whose potential and expectations cannot be met by reference to the recognition of individual rights alone. In the main, such recognition is offered grudgingly, reflecting a minimalist stance, which seeks to extend the tradition of individual rights into a multicultural context. Such extensions tend to obscure the key issue of group tension, namely the ability of the minority to preserve and, if possible, develop its own group characteristics and desires in the face of state-inspired assimilation.

Two sorts of argument are posed to counter the "special pleading" of con-stituent differentiated groups in the contemporary world (Williams, 1993a). The first contends that the prime duty of the democratic state is to treat all of its citizens equally, regardless of racial, national, ethnic or linguistic origin. The state should be neutral or at least blind as to the ethnic origin of the supplicant. Conversely, it can be argued that minorities should not require "extra rights" if the necessary democratic guarantees are in place. Both inter-pretations are understandable in a political context, which stresses the role of the reformed state as the agent and co-ordinator of radical change. Thus the growth of democratic representative power in, for example, Central Europe enables the state to pose as the guardian of civic rights, while individualism strives to triumph over collectivism in terms of human rights, social justice and economic productivity.

The challenge to liberal democracies is both real and very pressing, but what does equal representation mean if public institutions do not recognise particular identities, and allow only for general or universal recognition of shared interests based upon civil and political liberties, education, health care and economic participation? Public recognition of the worth of constituent cultures, as *permanent* entities in society, is what is at stake in liberal democracies. For many engaged in the politics of their group's survival, this is precisely what democracy should guarantee in practice as well as in principle. When it refuses to engage in the politics of recognition, liberal democracy appears arrogant and denies the life-enhancing spirit upon which all forms of democracy are based. It accentuates fragmentation and anomie within society, ultimately leading to various forms of disengagement from public life and community responsibility. Democratic "citizenship develops its force of social integration, that is to say it generates solidarity between strangers, if it can be recognised and appreciated as the very mechanism by which the legal and material infra-structure of actually preferred forms of life is secured" (Habermas, 1996, p. 290).

The real difficulty for such interpretations lies in maintaining the active participation of all citizens in the ensuing political process. It is far too tempting for many to yield responsibility and to opt out of formal politics altogether, joining instead informal pressure groups or single-issue movements, meanwhile leaving proponents of the community drained of their energies to mobilise and agitate on behalf of all. A concern for an active participatory democracy is surely relevant in most developed societies, where talk of "the hollow state" and of "the democratic deficit" reveal the shallowness of the general public's trust in professional politicians (Williams, 1994). There is, moreover, an urgent need to establish democratic credentials in the more "liberal" post-Communist societies after forty or so years of state totalitarianism. But the pristine democratic principles of co-equality, majoritarian tolerance, and freedom under the law to reproduce individual or collective identity, have not necessarily guaranteed nor satisfied minority aspirations in Western European societies. In Central and Eastern Europe, there is even less consensus about the nature of mass society, let alone the legitimacy of selected minorities in multi-ethnic societies (Williams, 1997b). Social justice is not necessarily served by a compliant reliance upon a constitutional majority, whether it acts in a benign manner or otherwise. Indeed the contemporary situation in Central and Eastern Europe is enigmatic, many previously warring factions apparently converging on a new conformity. This threatens, however, to be every bit as stultifying as the old system, as new forms of radical dissent are marginalised. We may be set for a new round of language and other related conflict as geo-strategic considerations clash with the emancipatory demands of mobilised minorities.

This situation arises because reconstructing societies face two opposing notions of justice. While one holds that justice is the apportioning of rewards to groups on the basis of proportionality, the other suggests that justice should consider the established rights of individuals, regardless of national origin, language, religion or any other diacritical cultural marker (Glazer, 1977). In an individualistic society, the majority would favour merit as a guiding principle of selection. The various constituent minorities would counter, however – and with some justification – that this merely reproduces their marginalised and pejorative position as permanent dependencies. If the state adopts a diffusion perspective of ethnic change, viewing group identities as malleable and group membership as a purely private affair, it will conceive of group rights as a barrier to minority assimilation and as a basis for maintaining permanent divisions within the state (Glazer, 1977). Conversely, if the state conceives of its constituent cultural groups as forming part of an established ethnically plural society, then it must legislate and act to demarcate the rights of each group.

None the less, a profound difference exists between the stated policies of governments towards minorities, as enunciated, for example, at international conventions, and the actual treatment of differentiated citizens at the local level. It is unduly facile to rest content with either individualist or collectivist paradigms of language contact management. Liberalism is not a neutral ideology. The liberal democratic state is much more than a referee for the warring factions contained within its bosom. Thus rather than presume that one universal solution exists to the question of managing ethnic pluralism in Europe and elsewhere, it is more instructive to draw attention to the sheer variety of assumptions about the nature of majority – minority relations inherent in models of ethnic integration. One of the most important is a scheme developed by Kallen (1995) and sketched out in Table 3.1.

This conceptualisation, which informs the remainder of the discussion in the chapter, envisages a four-fold model of integration. The first is the "melting pot" model, with its emphasis on integration and the creation of one nation/one people. In theory, this system should produce a non-discriminatory national identity. Second, the "mosaic" model refers to the cultural pluralism of a nation comprised of many peoples and cultures. Presently more applicable, perhaps, to the extra-European world, this model leads to hyphenated ethnic-national identities in societies that do not depend on institutionalised discrimination. It is possible to envisage, therefore, a future Europe comprised of Irish-Europeans, German-Europeans and so on, imitating the situation that still pertains in the United States. Third, "dominant conformity" which effectively describes the formation of nation-states in Europe, where a dominant culture and people frame the state in its

Table 3.1 Assumptions behind models of integration

Variables	Melting Pot (Integration)	Mosaic (Cultural pluralism)	Dominant conformity (Absorption)	Paternalism (Colonialism)
1. Societal Goal: Ethnicity and Nationality	One nation/one people/one culture	One nation/many peoples/many cultures	One nation/one people/one culture (dominant)	One dominant nation/people/ culture subordinated minorities
2. Symmetry/ Asymmetry of political, economic and social power	Symmetric (population relatively equal)	Symmetric	Asymmetric (dominant population is superordinate)	Asymmetric (dominant population monopolizes power)
3. Ethnocentrisim willingness/ability to maintain/shed	Low ethnocentrism willing and able to shed distinctiveness	High ethnocentrism willing and able to maintain distinctiveness	*Dominant*-high ethnocentrism willing and able to maintain distinctiveness *minorities*-low ethnocentrism willing and able to shed distinctiveness	*Dominant*-high ethnocentrism willing and able to maintain distinctiveness *minorities*-low ethnocentrism unable to shed distinctiveness (racial/ascribed)
4. Levels of prejudice and discrimination	Non-discriminatory low or absent prejudice	Prejudice and discrimination not institutionalized	Institutional and cultural discrimination; level of prejudice and discrimination *dominant*-high, intolerant *minority*-low (willing to conform to majority norms)	Institutional, cultural, structural discrimination; level of prejudice and discrimination: *dominant*-high, intolerant *minority*-stigmatised permanently

61

5. Criteria for social mobility	Achieved	Achieved	Achieved and ascribed	*Dominant*-achieved *within* stratum *minorities*-ascribed status is permanent: no mobility
6. Spheres of ethnocultural distinctiveness	None	Variable *public* (polit-ical/economic/linguistic pluralism) *private* (multiculturalism) *territorial* (nationalism)	*dominant*-public and private *minority*-acculturation required	*dominant*-public and *minority*-deculturation promoted/partial acculturation required
7. Collective identity	National identity (de-ethnicized)	Hyphenated-identity (ethnic-national)	national identity =dominant ethnic identity	*dominant*-national entity+dominant ethnic identity; *minority*-negative valence of marginal identity
8. Human Rights	Individual human rights	Individual and collective rights (collective, cultural and collective, national)	Individual rights of minorities predicated on dominant conformity; collective rights of dominant group entrenched at societal-wide level	*Dominant*-individual and collective rights *minority*-no human rights, systematic violation of rights

Source: Adapted with permission from Kallen, 1995, pp. 164–5.

own image and discriminate institutionally against minorities. Finally, we have the "paternalistic" model which describes the relationships between coloniser and colonised, with a dominant nation, culture or people imposing its values on subordinated minorities. This model effectively describes the history of states such as Ireland or Poland and, although no longer applicable, its legacy can still be detected in the national constructions of such states.

The politics of equal respect in multicultural societies

Kallen's model encapsulates the dichotomy between exclusive and inclusive definitions of civil rights. Contemporary Europe is facing a period of readjustment, following a series of structural transformations, which, cumulatively, have seen a greater recognition being accorded to its indigenous minorities. But what sort of multiculturalism are we discussing and how does it seek to promote the politics of mutual respect? Let us consider the difficulties of operating an ideology of multiculturalism within a model of liberal society, which purports to recognise more than the mere survival of cultures by acknowledging their permanent worth. The liberal assumption that "treating everyone alike" is the answer to structural inequality, and discrimination rests on a view of human nature that is deeply problematic, because it makes constant recourse to the "inner" humanity. While we are undoubtedly biologically one species, human differentiation is so contextualised that it would be absurd and pernicious to adopt a "oneness" approach in all situations, for so often that is a mask for the reproduction of hegemonic oppression. Rowan Williams puts it thus: "But human existence is precisely life that is lived in speech and relation, and so in history: what we share as humans is not a human 'essence' outside history, but a common involvement in the limits and relativities of history. The only humanity we have is one that is bound up in the encounter of physical and linguistic strangers" (Williams, R., 2000, p. 282).

A major difficulty in the post-modern period concerns the threat posed to communitarian democracy by the growth of special interest groups. The recognition of religious and linguistic rights has encouraged the belief that increased cultural pluralism is a reflection of increased mutual tolerance. Yet tolerance *per se* does not necessarily follow, for it depends upon which groups have received recognition for what purpose and in which contexts. A powerful analogy may be read over from the field of race relations. Some racial acts are overt, perverse and readily condemned within a liberal democracy. But racism, *per se*, is not overt and thus as Williams asserts it must be hidden; "it must be buried deep in our consciousness, needing to be excavated by suitable means" (Williams, R., 2000, p. 278) The oppression of the poor, and the oppression of the ethnically or racially distinct have in common one feature articulated by Ann Dummett (1973) and highlighted by Williams thus "the oppressor makes the claim to *tell you who you are*, irrespective of your intention, will, preference, performance. Only certain people have the right to construct an identity for themselves; others have their roles scripted for them" (Williams, 2000, p. 280).

> If a dominant culture (linguistic, ethnic, sexual) does in fact work by assuming the right to definition, it is hardly surprising if the reaction is "We don't need you to tell us what we are." Certain kinds of separatism are necessary to highlight the reality of a difference that has been over-ridden by the powerful conscripting the powerless into their story. Far from being a domesticated curiosity, whose strangeness or otherness is defused by absorption, functionalised by the dominant group, the disad-vantaged group must become *real* strangers, with a life manifestly *not* like that of their former masters. They must acquire or reacquire a kind of shared secret, a distinct human "dialect" bound up with a distinct group life. Oppressed groups have often done this even in the midst of their very oppression – secret languages, covert religious rituals, a subterranean scheme of authority relations within the group. Liberation has something to do with the presenting and owning in public of this reality of shared life behind and beyond the roles defined by the power-holders; and this means an accentuation, not an erosion, of difference – which is why racial justice and racial equality do not begin with "treating everyone alike."
>
> (Williams, 2000, p. 282)

There is at least one further complication. While some autochthonous (or indigenous) minorities are being treated according to policies, which assume pluralism as the basis of equality, other non-indigenous minorit-ies are being treated according to policies predicated on pluralism as the basis of non-equality. How do these two trends impact the one upon the other with regard to a liberalism of rights in language and religious matters?

Taylor (1992, p. 61) argues that the politics of equal respect embodied within the discourse of recognition, does not serve us well as we imagine. Instead, there is "a form of the politics of equal respect, as enshrined in a lib-eralism of rights that is inhospitable to difference". This "insists on uniform application of the rules defining these rights, without exception, and . . . is suspicious of collective goals". Taylor calls it "inhospitable" because the con-struct cannot "accommodate what the members of distinct societies really aspire to, which is survival". This is a collective goal, which will inevitably demand some variation in the kinds of law that are deemed permissible from one cultural context to another.

Clearly the dread hand of homogenisation can lie heavy on any attempt to maintain diversity through an appeal to universal considerations of human dignity and worth. Yet the filter process by which some decide the relative worth of others is far too imperfect. At its root lies an inherent paradox between the demands for equality and the forces for efficiency. As Taylor (1992, p. 71) contends:

> The peremptory demand for favourable judgements of worth is paradoxically – perhaps one should say tragically – homogenising. For it implies that we already have the standards to make such judgements. By implicitly invoking our standards to judge all civilization and cultures, the politics of difference can end up making everyone the same.

Taylor believes that the demand for equal recognition is unacceptable. Rather we require a more humble approach, which does not imply the pejorativisation of all other cultures. This, of course, presumes that cultural diversity is not only a growing feature of most societies, but also a positive and worthy feature. It has value both at the individual level of recognising human worth and also at a societal level, where it legitimises access to political power and frees participation in the democratic process. It follows that the ways of managing cultural diversity will vary according to why we think it has value.

A great stumbling block, however, in the recognition of equal worth is the operation of the market and bureaucratic state, which – in Taylor's view – "tends to strengthen the enframings that favour an atomist and instrumentalist stance to the world and others" (1991, p. 11). Community solidarity and public participation in the decision-making process are weakened and religious or ethno-linguistic groupings, intent upon their own survival, may be drawn closer into their own sub-cultures rather than forming a distinct part of the whole society, a process that accentuates the fragmented nature of mass society.

> This fragmentation comes about partly through a weakening of the bonds of sympathy, partly in a self-feeding way, through the failure of democratic initiative itself. Because the more fragmented a democratic electorate is in this sense, the more they transfer their political energies to promoting their partial groupings, and the less possible it is to mobilise democratic majorities around a commonly understood programme.
>
> (Taylor, 1991, p. 113)

Fragmentation and anomie seem to be winning the day for far too many previously committed citizens. And yet, in principle, they all possess the right of free association, free speech and political representation, the hallmarks of a modern democracy. Religious and linguistic distinctiveness rests both on special interest recognition and on the maintenance of a common social order, which affirm both ordinary life and also recognises its *limits*. This is an especially urgent consideration in South-eastern Europe and on the margins of Central Europe. In order to sustain religious and socio-linguistic pluralism here, as elsewhere, a re-definition of the essence of political engagement is required. Elshtain (1994, p. 79) argues that the affirmation of ordinary life has not been a primary passion of political philosophy but in order to retrieve that ordinariness we require a new socio-political project that tames and limits "the demands of sovereignty – both sovereign state and sovereign self". The politics Elshtain has in mind "shifts the focus of political loyalty and identity from sacrifice and control to responsibility" (1994, p. 79). In questioning whether a post-sovereign state politics is possible, Elshtain cites the writings of the President of the Czech Republic, Václav Hável, and urges us to forge civic identities in such a way that blood sacrifice is not so pervasive a demand and possibility. Hável's move from sacrifice to responsibility is best summarised in *Disturbing the peace* (1990) in which he argues that:

> We are going through a great departure from God which has no parallel in history. As far as I know, we are living in the middle of the first atheistic civilization. This departure has its own complex intellectual and cultural causes: it is related to the development of science, technology, and human knowledge, and to the whole modern upsurge of interest in the human intellect and the human spirit. I feel that this arrogant anthropocentrisim of modern man, who is convinced that he can know everything and bring everything under his control, is somewhere in the background of the present crisis. It seems to me that if the world is to change for the better it must start with a change in human consciousness, in the very humanness of modern man. Man must in some way come to his senses.
>
> (Hável, 1990, p. 11)

The politics of self-control does not mean, as some have implied, the removal of all limits on the human condition. Taylor offers a warning and a correction to some aspects of post-modernist thought when he writes:

> it is a thinking which moves from the undeniable fact that the aspiration to take responsibility involved in the displacement of *some* limits, to the conclusion that this aspiration inherently amounts to a rejection of *all* limits. In other words, it confounds the original aspiration and its aberrant form. This is a bad mistake, indeed, a potentially catastrophic one for us who cannot but share the modern identity.
>
> (Taylor, 1994, p. 233)

But there are other grounds for arguing that claims to an exclusive identity that shut people out are inherently contrary to the common interest of any democracy. Rowan Williams has drawn attention to the universal claim that, at root, a Christian doctrine of inclusivity is inherently political. By this he means that "Christian ethics can never be happy with a model of justice that is solely or even primarily reparative. The good or interest of the excluded matters not in itself but as the indispensable and unique contribution it constitutes to the good of all" (Williams, 2000, p. 263).

> The language of "rights" is an important *dialectical* moment in ethical discourse, but becomes sterile when it is divorced from a proper conception of the human good that has to be worked out in conversation with others. In that sense, strange as it may seem to put it thus, Christian ethics is relentlessly political, because it cannot be adequately expressed in terms of atomised rights invested in individuals or groups, but looks beyond to the kind of community in which free interaction for the sake of each other is possible. That means adjustment and listening; it means politics.
>
> (Williams, 2000, p. 263)

This is an important reminder that the issues with which we are concerned in this volume are the preserve of ordinary people. It may take international conventions, national parliaments and language policy agencies to implement the resultant rights, duties and obligations we are discussing. But the fundamental call to liberty and exercise of freedom are first and foremost an expression of communal living before they become transposed into political theory, theology or party doctrine. The "one" makes no real sense without the contextualised "many" and neither are fully intelligible without the many layers of hidden oppression being articulated and exposed.

Language policy and conflict in Europe

We now move on to consider the ways in which these socio-political forces are played out in linguistic terms and to assess the ensuing consequences for social policy and citizenship in the new Europe. As a mechanism for behaviour modification, language policy and planning depends largely on four attributes identified by Stewart (1968). These are the degrees of, standardisation, autonomy, historicity, and vitality. These characteristics of language freedom are critical in helping planners to evaluate existing language functions and to harness the dynamic cultural interactions that characterise many multilingual societies. Stewart proposes a typology of language (Table 4.1) which recognises the multiplicity of linguistic functions that can exist even within ostensibly one nation/one people/one culture states.

Most European societies have retained the language policies which were critical to the nineteenth-century project of constructing the territorial-bureaucratic nation-state. Consequently they face severe difficulties in matching their inherited institutional agencies and organisational structures to the reality of serving the legitimate demands of increasingly multilingual populations. Historically, we can identify four types of language policy implicated in the processes of European state formation. The first and most common – as found in France, Spain and Britain – reinforced political and cultural autonomy by giving primacy to one indigenous language and thus enforcing it, and no other, as the language of government, administration, law, education and commerce. In so doing, a number of goals were achieved simultaneously. Among these was the search for national integrity, the legitimisation of the new regime and its state apparatus, the re-establishment of indigenous social organisations, the reduction of dependence upon external organisations and influences, and the incorporation of all the citizenry in a wide range of para-public social domains. Foreign languages were reserved for the very specialised functions of higher education, international diplomacy and commerce.

A second type of language planning characterises those situations in which the "national" goal has been to maintain cultural pluralism, largely that the state might survive through containing its inherent tensions. Under this system, language was used to define regional associations rather than state or national citizenship. It is best exemplified in Europe by Switzerland's decentralisation, which incorporates cantonal unilingualism within a multilingual federal system, and the rigidly enforced division of Belgium between its Walloon- and Flemish-speaking populations.

The third form of language planning has occurred when a recognised minority was granted some degree of geographical distinction, based upon the territoriality principle of language rights. In Finland, for example, high levels of language contact along the west coast, marked religious uniformity, a strong tradition of centralised government, and the unifying effects of long-term external threats, led to a recognition that the minority Swedish-speaking population should be accorded official status. Following the 1922 Language Law, all communes were classified as unilingual Finnish, unilingual Swedish, or bilingual if they contained a linguistic minority of either group of 10 per cent or more; these classifications were revised after each decennial census to take account of changing linguistic geography (McRae, 1997). In comparative terms, the Finnish system of official bilingualism is characterised by a gross disparity in numbers, asymmetry in language contact, and instability over time, leading McRae to conclude that such institutional arrangements for language accommodation have been functional in terms of conflict moderation and management, but less so for language stability.

A fourth option – the modernisation of an indigenous tongue – is diagnostic of societies disengaging from colonial relationships and the cultural hegemony of a dominant state. This form of language planning was a key goal of the nationalist intelligentsia in Hungary, Ireland, Finland and Norway prior to independence, and remains critical to the political programme of nationalists and regionalists in Catalonia, Euskadi, Brittany and Wales today.

Each of these four types will be elaborated upon in the next chapter. For the moment it is enough to state that language planning in a multilingual society is not a precise instrument and is as capable of being manipulated as is any other aspect of state policy. Nevertheless, it is an essential feature of the economic and political restructuring of many states. The key issues are:

- who decides – and on what basis – such bi- or multi-lingualism is to be constructed?
- which languages are chosen?
- who benefits by acts of state-sponsored social and identity formation?
- how is language-related conflict managed and reduced?

Two conditions are necessary for competition to arise between language groups. First, the languages must share a common contact space, however defined, be it geographic, political, social, economic, cultural or religious in nature. Secondly, the relationship between these two languages must become the symbolic stakes of the competition, which takes place on the level of the shared space.

Laponce (1987, p. 266) has advanced the following four propositions about languages in contact:

- languages tend to form homogenous spatial groupings;
- when languages come into contact they tend either to specialise their functions or to stratify;
- the specialisation and the stratification of languages is determined by the socially dominant group;
- the social dominance of a language is a function of . . . the number of its speakers and the political and social stratification of the linguistic groups in contact.

How do minority interest groups influence the state structure so that it concedes certain rights, which are not requested by the majority? Concessions always follow contact and conflict, and may involve the use of a previously disallowed language within public administration and the legal system, or a religious-based education provision, or differentiated access to the media. Such reforms may be predicated on the basis of a personality or a territoriality principle or some expedient admixture of both (Nelde *et al.*, 1992).

Research in contact linguistics demonstrates that conflict cannot be resolved by means of a universal model for conflict reduction. On the contrary, procedures must be considered that are adaptable to each situation. Nelde *et al.* (1992) have argued that measures of linguistic planning, such as the principle of territoriality, are not in themselves sufficient to avoid conflicts, but they can soften the repercussions in the socio-economic, cultural and linguistic life of multilingual populations. They believe that many conflicts can be partially neutralised if the following conditions are observed:

- the territoriality principle should be limited to a few key areas like administration and education;
- the institutional multilingualism that emerges should lead to the creation of independent unilingual networks, which grant equal opportunity of communication to minority and majority speakers. These networks should also exclude linguistic discrimination connected with speakers of the prestige language;
- measures of linguistic planning should not be based exclusively on linguistic censuses carried out by the respective governments. Rather, they must genuinely take account of the situational and contextual characteristics of the linguistic groups;
- minority linguistic groups in a multilingual country should not be judged primarily on quantitative grounds. On the contrary, they should be awarded more rights and possibilities of development than would be due to them based on their numbers and their proportion to the majority.

Nelde *et al.* believe that according such equality to minorities by assuring them of more rights could result in fewer people adopting an intransigent ideological position, thereby lessening the infusion of emotionalism so often apparent in linguistic conflicts. One obvious conclusion is that unless far more attention is paid to the rights of lesser-used language speakers, then more conflict will ensue. Another is the potential loss of creativity and spontaneity mediated through one's own language(s), thus contributing to a quenching of the human spirit, and a reduction in what some have termed the ecology of "linguodiversity" (Skutnabb-Kangas, 1997; Williams, 1991). This latter reason alone may prove convincing to many. But need linguistic decline sound the death-knell for particular ethnic identities in Europe? As Edwards (1994) and Williams (1991) have argued, no necessary correspondence exists between linguistic reproduction and ethnic identity. Indeed cultural activities and symbolic manifestations of ethnicity often continue long after a group's language declines. None the less, increased interdependence at the European level implies more harmonisation for the already advantaged groups. In making multiculturalism more accessible, long-quiescent minorities will be rebuffed as they seek to institutionalise their cultures. It is not necessarily a tale of decline and rejection, however, for opportunities do exist to influence state and provincial legislatures and metropolitan political systems.

Linguistic hegemony

The project of European unity, combined with other macro-processes such as globalisation, poses a threat to conventional territorial relationships and simultaneously opens up new forms of inter-regional interaction such as cable television and global multi-service networks. However, choosing between the promotion of one or many languages in the educational domain and public agencies of new states is becoming less of a "free choice", as the increasing burdens of economic, social and cultural development crowd in on the limited resources available for language planning and its implementation. The increasing globalisation of economic, political and cultural relationships is one major constraint in language choice. But there is also the counter-trend of regional diversity, which emphasises the value of cultural diversity and the worth of each specific language, not least as a primary marker of identity. Concern over endangered languages in Europe has produced a re-examination of the relationship between culture, development and political identity (Williams, 1993b).

As a result of imperialism, neo-colonialism, the modernisation of technology and the globalisation of information flows, an air of acute inevitability surrounds the universalisation of hegemonic languages, primarily English, French and Spanish. Transnational languages have been significant elements of imperial rule since Classical times, and greatly influenced the spread of capitalism and the modern world system. English and French are also crucial to the development of former colonies, providing the basis on which these countries relate to the former metropolitan powers and to each other through the Commonwealth and *la francophonie* (Gordon, 1978; Williams, 1996b).

At the heart of the debate on European identity lies a consideration of the role of hegemonic languages as both symbol and instrument of integration. English – the premier language for international commerce and discourse – is used by over 1500 million people world-wide as an official language, of whom some 320 million have it as a home language (Crystal, 1987; Gunnermark and Kenrick, 1985). Should English be encouraged as the official language enabling most Europeans to communicate with each other? Or is it desirable to attempt to slow down its inevitable global spread? Critics claim that the spread of English perpetuates an unequal relationship between "developed" and "developing" societies. While access to information and power demands fluency, it also requires institutional structures, economic resources and power relationships. Tollefson (2001, p. 84) reminds us that:

> in order to gain access to English-language resources, nations must develop the necessary institutions, such as research and development offices, "think tanks" research universities, and corporations, as well as ties to institutions that control scientific and technological information. From the perspective of "modernising" countries, the process

of modernization entails opening their institutions to direct influence and control by countries that dominate scientific and technical information . . . the result is an unequal relationship.

The functions of English are nearly always described in positive terms. Language, and the ideology it conveys, is thus part of the legitimisation of positions within the global division of labour. However, attempts to separate English as a European bridge language or from its British and North American value systems are misguided, for English should not be interpreted as if it were primarily a *tabula rasa*. Any claim that English is now a neutral, pragmatic tool for global development is disingenuous, being:

> . . . part of the rationalization process whereby the unequal power relations between English and other languages are explained and legitimated. It fits into the familiar linguistic pattern of the dominant language creating an external image of itself, other languages being devalued and the relationship between the two rationalised in favour of the dominant language. This applies to each type of argument, whether persuasion, bargaining, or threats are used, all of which serve to reproduce English linguistic hegemony.
>
> (Phillipson, 1992, p. 288)

Such points emphasise that conflict is inherent in language issues and helps explain why multicultural education – far from encouraging the positive aspects of cultural pluralism – has hitherto been characterised by mutual antagonism, begrudging reforms and ghettoisation. Spatial segregation and social isolation have become mutually reinforcing patterns in far too many communities.

There are signs, however, within contemporary Europe that official languages are coming to terms with the realities of integration and globalisation. Of the major languages, German is likely to spread as a result of the revitalisation of Central and Eastern European commerce. It is Spanish, however, which seems set to be a major international, trans-continental bridge language. In global terms, if Spanish can be seen as a resource for socio-cultural growth as well as commercial gain, there could be a win-win situation rather than a zero-sum stand off between supporters of English and those of Hispanic-based bilingualism, especially in the Americas (Baker, 1996) – in its technological and commercial sectors. Renewed languages such as Welsh, Frisian or Basque have penetrated into new domains, such as local administration, education and the media. In contrast threatened minority languages such as Romany or Skolt Lapp will be further marginalised. Because of their high fertility rates, some groups are experiencing linguistic reproduction rates greater than one, and their prospects for survival look promising, especially in constructing an infrastructure for domain extension in education, government and broadcasting. Conversely, however, some

autochthonous language speakers are rapidly losing their control in traditional core areas as a result of out-migration, capital-intensive economic
development and increased mobility. The fact that lesser-used language
speakers have become highly politicised in the last thirty years should not
divert attention away from their fears of cultural attrition. So much of their
collective hopes and aspirations rest on the construction of an appropriate
political and socio-economic infra-structure.

An additional consideration is that many European migrants and refugees
who settled in another European country, often as a consequence of the
two World Wars, have lost the native language of their forebears. To them
markers such as diet, music or the visual arts, have replaced language as
the primary linkage with their wider cultural communities (Rystad, 1990).
Fundamental questions surround the symbolic bases of their culture and the
degree to which one may characterise residual elements as either authentic
or as expressing an integral identity. This is a major feature of Europe's
cultural heritage and will prove a testing ground for more sensitive and
flexible applications of any policy of multiculturalism. It is a problem most
acutely expressed in the recent re-discovery among many residents of Central
Europe of their German heritage and of their potential relationship with a
unified and re-invigorated German-dominated *Mitteleuropa* policy.

Perhaps the greatest challenge facing framers of European identity comes
from non-European migrants and their descendants, especially as globalising
perspectives will reinforce the need for link languages other than English
in this realm. Initially this will result from private and commercial-oriented
demands, but as the total size and significance of link languages – especially Islamic-related variants – grows, then there will be pressure to reform
public agencies and the educational system, particularly in France, the UK,
Germany, Belgium and the Netherlands. The increased presence of non-
nationals within European states will add to the alienated feelings of many
recent migrants that they do not belong by right to any particular state. As
Miles argues, the ideological notion of a "migrant" becomes embedded in
the reproduction of hegemony, especially in religious life:

> Once "we" all know who "the immigrants" are, and once the state has
> indicated that their presence is undesirable and that their numbers should
> be controlled or reduced, all uncritical and unreflexive use of the category
> legitimates the official definition and the related conspiracy of silence
> about all other immigrants whom the state does not "see" and who are
> excluded from public view.
>
> (Miles, 1993, p. 207)

Conclusion

Clearly the state is deeply implicated in the direction of change with
regard to multicultural policy. As society becomes more plural, and social

mobility increases, greater tensions occur between the functional provision of bilingual public services and the formal organisation of territorial-based authorities charged with such provision. These conflicts are exacerbated by immigration into fragile language areas, which leads to the public contestation of language-related issues as each new domain is penetrated by the intrusive language group. Such sentiments are hard to gainsay. The difficulty lies in determining what proportion of the public purse is to be expended upon satisfying the legitimate demands of this policy. Issues of principle, ideology and policy are frequently no more than thinly disguised disputes over levels of resource expenditure. One arm of government is involved in extending the remit of pluralism whilst another is reigning in the fiscal obligations to so act. Either way, dependent cultures are tied inexorably to the largesse of the state. Governments are obliged to maintain their support for many multicultural projects, albeit simultaneously signalling their intent to withdraw public finances and welcome private sector funding. Either way, the languages and cultures of visible minorities are in danger of being expropriated by external forces, while cultural dependency is being increased. As they become better organised, however, astute minority groups will press for greater recognition of their cultural rights, seeking the individual choice and empowerment to decide their lifestyle and future prospects as participative citizens. From this perspective, multiculturalism is a set of institutional opportunities for individual and group advancement in a competitive environment. In other words it becomes a platform for social progress.

The politics of mutual respect presuppose a historically well entrenched democratic order. The watchwords of the open society are redistributive social justice, participatory democracy and mutual tolerance. Majorities must always seek to temper their individual rights in the light of their collective impact on minorities. We must also address the implications of this balancing act, if we are to honour the full range of multilingual expectations and needs in Europe's major cities and densely populated regions. This in turn presupposes a political-juridical framework, adequate to ensuring that increased cultural contact will not lead to escalating conflict. Cultural communities are best represented when the state guarantees individual freedom of association and protection. "Cultural rights protect autonomy. They do this inasmuch as they look to guarantee the stability of the cultural environment within which the individual is able to exercise the capacity to make meaningful choices" (Kukathas, 1995, p. 241). Thus the urgent task of geographers, in association with others, is to locate the place of such cultural environments as constituents of European integration, and to identify the impact of policy on all citizens, regardless of the contested values that are ascribed to them.

4
Language Policy and Planning Issues in Multicultural Societies

State-Civil society relations

Issues of language choice and behaviour are integral to the social, economic and political stability of multicultural societies. This chapter explores the role of language policy and planning as instruments of social development and examines selected dilemmas faced by multilingual states as they seek to formalise language choice through a variety of implicit and explicit language-related reforms. It is my conviction that language planning can only be properly understood when seen as a form of socio-political intervention. Many take the view that language planning, as a discipline, has developed a certain objective detachment that allows it to be treated as if it were a form of scientific exercise. I accept that in certain aspects, such as corpus planning, translation and software development, such objectivity and precision is reached. However, language planning is in essence an extension of social policy aimed at behaviour modification. Given this it is essential that the broader social and political context, within which language planning is exercised, is fully acknowledged. Consequently the first part of this chapter discusses the various implications of recognising some languages at the expense of others within liberal democratic practices. It then suggests comparisons between the European and African experiences of language planning, before focussing on power differentials between hegemonic language groups and dependent language groups.

As one of the chief components of group identity and the means by which the ideas and techniques of social development are diffused, language has become one of the most sensitive issues of the contemporary world. It is estimated that some 6170 living languages (Mackey, 1991, p. 51), exclusive of dialects, are contained within the 187 or so sovereign states, and if we admit dependencies and semi-autonomous polities, the number rises to *c*. 200. Consequently there is a lack of congruence between the international political system and the cultural inheritance of its constituent citizens. This suggests that there will be a near-permanent crisis involving attempts to maintain linguistic diversity in the face of increasing linguistic standardisation in many parts of the world. Often language issues are an overarching mobilising factor within which other issues are pursued. Language-related tensions thus exacerbate normal socio-political strains. It follows that a sovereign state's language policy can be a key determinant of the degree to which political unity and the rate of economic "development" are achieved. If a language policy is harmonious and effective, it releases collective energies into other more profitable avenues. If on the other hand, it is authoritarian, divisive and dysfunctional, it can lead to alienation, pressures for regional separatism and ultimately to civil war or disintegration.

The multilingual character of most societies necessitates choices in communication at all levels from the individual to the state. Choice also implies conflict and tension, for one person's choice is another person's denial of opportunity; such is the competitive nature of languages in contact. The situation is complicated in many contexts because international migration and colonialism have introduced a new range of intrusive languages of wider communication (LWC) whose presence both challenge the indigenous languages and have a profound influence on the nature of the process of global development.

The state is central to any analysis of the impact of language policies on multicultural societies as the incorporation of ethnically differentiated territories has been a necessary precursor to the creation of the territorial-bureaucratic state. Normally incorporation strengthens central rather than local interests, and serves to threaten the material and spiritual sustenance which ethnic groups derive from the immediate locale. In consequence, patterns of state integration and development are often over-centralised, without a corresponding attention to the needs of the "periphery", except, of course, the need to integrate it politically and strategically. This has led to charges of core discrimination, peripheral marginalisation and the denial of group rights and cultural reproduction. For some this is a necessary product of global development. But should the price of economic and bureaucratic incorporation into the mainstream involve the denial of distinctiveness? Must we perforce sacrifice cultural autonomy for political-economic advancement in multicultural societies? For far too many subject peoples, state-integration has resulted in the conquest of ethnic territory, the denial of popular rights, and the external development of their ethnic homeland. Whether through forced out-migration as a result of land enclosure, such as Scotland in the eighteenth century clearances, or apartheid South Africa after 1948, of famine, Ireland in the 1840s, Sudan, 1980–1994; Ethiopia, 1984–1994, of resource exploitation, as happened to the Maori or Canada's First Nations and Inuit, rapid industrialisation, as in Euskadi in the late nineteenth century, most ethnic-linguistic minority groups perceive their territory as having been under threat in modern history.

Because institutional means of dissent are denied them, subject peoples invariably focus on cultural diacritical markers, such as language or religion, as a means of asserting their own separateness and demonstrating their resistance to external state and commercial incursions into their territory. If we accept that most ethnic-linguistic groups are relatively underdeveloped economically and politically, it is clear that questions of language, culture and identity are not merely supplementary to the more routinised socio-economic concerns of development. They can constitute the very essence of a subordinated group's relationship with the state in whose name the dominant group exercises power and control. As group identity and power differentials are rooted in their environment and expressed through material acts of construction or change, it is not surprising that any threat to the immediate territory of a subordinated group is interpreted as a challenge to their culture and group survival. Place, boundaries and territory are critical in the process of control and development and their appropriation by external agencies has a long history related to the extension of state hegemony and strategic, capital projects of "state-building" and "nation-formation", which are essentially contestations over space. The various ways in which this may be organised are summarised in Table 4.1.

In this schema, which combines typologies elaborated by Lijphart and Lehmbruch, systems of governing may be categorised as being organised according to basic principles: the way in which political relations are organised – majority rule or consociation (Lijphart) and conceptualised – according to a principle of the common good or of individual interests (Lembruch). This leads to a matrix of four possible modes of governance each with its own country or system exemplar: statism (France); corporatism (Switzerland and Germany); pluralism (United States); and network governance (EU). Kohler-Koch's typology is useful as it illustrates that there exist a variety of state traditions and also that the EU is not simply a system of governance *sui generis* but can be analyzed comparatively in the context of these state traditions.

Table 4.1   A typology of modes of Governance

		Organising principle of political relations	
		Majority Rule	**Consociation**
Constitutive logic of the polity	Common good	*Statism*	*Corporatism*
	Individual interests	*Pluralism*	*Network governance*

Source: Beate Kohler-Koch (1999), reproduced in Loughlin and Williams (2007).

The principle of equal recognition in liberal democracies

By the late twentieth century our conception of the rights of subjects and citizens had evolved such that the principle of *freedom from* state direction or oppression in religious or linguistic matters had given way to a demand for *freedom to* be represented on the basis of equality within society as the determining essence of the participative state. Nowhere are these rights so fiercely conjoined and attacked than in the question of ethno-linguistic identities in the modern state. How to promote the mutual respect of individuals as they identify with particular social groups is a key challenge facing language policy.

The new politics of recognition is a belated attempt to compensate for the systematic exclusion of groups from the decision-making structures of society. Previous attempts to specify the rights and obligations of minority cultures often presumed that no permanent change would result from such reforms. A basic tenet of liberal democracy was that legislation to clarify the meaning of minority rights would not overly interfere with mainstream political business and economic development. But the current transition from representative democracy to participatory democracy, at least within parts of the European Union, requires the decoupling of the state majority from its hegemonic position (Habermas, 1996, p. 289). The framers of the European experiment must search for a binding substitute for the initial state nationalism which determined the process of nation-building.

Our conceptions of human rights have been formulated in an increasingly comprehensive manner to include elements, which earlier theorists would have considered to have lain outside the proper remit of the citizen-state relationship. This relationship is central to the analysis since liberal democracy avers that citizens are entitled to certain minimum rights, chiefly those of participation in and protection by the state. However, the changing nature of the state, both as ideology and praxis, has encouraged a more pluralist view of its responsibilities.

The conventional, individual rights approach is that the state should not discriminate against or be in favour of particular sub-groups, however they may be defined. This is justified by majoritarian principles of equality of all before the law, and is implemented through legislation enabling equal opportunity for socio-economic advancement to be based upon merit and application. The fact that many states persistently discriminated, by law, against Jews/Catholics/Protestants/Romany in most multi-faith societies should never be marginalised in this discussion, for so often the state has exercised a malignant effect upon minorities, thereby blighting their historical development. Even when individual rights regimes have been extended to cover the interests of national minorities, they are rarely satisfied with such provision. Kymlicka (2001) cites three particularly contentious issues: decisions about internal migration/settlement policies, decisions about the boundaries and powers of internal political units, and decisions about official languages. The partial improvement in the treatment of minorities and the resultant constructive dialogue between representatives of the various interest groups and governmental agencies at all levels in the political hierarchy of Canada and Western Europe offers a more realistic basis for the future enactment of minority rights.

Alternatively, the group rights approach, favoured of late, recognises that there are permanent entities within society whose potential and expectations cannot be met by reference to the recognition of individual rights alone. Such recognition is offered grudgingly, and reflects a minimalist stance that seeks to extend the individual rights tradition into a multi-cultural context. Such extensions tend to obscure the key issue of group tension, namely the ability of the minority to preserve, and if possible, develop its own group characteristics and desires, in the face of state inspired assimilation (Williams, 1989a, 2000b). Eisenberg (1998) illustrates from the Canadian North how the debates over Aboriginal rights have been distorted by the construction of the dualism between Western "individualism" and Aboriginal "collectivism". By framing the debate thus, the real issue is masked, namely the ongoing effects of political subordination through colonisation which progresses the majority's unilateral attempts to undermine the minority's institutions and powers of self-government (cited in Kymlicka, 2001, p. 77).

When beleaguered groups protest that their voice is often ignored in favour of the greater needs of society, they are being thwarted by a perversion of majoritarian democracy. Three sorts of argument are posed to counter the "special pleading" of constituent differentiated groups in the contemporary world (Williams, 1993a, p. 95). The first argues that the democratic state has a duty to treat all its citizens equally, regardless of racial, national, ethnic or linguistic origin. Hável (1991) maintains that minorities should not need "extra rights" if the democratic guarantees are in place, an understandable interpretation in the Czech political context which stresses the role of the reforming state as the guarantor of individual freedoms. The second argument, heard most forcibly in the USA and France, is that minorities should meld over time into mainstream society.[1] But the greater recognition of the worth of constituent cultures, as *permanent* entities in society, is precisely what is at stake for those engaged in the politics of their group's survival within liberal democracies. When liberal democracy refuses to engage in the politics of recognition, it appears arrogant and denies the life-enhancing spirit upon which all forms of democracy are based. It accentuates societal fragmentation and anomie, ultimately leading to various forms of disengagement from public life and community responsibility. For "democratic citizenship develops its force of social integration, that is to say it generates solidarity between strangers, if it can be recognised and appreciated as the very mechanism by which the legal and material infra-structure of actually preferred forms of life is secured" (Habermas, p. 290).

The third argument suggest that collective rights or community rights are difficult to articulate in constitutional-legal terms and leads to obfuscation over both the target language and the defined holders of such rights. As we shall see in Chapter Nine, if the protection of French in Quebec belongs to a collectivity, which is it? The francophone Quebecers, the population as a whole or the State of Quebec represented by the Attorney General? Marc Chevrier (2003) has teased out these relationships and argues that government policy must find a way to navigate between the conflicting impulses to protect, proscribe and encourage via legislation and marketing campaigns in Quebec.

The integrative challenge is in maintaining the active participation of all citizens in the resultant political process. It is tempting for many citizens to yield responsibility and to opt out of formal politics and to opt in to informal pressure groups or single-issue movements, leaving proponents of the community drained of their energies to mobilise and agitate on behalf of all. A concern for an active participatory democracy is surely relevant in most developed societies, where talk of "the hollow state" and of "the democratic deficit" reveal the shallowness of the general public's trust in professional politicians (Williams, 1994).

There is also an urgency to establish democratic credentials in the more "liberal" post-communist societies after fifty or so years of state totalitarianism. But the pristine democratic principles of co-equality, majoritarian tolerance, freedom under the law to reproduce individual or collective identity, have not necessarily guaranteed nor satisfied minority aspirations in Western European societies. In Central and Eastern Europe there is even less consensus about the nature of mass society, let alone the legitimacy of selected minorities in multi-ethnic societies. Social justice is not necessarily served by a compliant reliance upon a constitutional majority, whether it acts in a benign manner or otherwise. Indeed the contemporary situation in Eastern Europe is enigmatic, for many previously warring factions seem to be converging on a notion of a new conformity, which threatens to be every bit as stultifying as the old system, as new forms of radical dissent are squeezed out of the picture. We are set for a new round of language-related conflict as geo-strategic considerations clash with the emancipatory demands of mobilised minorities.

It is too facile to rest content with either individualist or collectivist paradigms of language legislation. Liberalism is not a neutral ideology. The liberal democratic state is much more than a referee for the warring factions contained within its bosom. Thus rather than presume that there exists one universal solution to the question of managing ethno-linguistic pluralism, it is more instructive to draw attention to the sheer variety of assumptions about the nature of majority-minority relations inherent in models of social integration as we saw in relation to Kallen's formulation above at Table 3.1. Kallen's (1995) analysis has set forth an incisive account of inductive and deductive models of social reality, which conceives ethnic integration as a "social doctrine that provides guidelines for the attainment of an ideal mode of accommodation of ethnic diversity in society".

Within Kallen's four models of melting pot, mosaic, dominant conformity and paternalism we have a differentiation between exclusive and inclusive definitions of civil rights. Europe and North America are witnessing a series of structural transformations that accord greater recognition to minorities. How do various forms of multiculturalism seek to promote the politics of mutual respect? Let us consider the difficulties of operating an ideology of multiculturalism within a model of liberal society that purports to recognise more than the mere survival of cultures by acknowledging their permanent worth.

The extreme delicacy of a rights-based approach to language policy is well recognised. "Equality of rights is the precondition of recognition, but it is not sufficient to ensure it." (Ignatieff, 2000, p. 86). In similar vein, Tollefson (2001, p. 197) argues that "Language rights are a fragile base for language policy, . . . constant struggle is necessary to protect rights, even in a country with a long historical commitment to – and a federal structure which supports it – a pluralist language policy."

The modern recognition of religious and linguistic rights has encouraged the belief that increased cultural pluralism is a reflection of increased mutual tolerance. Yet tolerance *per se* does not necessarily follow, for it depends upon which groups have received recognition for what purpose and in which contexts. A major difficulty here is the threat posed to communitarian democracy by special interest groups. A further complication is that many indigenous minorities are being treated according to policies predicated on pluralism on the basis of equality, whilst non-indigenous minorities are treated according to policies predicated on pluralism on the basis of non-equality. How do these two trends impact the one upon the other with regard to the recognition of rights in citizenship and language matters?

It follows that the ways of managing cultural diversity will vary according to why we think it has value.[2] Ignatieff (2000, p. 87) argues that the real difficulty about such recognition turns on the question of whether it means acquiescence, acceptance, or approval. Demands for equal rights have become demands for approval and anything less than full approval by the majority denies the equal worth of the former discriminated party. In turn the rights revolution can "engender a coercive culture of ritualised, insincere approval. So political correctness becomes a code word for a new form of moral tyranny: the tyranny of the minority over the majority" (p. 88).

When applied to current Canadian constitutional bargaining Ignatieff argues that the politics of mutual recognition need not necessarily lead to fragmentation if the politics of reciprocity is engaged.

> This goes beyond balancing rights. It also means balancing acts of recognition. At the moment, the Canadian majority feels that is faced with multiplying demands for recognition from various minority groups,

without these groups accepting any obligation to recognize the majority. This is the heart of the bitterness in English Canada over Quebec. It is the feeling that the Canadian majority is being asked to concede recognition of Quebec's distinct status without earning any commensurate recognition of Canada in return. This perceived inequality of recognition has led many English Canadians to refuse to be party to further concessions. What has proved insupportable is not the nature of Quebec's demands, but the threat of separation that accompanies the demands. Give us what we want or we will go is not a form of recognition but an expression of contempt. (p. 122)

Ignatieff (p. 63) interprets the history of modern Canada as the story of the unwillingness of the majority to discard the connection between equality, individual rights, and group assimilation. In response to francophone demands, Trudeau chose to emphasise the rights, not of one territorial community, Quebec, but rather the rights of individuals throughout the state. His programme of coast-to-coast bilingual federal services provided a commitment and a context to language policy and planning. But its basic premise, namely the recognition of individual rights within a programme of civic equality, was not enough. It failed "to recognize and protect the rights of constituent nations and peoples to maintain their distinctive identities" (Ignatieff, 2000, p. 66). The Québécois response involved a territorial imperative, even though the rhetoric was couched in increasingly non-territorial, non-ethnic, terms, on the basis of an inclusive civil society. Kymlicka (2001, p. 79) points to the centrality of a language group exercising territorial hegemony when he writes that

There is evidence that language communities can only survive inter-generationally if they are numerically dominant within a particular territory, and if their language is the language of opportunity in that territory. But it is difficult to sustain such a predominant status for a minority language, particularly if newcomers to the minority's territory are able to be educated and employed in the majority language (e.g. if newcomers to Quebec are able to learn and work in English).

We shall focus on the territorial ramifications of language policy below, but first we need to examine the varieties of language policy that influence inter-group contact in selected states.

Varieties of language policy and planning

As modern global control is increasingly related to language functions we may ask how are these overarching socio-political forces played out in linguistic terms and with what consequence for social policy, democracy and citizenship? As a mechanism for behaviour modification, language policy and planning depends largely on four attributes identified by Stewart (1968). These are the degrees of standardisation. autonomy, historicity, and vitality. These characteristics of language freedom are critical in helping planners to evaluate existing language functions and to harness the dynamic cultural interactions that characterise many multilingual societies.

As early as 1951, UNESCO developed a typology of the range of choice available to language planners which has been in use for two generations. It includes the following categories:

1. **indigenous language** – the language of the original inhabitants of an area
2. **lingua franca** – a language used habitually by people who have different first languages so they can communicate for certain specific purposes
3. **mother tongue** – the language one acquires as a child
4. **national language** – the language of a political, social, and cultural entity
5. **official language** – a language used to do government business
6. **pidgin** – a language (formed by mixing languages) used regularly by people of different language backgrounds
7. **regional language** – a common language used by people of different language backgrounds who live in a particular area
8. **second language** – a language acquired in addition to one's first language
9. **vernacular language** – the first language of a group socially or politically dominated by a group with a different language
10. **world language** – a language used over wide areas of the world (a "language of wider communication" or LWC) (UNESCO, 1951, 689–90).

Though useful in a heuristic sense such typologies are open to criticism. Kay (1993), for example, argues that they are too imprecise to be used in any specific place or context. One may also query how "original" a language must be to be classified as indigenous, and why a vernacular language is associated with subordination in the UNESCO classification, as if a dominant group could not also possess a vernacular language. Such imprecise definitions, however, were commonplace in the initial stages of language planning, which often transferred European or North American models of social and linguistic behaviour to African, Asian or Latin American contexts.

Stewart (1968) proposes an alternative typology of language, which recognises the multiplicity of linguistic functions that can exist even within ostensibly one nation/one people/one culture states.

• official languages;
• provincial languages (such as regional languages);

- languages of wider communication (LWCs), which are used within a multilingual nation to cross ethnic boundaries;
- international languages, which are LWCs used between nations;
- capital languages (the means of communication near a national capital);
- group languages (often vernaculars);
- educational languages (used as the media of education);
- school-subject languages (those taken as second languages);
- literary languages (for example, Latin or Sanskrit);
- religious languages (such as Islamic Arabic).

At independence many developed societies retained the language policies which were critical to the project of constructing the territorial-bureaucratic nation-state. Consequently they face severe difficulties in matching their inherited institutional agencies and organisational structures to the reality of serving the legitimate demands of increasingly multilingual populations. Historically, we can identify four types of language policy implicated in the processes of state formation. The first and most common – as found in France, Spain and Britain – reinforced political and cultural autonomy by giving primacy to one indigenous language and thus enforcing it, and no other, as the language of government, administration, law, education and commerce. In so doing, a number of goals were achieved simultaneously. Among these was the search for national integrity, the legitimisation of the new regime and its state apparatus, the re-establishment of indigenous social organisation (often, but not necessarily incorporating an established religion), the reduction of dependence upon external organisations and influences, and the incorporation of all the citizenry in a wide range of para-public social domains. Foreign languages were reserved for the very specialised functions of higher education, international diplomacy and commerce.

A second type of language planning characterises those situations in which the "national" goal has been to maintain cultural pluralism, so that the state might survive through containing its inherent tensions. Under this system, language was used to define regional associations rather than state or national citizenship. It is best exemplified in Europe by Switzerland's decentralised system, which incorporates cantonal unilingualism within a multilingual federal system, and the rigidly enforced division of Belgium between its Walloon- and Flemish-speaking populations.

The third form of language planning has occurred when a recognised minority was granted some degree of geographical distinction, based upon the territoriality principle of language rights. In Finland, for example, shared historical context, high levels of language contact along the west coast, marked religious uniformity, a strong tradition of centralised government, and the unifying effects of long-term external threats, led to a recognition that the minority Swedish-speaking population should be accorded official status. Following the 1922 Language Law, all communes were classified as unilingual Finnish, unilingual Swedish, or bilingual if they contained a linguistic minority of either group of 10 per cent or more; these classifications were revised after each decennial census to take account of changing linguistic geography (McRae, 1997). In comparative terms, the Finnish system of official bilingualism is characterised by a gross disparity in numbers, asymmetry in language contact, and instability over time, leading McRae to conclude that such institutional arrangements for language accommodation have been functional in terms of conflict moderation and management, but less so for language stability.[3]

A fourth option – the "modernisation" or revitalisation of an indigenous tongue – characterises societies disengaging from colonial relationships and the cultural hegemony of a dominant state. This form of language planning was a key goal of the nationalist intelligentsia in Hungary, Ireland, Finland, and Norway prior to independence, and remains critical to the political programme of nationalists and regionalists in Catalonia, Euskadi, Brittany and Wales today.

Clearly language planning in a multilingual society is not a precise instrument and is as capable of being manipulated, as is any other aspect of state policy. Nevertheless, it is an essential feature of the economic and political restructuring of many states. The key issues are:

- who decides – and on what basis – such bi- or multi-lingualism is to be constructed?
- which languages are chosen?
- who benefits by acts of state-sponsored social and identity formation?
- how is language-related conflict managed and reduced?
- how is language planning to be related to all other forms of social intervention?
- how do citizens respond to reformed language regimes?
- how do such reforms relate to international trends in education, human rights, freedom of mobility of labour and skills acquisition?[4]

Space does not permit a detailed evaluation of the various models and methods that underpin language planning systems.[5] Nevertheless, by employing a series of illustrative tables some insight into language planning aims and models may be gained. The first and fundamental insight is that language planning processes conventionally may be viewed either from a predominantly societal (status planning) or language (corpus planning) focus.[6] Table 4.2 charts Einar Haugen's formulation which can be used either to focus on language policy and its implementation or on language teaching and development (for details see Kaplan and Baldauf, 1997, pp. 28–58).

Table 4.2 Haugen's (1983, 275) revised language planning model with additions

	Form (policy planning)	Function (language cultivation)
Society (status planning)	1. Selection (decision procedures)	3. Implementation (educational spread)
	a. problem identification	a. correction procedures
	b. allocation of norms	b. evaluation
Language (corpus planning)	2. Codification (standardization procedures)	4. Elaboration (functional development)
	a. graphization	a. terminological modernization
	b. grammatication	b. stylistic development
	c. lexication	c. internationalization

Haarman (1990) has added a behavioural dimension to such considerations, arguing that as status and corpus planning are both productive activities, what is missing is the perceptual filter by which people relate to the *prestige* factor of language planning. Haarman also emphasises the multilevel contexts within which language policy has to be received and implemented by the target audience. Thus Table 4.3 is an attempt to inject promotional and contextual elements to status and corpus planning.

In their excellent overview of the discipline, Kaplan and Baldauf (1997), provide a summary of the various aims which underpin language

Table 4.3 An ideal typology of language cultivation and language planning (Haarmann, 1990, 120–1)

	Ranges of language planning		Ranges of language cultivation	
	Activities of government	Activities of agencies	Activities of groups	Activities of individuals
Status planning	4.1	3.1	2.1	1.1
Prestige planning	official promotion	institutional promotion	pressure group promotion	individual promotion
	↑	↑	↑	↑
Corpus planning	4.2	3.2	2.2	1.2
	↓	↓	↓	↓
	Level 4	Level 3	Level 2	Level 1
Maximum	Efficiency in terms of the organizational impact Minimum			

Source: Reproduced in Kaplan and Baldauf (1997), p. 50.

planning. How plausible such schemes are depend in large part on the political context within which such goals are to be realised, and thus the next
section focuses on the alternative methods of implementing the principles
of language rights (see Table 4.4).

Table 4.4   A summary of language planning goals

Macro level[a]	Alternative formulations	Example[e]
Language purification		
External purification		
Internal purification		French e[5]
Language revival	Language revival[c]	Hebrew[e]
	Restoration	
	Transformation	
	Language regenesis[d]	
	Language revival	
	Revitalization	
	Reversal	
Language reform		Turkish[e]
Language standardization	Spelling and script standardization[2]	Swahili[e]
Language spread		
Lexical modernization	Term planning[b]	Swedish[e]
Terminological unification	Discourse planning[c]	
Stylistic simplification		
Interlingual communication		
Worldwide IC		
Auxiliary languages		
English LWC		
Regional IC	Regional identity[b]	
Regional LWC	National identity[b]	
Cognate languages IC		
Language maintenance		
Dominant LM		
Ethnic LM		
Auxiliary code standardization		
Meso level planning for[b]		
Administration: Training and certification of officials and professionals		
Administration: Legal provisions for use		
The legal domain		
Education equity: Pedagogical issues		
Education equity: Language rights/identity		
Education elite formation/control		
Mass communication		
Educational equity: Language handicap[f]		
Social equity: Minority Language access[f]		

a. Nahir (1984). b. Annamalai and Rubin (1980). c. Bentahila and Davies (1993). d. Paulson *et al.*
(1993). e. Eastman (1983). f. Kaplan and Baldauf (1997).
Source: Kaplan and Baldauf (1997), p. 61.

Personality and territoriality principles of language policy and planning

Conventionally language policies are predicated on either a personality or territoriality principle of planning.[7] Two conditions are necessary for competition to arise between language groups. First, the languages must share a common contact space. Secondly, the relationship between these two languages must become the symbolic stakes of the competition, which takes place on the level of the shared space. Laponce's (1987, p. 266) four propositions about languages in contact bear repetition:

- languages tend to form homogenous spatial groupings;
- when languages come into contact they tend either to specialise their functions or to stratify;
- the specialisation and the stratification of languages is determined by the socially dominant group;
- the social dominance of a language is a function of the number of its speakers and the political and social stratification of the linguistic groups in contact.

Research in contact linguistics demonstrates that it is unprofitable to search for a universal model for conflict reduction. On the contrary, procedures must be considered that are adaptable to each situation.

The recognition of the need to honour rights and plan language services normally involve the use of a previously disallowed language within public administration and the legal system, a religious-based education provision, or differentiated access to the media. Such reforms may be predicated on the basis of a personality or a territoriality principle or some expedient admixture of both, but they are not in themselves sufficient to avoid conflicts. Research in Canada, Belgium, Finland and Switzerland (Domenichelli, 1999; McRae, 1997; Nelde *et al.*, 1992) suggests that some conflicts can be partially neutralised if the following introduced in Chapter Three conditions are observed:

- the territoriality principle should be limited to a few key areas like administration and education;
- the institutional multilingualism that emerges should lead to the creation of independent unilingual networks, which grant equal opportunity of communication to minority and majority speakers. These networks should also exclude linguistic discrimination connected with speakers of the prestige language;
- measures of linguistic planning should not be based exclusively on linguistic censuses carried out by the respective governments. Rather, they must genuinely take account of the situational and contextual characteristics of the linguistic groups;

- minority linguistic groups in a multilingual country should are not be judged primarily on quantitative grounds. On the contrary, they should be awarded more rights and possibilities of development than would be due to them based on their numbers and their proportion to the majority (Nelde *et al.*, 1992).

Nelde *et al.* believe that according such equality to minorities by assuring them of more rights could result in fewer people adopting an intransigent ideological position. Unless far more attention is paid to the rights of lesser-used language speakers, then more conflict will ensue.[8] It is a matter of some considerable debate as to whether territorial principles of language protection, in general, offer adequate means to bolster language loss and whether language legislation in, for example, Quebec has enabled successive governments sufficient control to regulate language choice and behaviour within their purview.[9] Chevirer (2003) discusses the options for Quebec emphasising Dion's (1992) conclusion that the personality solution should be adopted throughout Canada except in Quebec where territorialism should be acknowledged as a political fact. Such asymmetrical paradigms mask the more substantive issue which is that federal systems attempt to contain, rather than energise, a coast to coast francophonie population and Chevrier, like Castonguay (1999b), and Cardinal (2000) is particularly acerbic in his portrayal of the impact of federal policies on French language maintenance, even if supporters of the federal programmes would argue that the intent was not to subvert, but to maintain, the French fact throughout the state.

What is not subject to debate is the fact that Quebec's move toward a territorial specification of language choice and regulation has been challenged as being discriminatory from a Canadian majoritarian point of view, as discussed below in Chapter Nine. Such demands for language rights and territorial control, as Kymlicka (2001, p. 79) makes clear, are taken as evidence of the minority's "collectivism". But the minority are merely seeking the same opportunities to engage in public life and the economy that the majority take for granted. In their own way, majorities are just as collective, perhaps more so, for they have internalised such values as "common sense" notions of democratic civility, while simultaneously denying such values to minorities.[10]

Language erosion also involves the potential loss of creativity and spontaneity mediated through one's own language(s), thus contributing to a quenching of the human spirit, and a reduction in what some have termed the ecology of "linguodiversity" (Skutnabb-Kangas, 1997; Williams, 1991a). This reason alone may prove convincing to many. But need linguistic decline sound the death-knell for particular ethnic or immigrants identities in Europe or North America? No necessary correspondence exists between linguistic reproduction and ethnic/immigrant identity (Edwards, 1994; Williams, 1991). Indeed cultural activities and symbolic manifestations of identity often continue long after a group's language declines. None the less, increased interdependence at the superstructural level implies more harmonisation for the already advantaged groups. The EU has harmonised state and community policies so as to strengthen its majority language regimes, which when combined with other globalising processes, open up new forms of inter-regional interaction such as cable television and global multi-service networks, but also poses a threat to conventional territorial relationships of both regional and immigrants minorities.

A further difficulty is the lack of adequate data by which to analyse demo-linguistic trends, and the attempt by government agencies to put a positive gloss on official language trends. Extra and Gorter (2001, pp. 7–16) have raised the issue of the criteria used for identification of population groups in multicultural Europe. They argue that data on Regional Minorities (RM) is recorded on the basis of (home) language and/or ethnicity while that on Immigrant Minorities (IM) is on the basis of nationality and/or country of birth. Due to the decreasing significance of nationality and country of birth criteria in the EU it is probable that the combined criterion of self-categorisation and home language will characterise future language planning policy. However, one should be alert to the political implications of choosing certain criteria by which to include and exclude residents in specific programmes. Consequently the advantages and disadvantages of various criteria are outlined in Table 4.5 below and their implications for

Table 4.5 Criteria for the definition and identification of population groups in a multicultural society

Criterion	Advantages	Disadvantages
Nationality (NAT)(P/F/M)	• Objective • Relatively easy to establish	• (Intergenerational) erosion through naturalization or double NAT • NAT not always indicative of ethnicity/identity • Some (e.g. ex-colonial) groups have NAT or immigration country
Birth-country (BC)(P/F/M)	• Objective • Relatively easy to establish	• Intergenerational erosion through births in immigration country • BC not always indicative of ethnicity/identity • Invariable/deterministic: does not take account of dynamics in society (in contrast to all other criteria)
Self-categorization (SC)	• Touches the heart of the matter • Emancipatory: SC takes account of person's own conception of ethnicity/identity	• Subjective by definition: also determined by language/ethnicity of interviewer and by the spirit of times • Multiple SC possible • Historically charged, especially by World War II experiences

Table 4.5   (Continued)

Criterion	Advantages	Disadvantages
Home language (HL)	• HL is a most signific-ant criterion of eth-nicity in communic-ation processes • HL data are corner-stones of government policy in areas such as public information or education	• Complex criterion: who speaks what language to whom and when? • Language not always core value of ethnicity/identity • Useless in one-person house-holds

P/F/M = person/father/mother.
Source: Extra, G. and Gorter, D. (2001), p. 9.

the EU and Canadian/Quebecois dialogue which follows should not be lost, especially if the discussion is informed by the insightful analysis of census-interpreters. Take, for example, Canada where Statistics Canada has chosen to define and interpret official language data in a certain manner which allows successive Federal governments to place a more positive gloss on offi-cial language policy than is warranted by reality. Castonguay (1997, 1999a) points to trends such as the demographic advantage of English, the collapse of Canada's French-speaking population, the impact of allophone language shift and the increasing anglicisation of francophones outside of Quebec as evidence that the "personality principle" approach to official bilingualism is inherently assimilationist, thus subversive. Cardinal (1999) offers a caution-ary rider to such trends, arguing that the federal language regime has placed francophone minorities outside Quebec in an unhealthy state of depend-ency on government and the courts. The acute political point she makes is that they thereby become part of the Trojan Horse federal strategy *vis- à- vis* Quebec as discussed by Castonguay (1999a) and Williams (1981, 1996b).

> The quid pro quo for this federal generosity toward official-language minorities has been that they accept being used-especially when the Lib-erals are in office- as accomplices in campaigns deigned to undermine Quebec's demands on language and other matters. Such a situation pre-vents the building of links with Quebecers. It accentuates the fragility of the small francophone communities outside Quebec since they are in con-stant political conflict with the overwhelming majority of the Canadian francophone population- who are Quebecers.
>
> (Cardinal, 1999, p. 84)

The emancipation of long-discriminated minorities has also to be set within the context of an enabling infra-structure which allows them to use their new found rights. However, deciding between the promotion of one or many languages in public services or in the educational domain is becoming less of a "free choice". The increasing burdens of economic, social and cultural development crowd in on the limited resources available for language planning and its implementation. This was demonstrated by the 2004 EU enlargement where an additional 60 languages now fall within the remit of European governments and NGOs. These comprise border minority languages, autochthonous languages (Kashubian in Poland, Carpatho-Rusyns in Slovakia), partially migrant languages (Russian in the Baltic States), official languages (Maltese in Malta) and linguistic islands (the Tartars). There is also the trend toward regional diversity, which emphasises the value of cultural diversity and the worth of each specific language, not least as a primary marker of identity.

In the EU ethno-linguistic minorities have reacted to these twin impulses by searching for European-wide economies of scale in broadcasting, information networking, education and public administration, establishing their own EU networks and entering into new alliances to influence decision-making bodies. They believe that by appealing to the superstructural organisations of the EU for legitimacy and equality of group rights, they will force individual states and the Community to recognise their claims for political/social autonomy within clearly identifiable territorial/social domains.[11]

But the wider question of the relative standing of official languages makes political representatives wary of further complicating administrative politics by addressing the needs of approximately 55 million citizens who have a mother tongue, that is not the main official language of the state which they inhabit. Historically, the recognition of linguistic minority demands is a very recent phenomenon. Since 1983, the European Commission has supported action to protect and promote regional and minority languages and cultures within the EU.[12] As we shall see in Chapter Five there has been a significant change of policy on behalf of the EU in respect of certain aspects of language promotion and democratic empowerment of long beleaguered minorities.

Each EU enlargement in 1995, 2004 and 2007 has presented new operational and translation challenges to the machinery of EU multicultural communication. It has also had real commercial and power implications for access to information, creating markets and the spread of capitalism. At the heart of the debate on European identity lies a consideration of the role of hegemonic languages as both symbol and instrument of integration. English – the premier language for international commerce and discourse – is used by over 1700 million people world-wide as an official language, of whom some 320 million have it as a home language (Crystal, 1987; Gunnermark and Kenrick, 1985). Should English be encouraged as the official language enabling most Europeans to communicate with each other? Or is it desirable to attempt to slow down its inevitable global spread? Critics claim that the spread of English perpetuates an unequal relationship between "developed" and "developing" societies. While access to information and power demands fluency, it also requires institutional structures, economic resources and power relationships.

Because of high fertility rates, some groups are experiencing linguistic reproduction rates greater than one, and their prospects for survival look promising, especially in constructing an infrastructure for domain extension in education, government and broadcasting. Conversely, however, some autochthonous language speakers are rapidly loosing their control in traditional core areas as a result of out-migration, capital-intensive economic development and increased mobility. Modernised indigenous languages, such as Irish or Catalan, are capable of expansion but are unlikely to displace hegemonic languages, especially within the civil service, or technological and commercial sectors. Renewed languages such as Welsh, Frisian or Basque have penetrated into new domains, such as local administration, education and the media, but even here much of this activity is tokenistic or reaches only the superficial structures of society. In contrast threatened minority languages such as Romany or Skolt Lapp will be further marginalised. The fact that lesser-used language speakers have become highly politicised in the last twenty years, should not divert attention away from their fears of cultural attrition.

An additional consideration is that many migrants who settled in another European country, often as a consequence of two World Wars, have lost the native language capacities of their forebears. For them diacritical markers, such as diet, music or the visual arts have replaced language as the link with the wider cultural community. Fundamental questions surround the symbolic bases of their culture and the degree to which one may characterise residual elements as either authentic or as expressing an integral identity. This is a major feature of Europe's cultural heritage and will prove a testing ground for more sensitive and flexible applications of any policy of multiculturalism, for it calls into question the use of the mother tongue as the key marker of identity. This is most acute in the recent re-discovery among many residents of Central Europe of their German heritage and of their potential relationship with a unified and re-invigorated German *MittelEuropa* policy.

Perhaps the greatest challenge facing framers of European identity comes from non-European migrants and their descendants, especially as globalising perspectives will reinforce the need for link languages other than English in this realm. Initially this will result from private and commercial-oriented demands, but as the total size and significance of link languages – especially Islamic-related variants – grows, then there will be pressure to reform public agencies and the educational system, particularly in France, the UK, Germany, Belgium and the Netherlands. The increased presence of non-nationals within European states will add to the alienated feelings of many recent migrants that they do not belong by right to any particular state.

Clearly the state is deeply implicated in the direction of change with regard to multicultural policy. As society becomes more plural, and social mobility increases, greater tensions occur between the functional provision of bilingual public services and the formal organisation of territorial-based authorities charged with such provision. These conflicts are exacerbated by immigration into fragile language areas, which leads to the public contestations of language-related issues as the intrusive language group penetrates each new domain. Such sentiments are hard to gainsay. The difficulty lies in determining what proportion of the public purse is to be expended upon satisfying the legitimate demands of this policy. Issues of principle, ideology and policy are frequently no more than thinly disguised disputes over levels of resource expenditure. One arm of government is involved in extending the remit of pluralism whilst another is reigning in the fiscal obligations to so act. Either way, dependent cultures are tied inexorably to the largesse of the state. Governments are obliged to maintain their support for many multicultural projects, albeit simultaneously signalling their intent to withdraw public finances and welcome private sector funding. Either way, the languages and cultures of visible minorities are in danger of being expropriated by external forces, while cultural dependency is being increased. As they become better organised, however, astute RM and IM minority groups will press for greater recognition of their cultural rights, seeking the individual choice and empowerment to decide their lifestyle and future prospects as participative citizens. From this perspective, multiculturalism is a set of institutional opportunities for individual and group advancement in a competitive environment. In other words it becomes a platform for social progress as we shall see in the next chapter.

The politics of mutual respect presuppose a historically well-entrenched democratic order. The watchwords of the open society are redistributive social justice, participatory democracy and mutual tolerance. This in turn presupposes a political-juridical framework, adequate to ensuring that increased cultural contact will not lead to escalating conflict. Cultural communities are best represented when the state guarantees individual freedom of association and protection.

Conventionally language policy analysts have concentrated on the needs of immigrant populations once they have arrived in Europe or North America without paying too much attention to the linguistic and socio-political backgrounds of their country of origin. Yet this is a major weakness in our thinking for the repertoire of languages and socialisation experiences of migrants can be a major determinant of their subsequent behaviour. Let us therefore explore some aspects of language planning practice as it has emerged in the context of modernisation and development in parts of Africa and Asia.

Language planning as an instrument of development: African and Asian perspectives

Many of the modernisation processes observed in Europe since the *Aufklärung* have been repeated in the so-called "developing world". Development theory often assumes that language-choice behaviour is utilitarian and rational and can be measured through techniques such as a cost-benefit analysis of language switching. It also assumes that the broad tenets of modernisation theory influence patterns of language maintenance and shift. Eastman (1983, p. 148) has summarised the development assumptions of language planning which may be modified as follows:

- people with language skills are favoured over those without; people with linguistic disabilities are held back in economic advancement;
- population increases via birth rate *or* migration affects the relative strength of languages or speech varieties;
- a quality increase as well as a quantity increase in per capita growth requires an expansion of linguistic knowledge; that is, people need to know and use more of a language as they acquire more and better goods;
- people need to be aware of, and know how to use, different language features (such as social dialects, special vocabularies, argots, jargons, or special-purpose languages) to adjust to changes in professional and industrial growth;
- international trade requires people to be able to use and have access to Languages of Wider Communication;
- linguistic homogeneity adds to the ability of people to cross occupational, industrial and status lines;
- where the spread of modern economic growth is sequential, modern linguistic growth is also sequential. The need for vocabulary development makes it likely that the world languages will be chosen for adoption in preference to attempts to enhance local languages (Eastman, 1983, p. 148).

Value recognition is not an essential part of language planning, although one might argue that it should be, for how can planning of any kind be effective without explicit recognition and practice of this principle? Hegemony prevails and will continue to do so until minority people band together and form some kind of common front to have their perspectives incorporated in the development planning process. This will involve a clash of discourses and a conflict over the very definition of what counts as the problem that development is seeking to overcome. From a local, community perspective the problem may be a lack of real power to transform their immediate situation. From the point of view of the central state apparatus it may be that ethno-cultural differences are perceived as an impediment to the creation of a state-wide programme of economic development where institutional agencies can redefine the populus as workers and consumers regardless of ethnic criteria. The commodification of identity is thus an essential feature of economic and political restructuring in the advanced stage of the development of organic capitalism when production and consumption in the semi-periphery remain so unbalanced.

Conscious of this ideological struggle, some language planning and development studies theorists have recognised the contextual effects on language maintenance and language loss and have sought to incorporate environmental and politico-economic factors more directly into their analyses (Williams, 1991). This bodes well for a realistic, holistic assessment of language change in developing societies. However, any attempt at language planning will depend on the resources available and the capacity of the public sector and educational system to realise the explicit goals of policy. Structural adjustment in most of Africa has exasperated the lack of a settled civil society and too often language promotion is linked to exhausted nationalism or to a variant of elite manipulation of the masses advocating an anti-neoliberal philosophy. Rising debt and the inability of many states to renegotiate their role within the global pattern of uneven development has damaged many of the earlier grand designs, partly because of an over-accumulation problem, partly because hard currency financing renders economies vulnerable and partly because many political leaders have "talked left and acted right" when it comes to their dealings with the World Bank or the IMF.

Creating order out of such a complex array of factors is a daunting challenge. Yet the work of Conklin and Lourie (1983), summarised by Baker (1996, 2006), offers a very useful framework and balance sheet for the factors

Table 4.6 Factors encouraging language maintenance and loss

Factors Encouraging Language Maintenance	Factors Encouraging Language Loss
A. Political, social and demographic factors	
1. Large number of speakers living closely together.	Small number of speakers well dispersed.
2. Recent and/or continuing in-migration.	Long and stable residence.
3. Close proximity to the homeland and ease of travel to homeland.	Homeland remote or inaccessible.
4. Preference to return to homeland with many actually returning.	Low rate of return to homeland and/ or little intention to return and/or impossible to return.
5. Homeland language community intact.	Homeland language community decaying in vitality.
6. Stability in occupation.	Occupational shift, especially from rural to urban areas.

Table 4.6 (Continued)

Factors Encouraging Language Maintenance	Factors Encouraging Language Loss
7. Employment available where home language is spoken daily.	Employment requires use of the majority language.
8. Low social and economic mobility in main occupations.	High social and economic mobility in main occupations.
9. Low level of education to restrict social and economic mobility, but educated and articulate community leaders loyal to their language community.	High levels of education giving social and economic mobility. Potential community leaders are alienated from their language community by education.
10. Ethnic group identity rather than identity with majority language community via nativism, racism ethnic discrimination.	Ethnic identity is denied to achieve social and vocational mobility; this is forced by and nativism, racism and ethnic discrimination.
B. Cultural factors	
1. Mother-tongue institutions (e.g. schools, community organizations, mass media, leisure activities).	Lack of mother-tongue institutions.
2. Cultural and religious ceremonies in the home language.	Cultural and religious activity in the majority language.
3. Ethnic identity strongly tied to home language.	Ethnic identity defined by factors other than language.
4. Nationalistic aspirations as a language group.	Few nationalistic aspirations.
5. Mother tongue the homeland national language.	Mother tongue not the only homeland national language, or mother tongue spans several nations.
6. Emotional attachment to mother tongue giving self-identity and ethnicity.	Self-identity derived from factors other than shared home language.
7. Emphasis on family ties and community cohesion.	Low emphasis on family and community ties. High emphasis on individual achievement.
8. Emphasis on education in mother tongue schools to enhance ethnic awareness.	Emphasis on education in majority language.
9. Low emphasis on education if in majority language.	Acceptance of majority language education.
10. Culture unlike majority language culture.	Culture and religion similar to that of the majority language.
C. Linguistic Factors	
1. Mother tongue is standardized and exists in a written form.	Mother tongue is non-standard and/or not in written form.
2. Use of an alphabet which makes printing and literacy relatively easy.	Use of writing system which is expensive to reproduce and relatively difficult to learn.

3. Home language has international status.	Home language of little or no international importance.
4. Home language literacy used in community and with homeland.	Illiteracy (or aliteracy) in the home language.
5. Flexibility in the development of the home language (e.g. limited use of new terms from the majority language).	No tolerance of new terms from majority language; or too much tolerance of loan words leading to mixing and eventual language loss.

Source: Reproduced with permission from Baker (2006), pp. 76–77. Adapted from Conklin and Lourie, 1983.

influencing language maintenance and loss. Table 4.6 illustrates the complexity of the issues involved, but I would argue that all three sets of factors need to be addressed simultaneously if a practical set of proposals is to be constructed in any particular context. In addition, as with nearly all examples of language planning schema, it also needs to identify the role of language in economic development and modernisation.

A staggering range of variables faces the language planner concerned with mobilising the state's educational system in order to produce functional bilingual or multilingual citizens. There is enough case-study experience in the literature for us to be able to predict weak and strong forms of education for bilingualism and biliteracy. Table 4.7 illustrates the available range that will be illustrated below by reference to specific examples in East Africa and Western Europe. It is my contention that the construction of an articulate bilingual or multilingual citizenry is an essential prerequisite of a developing state. Only when we can anticipate the utilitarian power of a language in particular economic contexts can we begin to talk of the pragmatic links between language processes and development processes.

Types of language choice

"Africa invented language; Asia sacralised language; and Europe universalised it" claim Mazrui and Mazrui (1992, p. 96). Africa's triple linguistic heritage makes it an acute case of linguistic dependency even though Mazrui and Mazrui argue that the cultural interplay between *indigenous*, *Islamic* and *Western* legacies has promoted a functional complementarity within the continental array of languages.

A central issue for developing countries is what should be the relationship between colonial languages and indigenous African languages? The question is just as urgent in Tanzania, where Kiswahili, rather than a European language is promoted nationally. Conventionally multilingual approaches to communication are adopted in such societies. How is this promotion of language spread best formalised in policy? What steps would be necessary to

Table 4.7 Weak and strong forms of education for bilingualism and biliteracy

Type of programme	Typical type of child	Language of the classroom	Societal and educational aim	Aim in language outcome
Weak forms of education for bilingualism				
Submersion (structured submersion)	Language minority	Majority language	Assimilation	Monolingualism
Submersion with (Withdrawal classes/ sheltered English)	Language minority	Majority language with "pull-out" L2 lessons	Assimilation	Monolingualism
Segregationist	Language minority	Minority language (forced, no choice)	Apartheid	Monolingualism
Transitional	Language minority	Moves from minority to majority language	Assimilation	Relative monolingualism
Mainstream with foreign language teaching	Language majority	Majority language with L2/FL lessons	Limited enrichment	Limited bilingualism
Separatist	Language minority	Minority language (out of choice)	Detachment/ autonomy	Limited bilingualism
Strong forms of education for bilingualism and biliteracy				
Immersion	Language majority	Bilingual with initial emphasis on L2	Pluralism and enrichment	Bilingualism and biliteracy
Maintenance/heritage language	Language minority	Bilingual with emphasis on L1	Maintenance, pluralism and enrichment	Bilingualism and biliteracy
Two-way/dual language	Mixed language minority and majority	Minority and majority	Maintenance, pluralism and enrichment	Bilingualism and biliteracy
Mainstream bilingual	Language majority	Two majority languages	Maintenance, pluralism and enrichment	Bilingualism and biliteracy

Note: (1) L2 = Second language; L1 = First language; FL = Foreign language. (2) Formulation of this table owes much to discussion with Professor Ofelia García.

Source: Reproduced by permission from Colin Baker (1996), *Foundations of Bilingual Education and Bilingualism* (Multilingual Matters: Clevedon, Avon). Adapted from Conklin and Lourie (1983).

ensure that multilingual strategies in, for example, education, are not again hi-jacked by an élite? (Robinson, 1994).

New political, economic and cultural forces have infused a spirit of linguistic competition in social domains and have created different socio-linguistic dynamics and formations. These changes are important, because recent strands of development theory are increasingly "concerned with the impact of development on groups which are distinguished through *cultural* criteria rather than by their function in the production process" (Hettne, 1984). If true, how does cultural complementarity and competition affect the process? The determining factor is, of course, colonial history and peri-colonial contemporary reality. Africa, no less than any other part of the world, is differentially integrated into a global division of labour that is mediated through ideology and culture. But the language of this integration is primarily Western, essentially English or French, or Afro-Islamic, particularly Arabic. Thus whilst Afro-Islamic or Western languages are transnational or national in their communicative range, most Afro-ethnic languages are sub-national, and limited to specific regions within state boundaries.

This suggests that as development relates to the global division of labour and international/universal technologies, then transnational languages are essential to development and indigenous languages are a barrier hindering access to the wider world. However, such implications are politically unacceptable, and therefore states must search for a modern version of a "hybrid" communication system which relate both to the heritage of traditional cultures and to global structures and opportunities. A language which is capable of embracing both requirements is thus essential and should be the one with the greater versatility, vocabulary and functional utility (Kay, 1993).

When the question is whether to use an LWC as a "national" and "official" language, planners should consider the six socio-political variables that characterise three modal types of "nation" (Eastman, 1983, pp. 58–59). Fishman (1969) argues that whether a "nation" is modal type A, B or C depends largely on whether nationism (instrumental attachment and operational efficiency) or nationalism (ethnic authenticity and sentimental-primordial attachment) is the goal.

As is evident from Tables 4.8 and 4.9, A-modal nations initiate language choices so that they may integrate a linguistically heterogeneous area with a primarily oral rather than written tradition. Eastman (1983, p. 13) comments that many developing states are of this type and frequently choose an LWC as an official and as a national language. Often indigenous language standardisation is also initiated so that people can learn to read and write their first regional language as well as the LWC, as is illustrated through the promotion of six regional languages together with the employment of English and French in Cameroon.

Type B nations are called uni-modal and are characterised by an indigenous language with a literary tradition, plus an LWC usually dominant because of

100

Table 4.8 Types of language choice (modified from Fishman,1969a, 192)

Features	A-modal nations (Type A)	Uni-modal nations (Type B)	Multi-model nations (Type C)
1. Is there a Great Tradition?*	No	Yes	Many
2. Reason for selection of national language	For political integration	For nationalism	For compromise
3. Reason LWC is used	As a national symbol	For the transition	A unifying force
4. LP activity to be done	Standardization	Diglossia	Modernization
5. Is bilingualism a goal?	No	Yes, but situational	Yes
6. Is biculturalism a goal?	No	Yes, but situational	Yes

* The term Great Tradition refers to a literary tradition of long standing thought to be great by the people who have it, and considered a part of their cultural heritage.
Source: Eastman (1983), p. 13.

Table 4.9 Varieties of language situations

Situation of LANGUAGE CHOICE (National)	Situations of LANGUAGE FUNCTION (Social)
1. Indigenous	1. Official language
2. Lingua franca	2. Provincial language
3. Mother tongue/first language	3. School-subject language
4. National language	4. Group language
5. Official language	5. Language of wider communication
6. Pidgin	6. International language
7. Regional language	7. Capital language
8. Second language	8. Literary language
9. Vernacular language	9. Educational language
10. World language	10. Religious language

Variables affecting LANGUAGE TYPE	Variables Affecting MODAL NATION TYPE
1. Standardization	1. Great tradition
2. Autonomy	2. National language rationale
3. Historicity	3. LWC rationale
4. Vitality	4. Type of LP activity
	5. Bilingualism
	6. Biculturalism

Variables Affecting the LANGUAGE-NATION RELATIONSHIP
1. Type of national language (endo-or exoglossic)
2. Status of languages within the nation
3. Juridical status of speech communities in the nation
4. Numerical strength of speech communities in the nation.

Source: Eastman (1983), pp. 59–60.

former colonial policy. The intelligentsia and employees of the bureaucratic-territorial state tend to favour the LWC, while the indigenous language with the literary tradition is promoted as both the symbol and the substance of nationalist mobilisation. Swahili's challenge to English in Tanzania well exemplifes the uni-modal nation's choice of national language.

Type C nations are multi-modal and have a range of competing languages with their own literary traditions. The selection of one all-purpose indigenous national language undoubtedly creates tension, especially in the ranks of supporters and speakers of the discriminated languages, but this may be a necessary price to pay for communicative efficiency in the new state. In multi-modal nations, bilingualism or trilingualism is a political goal, and in the case of India, for example, the indigenous national, all-state language Hindi has been championed at the expense both of other regional Indian languages and to a lesser extent, at the expense of English, the LWC.

Developing this distinction between "nationism and nationalism", Fasold (1988) has distinguished three main functions of national languages: (1) nationalist/national, or identificational; (2) nationist/official or administrative and (3) communicative. Brann (1991) has added a fourth element, the territorial or "son-of-the-soil" function, and suggests that in most former colonial situations new states must take account of all four criteria – territoriality, communality, representation and status when choosing one or several "national" languages.

The difficulty facing politicians and language planners in Africa is that very few indigenous languages are capable of satisfying both preservation and modernisation. Thus Mazrui and Mazrui (1992, p. 89) aver that the proportion of Afro-ethnic languages that have the potential to be truly national or transnational is rather small. They include Amharic (Ethiopia and Eritrea), Bemba (Zambia and Zimbabwe), Kituba (Zaire and Congo), Lingala (Zaire, Congo, Angola, Central African Republic, Sudan and Uganda), Lwena (Angloa, Zaire and Zambia), Nyanja or Chewa (Malawi and Zambia), and Sango (Central African Republic, Cameroon, Chad, Congo and Zaire). Such claims are open to question, but what is not in doubt is that many attempts are currently being made to redefine indigenous languages as "national" languages, which could become the common inheritance of most or all of the citizens of post-independent states.

It is often argued that speakers of Afro-ethnic languages tend to be mostly rural in terms of their core area of demographic concentration and linguistic value (though this is not true of Amharic, for example). This gives them an authenticity in both time and space, and a certain literary and psychological legitimacy in that most Afro-ethnic language speakers "tend to regard the rural homeland as their real home" (Mazrui and Mazrui, 1992, p. 90). However, functionally it limits their geographical spread and domain usage in an increasingly technological world. Examples of urban African concentrations that are growing quickly tend to weaken this claim, but the principle of low relative utility for Afro-ethnic languages in an increasingly inter-connected world holds true. In contrast most Afro-Islamic languages depend upon the dynamics of urbanisation; they prosper as regional *lingua francas* serving commerce, politics and leisure pursuits. Thus the top five *linguae francae* in terms of speakers are all Afro-Islamic languages, namely Arabic, Kiswahili, Hausa, Fulfulde and Mandinka, with the first three named growing at the expense of the latter (Mazrui and Mazrui, 1992, p. 90).

By and large African societies have retained the repertoire of language policies that they inherited from their colonial past. In consequence many societies are faced with severe difficulties in matching their institutional agencies and organisational structures to the reality of serving the legitimate demands of a multilingual population. As a central feature of postcolonial development, language planning has become a crucial tool of "state-formation" and "nation building". The key question was whether the national linguistic communication was to be based upon the use of indigenous or foreign languages. The new state may either seek to promote one exclusive "national" language, at the expense of all others– the "one-nation-one language plan" – or it may seek to recognise important languages within its boundaries and employ one or more for official functions, that is the "one-nation-more than one language plan" (Eastman, 1983; Stewart, 1968).

As we have seen, the first type of plan was common in European state formation, as in the French, Spanish and British versions of "national" development. It is best represented in Africa by post-war Rhodesia and to a lesser extent by Tanzania's political determination to create a "national" culture by replacing English with Swahili as its "official" language. Other examples of endoglossic nations would be Somalia (Somali), Sudan (Arabic), Ethiopia (Amharic) and Guinea (which has employed eight languages, Fula, Manding Susu, Kisi, Kpelle, Loma, Basari and Koniagi) (Heine, 1992, p. 24).

Such endoglossic policy seeks to institute political and cultural autonomy by giving an indigenous language full opportunity to be developed as the language of government, administration, law, education and commerce. This policy strengthens national integrity, the legitimisation of the new regime and of its state apparatus, the re-establishment of indigenous social organisation, the reduction of dependence upon Western organisations and influence and the incorporation of the citizenry in a wide range of para-public social domains. Again foreign languages are reserved for higher education, international diplomacy and commerce.

Of those nations that do not practice an active endoglossic policy, Heine (1992, p. 24) cites Botswana (Tswana), Burundi (Rundi), Lesotho (Sotho), Malawi (Chewa), Ruanda (Kinyarwanda) and Swaziland (Swati). They may aim to encourage an indigenous language, but as most are derived from colonial units with centralised political organisation and one dominant

language, they tend to favour the use of the colonial language for official purposes. In this respect there is a wide gap between the rhetoric of the declared
national language policy and the actual experience of daily communication
in the colonial *lingua franca*.

The second type of language planning exists when the "national" goal is
to maintain cultural pluralism. It is best represented in Africa by the commitment of the Bureau of Ghanaian Languages to introduce eleven languages in
the education system, including three variants of Akan. A quite different
interpretation of such planning was the extension of the apartheid system
in the Republic of South Africa from the initial Bantustans to the creation of
the putative independent Homelands. Under this system language was used
to define national citizenship, even if language affiliation was an ascribed
label rather than a measurable attribute, as in the case of all the people of
mixed descent who by being allocated to a Homeland were automatically
denied South African citizenship. South Africa's over-concern with the fit
between language and political boundaries expressed in its homeland policy
(language=culture=homeland) derives from the cornerstone of the *Genoot-
skap van Regte Afrikaaners* (Fellowship of True Afrikaners), founded in 1875,
"our language, our nation and our land". Herbert (1992, p. 5) comments that
this trinitarian conception that formed the homelands tribalisation policy
stems from "the projection of the Afrikaner's sense of ethnic particularism
and linguistic chauvinism onto other people" (Van den Berghe, 1968, p.
221). A radically different version of the pluralist goal of achieving unity
through diversity has now been implemented in South Africa with the recognition of eleven languages to serve its enfranchised citizens. Current patterns
in residential segregation between English and Afrikaans-speaking citizens
show more positive trends as the Coloured, Indian and White population
challenge pre-apartheid urban distributions based upon socio-economic differentiation and educational criteria. Indigenous African language groupings
vary, but in most cities tri-lingualism is the norm, with speakers from the
immediate rural hinterland strengthening the particular ethno-linguistic
mix. Only the industrial heartland of Galtung demonstrates a mix of all
eleven official languages to any significant degree. Thus language planning
in the RSA has had to come to terms with "national level", "regional"
and "metropolitan" level set of policies which simultaneously promote the
political and economic advantages of a language of wider communication
without necessarily damaging the ethno-lingusitic vitality of several smaller,
more vulnerable, language groups. Socialisation through formal education
is perceived as a key to such stability, however, it is doubtful if education
alone can perform such a task and consequently additional resources will
be required if a real language choice is to offered to citizens in domains as
varied as the health system, public administration and the legal system.

The "national language question" in Africa has always reflected the triumph of political zeal over the realisation of bilingual or multilingual

communicative competence. The will has always out paced the reach. In consequence one might argue that language planning in such cases is an acute expression of political social engineering. Yet Mackey avers "In the development of standard languages, edict has been less effective than example, the ideologies of the practitioners more powerful than the ideas of the planners" (Mackey, 1991, p. 56). The Tanzanian example would suggest that edict and example, ideology and plan must be synonymous if such planning is to be truly effective. That there are so few examples of effective planning in Africa suggests that there is very little consensus over both means and ends in this domain of language policy.

On the macro-scale, languages tend to specialise according to their utility and function. The trend is "that Afro-ethnic languages fulfil intra-ethnic communicative and social-psychological needs in non-formal, and many formal, domains of discourse. Afro-Islamic and Afro-Western language facilitate inter-ethnic communication and horizontal mobility" (Mazrui and Mazrui, 1992, p. 91). However, this old divide between vernacular and vehicular languages is no longer so tenable. One cannot simply juxtapose indigenous with exogenous, rural with urban, traditional with modern. Kay's (1993) powerful argument in favour of language and cultural displacement as a means of escaping structural poverty and the open prison of ethnic identity certainly seems like a rational justification for the encouragement of the "new African". His "pragmatic" solution of the adoption of English in multilingual Zambia, as elsewhere, as a language of wider communication appears rational. But is it reasonable? Is the North's globalising role in reforming African identity through technology, bureaucracy and ideology inevitable and therefore to be incorporated within development strategies and political policies? What are the consequences of adopting a Western language in multi-ethnic contexts on both the constituent ethno-linguistic groups and upon the universalising language "community"? Let us illustrate by asking whether English should be encouraged as the official co-equal or second language of many African states? Is it better to anticipate the inevitable or to resist the spread of English as the globalising language? What are the immediate implications of encouraging such global language spread in Africa?

One obvious consequence is the relative functional decline of many African languages, whose communicative power and symbolic purchase is reduced by changing socio-economic circumstances. Systematic exposure to external influences has revealed the limited functional utility of most African languages in a changing context. Breton (1991, pp. 172–174) avers that without energetic language defence policies, most African languages will be submerged within three generations. He recognises that the old pattern based upon language complementarity is being challenged by the pervasive spread of more functional "official" and inter-ethnic languages.

Today Africa is involved in a vertiginous breath-taking process of urbanization which has already lead to cities where all ethnic groups are mixed together, half of the population of many countries; there is the central "melting pot" whose pestle is the state language; there, there is nothing to compare with the old rural complementarity between vernacular and vehicular.

(Breton, 1991, p. 174)

Language dependency

The process of language dependency obtains at all levels of the socio-political and spatial hierarchy from the individual to the state and international level. Individuals have to perform daily cost-benefit analyses on the economics of language choice. This is not a new situation, as from ancient times traders and travellers throughout Africa exercised the same diglossic fluency as do modern taxi drivers in Cairo, or government officials in Lagos. But what changes the situation today is that the freedom of possibility of exercising such choice is increasingly determined by state-influenced infra-structural decisions. The individual and the state are conjoined by

the drastic law of economy which commands language development (for) here through language planning, psychology meets economics, and individual identity joins national design. The options faced by the man in the street are those of the man in power. Masses and governments, in this case at least, are alike – time and money are limited; emergency drives you in one way, the highway of modernity, which is a no return route.

(Breton, 1991, p. 174)

This lack of freedom and creativity is exacerbated when alternative power bases promote different languages for different reasons. Thus Tanzania and the apartheid Republic of South Africa were both cases where economic, commercial power required English, but political power promoted a rival tongue, namely Swahili or Afrikaans respectively. This lack of congruence added a further element to the already difficult process of modernisation.

The "new Africans", the "men of power", were until recently in a privileged position, in part, because of their command of a Western or other international language. Military, political and commercial leaders have exercised their multilingual skills to great effect such that the "credentials for ruling an African country are disproportionately based on a command of the Euro-imperial language. In Africa south of the Sahara it has become impossible to become a Member of Parliament or President without being fluent in at least one of the relevant European languages" (Mazrui and Mazrui, 1992, p. 84). The same observation can be made about senior executives in business, senior civil servants and academia.

Should the élite's diglossic capacity be extended to the masses? This is one of the biggest questions of social development policy. Kay argues that certain international languages should become available to all forthwith in order to liberate and develop people in Africa (Kay, 1993). In similar vein Carol Eastman has advocated an institutional diglossia with "English as a medium of instruction, at all levels, while at the same time encouraging first language in home, neighbourhood and regional activities" (Eastman, 1991, p. 148). Others may not be so persuaded by the functional necessity of massive language switching from African to European languages, therefore let us demonstrate a series of alternative answers to the key question of whether most Africans should possess, at the least, both an indigenous and an international language.

Alternative strategies

Pragmatists have a well-established pedigree in language planning. They urge the adoption of a universal language, such as English, in order to provide a "passport to the modern world". This perspective views ethnicity as a dualistic concept, reflecting both its potential for dynamic change and for reactionary conservatism. Because it is essentially a behavioural phenomenon reflecting acquired values, it can be manipulated for good or evil. Given the conviction that a Western language would better serve the developmental needs of sub-Saharan Africa than would an indigenous tongue, Kay (1993) has argued that "plural societies, in Europe no less than Africa, are better served by pragmatic, "neutral", *non*-racial and *non*-ethnic policies which are fairly cognizant of the nature and needs of all individuals, groups and peoples whom they serve". His Zambian illustration demonstrates that the people are divided by seventy two regional languages and united by one official language, English. "Like all human constructs, this language policy evidently is not without either history or ethnic origins; but it is pragmatic and seeks to serve the best interests of 8,000,000 people. English is their passport to the modern world" (Kay, 1993).

Such pragmatism, whether by design or default, is also encouraged by technological developments and by the globalisation of culture and economy (Williams, 1993b). There is an acute inevitability surrounding the universalisation of English and, to a lesser extent, of French. The question arises as to whether such inevitability is welcomed and adapted to specific "national", group and individual needs, or resisted and restricted only to the functional domains of an elite communication network, thereby perpetuating privilege and access to material and intellectual power bases?

Clearly the reasons why this form of pragmatism does not automatically endear itself to all is that both English and French symbolise and realise a colonial inheritance, and perpetuate a neo-colonial intellectual and political dependency. Virulent anti-colonial nationalism fed on this obvious manifestation of inequality and forced incorporation into a European imperial system. Post-colonial nationalism was faced with an acute dilemma of either rejecting the colonial instruments of subjugation, or somehow incorporating them into the new nation-state project, as described above by Hettne (1984). Kay (1993) counters this observation by arguing that Western languages *per se* were not instruments of subjugation *except* by their policies of exclusion. The stark choice facing educators was either to "revert to 'tribal obsolescence' or to 'modernise' – including the adoption of a <u>MODERN</u> (Western) language. Here we encounter a major misconception; it is the Tanzanian (Swahili) and RSA (Afrikaans) language policies which are the policies of subjugation." This attitude is intricately bound up with the perceived status differentials between constituent groups in the respective states.

The linguistic hegemony of English

Critics of English, as an instrument of imperialism and modernisation, claim that the spread of English perpetuates an unequal relationship between "developed" and "developing" societies because access to information and power does not depend solely upon language fluency. It also depends upon institutional structures, economic resources and relationships. Tollefson reminds us

> in order to gain access to English-language resources, nations must develop the necessary institutions, such as research and development offices, "think tanks" research universities, and corporations, as well as ties to institutions that control scientific and technological information. From the perspective of "modernising" countries, the process of modernisation entails opening their institutions to direct influence and control by countries that dominate scientific and technical information, the result is an unequal relationship.
>
> (Tollefson, 2001, p. 84)

The spread of English is also deeply implicated in the creation of new forms of inequality within societies. Most post-colonial societies are characterised by a dual institutional system, which though linked, nevertheless present different ranges of opportunities to their respective members in the conventional and modernised sectors. In a powerful critique of the role of ELT (English Language Teaching), Phillipson (1992, p. 270) has demonstrated how arguments used to promote English can be classified into three types based upon the language's

a) capacities: English-intrinsic arguments, what English *is*
b) resources: English-extrinsic arguments, what English *has*
c) uses: English-functional arguments, what English *does*

Each element is mediated by the structure of the world order in which English is dominant and each develops its own discourse which locates English *vis-à-vis* competing languages. Thus

> English-intrinsic arguments describe English as rich, varied, noble, well adapted for change, interesting etc. English-extrinsic arguments refer to textbooks, dictionaries, grammar books, a rich literature, trained teachers, experts, etc. English-functional arguments credit English with real or potential access to modernization, science, technology, etc.; with the capacity to unite people within a country and across nations, or with the furthering of international understanding.
>
> (Phillipson, 1992, p. 271–2)

The functions of English are nearly always described in positive terms. Whether the argument for its extension is couched in terms of persuasion, promise or threat, they represent various ways of exerting and legitimating power. This was well understood during colonial times and is reproduced today in more subtle, sophisticated ways as is demonstrated in the rhetoric of the British Council. When the British

> do not have the power we once had to impose our will ("sticks"), cultural diplomacy must see to it that people see the benefits of English ("carrots") and the drawbacks with their own languages, and then, consequently, want English themselves for their own benefit ("ideas"): "the demand is insatiable." And that means that British influence, British power has not diminished, because Britain has this "invisible, God-given asset". Thus "Britain's influence endures, out of all proportion to her economic or military resources."
>
> (British Council Annual Report, 1993, 1994. p. 9;
> quoted in Phillipson, 1992, pp. 286–7)

Language, and the ideology it conveys, is thus part of the legitimisation of positions within the global division of labour. Attempts to separate English from its British and North American value system are misguided, for English should not be interpreted as if it were primarily a *tabula rasa*. Any claim, that English is now a neutral, pragmatic tool for global development is disingenuous, because it involves a 'disconnection between what English *is* ("culture") from its structural basis (from what it *has* and *does*). It disconnects the *means* from *ends* or *purpose,* from what English is being used for. This type of reasoning

> is part of the rationalization process whereby the unequal power relations between English and other languages are explained and legitimated. It fits into the familiar linguistic pattern of the dominant language creating

Table 4.10 The labelling of English and other languages

Glorifying English	Devaluing other languages
World language	Localized language
International language	(Intra-) national language
Language of wider communication	Language of narrower communication
Auxiliary language	Unhelpful language
Additional language	Incomplete language
Link language	Confining language
Window onto the world	Closed language
Neutral language	Biased language

Source: Philippson, R. (1992), p. 282.

an external image of itself, other languages being devalued and the relationship between the two rationalised in favour of the dominant language. This applies to each type of argument, whether persuasion, bargaining, or threats are used, all of which serve to reproduce English linguistic hegemony.

(Phillipson, 1992, p. 288)

A summary of the manner in which English hegemony is "glorified" in a competitive situation is presented below in Table 4.10.

Such points emphasise that conflict is inherent in language issues and helps explain why bilingual and multicultural education – far from encouraging the positive aspects of cultural pluralism – has hitherto been characterised by mutual antagonism, begrudging reforms and ghettoisation. Attempts to overturn pejorative judgements about the normalcy of bilingual education or the promotion of minority languages as normal and as essential elements in society come up against powerful hegemonic discourses which negate the salience of such languages for general developmental issues and social intercourse. There are signs that such discourses are being challenged all over Europe and beyond (Phillipson, 1992; Skutnabb-Kangas, 1999), especially in relation to the urgent need to bring together basic human rights and economic rights within a more participative democratic process. The dilemma is encapsulated in this prescient quotation from the outstanding analyst in this field, Tove Skutnabb-Kangas, who writes:

Globalising access to information has enabled counterhegemonic forces to ensure that there is growing sensitivity to human rights. But at the same time there is also a growing inability to secure them by progressive forces in civil society. The gap between rhetoric and implementation is growing, with all the growing inequalities. Behind this lies the collapse of institutions of democratic political control of trade and capital. In this light, it is completely predictable that states commit linguistic genocide; it is part of the support to the homogenizing global market forces. . . . At present, though we can hope that some of the positive developments might have some effect, overall there is not much cause for optimism. We still have to work for education through the medium of the mother tongue to be recognized by states as a human right. And if this right is not granted, and implemented, it seems likely that the present pessimistic prognoses of over 90 % of the world's oral languages not being around anymore in the year 2100, are too optimistic.

(Skutnabb-Kangas, 1999, pp. 56 63)

Baker's concise attempt to capture ten varieties of such education in practice is encapsulated in Table 4.11.

Globalisation and European minorities

Ethno-linguistic minorities have reacted to globalisation and European integration by searching for European-wide economies of scale in broadcasting, information networking, education and public administration. They have also established their own EU institutions and bureaux and entered new alliances to influence EU decision-making bodies.[13] They believe that by appealing to the superstructural organisations for legitimacy and equality of group rights, they will force member states to recognise their claims for varying degrees of political/social autonomy within clearly identifiable territorial/social domains.

Logically, if globalisation and interdependence can enhance the productive capacity of majority "nation-state" interests, they can also be harnessed to develop the interests of lesser-used language groups. Historically the recognition of linguistic minority demands is a very recent phenomenon. In accordance with the resolutions of the European Parliament, Arfé (1981); Kuijpers (1987); Killilea (1994), the European Commission since 1983 has supported action to protect and promote regional and minority languages and cultures within the European Union. Equally significant we have a raft of legislation and declarations upholding the rights of minorities to use their languages in several domains (Williams, 1993c). However, linguistic minorities face many structural barriers to their full participation within the EU system.

The recent expansion of the EU in 2007 has increased the difficulties in translating multi-cultural communication and guaranteeing access to information and hence power for all groups. The real geolinguistic challenge is to safeguard the interests of all the non-state language groups, especially those most threatened with imminent extinction. A critical aspect of constructing these safeguards is access to knowledge, thus we need to ask and act upon the answers to questions such as who controls access to information

Table 4.11 Monolingual forms of education for bilinguals

Monolingual Forms of Education for Bilinguals

Type of Program	Typical Type of Child	Language of the Classroom	Societal and Educational Aim	Aim in Language Outcome
MAINSTREAMING/ SUBMERSION (Structured immersion)	Language minority	Majority language	Assimilation/ subtractive	Monolingualism
MAINSTREAMING/ SUBMERSION with Withdrawal classes /Sheltered english /Content-based ESL	Language minority	Majority language with "Pull-out" L2 lessons	Assimilation/ subtractive	Monolingualism
SEGREGATIONIST	Language minority	Minority language (forced, no choice)	Apartheid	Monolingualism

Weak Forms of Bilingual Education for Bilinguals

Type of program	Typical type of child	Language of the classroom	Societal and educational aim	Aim in language outcome
TRANSITIONAL	Language minority	Moves from minority to majority language	Assimilation/ subtractive	Relative monolingualism
MAINSTREAM with Foreign language teaching	Language majority	Majority language with L2/FL lessons	Limited enrichment	Limited bilingualism
SEPARATIST	Language minority	Minority language (out of choice)	Detachment/ Autonomy	Limited bilingualism

Table 4.11 (Continued)

Strong Forms of Bilingual Education for Bilingualism and Biliteracy

Type of program	Typical type of child	Language of the classroom	Societal and educational aim	Aim in language outcome
IMMERSION	Language majority	Bilingual with initial emphasis on L2	Pluralism and enrichment. Additive	Bilingualism & biliteracy
MAINTENANCE/ HERITAGE LANGUAGE	Language minority	Bilingual with emphasis on L1	Maintenance, pluralism and enrichment. Additive	Bilingualism & biliteracy
TWO WAY/ DUAL LANGUAGE	Mixed language minority & majority	Minority and majority	Maintenance, pluralism and enrichment. Additive	Bilingualism & biliteracy
MAINSTREAM BILINGUAL	Language majority	Two majority languages pluralism	Maintenance, & biliteracy and enrichment. Additive	Bilingualism

Note: L2 = Second Language; L1 = First Language; FL = Foreign Language.
Source: Reproduced with permission from Baker (2006), p. 215.

112

within the mother tongue and the working languages of European minorities?
Are such languages destined to occupy a more dependant role because of
superstructrual changes favouring dominant groups or will they achieve relative socio-cultural autonomy by adopting aspects of mass technology to
suit their particular needs.

Additional issues concern the adaptation of lesser used language speakers
to the opportunities afforded by changes in global-local networks, the growth
of specialised economic segments or services and of information networks
which are accessed by language-related skills. Accessibility to or denial of
these opportunities is the virtual expression of real power in society which
must be taken on board in any discussion of the politics of regional cultural
representation. The general pattern is expressed thus by Castells (1997) in
his monumental three-volume study, *The Rise of the Network Society*:

> *Cultural* expressions are abstracted from history and geography, and
> become predominantly mediated by electronic communication networks
> that interact with an audience and by the audience in a diversity of codes
> and values, ultimately subsumed in a digitised, audio-visual hypertext.
> Because information and communication circulate primarily through
> the diversified, yet comprehensive media system, politics becomes
> increasingly played out in the space of the media. The fact that politics
> has to be framed in the language of electronically based media has
> profound consequences on the characteristics, organisation and goals of
> political processes, political actors, and political institutions. Ultimately,
> the powers that are in the media networks take second place to the power
> of flows embodied in the structure and language of these networks.
>
> (Castells, 1997, p. 476)

Why is a common language so often seen as essential to "nation-building"
or state development? If conflict is such a predictable outcome why not opt
for linguistic and cultural pluralism as a dominant ideology? Is it merely
a post-imperial reaction to a European model of state formation and citizen socialisation? Is the faculty of imitation and the search for legitimacy
through national congruence, so strong as to impel political elites on such
a conflict-ridden trajectory?

The answer is surely that language is power to confer privilege, deny opportunity, construct a new social order and radically modify an inherited past
which is not conducive to the pursuit of hegemonic aims. Language choice is
thus a battleground for contending discourses, ideologies and interpretations
of the multi-ethnic experience.

> At a deeper level, the material foundations of society, space and time
> are being transformed, organised around the spaces of flows and time-
> less time. Beyond the metaphorical value of these expressions a major

hypotheses is put forward: dominant functions are organised in networks pertaining to a space of flows that links them up around the world, while fragmenting subordinate functions, and people, in the multiple space of places, made of locales increasingly segregated and disconnected from each other. The social construction of new dominant forms of space and time develops a meta-network that switches off nonessential functions, subordinate social groups, and devalued territories. By so doing, infinite social distance is created between this meta-network and most individuals activities and localities around the world. The new social order, the network society, increasingly appears to most people as meta-social disorder. Namely, as an automated, random sequence of events derived form the uncontrollable logic of markets, technology, geopolitical order or biological determinations.

(Castells, 1997, p. 477)

As a result of imperialism, neo-colonialism, the modernisation of technology and the globalisation of information flows, there is an acute inevitability surrounding the universalisation of hegemonic languages, such as English, French or Spanish. Transnational languages have been significant elements of imperial rule since Persian, Greek and Roman times and greatly influenced the spread of capitalism and the modern world system. The roles of English and French are crucial to the development of former overseas possessions, by relating former colonies to the motherland and to each other through the Commonwealth and *la francophonie* (Bostock, 1988; Gordon, 1978; Williams, 1996b). Should this inevitability be welcomed or resisted being restricted to élite communication networks, thereby perpetuating privilege and access to material and intellectual power bases?

Key domains: education, public administration and the economy

Within the European system, official languages, other than Russian, French, German, Spanish and Italian, are coming to terms with the reality of specifying their specific domain competence in spheres as varied as education, international jurisprudence, military technology and logistical planning, international environmental co-ordination and human rights. Of the major languages German has experienced a definite spread effects as a result of its revitalised East European commercial and foreign policy. However, it is Spanish which is set to be a major international, transcontinental bridge language. In comparative terms, is Spanish can maintain its growth within the European economy and education system, it could become a most significant LWC to link Europe and the Americas.

As a result of all these tendencies there is growing pressure for a pan-European educational policy in which

> isolated instruction in separate foreign languages should be replaced by instruction for multilingual communication. This requires training in the ability to quickly shift actively or passively from one language to another. In order to make accessible as many European languag es as possible, each European school should teach the following languages:
>
> a) the student's mother tongue
> b) the world's language (English)
> c) a language from a language family that does not include the student's mother tongue (i.e. a Romance or Slavic language for Germans, a Germanic or Slavic language for French, a Germanic or Romance language for Poles, etc.).
>
> (Posner, 1991, p. 134)[14]

Specialists stress education's potential in promoting cultural awareness which is predicated on the following assumptions (from Baker, 1996, p. 379):

1. There is a fundamental equality of all individuals and all minority groups irrespective of language and culture.
2. In a democracy, there should be equality of opportunity irrespective of ethnic, cultural or linguistic origins.
3. Any manifest or latent form of discrimination by the dominant group against minorities requires elimination.
4. A culturally diverse society should avoid racism and ethnocentrism.
5. While generalisations about cultural behaviour may be a natural part of humans making sense of their world, cultural stereotypes are to be avoided.
6. Minority cultural groups in particular need awareness of their culture as a precondition and foundation for building on intercultural awareness.
7. In mainstream monocultural education, language minority parents tends to be excluded from participation in their children's education. In multicultural education parents should become partners.
8. A pluralist integration is established by interaction and not a mosaic, by intermingling and a discovery of others to improve mutual understanding, break down stereotypes, while increasing self-knowledge and self-esteem.

Does promoting a common educational approach imply that ultimately the European Union will become the first post-modern, post-sovereign multicultural system of the twenty-first century? For the optimist this emphasis on accommodation, openness and diversity is an expression of a highly developed pluralist society that demands mutual respect and tolerance of its constituent cultures. For the pessimist such openness is a recipe for continued strife, inter-regional dislocation, inefficient government and the artificial reproduction of often misleading cultural identities that deflect attention away from more pertinent social categories. Rather than being a springboard for action such a conception is seen as an open prison which will hamper the unfettered development of the individual in a free and burgeoning society.

The basic issue relates to the relative autonomy of constituent groups within any European policy of multiculturalism. What started as an attempt to preserve a common Western heritage now has to adjust to the reality of managing divergence in a multiracial society. How vibrant are Europe's constituent cultures? How dependent are they on official patronage? Are they self-sustaining or are many perpetuating a generation-specific conception of a sub-culture, subsidised by public coffers? Clearly such questions draw attention to the dualistic relationship of culture and the modern state. Most minority cultures are increasingly dependent upon the state for legitimising their access to the media, for granting them permission to establish bilingual or religious-based schools, for upholding in law several of their key fundamental values and principles. However, when language and the culture it represents become institutionalised in new domains via new agencies, such reforms change the relationship between the individual and the state. Power for enfranchisement is the key to how successful such a relationship will be in serving the needs and expectations of a multicultural society.

It is imperative that European integration should take account of minority rights, without halting the emergence of new forms of ethnic and cultural identification. Only if people are incorporated within the process on equitable terms will the development of society operate at a reasonable political level, otherwise it is the tyranny of the powerful masquerading as progress and social change. In tackling the underlying fears and aspirations of the language reformers we need to ask a further set of questions.

1. What are the key needs for language development in Europe?
2. Whose interests are served in language development?
3. To what extent is democracy undermined by the unsatisfied aspirations of threatened language groups?
4. Are OLS (Other Language Speakers) considered as competitors to autochthonous groups in the crowded arena of minority rights?
5. Are the non-territorial claims of OLS groups sufficiently well developed to have a socio-spatial impact in local services and public provision?
6. What is the role of language in education for the adequate rendering of social services and how does one avoid creating a demand for particular languages at the expense of others?
7. What are the different critical masses required for particular services/classes/liaison?

8. In considering various levels of governmental recognition of language needs-in which domains are there well recognised multi-cultural rights, in which is differentiated service-provision still a privilege, and in which domains is there unlikely to be any progress whatsoever?
9. How do the central agencies of social reproduction, such as the law, education and health, relate to the increased demands of pluralism and strive to satisfy such demands within a multicultural system?

In tackling such questions pessimists argue there is little chance for the reconciliation of starkly contrasting ethno-linguistic pressures. Conflict is inherent in the situation and far from encouraging the positive aspects of cultural pluralism multicultural education hitherto has been a history of mutual antagonism, begrudging reforms and ghettoisation, where spatial segregation and social isolation have become mutually reinforcing patterns in far too many communities. The drift toward single-issue politics and fragmentation cannot be adequately captured through conventional theorising based around the grand ideas of the nineteenth century. This is why much of the earlier discussions centred upon Charles Taylor's critique of democratic involvement within divided societies is so timely and urgent.

Conclusion: Language policy and planning in comparative perspective

How do these considerations inform the analysis of language policy and planning discussed in the remainder of this volume? Cognisance has been taken of the following factors that determine the range of possibilities for language policies within multicultural societies:

- The state-system and political infra-structure
- Models of social integration and state-civil society relations
- Evolution of language legislation
- Personality and territoriality principles of language service provision
- Education's key role in socialising citizens and immigrants alike
- The linguistic hegemony of English
- The rise of the network society
- Types and strategies of language choice
- The economic and political resources needed to implement different types of language policy
- Conflict resolution through language policy and economic development.

Taken together these are some of the suggested parameters by which language policy may be translated into social practice. But language policy, as successive chapters in this volume will testify, is reflective of fundamental political and philosophical differences which revolve around the tension between the state, the collective good and the individual citizen. Calls for tolerance and mutual understanding abound. But they do not necessarily translate into vital, active support for the promotion of target languages wherever they are spoken in a designated set of spaces. Consequently, the struggle continues, and the geo-linguistic facts do not give comfort to those who would argue that shared sovereignty is the best guarantor of a threatened language's survival. Many will pin their hopes on reconciliation and heed Ignatieff's (2000, p. 134) call for the construction of a shared common truth. Others will argue that interdependence and partnership merely serve to perpetuate dependency, however much it is dressed up in the language of equal rights and an overarching legitimate legal order. For my part, coping rather than controlling seems to be the watchword for the twenty first century in most of the cases discussed below. It is my conviction that interpretations such as these help us realise the magnitude of the forces we are seeking to change and the inherent fragility of socio-linguistic realities in plural societies.

Notes

1. An example of the intransigence of the French system in this respect is the decision of the French Court (November 2001) to strike down as unconstitutional an agreement between the Ministry of Education and the Breton schools movement, Diwan. The court declared that French was the sole official language of the state, and this has obvious implications for language use in Alsace, North Catalonia, North Euskadi and Occitania, to say nothing of the condition of Arabic and other "immigrant" languages.
2. In discussing these value conflicts in the Canadian context, Ignatieff (2000, p. 134) reveals the crux of the problem "The real issue is that we do not share the same vision of our country's history. The problem is not one of rights or powers, but one of truth. We do not inhabit the same historical reality. And it is time we did. For two generations, English Canada has asked, with earnest respect, 'What does Canada want?' Its time for English Canada to say *who* we are and what *our* country is. The answer is: we are a partnership of nations; a community of peoples united in common citizenship and rights. We do possess a common history, and like it or not, we had better begin to share a common truth."
3. See the work undertaken by the From Act to Action research team.
4. Communicative labour-market skills are grossly under-valued in language planning.
5. I favour Robert Cooper's broad definition of language planning, which states that "language planning refers to deliberate efforts to influence the behaviour of others with respect to the acquisition, structure, or functional allocation of their language codes. This definition neither restricts the planners to authoritative agencies, nor restricts the type of target group, nor specifies an ideal form of planning ... Finally, it employs the term influence rather than change inasmuch as the former includes the maintenance or preservation of current behaviour, a plausible goal of language planning, as well as the change of current behaviour" (Cooper, 1989, p. 5).
6. Many critics argue that such a division is artificial and untenable and that the sequence in Haugen's model is too idealistic to be of any practical worth.

7. However, many critics argue that this is a naïve division, which can lead to confusion and conflict as language behaviour, and demographic trends nullify the principles upon which original language policy was predicated.

8. As will be suggested later in Chapter Nine below, the status of language rights in Canada is now fundamental to the constitutional principles of political life. They are thus less amenable to the asymmetrical, territorial solutions that are advocated by critics of the current policy.

9. On this see the discussion in MacMillan (2003) especially his key point that "The Quebec language legislation offers ample testimony that the Quebec government already possesses the main factor in language survival, namely political control over language within its territorial space. In conjunction with its other strengths, the French language exercises control of the education system, and experiences widespread use through the family, community and economic life" (Palgrave MacMillan, 2003, p. 108).

10. Kymlicka puts it thus "In reality, the anglophone majorities in both the United States and Canada zealously guard the right to live in a state where they form a majority, and their right to have English recognised as a language of public life. This defence of boundaries and linguistic policies of existing nation-states is as 'collectivist' as the demands of minorities for protection of their self-government and language rights" (Kymlicka, 2001, p. 79).

11. Robert Mugabe of Zimbabwe illustrates this tendency throughout the nineties. In an attempt to appease several dissenting groups he provided a monthly pension to the war veterans, engaged in wide spread land reallocation which implicated over 800 white farms. In the global capitalist crisis he reduced exchange controls which led in 1997 to a 74 per cent crash of Zimbabwe's currency. Four consequences followed: 1) imported inflation; 2) a rise in VAT; 3) the IMF riots; 4) rises in petrol prices and transport fares triggered an "autonomist" response which in December 1997 led to the worst melt-down in its history. Black Friday was followed by Red Tuesday. Mugabe responded by utilising 38 per cent of export earnings as foreign debt repayment. Source: Patrick Bond, seminar on Zimbabwe, Oxford University, 15/2/2002.

12. In 1996 some four million ECU's was allocated to European socio-cultural schemes. Equally significant is a raft of recent legislation and declarations upholding the rights of minorities to use their languages in several domains (*Declaració de Barcelona*, 1996; Williams, 1993b).

13. A good example is the establishment of a European network of language planning agencies in October 2001 at the instigation of the Basque Government and the Welsh Language Board. This brought together civil servants and professional language planners from Foras na Gailge, Ireland, Folktinget, Finland, the Fryske Akademy, Friesland, Netherlands, the Language Planning Departments of the Basque Country, Galicia and Catalonia, Spain, the Welsh Language Board, UK and EBLUL. Three results may be reported: 1) initially the Basque Government and then the Welsh Language Board has provided the secretariat for this network, 2) the EU has recognised the legitimacy of involving this network in their language policy deliberations and 3) the emergence of a new operating structure whereby EBLUL will concentrate more on the relatively poorly represented linguistic minorities within the EU particularly in Central and Eastern Europe, while the European Language Planning Boards will co-ordinate the activities of responsible government agencies. See www.languageplanning.com.

14. This general maxim is laudable, and would need to accommodate the situation of lesser-used language speakers such as Breton, Catalan or Friulian, for whom the state language would be co-equal with the mother-tongue instruction.

5
Enhancing Linguistic Diversity in Europe: Cross-Cutting Themes

Supra-National language promotion

Elements within European society have embarked on a mission to create a common structure out of an uncommon mélange of languages. I have already discussed a number of innovative and challenging ways in which this search for a common structure is both a realisable goal and an ever-changing impediment to successful democratic citizenship. Actors as varied as state governments, the European Union and Parliament, multilateral interest groups and regional level authorities contribute both to the policy agenda and to the construction of the infra-structure whereby languages can be accommodated within a complex network of agencies. But the underlying concern I want to address is what holds these various, at times, quite conflicting perspectives, together? Clearly there is no single answer, nor even a set of adequate answers, to which one can turn to for advice and leadership. Nevertheless, there is, I believe, a constant need to look beyond the obvious, the immediate, the pressing concerns of political expediency, when addressing minority and immigrant language issues on a broader European canvass.

In some domains we have succeeded in reversing language shift and in establishing new opportunities wherein the lesser-used languages may be used. Such opportunities have been fashioned out of the creative tension between two key processes. The first, centrifugal, process is the decentralist challenge of the "ethnic revival" which has characterised the past generation. The ethnic intelligentsia in many of the lesser-used language regions of Europe has stressed the organic authenticity of language. Their focus on the inviolability of the ethnic homeland has given a literal interpretation to the search for roots in the soil, community and landscape of one's own people. As we saw in Chapter Two much of the justification for bilingual education, self-government and economic self-sufficiency derives, in large part, from the ideological thrust of nationalism. The second, centripetal, process is the internationalisation of language, described by Mackey (1986) as the "definitive liberation of language from its traditional bounds of time and space . . . when language is no longer inevitably attached to spatial boundaries as it was in the past, when its speakers had to be limited to one or a few areas of the globe". Telecommunication changes and mass migrations have empowered world languages, such as English and French, to perform critical inter-communicative roles, which are historically predicated upon the economic power of mature capitalism. But they also derive immense power from the extension of digital technology, Mini-Satellite T.V. and interactive computing systems to the farthest reaches of this globe. Technology further empowers such languages as essential means of communication and endows them with a cumulative relative advantage vis-à-vis all other languages.

The key question then becomes whether "smaller" languages such as Irish, Lithuanian, Welsh and Breton can benefit from the same liberation from time and space? Whether they too can be technologically empowered so as to compensate for the loss of domain-related and territorial dominance? Further, we need to know whether there is a relationship between decentralist localism and globalisation? If there is, how do both processes at either end of the continuum mediate what happens within mainstream society? Is the former process a primordial reaction to cope with the new threats and demands of the latter? Put in its most fundamental form, does the increased internationalisation of global means of communication, such as those which advance English, inevitably threaten the ability of many other less-favoured languages to survive and compete well into the future?

The technological trends underpinning European integration suggest that there are alternative outcomes in relation to the interaction of language, ethnic identity, territory and the state system. First, developments in commerce and the international political economy together with those in education, entertainment and tourism, aided by mass communication technology, have reinforced the dominance of English for both native and non-native speakers. English has achieved a critical self-sustaining mass as the lingua franca of Europe. Today this has little to do with coercion or imperial overstretch, for as Wright argues,

> the millions of second language speakers and would-be speakers cannot be accounted for by straightforward coercion nor even through direction; the mass results from the incremental effect of individuals deciding that English is of advantage to them, as the prime language of social promotion in a globalising world. Thus we have a classic situation of hegemony in the Gramscian sense; those disadvantaged by their non-native speaker position contribute to their own disadvantage by their consensual behaviour. If they refused to acquire English, they would halt the imbalance that deprives them of the advantage of the native speakers. However, they

perceive that to do so unilaterally would cut them off from global networks and systems that can bring them political advantage, professional reward or economic benefit, and so do not make that choice.

(Wright, 2004, p. 156)

This has led advocates of French, German and Spanish to re-negotiate their positions within the educational, legal and commercial domains of an enlarged Europe. Fears of Anglicisation ushering in greater North American and Japanese influence has stimulated a great number of initiatives designed to harness or at least manage the dominance of English to tolerable levels. Among the plethora once can discern alternative propositions; 1) that harmonised educational systems within the EU should encourage all students to acquire two foreign languages; 2) that a first foreign language should be obligatory; 3) that English should be taught as a second foreign language, but never as a first; 4) that less information and cultural loss would occur if the principle of multilingualism could be instituted in most supra-national public and governmental affairs.

Such considerations are discussed regularly by international and state agencies as varied as NATO, the Council of Europe, the EU Socrates and Comenius Programmes, Immigrant Language Testing Regimes and Local Education Authorities.[1] Most overarching frameworks and schemes tend to promote the interests of state languages only, or are designed to modify the impact of the dominance of English. Such propositions do not take into account the situation of autochthonous language groups, such as the Basques, Bretons, Irish and Welsh, who might be further marginalised in an increasingly complex and competitive social order (Williams, 1998b, p. 270). In order to escape such double marginalisation, their main hope appears to lie in establishing regional bilingualism as the dominant pattern in education, public administration, media and the law. However, ethnic mobilisation is so often a surrogate for issues such as political struggle, economic deprivation and psychological adjustment that the salience of identity is likely to increase as the EU avers a more open, pluralistic society. A major challenge is interpreting the disjuncture between formal political units and the social behaviour of increasingly autonomous and individualistic citizens. Within the stronger jurisdictions, such as Catalonia, Euskadi and Wales, this hope is being realised. But this positive development should not blind us to the reverse trends of attrition and collapse which characterise too many of the lesser-used languages within Europe.

The current thrust for linguistic pluralism, for preserving European diversity, inevitably places a huge responsibility on the various educational systems to deliver these new political ambitions. Education has long been the prime socialisation agency of advanced modernising states. Accordingly it is teachers that occupy the front line of bilingualism and multiculturalism in Europe. Curriculum and language planners may set the agenda, but it is the teaching profession which is best armed to deal with the particular needs of children and students within an increasingly multicultural Europe. In consequence, the teaching profession constitutes the core of any society's information network. But from time to time, it can be unfairly burdened should popular expectations presume that it, above all other elements, should be primarily responsible for the transmission of a designated range of languages and cultures. Within both RM and IM classes, quite unanticipated consequences of inhabiting increasingly multilingual societies are being faced. Thus educational planners used to dealing with curriculum development and teacher training issues are also now becoming more sensitive to the issues of personality development and the social psychological adjustment of children with mixed identities living within pluralist environments.

But in addition to being exposed to primary instruction in two or more languages, pupils at bilingual schools also engage in self-reflective assessment of the relationship between their individual bilingualism and their collective social identity. Sometimes it is very obvious that significant groups within multicultural societies neither accept nor respect the particular sort of education which bilingual or multilingual children are receiving. Tension and social conflict often accompany initial attempts at establishing a bilingual educational system, especially if the rationale of the reform is to compensate for the previously discriminatory experience suffered by a particular section of society. As we shall see this is a particular concern of many advocates of Basque or Irish-medium education, where despite upwards of 1500 hours of language instruction within an average school career, many students fail to master the basics of the language. A common feature of many such contexts is for the hegemonic language to dominate the social activities of the students outside the class-room such that Spanish or English becomes the default language of social interaction.

Some language groups face a more positive future if they can use this international spur to democratic participation in public affairs, by encouraging representation within decision-making bodies at all levels from the local, to the supra-state level. Parallel developments within international law, especially those which advance the human rights paradigm, also benefit members of linguistic minorities. Initially the major international human rights instruments, such as the United Nations *International Covenant on Civil and Political Rights* ("ICCPR")[2] and the Council of Europe's *Convention for the Protection of Human Rights and Fundamental Freedoms* ("ECHR")[3] had a limited impact on linguistic minorities. The growth of European legislation on the Protection of National Minorities, or the Council of Europe's the Framework Convention and European Charter for Regional or Minority Languages, requires states to take positive measures to support access to minority-language education and administrative services. However, reliance on this form of supra-structural promotion of rights could provide a false dawn of optimism, if it is not also accompanied by a parallel sub-structural reform of many aspects of life within multicultural societies at regional, metropolitan and local levels.

The provision of new rights should be accompanied by investment in an enhanced capacity to use the opportunities and deliver the services to which the right pertain. Yet this hardly ever happens in an orderly, systematic manner. This calls into question the sufficiency of the rights-based approach to democratic participation as the definitive model of minority protection and empowerment. In my view it is essential that innovations in language planning regimes, such as those currently being undertaken in, for example, the Basque Country and Wales, be fully honoured and funded by the local state. Because these are "true *Abstand*" minority languages (Trudgill, 1993), what happens to the struggling minority in these two countries is a predictor of the linguistic fortunes of other groups, including those such as Norwegian and Danish who are bolstered by their own state, but nevertheless face the same external competition from languages of wider communication. This is why bodies such as the European Parliament, the Council of Europe, the European Cultural Foundation are engaged in a fundamental political assessment of linguistic diversity in Europe, asking to what extent the international agencies can sustain all the competing language interests within a representative, but effective, European political system. We shall examine current attempts to develop EU-wide language networks in the final chapter.

The conventional way in which solutions to language diversity are framed is to ask the question "Which Languages for Europe?" Various models have been proposed and several practical solutions were recommended by the European Cultural Foundation and the European Parliament limited-life working panel established to address this theme (ECF).[4]

Virginie Mamadouh of Amsterdam University has argued that rather than ask such questions, a more pertinent question is "How should the mediation between speakers of different languages be organised?" She has explored an answer by reference to grid-group cultural theory and has demonstrated how policies and practices are the result of competition between different rationalities and therefore depend on the influence, strategies and alliances of their adherents (Mamadouh, 2002).

In 2007 the EU had 28 official and working languages and a plethora of vital languages spoken by its population. The recent accession states of Bulgaria and Rumania have contributed their own suite of language-related opportunities and challenges. Consequently future language policies will have to deal with a varying geometry of multilingualism which is reasonably well known. What is not recognised so well is what Mamadouh (2002) has termed the dual influence of language diversity both on national identities and on the ability of citizens to access supranational and transnational decision-making processes. Too often discussions on the relevance and practicality of championing linguistic diversity are couched at the global or state level, whereas such issues are best discussed simultaneously at all seven scales in the hierarchy, namely 1) Pan-European; 2) Macro-Regional; 3) State; 4) National/regional; 5) Metropolitan/local; 6) Ethnic, cultural or interest group; 7) Individual citizen/subject/immigrant, level of analysis. At each level in the scale hierarchy a different combination of ecological, holistic and geolinguistic applications will be required to facilitate policy. I am conscious that there exist excellent treatments of linguistic diversity from a legal (Trifunovska, 2001), sociological (Extra and Gorter, 2001) and statistical (Euromosaic, 2004) perspectives. I want to supplement such studies by offering a holistic perspective.

Holistic perspectives

My central argument is that we need to give more prominence to the study of human ecology and planning in order to understand and situate language-related issues and then to apply holistic methods and perspectives to the formulation of policy. Human ecology is generally defined as the study of interactions of organisms (including *homo sapiens*) and the environment. If we extend the biophysical environment to encompass human behaviour as adaptation to stimuli then we also introduce the concepts of governance, human health and well being. The key terms within this formulation and interpretation are *"language in context"* and the adoption of a sensitive approach to *"environmental considerations in language planning"* (Williams, 1991).

McHarg (1998) has advised that planning consists of the formulation of hypothetical alternative scenarios. Human ecological planning refers to the physical, biological and cultural regional/spatial contexts, but it is rarely operationalised as such, for language planning, by and large, pays lip service to the physical and biological sciences, ecology, ethnography, anthropology and epidemiology. As we saw in Chapter Four, it concentrates on linguistics, education, economics, sociology and political structures.

Nevertheless it is important to recognise that the major determinant of any allocation process in terms of planning resources is the value system and context of the problem identifier and solver. This is why holistic perspectives need to be emphasised because unless the decision-maker is suitably briefed, she/he will marginalise the significance of context for languages in society and will opt for thematic, partial and sectoral solutions to policy issues.[5]

Holistic language planning should aspire to regulate the behaviour of linguistic minorities in a self-sustaining manner by creating fit environments and adapting these by virtue of syntropic-fitness-health measures. The opposite, alternative policy option would imply entropic-misfitness-morbidity, which ultimately leads to language death.

Edwards (2002) has reminded us that such perspectives derive from a specific concern for the preservation and continuation of endangered languages, which in turn is underpinned by an emotional attachment to diversity.

Consequently, I recognise that holism, like ecology, is subject to bias. It depends upon which holistic thought and action is being advocated, by whom, for whom and under what precise conditions.[6]

Why then do I believe that linguistic diversity is a valuable thing, and what conditions are necessary for it to thrive? Why do we who are active within the language and minority rights networks seek to promote an alternative vision of European linguistic diversity to that which is advanced by the major economic actors and international organisations? Edwards (2002) asserts that we do so because we recognise that diversity is good in itself, because it involves a preference for heterogeneous landscapes and an aesthetic appreciation that values multidimensional perspectives.[7]

He also asserts provocatively that guilt is a powerful motivating factor at work because the champions of such diversity often emanate from outside the communities concerned![8] He challenges us to ask two self-reflective questions; a) isn't it, at the very least, disingenuous not to acknowledge such motivations? And b) are they not more likely to persist because of their cathartic value than because of any useful consequences for the intended beneficiaries?[9]

But how might endangered languages be supported? It might be argued that we could be more sympathetic to the formal shortcomings of the new ecology (read holistic perspectives) if its assumptions and programmes seemed to make a significant difference on the ground. The difficulties of language maintenance are by now very well known, but the central justification for emphasising greater holistic perspectives is that maintenance and revitalisation efforts rely on much more than language, education and culture. And yet too few of our language planning agencies are really able to grapple with the multifaceted elements required, being limited to social mobilisation programmes, educational initiatives and marketing campaigns.[10] Hence they are bereft of any structural, and hence lasting, influence on issues of mainstream economic growth, regional development policy, labour migration, investment strategies and the like, all of which influence the vitality (or morbidity) of language networks and communities. Language planners conventionally cite the extra-linguistic impediments to effective policy implementation, but rarely engage such factors head on, presuming that they fall within the remit of other professional disciplines.

It is thus tempting, as Edwards does in regard to the value of the "new ecology", to argue that our understanding of diversity and linguistic endangerment has not been enhanced. He avers that "we are no nearer a strong logical base for the support of diversity, nor are we any closer to effective methods of maintenance – ones that is, that are neither too draconian or undemocratic, nor workable only in highly restricted contexts" (2002, p. 3). I accept that this is a major challenge which is only now being tackled by the more mature, astute language planning bodies in Europe. But even when contemporary opinion offers some comfort in arguing that linguistic globalisation stimulates counter-measures in support of local identities,

Edwards posits that this ebb and flow will produce more and more indigenised "Englishes" as varieties develop in divergent ways.[11] We may ask if the inevitability of such trends renders any countervailing measures to support lesser-used languages as worthless. To put it in a nutshell, is most of what we have discussed to date in this volume an expression of wish-fulfilment, more concerned with vanity, with the massaging of minority egos than with social justice and enhancing the quality of life? Edwards would maintain his challenge by reference to the following implications:

> (i) while it is impossible to accurately assess the possibilities here the historical record is suggestive; (ii) an implication may be that the social trends of the broadest sort, operating both temporarily and geographically, completely dwarf language-planning efforts (with the provisos noted above); (iii) a further implication may be that we will always have linguistic and cultural diversity-perhaps more at some times than at others, and perhaps having to coexist in new ways with globalising tendencies – although the *forms* of that diversity may alter.
>
> (Edwards, 2002, pp. 3–4)

This is a salutary reminder, if one were needed, of how inadequate are the forces ranged against the hegemonic advance of major languages, by the champions of linguistic diversity and minority rights. Yet we know how difficult the challenge is, we have lived it for many generations.

Let me progress the argument by reference to several cross-cutting themes which challenge policy-makers throughout Europe. As a geographer my professional bias is to start with those regional contexts wherein the target language may be protected, promoted and used in employment. Three contrasting examples taken from Ireland, Wales and the Basque Country will illustrate the various approaches which have been adopted to secure some degree of stability and prosperity for lesser-used languages. If some inroads can be made to stabilise routine spaces and contexts for minority language use, then such opportunities should have a reinforcing effect on language choice and functions.

Models of regional development

The Gaeltacht Authority in Ireland, Menter a Busnes in Wales and the Mondragon co-operative movement in the Basque Autonomous Community offer contrasting examples of regional employment initiatives and models of spatial planning which have had mixed fortunes in marrying regional development and applied language planning.

The first model is spatially defined territorial language planning, whereby the authorities seek to identify and define parts of the state for special attention. In 1922 the newly independent Irish state launched a comprehensive strategy for the restoration of Irish as a national language. Irish speakers were given preference in public service positions such as Gardai, Army Officers, teachers and civil servants, thereby creating a new middle-class element to supplement the Irish-speaking population. The 1937 Constitution gave recognition to two languages, Irish and English, but declared Irish as the first official language. There followed a policy of incremental reform to establish State initiatives to promote the use of Irish, to stabilise Gaeltacht communities and to encourage a nationwide system of voluntary language organisations, the most prominent of which is Comhdhail Náisiunta Na Gaeilge.

Government initiatives, particularly its rural development policies, did not stabilise the Irish-speaking communities and as a result of improved education and economic development large numbers of Gaeltacht residents quit the predominantly Irish-speaking areas for employment opportunities in urban, anglicised locales.[12] But though required to use their Irish language skills in a professional capacity, many of the incipient middle-class chose not to reproduce their language within the family or the new urban neighbourhoods, although of course they continued to use Irish when they returned to their home communities. Nevertheless the government committed itself to a two-pronged attack to arrest the decline of Irish. The first policy was to define and preserve the Irish-speaking areas, the Gaeltachtai hoping thereby to bolster the already fragmented Irish-speaking districts. The second policy initiative was to increase the number of Irish-speaking inhabitants primarily through the statutory education system. The Gaeltacht had long been subject to interventionist planning which sought to attract suitable economic development to stabilise the Irish-speaking population. But from its inception the delimitation of the Gaeltacht was flawed both in terms of offering a platform for regional development and as an ideological resource for language revitalisation (Williams, 1988a, 1991). As we shall see in detail in Chapter Seven, the implementation of government policy was characterised by a lack of policy precedent, of socio-spatial planning, of census interpretation experience, of conceptual awareness and of theoretical sophistication (Hindley, 1991, p. 92). There was no awareness of fundamental patterns of sociolinguistic behaviour, nor of the maintenance of networks so essential for language survival. There had been no conceptual exploration of the territorial or individual alternatives in language planning strategies, nor indeed had much need been felt for language planning in the English-speaking world to which all *Irish*-speaking scholars belonged.

For some sixty years the various reforms and initiatives had not transformed the Gaeltacht into a dynamic, self-sustaining Irish-speaking entity, how could they given the poor base and shaky premises upon which this enterprise had been conceived? Nevertheless the Gaeltacht remained an integral part of both government strategy and activist thinking, so much so that when the need for a national action plan for Irish was spelled out in the late-eighties by Board na Gaeilge, special attention was paid to the role of the Gaeltacht within national planning for Irish (Board na Gaeilge, 1988). Many of the strategic policy initiatives identified then have now been implemented, albeit within the context of a healthier Irish economy. In 1988 it was reported that only *c*.5 per cent of the Irish citizens use Irish extensively in their homes, neighbourhood or at work, although a further 10 per cent of the population use Irish regularly if less extensively. Weak rates of language reproduction lead the authors of the report to suggest urgent remedial action along the following lines. They argued that the state should take the initiative in changing the operating context of Irish usage and in changing the popular consciousness about Irish identity. In essence the state should recreate an ideological basis for Irish language loyalty and learning. To this end the report advocated that Board na Gaeilge be given wider powers to counter the generally marginalised position of Irish within other government agencies. It argued that central government itself, through its discourse, sense of complacency and lack of leadership, was one of the key agencies militating against promotional measures on behalf of Irish. Second, the report called for a popular cultural movement, both to resist provincialism and the downgrading of Irish, and also to act as a fulcrum for the re-creation of virile Irish-medium social networks. Third, the basic rights of Irish speakers in their dealings with state agencies needed much greater specification. While Article 8 of the Bunreacht na hEireann established the constitutional standing of both official languages, there was little in the Irish system which set out the detailed practical legislative provisions. Calls for a revised Irish Language Act were eventually heeded and a new Official Languages Act together with the Office of Commissioner for the Irish Language (An Coimisinéir Teanga) were established in 2003. Legislating for the right to use Irish without also investing in the infra-structural support which sustains the language is partial so that I take such investment to be the key element for the realisation of language choice in a multilingual society. Four other needs were identified, to give legal effect to the concept of the bilingual state; to strengthen Irish in the public service; to increase the visibility and usage of Irish in the state-sponsored media and to arrest the decline of Irish in the Gaeltacht (Bord na Gaeilge, 1986).

Since 1988 the main government agencies the Department of the Gaeltacht, Udaras na Gaeltachta and the Bord na Gaeilge have been accused of failing to achieve a high degree of policy integration. The principal actor in the Gaeltacht, Údarás na Gaeltachta, was established in 1979 as a successor agency to Gaeltarra Éireann, and received €32.7 million from the DCRGA in 2003 (DCRGA, 2004c). Údarás-assisted companies employed 7346 workers, some 19.1 per cent of the Gaeltacht workforce of 38,433 people, together with 4220 part-time/seasonal employees (Údarás na Gaeltachta, 2004). Despite having had some success in attracting a variety of industries to one of Europe's most marginal locations, Údarás has also been constantly criticised for not fulfilling its language promotion remit. Indeed on several occasions it has accelerated the very process of Anglicisation it was designed in part to ameliorate (Williams, 1988a; Hindley, 1991; Ó Cinnéide *et al.*, 2001).[13] Conscious of these lacunae, Údarás currently directs 20 per cent of its capital budget toward language-related activities, but the majority of its expenditure is still on fairly conventional economic development. While it would be fair to say that co-ordination between and within organisations has not always been as smooth as might have been expected, there appears to be a fresh and genuine determination to tackle the following underdeveloped issues: more robust regional development policies within the Gaeltacht which were sympathetic to the need to stabilise Irish-speaking communities and networks; the integration of migrants into the Irish-speaking networks of the Gaeltacht; greater emphasis on the media as a resource for integrating Gaeltacht residents and Irish language speakers outside the Gaeltacht; more dynamic models of language learning; the promotion of Irish as an economic resource; and the expansion of the work of Gaelscoileanna.

Each element has witnessed growth and the area surrounding Galway in particular has experienced a mini-revival in terms of its sociolinguistic vitality. But there remains the recognition within Údarás, Foras na Gaelige and other Irish promotional bodies that, unless a sustained campaign is mounted to transform Irish as the default language of the Gaeltacht, so much good work will have been wasted.[14] Providing opportunities to use the language is one thing, influencing people's behaviour to maximise that potential is quite another. This is made even more acute as Foras na Gaeilge has yet, to date, to undertake serious work within the Gaeltacht.[15] Now would seem an opportune time for the integrated, inter-departmental planned promotion of Irish to take place across all state agencies.

Wales has rejected the Irish model whereby official language districts are designated for special attention. This despite strong and persistent calls by pressure groups, such as Adfer in the seventies and eighties and Cymuned today. It illustrates a second model which seeks to transform the economic and skills potential of a language group from within by promoting entrepreneurial activities and community development initiatives. The main agencies are the National Assembly's Economic Development Department (having incorporated the Welsh Development Agency in 2004), Menter a Busnes (Enterprise and Business), Antur Teifi and the Mentrau Iaith (Language Enterprise Initiatives). Menter a Busnes has adopted innovative approaches to the challenge of promoting self-directed and targeted economic development and cultural change. Its aims and objectives since 1989 have been to:

- maximise the economic potential of Welsh speakers;
- create and operate a long term action based programme to make sure that Welsh language culture adapts itself creatively in terms of economic attitudes and activities;

- to increase considerably the number of Welsh speakers who develop companies that already exist; work in and manage businesses of all kinds; invest in businesses; establish new ventures; initiate economically-based activities in the community; operate in a wider range of sectors; and manage effectively in a variety of situations.

The practical means by which Menter a Busnes translate these aims into reality include comprehensive business and management training programmes; schools and adult education seminars on business enterprise opportunities, vocational training; agricultural enterprise and marketing information packs; promoting empirical research and policy initiatives; EU inter-regional projects co-ordinated by Agora, with an emphasis on cultural tourism and farm diversification; promoting new forms of bilingual intervention in both the rural and urban contexts (Menter a Busnes, 1997).

The National Assembly's involvement is to build up infra-structural capacity, to co-ordinate economic and cultural initiatives through its administration of Objective 1 funding, the application of Wales Spatial Plan and a plethora of tourist developments, some of which emphasise the theme of cultural and linguistic heritage.

The 23 Mentrau Iaith are involved in community-level area-based projects and represent the local expression of national network of language enterprise agencies. Each Menter Iaith is unique and is designed to reflect the needs and priorities of the community it seeks to serve.[16] However, they all share common aims which are:

- to create social conditions that would foster positive attitudes towards the Welsh language and an increase in its use;
- to institutionalise the use of Welsh as a medium of social and institutional communication;
- to highlight the close relationship between language and attitudes which relate to quality of life and socio-economic issues.

The main role of the first agency, *Menter Cwm Gwendraeth*, was to create a sound economic base for Welsh and to encourage local enterprise by co-ordinating economic policies and training programmes initiated by various government agencies and local authorities (Campbell, 2000). By establishing a Welsh language business club, *Menter Cwm Gwendraeth* supported indigenous Welsh-speaking businesses and provided them with the skills and confidence to succeed in an increasingly competitive market. Similarly Welsh language training programmes have been put on to develop the linguistic skills of employees, especially those who are in direct contact with the public. Translation services have also been provided to support the use of the Welsh language in the private sector along with seminars on language awareness and sensitivity and courses for dealing with the Welsh language media.

Given that much of Wales is economically disadvantaged, the community development programmes also offer an additional tool for tackling social exclusion. Too many disadvantaged groups such as single parents, retired miners or poorly educated young people – by lacking confidence and having a negative self-image – can remain excluded, alienated and unable to participate in the mainstream of community life. Thus the Mentrau conception of community development is about:

- tackling social exclusion
- developing people skills
- increasing community participation
- encouraging community empowerment
- increasing confidence and self-esteem
- accessing knowledge and information
- developing skills in decision-making and advocacy
- capacity building.

The main objectives of Mentrau activities in this respect are to:

- enable communities to identify their needs and aspirations and highlight the extent to which these are currently being met by various agencies.
- undertake a social audit and profile outlining weaknesses or gaps in provision by mainstream agencies.
- set up village fora to increase community participation in decision-making processes.
- enable agencies to help communities prioritise their needs and aspirations.
- help the community to draw up a strategic action plan.
- identify and access funding from various sources.
- facilitate community capacity building through developing people's skills, knowledge, experience and confidence.
- encourage the establishment or enhancement of effective inter-agency partnerships.
- assist in implementing direct-benefit projects to do with capital expenditure programmes, training, environmental improvements, job creation, health awareness programmes and crime prevention schemes (for details see Campbell, 2000).

Such a nation-wide network of Mentrau Iaith is relevant because:

- in situations characterised by strong language potential but weak socio-linguistic networks, which would otherwise lead to fragmentation, they offer a significant socio-psychological fillip for the reproduction of the language.

- as local language co-ordinating bodies, they can create new partnerships between the National Assembly, the Welsh Language Board, local government, statutory public bodies, health trusts and voluntary agencies and private companies.
- they can encourage the use of Welsh in hitherto limited domains and that without them constituting part of the official administration of any district.
- they can initiate novel and pioneering forms of encouraging the use of Welsh and take advantage of social and institutional opportunities as they arise.
- the great strength of Mentrau Iaith is that they seek to serve the needs of the local community and encourage a shared responsibility for the language's future.
- they are viewed as pioneering interventionist agencies which seek to change expectations, create new networks and enable communities to regain ground which they have lost in linguistic terms.
- they are also perceived as worthwhile, cost-effective agencies engaged in the process of community regeneration (Williams and Evas, 1997; Campbell, 2000; Williams, 2000d).

More recently the Mentrau have been joined by a second tier of language agencies, the Area Development Schemes, which seek to harness all the agencies related to the provision of Welsh-medium services within one small area.[17] Each location provides a local area action plan which stipulates how micro-level language promotion is to be achieved within which time-frame and targets.

A third model is the creation of indigenous social and economic capital funding, so as to sustain fragile or threatened communities. Basque private sector language initiatives and programmes have played a vital role in the revitalisation of the Basque language, and it is only rather recently that such funding has been accompanied by significant government investment. Within the Basque Country the Mondragón co-operative movement represents the most effective agency for economic transformation. This was founded in 1956 in Arrasre, Gipuzkoa, by five graduates of the local Polytechnic.[18] They established a local credit union, the Caja Laboral Popular in 1959, which financed the initial establishment and subsequent growth of a number of Small and Medium-sized Enterprises, (SMEs), such as Fagor Electrónica, Fagor Ederlan and Danobat. Three principles underlay the development of the movement: 1) an adherence to co-operative participatory democracy and self-management; 2) a concern to promote the Basque language, both as a symbol of identity and as a means of social communication within the companies of the region; 3) a consciousness that the Spanish state, both contemporaneously and historically, could not be relied upon to tackle many of the issues which workers and citizens in the Basque Country faced. Thus an element of economic self-sufficiency and brand loyalty was created, which was manifested through granting discounts at Eroski supermarkets or on Fagor electronic "white" appliances, while parallel developments in health insurance and pension funds at Lagun Aro were encouraged. The movement also invested heavily in the promotion of the Basque-medium *ikasolas* and eventually in the creation of Mondragón University to serve both the educational needs of the region and to reduce the hemorrhaging of young talented people. The Mondragón Cooperative Corporation is now the Basque Country's largest corporation, the seventh largest in Spain and the world's largest worker co-operative. It consists of over 150 companies, ranging from manufacturing and engineering interests, to retail, financial and educational activities. Its supermarket cooperative, Eroski, is the largest Spanish-owned retail food chain and the fourth largest retail group in Spain. In 2002 the MCC contributed 3.7 per cent towards the total GDP of the Basque Country. It has *c*.60 industrial plants abroad, several of which are located in Latin America.[19]

The decision-making body is the 650 member Co-operative Congress, whose delegates are elected from the constituent co-operatives. The annual general assembly elects members to a governing council which has day-to-day management responsibility and appoints senior staff. For each individual business, there is also a workplace council, the elected President of which assists the manager with the running of the business on behalf of the workers. Ten principles characterise the initiative, namely open admission, democratic organisation, the sovereignty of labour, the instrumental and subordinate nature of capital, participatory management, payment solidarity, intercooperation, social transformation, universality and education.

Education has been central to MCC and its development, and it was the cooperative movement which promoted the gradual introduction of Basque as a medium of instruction within the primary, then secondary and finally the tertiary level. Mondragon Unibertsitatea, established in 1997, is comprised of three faculties, each of which emerged from three cooperatives – engineering (established in 1943), business and management (1960) and humanities and education (1976). The university operates from three campuses in Oñati, Eskoriatxa and Mondragón and is supported by a series of Technological Research Centers. It is currently evaluating the effectiveness of a major initiative whereby each student, by the time they graduate, will be proficient in Basque, Spanish, English and the use of IT.[20] The vast majority of its students has come from the *ikastolas* movement and will seek employment from within the BAC. The Humanities Faculty, HUHEZI, concentrates on teacher training, on enterprise training for management positions, on multilingualism and education.[21] The Faculty is committed to the normalisation of Basque, principally through the *Ulibarri* project supported by the

Basque government and by the evaluation of other local projects such as BAZARA and HIZPRO.[22]

Given the oppression of the Basque people and their culture during the Franco period, it is not surprising that private sector and voluntary initiatives characterise the Basque struggle more than perhaps most other western European cases. The resultant language organisations may be divided into three types of movement, according to Gardner (2000), namely technical-entrepreneurial, professional-cum-trade union and citizen-activist.[23] In the first group he includes modern Basque language cultural companies, such as the terminological centre *UZEI*, local Basque language publishers, private language schools *ikastolas*, Basque language press, and language planning consultancies working in the private sector. These almost invariably set up within a conscious language planning perspective, sometimes as non-profit making bodies, sometimes in pursuit of profit. He argues that, as yet, there are few examples of the professional associations and trade union groups, but the most effective has been the union of Basque-speaking lawyers, who advocate the establishment of Basque language courts. The third group includes, amongst others, *Euskal Herrian Euskaraz*, a small association of activists, well-known throughout the Basque Country for its confrontational tactics in favour of Basque. More powerful and, on the whole, more attractive he argues, to the majority of the population are the numerous grass roots Basque language associations, located in specific towns, villages or small geographical areas.[24] Many of these have spawned initiatives belonging to the first group, particularly in the sphere of local mass media. A good example of this would be the Goièra Communication Group which has grown from the production of a small newspaper to managing a TV and radio station, web sites and broader publication interests.[25]

A recent noticeable development has been the banding together of many of these non-governmental organisations in a single umbrella organisation called *Kontseilua*. The private, non-governmental sector offers a relatively vigorous example of community and industrial initiatives in favour of the promotion of Basque which has come to realise that their cumulative efforts will be greater by advocating co-ordinated, integrated action.

However, the relationships between government language planning and private sector initiatives has been difficult within the Basque country. Gardner *et al.* (2000, p. 331) cite the pivotal role of the coordinating bodies that the private sector has developed. For example, *EKB*, set up in 1983, at times seemed to act as a shadow language planning body, often critical of the Basque Government, particularly of the failure to produce a thoroughgoing strategic plan for the language. This demand went unsatisfied until 1999 when the Basque Government made its plan public.[26] By then *EKB* was winding down, giving place to the broader based, rather more cooperative *Kontseilua*. The new ambience was reflected in the recent increase of the number of members from NGO's on the Advisory Council for Basque. Nevertheless there is still much to be done to co-ordinate both public and private sectors and to integrate language planning with other forms of planning. The current system is conscious of this deficiency and is seeking remedial action to strengthen the full impact of interventionist programme.

Three models, reflecting three methods of promoting the economic and regional context which sustain language use and vitiates its relevance within specific domains. However, each of these models reflects the particular political circumstances which permitted or forced such developments. None of them was based upon language planning principles or practice, and each of them grew organically and justified their position within the range of promotional activities because they went unchallenged for so long. With the rise of regional government a more professional and integrated approach has been developed to which we now turn.

Regional government initiatives

A second cross-cutting theme is how region-level governments harmonise their language policy and planning initiatives within specific programmes and throughout the region's public administration. The best example is the Catalan government's commitment to improve the capacity of the local state to deliver bilingual services, to institutionalise the use of Catalan and to adapt key elements of its educational and health provision to the fresh challenge of a new wave of migrants in the past decade.

The Catalan Language Planning System, derived from the General Directorate of Language Policy established in 1980, is a well-developed institutional frame for the co-ordinated action of governmental departments and their interaction with civil society (Puigdevall i Serralvo, 1997). Paralleling the political support for Catalan there has been heavy investment in professional language planning training with some 600 "*tècnics de normalització lingüística*" (professional language planners) working within the public administrative system.

Following the establishment of the DGPL,[27] other agencies were created to bolster the role of Catalan as an official, working language of the regional state. These include the *Servei d'Assessorament Lingüístic* (Language Advisory Service), *Servei de Normalització Lingüística* (Language Promotion Service) and the *Institut de Sociolingüística Catalana* (Institute of Catalan Sociolinguistics) which are answerable to the Sub-directorate General. The Advisory Service was charged with the promotion of the quality of the Catalan language, used by public and private organisations alike, and the promotion of the teaching of Catalan both in areas with special needs and overseas. The Promotion Service is responsible for the promotion of Catalan in all areas of social activity through marketing campaigns and other means. The Institute is a centre for research and expertise in sociolinguistics, which has the function of monitoring, documenting and evaluating the results of language policies undertaken by the DGPL. It also undertakes research within various sectors of the society and economy and is a major resource tool for evaluating and monitoring the sociolinguistic situation of Catalan.

In addition, as Puigdevall i Serralvo in Gardner *et al.* (2000) makes clear all government departments have a language unit[28] which have the dual function of advising civil servants on linguistic matters and of diffusing specific terminology within organisations and various professional bodies linked to each sector of activity. The Generalitat has created a network of organisations in order to co-ordinate and draw together all these internal services to:

- guarantee the even application of the linguistic normative among every department (Technical Commission for Language Policy);
- inform the DGPL on actions concerning language policy undertaken by the different departments; to both the accomplishment of the language use legislation in the Administration and the norms about the knowledge of Catalan among civil servants and to supervise the correct and uniform use of terminology in close collaboration with the Termcat (The Technical Network);
- advise the DGPL on matters relating to the administrative and judicial language (The Advisory Commission for Administrative language);
- devise and organise examinations for the award of general and specific certificates of proficiency in Catalan (Permanent Board) (p. 351).

There are also language units in the territorial representation of the Generalitat in all four of the provincial capitals of Catalonia. Evaluation of the impact of government initiatives is undertaken by regular, professional surveys such as "El Coneixement del Català, 1996" by Farràs i Farràs, Torres i Pla and Vila i Moreno (2000) which offers a sophisticated sociolinguistic analysis of the linguistic behaviour of the Catalan population.

For some two decades the system developed to adjust to fresh challenges and to diffuse best practice within language policy and language planning throughout the local government sector. However, at the turn of the century it was felt that a fresh initiative and political impetus was needed to re-energise the official promotion of Catalan. This was occasioned by a change of government in November 2003 when a coalition of three parties (Catalan Socialists, the Catalan Republican Left and the Greens) ruled the Generalitat. Consequently the system was re-organised as illustrated in Figure 5.2. whereby the DGPL was upgraded into the Secretariat for Language Policy, and moved from the Department for Culture to the vice-presidency's Cabinet Office.[29]

Puigdevall i Serralvo (2006) has identified several significant changes in the revised organisational structure. First, as the Language Policy unit grows in complexity it is necessary to have better co-ordination both internally and territorially within a revised Departmental Co-ordination Section.

138

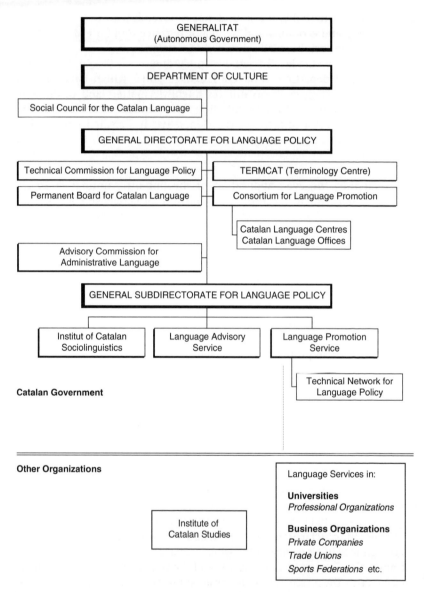

Figure 5.1 Organization chart of language policy of the autonomous Government of Catalonia (1980–2005)
Source: Puigdevall i Serrlavo (2000), p. 350.

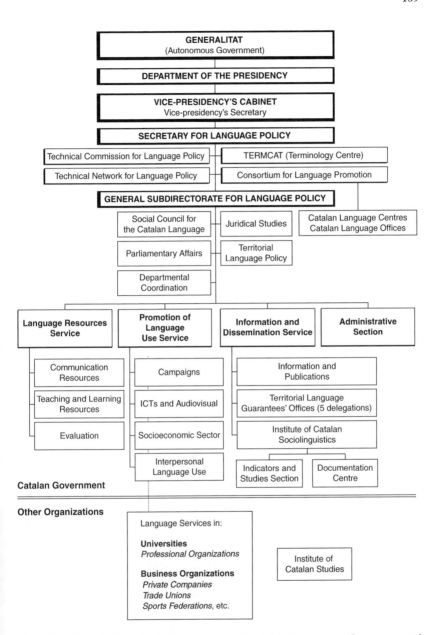

Figure 5.2 Organization chart of language policy of the autonomous Government of Catalonia (From 2005)

Second, the Parliamentary Affairs and Juridical Sections follow more closely parliamentary and political activity, giving a new impetus to the Social Council for the Catalan Language and providing legal advice to the government in the field of language policy. Third, the Language Resource Service replaces the Language Advisory Service. Its main aim is to devise and diffuse resources which will facilitate the use of Catalan. These include new teaching resources so as to instruct late arrivals and immigrants, a variety of tools in the field of language engineering and the provision of official certificates which conform to the new European framework of language evaluation. Fourth, the Promotion of Language Use Service replaces the Language Promotion Service. Its aim is to promote Catalan within information and communication technologies (ICTs) and to increase its regular use within the media, aspects of the economy and within informal and interpersonal networks more generally. The Information and Dissemination Services is charged with informing civil society and government circles alike of the activities and findings of the SPL. At the core of the department lies the Institute of Catalan Sociolinguistics which is responsible for evaluating the effectiveness of language policy. There is also a new section, created as a result of collaboration between the SPL and the Department of Commerce, Consumers and Tourism, known as "*Oficina de garanties lingüístiques*" (Language Guarantee's Office) which has five offices throughout the region. The *Oficina* functions as a one-stop-shop for the public to enquire about their language rights and to lodge official complaints about non-compliance with the language law by companies, institutions and other organisations. The *Oficina* forwards complaints to the appropriate department which will carry out an inspection and if necessary levy a fine. The *Oficina* also offers legal advice and resources whereby the use of Catalan may be improved within companies where there have been complaints. Additionally, it has a proactive role in analysing and proposing actions in the areas or sectors where there is significant evidence of non-compliance and/or complaints. Thus the improved infra-structure represents both an increased determination to make language policy work and the allocation of additional resources to support the monitoring, evaluation and regulatory functions this implies.[30] In order to improve inter-departmental consistency the revised Technical Commission for Language Policy has initiated a programme whereby each department of government takes responsibility for promoting Catalan within its own domain.[31]

A second reform was to mount a series of promotional programmes so as to revitalise the languages's struggle. This was a reaction both to an increased sense of apathy by sections of society (especially younger members) and to a realisation that immigration to Catalonia was increasing its multicultural character, several aspects of which favoured Spanish at the expense of Catalan.[32] Having faced one wave of in-migration, largely from southern Spain in the late sixties and seventies, Catalonia is currently facing a second wave of migrants, largely from North Africa, Latin America and other parts of Europe.[33] Early in 2006 there were a reported 700,742 immigrants living in Catalonia, and these constituted 10.6 per cent of its population. This diversity of origin also means a great multiplicity of languages. Currently some 66 different languages are spoken in Catalonia and the diversity is growing. This new reality has prompted calls for measures which will facilitate the learning of Catalan by the immigrant population and to persuade the fluent Catalan population to speak Catalan to newcomers rather than their default practice which is to use Spanish first.

Thus in 2004 the SPL produced an Action Plan, inspired by two campaign slogans,

"make it easier to live in Catalan" and "also in Catalan, in Catalan first". The Action Plan contains six goals which aim to:

1. Make it easier for everyone to learn Catalan, especially for newcomers.
2. Promote the informal use of the language.
3. Guarantee a wide range of goods, products and services in Catalan.
4. Guarantee the right of Catalan speakers to live their lives through the Catalan language.
5. Increase the collaboration between all Catalan-speaking territories in order to advance the status and use of the language.
6. Enhance the status of Catalan both within Spanish and European Institutions.

Five target areas for action were identified, namely 1) the interpersonal, informal use of Catalan; 2) newcomers and new citizens; 3) information and communication technologies; 4) the socio-economic sector and 5) Spanish and European institutions. Tackling each of these issues is compounded by increased globalisation, persistent in-migration, greater multilingualism and the growth of English as a lingua franca.

Within Catalonia, and particularly within Barcelona, home to speakers of more than 200 different languages, the urgent challenge is how to cope with the integration of such a diverse population increase without simultaneously loosing sight of the need to promote Catalan as the language of social inclusion. One very practical illustration is the necessity to serve multilingual patients within the Catalan Health System. Differences of languages, lifestyles, cultures, traditions, religions, ways of interpreting health and illness, can all create barriers and hinder effective treatment from within the health service. Consequently the Catalan Health System established the Directive Plan of Immigration to devise and administer new strategies for dealing with its increasingly plural population. Three aspects were given special attention, namely welcoming, mediation and training. The Welcoming Plan seeks to ease access and understanding of the services on offer by extensive use of translated material and documentation. The Intermediation Plan employs mediators within the health system to establish communicative confidence and maximise the amount of information exchanged between patient and the professionals. The Training Plan seeks to impart to professionals a higher degree of competence (especially in cross-cultural matters) in dealing with the immigrant population. Taken together these three initiatives, derived largely from long established practice within the UK National Health System, improve the quality of Health Service-Patient Care relationship.

At a Mercator conference in Barcelona, 19–21 October 2006, representatives of the Catalan Health Service identified several problems which such initiatives have yet to overcome.[34] I believe that these are germane to many other multicultural societies in Europe, whose health service is serious about respecting the integrity and human dignity of each of its patients qua individuals and not just as a representative category of patient type. The most fundamental issue as reported by Tona Lizana of the Department of Health is of course, engaging with the health system in the first place. Increased bureaucracy, the needs for accurate and updated data all require personal identification records to be established. Far too often some migrants shun the health service for they fear that such contact will lead to official recognition, police action and possibly deportation or a prison sentence. Thus the first barrier to overcome is that of accessing the health care system in order to be registered, to be given an ID and a Health Card. The second issue is establishing trust between patient and professional caregivers. The third is overcoming several cultural filters that prevent the patient from presenting the exact nature of an illness or a medical condition. This is why the cultural mediators, adopted in both Catalonia and the UK, are so vital for they can often interpret, literally both the language being used and the nuanced cultural connotations, which accompany the reporting of ailments and the diagnosis. The fourth is the issue of language itself and the need for accurate translation at all stages of the diagnostic, treatment and post-treatment stages. Understandably perhaps patients tend to access the services of a mediator at the point of initial contact with the medical experts, but once the treatment is progressing, particularly within a hospital environment, the patient may or may not understand the exact requests made upon him/her and this obviously increases stress all round. The fifth issue is the attitude of the health professionals themselves. Speakers at the Mercator conference reported that in many cases the specialists resented the presence of the mediator, and although they recognised that without such intermediaries, mutual understanding would not be achieved, that nevertheless such mediators were considered a nuisance or a drag on proceedings. At other levels in the health system, medics, nurses, care givers, ancillary staff, cleaners, caterers etc. were as representative of normal Catalan society as any other group of workers, and thus there was likely to be an element of cynicism, intolerance and racism at the presence of foreign patients within the system displayed by some. This is why the training programme for all staff was so important, not just the acute medical staff.

Illustration of initiatives in action was given in three case studies. Tai Mooi Ho (Hospital del Mar, Barcelona) provided first hand evidence on how her hospital sought to overcome the language barriers. The authorities were conscious that unless a great effort was made by all concerned, the language difficulties would result, unintentionally, in inappropriate treatment and a resultant diminution in the standards of health care received by the patient. The prime response was to improve the training for health professionals to make them far more competent in this field and to establish an effective and mutual way of communication. A second response was to conduct on-going research into the ways in which such procedures were working. A third was a scoping exercise to seek examples of good practice from other parts of the world and to apply them to Catalonia.

A second illustration was provided by Sid Ahmed Baba El Hebli (The Health and Family Association, Barcelona). Working as and with other cultural mediators in the Lleida region, the presenter reported on a marked improvement in the quality of the immigrant patient-professional interaction and care over the most recent years. This he attributed to a new framework, which gave attention to the following maxims:

1) That the immigrant is not deprived from the symbolic interaction with others;
2) That suitable access to different public services is made easy to guarantee an optimal inclusion-integration within the host society;
3) That the immigrant is allowed to express his or her doubts, sorrows, beliefs, traditions, habits and cultural values;
4) That he or she is assisted in understanding and make him or herself understood facilitating a mutual approach between him or her and the health professionals in order to ensure a suitable care without misunderstandings and/or cultural transgressions;
5) That necessary information/training is given to foster personal autonomy. This overall increase in competence is attributable, in part, to the fostering of the role of cultural mediators within the system.

A comparative perspective on such issues, drawn from four European models of cultural mediation, was presented by Jacob Als Thomsen (Copenhagen University) who reported that different European approaches to cultural mediation are closely linked to interpretations of patient rights and general policies of integration. In the Danish case an analysis of interviews conducted with seventy health professionals revealed that the adoption of cultural mediators in the process did improve communication, that patients valued this intervention, that such strategies influenced the quality and the duration of the treatment and that although there were generally very positive things to say about the method, there were also some negative implications. The cultural mediators themselves often felt that they played the role of the key linking person in the process, but in many cases had reported that they felt humiliated by the attitude and behaviour towards them of some medical personnel. Most of these viewed mediators as a burden, slowing down the interview and making "bad" patients worse.

The comparative study reported the main benefits as follows: 1) there was more equality of treatment regardless of the origin of the patient; 2) better recovery rates; 3) more satisfied patients; 4) more satisfied professionals who felt that they experienced less frustration and fewer conflicts with their patients. But the study also revealed some unintended consequences also. Thus in one, unidentified city, with four hospitals, only one of which employed cultural mediators, a large proportion of the "ethnic" "foreign" or "immigrant" population attended that one hospital and shunned the other three. In another case where a Chinese cultural mediator was employed significant number of patients of Chinese extraction presented themselves for treatment, even though in most cases they were not physically ill. The explanation given was that such people felt lonely, or lost, or sought expert advice on some aspect of their new life in the city, but that rarely, if ever did these concerns have a medical foundation. I would add that in many cases if the role of the cultural mediator is widened to counter depression, dissonance or lack of self-worth then that is a very positive illustration of preventative medicine. However, the hard-pressed cultural mediators are not, by and large, charged with such duties.

The underlying strategic issue of all these examples was whether or not the provision of additional services for an increasingly multilingual population necessarily undermined the attempts to normalise Catalan (or any other official "national" languages).[35] It was evident that unless and until an adequate and robust strategy for dealing with such patients in Catalan was established, then inevitably Spanish would be the default language. A move to labelling prescription drugs, signage, information packs and general medical orientation in five languages had improved matters, but there was still considerable inconsistency in the system as regards the ability of patients to access all services in the language of their choice. It was recognised that the challenge would increase as both the rate and source area of immigration would change and as Catalonia became a more multicultural society. However, it was very evident that within the more advanced current practices in Catalonia there was both a concern for personal dignity and the attention to the whole person, not to just the clinical diagnostic ailments or conditions. When one adds to the normal concerns of an indigenous patient (and his/her family) undergoing treatment the additional issue of language difficulties or language incomprehension, then it becomes even more of a test of a humane society, as to how such people are treated in the most dignified way possible. Too often in our concern with language as system or language as practice, we can forget the very real human needs which are put at risk by adopting too strident a linguistic policy which favours some at the expense of others.

On June 18, 2006, 48 per cent of the Catalan electorate voted in a referendum to renegotiate Catalonia's relationship with Spain. The package negotiated between Madrid and Barcelona was one further act in the evolving functional federalism of contemporary Spain. The powers of the autonomous communities are largely determined by statutes that are negotiated by Madrid and the respective community rather than by constitutional reform. In the 2006 negotiations a large part of the new deal related to the further devolution of power to Catalonia within certain subject areas, such as agriculture, water, banks, trade, external relations, and most sensitively of all, language and identity. The Catalan government had proposed a text that explicitly recognised the "Catalan nation" and asserted Catalonia's uniqueness and the precedence of its laws (Anderson, 2006).[36] In the end Barcelona accepted a heavily negotiated, non-judiciable, preambular clause that takes note of two different views: namely that Catalonia's Parliament has defined its territory as a "nation" while the Spanish constitution "recognises the national reality of Catalonia as a nationality" (Anderson, 2006, p. 15). The agreement declares, "Catalan is the official language of Catalonia", while that of Spain is Spanish. It declares that each individual in Catalonia has the "right to use and the right and duty to know the official languages". The language is both a symbol of Catalonia's uniqueness and a reminder to Spain of a link to a premodern state existence in which the Catalan elite enjoyed independence. A very practical manifestation of this desire for cultural autonomy and fiscal autarky is Catalonia's persistent attempt to negotiate a financial deal similar to that of the Basque Country and Navarre, where it is the "regional" government which collects all personal, corporate and sales taxes and returns an agreed proportion to Madrid. An extension of this model which would result in Madrid being more dependent upon the autonomous communities, especially the richest of them all, Catalonia, was unacceptable to Prime Minister Zapatero.[37]

Be that as it may, Catalonia demonstrates several of the more innovative and sympathetic ways in which to manage the linguistic diversity of its residents, many of whom may serve to undermine its attempts at normalising Catalan alongside Spanish as a language of public services.

Legislative reforms and the implementation of rights

A third theme is the use of strong legislative reforms to create opportunities to use a formerly discriminated language in new contexts. However, creating an opportunity does not necessarily guarantee that the full spirit of the law will be honoured in the delivery of services or indeed in the increased use of such opportunities by citizens. Let me illustrate by reference to the recent Basque experience. The adoption of a new Spanish Constitution in 1978 marked a turning point in the transition to democracy after Franco's death in 1975. The Constitution is divided into 11 parts or "titles" – which are in turn sub-divided into 169 numbered articles organised into "chapters" and "sections".[38]

The 1978 Spanish constitution marked a major transformation in the legal situation of its constituent languages. Gardner in Gardner *et al.* (2000) reminds us that Article 3 states:

1. Castilian [Spanish] is the official language of the Spanish state. All Spaniards have the duty to know it and the right to use it.
2. The other languages of Spain will also be official in the corresponding Autonomous Communities [i.e. regions] in accordance with their [the regions'] statutes.
3. The wealth of different linguistic modalities of Spain is a cultural heritage which shall be the object of special respect and protection.

Paragraph 2 of the above article was, in fact, further developed in both the BAC and Navarre.

In Navarre the founding law of the region[39] contains the following precepts (article 9):

1. Castilian [Spanish] is the official language of Navarre.
2. Basque shall also have the character of official language in the Basque-speaking areas of Navarre
   A charter law shall determine the aforementioned areas, shall regulate the official use of Basque and shall organise the teaching of this language within the framework of the general legislation of the state.

The subsequent Navarrese law on Basque[40] established three zones:

• a Basque zone in the north of Navarre, which corresponds to the present day extension of the traditionally Basque-speaking area;
• a mixed central area including Pamplona, capital of the region, where numerous Basque speakers live;
• a non-Basque area in the south of the region, where percentages of Basque speakers are much lower and where part of the territory at least has never been Basque-speaking.

The rights of speakers in the Basque-speaking zone are similar to those who live in the BAC as described below. In the mixed area, citizens have the right to use Basque with the administration, but there is no guarantee of a response in that language. There the public authorities may optionally require knowledge of Basque of certain civil servants, while teaching of and in the Basque language is optional. In the Spanish-speaking area, citizens dealing with the administration in Basque may be required to present a translation; while in education, the teaching of Basque as a subject, but not as medium, is financed by the administration. Gardner concludes that the law is directed at maintenance, not normalisation in its habitual Spanish state sense of gaining speakers and domains.[41]

In the Basque Autonomous Community mention of Basque in the Statute of Autonomy was included in the following form (article 6):

1. Basque, the Basque people's own language, shall have, like Spanish, the character of official language in [the Autonomous Community of] the Basque Country and all its citizens have the right to know and use both languages.
   (...)
2. Nobody shall be discriminated for reasons of language.[42]

The article also anticipates a law for the normalisation of Basque, through the operation of the Royal Academy of the Basque Language as an official consultative body, and authorises the BAC to propose international agreements for the protection and promotion of the language. Initially this led to closer collaboration, with the Quebec language planning agencies, and later with other European language boards as discussed in Chapter Ten. The law is intended as a central instrument of RLS and includes specific measures for a number of domains commonly tackled by such legislation: education, the media, administration, justice and so on. The approach adopted in the legislation is based primarily on the principle of personality, though there are also minor elements of territoriality visible, particularly in the Navarrese legislation.[43]

In common with other cases, much of the drive for language promotion in the BAC has come from nationalist parties and from committed volunteers.[44] But in contrast to Wales and Quebec, nationalists have constituted a majority in the Basque Parliament since its inception in 1980, although the proportion of votes seems to be falling slowly since the mid 1980s.[45] The Basque Government has frequently been a coalition, but the dominant party is always nationalist as reflected in the fact that the government's *lehendakari* or president has always been a nationalist. In the run up to the passage of the 1982 language normalisation legislation, the nationalists were aware of the need to seek a broad consensus and the resultant law obtained support from the Spanish Socialist Party, though not from the state-wide centre right Popular Party.[46] However, Gardner reports that this relative consensus has largely come to an end, as the new policies begin to alter the *status quo*. Further the very close relationship between nationalism and language has alienated many within the other parties who tend to view any attempt to promote the language as a surrogate for nationalist empowerment. Consequently there is a history of rejection of some or all pro-Basque language legislation and policies by some of the opposition parties.[47]

Despite this there is no doubt that the Basque framework establishes a strong statutory underpinning for language policy measures. However, creating the opportunity is one thing, implementing the language reforms is quite another, as it is subject to great variation in interpretation and application by governmental agencies of a lower order (departments of the regional government, provincial [i.e. county] councils, town and village councils ...) or in Spain by the behaviour of agencies under the control of the state-wide government. Building capacity so as to implement government plans and schemes so often lags behind the declaration of rights, yet clearly if such rights are to be fully honoured then significant training in language awareness and investment in improving language and organisational skills has to be instituted.

Take, for example, the 1982 Law for the Normalisation of the use of Basque by which citizens have the right to address any Government body in the BG's territory in Basque and be dealt with in Basque. The law insists that the administration is bound to attend to citizens in the official language of their choice and, where it is unaware of their choice, to provide information in both languages.[48] Given that when the act was passed the administration in the Basque Autonomous Community was not in a position to comply fully with the new law, gradual implantation has been provided for in two officially planned ways: one is the language profile scheme and the other the authority-wide language schemes, called *erabilera-planak*, that is, plans of language use.

Within the language profile scheme all posts in regional administration have a number of published requisites (level of education required, subject studied, good health, lack of a prison record or whatever ...). To these requisites the 1989 Public Service law added two extra ones, to be published in the official gazette(s) along with the others:

- the level of Basque required to carry out the functions associated with that post (at present one of four levels, to be proved by exam).
- the date, if any, by which the holder of the post must prove that she/he has attained the required level.

The Basque Government runs several language schemes. Here I refer to its core scheme involving just over 6000 employees carrying out tasks which derive from internal workings of the civil-service.[49] It would appear that the scheme is not effective and does not deliver a comprehensive service by which citizens may engage with the administration in the language of their choice. We may ask whether the policy objectives are appropriate. According to an informant's own opinion the law, as outlined above, is perfectly adequate in present circumstances. It spells out that the administration must attend people in the official language of choice and, if that choice is unknown, in both; further, the rule must be gradually implemented.

Why then are the results of the BG scheme to be considered unsatisfactory? The Basque Government itself when reporting on its results for the 1998–2002 period admitted that it had not achieved its objectives. It reported specifically that:

1) the number of posts created does not reach the level of Basque specified,
2) the number of posts with a date of compulsion is low as compared to the number of posts which should have such a date,
3) the low number of permanent post holders in posts with date of compulsion having certified achievement of required level,
4) the number of administrative units with bilingual status.

Consequently a major criticism is that if the primary objective is to provide an official service to citizens in the language of their choice, then the system should be, in addition to measuring increase in officials' knowledge, also measuring how far citizen demand is being satisfied both orally and in writing.[50] This appears not to be a priority for any agencies within government.

Ultimately, the Basque Government has concentrated on increasing knowledge instead of use. That is, it has sought to emphasise input at the expense of output or delivery. Why is this and what are the barriers to the reform process? There is no single factor which can be identified, rather an accumulation of details identified by informants, such as the following:

Bureaucratisation: the whole scheme has spawned an immense amount of regulations and paperwork, forever postponing the time for real action. The obsession with cover-all-contingencies in detailed planning has delayed the introduction of simple, effective, immediately applicable measures.

Plans have not been made: no government department actually produced a plan during the 1998–2002 period. In spite of all the planning apparatus being in place (regulations about how to, officials in most departments dedicated full-time to the task ...), in spite of viability reports in most departments (data collection ...), no plan was actually completed and, hence, none implemented. In the meantime, no interim measures were implemented, except the provision of language training for officials and the subsequent exams.

Interest conflict: some departments aren't really interested in taking the planning on board. In particular, assignation of dates of compulsion gives rise to conflict, as this reduces the opportunities for a department to manipulate personnel movements. Thus conflicts frequently arise between departments wishing to assign a particular date and/or level of Basque to a post and the Sub-department of Language Policy, which oversees the system and checks that departments are conforming to the rules of the game.

Lack of mainstream leadership: it is one thing to focus on the Sub-department of Language Policy's interest in doing things "right"; it is quite another to ask whether the politicians in each department are really interested in or bothered about carrying out government language policy. Lip-service is almost invariably paid to the policy, but in some cases precious little done. In such cases the language planning officials, often in junior positions, have little power to push through the planning agenda and implementation, without proper management backing.

Civil servant interests: the fact that an official learns Basque in no way guarantees willingness to use it. Certification is sufficient to improve one's chances of promotion. There is no follow-up to ensure that government-paid language training actually leads to language use: sometimes it does, sometimes not.

Widespread misunderstanding of objectives: many officials believe that the object of language planning in the Basque Government is to ensure that all texts are bilingual. Thus, it doesn't matter what the citizen's language of choice is: they will automatically get a bilingual reply. This, insiders believe, is extremely damaging: if Basque is to survive it must have communicative value. If the Spanish text is alongside, the Basque text is likely to lose that value a) because recipients, unless young, almost invariably find the Spanish text easier to read; b) because the Basque text is often a mere translation, usually less well written and comprehensible. If, on the other hand, a monolingual Basque text is provide for a client or a customer, then officers will have to make sure of its comprehensibility before sending it; the text, moreover, becomes communicative, ceasing to be merely symbolic.

Insufficient attention to bottom-up aspects of planning: there seems to have been no attempt to involve officials in the planning, no attempt to harness their good will, where it exists. The Basque Government's application of its scheme is a classic top-down case of planning, purveyed through the specialist language planners. This is probably related to overall top-down culture in the Basque Government, where modern management methods seem to be relatively little known.

Lack of information: if the administration is to respond to the citizens in the language of their choice, then it must have knowledge of that choice. The Basque Government has created virtually no instruments to ensure that knowledge. Indeed, the bilingual-reply system mentioned above means that one does not have to pay attention to that choice. Even if one official knows what the choice of a particular citizen is today, that is no guarantee that she/he will know next week, nor that any other official will know. The solution to this problem seems, according to informed insiders, to lie in the creation of a language-choice register, whereby citizens can register their language choice; if computerised, all those Basque Government computer produced letters could then be monolingual according to that choice.

The problem in no way seems to be related to lack of resources: there are substantial sums available for civil servant language training, there are a fair number of full-time planners, translators; other assistance is given (on-line dictionaries, terminology bank, spellchecker, computer programmes in Basque . . .). It appears that there has simply been insufficient attention paid to evaluation and to the need to deliver what government rhetoric claims is the citizen's rightful expectation – the delivery of government services in the language of one's choice.

This is even more surprising as the Basque government has a very well earned reputation for promoting Basque immersion, bilingual education and adult teaching across the statutory and non-statutory sectors.[51] Strong acquisition planning has, however, produced three unanticipated consequences according to Zalbide *et al.* (2005, p. 120). The first is that the mother-tongue factor is not sufficiently taken into account, and as L1 and L2 learners are often taught together the tendency is for L1 Basque students to gravitate towards the L2 Spanish norms. Second, the relative success of teaching Basque as a second language has led paradoxically to non-native speakers outnumbering natives in areas where the latter were demographically weak. Third, there is a strong trend for society's negative attitudes to provide disincentives towards the maintenance of Basque and this is a classic feature among adolescents who report on their increased language switching to Spanish.

This is compounded by the relative fragility of Basque language acquisition by many adolescents within the statutory education sector. Specialist argue that a concentration on increasing numbers receiving an element of instruction in Basque has overshadowed the need to evaluate the quality of Basque learned and used by students. In an attempt to answer the question do young people learn Basque by the time they complete their statutory education, the Department of Education of the Basque Government initiated a study of the Basque language levels of sixteen-year – olds in Compulsory Education in the BAC. In the study, published in 2005, 1191 students in Models B and D took a test comparable to the English First Certificate exam (744 students from 39 Model D classes and 447 from 24 Model B classes).[52] All the students were tested for listening comprehension, reading comprehension and writing. To test speaking, a random sub-sample of 243 students was taken (120 in Model D and 123 in Model B). In the event the study was limited to Model B and D schools, because in a pre-study test of the two best Model A schools, not a single student passed the test.

The results obtained were as follows; the *failure* rates were 100 per cent in Model A, 67 per cent in Model B and 32 per cent in Model D. Thus even in the most Basque-intensive school model almost one-third of the students failed the test. Thus as far as quality parameters are concerned it cannot be said that the objectives set by legislation, such as the Basic law Regulating the Use of Basque (19.1982), have been met (Biteri *et al.*, 2005, p. 14).

In theory, education provides the skills and legislation provides the opportunities, but other factors are likely to affect the future of Basque, not least of which is globalisation. This is likely to happen in four distinct ways according to Zalbide *et al.*

- the increasing movement of Basque speakers, particularly those with medium to high level qualifications, to other parts of Spain (and France) and even elsewhere in Europe in the pursuit of their professional career will ensure a continual "brain drain" amongst the most highly trained Basque speakers, not to mention the effects of increased mobility on the development of the private life of many Basques;
- the increasing presence of immigrants and their languages provides a new challenge for Basque, as the degree of the immigrants' linguistic integration in uncertain;
- the growing presence of English in the Basque Country as the language of modernity and wider communication means that it will increasingly compete with Spanish and French (and to a much lesser extent Basque) for functions basically related to modernity, pop consumerism and technological advances;
- in the face of globalisation many feel the need for a more rooted, particularised identity; in the Basque Country that need for a counterweight to globalisation may strengthen such people's positive evaluation of Basque (Zalbide *et al.*, 2005, p. 124).

In order to maintain the momentum in this unequal struggle, a strong dose of reality and a new consensus is needed. Prioritising where limited energy and resources are to be located would be a necessary first step in language planning, for at present the system seems to be overreaching itself in an attempt to be as inclusive as possible.

Several basic tenets of language politics are in need of urgent revision and public debate if the language struggle is to overcome many of the weaknesses identified herein. A central difficulty is the ideological inheritance of Basque nationalism which argues both that a monolingual Basque Country is not only possible, but also desirable, and that full independence is the only means by which this goal will be achieved. This orthodoxy denies the current praxis of inhabiting a bilingual society and minimises the current possibilities short of independence. Both of these views are worrying, for the contending discourses render a deep challenge to democratic representation and participation of all within Basque society. In short it calls into question who are the "we" or the "us" who constitute the core of Basque identity.

Four direct challenges to orthodox assumptions have been laid down by reformist language loyalists, who seek to review basic assumptions, among which are:

- The confusion about what is Basque, both in regard to territory and ethnicity;
- The recognition of other language communities;
- The use of simplistic historicist pseudo-arguments;
- The assumption that political independence is the most reliable route to (or, in its strong version, a necessary but insufficient condition for) ensuring the survival of Basque (Zalbide *et al.*, 2005, p. 126).

If the internal Basque discourse needs revision so too does that of the Spanish and French state and their attack on language loyalists. Of particular concern are the ways in which five themes have been manipulated for political ends with the cumulative effect of marginalising the position of Basque. The themes are:

1. Unrestricted *hispano-conformity*;
2. Invisibility of the Basque speech community and its concerns;
3. Pseudo-historical arguments;
4. Other simplistic arguments;
5. The European dimension.

Zalbide *et al.* expand on each of these themes, but for now it is sufficient to be reminded by them that the Basque situation may be considered a test case for similar minorities in Europe. They advise that

> if the Basques fail in these relatively favourable circumstances to maintain their language, others will surely feel pessimistic about their own chances of doing so. But then, the death of Basque has frequently been prophesised, burial dates have come and gone and Basque has so far survived, due in no small part to the deeply entrenched loyalty and tenacity displayed time and again by its speakers.
>
> (Zalbide *et al.*, 2005, p. 139)

The limits of language planning intervention

Each of these three themes, regional development, regional government initiatives and legislative reform, has demonstrated that there are limits to language planning intervention. Some limits derive from raw political antagonism, some are structural and organisational, and some are deeply embedded within the expectations and behaviour patterns of citizens. But all of these limits and interpreted from within specific discourses. This leads Williams and Morris (2000) to focus on the clash of discourses which have been analysed in relation to language promotion and planning. They argue that language planning intervention from a market perspective is a highly irrational activity in

> the orthodox conception of language planning, where planning is viewed as the intervention of the state in order to overcome market forces on the ability of the group to reproduce itself. . . . language planning also seeks to conform with a conception of rational organization, but given the opposition between planning and the market, the implication is that the market system is irrational as least insofar as it acts in opposition to the idea of a democratically elected government rationally to control the destiny of those who-presumably on rational principles-have elected it into office.
>
> (Williams and Morris, 2000, p. 249)

These remarks are a salutary reminder of the inability of limited planning to effect wholesale change. Nevertheless, astute, well-developed initiatives can make a significant difference to the vitality of indigenous linguistic minorities. That our individual efforts are clearly not enough goes without saying, hence the need for co-operative ventures at the European level. There is also the need to adopt general rules of good practice and to increase the amount of knowledge and procedures which are exchanged among language boards, planners, decision-makers, and perhaps most important of all, line-managers within specific departments charged with the delivery of language-specific services.[53]

Implications: Elements of good practice

Rule 1. Always involve the target speakers/users of services as much as possible in the language planning decision-making process.

Rule 2. Engage the participation of inter-departmental agencies to realise language planning aims and programmes.

Rule 3. Seek to introduce horizontal forms of governance where feasible, but expect only partial success given the tendency to centralise and bureaucratise language-related activity.

Rule 4. Anticipate and resolve to overcome the barriers, vested interests, traditional thought and practice that arise from inter-departmental turf-wars and boundary disputes.

This means that the language planning agencies must recognise themselves as part of the problem as well as being part of the solution. Not always an easy consideration when many technocrats feel themselves to be "up against it" when it comes to representing the interests both of their departments and of their constituents in hard pressed competitive administrative systems. We shall return to these issues in the final chapter.

Navigating into the EU mainstream

I have concentrated on examples taken from the more robust regional minority (RM) contexts of Western Europe yet even here we see how difficult it is to turn political rhetoric and language legislation into improved bilingual public services. Much of this difficulty results from the adherence of state bureaucracies to fairly conventional ways of managing public services. It reflects part of a wider conflict, described by Mar-Molinero and Stevenson (2006, p. 2) as deriving from a conflict between "the stubborn persistence of the Herderian conception of the axiomatically monoglot nation on the one hand, and the constantly shifting multilingual constellations of European states on the other". By focussing on the contradictions between monolingual ideologies and multilingual practices it is possible to identify those areas of policy formulation which reinforce the legitimacy of the hegemonic languages, such as English, French and German, and undermine the salience of so-called lesser-used languages such as Basque, Irish or Welsh. It is also claimed that such practices undermine the "post-nation" European credos of pluralism and diversity. Yet paradigms are shifting and events are progressing the cause of linguistic diversity in ways which would have been considered impractical a generation ago.[54]

There are four reasons for arguing that the EU has adopted a radically different stance towards integrating RM and to a lesser extent IM language groups into its diversity portfolio. The first is that the threat posed to the state system by linguistically tinged, antipathetic and hostile separatist political movements has declined. Thus while in the seventies and eighties Corsica, Northern Ireland and the Basque Country were considered to be clear examples of the failure of state integration, by today, minority language recognition is an established fact, as is the right to be different. Second, the maturation of sub-sate responsible government in, for example Flanders, Catalonia and Wales, has not only witnessed the establishment of alternative language regimes, but has also turned these governments and administrations into active players on the European stage, well capable of influencing policy and demonstrating proven ways of enhancing both democracy and the delivery of linguistically specific services to citizens. Third, the successive enlargements of the EU have forced Brussels-based policy makers to devise more inclusive and innovative Pan-European policies which do not consciously discriminate against the smaller "official" communities which are ostensibly equal partners in the European project.[55] Fourth, in an attempt to re-define Europe, and to widen and deepen its own legitimacy, the EU has recognised the great wealth of common European experience represented by the historically disadvantaged political sub-units which are now being given a voice. This is undertaken both to strengthen the commonality of economic, religious, social and linguistic roots and for "fear of something worse", namely the rise of non-European faith communities and their own increasingly strident demands to be recognised as permanent constituents of Europe, qua Europeans, and not as geographical extensions of Islam or Sikhism. Far better, it is argued, to allow some element of Basque sub-state "ethnic" or Catalan "national" representation within common European structures and thereby incorporate their energies and drive into a common purpose, than to risk alienation and obfuscation by trying to tackle the demands of both RM and IM communities simultaneously. In a darker mood one can be forgiven for concluding that the RM experience and agencies will be used as both an exemplar and as the responsible partners for aiding the transition of some IM groups, thus shifting the burden of responsibility, if not of tolerance and co-operation, from majoritarian shoulders!

Yet it need not necessarily be so, for as we shall report in the final chapter there are very significant moves to improve considerably the lot of both RM and IM speakers within the European Union.

Notes

1. For an interesting international example concerning the linguistic training of educational leaders and managers see the Comenius 2.1 Project TERRA: Inter-cultural curriculum. http://www.Skole.Karmoy.Kommune.no/partners.htm.
2. Adopted and opened for signature, ratification and accession by UN General Assembly resolution 2200 (A) (XXI) of 16 December 1966, and entered into force on 23 March 1976.
3. Eur. T.S. 5, adopted and opened for signature on 1 November 1950, and entered into force on 3 September 1953.
4. I was a member of this working panel.
5. I accept that in many contexts it is not possible to apply a strict spatial criteria to the minorities in question, but I would maintain that there is nearly always a spatial context to policy, it depends upon what scale the policy is being applied.
6. This is particularly acute at the international level for organisations such as the European Union, The Council of Europe, The International Court of Justice, The World Labour Organization, NATO, all advance systematic programmes for language policy, but have not been well disposed to contextual or environmental analysis as part of their thinking.
7. Is it any wonder then that so many promising initiatives fail, because the ground work in terms of measuring capacity, preparing for change and identifying the key contextual variables is so often not undertaken.
8. In my experience this is not generally the case as most activists are driven by a concern for social justice and the restitution of "wrongs" which have hindered the advancement of their group. I do accept that occasionally "committed" outsiders are far more concerned with the state of the endangered language groups than are many of the speakers, but to consider such outsiders as motivated primarily by guilt rather than a genuine concern, is harsh in my view.

9. This suggests a self-indulgent, rather than a pragmatic basis for action, which again in my experience is not the case with regards to most professional language planners and activists.

10. Clearly in very difficult circumstances such as those which face most Central and Eastern ethno-linguistic minorities, even accomplishing the introduction of such elements is a challenge which I do not seek to minimise. My comments here are addressed more to the by now well-established language planning agencies within the EU.

11. This does not preclude the simultaneous strengthening of variant standard Eng-lishes either. Witness the recent transfer of British call centre operations to India, mainly because of the low wage levels there for graduate employment, *c*.£10:00 per week as opposed to *c*.£151:00 per week in the UK, but also because of the communicative competence of the graduate workforce. Established international banks, British Airways and Prudential Insurance are but the latest to transfer parts of their call centre operations to the Indian sub-continent.

12. As Ó Riagáin (1997) makes clear in his study of language policy and social reproduction, government intervention "changed the 'rules' of the social mobil-ity process" (p. 275), creating an important middle-class sector with at least a moderate competence in Irish.

13. Although as Walsh (2005, p. 6) has indicated this is a contentious issue. The linguistic demand appeared to be met by Article 8(1) of the Údarás na Gaeltachta Act (1979), entitled "Functions of An tÚdarás" and second sub-section of Article 8 states that the Údarás "shall carry on, control and manage (either directly or, in any particular case, through a body corporate controlled by an Údarás) the industries and productive schemes of employment carried on, controlled or managed, directly or indirectly, by Gaeltarra Éireann" (Article 8(2)).

    Walsh observes that this ordering of "functions" gave the impression that pro-moting Irish was one of the organisation's objectives, and there is a perception that this is the case (see for instance, Ó Cinnéide *et al.*, 2001, 148; Ó hÉallaithe, 2004). However, two Attornies-General have advised the DCRGA in recent years that Article 8 (1) is not in fact a "function", but simple a preamble to the organ-isation's industrial functions, implying that Údarás does not have any function in relation to Irish. This is an astonishing development and one which Walsh questions astutely by asserting that, "it is reasonable to expect that 'the preser-vation and extension of the use of the Irish language as the principal medium of communication in the Gaeltacht' would be of paramount importance to Údarás na Gaeltachta. After all, if it were not for the Irish language, there would have been no need for organisations such as Údarás na Gaeltachta (or indeed, the DCRGA) in the first place" (Walsh, 2005, p. 6).

14. Despite the efforts of many countless hundreds volunteers, community activists, agencies and government, the task of revitalising the Irish language has proved greater than the resources and commitment hitherto shown. The basic fault seems to have been an over-optimistic assessment of the capacity of state intervention to restore Irish as a national language without a concomitant investment in socio-economic planning to bring about the necessary conditions to regulate the market forces which encouraged widespread Anglicisation. It is only recently that holistic, integrated policies are being attempted in the Gaeltacht region and it is too early to assess their full impact.

15. I am conscious of the various socio-political trajectories of Gaeltacht and non-Gaeltacht bodies and of the differing responsibilities for Irish language pro-motion which various Departments of State enjoy. Nevertheless it seems illogical

that this basic split appears to militate against the achievement of national language planning goals.

16. The Welsh Language Board guidance to all Mentrau is to undertake a systematic evaluation of the language situation which involves a full statistical, data-gathering audit of the most relevant evidence available to produce an area profile, detailing how and where the language is used in their community, and noting target areas for development. A second initiative, the Area Development Scheme, operates on a similar basis and requires an analysis of the social opportunities available to use the language and a detailed SWOT analysis to be used as a basis for developing pilot plans and as a monitoring framework.

17. Further information on Mentrau Iaith is available from www.mentrau-iaith.com while a critical assessment of their success is available in Williams (2000d). For the Area Development Schemes see the Welsh Language Board www.bwrdd-yr-iaith.com.

18. The inspiration for the movement was Father *José María Arizmendiarrieta*, who had arrived in Mondragon in 1941 and established a fledgling co-operative movement and a democratically managed Polytechnic School which in turn played a decisive role in the intellectual and commercial development of the co-operative movement. Five of its graduates formed the first co-operative enterprise in 1956, named ULGOR (now Fagor Electrodomésticos) after their surnames, which specialised in the production of domestic heating and cooking appliances.

19. Members seeking admission have to provide a buy-in capital contribution to the cooperative equal to about one year's base salary at the lowest level of employment before becoming a full member, which is usually financed by a loan from the cooperative bank. The most common criticism levied against the MCC is that it does not apply a consistent standard of membership rights throughout its network, especially in relation to its workers in Latin America.

20. Information derived from an interview with Arantza Mongelos Garcia, Head of International Relations, HUHEZI, Mondragon University, 20 September 2005.

21. The Humanitate eta Hezkuntza Zientzien Fakultatea (Faculty of Humanities and Education Sciences) based in Mondragon is increasing its provision of Basque-medium instruction across a wider range of subject areas as both the *ikastolas* and Model B schools continue to grow.

22. BAZARA is a secondary-school based project to build up Basque consciousness and contextualised history, while HIZPRO is a language project devoted to multiculturalism but with the Basque language firmly established at its core. Both projects were initiated by staff, parents and pedagogic specialists operating from the *ikastolas* secondary school at Arizmendi. I am grateful to the teaching staff who shared their vision and project details with me during a school visit on the 24 November 2006.

23. Following Agirrebaltzategi, p. 58.

24. Over seventy such organisations, large and small, were active in the BAC in 1999. (Information provided by sub-ministry for language planning of the BAC to Gardner, 2000.)

25. Information supplied by Jaxe Aranzabal at interview in Mondragon on 22 November 2006. The Goiera Group currently employs 55 people, and receives financial support from the Basque Government, the Mondragon Local Authority and from its subscribers.

26. See Eusko Jaurlaritza and Kultura Saila (1999).

27. For more information about the General Directorate visit its official web page at: http://cultura.gencat.es/llencat/.

28. Some of them make extensive use of the internet in order to make their services more accessible and easy to use. For instance the Department of Territorial Policies and Public Works (http://www.gencat.es/ptop/serveis/frllengu.htm); the Department of Industry, Commerce and Tourism (http://www.gencat.es/dict/serveis/servling/serveilingdef.htm) and the Department of Justice (http://www.gencat.es/justicia/llengua/).

29. Puigdevall i Serralvo (2006) explains that this move has given the Secretariat increased authority to co-ordinate, to impel and lead the language policy of all Government departments. The advantage of this increased coordination is that Departments are better acquainted with their specific sectors and key social agents. This makes it easier to implement specific actions to promote the use of language in all areas of society.

30. The budget shows a significant increase from 12,578,770 million Euros in 2000 to 17,517, 149 in 2004 (the first allocation by the new coalition government), to 21,715,035 in 2005. Data taken with permission from Chart 4 of Puigdevall i Serralvo (2006).

31. A key decision made by the General Secretaries was their determination to use Catalan when buying goods, products and services from external companies.

32. Puigdevall i Serralvo (2006) observes that the migrants to Catalonia in the 1950s and 1960s are growing older, while their second and third generation descendants are growing up in a society where Catalan has acquired a new prestige and currency. Because of the prevailing class structure, where Catalan was spoken more extensively by middle and upper-middle classes, the native language acquired concomitant status and prestige. For many Spanish-speaking immigrants from the early 1970s and onward, upward social mobility would involve acquiring a command of Catalan. However, despite their proficiency in Catalan and identification with the nation, there remains a sizeable, permanent Spanish L1-speaking community in Catalonia.

33. The geographic breakdown is as follows South America (39.03 per cent), Africa (28.86 per cent), Europe (23.42 per cent). The main country of origin is Morocco, followed by Ecuador, Colombia, Argentina, Romania and Peru. Catalonia hosts migrants representing 190 different nationalities.

34. The excellent conference was organised by Mercator/Ciemen and devoted to "Linguistic Rights as a Matter of Social Inclusion". For a full report visit www.ciemen.org/mercator website.

35. A number of issues were raised by the audience in response to these presentations. A key question was why were the medical professionals so reluctant to take the assistance offered by the cultural mediators? A second was to what extent this investment in Catalan-speaking cultural mediators served only the upper echelons of the medical service. For once the patient was on the ward, or dealing with the auxiliary staff, so much of the conversation would be conducted in Spanish. A third was that if a patient registered in either Catalan or in Spanish to what extent could that respective language choice be guaranteed at all stages in the medical treatment process?

36. Both the timing and impact are similar to the Canadian initiative to recognise Quebec as a nation within Canada, except that in the Canadian case it came directly from the Federal government.

37. Anderson (2006) comments that successive rows over what exactly was agreed in the June 2006 settlement will drag on over the next years and will be complicated by the differential impact of EU assistance funds for the period 2007–2011.

38. Ross (2002, p. 21) reports that Adolfo Suárez's initially wanted to have government lawyers draft the document, without reference to a popular vote. His hand was forced by the results of the 1977 election which left him dependent upon the opposition who forced him to employ the constituent assembly (*cortes constituyentes*) as the principal instrument for drafting the constitution. They delegated the task to a seven-man cross-party committee whose members became known as the "Fathers of the Constitution" and they delivered an agreed text to be submitted to a referendum held on the 6th of December 1978. It received the support of 88 per cent of those who voted. However, in the BAC, although three quarters of the votes case were favourable, the low turnout (49 per cent) meant that these represented just over a third of the eligible electorate.
39. Literally, the Organic Law for the Restoration and Improvement of the Charter Régime of Navarre.
40. Published in the Official Gazette of Navarre on December 17th 1986.
41. Gardner in Gardner *et al.* (2000) writes "If I may be permitted to introduce an element of evaluation, I would go as far as saying, that in spite of the fact that this law occasionally goes as far as using the expression "normal use" (art. 1.1.) and speaking of "protecting the recovery and development of Basque in Navarre" (art. 1.1.b), it is clear from the framework that the object is more one of maintenance or conservation of Basque in the Charter Community [of Navarre] than of setting in motion a process of language normalisation within a régime of effective bilingualism; more a case of halting the process of regression at the moment of initiating this piece of legislation than of promoting its reversal" (Cobreros, p. 145).
42. Gardner's translation. An alternative translation, along with translations to other state languages of the EU including Irish, can be found in Berriatua (1983).
43. The one modest element of the use of the territoriality principle in BAC legislation, to wit the right of local councils in predominantly Basque-speaking areas to use Basque only, was declared unconstitutional by sentence 82/1986 of the Constitutional Court of Spain.
44. Here we may cite the heroic efforts of parents in regards to the *ikastolas* movement while Gardner (2000) emphasises the role of the non-governmental grass roots organisations, especially the *Euskaltzaindia* or Royal Academy of the Basque Language, now largely funded with public money, stands out for its role in many aspects of Basque language promotion up until the early 1980s. Since then it has concentrated on its corpus planning role, passing most of its teaching, examining and cultural organising roles on to specific public and private bodies, whilst retaining an overview of status planning for Basque.
45. For data on elections in the BAC, visit www.eustat.es (Eustat is the Basque Government's statistics organisation).
46. See Cobreros (1989), p. 101.
47. Gardner reports that the insistence by some nationalists to strengthen the differentiation between "them" and "us" (i.e. between Basque and Spanish) has had consequences in corpus planning, as it has led to purism in vocabulary, neologisms being coined on the basis of really or supposedly authentic Basque roots avoiding any Romance input. This purism, though satisfying for the élite proposing it, has not facilitated the spread of new vocabulary and has possibly alienated some users (Gardner *et al.*, 2000, p. 326).
48. For statistics on the situation of the Basque language, visit the Basque Government website at www.euskara.euskadi.net and select the EAS statistics bank: the text is also available in English.

49. It leaves asides specific schemes for education, health sector, police and the administration of justice.
50. The vitality of the oral tradition, especially in gastronomy, sport, music and dance is unquestionable. However, Basque lacks the authentication tradition of Welsh or Catalan, because of the relative weakness of its literary tradition, particularly a lack of a strong standardised religious Basque and the failure of local elites to use written Basque (Zalbide *et al.*, 2005, p. 125).
51. For a prescient overview of Basque education see Zalbide (2005).
52. In the BAC, Model A refers to schools which use Spanish as the medium of instruction, but Basque is taught as a subject and students are expected to understand Basque well, to be capable of giving basic explanations in every day situations, to develop a positive attitude towards the Basque language and to be capable of integrating into Basque-language environments. Model B schools employ both Spanish and Basque for teaching purposes on a roughly half to half ratio. Model D schools are Basque-medium with Spanish taught as a subject.
53. I can guarantee that most technocrats and civil servants will declare that they follow these rules implicitly. If so, why do we encounter so much difficulty in realising our collective aims and objectives?
54. Having said this I recognise that I and many others were thinking along these very lines a generation ago. What has changed is the political will and capacity to realise these aims as public policy within an EU context which pushes subsidiarity.
55. I am thinking of Estonia, Latvia, Slovenia, Malta and the like. It was the recognition of these smaller languages as EU official languages which prompted the civic campaign in Ireland to have Irish recognised as an official EU language, which came into force on the 1st of January 2007.

6

Securing "Official Bilingualism": From Special Pleading to Deliberative Democracy?

Introduction

This chapter interprets the ideological, political and legal implications of incorporating "official bilingualism" as a key policy objective within parts of the UK, Ireland and Canada. It will do so by examining the transition from a minority dependency situation to one of a more inclusive, if not quite deliberative, democracy. This involves, *inter alia*, discussions of interest group pluralism and deliberative democracy, the effectiveness of language legislation, the promotion of an equality agenda and the impact of asymmetrical devolution.

Proponents of official bilingualism within the "so-called Celtic fringes" of the British Isles defend a common ideal, namely that democratic politics should incorporate considerations of language equality and promotion as a routine matter of state activity. Hitherto, the defence of the Celtic languages has been characterised as a struggle for survival, recognition and equality. By today the infra-structural developments necessary to enable both Wales and Ireland, if not Scotland and Northern Ireland, to function as bilingual societies has been assembled. But such developments are arrested by the putative incoherence of the ideal of official bilingualism. Wales and Ireland illustrate more general European trends, whereby the national languages have secured official status and have been given a great deal of attention, yet still face an uncertain future. Added to this is the regrettable, if understandable, fact that individual and social behaviour has not taken full advantage of the opportunities created by language revitalisation efforts. These have revolved around greater *institutionalisation*, that is, ensuring that the languages are represented in key strategic areas such as law, education, and public administration, together with *parallelism/normalisation*, that is, extending the use of the languages into the optimum range of social situations, including the private sector, entertainment, sport and the media.

Proponents of "official bilingualism" argue that at last the recalcitrant state is incorporating language promotion, together with bilingual service provision, as a routine policy dimension within the equal opportunities agenda of a pluralist democracy. Opponents have denigrated such advances as a sop to the special pleading of a declining minority. The minority are accused of constructing an elite network of privileged bilinguals, of operating an exclusionary labour market and of abusing their power and influence to discriminate against the silent majority.

At the heart of the struggle for minority promotion there is a dual concern. How to wrest further concessions, qua rights, from an unresponsive majority? And how to convince the target audience that official bilingualism is a practical pursuable policy objective?

A second aim of this chapter is to examine how the differing political contexts within the British and Irish states conduce to the implementation of declared language policy. Detailed evaluation of the merits of various policies by region is undertaken in Chapters Seven and Eight. Each context discussed involves both a different relationship between the indigenous language and the inhabitants, and between the nation and its role within a historical British and Irish political and socio-legal framework. The broader characteristics of state development have been examined superbly by Kearney (1989), Colley (1992), Davies (2000) and Bryant (2006). However, few scholars have focussed on a comparative language dimension as a key component of state and sub-state differentiation.

Since achieving independence in 1922 the Irish state has sought to promote Irish as an official language with varying degrees of success in different domains and periods. More recently the post-devolution settlement in Wales since 1999 has recognised official bilingualism as a socio-political reality, and has sought through National Assembly policies to strengthen and deepen societal and institutional bilingualism. By contrast, Northern Ireland and Scotland have demonstrated lesser degrees of support for their own indigenous languages, and have not yet succeeded in convincing enough of their residents to become functional bilingual citizens. Consequently issues of indigenous or regional minority (RM) language in law, politics and governance remain diverse and problematic throughout these isles.

Welsh, Irish and Gaelic are currently undergoing different impulses of revitalisation as a result of conscious language planning, and changes reflecting broader constitutional parameters. However, the twin processes should not be conflated. Revitalisation policies have been a feature of the Celtic context for quite some time, but they have been given greater political impetus and additional resources only as a result of asymmetrical devolution and new forms of governance. Despite their increased institutionalisation, however, the long term prospects of success are not assured as the Celtic languages have been experiencing a steady decline throughout the twentieth century (Pryce and Williams, 1988; Withers, 1988a, b; Hindley, 1990).

Table 6.1   Recent census data on language change

Wales	Welsh	(1991)	*c.* 508,098 (18.6%)
		(2001)	*c.* 575,604 (20.5%)
Scotland	Gaelic	(1991)	*c.* 65,978 (1.37%)
		(2001)	*c.* 58,562 (1.21%)
N. Ireland	Irish	(1991)	*c.* 142,003
		(2001)	*c.* 167,490 (9.98%)
	Ulster Scots	(2001)	*c.* 100,000
Ireland	Irish	(1991)	*c.* 1,095,830
		(1996)	*c.* 1,430,205 (353,663 fluent)
		(2002)	1,570,894

Source: General Register Office for Scotland, Wales and Northern Ireland; Government of Ireland Census Results.

Two issues dominate their chances of survival: one is demographic change, the other is language competence. In several instances, as Table 6.1 indicates there has been substantial growth in the numbers capable of speaking two of the Celtic languages, but sociolinguistic evidence suggests that many of these speakers lack confidence or the willingness to use their primarily school-gained competence in real life situations. The real challenge is to transform this potential into a lived reality.

The bare bones of the most recent census results for 2001 are indicated in Table 6.1.

Two things are evident: that demographic mass is the greatest influence on the vitality of the respective language groups; and that in all cases the Celtic language speakers form a numerical minority, which may not necessarily constitute a self-conscious and coherent entity within society.[1] Even though we are careful not to treat census language categories as if they were undifferentiated social groups, nevertheless we can still make meaningful observations about the structural trends which characterise such aggregate populations.

Structural commonalities

Speakers of the Celtic languages face similar structural characteristics, the most germane of which are the failure of inter-generational language transmission, community fragmentation and limited educational opportunities in the chosen language. Let us consider family transmission and community fragmentation first. Until the mid-twentieth century reasonable rates of language reproduction within the family, combined with relative isolation and locational disadvantage, had sustained viable ethno-linguistic communities. But economic growth, improved transport access and infra-structural developments, urbanisation and modernisation, together with greater participation in further and higher education, triggered increased rates of both in and out migration. This demographic transformation challenged the hegemonic role of the local indigenous language and accelerated its decline. Thus a classic process of language shift occurred which occasioned the atrophying of self-sustaining communities and their associated cultures. Such situations become particularly acute when survey evidence reveals that in many mixed language families (more than a half in Scotland and Ireland and about a half in Wales) where only one parent speaks the target language, the children tend not to be able to speak Gaelic/Irish/Welsh. Both voluntary and official attempts to reverse such trends have been criticised as being interventionist and artificial, running counter to the neo-liberal paradigm which so influenced much of state policy in the late twentieth century. Thus revitalisation efforts and ameliorative policies run into difficulty at both an ideological level and at the level of practical implementation (Williams, 2000a). Of acute concern are the lacklustre efforts to promote greater economic diversification and indigenous entrepreneurial activity, to set planning controls in order to curb developments which are perceived as damaging to the local "threatened" community, to tighten regulation of the local property market, and to target investment to improve the range and skill level of local school leavers.

Given that the family and the community were unable to reproduce the indigenous languages at rates considered necessary to long term survival, formal bilingual education was pioneered from the early sixties onwards. Within the four national education systems there is a wide range of experience of bilingual education, some elements of success, and also a great deal of frustration engendered by many false dawns. Wales is the most promising context with spectacular gains in promoting many types of bilingual success, but even here significant proportions completing primary education as L1 Welsh speakers commence secondary education as L2 speakers. Bilingual teenagers, especially males, use Welsh less frequently as they grow older. The proportions who undertake further and higher education through the medium of Welsh are very small. Jones (2004) has offered a trenchant criticism of the failure of the University system in Wales to provide minimal, let alone adequate, Welsh medium provision for its student population. But there is little sign that any one in authority is acting to remedy this weakness. The situation is far worse in Northern Ireland and Scotland.

Interest-group pluralism and deliberative democracy

Within the wider discourse on language rights it is commonplace to assert that the promotion of the Celtic languages is a classic example of interest-group politics. Special pleading by historically disadvantaged linguistic minorities has lead to the gradual wresting of concessions and rights from a disinterested central state and a quiescent international legal order. So long as the inhabitants of Scotland, Wales and Northern Ireland did not possess a measure of self-rule with their own national decision-making bodies, this was an understandable position. The supplicant subject rather than the empowered citizen was, after all, a comfortable position for many to adopt, because ultimate responsibility for the fate of one's own language lay outwith the immediate political context. But with the transfer of selected powers to devolved national parliaments and assemblies, responsibility for language policy and all the attendant props which sustain various networks of speakers and institutions were now capable of being embedded within civil society and its elected representatives. I have previously argued that greater attention should be paid to the principles of deliberative democracy where reasonableness and partnership would seek to render political solutions publicly acceptable (Williams, 1996c, 1998c). I want to develop this argument by suggesting that the next logical step in the promotion and regulation of language policy should be a serious attempt to involve all the stakeholders in the broader discussion surrounding governance. I do not believe that current attempts in Wales, for example, to host a six monthly Language Forum as the "voice of the people" is anything more than a sop. In order to build up a critical capacity of informed and responsible activists, arrangements have to be made to engage, entitle and empower a wide range of interested parties to contribute directly to the formulation of language policy themes and priorities. The Welsh Language Board believes that it has gone some way to achieving this through its regular consultation with its many partners, but such an arrangement leaves out the routine input of language pressure groups such as Cymdeithas yr Iaith Gymraeg, Cymuned and Cefn and does not come close to being an adequate substitute for a deliberative civil society.

I recognise that the principles of deliberative democracy, though attractive, are hardly an everyday notion in the minds of most of the participants. Consequently there is a need to make explicit the merits of such an approach. This is particularly so in view of the strength of the powers of the Parliaments and Assemblies within asymmetrical federalism.

Towards deliberative democracy?

The dominant mode of political representation within the UK remains participatory democracy. But in one policy field, namely language policy and planning, I want to advance the argument that demands for deliberative democracy are growing apace, especially in Wales. Let me outline the key features of deliberative democracy. Christiano (1999) writing in a major collection of essays devoted to reason and politics (Bohman and Rehg, 1999), has argued that democratic decision-making ought to be "grounded in a substantial process of public deliberation, wherein arguments for and against laws and policies are given in terms of whether they advance the common good of citizens and justice of the political society" (p. 243). Writing in the same collection Cohen (1999) has argued that at the heart of deliberative democracy is "the fact of reasonable pluralism" which establishes a substantive conception of politics. This, the editors explain, "contains a very specific interpretation of egalitarian and liberal values of rights and liberties" (Bohman and Rehg, 1999, p. xxvi). Deliberative democracy goes well beyond a procedural conception of justification so as to embrace "a wide guarantee" of religious, moral and expressive liberties.

Proponents of deliberative democracy tend to point to the impact of referenda on the process and efficacy of governance and argue that if deliberative polls or deliberative days could be linked to the policy formation process then a far stronger and informed public opinion would be harnessed. My argument is that one does not necessarily have to have referenda or citizen fora to qualify as being deliberative and engaged. There are other multiple possibilities as discussed by Saward (2003) as follows:

- In specially constructed micro-forums ... where a small representative sample of people debate and in some cases vote on issues (deliberative polls, citizens' juries etc);
- Within political parties;
- In national and other parliaments;
- In supra-national committee networks such as those in the governing structures of the European Union;
- Within private or voluntary associations;
- Within courts; or
- Within a diverse "public" sphere of "protected enclaves" or "subaltern counterpublics", in other words, oppressed groups in society (Saward, 2003, pp. 123–4).

Held has summarised the chief features of this form of democracy as follows in Table 6.2.

Deliberative democracy has received some attention of late, especially within political philosophy. I am not aware that it has been used widely in language policy and language planning or applied to the cases discussed in this volume, although I believe that it has much to offer. The salience of inclusion as a determining characteristic of deliberative democracy renders it a fitting framework for our discussion. Let me illustrate. The very fact, for example, that within the National Assembly, Welsh speakers are both a legitimate constituency and a target group for public policy reflects a new definition of the changed political order. The Education and Culture Committees of the National Assembly routinely debate language and language-related issues and invite experts, both from within

Table 6.2   Forms of deliberative democracy

"Deliberative democracy

Principle(s) of justification

   The terms and conditions of political association proceed through the free and reasoned assent of its citizens. The "mutual justifiability" of political decisions is the legitimate basis for seeking solutions to collective problems.

Key features

Deliberative polls, deliberative days, citizens' juries	renewing representative democracy
E-government initiatives from full on-line reporting to direct access to representation E-democracy programmes including on-line fora Group analysis and generation of policy proposals Deliberation across public life, from micro-fora to transnational settings	
New uses of referenda tied to deliberative polls, etc.	radical, deliberative participatory democracy

General conditions

   Value pluralism
   Strong civic education programme
   Public culture and institutions supporting the development of "refined" and "reflected" preferences
   Public funding of deliberative bodies and practices, and of the secondary associations which support them

---

Source: Held (2006), p. 253.

the UK and beyond, to submit evidence on a wide range of matters from immersion education to software development for multilingual computer platforms. Such exposure and constructive deliberation was not a feature of pre-devolution days.

   Similarly the Welsh Language Board holds public meetings in a different part of Wales every six weeks. It hosts specialised fora on terminology, community development, youth work and marketing, and seeks to involve its many partners in the determination of policy. Not only does this increase the legitimacy of the Language Board, but it also gives the real impression to many actors that they have been empowered by this process, of which more will be said below. The same has been true historically of Irish speakers in relation to periodic initiatives by agencies of the state.

   However, the recognition of RM speakers as a permanent entity within the polity poses challenges for the majority who must accommodate to this new reality and construct reasonable guarantees together with the minorities which will allow for harmonious relations. Why are such guarantees necessary? Historically the lack of such guarantees for the Catholic Irish-speaking minority in Northern Ireland should be evidence enough that without some degree of mutually recognised right to exist, to participate and to share power; stable relations between communities are unlikely to develop.

> Thus such guarantees are to ensure full membership to all citizens in the sovereign body that exercises power. Thus, deliberative inclusion can be justified as a requirement of liberty of conscience, itself guaranteed by the deeper political values of freedom and equality. The substantive values of freedom and equality thus extend such guarantees beyond the political-deliberative process itself. Indeed, the very disagreements that are an ineliminable feature of a democratic community of free and equal citizens demand "wide" liberties of conscience, religion and expression by denying the community or the majority the legitimate power to enforce its contingent consensus on moral matters. The fact and origins of disagreement demand limits on public reason, as Rawls has argued; but these limits also imply substantive solutions to pressing matters of moral conflict and political legitimacy. Reasonableness is thus a central norm to be built into deliberative procedures.
>
> (Bohman and Rehg, 1999, pp. xxvi–xxvii)

The "reasonableness" of incorporating the Celtic languages within the affairs of the local state becomes, not only a fulfilment of expressive liberty, but also a central plank within an equal opportunities agenda. If in time this can be allied to policies adopting a holistic perspective as outlined in Chapters Five and Ten then the revitalisation efforts currently undertaken are far more likely to have a lasting impact on the prospects for survival and growth.

Nevertheless, as Loughlin and Williams (2007) argue, there are ideological undercurrents in the transformation of minority language speakers from supplicants to empowered citizens. Three critical issues, which influence the current relationship between the citizen and the state, need careful scrutiny. The first is the logic of the neoliberal discourse which avers that the contemporary state is an enabling agency, which by seeking to minimise citizen dependency on the state apparatus releases the full potential of its citizenry. This is to be done by shifting a range of social responsibilities from the welfare state back to the realm of civil society. Nominally this shift is about the empowerment of civil society and the strengthening of the capacity of para-public and voluntary agencies to deliver services formally provided by the state. But as Marquand (2004) has demonstrated, all too often this leads to a diminution of the quality and frequency of services and to the disenfranchisement of the poorer, marginal sections of society.[2]

The second issue is the related notion of community empowerment and language planning intervention. I have previously argued that

> instilling a sense of ownership within communities which have been ravaged by successive waves of deindustrialization, social fragmentation and economic collapse is a huge challenge ... the key question is to what extent such a challenge can, or should, be met by organizing around the issue of language decline and revitalization. Apart from the disingenuous nature of government policy, shifting responsibility, without releasing sufficient resources to maintain community development, there is also the question of structural tension and mutual suspicion between the state and civil society and between factions within society. These arise when questions of ownership of a social process are engaged and challenged, especially when languages in contact are also languages in competition.
>
> (Williams, R., 2000, p. 222).

Empowerment is an attractive notion but all too often such initiatives turn out to be illusory or transitory or both.

The third issue is the discourse of language planning within which many of the contradictions of the neoliberal perspectives have become embedded. Williams and Morris (2000) have offered a trenchant criticism of its foundational principles such as "enabling", "participation", "development" and the like. They have argued that only when language planning efforts are based on a thorough understanding of the social construction of meaning and its relationship to discursive processes as social practice will the current opposition between the market and planning be reduced. Writing in the late nineties they did not see much evidence of such understanding within the language agencies they were analysing. If this is hard enough for indigenous minorities within liberal democracies it is much more challenging for both RM and IM in the emerging democracies of the eastern and south eastern margins of Europe.

The EU is redefining its political aspirations, in part as a response to the enlargement process and in part in an attempt to face the challenges of China, India, and as a consequence of economic globalisation and foreign policy pressures (Alexander, 2005). Challenges to a state's rejection of identity and official denial of citizenship, together with issues of inclusion and exclusion are increasingly being referred to national tribunals and are subject to international legal pronouncements. Protecting threatened identities has become a significant feature of the political agenda in many European societies, and the use of threatened identities as a violent and non-violent political instrument has risen tremendously.

Language issues are directly related to questions of citizenship, education, socialisation and participation especially in the public sphere. Some states are turning towards language testing regimes as a way of controlling both the quantity and the skills levels of potential in-migrants. There is also tremendous pressure on institutions within the EU to simplify and harmonise the range of services offered within a particular suite of languages. However, considerations of post-sovereign interaction in the Europeanisation of public affairs render formal language planning increasingly difficult. This is because the post-Enlightenment notions of inclusive citizenship are breaking down in the face of market segmentation and apparent consumer empowerment. This leads to a tension between commonality and fragmentation, between the basic needs of state socialisation, including communicative competence in state-designated languages, and the reality of individual choices and the community-orientation of many interest groups. A major concern is access to public services by marginalised groups. But as Marquand (2004) has cautioned "the barriers that once protected the public domain from the market and private domains grew up piecemeal, but it does not follow that they can be renewed in the same manner. In the twenty-first century, the inexplicit, half-conscious incrementalism of the late nineteenth century is unlikely to be enough" (p. 148).

Within selected European regions the previously disadvantaged minority have become the locally powerful majority, and typically express their new found power to promote a lesser-used language, such as Euskerra in the Autonomous Basque Country, or in establishing a bilingual education system as in Gwynedd County Council in Wales. Understandably such a reversal of fortunes for minority groups is challenged by factions within the majority. The minority often counter in private "having suffered for centuries at the hands of the majority it is our turn now". But we cannot accept automatically that the resolution of claims based upon a perceived historical grievance is necessarily conducive to democratic justice.

Gutman (2003) has argued that

> democratic justice entails treating all individuals as civic equals with equal liberty and opportunity. Granting identity groups sovereignty or other significant political powers regardless of the way they treat individuals would mean subordinating individuals to their cause. Subordinating individuals to groups is another name for tyranny.
>
> (Gutman, 2003, p. 193)

To reduce this malaise one needs to establish a firm defence for the appropriate role of identity groups in society. This involves recognising that individuals join identity groups for a variety of reasons, some of which are:

- To publicly express what they consider an important aspect of their identity;
- To conserve their culture, which they identify with the group;

- To gain more material (and other) goods for themselves and their group (whether justified or not);
- To fight in a group for or against discrimination and other injustices;
- To receive mutual support from others who share some part of their social identity; and
- To express and act upon ethical commitments that they share with a group (Gutman, 2003, p. 210).

For the majority in a democracy there is a very thin line between applauding and denying several such claims by identity groups; whereas for many members of such identity groups these claims are central to their political action. Language issues in the UK. Ireland and Canada are a case in point. This is why systems of governance have to balance both the legitimate demands of the identity groups and the expectations of the majority that they will not necessarily be disadvantaged by the recognition of alternative claims in a liberal democracy.

> Citizens who are concerned about democratic justice need to distinguish the better from the worse while recognizing that the aims of abolishing identity groups or elevating them above basic individual rights would threaten the very cause of democratic justice that they wish to be defending.
>
> (Gutman, 2003, p. 211)

One bulwark for the defence of justice is of course, the legal system. We are conscious that while in Canada, the courts are a major bastion for the protection and indeed the promotion of official language minorities, in Britain and Ireland the legal system is a relatively underdeveloped instrument for the articulation of language rights and services (Williams, 2003, 2006b). Yet, however underdeveloped, language-related legislation is a *sine qua non* for the establishment of a binding commitment by the state to honour the putative rights of speakers of officially recognised languages. It is also the basis by which the growth of deliberative democracy is enabled. Let us examine how such issues have played out in each of the four national contexts under discussion.

Language legislation

The most telling reason why language legislation is important is that it contributes to the official recognition of the language in question and legitimises it within the administrative procedures of government. The relationship between law, public opinion and bureaucracy has been framed, since Dicey's days, as an abiding tension between ideas associated with individualism and those associated with collectivism. A more specific focus, the relationship between language, law and politics, has tended to be treated in terms of the challenges which flow from contradictory notions of national identity and ethnicity, which threaten most legal boundaries and confident social boundaries (Campbell, 2003). Analysis of such tensions in Canada (Newman, 2007), the UK (Roddick, 2007) and Celtic contexts (Williams, 2003) reveals deep divisions over fundamental and subversive issues and remind us that any particular piece of legislation in itself is not a value-neutral instrument. Neither should it be considered as being automatically effective in securing the goals of legislators, whether benign or not. In the Celtic and Canadian cases which follow, the issue of implementing language legislation is currently dominant.

Robert Dunbar (2006a) has presented a prescient overview of the need to measure language legislation in terms of its effectiveness and it is to his analysis that I will turn in this preliminary discussion of legislation.[3] He argues that effectiveness should be assessed from the formal perspective of making sure that the specific requirements of legislation are met. But this alone is insufficient if it ignores the wider perspective of ensuring that the overall regime which is created by the legislation is being implemented. Such legislation should seek to enhance the linguistic vitality of the minority language community more generally. He avers that a legislative regime which is separated from actual day-to-day language behaviour is not a particularly useful one and could in fact become dangerous for the target group.[4]

The contextual effect of language laws is germane because if the institutions which impact upon a minority language community were supportive of, and responsive to, their needs, and speakers were energised in support of their language, legislation would hardly be necessary at all. In far too many cases basic legislation is accompanied by fine political rhetoric which masks the failure of the administrative system to honour the putative rights and expectations of its citizens. In consequence legislation is necessary for minority languages precisely because the environment in which speakers of minority languages exist generally does not tend to be supportive. Institutions, such as local government, hospitals, public schools tend not to be robust providers of bilingual services, or if they are, the service is very halting and dependent upon key individuals, the vagaries of employment policies and other priorities within the system.

Dunbar reminds us that both the public sector and the private sector tend to give priority to the needs and desires of the larger constituencies. The smaller the linguistic minority the more marginal are their linguistic concerns. Tolerance and goodwill are often in short supply. As we saw earlier it is too facile to assume that minorities always support innovative measures or that they are equally comfortable in addressing officialdom in non-hegemonic working languages.

Speakers of minority languages are often not energised in support of their language. They are often bilingual, and in many linguistic domains, may have a greater competence in the majority language. They are used to a world in which their language is not recognised. They often have profoundly negative attitudes towards their language, inculcated by the dominant institutions in their daily lives. In these circumstances, legislation is usually the best, if not the only, guarantee that the needs of linguistic minorities will be considered.

(Dunbar, 2006b, p. 2)

Why is language legislation important according to Dunbar? First, it can, and should, induce changes in the linguistic behaviour of those organisations to which it applies. It can set standards for the provision of minority language services, as we shall see in Chapters Eight and Nine. Second, it can, and should, induce changes in the linguistic behaviour of speakers of the minority language itself. It can assist in the acquisition of the language, and in deepening command of the language across a range of domains. It can increase opportunities for the use of the language. It can increase the visibility and prestige of the language. The provision of minority language services will create job opportunities for speakers, and this both contributes to the enhancement of prestige and to incentives for acquisition. Third, if properly structured – implementation via enforcement – it can allow members of the minority language community to take action to address failures in delivery of such services. Fourth, it creates a different normative environment, and allows the behaviour of organisations to be critically assessed by the public, the press, and politicians in a different and more demanding light.

Different approaches to the question of legislating for the protection and promotion of minority languages have a different potential for effecting change. Conventionally a hierarchy of approaches is adopted whereby internationally binding legislation is given primacy. The most significant international treaties which create important rules relating to minorities are the United Nations' *International Covenant on Civil and Political Rights* (the "ICCPR"), 1996; the declaration on the Rights of Persons Belonging to National, Ethnic, Religious and Linguistic Minorities, 1992; In Europe there are the Council of Europe treaties such as the *European Charter for Regional or Minority Languages* (the "European Charter"), 1992, the *Framework Convention for the Protection of National Minorities* (the "Framework Convention"), 1995; together with the Parliamentary Assembly Recommendation 1383 on Linguistic Diversification, 1998. More recently there is the *European Convention on Human Rights* (the "ECHR"). Documents of the Organization for Security and Cooperation in Europe have also been critical, such as the Document of the Copenhagen Meeting of the Conference on the Human Dimension of the CSCE, 1990; and the Oslo Recommendation Regarding the Linguistic Rights of National Minorities and Explanatory Note, 1998. Region-specific activities include the Council of the Baltic Sea States protection of persons belonging to minorities, together with the establishment of a Commissioner, Prof. Ole Espersen, to promote democratic development and the protection of human rights, including the rights of persons belonging to minorities.[5] A second more recent development is the Central European Initiative which produced an instrument for the protection of minority rights at its Turin meeting on 19 November 1994 (Trifunovska, 2001, p. 333).

Such instruments are deemed to be critical and in many cases mutually supportive, for they establish a body of conventions, instruments and law which can have major implications for the protection of minorities. But they also have purchase as a useful reference framework for supplicants rather than being merely an expression of state policy on language legislation.

A historically salient order is that which expresses state sovereignty. Minority languages can, for example, be recognised under the national constitution or basic law. This is an approach taken in Canada and Ireland, as well as Finland,[6] Belgium and Switzerland.[7] Similarly, minority languages can assume official status within particular territories of the state: examples include the Statute of Autonomy of Catalonia and of the Basque Autonomous Community in Spain, the Government of Wales Act 1998 in the UK, and the special autonomy regimes created in places such as South Tirol in Italy and the Åland Islands in Finland.

Specialists argue that great care needs to be given to how language regimes translate new opportunities into legally binding obligations. Thus it is important to recognise that legislation does not necessarily mean the creation of "rights" for speakers of minority languages. As we shall see in Chapter Eight, the Welsh Language Act 1993 involved the creation of very few identifiable rights, for it relied on Language Plans as the means by which a bilingual service would be provided. But is nevertheless relatively effective as an empowering, if not an enforcing, instrument.

Dunbar cautions that even when a "right" is established there may be severe difficulties in its implementation. These relate to technical issues such as imprecise wording or a right may be subject to a range of qualifications or conditions. In other circumstances the right-holder *may* have a remedy, such as going to court or seeking the assistance of an ombudsman or public defender, but such remedies may also be subject to great cost, unacceptable delay, obfuscation within the system and the unerring tendency of some regimes to subject such rights to administrative discretion.[8] It may also be that "rights" allowed at one level of jurisdiction are subsequently challenged, and at times overturned at a higher level of jurisdiction, as has happened in the Canadian context (Braën, Foucher and Le Bouthillier, 2006).

Kymlicka (1995, p. 2) has argued that language issues, and particularly rights, are central to both individual freedom and political community. We return again to the relationship between the individual and the community, the one and the many. But the notion of community is itself problematic.

Hartney (1995) has discussed to what extent communities can be said to exercise rights over and above those which are held by individuals. He concludes that there are no moral rights which inhere in collective entities and thus the primary need is to specify the relationship between arguments in favour of individual rights, collective rights and community survival or well being.

With reference to Canada he argues that 1) communities are important for the well being of individuals, 2) that legal rights can vest in collective entities, and that there may be substantive reasons for endowing communities with them, and 3) that it is conceivable that members of communities could have individual moral rights to the preservation and protection of their communities. He avers that claiming that moral rights can inhere in collectivities leads to confusion and to moral mistakes. He illustrates this by assessing different arguments that are meant, in his opinion, to justify legislation restricting the use of English in Quebec.

The first argument is that "while members of the English-speaking majority in Quebec possess certain individual rights, the French-speaking majority also have rights, that these rights are collective, and that they over-ride the individual rights of the English-speaking minority." As we shall see in Chapter Nine this appears to be an unassailable position for the Quebecois majority and guarantees their primacy within their own province or local state. It is also the logic adopted by the Catalan government, and resonates with many of the aspiring stateless nations in a post-sovereignty era as discussed by Keating (2004) and Kymlicka (2001).

However, Hartney cautions that this argument often

> takes the form of an appeal to "democracy" and majority rule, to the "collective rights" of the majority to see it's preferences prevail. In summary then, (1) it is the majority which is supposed to have these collective rights, (2) they are rights against the minority; and (3) they override the individual rights of this minority. This is nothing more than the claim that "society" or "the majority" has rights against minorities and individuals, and as such, is untenable.
>
> (Hartney, 1995, p. 221)

The second argument conceives of French-speaking Quebeckers as a minority within Canada, and it is as a threatened minority that they possess collective rights to survival: these rights then justify a special status for Quebec within Canada, and ultimately legislation restricting the use of English within Quebec. This is roughly the position examined below in Chapter Nine and has become the orthodox justification from successive Quebecois governments for the adoption of a certain type of language regime.

Hartney adduces that "(1) the collective rights belong to a minority; (2) they are rights against the majority within Canada (and secondarily against the anglophone minority within Quebec); and (3) they override the individual rights of Anglo-Quebeckers." Hartney readily concedes that the survival of French in Canada is important, and that this fact induces governments to act in favour of the preservation of the rights of individuals who speak French which may prejudice the interest of some at the expense of others. However, he observes that

> the only way to determine which interests are to prevail is to determine the importance of the interest for the lives of the individuals affected and the number of individuals affected. The weight of the interest of the preservation of the French language is no greater than that of the individuals concerned. The use of the term "collective right" here is a rhetorical device intended to give greater weight to the francophone interests than would otherwise be the case" (p. 222).[9]

He concludes his analysis with a warning that often the term "collective right" can be used to give *less* weight than is intended to the group whose interests it is meant to protect.

A final feature of language legislation is that it applies primarily to the public not the private sector. In consequence much of an individual's social, commercial and leisure activities are left untouched by legislation. This fragmentation in the reach of language legislation is very understandable. Were the vast majority of opportunities created by recent language acts taken up by the target group then so many of our fragile minorities would be in a far stronger position than they are currently. Thus creating new language related services and responsibilities is one thing, securing their full use is quite another. Consequently many critics argue that it is far better to adopt an evolutionary perspective on language reform and advise against tackling directly the more difficult issue of influencing the private sector with respect to language rights and obligations. This view is current in Wales, although as we shall see in Chapter Nine, there are strong arguments for bringing parts of the private sector within the remit of revised language legislation.

Understandably, if perhaps erroneously, legislation like Quebec's Bill 101, the *Charter of the French Language*, is comparatively rare. Dunbar advises that regulation of language use in the private and voluntary sectors implies a level of language intervention that governments, and even many minority language activists themselves, are often reluctant to consider. Both advocates and opponents recognise that enforcement legislation creates a new climate within which companies are required to operate.

> A reluctance to engage in explicit compulsion is understandable, but it also limits the range of legislative options, and of the potential impact of language legislation. Leaving the provision of minority language services

in the private and voluntary sectors to the goodwill and enlightened self-interest of actors in those sectors carries the same risks that apply to the abstention from legislating in respect of the public sector.

(Dunbar, 2006b, p. 6)

Neither is it inevitable that public sector legislation will be followed by that which applies to the private sector. It is far more likely that elements within the private sector will adopt several of the features of formal legislation, *as if* it applied to aspects of their work, as has happened in the case of former public utilities, such as gas, electricity and water which are now private and offer a degree of customer service and billing which is language choice specific.

The relationship between legislation, individual language choice and human rights is a dynamic field of enquiry to which we shall return in Chapter Ten.

Language equality: An evolving discourse

If legislation is often slow to capture a new sense of reality, the public discourse on minority cultural rights is often too quick to celebrate the gains and virtues of minorities within a pluralist democracy. In modern discussions of minority achievements we are presented with the claim that certain forms of bilingual education are superior to "majority" mainstream education, that having two or three languages at one's disposal increases the quality of life and leads to a greater range of employment choices in the market place. Yet the rhetoric often serves only to boost the ego of the already fragile minority and leaves many within the majority severely underwhelmed. If any political demands for national self-determination or threats of secession are associated with minority gains in civil society, then it may be in the interests of most political factions to play down the historical relationship between language gains and nationalist mobilisation.

Astute interpreters of the minority's predicament have recognised the negative impact which may derive from too close an association between language revitalisation and nationalist rhetoric. By appealing to common European norms and values, especially the maxim of unity in diversity, they have sought to reframe the debate in terms of issues of inclusivity and democratic pluralism. Thus the ideology of liberal equality has sought to displace the old nationalist orthodoxies we examined in Chapter Two. This has the double effect of separating the language agenda from an exclusionary nationalist orientation and of plugging in to the European mainstream, by emphasising the common European heritage of Catalonia, Galicia, Flanders and the like.

In Britain and Ireland, despite a diversity of approaches adopted in the management of language and governance, indigenous language issues are

Table 6.3 The changing nature of the debate

From	To
Struggle	Normalization
Discrimination	Current equality
Protect unique language	Promote bilingualism or multilingualism
"Nationalist" ideology	Inclusive pluralism
Marginal dependency	Self-reliance/governance
Minority special pleading	Equal opportunity
Language as a divisive issue	Language as integral
Cultural justification	Socio-economic rationale
Preoccupation with education	Holistic thinking
Para-public employment	Economic marketing
Compensation-deficit	Structure and planning
Reactive policy	Purposive growth
Historical orientation	Future prospects

increasingly incorporated into the equality agenda. The most significant change has been a shift from minority special pleading to the routine consideration of language-related issues as part of participative government. Table 6.3 summarises the main changes in the discourse

Wales and Ireland are further along this transformation than are Scotland and Northern Ireland, yet I would argue that if a true deliberative democracy is to be entertained, then all questions of language rights and obligations should be framed within an inclusive, pluralist framework. This involves constitutional reform, language legislation, citizen empowerment and the adoption of broader holistic perspectives. Roddick's (2002, p. 38) assessment of the changing constitutional context is illustrative of the principles of deliberative democracy.

> Parliament's more liberal and tolerant attitude towards the different nations of the UK is demonstrated by the devolution statutes. Its respect for the individual is demonstrated by its introduction of the *Human Rights Act,* the *Freedom of Information Act* and the *Race Relations (Amendment) Act.* Together these represent a colossal change. We have a modern democracy based on involvement, openness, accessibility, scrutiny, accountability, privacy and respect. These are the essential elements of a modern democracy.

Civil society and the economy are also being nourished by post-devolution developments. What is exiting about such developments is that individuals and interest groups, who prior to devolution would not necessarily have seen themselves as having an input into the public debate, are now convinced that they have some form of conduit and possible influence on the conduct of national affairs. This is the essence of the fledgling deliberative democracy we are witnessing.

Yet so much of this activity poses a puzzle, a conundrum, for it is central government which has been driving this more inclusive pluralism and openness. Mindful of the withdrawal of popular participation within civil society, government has been keen to create a system of involvement and consultation, whereby interest groups are encouraged to shoulder the responsibilities for restoring a "healthy social fabric". Yet as Johnson so tellingly observes it is government policy itself, allied with the extension of regulation and legal obligation, which has emasculated so many participants, "so that many activities which previously could be tackled by voluntary groups have been put out of their reach by the complexity of conditions to be observed and high costs" (Johnson, 2004, p. 298). Further, there has been a significant increase in centrally established and steered funding agencies, many of them established to promote social tasks or ameliorate specific problem areas. Language Boards are a case in point; as are the numerous cultural agencies which seek to address a wide range of issues, often well beyond their original remit. Yet as Williams (1993b) warned there is a real danger in linking a minority cultural infra-structure too closely to the dictates of the local state.

The growth of deliberative democracy is stifled by such trends.

"This is such a widespread phenomenon now that it is possible to discern the emergence of a managed or guided pluralism under which apparently independent social organisations are brought under the ambit of the policy objectives and priorities of national government. Once again, such developments may bring benefits in some spheres of social life and for particular groups in society, but they are unlikely to encourage the sort of vigorous independent pluralism which is so often seen under the customary constitution as a significant factor in a pattern of checks and balances derived from the structure of society itself and strong enough to impose limits on the exercise of power by ministers and their agents".

(Johnson, 2004, p. 300)

Asymmetrical devolution and its consequences

The UK's devolution settlement is a work in progress. The devolution statutes – the Scotland Act 1998, the Northern Ireland Act 1998 and the Government of Wales Act 1998 – introduced three new devolved assemblies: the Scottish Parliament, the Northern Ireland Assembly and the National Assembly for Wales. Each assembly is unique, they vary in their size and composition, their law making powers, their internal organisation and structure, their relationship with local government and other public agencies, and of course their relationship with Whitehall. Yet each operates under the sovereignty of the Westminster Parliament. Thus although some are tempted to describe this settlement as a form of federalism, in truth the centre is dominant, especially as it also legislates for England which comprises 87 per cent of the population of the polity.

A major research enquiry, "Devolution and Constitutional Change", sponsored by the ESRC, has concluded that devolution has opened up a new scope for policy innovation. Each part of the UK now has a differentiated policy process which is likely to grow because the devolution arrangements are highly permissive of policy divergence. Country specific initiatives such as free long term care for the elderly, abolition of University tuition fees and proportional representation for local government elections in Scotland have been complemented in Wales by the establishment of a Children's Commissioner, the phased abolition of NHS prescription charges, and the promotion of official bilingualism, and in Northern Ireland by the provision of free public transport for the elderly, a comprehensive equality policy and proposals for local government reform. Asymmetrical devolution also encourages bilateral rather than multilateral (UK) discussions of policy ideas so that UK – Scottish discussions may have different outcomes than UK – Welsh discussion. Intergovernmental coordination is a major challenge for it is weakly institutionalised.

The key to these dynamic relationships is legislative competence and financial muscle. The devolution and public policy summary overview (ESRC, 2006) argues that the financial settlement underpinning devolution is also permissive.[10] The UK Treasury adopts an adjusted Barnett Formula to fund devolution via an unconditional block grant. The administrations within the devolved territories are not bound to deliver UK-wide policy objectives and the UK government has no mechanism within the fields covered by the block to "buy" its way into devolved autonomy to meet such objectives (ESRC, 2006).

While such an arrangement might appear to give maximum freedom of movement to the autonomous territories, it does suffer from a number of operational and constitutional difficulties. The principal failing to be discussed in this volume concerns the lack of an overall vision as to how the whole system fits together and can be calibrated to derive maximum benefit to all citizens of the UK. Current arrangements are based on incremental reform rather than systemic logic. Intergovernmental relations have been characterised in the main by informality and a willingness to co-operate at many levels of the administrative hierarchy. There are signs that after devolution the highly fragmented way in which individual departments operated has given way to a more cohesive and disciplined approach. But this has not involved wholesale changes to the internal organisation or administrative processes of the UK government. This is because a largely pragmatic and instrumental approach to departmental autonomy has been the norm. Trench (2005, p. 199) has argued that central controls or check have, traditionally, been very limited. They are driven both by the central sources of legal advice (the Law Officers, the Treasury Solicitor and Parliamentary Counsel) and the co-ordinating machinery of the Cabinet Office in exercising the Cabinet's unifying doctrine of collective responsibility. In truth, avers Trench, "the response of the UK state to evolution in many other respects has been minimal change, made incrementally, pragmatically, and only as necessary to accommodate the direct and immediate implications of the changes devolution constitutes" (Trench, 2005, pp. 224–5).

As a result there are a number of unintended consequences and inequalities within the system which have yet to be tackled. For instance, many policy issues decided by Westminster for England have knock-on consequences for Scotland and Wales. The ESRC study reports on health issues for Scotland and Wales, "here devolved health policy all too easily ends up getting judged by targets Westminster has set for England" (ESRC, 2006). Similar judgements could be made on a range of supposedly devolved policy issues. Compounding this spill-over effect is the lack of policy-making capacity within the civil service, certainly in Wales and Northern Ireland, and to a lesser extent in Scotland also. A third issue is the question of realpolitik. So long as Labour dominate the government of the devolved territories and rule at Westminster, certain problems can be settled through internal party mechanisms. But once a different configuration is in place inter-governmental relationships will be far more susceptible to inter-party conflict. Yet one would not wish to deny the fact that devolution has opened up new spaces and engaged new actors and agencies in the policy-making process. Surely a major plus for democratic participation in these isles?

Devolution has also stimulated closer co-operation with the Irish Republic, both within an all-Ireland context and within the framework of the Irish-British Council. The dawning of a fragile peace in the north of Ireland is a major plus. But making sense of these new inter-governmental arrangements is not easy, neither is it clear what the major gains made are.

Conclusion

In order for the Celtic languages, and to a lesser extent Ulster Scots, to flourish both domestically and in the context of a new set of relationship between National Assemblies/Parliaments, the Irish-British Council, European Institutions and other international bodies, I believe that additional initiatives should be pursued as follows:

- Active participation in joint language policy initiatives.
- Joint representation of the needs of lesser-used languages both at a national and EU level.
- The transfer of good practice in bilingual education, community development and economic regeneration.

- The recognition of the need to implement more radical, innovative ways of addressing language-related issues.
- Ensuring the full implementation the European Charter for Regional and Minority Languages (Council of Europe).
- Expanding National Assembly for Wales concordats with Catalonia and Brittany to other EU regions.
- Maintain the Welsh Language Board's leadership in steering the network of European Language Authorities to influence EU decision-making and to exchange good practice in language planning.
- Contribute to the democratic practice of an enlarged European Union.
- Develop relationships with Canadian and other "Commonwealth" legislatures/partners.
- Investigate the role of Language Commissioners world-wide so as to provide good practice exemplars which could be adapted for the UK and other European states (Williams, 2000).

Within and between the "Celtic" nations three urgent needs present themselves. The paramount need is for greater investment and vision in bilingual education. This involves the development of a range of bilingual schools, attractive texts and resources, the training of teachers, while the introduction of optional (or mandatory) Gaelic/Irish/Welsh lessons in all state-funded schools needs to be tackled afresh. Second, community development experience, particularly in Scotland and Wales, suggests that individuals need direct government support to enable them to establish and maintain certain community networks which enhance the vitality of their bilingual/multicultural heritage. This could take the form of language enterprise agencies (Williams, 2000), the creation of a more visible bilingual landscape through public signs, the development of resource centres, the adoption of stress-free teaching methods for adult learners, media developments and collaborative projects in Northern Ireland, Scotland and Wales with colleagues in the Republic of Ireland. Finally, it is imperative that the Parliaments and devolved Assemblies and their respective civil servants declare clear, consistent and realisable roles for language policies which are fully funded, mainstreamed and monitored effectively; else the fledgling deliberative democracy we have identified will flatter only to deceive. Effective governance requires a responsive government and a committed citizenry. The devolution process offers this prospect, but at times shows worrying signs of being transformed into a colonial leviathan.

Notes

1. I do not discuss Manx or Cornish, despite there being significant developments in both cases. For Manx the growth of primary and adult education bodes well. For Cornish the findings of the Commission established by the Cornish Language

Partnership to report on a single written form and to develop a strategy for the next period will be very critical. I should add that I am a member of the Cornish Commission.

2. I have previously explored the disingenuous nature of such ideological pulses in relation to language policy in the UK, Canada and the USA (Williams, 1996; 1998; 2000).

3. I am grateful to Robert Dunbar, my colleague in Celtic Studies at Aberdeen University, for his permission to use this material and for many stimulating discussions over the years we have been friends.

4. He is conscious of the limitations, and even the dangers of legislation, for "laws create a framework for human behaviour, and they can have a powerful impact on shaping human behaviour. However, laws are only instruments, and sometimes they are fairly blunt instruments. Human behaviour is always far more complex than any law, and even good laws rely on human beings in order to have an effect. Any legislation which attempts to shape human behaviour can also have unintended results, and sometimes these results can even run counter to the aim which the law seeks to advance" (Dunbar, 2006, p. 2).

5. Though significant, the Commissioner cannot make decisions which are binding on member states, although he can bring his recommendations to the attention of the Council. For a detailed explanation, see Trifunovska, (2001), pp. 319–27.

6. Section 14 of the Finnish Constitution Act of 1919 provides that Swedish is the second national language; it also provides at paragraph 3 that Sami, Romanes and "other groups" have the right to maintain and develop their own language and culture.

7. Under Article 4 of the Federal Constitution of Switzerland of 2000, there are four official languages, German, French, Italian and Romansh. For a brief overview of the legislative position of Romansh, see Gross (2004) and visit www.kultur-schweiz.admin.ch. For the legal position of Romansh within the Canton of Graubünden, see Gross (pp. 41–2).

8. Dunbar adds that they can also "result in the misapplication of relatively scarce resources, including the most scarce resource of all – speakers of the minority language itself. Minority language revitalisation usually requires very finely and sensitively-tuned strategic interventions, and a rights regime generally does not allow for such interventions."

9. Hartney also discusses the case of the *Attorney General of Quebec v. Quebec Association of Protestant School Boards*. For details, see pp. 222–3.

10. This report was written largely by John Adams, the overview document was written by C. Jeffrey, see ESRC, 2006.

7
Celtic Language Regimes and the Basis for Deliberation

Michael Ignatieff has advised that "we need to stop thinking of human rights as trumps and begin thinking of them as a language that creates the basis for deliberation" (Ignatieff, 2001, p. 95). He rejects foundational thinking about human rights as a kind of secular belief system or idolatry and urges that we seek to build support for human rights on the basis of what such rights actually *do* for human beings. A nested hierarchy of general and specific rights are now operational within the international order, the sovereign state and those sub-state agencies charged with the delivery of language-related services. In consequence rights and obligations will increasingly be protected and upheld by overlapping jurisdictions. In some jurisdictions, such as the EU, this will require increased shared sovereignty while in others, such as many of the emerging states, it will require the strengthening of state sovereignty as the guarantor against tyranny, civil war and anarchy. In either case specifying under what conditions minority rights are to be recognised and then implemented requires a toleration of diverse means of managing majority–minority relations, even within the same state jurisdiction. Equality of recognition does not necessarily imply unanimity in treatment. Thus it is that within the UK and Ireland variants of Gaelic have been subject to quite astonishing degrees of differential treatment and even today there is no uniform response to the issue of rebuilding the Celtic languages (Ó Néill, 2005).

We have already considered whether or not majoritarian democracy is favourable to minority rights and to language rights in particular. We recognise that political legitimacy is always local, in other words regardless of the acceptance of international conventions and even governmental pronouncements, it is often the case that governance without conviction and reticence to empower minorities lies at the heart of the reluctance to implement minimal reforms. Nowhere is this more true than in the treatment of the Irish language within Northern Ireland and to a lesser extent that of Gaelic in Scotland. Let us therefore contrast the fortunes of Gaelic and Irish within the UK jurisdiction with that of the treatment of Irish within the Republic of Ireland's jurisdiction.

Scotland

Within the Celtic parts of the UK, Scotland offers a marked contrast to Northern Ireland and Wales. It has an established set of national institutions, a distinguished history of achievement in all the major sciences and arts, it has played a major role in the expansion of the British Empire, so much so that many of the British Canadian institutions and practices discussed later in this volume are in fact distinctly Scottish in origin. Scotland is characterised by a robust civil society and an engaging history of robust democracy. However, unlike Welsh or Irish, *Gaelic* in Scotland tends not to be considered as the national language, because of its demo-linguistic history and marginalisation since the fourteenth century and the persistence of the Highland/Lowland divide.[1] The failure of the Jacobite Rebellion culminating at Bonnie Prince Charlie's defeat at Culloden in 1746 had major repercussions for Gaelic culture, including forced eviction from the land, overseas migration and the collapse of the Clan structure as a semi-autonomous system within the burgeoning British state. How different Gaelic culture might have been today had not the Hanoverian hegemony penetrated so deeply into the Highland social system.

Architects of language revival are often very conscious of the historical legacy with which they have to deal. But under any definition the Highland clearances were a profound form of ethnic cleansing carried out by a ruthless regime in which the British Army committed some of the worst atrocities ever witnessed on British soil. Well established Highland/Lowland, Scottish/English, Catholic/Protestant divides were exacerbated by internal schisms and overlapping loyalties within the leading Gaelic families and political leaders. As a consequence the past three centuries have been particularly acute for *Scottish Gaeldom* and it is no surprise at all that significant elements of the economy and culture have suffered major reversals.[2]

Today non-*Gaelic*-speaking Lowland Scots often feel that *Gaelic* has little to do with them despite evidence to the contrary in personal names and place names. The Gaelic language, unlike Welsh in Wales or Irish Gaelic in Ireland, was not part of a patrimony, lost, imagined or otherwise according to some historians. This ideological divide has been exacerbated by three centuries of Whig history and historicism, and the acceptance of what some call a "teutonist" ideology. Allied to this is a majoritarian perception, correct or otherwise, that much of the Gaelic culture is imbued with anti-modernist perspectives. This allows them not only to disavow any responsibility for its fate but to distance themselves from the core values which it is claimed Gaelic culture espouses. Thus rather than being seen as a Scottish variant on Celtic language shift, conventional labour and economic historians argue that it is more profitable to interpret this complex relationship between majority and minority, as a form of ethnic re-definition.[3] Consequently this limits the extent to which devolution itself promises a *prima facie* improvement in the situation of Gaelic.

Celtic Scholars and Language Planners, among others, counter that this interpretation should be qualified as a result of the "Gaelic renaissance" of recent decades. Oliver (2005) argues that

> this renaissance does not strictly describe an organised or uniform movement; it better describes the emergence over time of a growing appreciation of indigenous culture (particularly since the 1960s with the growth of identity politics and popularisation of "folk" culture in western societies) and a parallel growth of Gaelic language activism in Scotland. This combination of activism with an enlivened awareness of local and national heritage has lead to a greater sympathy for the Gaelic language, and subsequent revitalization programmes have evoked and strengthened the concept of Gaelic Renaissance.
>
> (Oliver, 2005, p. 1)[4]

McLeod (2005, Private Correspondence, 3rd November) avers that the Gaelic renaissance is linked to interpretations of "Scottishness" and the politics of Scottish national identity. In recent decades Gaelic has become established as one element, albeit often a relatively minor one, in general public perceptions of "Scottishness". However, the fact remains that the relatively small size of the Gaelic-speaking population militates against its being seen as an integral element of society.

Recent survey research data tends to demonstrate a positive support for the welfare of Gaelic (Table 7.1). Thus the "mruk" survey published in September 2003 showed that 66 per cent of the respondents (a national sample of 1020 adults – apparently none of them Gaelic speakers) agreeing or strongly agreeing with the proposition that "Gaelic is an important part of Scottish life and needs to be promoted" as against 13 per cent disagreeing or strongly disagreeing.

We need not place too much store by such results, other than them acting as a useful boost for the marketing campaign surrounding Gaelic language promotion. Stronger survey evidence is articulated regularly in Ireland, Wales and Canada, but this does not necessarily translate into action, individual behavioural modification, language learning or policy reform. In fact such mass survey evidence can often mask the complexity of the language-identity nexus. Oliver's analysis of Gaelic identities (2005) suggests that despite the evidence derived from a more inclusive Gaelic Renaissance[5] there persists the idea of a symbolically and culturally bounded *Gàidhealtachd*, with related notions of the traditional, of *Gemeinschaft*, and rankings of the "authentic". His interview data suggests that the external and instrumental interpretation of Gaelic language competence (i.e., "Gaelic speaker") as a marker of a cultural Gaelic identity is over-simplistic. This implies that

Table 7.1   Market research on Gaelic, mruk, September 2003

Statement One: 'Gaelic is an important part of Scottish life and needs to be
  promoted'
Strongly agree 25%
Agree 41%
Neither/nor 13%
Disagree 9%
Strongly disagree 4%
Don't know 8%

Statement Two: 'Bilingual education and education through the medium of Gaelic
  should be promoted and expanded'
Strongly agree 23%
Agree 41%
Neither/nor 17%
Disagree 6%
Strongly disagree 3%
Don't know 10%

Statement Three: 'More Scottish people should attempt to learn Gaelic'
Strongly agree 22%
Agree 37%
Neither/nor 17%
Disagree 10%
Strongly disagree 4%
Don't know 10%

Source: Market research on Gaelic, mruk, September 2003

measures of the health of the Gaelic language should not be predicated
on quantitative analysis alone, and localised contextual factors are potentially more relevant in perpetuating the language than ascribed language
ability. Further related is the question of how much the evidenced contingencies of Gaelic identities are a symptom of, or contributor to, the
decline of Gaelic-speaking areas?

(Oliver, 2005, pp. 12–13)

A crucial conundrum for language promoters is the finding that

young Gaelic speakers are more conscious of identities other than those
traditionally associated with Gaelic-speaking communities. That being so,
in a changing Scotland, the Gaelic language (and its cultures and identities) is now even more open to appropriation, as a symbolic "marker" of
being Scottish, or allegiance to Scotland. This may help strengthen Gaelic-
medium education but it may not promote language use, or strengthen
Gaelic identities.

(Oliver, 2005, p. 13)

Further, he asserts that Gaelic-medium education may now be acting as a substitute for the use of Gaelic at home for many young people.[6] He believes that Gaelic is used more pragmatically and instrumentally, as a part-element in the negotiation of *Gesellschaft*, hence the ambiguity of Gaelic identities.[7]

For these and other reasons, McLeod (2005, Private Correspondence, 3rd November) believes that by the early twenty-first century Gaelic had become an ambiguous national language, with the predominant attitude being one of mild, vague support, even as a long-standing discourse of contempt (what Gaelic speakers know as *mì-rùn mòr nan Gall*) continued to resonate. Mild, vague support and symbolic valuation will certainly not be enough to maintain Gaelic as a living language in Scotland. Whether views have shifted enough to bring about genuine language revitalisation remains to be seen.

Yet we know that views are contextualised and often respond to currents in mainstream economic and socio-political life. Consequently it would be expected that the restoration of a Scottish Parliament would be a milestone event in the revitalisation of Gaelic. The arguments for a Scottish Parliament did not occasion the same levels of commitment to the development of Gaelic as happened to Welsh in Wales. Until devolution, distinctly Scottish institutions such as a separate legal system, the Presbyterian/Calvinist national church, and the education system, with their attendant ideologies, had all been crucial in strengthening national identity.[8] Scottish civil society is a far more developed construct than its Welsh or Northern Irish counterpart. But language has not figured as a central plank either of identity or of society.[9] In fact it was commonplace to argue that neither Gaelic nor the Scottish dialect of English now termed Scots would achieve salience in national politics. Neither, for example, received any mention in the *Scotland Act*, 1998. There is some provision for Gaelic in the Standing Orders of the Scottish Parliament (Scots gets none at all), and there have been some titular concessions to Gaelic, as in an evolving and a systematically bilingual Parliament, the appointment of two Gaelic officers, and the occasional use of the language in a number of functions of national importance.[10] Yet Oliver (2005, p. 2) suggests that together with the symbolic use of Gaelic on building signage, the Internet and other "signposts", such reforms can be seen as "a way of branding the nation but it also functions as a means of social inclusion, to provide for those who wish to use the language ... (and that) the Gaelic language has been symbolically appropriated at a national level." Conventional interpretations then need to be recast as a result of the greater articulation of Gaelic identity as a national resource and as a consequence of a changing discourse concerning the role of Gaelic in national life.[11]

However, the very limited scale of the Gaelic-speaking population at only *c*. 58, 562 (1.21 per cent) in 2001 makes language policy both more urgent and complex. Speaking, reading, and writing are claimed by only 66,063 persons, understanding, by an additional 27,219. As many as 37,022 respondents, who could not speak Gaelic reported that they could understand, read or write Gaelic, or possess some combination of skills (MacKinnon, 2003). There is some encouragement in that the rate of language decline is slowing. MacKinnon (2003) reports that there was an annual decrease between 1981 and 1991 of 1333; and of 701 per annum between 1991 and 2001. Yet Gaelic speakers are also dispersing. The Highland/Lowland split in 1891 was 72-28 in 1891. In 2001 it was 55/45. Dunbar (2005a) reports that by 1981, Gaelic was spoken by a majority only in the Western Isles, a new local authority area formed by local government reorganisation in the 1970s, where there were 23,446 Gaelic speakers (76.3 per cent of the population) and the Western Isles remained the only local authority with a Gaelic majority in 1991. Then the only areas with Gaelic-speaking majorities were the parishes of Kilmuir and Snizort in the Isle of Skye, and the Isle of Tiree in Argyll & Bute. By 2001 these had contracted further to Kilmuir parish in Skye only. Tiree, for example, just failed to reach the majority status at only 48.6 per cent (MacKinnon, 2005, Private correspondence, 15th November). However McLeod (2005, Private Correspondence, 3rd November) reminds us that there were several areas outwith the Western Isles with significant Gaelic-speaking populations, including Skye and Lochalsh, which was a formal administrative subdivision of the then Highland Region. By 2001, the number of Gaelic speakers there had fallen by almost 8000 to 15,811, representing only 59.66 per cent of the population. The percentage decline would have been sharper, except that the population of the Western Isles itself has been declining quite sharply, although now it is rising slightly, leading MacKinnon (2003), Dunbar (2003) and McLeod (2001) to argue that current policies are unable to stabilise Gaelic in the "heartlands" or the wider *Gàidhealtachd*.

Representing less than 1 per cent of all Scotland's statutory school-age students the paucity of educational opportunity also affects the low rates of literacy amongst Gaelic speakers.[12] The 1991 census showed that only 42,159 people, or 63.9 per cent of all Gaelic speakers aged 3 and over, could read Gaelic, and that only 30,760 people, or 46.6 per cent of all Gaelic speakers 3 and over, could write it. Since 1991, despite an expansion in Gaelic-medium education, fewer Gaelic-speakers – only 39,184 – could read the language, although they made up a larger percentage, 66.8 per cent, of all Gaelic speakers or 77.4 per cent of all Gaelic speakers aged 3 or over who could read the language. The number of Gaelic speakers who could also write Gaelic had, however, increased slightly over 1991, 31,235 people, or 53.3 per cent of all Gaelic-speakers aged 3 and over, could write the language. At its maximum some 27 per cent of primary pupils in Western Isles availed themselves of Gaelic medium education; this had declined to 23 per cent in 2004/2005 but rose again to 27.3 per cent for 2004/2005 and remains a very small number indeed elsewhere in Scotland.[13] However, McLeod (2005, Private Correspondence, 3rd November) notes that in Skye and Lochalsh the proportion is as high or higher than in the Western Isles, and there are other Highland areas (particular towns and villages) where the proportion would also be significant. In 2003–2004 there were 1972 primary school students studying through the medium of Gaelic at 59 schools which have Gaelic-medium classes and at the sole all-Gaelic-medium school, located in Glasgow. A further 288 students undertook some of their education through the medium of Gaelic at 15 secondary schools. In 2006–2007 this had risen to 2068 primary school pupils in 61 schools together with 307 secondary pupils attending 18 secondary schools.

Gaelic medium television and radio are successful but reach a small audience. Between 1990 and 1996, the Gaelic Television Fund was administered by *Comataidh Telebhisein Gàidhlig* (CTG), the Gaelic Television Committee. This enabled it to fund extra hours of Gaelic television. Under the Broadcasting Act 1996 the CTG became *Comataidh Craolaidh Gàidhlig* (CCG), the Gaelic Broadcasting Committee, and was given the additional remit to fund Gaelic radio programmes. *Radio nan Gaidheal,* Gaelic radio, is broadcast by BBC Scotland (BBC Alba). According to Dunbar (2005a) the value of the fund distributed by the CCG (itself replaced in 2004 by a new body, *Seirbheis nam Meadhanan Gàidhlig,* the Gaelic Media Service, or the SMG) still stands at £8.5 million, meaning that its real value has been eroded by about a third since 1990. The CCG could only fund the production of programmes, but had to rely on broadcasters – the BBC and Channel 3 licence-holders in Scotland – to broadcast them. While the BBC has expanded its television output somewhat, the Channel 3 broadcasters are reducing their output and have signalled their desire to withdraw from their obligations. Both Westminster and Holyrood accept the case for a dedicated digital Gaelic television channel and have been involved in long standing debates over funding illustrating another facet of devolution-related complications. The service became operational during 2007.

The Scottish Executive gives financial support to a number of Gaelic organisations, initially through *Comunn na Gàidhlig,* the Gaelic development body, which was set up in 1984 to promote and develop the Gaelic language and culture and now through *Bòrd na Gàidhlig.* Between 1995 and 2003, CNAG had organised an annual *Còmhdhail* (Congress) to discuss and develop national policies for Gaelic. *Comunn na Gàidhlig's* views on legislation and governance are detailed in its "Secure Status for Gaelic" (*Inbhe Thèarainte dhan Ghàidhlig*), and in July 1999 its "Draft Brief for a Gaelic Language" Act (*Dreach Iùl airson Achd Ghàidhlig*). In 2000, the MacPherson Report, commissioned by Scottish Ministers, recommended that a Gaelic Development Agency should, *inter alia*, facilitate the process of secure status for the language. This was given more substance by the report of the Ministerial Advisory Group on Gaelic, chaired by Professor Donald Meek which also presented the case for a Gaelic Language Act.[14] The commitment to provide secure status for Gaelic through a Gaelic Language Act was confirmed in the "Partnership Agreement for a Better Scotland", and then in the First Minister's statement on the Executive's legislative programme.[15] The "Partnership Agreement for a Better Scotland" promised high level commitments which relate to Gaelic and Scots as follows:

- "We will develop a new focus for Scotland's languages recognising both our heritage and our diversity."
- "We will legislate to provide secure status for Gaelic through a Gaelic Language Bill."
- "We will introduce a national strategy to guide the development and support of Scotland's languages, including British Sign Language and ethnic community languages."
- "We will continue to invest in Gaelic-medium education, including the provision of more teacher training places."[16]

On the 14th of June 2002 Michael Watson, the Minister with responsibility for *Gaelic*, signalled that his government was establishing a *Gaelic* Language Board and a small-unit of *Gaelic*-speaking civil servants within the Executive to deal with *Gaelic* matters.[17] Language activists and some politicians welcomed this but pressed for the passing of a *Gaelic Language Act* as recommended by the *Meek Report*.[18] This was achieved on the 21st of April 2005 when the Scottish Parliament passed the Gaelic Language Bill.[19] The Gaelic Language (Scotland) Act 2005 received Royal Assent on 1 June 2005. and was implemented on the 13th of February 2006.[20]

The main provisions of the Act are as follows:

- the establishment of the Gaelic development agency, *Bòrd na Gàidhlig*, which is required to exercise its functions with a view to securing the status of the Gaelic language as an official language of Scotland commanding equal respect to the English language;[21]
- the requirement for the development of a National Gaelic Language Plan to set out a blueprint for future Gaelic development (and within that plan, the development of a national Gaelic education strategy) across Scotland;
- the ability for *Bòrd na Gàidhlig* to require individual Scottish public bodies to prepare and implement a Gaelic language plan which will set out how they will use the Gaelic language in connection with the exercise of their functions;
- the ability for *Bòrd na Gàidhlig* to issue guidance to public bodies on the development of Gaelic education; (The Gaelic Language (Scotland) Act, 2005).

The Parliament's Education Committee, not the Gaelic lobby, was responsible for the potentially very useful addition to the Act that public bodies developing Gaelic plans must have regard not only to "the extent to which the persons in relation to whom the authority's functions are exercisable use the Gaelic language" but also, crucially, "the potential for developing the use of the Gaelic language in connection with the exercise of those functions." Parliamentary scrutiny of the passage of the Act has been described as "mature and constructive" (McLeod, 2005, Private Correspondence, 3rd November). The initially mixed reactions to the Executive's draft bill and significantly improved substance of the Act as enacted, demonstrates how the establishment of the Parliament has been beneficial to Gaelic (McLeod, 2005, Private Correspondence, 3rd November). Parliamentary scrutiny has also made the government more accountable and has influenced the development of more robust policies regarding the promotion of Gaelic. *Bòrd na Gàidhlig's*, first Chairman Duncan Ferguson reacted thus to the passage of the Gaelic Language Act:

> This is a truly significant moment in the history of the Gaelic language and culture. Today Gaelic has been officially recognised as an important and valuable part of the living culture of a thriving new Scotland, and we are delighted to welcome the advent of the Gaelic Language Act. Today is an occasion for celebration, congratulations and thanks to all those people who have worked for Gaelic over so many years. It is also a time to look to the future, to a new and confident generation of Gaelic speakers, to new opportunities to learn and to use Gaelic, and to a greater understanding and respect for the Gaelic language and culture.
>
> The Gaelic Language Act recognises Gaelic as an official language of Scotland, commanding equal respect with English. The Act establishes *Bòrd na Gàidhlig* as part of the framework of government in Scotland and requires the creation of a national plan for Gaelic to provide strategic direction for the development of the Gaelic language.
>
> It gives *Bòrd na Gàidhlig* a key role in promoting Gaelic in Scotland, advising Scottish Ministers on Gaelic issues, driving forward Gaelic planning and preparing guidance on Gaelic education. The Act also provides a framework for the creation of Gaelic language plans by Scottish public authorities.

Bòrd na Gàidhlig's mission is to ensure a sustainable future for the Gaelic language and culture in Scotland which it hopes to ensure through the following aims:

> Increase the number of speakers and users of Gaelic;
> Strengthen Gaelic as a family and community language;
> Facilitate access to Gaelic language and culture throughout Scotland;
> Promote and celebrate Gaelic's contribution to Scottish cultural life;
> Extend and enhance the use of Gaelic in all aspects of life in Scotland.
> *(Bòrd na Gàidhlig, 2005, p. 4)*

Eight Board members, together with an experienced Chief Executive and his staff, progress the Board's Operational Plan for the medium term. On the 1 February 2006 as a result of its new statutory status a new Bòrd was established committed to similar priorities as the Welsh model, namely initiating partnership ventures, gaining support from Local Authorities, developing Gaelic-medium education and extending broadcasting. The current priority is to implement the Gaelic Language Act, and a National Plan for Gaelic which will establish a number of statutory Language Schemes,[22] and evolve a distinctly Scottish national model for language planning. Campbell (2006) has identified the three pressing tasks as seeking community and governmental financial support for the National Plan so that its strategy can be fully realised. This requires a promotion and marketing thrust so that the general public are aware of the new opportunities, and then a programme of review and evaluation both to improve the service and to satisfy governmental audit requirements.

A second task is to agree the Gaelic Language Plans with the public organisations identified under the National Plan. It was envisaged that about ten such Plans would be implemented annually and in October 2006 the first 27 bodies were named and were required to agree Language Plans during the next three years. The model follows the Welsh experience of providing initial guidance from the Bòrd, a round of public consultation and then, if satisfactory, full agreement leading to the third stage of implementation.

The third task, that of delivering bilingual services, will test the capacity of partner organisations to operate an acceptable Gaelic system. Unlike the Welsh experience which was limited by statute to the public sector, the Gaelic Language Plans are more flexible and will involve a close collaboration between public, private and voluntary sector. Given the small scale of the Gaelic target audience this is both more necessary and feasible than it is in Wales. Thus new initiatives and investment in training policies, language skills acquisition and networking in the Arts, Broadcasting and Local Government will characterise the initial phase of Language Plan implementation. A strategic goal is to take full advantage of the additional opportunities which will be presented by the forthcoming Scottish Year of Highland Culture.

Even at this early stage three likely issues need discussion. The first is the nature of the partnerships being established. There is an acute danger that they will be grant dependent upon the Bòrd and thus in order to transfer real responsibility and build up community empowerment, the Bòrd will have to adopt a very sophisticated strategy of managing the initial delicate relationships without appearing to dominate and control them in perpetuity. Secondly, there is the acute observation that proving a range of new opportunities is one thing, getting citizens to use the new opportunities and to switch to Gaelic from English is quite another. Despite increasingly favourable attitudes towards the adoption of Gaelic in education, the health services and broadcasting, actual language behaviour change is more resistant, not surprising given the dominance of English, its hegemonic position and its all powerful technical apparatus in terms of vocabulary, patterns of speech, software, etc. Thus not only will the Bòrd have to re-educate many of its constituent audience it will have to secure that the necessary infra-structure capable of realising these opportunities as meaningful social interactions is put in place. This involves a co-dependency between the Scottish Executive, the Bòrd and the many disparate parts of the language service industry which are capable of training teachers, teaching adults, providing Gaelic software and publications, in-service professional training, changes to civil service operations, the provision of bilingual official forms, templates, on-line enquiries and submissions and the like. All this is beyond the capacity and remit of the Bòrd at present, and will require significant political leadership and inter-agency investment to bring to fruition.

It is too early to assess the impact of the new Gaelic Language Act, but it is certain that Scottish devolution has given a platform for the discussion of indigenous issues. Whereas *Gaelic*, when seen from the majoritarian perspective, might have been regarded as a "regional" rather than a "national" issue, this is no longer the case. Thus McLeod (2005, Private Correspondence, 3rd November) argues that in terms of Glasgow, which is now quite keen on promoting itself as a Gaelic "power centre" in terms of education, media and culture, a "local" approach has to be interpreted as a very new version of "Gaelicness." In common with many other revitalised languages, Gaelic appears to be occupying new spaces and using new networks and connections to sustain its social communication functions.

When coupled with the "rights" discourse which the *Human Rights Act* has ushered in and the new minorities discourse on "multi-culturalism, citizenship and development" which the *European Charter on Regional and Minority Languages* may be able to advance, there are now some ideological bricks and mortar out of which a coherent *Gaelic* policy and identity may be fashioned (Dunbar, 2001b). As Oliver advises

> Gaelic use can be strengthened and increased through the reimagining of Gaelic identities; and *vice versa* Gaelic identities will be revitalised and reimagined through the increased use of Gaelic. This would coincide with the normalisation of the language, with measures to build up everyday language use in community contexts, beyond the instrumental function of formal education structures and settings; where persisting notions of the traditional *Gàidhealtachd* would become more fluid, conceiving *Gesellschaft* as a dynamic and alternative context for maintaining Gaelic identities.
>
> (Oliver, 2005, p. 13)

But time is running out for language transmission within fragile *Gaelic* communities and the progress in bilingual education does not offer a substitute for the organic reproduction of a total culture. Nevertheless it is encouraging that pupil numbers in Gaelic-Medium Primary schools in 2004–2005, exceeded 2000 for the first time while over 3500 pupils study Gaelic as a subject in secondary schools. A major step forward is the opening in 2006 of the first dedicated all-through (age 3–18) Gaelic-medium school facilitated by a £2.75m grant from the Scottish Executive.

The Minister for Education and Young People had issued draft Guidance under section 13 of the Standards in Scotland's Schools Act 2000 for consultation in the summer of 2004. The aim of the Guidance Paper is:

- to ensure education authorities have a policy statement on Gaelic education;
- to encourage a consistent approach to Gaelic reporting under the 2000 Act
- to inform parents and Gaelic interests of their entitlement to Gaelic-medium education in each education authority area.[23]

In August 2004, the Minister for Education and Young People also established a Gaelic Secondary Information Communication Technology Implementation Group, to look specifically at the needs of the Gaelic secondary education sector and to formulate proposals to enable expansion of this sector. The Group has been asked to formulate proposals in the following areas:

- Decide which subjects and which stages to focus on.
- Commission the preparation of course materials working with Learning and Teaching (Scotland).
- Establish the delivery mechanisms and locations for Gaelic ICT subject delivery.
- Consider the professional development needs of teachers to assist the delivery of courses.

A second initiative was the Gaelic-medium Education Teachers Short-life Action Group Guidance on Gaelic Education.

In February 2005 the Education Minister, Peter Peacock, established an Action Group to make recommendations on the following aspects of the recruitment and training of Gaelic teachers; Existing Teacher Education Opportunities; Professional Preparation of Gaelic-medium Teachers; Professional Support for Gaelic-Medium Teachers. A new degree course for Gaelic teachers hosted by Strathclyde University and the UHI Millennium Institute produced its first graduates in 2005. At Aberdeen University a revitalised Department of Celtic Studies has attracted several language planning specialists and is capable of contributing research-based evidence for Gaelic policy formulation. The networking, educational and research centre activity at Sabhal Mòr Ostaig focuses on applied public policy and linking language issues with regional development. This offers a much needed focus for action research which feeds directly into the policy concerns of both the Highland Council and the nation and builds up capacity within the Gaelic-speaking professional community. Recently joint planning by several universities has lead to a series of much-needed initiatives to fund a team-based approach to Gaelic revitalisation. The SGRD bid has identified the three themes of Gaelic as a family and community language, Gaelic in education and policies for Gaelic as central to all their activities.[24] Cutting across these themes are the two transversal themes of Gaelic identity and self-confidence and Gaelic language use. It is too early to assess the impact of these initiatives but it is encouraging that such co-operative evidence-based research is now being funded and driven by committed professionals.

Despite these initiatives there remain deep-seated structural concerns which, as McEwan-Fujita (2005) reports, are not assuaged by the neoliberal ideologies and the actual practices of governance on language planning in the Highlands and Islands. Her evaluation of the language development programme "Gaelic in the Community Scheme" suggests that far from enhancing the use of Gaelic, "the adoption of neoliberal development practices can negatively impact Gaelic language-planning, even as they seem to facilitate the creation of language-planning programmes" (p. 161).[25] This is a contentious issue and one which needs to be addressed for it echoes similar criticisms of many of *Údarás na Gaeltachta* programmes in Ireland as discussed below.[26]

Scotland has taken significant steps to ameliorate some of the democratic deficiencies surrounding the treatment of Gaelic, but faces a Herculean task in restoring Gaelic as a vibrant community language in many conventional contexts, even as fresh hope is offered by the construction of new networks of speakers in new domains.[27] Asymmetrical Devolution and the attendant Constitutional Settlement was designed to address the legitimacy deficiency within the UK's outer regions. Under the Scotland Act 1998, the Scottish Parliament enjoys a general power to make laws within its legislative competence. The passing of the Gaelic Act of 2006 marked a new stage in language governance within these isles, although its remit is limited to "national" rather than "UK wide" affairs in comparison with the Westminster Welsh Language Act of 1993 legislation which established the Welsh Language Board. This limits the scope of the Gaelic Act for it does not cover many significant UK departments and agencies which have a remit and service provision in Scotland. This may be one of the unanticipated side effects of devolution and will doubtless create a series of quasi-constitutional and territorial bureaucratic uncertainties as the devolved assemblies acquire greater primary legislative powers.

My view is that Scottish devolution has created a fresh impetus and by implementing the Gaelic Act of 2006 has created a statutory obligation to act in support of Gaelic. This recognition is both symbolic and practical. It is symbolic in that it recognises that the responsibility for the future of Gaelic is a national political matter and not one which can be hived off only to a Parliamentary Committee or a new specialist agency. It is eminently practical in that it provides both a statutory body and initial requisite resources to implement the National Plan for Gaelic. In that one respect the governance of the language augurs well if *Bòrd na Gàidhlig* partnerships and political initiatives can influence behaviour and boost confidence in the actual use of Gaelic in worthwhile domains.

Language and public policy in Northern Ireland

For both scholar and politician alike, Mac Póilin has warned that images of the Gael and descriptions of the essence of Irish culture and language can mutate from being useful interpretations to becoming prescriptive simplifications.

> The process of defining has itself an inbuilt weakness, in that a definition is always in danger of turning into a self-sustaining prescription, which is in danger of being turned into an orthodoxy, and an orthodoxy, if it is not careful, can finish up as a slogan-the ultimate simplification. This tendency towards prescriptiveness is of course a permanent temptation for ideologues, and we have seen ideologues with agendas of their own moulding the image of the Gael from the earliest times.
>
> (Mac Póilin, 1994, pp. 20–21)

Up until the late sixteenth century Irish was the main language used in Ireland. The Tudor incursions had lead to the displacement of many aristocratic Gaelic-speaking families and their replacement by a largely English-born land-lord class. Gaelic Ulster lost its self-sustaining order with the Flight of the Earls in 1607. The new bureaucratic-military order had far-reaching consequences for the survival of the Irish language which as Elliott narrates "goes into rapid decline from the 17th century, not because of oppression but because the new legal system required the populace to come to terms with the English word and the written document" (Elliott, 2000, p. 126). Life under the penal laws was more concerned with property and land, the stirrings of an international economy and the promotion of Protestant patriotism.

> For much of the eighteenth century, Ulster Catholicism seemed quiescent and de-politicised ... the penalisation of the Irish language and culture was a thing of the distant past and for much of the eighteenth century

the Protestant gentry not only participated in traditional Irish pastimes but promoted a major revival.

(Elliott, 2000, p. 214)

Throughout the nineteenth century, Irish witnessed a dramatic decline. By 1851 Gaelic was spoken by only 6.8 per cent of Ulster's population; by 1911 only 2.3 per cent, the majority of whom lived in Donegal and Antrim (Elliott, 2000, p. 368). Yet Native Irish speakers were recorded in County Tyrone until well into the nineteen sixties.

It is a commonplace to ascribe much of the decline in the fortunes of Irish to the fall-out from the struggle for independence and the Civil War. In 1912 Ulster rejected Home Rule. The radical political movement comprised of Sinn Féin, the Gaelic League and other interest groups opposed to the temporising over the postponement of Home Rule, decimated the Home Rule Party in the 1918 elections.[28] The Sinn Féin MPs abstained from taking their seats in Westminster and formed a provisional government in Ireland giving priority to the establishment of a Department of National Language with the then president of the Gaelic League as Minister. In December 1921, after nine month of hostilities, a treaty was concluded with the British government establishing the Irish Free State in 1922 but enabling the six counties of Northern Ireland to remain within the United Kingdom. It is hard to be precise on what effect these events and the ensuing Civil War had on the development of Irish language policy. Ó Riagáin (1997, pp. 12–15) offers the interpretation that so much of the energy and personnel which might have gone into a virulent construction of an Irish-speaking state was actually dissipated in the nationalist political struggles, thus there was no guarantee that any successful party would have transformed the pre-Civil war rhetoric into robust language policy. Indeed it could be argued that "the pro-treaty group who formed the early governments were, as a result, anxious to demonstrate their credentials and chose Irish language policy as the means to this end" (Ó Riagain, 1997, p. 14). Others would counter that as a particular. (Pro British) side won the Civil War, the new state took on board "lock stock and barrel" the British form of a Legal System and Education System, just like other former Colonies like India and Pakistan did in the fifties! Nor did it dare challenge the hegemony of the Roman Catholic Church in the education system ... the RC Church was of course wedded to English-medium education (Ó Gribín, 2006).

For Ulster itself anti-Catholicism and opposition to Home Rule was a strong part of the explanation (Brewer and Higgins, 1998).[29] But the seeds of decline were sown long before the late nineteenth century. Akenson comments that

it was fashionable to explain the Irish people's rejection of the Irish language as a result of the three-pronged attack by the Irish national school system (which, until the early twentieth century did not permit a bilingual program), to the activities of Daniel O'Connell (the liberator made his speeches in English and showed no concern for preserving the language of the people), and to the Catholic Church (whose priests for the most part showed a marked preference for English). Such suggestions miss the point that the Irish peasantry was shrewd enough to read the economic signs of the times ... So, with a rational and a prudent calculus, the speakers of Gaelic in Ireland chose to learn English.

(Akenson, 1988, pp. 135–6)

Such views are contentious and suggest a level of empowerment which the common people simply did not exercise. Anglicisation here, as in Wales, was a top-down process of state assimilation; the masses were largely powerless in the face of such tremendous political, economic and religious forces.

After partition the teaching of Irish in Northern Ireland was a controversial issue, being hailed as an "excuse for Republican or Catholic indoctrination", a "useful pastime", but "useless in commercial terms", and ultimately counter-productive to the forging of a Unionist, British hegemony.[30] Irish language instruction was largely confined to the Catholic school system and the separate educational systems contributed to the "dialogue of the deaf" between the two communities. Little wonder then that by the 1991 Census only some 142,000 people in Northern Ireland had some knowledge of the Irish language. By 2001 this figure had risen to 167,490. Today the vast majority of speakers are identified with the nationalist community where the language is taught as a subject in most Catholic secondary schools, but not to every pupil and only a small proportion sit "A" level Irish. Significant proportions are adult learners of the language.[31] Partly as a reaction to the Gaelic language movement a campaign emerged in recent years for recognition of the Ulster Scots linguistic tradition.[32]

On 4 June 1998 the UK Government announced its intention to sign the Council of Europe *Charter for Regional or Minority Languages*. On 2 March 2000 the UK Government signed the Charter recognising Irish, Scottish Gaelic, Welsh, Scots and Ulster-Scots for Part II. It thereby committed itself to apply the general principles and objectives of recognition and non-discrimination. The Charter was ratified on 27 March 2001, and came into force on Monday 2 July 2001.

Upon ratification, the UK Government specified Irish, Welsh and Scottish Gaelic for Part III of the Charter – *Measures to Promote the Use of Regional or Minority Languages in Public Life etc* ... The Northern Ireland Executive has a responsibility to ensure that the Charter is observed and implemented in Northern Ireland in respect of devolved issues and to inform the Foreign Secretary, who in turn reports to the Council of Europe on the implementation of the Charter. By December 2005 the Charter's Committee of Experts had paid their second scheduled visit to Northern Ireland to seek evidence from officials, NGOs and the general Public as to how the measures were being implemented.

Similarly the *Education (Northern Ireland) Order* 1998 places a duty on the Department of Education for Northern Ireland to encourage and facilitate the development of Irish medium education. Gaelic is taught in only a minority of primary schools although the CCEA (Council for the Curriculum, Examination and Assessment) is currently developing plans to introduce languages to the curriculum at Key Stages 1 & 2. The department is currently funding eleven Irish medium schools (nine primaries and two secondary) with approximately 1,900 pupils. At second level, in most schools in the Catholic sector and a small number in the integrated sector, Irish is studied alongside other European languages. Pupils may opt to study either Irish or another European language at GCSE/AS/A2 level. After French, Irish is the most popular second language taught in second level schools in Northern Ireland. The gradual implementation of the strategic development plan of Comhairle na Gaelscolaíochta will result in additional schools being established. By contrast there are no current demands from within the school system for Ulster-Scots to be taught.

The Good Friday Agreement contains undertakings that the Government would explore the scope for achieving more widespread availability of (TG4) *Teilifís na Gaeilge* in Northern Ireland, and seek more effective ways to encourage and provide support for Irish language film and television production in Northern Ireland. The Department of Culture, Arts and Leisure has lead responsibility for developing agreed language policies and guidance on language issues to other Departments within the Executive. Linguistic diversity is a relatively new policy area and has emerged from the Good Friday Agreement which commits the Government to:

> recognize the importance of respect, understanding and tolerance in relation to linguistic diversity, including in Northern Ireland, the Irish language, Ulster-Scots and the languages of the various ethnic minority communities, all of which are part of the cultural wealth of the island of Ireland.

In strict political terms there are far more important clauses in the Agreement which have far reaching implications, depending upon how they evolve. For example, under the heading "Constitutional Issues" it is stated that

> The participants endorse the commitment made by the British and Irish Governments that, in a new British-Irish Agreement replacing the Anglo-Irish Agreement, they will: affirm that whatever choice is freely exercised by a majority of the people of Northern Ireland, the power of the sovereign government with jurisdiction there shall be exercised with rigorous impartiality on behalf of all the people in the diversity of their identities and traditions and shall be

founded on the principles of full respect for, and equality of, civil, political, social and cultural rights, of freedom from discrimination for all citizens, and of parity of esteem and of just and equal treatment for the identity, ethos, and aspirations of both communities; recognise the birthright of all the people of Northern Ireland to identify themselves and be accepted as Irish or British, or both, as they may so choose, and accordingly confirm that their right to hold both British and Irish citizenship is accepted by both Governments and would not be affected by any future change in the status of Northern Ireland.[33]

The Government envisages the Northern Ireland Assembly to undertake the following measures in respect of promoting Irish.

In the context of active consideration currently being given to the UK signing the Council of Europe Charter for Regional or Minority Languages, the British Government will in particular in relation to the Irish language, where appropriate and where people so desire it:

- take resolute action to promote the language;
- facilitate and encourage the use of the language in speech and writing in public and private life where there is appropriate demand;
- seek to remove, where possible, restrictions which would discourage or work against the maintenance or development of the language;
- make provision for liaising with the Irish language community, representing their views to public authorities and investigating complaints;
- place a statutory duty on the Department of Education to encourage and facilitate Irish medium education in line with current provision for integrated education;
- explore urgently with the relevant British authorities, and in co-operation with the Irish broadcasting authorities, the scope for achieving more widespread availability of *Teilifís na Gaeilge* in Northern Ireland;
- seek more effective ways to encourage and provide financial support for Irish language film and television production in Northern Ireland; and
- encourage the parties to secure agreement that this commitment will be sustained by a new Assembly in a way which takes account of the desires and sensitivities of the community.

The Linguistic Diversity Branch, which began work in February 1999, had a total of eight staff, but did not have a grant making capacity.

In terms of language and governance the most tangible element to emerge from the Good Friday Agreement was an all-Ireland agency for language policy. The North/South Language Body, known in Irish as *An Foras Teanga* and in Ulster Scots as *Tha Boord o Leid* was established by the *North/South Co-operation (Implementation Bodies) Northern Ireland Order*

1999 which came into operation at devolution. The NSLB has twenty-four Board members, two joint Chairpersons, and is comprised of two separate agencies, *Foras na Gaeilge* and *Tha Boord o Ulster Scotch*. The NSLB has a duty of promoting the Irish language; facilitating and encouraging its use in speech and writing in public and private life in the South and, in the context of Part III of the *European Charter for Regional or Minority Languages*, in Northern Ireland where there is appropriate demand; advising both administrations, public bodies and other groups in the private and voluntary sectors; undertaking supportive projects, and grant-aiding bodies and groups as considered necessary; undertaking research, promotional campaigns, and public and media relations; developing terminology and dictionaries; supporting Irish-medium education and the teaching of Irish.

Ulster Scots is recognised as a variant on the Scots language for purposes of Part II of the Council of Europe *Charter on Regional or Minority Languages*. *The North/South Co-operation (Implementation Bodies) Northern Ireland Order* 1999 provides that Ulster Scots is to be understood as the variety of the Scots language traditionally found in Northern Ireland and Donegal and has established an Ulster Scots Agency.[34] The NSLB has the following functions in relation to Ulster-Scots language and culture: promotion of greater awareness and use of *Ullans* and of Ulster-Scots cultural issues, both within Northern Ireland and throughout the island.[35]

Tha Boord o Ulster Scotch released its *Heid Ploy* (Corporate Plan), on 2 January 2001 consisting of four themes: 1) Supporting Ulster-Scots as a living language and promoting its use and development; 2) Acting as a key contributor to the development of the Ulster-Scots culture; 3) Establishing partnerships with the education and community sectors to promote the study of the Ulster-Scots language, culture and history; 4) Developing the public's understanding of the Ulster-Scots language and culture. An amount of £1.4 million was allocated to implement these schemes. In the year prior to devolution (1999/2000) Government support in Northern Ireland for projects with an Irish language dimension grew to over £10 million (including. £8 million for Irish medium education). In the same period funding for Ulster-Scots was £118k.[36]

Language governance implications for Northern Ireland

A measure of legal recognition and protection is now in place. However, in order for Irish Gaelic to flourish as a vehicle for the communication of ideas, skills and a pluralist culture, it is essential that new networks and a new set of institutions be established which enable the target language to be embraced by all in society should they so choose. Thus issues of the development of Irish-medium schools, attractive texts and resources, the training of teachers, the introduction of optional (or mandatory) Irish lessons in all state-funded schools need to be tackled afresh, with a great deal of respect for the existing institutional arrangements based within Roman Catholic networks. However, logic alone suggests that if Irish is always to be associated with Catholic cultural imperatives it will not serve as a bridge or a platform upon which more cross-cutting networks can be established. Thus it is imperative that DENI re-consider the whole issues of language choice within the educational system, including the training of teachers and the location of resource centres. This is critical so that a free choice may be offered to every non-Irish-speaking citizen to benefit from a bilingual experience either for themselves in adult education or more probably for their children.[37]

Language policy making in Northern Ireland has been something of a unique endeavour, largely prompted by political expedience and reliant on the insights of committed individuals. During the past two decades the Ultacht Trust has devoted a great deal of attention to the promotion of Irish and community development within the north. More recently POBAL has made important contributions in both setting the agenda and in providing reasoned, evidence-based arguments for a range of Irish language policies, the cutting edge of which is their case for an Irish Language Act for Northern Ireland (POBAL, 2006a).

I share the conviction that Irish should be designated as official language in Northern Ireland (although this begs the question as to whether or not English is an official language). This would be an action to ensure official status first and then consequently to stimulate increased use. This would be a very important symbolic statement on behalf of the Irish language and a means of emphasising the UK Government's commitment to, and objectives for, Irish. But in addition to supporting the symbolic element there is also a far more practical set of considerations and overall justification for supporting "The Irish Language Act for Northern Ireland". Let me present six reasons for this assertion:

1. First it is needed – it is time that relevant elements of Irish linguistic rights be put on a statutory footing.
2. Irish is the historical indigenous language of Ireland and thus cold logic suggests that it should be recognised within its own unique spaces.
3. The Irish language has become part of the "Equality Agenda", consequently language rights need to be developed in line with more established rights in such policy areas as Antiracism, Sexual Equality, Disability and so on.[38]
4. A number of European trends are leading towards a more comprehensive definition of civil, social and economic rights. This is in reaction to a number of various developments e.g. globalisation and the evolution of the responsive nation-state infused as it is with strands of a social market doctrine.

5. Developments in Wales, Scotland and in the south of Ireland all point to a greater awareness of the relevance of statutory language regimes. The current Coimisinéir Teanga or Language Commissioner might be joined in Wales by either a Language Adjudicator or a Commissioner to deal with complaints from the public and to investigate how Government departments are adhering to their statutory Language Schemes.
6. The declaration that Irish is an official language of the European Union opens up new opportunities for its employment in an increased range of formal domains, including inter-state partnerships and international contacts.

Key questions

1. What kind of legislation is needed?
2. Is there to be one comprehensive Irish language act and/or a number of strategic measures as devolution develops?
3. Should there be an Official Languages Act? An Act which declares both English and Irish as Official Languages?
4. What will be the relationship between Westminster Legislation and the Northern Ireland Assembly Legislation on the Irish language and the Assembly's consequent greater involvement in this unique policy area?[39]
5. How will legislation and new patterns of co-operative working stimulate a change in the linguistic behaviour of citizens, customers and employees? Clearly opportunity, habit and choice are intimately interconnected in this sphere.
6. How will the granting of official status influence the activities of a number of all-Ireland bodies, specifically the NSMC and the An Foras Teanga/Tha Boord o Leid, the North/South Language Body?

Linguistic rights

There are strong political reasons for supporting bilingualism and multi-lingualism in Europe. But the precise conditions under which particular languages receive state support at some level and not at others remains largely a function of political expedience and statecraft. Undoubtedly language awareness has increased tremendously in all sorts of ways in the past five decades. Thus the European Union has declared itself committed to the promotion of linguistic diversity. In the "Treaty establishing the European Community" Article 151.1 we read that "The Community shall contribute to the flowering of the cultures of the Member States, while respecting their national and regional diversity and at the same time bringing the common cultural heritage to the fore."[40]

However, until very recently, little of this commitment was channelled into a greater specification of the language rights of lesser-used speakers per se. Yet there are instruments which encourage language awareness and policy action within the context of lesser used languages.[41] The most significant is the Good Friday Agreement and more recently the St Andrew's Agreement. At a European level the European Charter for Regional or Minority Languages is highly relevant.[42] The UK government is a signatory state and the Charter monitoring process has now entered its second round of consultation. In 2006 the UK Government submitted review evidence to the Council of Europe on its implementation of the Charter, and various groups and bodies shared an important opportunity to submit evidence to the Council of Europe and its visiting Committee of Experts. This is an important discussion at the European level regarding language policy within Northern Ireland, the GB and Ireland. Other applicable international legal obligations of direct relevance to the 2006 POBAL proposals include the International Covenant on Civil and Political Rights, the European Convention on Human Rights and the Framework Convention of the Protection of National Minorities.

The Human Rights Act (1998) has also developed our understanding of the concept of individual basic rights. The Irish language is already part of the equality agenda in Northern Ireland but we have yet to be as ambitious in the case of Irish as in the case of other equalities. After a decade of promoting the need for language legislation, the stage is now set to take the next steps in establishing specific linguistic rights for individuals and making the Irish language an integral part of the anti-discrimination legislative agenda. Such a step is necessary to show that we are serious about safeguarding the Irish language. Northern Ireland would thus be in conformity with other parts of the UK such as Scotland and more particularly Wales where the Welsh Language Act (1993) places a duty on public bodies to treat Welsh and English on the basis of equality when providing public services.[43] The prime instrument for achieving this are the contents of language schemes prepared by public bodies and agreed by the Welsh Language Board.[44] By and large this has been a very effective method of promoting Welsh and of making bilingual services available to the general public. But all this has been achieved in Wales in the absence of a detailed specification of particular language rights. That this has been possible is due to the relatively large number of Welsh speakers, an increased good will on the part of the central and local government and the skill and sophistication of the central language planning agency, the WLB, in knowing how to handle a challenging set of reforms within the public sector. Current developments in Scotland, as noted above, reinforce this need for the transference of best practice from one context to another and to strengthen the network of agencies and pressure groups which seek great recognition for the rights of lesser used language speakers.

POBAL's (2006a) draft Irish Language Act is a most comprehensive document and a genuine historical milestone in the promotion of the Irish language. The detailed provisions cover the implementation of the proposed act in spheres such as the Northern Ireland Assembly, local authorities, the administration of justice, public services, employment, education, the media and the enforcement of rights and obligations under the act.[45]

The fundamental weakness of the current system is that there in no clear official declaration as to what role Irish is expected to play within the society of the north of Ireland. One trend elsewhere is to promote institutional rights in terms of the delivery of services to the public. Yet the trend favoured within the POBAL document is to argue for a strongly rights-based approach more akin to Canada than to Scotland or to Wales.

Yet the Welsh example demonstrates that although they may not have individual language rights, they do have government support to enable them to establish and maintain certain community networks that enhance the vibrancy of a bilingual heritage. In Northern Ireland this could take the form of language enterprise agencies (akin to the Welsh *Mentrau Iaith*), the creation of a more visible bilingual landscape through public signs, the development of resource centres, the adoption of stress-free teaching methods for adult learners, media developments and collaborative projects with colleagues in the south of Ireland, Scotland and Wales. Research into the patterns of Irish and Ulster Scots's language use is needed to ascertain processes and problems. This would likely focus on youth culture and on extra-curricula activities. But it would also need a great deal of work on the specification of the relationship between bilingualism and the economy so that future employment prospects might be considered in tandem with socio-cultural considerations.[46]

It is time to build on these comparative foundations and establish worth-while legislative rights for Irish speakers, based on specific aspects of public service provision. Because Northern Ireland cannot yet rely on several of the factors which obtain in Wales and to a lesser extent in Scotland, it must resort to a more formal specification of language rights under a Language Act together with the enforcement capacity of a Language Commissioner. Given this it would be timely to establish statutorily that individuals have the right to receive Irish-medium education, the right to use Irish in a number of cases in dealing with the Health System, or in the workplace, the right to correspond in Irish with bodies which come within the scope of the proposed Irish Language Act, and to receive correspondence or information from them through the medium of Irish.

I also believe that it is important to mirror the duty to provide a service with the right to receive it. This principle is the basis of linguistic planning in a number of countries – but is almost completely absent in Wales. The exception to this situation is the right to a hearing through the medium of Welsh in a court of law. Those bodies responsible for providing this partic-ular service have planned action in a timely way to meet the requirements of the Act. The legislation makes it clear that they have a duty to provide the service – and that individuals have the right to receive it. In the short term some rights can be addressed by buying in expertise from the private sector, notably written translation (web sites, forms, etc.) whilst the provision of bilingual staff will take more time and involve recruiting such staff and replacing monolingual staff that leave or retire with such people. But this involves both a significant investment and language awareness training programme. Currently there are severe doubts as to whether the public administration in Northern Ireland is equipped to deal with these issues.

I also commend the concept of integrating the Irish language and its affairs as an integral part of the anti-discrimination legislative agenda. Dealt with in this manner the Irish language would be less likely to be considered as a cause célèbre or a political football. To my mind this is a rational way of tidying up a legislative landscape which has to deal with historical inequalities and a lack of action in the past. This, I assume, is part of the concept of the institutionalised of the Irish language.

Current British and Irish experience in language planning suggests that arrangements in Wales and more recently in Ireland are particularly good at fostering the capacity to prepare Language Schemes, but that the present systems are not as effective in terms of supervising and ensuring implementation of the schemes.[47] For example, the 1993 Welsh Language Act's hold on Crown Bodies, such as UK Government departments (including the Assembly for Wales Government) and a number of its agencies, is a clear example of the weakness of the existing legislation. The Welsh Language Board's powers to require bodies to prepare, and then to approve Language Schemes do not apply to Crown Bodies. We see similar failings in respect of the Board's ability to review the content of schemes and, in the case of the Government, the power to enforce the implementation of Schemes. Instead, the goodwill of Crown Bodies must be relied upon. This goodwill manifests itself in the fact that Crown Bodies, on average, take twice as long as other bodies to prepare language schemes. On other occasions Crown Bodies have refused to implement the content of their Language Schemes – and political intervention at the highest level was necessary to rectify the situation.

This is neither acceptable nor reasonable. Consistency and clarity are needed, and the same expectations and standards should be placed on Crown Bodies as on other public bodies. The Assembly Government has already provided evidence to the Richard Commission setting out how it would be possible to bring Crown Bodies entirely within the scope of the 1993 Act. Under Section 10 of the 1993 Act, the Assembly is required to obtain Westminster's approval for any amendments to the Board's statutory guidance on the preparation of Language Schemes. In the wake of devolution, and considering that the National Assembly leads in this policy area, I believe it would be appropriate and timely for the Assembly to have the power to approve any change to statutory guidance on the preparation of Language Schemes.

As the POBAL (2006) proposals make clear there is an urgent need to specify the exact nature of language rights in the services provided by both the public and private sectors. But I would urge caution here because precision in the interpretation and application of rights will be difficult given the complexity of the current socio-economic context. There is some merit in the argument that sometimes a lack of precision makes the idea more acceptable to the "other side" and allows flexibility on the part of those who want to make changes. The interpenetration of different sectors also makes it very difficult to define the boundaries of a particular service, apart perhaps from fairly simple things like face-to-face commercial interactions in a shop or a public house. Anticipating language-related behaviour becomes increasingly complex with the increase in the mixed market and telecommunications, and as individually orientated behaviour rather than mass or community behaviour increasingly becomes the norm. So it is appropriate to take a more thematic rather than a sectoral view, and to consider the nature of the services provided to the public. A classic example of this thematic approach would be the role of recently privatised water companies. They provide a public service through the private sector. The Government of Wales has already accepted this principle in part through its decision to bring water companies under the ambit of the existing 1993 Language Act. Once the Government has completed its work in relation to utilities, it would be appropriate to consider and discuss whether the act (or new legislation) should be extended to other spheres of activity, such as banks and insurance companies. I believe that the National Assembly should have the power to designate groups of particular bodies in relation to linguistic legislation, as was done in the case of the water utility companies.

Language Regulator or Commissioner?

The idea of establishing a Language Commissioner for selected Celtic languages is something I have supported since 1973 when I did my first research work in Canada on linguistic planning and the language struggle in Quebec. But does Northern Ireland need a Commissioner for the Irish Language or a Language Commissioner? This I believe to be a significant option given that the Irish language bodies have a 32-county remit now. The latter could conceivably have a far wider and inclusive role than the former and could conceivably have a joint cross-border remit with the Irish Republic's Language Commissioner in specific circumstances. If a Commissioner for the Irish Language is established, will this person act as a public advocate who promotes and challenges, or will the Commissioner's office be restricted solely to investigating and reporting on the failings of the system?

POBAL's current legislative initiative favours the creation of an Irish Language Commissioner for Northern Ireland.[48] The office holder is to be appointed by the Secretary of State for the reasons given below. It is envisaged that the Commissioner would also have some policy-making functions, and could make recommendations on a wide range of matters relating to the Irish language in Northern Ireland. The Commissioner's central role, however, will be the investigation of complaints normally as a response to citizen involvement and occasionally on the Commissioner's own initiative into failings of the system. An additional element is the further right of appeal to the courts[49] and the requirement that the Commissioner consult and liaise with An Coimisinéir Teanga in the south of Ireland (whose remit over NI could also be negotiated) and with Foras na Gaeilge, to ensure maximum cooperation.

Now it is possible that if the UK government establishes a regulatory regime to monitor and implement the proposed Irish language Act, it would not necessarily favour establishing the office of Irish Language Commissioner. It may favour the appointment of a "regulator" who will intervene as and when a significant dispute arises. There is a risk that the "regulator" would concentrate only on the essential matters under the ensuing legislation, and that other parts of the work of actuating and promoting Irish would be lost within the office of the Assembly's Administrative Ombudsman.

For this reason it is vital that any proposed "regulator" be an independent voice for the implementation of the Act or any revised legislation. This appointment should be for a fixed term, and should be made by the Secretary of State initially, but in time by the Northern Ireland National Assembly rather than the Assembly Government. This would follow the pattern in the UK as regards the Public Services Ombudsman and the Auditor General. It should be ensured that the proposed "regulator" has the appropriate powers and resources to undertake his/her duties in a timely and effective fashion.

I believe it is vital that the "regulator" also has the defined role of supervising and implementing the Linguistic Legislation, in the exact same way as the other responsibilities provided, such as race and disability. In time, of course, one could envisage a network of Language Commissioners from Canada, Ireland, Wales, Northern Ireland and other parts of the world working together and then sharing their common experience with Commissioners in other policy spheres, such as Administration, Children, the Elderly, Health and Welfare and so on.

Should the idea of an Irish Language Commissioner for Northern Ireland be turned down as being premature or inoperable then it is quite logical to call for the establishment of a UK-wide Language Commissioner who would be responsible for the enforcement of language rights and duties in respect of all the languages which fall under international treaty obligations. These would include the Good Friday and St Andrew's Agreements, the European Charter for Regional or Minority Languages, the Framework Convention on the Protection of National Minorities, various Human Rights treaties and the

International Covenant on Civil and Political Rights as discussed below in this document.

A charter and forum for the Irish language

As well as a new Language Act, the production of an Irish Language Charter would be a significant statement in respect of rights in education, the economy, public services, and the media and so on. This I believe is the appropriate place for political and social statements about the nature and role of the Irish language in Northern Ireland.

It follows that if civil society is to be actively involved in the policy and planning aspects of Irish language promotion then there should also be established a democratic and inclusive forum to discuss the Irish language. At the very least, a proposed Irish Council or Forum (which should meet regularly throughout the year) should have an essential role in offering evidence, and in giving a voice to all, particularly those whose views are not otherwise expressed through formal political or civil society channels. But what would be the exact nature of the Council's function and responsibilities? How effective would it be? How would key decisions of the Forum be transferred into government policy? These are matters for debate and reflection, but in my view if the proposed legislation is to be both workable and effective, there has to be a permanent common ground above and beyond the Northern Ireland Assembly where issues germane to the well being and promotion of Irish are handled. Regardless of which consultative model is adopted I propose that there should be a small committee of specialists who would garner the better suggestions, including those from the Forum/Council, and convert them into practical proposals which politicians could absorb and then implement in their development of a more bilingual society. Another obvious element of these proposals, of course, is that pieces of legislation would have to be bilingual; this would complement the unique nature of the informal constitution and various initiatives in using the Irish language in new areas for the first time.

Others may argue that instead of establishing yet another body it would be much better to give a new role to Foras na Gaeilge, together with the financial backing needed to normalise use of the language. Perhaps an Official Language Consumer Rights Body could also be formed to oversee public satisfaction etc with progress towards bilingualism?

Naturally, all this raises fundamental questions regarding the devolution settlement and the ongoing transfer of powers and responsibilities within the UK. In Wales current plans to strengthen the National Assembly have elicited several challenging proposals vis-á-vis the role of the Assembly in legislating on behalf of the Welsh language. In time the implications of the full devolution of powers to legislate on the Welsh language for United Kingdom bodies which provide services in Wales would also have to be

212 Linguistic Minorities in Democratic Context

considered. The same would hold true with respect for the use of Irish by Northern Irish departments and in relation to other UK departments providing services to citizens in the north. The restitution of full devolution was quickened by the holding of Northern Ireland Assembly elections on the 8th of March 2007. The Democratic Unionist Party (36 seats) and Sinn Féin (28 seats) emerged as the clear winners, eclipsing both the Ulster Unionist Party (18 seats) and the SDLP (16 seats) who were for so long the main players within the system. There is a possibility that an Irish language Act for Northern Ireland will be passed soon at Westminster, or in time, at Stormont.

The acid test of the adequacy of these legislative proposals is how they will lead to an increased use of the Irish language in everyday life. The symbolic nature of language recognition is an important factor, so too is raising language awareness, so that any citizen may avail themselves of the new opportunities afforded by bilingual education and bilingual public services. But the key to language promotion is transmission and usage. Legislation by itself will not guarantee increased use within family transmission or usage. But it will provide an enabling and empowering framework within which other policies can operate. I look forward to a time when not only genuine language choice will be available, but that significant numbers of citizens will actually make determined use of that choice, and thereby add to the quality of their daily life and to the rich diversity of their society.

Ireland

The formal Act of Union of 1800 has been described by Boyce as a conundrum in that it was intended by Pitt the Younger to confer on the Roman Catholic majority of Ireland certain political rights, critically the right to sit in Parliament in London. Yet simultaneously "assurances were made to the Protestant minority, and more particularly the landed gentry whose parliament was politicised out of existence between 1799 and 1800, that the Union would secure them in the rights and safety that their own political control of Ireland could no longer guarantee" (Boyce, 1988, p. 4). MacDonagh adds that as Irish nationalism grew "it was argued that in 1800 neither parliament represented, in any acceptable sense, the peoples involved; and as popular sovereignty as the source of political authority gained in estimation in the nineteenth century, so the Act of Union became more vulnerable" (Mac Donnagha, 1977, p. 14). British "miscalculations" and Irish denials of the legitimacy of the terms and implications of the Union in an increasingly free trade economy turned around issues of land ownership, protectionism, the failure to nurture and attract capital, the defence of religious interests, the abandonment of insulated Irish decision-making and the introduction of the direct exercise of power from London. But language was not a prominent feature of the discourse until the end of the century, and even then its actual role within society was highly debatable.

However, a central feature of the nineteenth century *Gaelic* revival and the move towards independence, achieved by the Treaty of 1921, was the need to distance and further differentiate Irish culture and values from British mores and interests. The three most prominent agencies for cultural liberation in the national struggle were Catholicism, the land and the language. In 1922 the newly independent state launched a comprehensive strategy for the restoration of Irish as a national language. Irish speakers were given preference in public service positions such as *Gardai*, Army Officers, teachers and civil servants, thereby creating a group of state employees with an ability to speak Irish, who could bolster the existing middle-class Irish-speaking population. Nevertheless it should be recalled that the majority of native speakers would have been fishermen, labourers and small farmers.

Article 4 of the first constitution in 1922 made Irish and English official languages.[50] The 1937 Constitution gave recognition to two languages, Irish and English, but declared Irish as the first official language. There followed a policy of incremental reform which sought to establish State initiatives to promote the use of Irish, to stabilise *Gaeltacht* communities and to encourage a nation-wide system of voluntary language organisations, the most prominent of which is *Comhdhail Náisiunta Na Gaeilge.*

State support for agriculture did not stabilise the Irish-speaking communities and as a result of education and planning policies large numbers of *Gaeltacht* residents quit the predominantly Irish-speaking areas for employment opportunities in urban, anglicised locales. To arrest the decline of Irish the government committed itself to a two-pronged attack which focussed on territorial defence and educational reform. In seeking to define and defend the fragmented Irish-speaking areas, the *Gaeltachtai*, the government opted for a "common sense" solution to protect Irish within its remaining heartlands. This approach is echoed in calls in Wales to defend *Y Fro Gymraeg* and in Scotland to defend the *Gaidhealtachd*, concepts which Withers (1988b, p. 4) reminds us are merely "abstract terms, not ordinary place names, and the areas they designate are not drawn with precise boundaries."

The 1926 Gaeltacht Commission, set up by the Free State Government, undertook the task of compiling the attitudes of people in Irish-speaking regions of the State, and defining the boundaries of Irish-speaking districts (Tuarascáil Choimisiún na Gaeltachta, 1926). The Commission reported on the population's capacities in Irish and undertook an economic analysis of Gaeltacht areas, expressing particular concern at the demise of Gaeltacht areas such as east Sligo, south Kilkenny, southwest Cork and much of Mayo.

The territorial shrinkage of the Gaeltacht between 1851 and 2001 stands in marked contrast to the Official Gaeltacht as represented on Figure 7.1.

Hindley (1990) has advanced five lessons, which with hindsight might have made the Irish language policy less dependent upon ill-advised

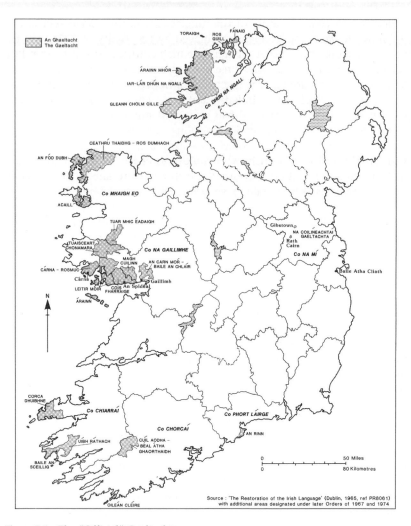

Figure 7.1   The "Official" Gaeltacht
Source: Williams, 1988a, p. 281.

territorial language planning. The implementation of government policy was characterised by a:

1. Lack of policy precedent. There were no precedents in 1925 for any attempt to revive a national language, which had already become a minority tongue within its own national territory.

2. Lack of socio-spatial planning. There were no precedents, other than native reserves in the colonies, for demarcating minority language areas in order to preserve their cultural identity – except when as at Versailles the minority was a majority elsewhere.
3. Lack of census interpretation experience. There was little experience of the inadequacy of census enumeration of language ability as a guide to language use or genuine command.
4. Lack of conceptual awareness. There was no awareness of such concepts as "critical mass" below which a language ability as a guide to language could fall in numbers or proportions only at its extreme peril, nor of village and urban "systems" command of Irish, at least one of which was essential for language survival.
5. Lack of theoretical sophistication in terms of policy options. There had been no conceptual exploration of the territorial or individual alternatives in language planning strategies, nor indeed had much need been felt for language planning in the English-speaking world to which all *Irish*-speaking scholars belonged.

Irish language activists feel that Hindley was being far too harsh but in many ways language policy continues to grapple with these same issues three generations on. Walsh (2002), for example, presents an interpretation of the original and contemporary debates surrounding the existence of the Gaeltacht in his *Díchoimisiúnú Teanga: Coimisiún na Gaeltachta 1926*.

Walsh revisited the main themes of the original Commission, namely the survival of the Irish language, emigration, education, administration and the economy. His data was compiled from 26 meetings organised nation-wide with over 100 Irish speakers being interviewed. In several respects they voiced the same concerns as did the original 1926 respondents. An official enquiry into the state of the Gaeltacht Tuarascáil Choimisiún na Gaeltachta (2002) advanced the following recommendations several of which have by now been enacted:

1. The immediate enactment of an Official Languages Equality Bill which will define the language rights of citizens and ensure that all public services will be available through Irish as of right to the people of the Gaeltacht and to the Irish-speaking community.
2. The availability of a comprehensive education system at all levels – nursery, preschool, primary level, second level, third level, professional education and lifelong learning – in which priority will be given to Irish as the first language within the Gaeltacht.
3. Secure the status of an official working language for Irish within the European Union.
4. The establishment of a dedicated Third Level Education Unit for Irish Language sociolinguistic studies and language planning, including

teaching and research, with appropriate resources and funded by the Higher Education Authority.

5. The formulation by the Government of a State policy to revive Irish as a national language.
6. The development and implementation of a National Plan for Irish containing clearly defined targets and illustrating the role of the Gaeltacht in the national effort.
7. The Official Languages Equality Act to affirm the rights of the individual to services through Irish and to this end that there be provision for an office of Language Commissioner as a part of the Act.
8. That every office of the State located in the Gaeltacht function through the medium of Irish and that Irish be the normal working language of such offices.
9. The development of a National Language Planning System based on best international practice Tuarascáil Choimisiún na Gaeltachta (2002).

Turning back to the initial efforts at language planning more fertile soil was the control of the national education system to bring about language stabilisation. In the 1920s Eoin Mac Néil was very conscious that one should not place an undue burden on the school system to bring about a revival. Nevertheless as Minister of Education he was to preside over the legislative steps which made such dependence both possible and inevitable. Ó Gadhra (1999, p. 7) phrases the dilemma thus:

> Central to this language restoration policy was the idea that it was possible to restore Irish through the schools-with little thought being given to matters like incentive, or the simple linguistic reality we now all accept i.e. teaching Irish even well in the class is NOT sufficient. You need motivation, you need planning; you need political support and moral support from leaders and role models. Above all you need to place an emphasis on chances to use the language you have learned, written and oral. Above all else, you have to convince the native Irish speakers of the value of their own heritage which they must be encouraged to hand on to their own children and indeed to everybody else who is interested.

That challenge was not faced then and still remains problematic now, despite a range of reforms undertaken to safeguard the Irish language, including in:

1913 Irish became compulsory for matriculation to the National University;

1922 Irish was designated the "national language" and competence in it became compulsory for entry to the civil service, police and army;

1926 The Official *Gaeltacht* was defined and demarcated;
1937 The status of Irish was reaffirmed in the Constitution;
1943 *Comhdháil Náisiúnta na Gaeilge* was funded as a co-ordinating agency for voluntary language organisations.

In terms of the designation of the Official *Gaeltacht*, Nic Craith (2006, Private Correspondence, 13th October) has suggested to me that there is a school of thought which argues that the drawing of the boundaries implies that people in these areas could lives their lives as Gaelic-speakers and leave the rest of the nation to the business of getting on with "modern" life. It is debatable as to whether or not the official boundaries hindered the cause of language revitalisation, and is one of the principal reasons why so many in Wales reject similar calls to codify *Y Fro Gymraeg* and its presumed consequence of linguistic territorial fragmentation.

Figures 7.2 and 7.3 show the number and percentage of Irish speakers by county, 1961–1981. This was a crucial period as it reflected a transition from a largely education-based language transmission policy to one where more comprehensive language planning policies were initiated. The growth in Irish-speakers in Cork and especially Dublin reflect their third level and public sector developments. Dublin and its journey-to-work hinterland dominates the pattern although there remain substantial thresholds in Galway and Cork. Elsewhere from the early 1960s onwards the declining viability of the family-farm sector, the out-migration of the young and low levels of participation in tertiary education necessitated a change of economic policy. Most of the drop of population in the predominantly Irish-speaking areas was the result of long term emigration rather than internal migration. There were Irish-speaking communities in Boston, New York and Chicago and many of the larger cities in the UK. There was some reversal in the 1970s and again since the 1990s as a result of improvements in the Irish economy.

Instead of adopting protectionist agricultural policies and concentrating on the internal market, Ireland developed the export market together with its small and medium sized enterprises. In this modernising context severe doubts were raised as to the linkage between educational success, competence in Irish and entry into parts of the labour market. Consequently in 1973 Irish ceased to be a compulsory examination requirement for the Leaving Certificate at the conclusion of secondary education and for entry to the public service.[51] Ó Riagáin (1997) demonstrates the painful disjunction between economic policy and language policy, because such socio-economic mobility as was available depended on inherited economic capital in the form of family land-holdings or small shops; the incentives for Irish built into the educational and government-employment systems affected relatively few young people.

The government continues its support for all-Irish schools but has weakened the rule that all secondary students should learn Irish and the

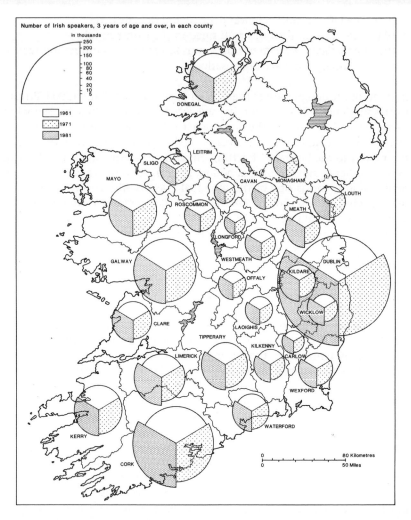

Figure 7.2   Numbers of Irish speakers aged 3 years of age and over in each county
Source: Williams, 1988, p. 292, calculated from the Irish census of population for 1961, 1971 and 1981.

Irish language requirement for second level teachers. Re-structuring of the National University has also meant changes to the role of Irish as a necessary requirement for University entry. All second level students must take Irish. Some may and have sought an exemption and the numbers who have adopted this have increased significantly.

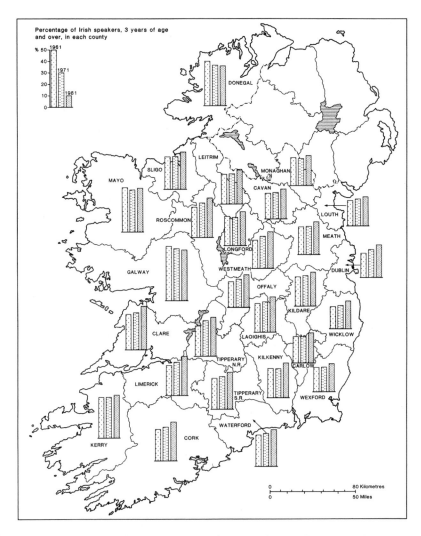

Figure 7.3 Percentage of Irish speakers aged 3 years of age and over in each county
Source: Williams, 1988, p. 293, calculated from the Irish census of population for 1961, 1971 and 1981.

The principal features of twentieth century language policy and the need for a national action plan was spelled out in the late eighties by *Board na Gaeilge* (1988). The strategic policy initiatives identified then are still valid now, albeit within the context of a healthier Irish economy. It was reported that only around 5 per cent of Irish citizens use Irish extensively in their homes, neighbourhood or at work, although a further 10 per cent of the population use Irish regularly if less extensively. Weak rates of language reproduction lead the authors of the report to argue that the state should take the initiative in changing the operating context of Irish usage and in changing the popular consciousness about Irish identity. The state should also recreate an ideological basis for Irish language loyalty and learning. The report advocated that *Board na Gaeilge* be given wider powers to counter the marginal position of Irish within government agencies, arguing that central government itself, through its discourse, sense of complacency and lack of leadership, was one of the key agencies militating against promotional measures in support of Irish.

The report also called for a popular cultural movement, both to resist provincialism and the downgrading of Irish, and to act as a fulcrum for the re-creation of virile Irish-medium social networks. In addition the basic rights of Irish speakers in their dealings with state agencies needed much greater specification. While Article 8 of the *Bunreacht na hÉireann* set out the constitutional standing of both official languages, there was little in the Irish system which set out the detailed practical legislative provisions. Infrastructural provisioning and planning, a key element for the realisation of any relatively free language choice in a multilingual society, were to include giving legal effect to the concept of the bilingual state; strengthening Irish in the public service; increasing the visibility and usage of Irish in the state-sponsored media and arresting the decline of Irish in the *Gaeltacht.*

The Department of the Gaeltacht, *Udaras na Gaeltachta* and the *Bord na Gaeilge* have been accused of failing to achieve a high degree of policy integration in tackling the chief issues which remain, namely: the relationship between Irish language speakers within and outside the *Gaeltacht*; migration; language learning; traditional conceptions of the role of the Irish language in society and economy; television and the media occupying an important niche; the *TG4* television station; Irish as an economic resource; and the work of *Gaelscoileanna.*[52]

Despite communal and government efforts, the task of revitalising Irish has proved greater than the resources and commitment hitherto shown. The underlying fault is an over-optimistic assessment of the capacity of state intervention to restore Irish as a national language without a concomitant investment in socio-economic planning to bring about the necessary conditions to regulate the market forces which encouraged widespread Anglicisation.

In 1991, some 1,095,830 persons (32.5 per cent of the population) were returned as Irish speakers in the Census of Population. National percentages mask wide regional and class variations. The designated Irish-speaking areas, the Gaeltacht, contain only 2.3 per cent of the state's population, but fully 45 per cent of all Irish-speaking families. By 2002, as Table 7.2 indicates, total Irish speakers had risen to 1,570,894 (41.9 per cent of the population). The low points during the period 1861–2002 were in 1926, when only

Table 7.2 Persons, males and females aged 3 years and over, classified by age group and ability to speak Irish in 2006

Age Group	Total	Ability to speak Irish			Irish speakers as a percentage of total
		Irish speakers	Non-Irish speakers	Not stated	
Persons					
3–4 years	120,050	14,773	93,122	12,155	13.7
5–9 "	285,325	171,290	105,795	11,240	61.8
10–14 "	273,672	194,337	73,846	5,689	72.5
15–19 "	290,257	184,847	101,016	4,394	64.7
20–24 "	342,475	149,122	185,613	6,740	44.4
25–34 "	722,439	264,516	443,726	14,197	37.3
35–44 "	623,434	204,541	407,991	10,902	33.4
45–54 "	521,813	191,600	321,093	9,120	37.4
55–64 "	407,055	138,483	259,891	8,681	34.8
65 years and over	467,926	143,281	307,081	17,564	31.8
Total	4,057,646	1,656,790	2,300,174	100,682	41.9
Males					
3–4 years	61,193	6,784	48,083	6,326	12.4
5–9 "	147,984	84,914	57,249	5,821	59.7
10–14 "	140,504	95,247	42,265	2,992	69.3
15–19 "	148,241	86,448	59,301	2,492	59.3
20–24 "	172,766	65,262	102,493	4,011	39.3
25–34 "	366,739	114,936	242,741	9,062	32.1
35–44 "	315,249	88,414	219,921	6,914	28.7
45–54 "	262,533	87,836	169,227	5,470	34.2
55–64 "	205,504	65,680	134,903	4,921	32.7
65 years and over	207,095	60,546	139,523	7,026	30.3
Total	2,027,808	757,067	1,215,706	55,036	38.4
Females					
3–4 years	58,857	7,989	45,039	5,829	15.1
5–9 "	140,341	86,376	48,546	5,419	64.0
10–14 "	133,368	99,090	31,581	2,697	75.8
15–19 "	142,016	98,399	41,715	1,902	70.2
20–24 "	169,709	82,860	84,120	2,729	49.6
25–34 "	355,700	149,580	200,985	5,135	42.7
35–44 "	308,185	116,127	188,070	3,988	38.2
45–54 "	259,280	103,764	151,866	3,650	40.6
55–64 "	201,551	72,803	124,988	3,760	36.8
65 years and over	260,831	82,735	167,558	10,538	33.1
Total	2,029,838	899,723	1,084,468	45,647	45.3

* Excluding not stated.

540,511 speakers were recorded and immediately after the Second World War when only 588,725 speakers were identified. Table 7.3 also reveals the regional distribution of Irish speakers by province for the period 1861–2002. This suggests a remarkable proportionate growth in Leinster from only 2.4 per cent in 1861 to 38.2 per cent by 2002. Connacht has witnessed several fluctuations but has maintained its pre-eminent position and currently some 48.5 per cent of its population record themselves as Irish speakers. Yet numerically the population has almost halved down from 409,482 in 1961 to 216,128 by 2002.

The 2006 census reported that there were 4,057,646 Irish speakers (41.9 per cent) of the population. What is fascinating and of long term significance is that the highest numbers of Irish speakers in any of the decennial cohorts is within the 25–34 age group, at 264,516. This is significant in two respects, it is the child-rearing stage and thus one can anticipate a steady demand for Irish medium education from many within this cohort, and secondly, numerically it is double the size of the 55–64 age group (at 138,483). This represents both the capacity of the education system in transmitting language skills, if not always language choice, and indicates the strength of the Irish economy in being able to absorb a larger proportion of its population at home, rather than witness the mass emigration of former years.

Turning to the Gaeltacht some 89,260 residents were recorded as living there in 2006, of whom 62,959 (71.4 per cent) were Irish speakers. The census investigated the frequency of speaking Irish by age group and Table 7.4 reveals additional information related to differential patterns of speaking Irish within and outwith the education system, together with daily, weekly and infrequent use of spoken Irish. In total of the 62,959 residents who spoke Irish, some 13,718 spoke it daily only within the education system, while a further 5,167 also spoke it outside the education system. Aside from the educational domains, 17,613 residents reported they spoke Irish daily, 6,462 did so weekly and 14,633 did so less often. Admittedly we are dealing with small numbers relative to the national total, but such patterns are significant given the Gaeltacht's special status and oft-referenced integral role within the national plan.

The age distribution of current Irish speakers is also significant. The school age effect is obvious as the proportion speaking Irish aged 3–4 jumps from only 10.3 per cent to 52.3 per cent for the primary age group 5–9 and is even higher for the early years of high school aged 10–14 years at 68.7 per cent. Thereafter it declines successively at each age group down to only 31.2 per cent for those aged 65 and over. This is in contrast to the Welsh situation where the younger and older age groups show relatively high proportions of speakers while it is in the 25–55 age groups where the lowest proportions are recorded.

Collecting data on the numbers attending Irish-medium schools at both primary and second level is hampered by the fact that two separate agencies,

Table 7.3 Irish speakers and non-Irish speakers in each province at each census since 1861

Year	State Irish speakers	State Non-Irish speakers	Leinster Irish speakers	Leinster Non-Irish speakers	Munster Irish speakers	Munster Non-Irish speakers	Connacht Irish speakers	Connacht Non-Irish speakers	Ulster (Part of) Irish speakers	Ulster (Part of) Non-Irish speakers
					All ages					
1861	1,077,087	3,325,024	35,704	1,421,931	545,531	988,027	409,482	503,653	86,370	431,413
1871	804,547	3,248,640	16,247	1,323,204	386,494	1,006,991	330,211	516,002	71,595	402,443
1881	924,781	2,945,239	27,452	1,251,537	445,766	885,349	366,191	455,466	85,372	352,887
1891	664,387	2,804,307	13,677	1,174,083	307,633	864,769	274,783	449,991	68,294	315,464
1901	619,710	2,602,113	26,436	1,126,393	276,268	799,920	245,580	401,352	71,426	274,448
1911	553,717	2,585,971	40,225	1,121,819	228,694	806,801	217,087	393,897	67,711	263,454
1926	543,511	2,428,481	101,474	1,047,618	198,221	771,681	175,209	377,698	68,607	231,484
					3 years and over					
1926	540,802	2,261,650	101,102	978,536	197,625	718,068	174,234	348,964	67,841	216,082
1936	666,601	2,140,324	183,378	966,434	224,805	668,030	183,082	315,322	75,336	190,538
1946	588,725	2,182,932	180,755	1,017,491	189,395	672,660	154,187	309,638	64,388	183,143
1951	716,420	1,919,398	274,644	964,383	228,726	567,613	148,708	246,592	64,342	140,810
1971	789,429	1,998,101	341,702	1,055,160	252,805	573,308	137,372	231,960	57,550	137,591
1981	1,018,413	2,206,054	473,225	1,202,292	323,704	612,526	155,134	244,264	66,350	148,972
1986	1,042,701	2,310,931	480,227	1,274,353	337,043	630,434	158,386	250,474	67,045	155,670
1991	1,095,830	2,271,176	511,639	1,264,188	352,177	612,988	162,680	242,091	69,334	151,909
				New question (3 years and over)						
1996*	1,430,205	2,049,443	489,703	1,155,696	451,129	541,616	201,195	215,809	88,178	136,322
2002*	1,570,894	2,180,101	768,404	1,245,467	493,500	561,683	216,128	229,844	92,862	143,107

* A new question on ability to speak the Irish language and frequency of speaking Irish was introduced in the 1996 Census of Population. The new version of the questions marked a major departure from the version used in previous censuses. The version used in those years asked respondents to write "Irish only", "Irish and English", "Read but cannot speak Irish" or to leave blank as appropriate. The version introduced in 1996 was retained unchanged for 2002. Non-respondents on ability to speak Irish (i.e. not stated), who were explicitly identified in 2002, are included in the category "Non-Irish speakers" in the above table.

Source: Census 2002 Irish language, Government of Ireland, page 11.

Table 7.4 Irish speakers aged 3 years and over within the Gaeltacht classified by frequency of speaking Irish and age group

	Total	3–4	5–9	10–14	15–19	20–24	25–34	35–44	45–54	55–64+	65+
All Gaeltacht areas	62,959	1,213	5,401	5,888	5,638	3,900	7,338	8,351	8,893	7,162	9,175
Speaks Irish within education only	13,718	499	3,399	3,573	2,376	371	627	689	774	617	793
Speaks Irish also outside education	5,167	178	1,005	1,051	780	158	382	490	484	329	310
Outside education, daily	17,613	332	492	566	814	989	2,187	2,765	3,080	2,686	3,703
weekly	6,462	84	184	256	395	494	857	1,118	1,095	904	1,075
less often	14,633	83	192	286	853	1,314	2,294	2,465	2,594	2,045	2,507
never	3,991	1	30	76	312	483	856	681	689	390	473
not stated	1,375	36	99	80	108	92	135	143	177	191	314

Source: Census of Ireland, 2006.

(one Gaeltacht and the other non-Gaeltacht) are responsible for the provision and collation of data. The Gaeltacht has both a nationalist symbolic and very real resource significance for the transmission of the Irish language and culture. But it is not without its critics today as yesterday. Three criticisms are levelled at the Gaeltacht. First that it is an historically ill-conceived and ill-defined territorial base for the delivery of Irish-medium services. Secondly that a great deal of complacency and duplication of effort characterises those governmental and economic agencies which operate within and on behalf of the Gaeltacht. Thirdly that the educational system within the Gaeltacht is less effective than it might be in sustaining high levels of fluency in Irish.

A "Study of Gaeltacht Schools"[53] (Mac Donnacha *et al.*, 2005) contains the most recent information on the nature of education within Gaeltacht schools. Under the provisions of the Education Act, 1998, the Gaeltacht is defined as those areas which are recognised as Gaeltacht areas under the provisions of the Ministers and Secretaries (Amendment) Act, 1956, and Section 9(h) of the Act states that the functions of a school located in a Gaeltacht area, include contributing "to the maintenance of Irish as the primary community language".[54]

Mac Donnacha reports that a complex linguistic situation is compounded by the fact that because the majority of Gaeltacht schools are small it is more difficult to accommodate the needs of pupils with a wide range of linguistic abilities. In addition Gaeltacht schools are being supported within a system that is designed to support the English-medium education sector.

"This results in existing systems and processes being adapted for, and sometimes being imposed upon, Gaeltacht schools and pupils, with very little effort being made to develop systems and processes appropriate to their needs" (Mac Donnacha, p. 2). Thus of the 143 Gaeltacht primary schools (with 9,556 pupils) the majority (69 per cent) are small 1–3 teacher schools. In two thirds (66 out of 98) of these schools in the period 1998–2002, the number of pupils decreased and in 58 of these schools, the decrease was in excess of 10 per cent while the number of pupils decreased by more than 30 per cent in 18 of the 1–3 teacher schools. In addition Gaeltacht primary schools find it difficult to recruit teachers; thus in the period 2001–2003, 18 per cent of the posts advertised in Gaeltacht primary schools were not filled and in 68 per cent of the positions advertised three applications or less were received. MacDonnacha's report also provides data on fluency levels,[55] the language of instruction in different types of schools, teaching aids and teacher recruitment issues. At secondary level the problems of falling schools rolls within many of the 20 secondary schools are accompanied by a number of factors.[56] One is mobility and home sociolinguistic context for whereas 91 per cent of primary schools pupils live within the Gaeltacht, only 82 per cent of post-primary pupils live within the Gaeltacht.[57] The other is teacher recruitment. A third is the relatively disappointing levels of fluency gained by many students in Category C schools as they leave secondary education.[58] It is thus clear from the report that schools are not achieving all of the expected language related objectives in every case.[59] They report that a quarter of pupils leave Gaeltacht primary schools with only a reasonable level of Irish and that approximately 10 per cent of pupils leave primary schools with little or no Irish.[60] At Leaving Certificate level 18 per cent of pupils have only a reasonable level of Irish and 10 per cent of the pupils have little or no Irish. In addition, as is so often reported in Celtic contexts, English is the main language used by pupils in normal conversational interactions in the vast majority of Gaeltacht schools. Unless remedial action is taken soon it is likely that the situation will worsen within the next twenty years.

Radical recommendations follow from this investigation, principally that the current definition of Gaeltacht schools located within the official boundaries of the Gaeltacht be reviewed and that they be restructured so as to offer one of three options:

- A first language education model with Irish as the medium of instruction.
- An immersion education model with Irish as the medium of instruction.
- A first language education model with English as the medium of instruction (p. 18).

In turn these options should imply:

> That clear and objective guidelines, criteria and benchmarks are developed to clarify what is the acceptable educational, language planning and administrative best practice within each of the above education models, and that these shall be used in the future as the basis for:
> - The evaluation of Gaeltacht schools.
> - The pre-service and in-service training of teachers who teach in Gaeltacht schools.
> - The design and implementation of the primary and second level schools' curriculum for the Gaeltacht.
> - The way in which educational support services are delivered in Gaeltacht schools (p. 18).

The greatest need is for the integration of the various services on offer, a reflection of the increasingly holisitic perspective in language planning and language policy (Williams, 1991). Thus the report recommends that "the Gaeltacht be dealt with as a separate educational sector comprising the primary level and second level Gaeltacht schools that teach through the medium of Irish along with the support and advisory services." It also suggests the establishment of a designated Gaeltacht Education Inspectorate[61] with designated units of the educational support services currently providing support services to Gaeltacht schools and the establishment by *An Chomhairle um Oideachas Gaeltachta agus Gaelscolaíochta* of a regional centre in each of the major Gaeltacht regions. Beyond the school confines the report also suggests that a comprehensive youth service be established in the Gaeltacht to increase access for young people to Irish-medium fun, leisure, music, sport and cultural activities.

The report ends with a dire warning for the "the future of the Gaeltacht is inextricably linked to the future of the Gaeltacht education system. As a result, if the perilous current state of Gaeltacht education is not resolved, the future of the Gaeltacht itself is threatened" (Mac Donnacha, 2005, p. 24).

Outside the *Gaeltacht* by 2006 Ireland had 260 voluntary Irish medium playgroups serving 2,500 children; 131 Irish medium primary schools, and 35 post-primary schools serving some 22,000 children (see Figure 7.4). Too little effort has been expended on the professional/vocational elements of Irish medium education, giving rise to fears over a general decline in standards of written Irish particularly in relation to authenticity of expression in both public and private sector employment. Irish is still necessary for Matriculation for the National University of Ireland (probably what has kept it as a subject right through secondary school).[62] The newer universities Dublin City University and Limerick require Irish or English for entry. Trinity College never had an Irish requirement.

227

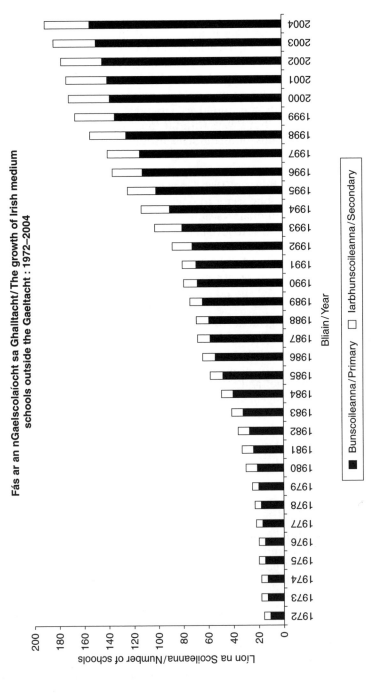

Figure 7.4 The growth of Irish-medium schools outside the Gaeltacht
Source: By kind permission of Gaelscoileanna, see www.gaelscoileanna.ie.

Elements of holistic language planning belatedly characterise the Irish experience. But for far too long it was assumed that dedicated language initiatives, based in part on good will and in part on a symbolic adherence to Irish as a token of national identity, would suffice. The reality, of course, is far more complex and we accept Ó Riagáin's view that language policies "cannot be treated as an autonomous, independent factor" (p. 283). They must be related to trends and initiatives, grounded in the socio-economic context of every-day life, but always with the force of State legislative power and redress if public organisations and state institutions are to respect citizen language rights.

Once again we return to the centrality of legislation in legitimising new statutory norms as the hopes of Irish language planning today rest on the re-invigoration of the public sector through the passage of a new Irish Language Act. In 1998 Comhdháil Náisiúnta na Gaeilge argued that there is a need for a Language Act so as to give practical effect to the existing language rights of citizens. It recommended that the new Act should: "Define and set out the State's duties and obligations in respect of the Irish language and give effect to the rights of citizens in relation to that language." It also advocated that the new Act should provide for:

1) Institutional arrangements concerning the implementation of the said rights and duties.
2) Amendments to existing legislation and Government schemes to ensure that they are in accordance with the status of Irish as the "national language" and the "first official language".
3) Institutional arrangements to ensure that all legislation enacted in the future is in accordance with the status of Irish as the "national language" and as the "first official language".
4) The establishment of structures that will be responsible for the execution and implementation of the Act and for ensuring that State services through Irish are freely available to Irish speakers and *Gaeltacht,* communities.

(Comhdháil Náisiúnta na Gaeilge, 1998)

In April 2002 an *Official Languages (Equality) Bill, 2002*, was published comprised of five parts covering preliminary and general interpretations and regulations, the use of both languages in the House of *Oireachtas* and the administration of justice, the rights to deal with services from public bodies in the official languages, the establishment of an Official Languages Commissioner together with a final part relating to the role of the Ombudsman and issues of civil or criminal liability.[63] Critics argue that the final draft of the Bill bore little resemblance to the original and the word (Equality) was dropped following legal advice which was based on the primary status of Irish in the Constitution. The Commissioner does not have an Ombudsman

Status in Law but does have a role in the examination of the implementation of all legislation with provisions on the Irish language. While it is too early to interpret the impact of both the subsequent 2003 Official Languages Act and the Language Commissioner on the fortunes of the Irish language, these initiatives bode well and reflect a growing European-wide trend to deal with national and minority language rights in a far more systematic manner than hitherto. On the 13 June 2005 an additional fillip to the full recognition and wider use of Irish was its acceptance as the 21st official and working language of the European Union. From 1 January 2007, all key EU legislation has been translated into Irish. This decision was the result of a well supported campaign articulated in accordance with arguments presented in Ó Laighin (2004).

Foras na Gaeilge

A Language Commissioner, a new Language Act and a modified language planning agency Foras na Gaeilge are the tripartite pillars supporting Irish. Foras na Gaeilge, together with Tha Boord o Ulstèr-Scotch (the Ulster-Scots Agency), makes up An Foras Teanga/Tha Boord o Leid, the North/South Language Body, one of the implementation bodies established in accordance with the terms of British-Irish Agreement Act, 1999.[64] Foras na Gaeilge has the following statutory obligations:

- The promotion of the Irish language;
- Facilitating and encouraging the use of Irish in speech and writing, in public and private life in the South and, in the context of Part III of the European Charter for Regional or Minority Languages, in Northern Ireland where there is appropriate demand;
- Advising both administrations, public bodies and other groups in the private and voluntary sectors;
- Undertaking supportive projects and grant-aiding bodies and groups as considered necessary;
- Undertaking research, promotional campaigns, and public and media relations;
- Developing terminology and dictionaries;
- Supporting Irish-medium education and the teaching of Irish.

Foras na Gaeilge is responsible to the North/South Ministerial Council (NSMC) and in particular to the Ministers of Community, Rural and Gaeltacht Affairs and of Culture, Arts and Leisure.[65] Foras an Gaeilge consists of an NSMC-appointed Board, and an Executive. The Executive consists of three Directorates which are responsible for Education Services (education, publications), Development Services (public sector, the arts, communications, marketing, community and private sector) and Corporate

Services (corporate planning, finance, human resources, and information technology).[66]

Foras na Gaeilge's strategic plan is to achieve significant progress by 2011 in the following key areas:

- The numbers of people speaking Irish on a daily basis;
- The numbers of children who, by the age of four, are native Irish speakers or bilingual;
- The numbers of school-going children in quality Irish-medium education;
- Promote the provision of high quality youth and extra-curricular activities;
- The visibility and presence of Irish in the physical, social and cultural environment. The achievement of these goals should be greatly facilitated by the provisions of the Official Languages Act, 2003 in the South. Greater visibility and presence of Irish in signage in Northern Ireland will be encouraged under the European Charter for Regional or Minority Languages where appropriate demand exists. Greater use of Irish in other public notices/sign-posts e.g. in the private sector, will be encouraged;
- The use of Irish in existing Gaeltacht areas will be developed and expanded in partnership with the Department of Community, Rural and Gaeltacht Affairs and Údarás na Gaeltachta.

But Foras is also mindful of its dependency on others, particularly over three hundred statutory organisations, to realise these aims. The Chief Executive describes its position thus:

Foras na Gaeilge recognises that although the above goals are ambitious and challenging, it is through the achievement of such goals that the Irish language will become part of everyday life for more people on the island of Ireland. The vision will be kept under continuous review in the light of progress made and the monitoring of such progress will be underpinned by ongoing internal and commissioned research. The Corporate Plan will be subject to annual review, both to ensure it remains relevant, realistic and achievable and to measure progress against targets. Foras na Gaeilge is also mindful that it does not have full authority and responsibility for delivering on the vision set out above and a real concern is that athough Foras na Gaeilge is not prevented by legislation from operating in the Gaeltacht, it has not done so since its inception. This to my mind is a real hindrance to the implementation of a national plan for Irish. Its role, therefore, in addition to its policy advisory and executive functions, will also include advocacy and working in close consultation and partnership with the relevant government departments and organisations in both jurisdictions. Therefore, these key goals will be realised through incremental advances and working in partnership with other stakeholders. Indeed many of the objectives and strategies contained in our strategic develop-ment plan emphasise the importance of this partnership approach. This will require that Foras na Gaeilge retains the strategic flexibility to anti-cipate, cultivate and respond to changing circumstances. Our intention to involve all the stakeholders in the formulation of The Strategic Plan for Irish is perhaps the most obvious example of the leadership which Foras na Gaeilge can show in this area.

(Foras na Gaeilge, 2005)

Several of its partners would caution that it seems odd that the Foras has identified the strategic areas before involving all the stakeholders in the formulation of the Strategic Plan. Would-be stakeholders complain that this is a well-tried tactic and that the strategy, presented in September 2005, was as fait accompli, without any documentation and they were asked to sign up. By the beginning of 2006 they still awaited the documentation. Critics argue that this bears a strong resemblance to what happened in the 1980s when Bord na Gaeilge had Action Plans, and again the role of the voluntary sector was included, without the sector being consulted. The current Strategic Plan has been presented under varying guises between 2003–2006 and has mutated from being an internal Foras strategic plan to being a strategic plan for the Irish language. What most partners require is an agreed National Plan for the future of the Irish language with full government backing.

Foras na Gaeilge received €13.4 million from the DCRGA during 2003 (DCRGA, 2004b, p. 35) and €4.5 million from the Department of Arts, Culture and Leisure in Northern Ireland. In its initial years it has faced problems related to restructuring, to producing annual reports, to establish-ing a sense of "ownership" and partnership with elements of the voluntary sector.[67] It faces an ongoing problem of being threatened with re-location to Gaoth dobhair -Gwee dore in Donegal, following a statement by the O Cuiv the Minister for Community, Rural and Gaeltacht Affairs late in 2003 and repeated in October 2005.[68]

Another complicating factor is that Foras has to navigate its planned policy within the structures of two sovereign governments and their corresponding civil service traditions and socio-economic contexts. This duplication is made all the more difficult by the division of labour, not to say rivalry, within the Republic between Gaeltacht and non-Gaeltacht agencies. The principal actor in the Gaeltacht, Údarás na Gaeltachta, was established in 1979 as a successor agency to Gaeltarra Éireann and received €32.7 million from the DCRGA in 2003 (DCRGA, 2004, vii), Údarás assisted companies employed 7346 workers, some 19.1 per cent of the Gaeltacht workforce of 38,433 people, together with 4220 part-time/seasonal employees (Údarás na Gaeltachta, 2004, p. 24). Despite having had some success in attracting a variety of industries to one of Europe's most marginal locations, Údarás has also been constantly criticised for not fulfilling its language promotion remit. Indeed on several occasions it has accelerated the very process of Anglicisation it was designed in part to ameliorate (Williams, 1988b; Hindley, 1991; Ó Cinnéide et al., 2001).[69] Conscious of these lacunae, Údarás currently directs 20 per cent of its capital budget toward language-related activities, but the majority of its expenditure is still on fairly conventional economic development. There is a growing recognition within Údarás, Foras and many other Irish promotional bodies that unless a real sustained campaign is mounted to transform Irish as the default language of the Gaeltacht, then so much good work will have been wasted. Providing opportunities to use the language is one thing, influencing people's behaviour to maximise that potential is quite another. This is made even more acute as Foras has yet, to date, to undertake serious work within the Gaeltacht. I am conscious of the various socio-political trajectories of Gaeltacht and non-Gaeltacht bodies and of the differing responsibilities for Irish language promotion various Departments of State enjoy. But it would seem opportune for the integrated, inter-departmental planned promotion of Irish to take place. So much of what has passed before either in legislative terms, or in socio-economic and labour requirement terms have flattered, only to deceive.

This, together with a fresh debate on the role of compulsory Irish in the education system, has forced into the open a number of worrying trends.[70] In March 2005 An Coimsinéir Teanga, the Language Commissioner Seán Ó Cuirreáin, called for a national debate on the teaching of Irish. He pointed out that up to €500m and 1500 school hours are invested annually in teaching the language but that this did not transform potential into actual use because large numbers of children left school with a lack of fluency in Irish. On November 15th 2005 Fine Gael Opposition leader Enda Kenny called for Irish to be made an optional subject for Leaving Certificate pupils at secondary school.[71] He argued that

> Compulsion is a blunt tool. Forcing students to learn Irish is not working and is actually driving many young people away from a real engagement with this beautiful language.

Daily Ireland's editorial criticised the Fine Gael leader.

> The Official Languages Act, full recognition for An Ghaeilge as an official working language of the EU, robust planning policies in the Gaeltacht to protect the language and the creation of an all-Ireland body to promote Irish under the Good Friday Agreement are just some of the remarkable steps Irish has enjoyed in recent years. The Fine Gael proposal would be the first backward step in a remarkable renaissance of the Irish language over the past decade.

Hours before a mass protest in Dublin on November the 16th 2005 the Fine Gael leader and An Taoiseach, Bertie Ahern, debated the subject in the Dáil.

Raising the issue at Leaders Question Time, Deputy Kenny stated that "few subjects over the generations have been the target of so much hypocrisy and lip service as the Irish language." He asked,

> Does the Taoiseach as Head of Government, honestly believe that the compulsion element to what now exists actually assists in the learning of Irish and puts sufficient emphasis on it as a spoken language? ... If Irish is taught properly, using the skill and experience of teachers and the modern innovative methods available in teaching all languages, students will want to study the language at junior certificate because they understand it. These students can work and get married at 16, they can own and drive a moped, yet we tell them they must study this language.

The Fine Gael leader pointed out that the 2002 census showed that in the vast majority of cases, as soon as students finish the Leaving Certificate, they leave Irish behind them. "I want to do something about this and it is time that politically we take it by the scruff of the neck and reform the situation from top to bottom. It is not just a question of clinging to a 75 year old sacred cow that will not deliver."

In his response the Taoiseach pointed out that in 1973 the requirement for pupils to do the Irish language exam at Leaving Cert had been removed amid predictions that the dropping of the compulsion element would benefit the language.

> The decision in 1973, as I recall, was made on the basis that perhaps more people would speak Irish, but this was not the experience and that hypothesis did not hold up. As mentioned by Deputy Kenny, the statistics prove that when compulsory Irish at Leaving Certificate was removed from the equation, fewer people took the subject and that trend has continued down through the years. From a Government viewpoint my concern is that if Irish is taken out of the schools the amount of Irish will be even more limited in ten years time.

The Taoiseach later issued a statement attacking the Fine Gael stance.

> I believe that their proposals to downgrade the language is a regressive step, and one which will ultimately lead to a drop in the number of speakers of the Irish language. Instead of sidelining or downgrading the language in the education system, I believe that we should work to resolve the difficulties that exist so that we can continue the promotion and expansion of language.

> (Eurolang, November 24, 2005)

Thus several strands within deliberative democracy are calling into question key fundamental features of modern Irish society and this has lead to a repoliticising of the language issue. A strong legislative regime under the new Irish Language Act reinforced by a Language Commissioner with purchase to influence the system augers well. However, given the countervailing trends of opposition and of benign neglect the language regime has to be under-pinned by sustained, tangible, political support from the state if official bilin-gualism in Ireland is to be an every day, lived reality for many of its citizens.

Language governance implications in the UK and Ireland

Any consideration of the relationship between language, law and governance in the UK and Ireland must deal with the following, often dichotomous, difficulties in implementing agreed plans. Should we advocate policies which rely on:

1. Statutory obligation or good will only? There is a critical need for statutory obligation – good will is not enough if policy aims to provide a genuine choice of language service. This issue is a major stumbling block for North-ern Ireland and in the implementation of language legislation in Scotland, Wales and Ireland. The Coimisinéir Teanga has a vital role in this regard both in terms of his operation within his own jurisdiction and by offering a beacon of hope to the other jurisdictions discussed in this chapter.
2. Holistic versus sectoral language planning. "Joined up thinking" within and between government departments and their partner agencies in the community is a *sine qua non* of new forms of horizontal governance. "Holistic language planning" can so easily become "sectoral language planning" and the radical cutting edge of innovative policy is thereby lost.
3. Symbolic or practical language schemes? Agreed language schemes, at Parliamentary/Assembly and local authority level, can often become symbols of good intent rather than the provision of genuine services at the point of local demand/contact. There is a critical need to monitor the actual working of such schemes. Hence the need to tackle the twin issues of adequate resourcing of language schemes and target community implementation. Processes of empowerment, ownership, participation and partnership are far easier to assume as given rather than work on as part of infra-structural development of language planning.
4. Institutional or individual language rights? In whom are basic rights vested? Is it in individual citizens regardless of where they live or in institutions charged with implementing an equal opportunities policy? To what extent are notions of equality or equity tested in the courts in relation to language rights?
5. Public sector or plural sector approach? Initial language policy schemes are targeted at public sector institutions and educational domains. How-ever, to be truly effective, language schemes should have a medium term

aim of influencing language rights behaviour in most socio-economic contexts.

6. Top-down or bottom-up planning? How does the partnership between central and local agencies, vital community initiatives, the voluntary sector and the world of work, mobilise and reflect society's language-related energy to reinforce the central thrust of language schemes? There is an acute danger that in Scotland and Northern Ireland, if not Wales, that policy is driven only from above without any real local commitment.

7. There is often a tension between instrumentalists and analysts. In all cases of language revitalisation different priorities are promoted by advocates of front-line services and language teaching requirements, and others who also recognise that sound planning requires accurate trend and impact analysis, together with an effective audit and monitoring function of language planning. Consequently there is a temptation to launch language schemes without the necessary audit and monitoring functions of language planning.

8. Priorities of language governance agencies. To what extent are fledgling language governance agencies essentially a grant distribution operation? How do they evolve into becoming a genuine language planning and policy unit?

9. How effectively will the UK and Ireland's language agencies co-operate at a UK, Irish and European Union level to press for structural reforms and international recognition of their role in delivering multilingual policies?

10. Internal reticence within the civil service. Usually the biggest stumbling block to the implementation of language schemes is the reticence of civil servants not directly concerned with LP schemes. Two temptations loom large: a) to view all language-related issues as being the special responsibility of a designated governmental language agency only; (the ghetto approach) and b) to refuse to accept the legitimacy of cross-cutting language issues within key functions of the local state, for example, economic development, environment, health and social services (the head in the sand approach). Language awareness training coupled with firm political direction can overcome some, but not all, of this reticence.

The development of a fully comprehensive language policy is a project in social engineering which will require investment, training, encouragement and crucially, political conviction and power to act. In both the UK and Ireland four areas require urgent attention. The first is the official languages translation system. This involves training requirements and professional development implications, qualification and standardisation issues, aspects of style, prioritising tasks. The second is the whole field of bilingual education provision including levels of acquired bilingualism, teacher training requirements and recruitment, curriculum design and innovation, levels of resourcing, text, media and IT developments, the target language as a medium for teaching a range of subjects at different levels. The third is the language-choice behaviour of Assembly/Parliamentary members in terms of their linguistic competence, domain-specific behaviour, and their political effectiveness if they choose not to use English, the scope of the political institution's bilingual character, the levels of support for members in the discharge of their functions. The final field is the development of national language-related policy in terms of a promoting language schemes, mainstreaming language into an equality agenda, community relations, information, evaluation and research for evidence-based policy formulation.

Having seized the opportunities which structural reforms of the British, and to a lesser extent the Irish state have allowed, the next step is to promote bilingualism in as many avenues of daily life as is reasonable without ever loosing sight of the political fact that this is done under the consensual eye of the majority. But this presumes new forms of governance in which governments become catalytic, steering and sparking action rather than prohibiting change; community-owned, empowering rather than serving; and which are mission-driven, results-oriented and customer-focused. The bottom line is how well policy and practical politics safeguards the interests both of individual speakers and vital communities. And all of the argument presumes a continued will on behalf of individuals to fight for their rights and to demand of governments the freedoms to interact one with another in forms which we, as citizens, decide.

Notes

1. The following is an extract from the "Iomairt Cholm Cille" website at URL http://www.colmcille.net/content.asp?id=3&lang=1
   "The Gaelic world is bigger and more varied than a single region or country. Communities in Scotland, Ireland and the Isle of Man contribute to the Gaelic world and the Gaelic language. Gaelic speakers in the different areas share the same language in the broader sense; they also share similar challenges: the need to sustain a minority language, the need to sustain and develop Gaelic-medium education."
2. Gaeldom means the "Kingdom of the Gael" or *"Ríocht na nGael"* and extended "from Caithness to Kerry" or *"ó 'Cáiteamh go Ciarraí"*.
3. I am grateful to Alan Campbell, Rob Dunbar, Ken MacKinnon, Wilson McLeod, Éamonn Ó Gribín and Boyd Robertson for their observations and insights on the position of Gaelic. So far language issues have played a relatively small part in Scottish devolution. The role of Gaelic in nationalist discourse has been ambiguous, whereas institutions and ideologies have played the defining role in national self-definition. See Dunbar (2001a, 2006b).
4. For Oliver's work and those of other commentators on Scottish Affairs see: http://www.scottishaffairs.org/onlinepub/sa/oliver_sa51_spr05.html. I am grateful to Wilson McLeod of Edinburgh University for drawing this paper to my attention and for many other astute observations on the contemporary Gaelic Renaissance.

5. This would include developments in Gaelic-medium education, the Gaelic media, in government and through some national "signposts".

6. Oliver implies that this is an expected short-term scenario for a revitalisation programme of an endangered language, where many of the young people in Gaelic-medium education do not have Gaelic-speaking parents. Nevertheless, the use of Gaelic outside of school, the classroom even, is low. This is a common phenomenon also in Ireland and Wales.

7. Such as in Gaelic-medium education, when thinking about career opportunities. Yet Oliver recognises that for others, Gaelic *is* part of home life and the re-creating of *Gemeinschaft*. But he warns that "the further growth hoped for in Gaelic-medium education will introduce more young people to Gaelic who do not have Gaelic at home, adding to the dynamic of Gaelic identities, identities that in increasingly complex social contexts are subject to multiple competing identities as young people become adults, weakening the prospects for the future everyday use of Gaelic by these people" (p. 3).

8. Many dissent at the use of the term national in this context. Thus, for example, Éamonn Ó Gribín advises that "I'm worried at the term 'national' in this context. Is Scotland one nation or a multinational entity? I would say the latter, given that the Lowlanders viewed the Gaelic speaking people as foreign . . . as Irish. The Gael of course viewed the Lowlander as foreign also . . . as a 'Gall'. As discussed earlier the nationality of the Gael encompasses the two islands GB and Ireland (as well as the Isle of Man). The creation of a Scottish nationality or an Irish nationality should be seen in the context of post-French Revolution rise of modern nationalism" (Ó Gribín, 2006, Private Correspondence, October 14).

9. Ireland could be described as the "mother country" of the Scottish Gaels. Scottish and Irish Gaelic could be classed as dialects of the one Gaelic language. See Joep Leerssen, "Mere Irish and Fíor-Ghael", p. 264.

10. In May 2002 Alex O' Henley, the first officer for Gaelic, resigned his position in protest at obstructivism in the system and the lack of progress on the language front. In time he was replaced by two officers, a parliamentary officer and an outreach officer. For the use of Gaelic in the Scottish parliament see http://www.scottish.parliament.uk/.

11. Oliver addresses a central issue of minority language promotion when he questions "In retrospect, there are shades of the chicken and egg argument: is investment a result of this renaissance, or vice versa? Has the language moved into the public domain because it has been politicised or has it become more politic to support Gaelic because it has become more visible in the public domain?" (p. 3).

12. See MacLeod (2003) for a historical overview of the development of Gaelic Medium Education (GME).

13. I owe this detail to Ken MacKinnon who reports that the Western Isles Language Plan published in November 2005 contains this figure.

14. The Task Force on Gaelic reported in September 2000. It led to the establishment of the Ministerial Advisory Group on Gaelic (MAGOG).

15. This was the legislative programme agreed as the basis for the coalition between the Scottish Labour and the Scottish Liberal Democrats following the 2003 Holyrood election. It is interesting to note that the *Iaith Pawb* strategy in Wales was also the direct result of a Liberal initiative in a short-lived Liberal-Labour coalition within the Wales National Assembly. See publications library of www.welsh-language-board.org.uk.

16. See http://www.scotland.gov.uk/library5/government/pfbs.pdf.

17. In November 2002, a Member's Bill on Gaelic was introduced to the Scottish Parliament, which required certain public bodies to publish, maintain and implement plans based on the principle that the Gaelic and English languages should be treated on a basis of equality. The Education, Culture and Sport Committee of the Scottish Parliament took evidence on the Member's Bill. The evidence showed that there was strong support for a Gaelic Language Bill to secure and protect the Gaelic language. Although the general principles of the Member's Bill passed unanimously, lack of time meant the Bill fell towards the end of the last session of the Parliament.

18. MAGOG (2002) *A Fresh Start for Gaelic*. Report of the Ministerial Advisory Group on Gaelic, Edinburgh. See also the excellent papers by McLeod (2001), MacCaluim and McLeod (2001).

19. Education Minister Peter Peacock, who had ministerial responsibility for Gaelic, said: "This is a momentous day for Gaelic as we open a new chapter in the language's history. We have come a long way since the dark days of 1616 when an Act of Parliament ruled that Gaelic should be 'abolishit and removit' from Scotland. Gaelic is a precious part of our history and our culture and the Gaelic Language Act will help to ensure it can also be a flourishing part of our country's future. This Act will create both the context and the confidence for Gaelic to be passed on in families, promoted in schools and widely used in communities and workplaces. We already have growing numbers of young Gaelic speakers – thanks, largely, to the success and growing popularity of Gaelic medium education. Our challenge now is to nurture these youngsters and future generations ensuring they have continued opportunities to develop their language skills and, more importantly, to use them. That is what the Gaelic Language Act will do." Cited on the Scottish Executive's website: http://www.scotland.gov.uk/News/Releases/2005/04/21162614.

20. The progress of the Bill through Parliament is recorded on the Parliament's website at http://www.scottish.parliament.uk/business/bills/billsInProgress/gaelic Language.htm.

21. It is hard to find a definition of "equal respect" which is somewhat like "parity of esteem" as used in the "Belfast Agreement". Activists ask if this means equal to English, why then did they not pass an official languages Act.

22. McLeod (2005, Private Correspondence, 3rd November) explains that these are two separate obligations imposed by the Act, although obviously the "plans" in the Act [equivalent to the Welsh "scheme"] will be an important strand in the National Plan.

23. The terms of the draft Guidance can be found at http://www.scotland.gov.uk/ Topics/Arts-Culture/gaelic/17909/GaelicEdGuidanceConsult.

24. The Gaelic Research Network was proposed to the Societal and Public priority area within the Scottish Funding Council's SRDG provision and the Highlands and Islands Enterprise by a consortium lead by the UHIMI Millennium Institute on behalf of the Universities of Aberdeen, Sterling, Edinburgh, Glasgow and Strathclyde.

25. This, in part, is due to the use of both English and Gaelic registers of "development discourse" which may reinforce Gaelic-English diglossia and in part it reflects what the author asserts is the unexamined conception of "community", which can reduce the number of opportunities for Gaelic-English bilinguals to speak Gaelic. More recent evidence suggests that the scheme in its latter stages was better-funded and much more language-focused, but has now ceased due to the to cessation of EC funding.

26. Please note that the Irish Republic is merly a description of the type of government it is not the official name of the state which is "Ireland" in English and "Éire" in Gaelic. REF: URL http://www.taoiseach.gov.ie/upload/publications/ 297.htm Bunreacht na hÉireann (Irish Constitution) THE STATE Article 4.

27. Some commentators, such as Éamonn Ó Gribín (2006) argue that the Gaelic Act falls so far short of the status accorded Welsh that one would be foolish or naïve to believe that any substantial change will occur in the fortunes of the language as a result of Bòrd na Gàidhlig's efforts. Given the reluctance/refusal of Scottish politicians to give Gaelic and English equal official status in Scotland, perhaps it would have been better to have fought to secure it such a status in the "Highland and Islands" and maybe also in the large cities, and leave English or Scotch English to the Lowlands!

28. Sinn Féin's take over of the Gaelic League in 1915 and the predictable effect that this had (and still has) as regards attitudes to Gaelic amongst the Protestant and unionist traditions is also significant in this respect.

29. The introduction of the National School system (monolingual English-medium education at Primary level, what P.H. Pearse described as the "Murder Machine" http://www.ucc.ie/celt/online/E900007-001/text001.html) in Ireland and the attitude of the Roman Catholic Church are significant in this regard but space does not permit an extended discussion.

30. The Treaty was signed on the 6 December 1921. Harris (1993, p. 104) comments that the Catholic bishops supported the Treaty which allowed the six North-Eastern counties to opt out of the Irish Free State and conferred on the remaining twenty-six counties dominion status, which in reality was a greater degree of autonomy than that provided for by the Government of Ireland Act.

31. For details on the relationship between the Catholic Church, the foundation of Northern Ireland and the promotion of Irish see Akenson (1991), Elliott (2001) and Harris (1993).

32. There was no question on knowledge of Ulster-Scots in the *Census* held on 29 April 2001. For a comprehensive treatment of Ulster Scots from a linguistic perspective see Robinson (1997).

33. In other words the right to an Irish or even a Gaelic identity and citizenship is supposed to be given equal status to a British/English identity and citizenship. In the absence of legislation of course it is impossible to know precisely what "parity of esteem" etc. means. Gibben has advised that the recent appearance before the courts of a young teacher (Máire Nic an Bhaird) who spoke in Gaelic only to a member of the Police Service of Northern Ireland will cast some light on the matter (see URL: http://www.indymedia.ie/article/77335).

34. The Ulster Scots Language Society estimates 100,000 speakers in Northern Ireland. For context see Mac Póilin, A. (ed.), (1997): and Nic Craith, M. (1999). For details on the structure and grammar of the language see Robinson (1997).

35. The Irish Language Agency (*Foras na Gaeilge*) has its headquarters in Dublin (7 Merrion Square, Dublin 2), and a regional office in Belfast. The Ulster Scots Agency (*Tha Boord o Ulster Scotch*) has its headquarters at Franklin House, 10–12 Brunswick Street, Belfast, BT2 7GE. It claims that it "will act to position the Irish language such that it will be an integral part of daily life, widely used by speakers who are committed to, and comfortable with, its usage and accepted by all as a normal means of communication".

36. The funding available for the year 2000/2001 was £667k. Resources were made available for projects with a language dimension, which met the objective criteria of a range of mainstream programmes. In 2001/2002 funding of £11.42m was

available of which the Irish Language Agency received £10.12m and the Ulster-Scots Agency £1.3m. (Northern Ireland provided £3.5m of this.)

37. Logic suggests that in similar terms the exposure to elements of Ulster-Scots should be widened within the remit of the education authorities, but it is hard to judge the levels of demand.

38. Even if in several instances this is denied or adopted in a most recalcitrant manner. In Newry and Mourne District Council for instance, an EQA found that its Bilingualism Policy was problematic.

39. At the time of writing it is not known whether in fact Westminster of Belfast will be the sponsoring body of any new Irish Language Act.

40. The Treaty Establishing the European Community, Rome, 25 March 1957.

41. Some argue that it is a mistake to categorise Irish Gaelic as a Lesser-Used Language and demonstrate this by reference to Ireland's Minister Eamon O Ciuv's decision not to sign the Charter. It is the first official language of Ireland according to the Irish Constitution and Irish Citizens have the right to use the language in dealings with the State. In Northern Ireland Irish citizens have been guaranteed "parity of esteem" and the right to be Irish Citizens (or British or both). Such considerations may equally be applied to the Catalan government's view of its position along the European language continuum where despite being seen as the strongest of the lesser-used languages, does not have the state-backed support which Irish has at both state and international level.

42. For a comprehensive interpretation of the Charter and of its evaluation see Grin (2003).

43. The history of the legislative development of the Welsh language shows how lessons were learnt through experience in order to eradicate cases of linguistic inequality in the public sphere and to strengthen the status of the Welsh language over a period of time. The Welsh Courts Act 1942 permitted the use of the Welsh language in courts of law by individuals who would be at a disadvantage if they used the English language. The Welsh Language Act of 1967 increased the status of the Welsh language in the courts, and gave Ministers the power to prescribe bilingual versions of official forms. However, the Welsh language did not receive equal treatment in public life – and the chief aim of the 1993 Welsh Language Act was to rectify this inequality (see Williams, 1989a).

44. Having said that the implementation of such language schemes is largely inconsistent, and it is not clear to the public what they can expect to receive in terms of Welsh language services (for details of the schemes and a great deal of very useful information visit www.welsh-language-board.org.uk).

45. Not all language activists accept the strategy adopted by POBAL. I should add that I was involved both in the writing of the POBAL (2006) proposals and a speaker at the subsequent follow-up conference convened in Belfast on the 30th of November 2006. In this context one commentator has advised me privately that "The fact that the Draft asks for an Irish Language Act and not an Official Languages Act is a great mistake. The south of Ireland has an Official Language Act and this part of Ireland should have followed that example. Not only because of the rights of Irish citizens under the Good Friday Agreement but also because it disregards the *de facto* position of English as an official language. We are asked to support the vista of having Irish Gaelic recognised as an Official Language whilst no mention is made of the other official language (English the '*de facto* official' language!) By directing attention on Irish Gaelic and not on the concept of a 'bilingual society' we also open the doors to those who wish to kill the idea at birth. The Ulster Scots lobby will also have ammunition for their

agenda. .... What about quid pro quo for Ulster Scots" will be heard from every quarter? This lobby never sought parity with English and by removing Irish Gaelic from an English Gaelic bilingualism one is open to attack by the Ulster Scots lobby (confidential memo to the author, 2006).

46. My colleague Diarmait Mac Giolla Chriost has drawn attention to the Gaeltacht Quarter Report by Clive Dutton which envisaged a vibrant Irish-medium sector in Belfast. This may be viewed as a groundbreaking statement of the relationship between language and economic regeneration and is significant because it was commissioned by three departments of the Northern Ireland government.

47. One area where the legislation could be strengthened is by placing a duty on bodies to provide information as requested by the Welsh Language Board as part of any statutory investigation under section 17 of the Act into the lack of implementation of a language scheme. Bodies have exploited this and have refused to cooperate and provide the Board with basic information. So the statutory powers should be strengthened to this end.

48. The proposals in this section follow closely the model of the Canadian Commissioner for Official Languages, one of the most rigorous models for the enforcement of language rights and duties that is available, and the model that inspired to a significant degree the provisions of the *Official Languages Act 2003* and the Oifig Choimisinéir na dTeangacha Oifigiúla created thereunder.

49. While the right of appeal to the courts is that of the person making the complaint, it is proposed that the Commissioner can participate in such a court action and, with the approval of the complainant, may even act on the complainant's behalf.

50. The Constitution of the Irish Free State (Saorstát Eireann) Act, 1922 and the Public General Acts passed by Oireachtas of Saorstát Eireann during the year 1922 (Dublin: Stationery Office, n.d.).

51. FitzGerald (1991, p. 306) has this to say about his reasons for expediting this move: "The removal of the Irish language requirement for public service entry took several years to implement, but I got agreement to earlier action in relation to the exceptionally large intake of twenty-nine third secretaries into the Department of Foreign Affairs in 1974, with the result that no fewer than seven of this number came from Northern Ireland, drawn from both communities there. Few if any of these would have been able to qualify for entry into the foreign service but for the exemption from Irish."

52. In Autumn 2005 Údarás set up the company Óige na Gaeltachta Teo, especially to develop a youth service in the Gaeltacht regions.

53. *An Chomhairle um Oideachas Gaeltachta agus Gaelscolaíochta* commissioned *Oifig na Gaeilge Labhartha*, NUIG and *An Díseart*, to undertake a major study of Gaeltacht schools. Consequently between November 2003 and March 2004 a questionnaire was sent to every primary and post-primary school in the Gaeltacht, which sought information concerning, inter alia, the pupils, staff, accommodation and facilities of the school. The resultant interpretation and recommendations of the investigation are reported in Mac Donnacha *et al.* (2005). *An Chomhairle um Oideachas Gaeltachta agus Gaelscolaíochta* was established in 2002 under the terms of Article 31 of the Education Act (1998) with research as one of its statutory functions. Its mission statement is: "To fulfill effectively, professionally and at a high standard the responsibilities of An Chomhairle um Oideachas Gaeltachta agus Gaelscolaíochta for the development of the Gaeltacht and Irish medium sector and the teaching of Irish in all schools."

54. Mac Donnacha *et al.* (2005, p. 2) argue that a literature review of earlier reports on Gaeltacht education (namely Tuarascáil Choimisiún na Gaeltachta

(1926), Tuarascáil ar an mBunoideachas sa Ghaeltacht (1981), Tuarascáil an Chomhchoiste um Oideachas sa Ghaeltacht (1986), Gnéithe den Oideachas sa Ghaeltacht:Impleachtaí Polasaí (Muintearas 2000), Tuarascáil Choiste Comhairleach na nÓg (2001), and TuarascálachaChoimisiún na Gaeltachta (2002) Ó Cinnéide *et al.*, 2001) reveals that although the State has succeeded in developing an Irish-medium primary and post-primary education system there, the education sector faces major challenges due to the complex linguistic situation and the absence of an adequate support system.

55. Mac Donnacha reports that for the largest group of primary schools (69 Category C schools) instruction is through the medium of English for half or more of the lessons. These schools account for 4544 pupils (56 per cent of Gaeltacht primary school pupils). In general around a third of the pupils have a good level of competence, with some being fluent in Irish as they begin school or they attain such a level of competency during their school years. Circa one third have a reasonable level of competence in Irish as they begin school or they attain such a competency during their school years. The final third comprise pupils in the lower classes who have just started school with little or no Irish and those in the higher classes who fail to increase their level of competency in Irish during their school years.

56. The number of post-primary school pupils fell by 10 per cent between 1998 and 2003. This decrease is greater than the 7 per cent fall experienced by primary schools over the same period. Twenty three per cent of Gaeltacht post-primary school pupils were born or lived outside the Gaeltacht at some stage before attending school in the Gaeltacht; and 5 per cent were born or lived outside Ireland. This percentage is lower than the equivalent figures for primary level pupils, of which 26 per cent were born or lived outside the Gaeltacht and 11 per cent were born or lived outside Ireland. Mac Donnacha reports (p. 10) that this problem can only worsen.

57. The distribution of Gaeltacht secondary school pupils by county in 2004/2005 was as follows: Co.Kerry – 514 pupils in two schools; Co.Cork – 278 pupils in two schools; Co.Donegal – 468 pupils in three schools; Co.Galway – 1104 pupils in eight schools (an additional school failed to submit annual returns); Co.Mayo – 251 pupils in two schools; Co.Meath – 126 pupils in one school and Co.Waterford – 89 pupils in one school. I am grateful to Nóra Ní Loingsigh of Gaelscoileanna, Dublin who, at an interview on 21 October 2005, provided this data together with a copy of the Mac Donnacha report. The Department of Education and Science collects its own data from all schools on an annual basis and publishes statistics on an annual basis even if they are a year or two behind.

58. Thus 95 per cent of first year pupils in Category A post-primary schools are fluent or have a good level of competence in Irish as they begin their post-primary education. Principals reported that 71 per cent of 1st year post-primary school pupils in Category B schools were fluent or had a good level of competence in Irish. As in the case of the Category A schools, this percentage fluctuates slightly between 1st year and 6th year, at which stage 71 per cent are again considered fluent or have a good level of competency in Irish. Three times as many pupils begin 1st year in Category B post-primary schools with little or no competency in Irish as do in Category A post-primary schools (13 per cent in Category B, 4 per cent in Category A). Overall, a similar percentage, 12 per cent, of pupils with little or no Irish is recorded in 6th Year as is recorded in 1st Year in these schools.

59. The authors remind us that under the Education Act, 1998, the education system in the Gaeltacht has both educational and language planning objectives. "The educational objectives pertain to the constitutional rights of children, and in particular the aim that everybody living in the State shall be provided with a level and quality of education appropriate to their needs and abilities (Section 6(a) and 6(b) Education Act, 1998). The language planning objectives contained in the Act are set out in section 6(j) and state that every person concerned in the implementation of the Act shall have regard to the objective of contributing 'to the maintenance of Irish as the primary community language in Gaeltacht areas.' It is important to note, therefore, that this objective applies to the education system in general and is not limited to schools. This research project confirms that Gaeltacht schools are achieving some of these objectives in an effective manner" (Mac Donnacha, 2005, p. 16).

60. Thus pupils in Gaeltacht schools do not have access to Irish-medium support services from health boards or from psychological support services, except in a limited number of cases. Mac Donnacha concludes that these issues have been exacerbated in the absence of the development of clear school-level policies that would provide guidance for teachers dealing with the language planning and educational issues that arise in Gaeltacht schools.

61. This would function through the medium of Irish, support the development of best practice approaches to teaching and function under the auspices of An Chomhairle um Oideachas Gaeltachta agus Gaelscolaíochta but working with and reporting to the Inspectorate.

62. An internal review by the Senate of the NUI found that the Irish requirement was not a factor in prospective students not choosing NUI Colleges.

63. *Bille na dTeangacha Oifigiúla (Comhionannas), 2002, Official Languages (Equality) Bill*, Dublin: Government of Ireland, April 24th 2002.

64. A number of previously existing bodies and sections of Government Departments were subsumed into Foras na Gaeilge on its establishment, chiefly Bord na Gaeilge (the state Board for promoting the Irish language established by The Bord na Gaeilge Act, 1978 in the South), An Gúm and An Coiste Téarmaíochta, respectively the Irish language publication and the terminological branches of the Dept. of Education and Science in Ireland. Walsh (2005, p. 8) observes that the Irish state effectively ceded its sovereign responsibility for promoting Irish to a structure which is linked to the British state and to an unstable peace process in Northern Ireland (for a further discussion, see Ó Murchú, 2002).

65. Walsh (2005, p. 6) observes that the Republic of Ireland no longer has a state board to promote Irish. It is difficult to imagine the Irish government being willing to do this in any other area of national policy. For instance, the establishment of another cross-border body, Inter *Trade* Ireland, did not lead to the abolishment of any of the Republic of Ireland's public bodies with responsibility for business or trade (see British-Irish Agreement Act, 1999).

66. I am grateful to the then Chief Executive of Foras for granting me several interviews during 2004-5 and for arranging full and unfettered access to his core staff to discuss many issues during October 2005.

67. In 2004, a report by Trinity College Dublin and Comhdháil Náisiúnta na Gaeilge, the umbrella body for the voluntary sector, found that Foras was "competing" with the voluntary bodies rather than supporting them and that there was considerable confusion about what its precise role was (Donoghue, 2004; Ó Gairbhí, 2004). Comhdháil Náisiúnta na Gaeilge crticised Foras na Gaeilge for its "unsatisfactory and unprofessional approach". The chief executive, Conradh na Gaeilge,

244 Linguistic Minorities in Democratic Context

resigned in protest at the funding cuts, saying that she had "no confidence" in Foras na Gaeilge. For further details see Walsh 2005.

68. Many academic commentators and Government officials interviewed during the autumn of 2005 expressed astonishment at this continuing undermining of Foras's position, arguing that it is difficult to understand why Foras, Údarás and DCRGA would all need to operate from within the Gaeltacht, that it would be difficult to retain and recruit additional high quality staff in a move to Donegal but recognising that this move had little to do with national language planning and everything to do with patronage politics and the employment difficulties faced by the Gaoth Dobhair-Gweedore area which had lost near to 400 jobs in recent months.

69. Although as Walsh (2005, p. 6) has indicated this is a contentious issue. The linguistic demand appeared to be met by Article 8 (1) of the Údarás na Gaeltachta Act (1979), entitled "Functions of An tÚdarás" and second sub-section of Article 8 states that the Údarás "shall carry on, control and manage (either directly or, in any particular case, through a body corporate controlled by an tÚdarás) the industries and productive schemes of employment carried on, controlled or managed, directly or indirectly, by Gaeltarra Éireann" (Article 8(2)). Walsh observes that this ordering of "functions" gave the impression that promoting Irish was one of the organisation's objectives, and there is a perception that this is the case (see for instance, Ó Cinnéide et al., 2001: p. 148). However, two Attornies-General have advised the DCRGA in recent years that Article 8(1) is not in fact a "function", but simple a preamble to the organisation's industrial functions, implying that Údarás does not have any function in relation to Irish. This is an astonishing development and one which Walsh questions astutely by asserting that "it is reasonable to expect that 'the preservation and extension of the use of the Irish language as the principal medium of communication in the Gaeltacht' would be of paramount importance to Údarás na Gaeltachta. After all, if it were not for the Irish language, there would have been no need for organisations such as Údarás na Gaeltachta (or indeed, the DCRGA) in the first place" (Walsh, 2005, p. 6).

70. Fine Gael leader Enda Kenny announced on November 2005 that he wanted to make Irish more attractive to students rather than have them forced to study the language. Gaelscoileanna, Comhdháil Náisiúnta na Gaeilge and Foras na Gaeilge are among those who have joined Conradh na Gaeilge in expressing their disquiet at the Fine Gael proposals. With an election due within the next 2 years, and more likely sooner, Enda Kenny could be the next Taoiseach and his policy on Irish could indeed be government policy (Eurolang, 2005).

71. He told the Irish language daily Lá in November 2005 that it was wrong that children had to spend 13 years learning Irish. Adding that: "Using modern teaching methods I am sure that you can teach a child any language within 6 months. Instead of that children are being taught Irish for 13 years and they are still learning essays by heart for their Leaving Cert exams."

8
Welsh Language Policy and the Logic of Legislative Devolution

Wales is a conquered nation and like all conquered nations has suffered the consequences. But by contrast to several other European cases, Wales demonstrates a remarkable example of what might be called stealth ethnogenesis and the politics of resilience. It has refused to disappear from the pages of history and much of this refusal is intertwined within the struggle for the language.[1]

Wales has long been a context for language contact, conflict and shift. Indeed multilingualism is one of the abiding, if underemphasised, features of its historical development. Today Wales is seen as a reasonable model of bilingualism, but in earlier successive eras, the Romano-British (AD 43–c.410), early mediaeval (AD c.410–c.1100) and later medieval period (AD c.1100–c.1500) it could be argued that invasion, resistance and conquest have had a profound linguistic impact on the patchwork of kingdoms, territories and fealties owed by the Welsh landed classes. Many scholars from various disciplines have made the claim that Wales was largely defined, if not created, by external forces and legitimising narratives. Old orthodoxies about the residual British Celts being driven westward by successive hordes of Saxon invaders are now being challenged on both historical-linguistic and genetic grounds. What is not in dispute is the emergence of a remarkable indigenous culture which had to cope with Anglo-Saxon penetration, Viking incursions, the Norman suzerainty and subsequent Anglo-French conquest and the emergence of an English hegemony. Throughout these power struggles the Welsh language, its literature, legal conventions and social mores were challenged and transformed so that what emerged at the end of the late medieval period was an enriched, relatively robust and distinct national culture operating within a dependent political context. The twin anchors of this high culture were learning and religion which maintained the centuries-old link between Church affairs and the native literary tradition. Glanmor Williams identifies the most important constituents of this link as being the translation of parts of the Bible, the Creed, popular hymns and prayers, lives of the saints and works of devotion and mysticism (Williams, G., 1997, p. 12). "Thus was the continuity between the pre-Norman age and post-Norman experience maintained largely unbreached in the expression of popular devotion" (Williams, G., 1997, p. 12). The Bardic tradition also emphasised various religious themes related to piety, Christ's suffering and the last days, together with more contemporary concerns, notably post-conquest discontent, the travails of the Hundred Years War with France and the re-emergence of an independent Welsh spirit.

The Edwardian colonial conquest of Wales after 1282–1283 AD resulted in the annexation of Wales into England and was sealed in law by the First Statute of Westminster (1284).[2] Subsequently the gradual incorporation of the landed gentry throughout the later Middle Ages had transformed Wales from a rebellious periphery to a fairly conservative, if not quite domiciled, border region of England.[3] The splendid castles, much admired by tourists and locals alike, are a permanent reminder that Wales is a conquered territory, where a re-settled "alien" population dominated the urban hierarchy and sought to diminish the differences between the Welsh and the English. Despite the conquest, Welsh laws, Welsh local administration and religious customs prevailed such that the anticipated erosion of national differences between the native Welsh and foreign English was not progressing sufficiently quickly. Mann (2005, p. 58) reports how in 1509 the English burgesses of Conway, a plantation garrison town, petitioned for more discrimination against the Welsh. They complained "it is no more meete for a Welshman to bears any office in Wales-than it is for a frinchman to be Officer in Calis [Calais], or a skotte in Barwicke [Berwick]". Sadly for them their petition was sent to the first of the Tudors, King Henry V11, whose accession in 1485 had sealed a long process of aristocratic lateral assimilation and inter-marriage between English and Welsh lords.

His son, Henry VIII, enacted the Acts of Union 1536 and 1542, which formally incorporated Wales into the legal and political realm of England, imposing one administration, one law and one language. The Act's most significant clause in terms of the future of the language was to exclude Welsh from official life and require all public officialdom that was transacted in the "principality" to be in English. It said that no person who commanded only "the Welsh speech shall have or enjoy any manner of offices or fees within this realm". These Acts are often interpreted as a turning point in Welsh history when both state incorporation and linguistic exclusion dealt a double blow to the Welsh people. Yet as Mann (2005) observes, "while about 90 per cent of the Welsh monolingual population were now officially disqualified from holding public office, *they never held public office*. As in England, 90 per cent of the population did not count in politics" (p. 58). What mattered were the remaining ten per cent: the nobility, gentry, merchants, and guildsmen. English was already the language of officialdom and bureaucracy and the anglicised ruling cohorts in Wales had acquired English as a second language in order to prosper in the ascendant Tudor state. What operated was an early example of colonial language policy, reminiscent of post-imperial India and parts of Africa and not too dissimilar to the impact which English hegemony has today as a result of globalisation and advanced capitalism. But to see all this in terms of national displacement is to give undue emphasis to the nationalist vision of world order. Mann is correct in insisting, what several Welsh critics have noted, that what was involved in this institutional coercion was in part colonial exploitation by the English, in part class betrayal by Welsh elites. A similar pattern obtained as a result of "upper class withdrawal" from popular culture right across sixteenth to eighteenth century Europe. For example, the Bohemian nobility withdrew from Czech to German, educated Norwegians withdrew to Danish, Finns to Swedish. Mann described the *modus vivendi* of this process in Wales thus:

> But the Welsh-speaking gentry operated in a world in which bilingual-
> ism was the obvious strategy for advancement-and also the best way to
> provide protection for their retainers and their dependants. Welsh prag-
> matism was matched by that of the English. In 1563 the Anglican Church
> recognised that to convert Welsh people to Protestantism required a
> Bible in Welsh, the only language understood by the masses. This pro-
> ject encouraged literacy in Welsh ... English spread down to the lower
> classes. During the nineteenth century it made serious inroads into the
> Welsh language. Before then, assimilation was still lateral and elitist.
> Welsh, unlike Irish, was being voluntarily undermined from the top, class
> by class. This was becoming a stratified yet national state.
>
> (Mann, 2005, pp. 58–9)

Some degree of autonomous cultural reproduction was encouraged in the seventeenth century by the emergence of new religious movements, such as the Independents (Yr Annibynwyr) and the Baptists (Y Bedyddwyr), which paved the way for non-Established religious affiliations with their own social organisations, networks and denominational presses. Calvinistic Methodism dominated the next century with its emphasis on order, sobriety, piety and learning. The Methodist Church soon became established as the dominant religious force in large parts of the country. In the succeeding centuries, des- pite discrimination and persecution, dissenting religious groups flourished and encouraged a Trans-Atlantic, Welsh-medium network of correspondents, journalists, teachers, social and spiritual interpreters, that culminated in a period of late-nineteenth-century liberal radicalism. During the latter part of the nineteenth century rapid Anglicisation occurred as a result of industri- alisation and urbanisation. For the first time in Welsh history bilingualism became a mass phenomenon creating a new if relatively unstable sociolin- guistic pattern. New codes of worship, work, leisure and political beliefs were transmitted to an increasingly literate work force by a mass media created by print capitalism. The Welsh language was undoubtedly strengthened by the redistribution of a growing population consequent to industrial expansion. As industrialisation generated internal migration, the Welsh, unlike the Scots or the Irish, did not have to abandon their language and homeland for employment abroad, particularly by emigrating to the New World (Thomas, 1959; Williams, 1971). Consequently the large-scale rural-urban shift which took place within Wales was capable of sustaining a new set of Welsh institutions, which gave a fresh impetus to the indigenous language and culture, institutionalising them within new, modernising industrial domains.

This may be the principal reason why modern Welsh identity is more closely linked to the maintenance of language than any other Celtic case. Welsh culture was less reliant on the political and formal national institutions and has been reflected more through popular involvement in chapel-based social activities, choral festivals, *Eisteddfodau* competitions in music, drama and poetry, a brass band tradition, miners' libraries, and early national sporting federations. These manifestations were as much a redefinition of indigenous Welsh culture as they were the sharpening of a distinctly Anglo-Welsh identity and tradition.[4] However, this mutually-dependent Welsh and Anglo-Welsh popular culture has heavily influenced the nature of urban Welsh-medium culture, for, unlike rural Wales, such changes were operative within a set of formal, English-medium public sector and commercial domains.

At the beginning of the twentieth century English had emerged as the dominant language in Wales, primarily as a result of in-migration and state policy. Imperial economic advances and state intervention following the Education Act of 1870 and the Welsh Intermediate Education Act of 1889, bred a new awareness of English values, culture and employment prospects and gave a powerful institutional fillip to the process of anglicisation, which encouraged the transmission of Welsh identity through the medium of English. The standardisation of education and local government encouraged closer economic and administrative association with the rest of the U.K. Modernisation reinforced English and denigrated Welsh. Refusal to speak Welsh with one's children was a common enough reaction to the status differential which developed between the languages. How the masses welcomed this "liberation" from traditionalism and conservatism is best evidenced by the wholesale generational language shift in the period 1914–1945 (Pryce and Williams, 1988). English was perceived (and still is to a large extent) as the language of progress, of equality, of prosperity, of commerce, of mass entertainment and pleasure. The wider experience of Empire-building, understandably, made acquisition of English a most compelling feature and the key to participation in the burgeoning British-influenced world economy. Added to this was the failure to use Welsh in the wide range of newer speech domains which developed in all aspects of the formal and social life of the nation.

A prime vehicle of modernisation was the rapidly expanding communication network, which intensified in the late nineteenth century. Modernisation theorists stress the importance of physical and social communication in the development of self-conscious nations and in the process of cultural reproduction and replacement. In Wales, relative inaccessibility had provided some basis for cultural differentiation both within and between the socio-linguistic communities. However, the development of an externally derived transport and communication system served to reduce that isolation. Technology promised to overcome the friction of distance. The critical factors influencing the development of the transport system were defence and commerce in that the network was designed to facilitate through traffic from England to Ireland via Wales. The main railway routes ran east-west through the centre and along the northern and southern coasts respectively, with branch lines penetrating the resource-rich hinterland allowing the exportation of slate, coal and iron and steel products. This had the effect of integrating South Wales economically with the Bristol region, the Midlands and London, and North Wales with Chester together with the Lancashire conurbations focussed on Manchester and Liverpool. Wales lacked a metropolitan tradition and in effect, London, Birmingham and Liverpool fulfilled these functions. Welsh societies in these major conurbations, particularly London, were extraordinarily influential in determining events at home (Jones, 2001). Wales's poorly developed internal road and rail system did not conduce to the creation of a nationally shared space and territorial identification and led to economic initiatives being located either in better served British regions or attracted to Wales largely as a result of government subsidies and regional development grants.

As a consequence of both industrialisation and modernisation, political life in Wales reflected the radicalism of a working class mass struggling for representation, equality of opportunity and decent working and living conditions for themselves and their dependants. At the turn of the twentieth century the majority of voting males supported the Liberal Party. It was dedicated to social justice, to educational and health improvements under statutory regulation, to the Disestablishment of the Church of England in Wales, and to Home Rule all round for the Celtic nations, particularly in Ireland. In the Welsh-speaking parts of Wales, Liberalism was also a vehicle for cultural nationalism and for the development of a Nonconformist-influenced moral and social order.[5] During the early part of the twentieth century, under its charismatic, Welsh-speaking Prime Minister, David Lloyd-George, the Liberal Party was arguably the most influential political party on the world stage reflecting British Imperial power and interests. It was simultaneously the national party of Wales advocating self-government at home, whilst enslaving more and more indigenous people abroad in the name of God, King and Country. At the local level, the main conduit for spreading the Liberals, message of social reform and democratic representation was the Free Church or Nonconformist Chapel System which pervaded almost every settlement in Wales. The spectacular growth of the Nonconformist denominations following on from the Great Religious Revival of 1905 not only made Wales an outwardly more Christian society than hitherto but also influenced nearly every aspect of public behaviour and private life. Both in literary and scholarly terms, Welsh popular culture owes a great deal to the opportunities for self-expression and publication afforded by the various denominations.[6]

A minority resisted anglicisation and developed counter movements dedicated to the promotion of Welsh, inspired by intellectuals such as the Reverend Michael D. Jones, who led the small exodus to Patagonia (in Argentina) to establish a wholly Welsh migrant community (Williams, G., 1992). The Reverend Emrys ap Iwan was the first minister of religion to appear before a court of law and insist on the primacy of the Welsh language in legal proceedings in Wales. Dan Isaac Davies, the HMI (Her Majesty's Inspector) for Schools, advocated a greater use of Welsh-medium education. Thomas Gee, the publisher of such ambitious multi-volume Encyclopaedias as "Gwyddoniadur" was an advocate of mass circulation periodicals in Welsh. The most influential family of all was headed by O.M. Edwards, the university teacher, writer, publisher and first Chief HMI for schools in Wales, who tried to establish a more tolerant approach to bilingualism by attacking the injustice associated with the Welsh NOT within the school system (the practice, common in the nineteenth century, whereby teachers, at the request of parents and governors, punished pupils for using Welsh within the school). His son, Sir Ifan ab Owen Edwards, established Urdd Gobaith Cymru (The Welsh League of Youth) in 1922; it has become the largest mass movement in Wales encouraging children and young adults to develop skills, competence and leadership qualities in a variety of contexts, principally community work, *Eisteddfodau*, and sporting achievements.

In the liberal heyday, Wales established a set of national institutions that paralleled those in Scotland and Ireland. These include the federal University of Wales (established 1883); the National Library of Wales at Aberystwyth and the National Museum of Wales at Cardiff which were established in 1907; and the Church in Wales which was created following the Act of Disestablishment in 1920. A variety of cultural movements flourished, such as *Undeb Cenedlaethol Y Cymdeithasau Cymraeg* (the National Union of Welsh Societies), established in 1913, and *Urdd Gobaith Cymru* established in 1922. However, this emerging political-cultural infra-structure was largely dependent upon external factors and it was concluded that the forces which militated against the reproduction of a Welsh culture could only be mediated by a form of genuine self-government or home-rule. For the intellectual figures in the early language movement, culture, history and education were constant reference points. Their search for identity was predicated on a platform of struggle, recognition and legitimacy, as realised in a plethora of social reforms and cultural initiatives. In 1925 *Plaid Genedlaethol Cymru*

(The Welsh National Party) was formed in Pwllheli by intellectuals which included Saunders Lewis, a University lecturer and playwright, the Reverend Lewis Valentine, a Baptist Minister, and D.J. Davies an economist. Their initial concerns were the preservation of Welsh cultural and spiritual values primarily through the maintenance of a small-scale, predominantly rural, communitarian life-style.[7]

Cultural nationalism was profoundly influenced by Nonconformist principles, yet not exclusively so, for at a critical early juncture, nationalism's moral philosophy was deeply imbued by the Catholicism of several of its original leaders.[8] Yet in comparison with Catholic Ireland between 1880 and 1921 Wales did not succumb to the power of the gun in the name of national freedom, despite several attempts to use the Irish example as an inspiration.[9] Both the constitutional and "physical force" traditions contributed to the ideology that in order to be-reborn the Irish nation had to demand the sacrifice of martyrs for the cause. This common thread in romantic nationalism emphasised land, language, race, a common past and the necessity for open conflict in the struggle against the oppressors. In Wales there was an overriding commitment to non-violent principles in nationalism's thought and deed.[10] In contradistinction to most other political movements in the second phase of 1921–1939, pacifism and non-violent resistance characterised Welsh nationalism.[11] It articulated a popular belief in communal-oriented consensus politics under the two most influential Presidents of Plaid Cymru, Saunders Lewis, who was leader from 1926–1939, and advocated a combination of constitutional and unconstitutional direct action, and Gwynfor Evans, leader from 1945–1981, who was a committed pacifist and moved the party in the direction of total opposition to violence and war as a means of achieving self-government.[12] The Welsh language, national identity and Christianity dominated the early policy discussions.[13] It was only after 1932, that self-government was adopted as party policy as a means of achieving national self-respect and some semblance of autonomy within a dynamic European state system.[14] They were well aware of many other small nations in Europe being admitted to the League of Nations and while Plaid Cymru vacillated as regards the dominant European ideologies of Liberalism and Socialism, they wanted to reduce class antagonism and create a national community.[15] Early Welsh nationalists sought a redefinition of the evolving European order in moral not in materialistic terms.[16] However, whilst in the main the intelligentsia turned to the Celtic realm for moral inspiration and to post-Civil-War Ireland as an example of a successful national struggle, Saunders Lewis sought his authenticity in the larger context of a European, Catholic and Latin civilisation.[17] In his seminal lecture *Egwyddorion Cenedlaetholdeb*[18] he outlined his conception of Welsh national history, which was to be influential in subsequent justification both of the language struggle and party strategy. In medieval Europe individual cultures were nurtured and protected because their rulers deferred to a higher authority.[19] The growth of state nationalism had destroyed the civilisation of Wales, and of other small countries in Europe. Having usurped the moral Christian order from the sixteenth century onwards, state nationalism inaugurated a programme of state-nation congruence in the name of the people, covering a systematic exurpation of minorities under a veil of democratic rhetoric, which in time emphasised the principles of liberty and equality, if not always brotherhood, within the state's aegis. In order that his compatriots deliver themselves from the false consciousness of British imperialism and state nationalism, Lewis advocated that they promulgate a genuine nationalism as a necessary means by which Welsh culture would be nurtured within its own political institutions. Lewis justified the selection of Welsh as the critical battleground for political action because its continuance, despite centuries of state-inspired anglicisation, was proof of the Welsh having kept faith with the universal values of a pre-existent Europeaness. Wales should "demand a seat in the League of Nations, so that she may act as Europe's interpreter in Britain, and as a link to bind England and the Empire to Christendom and to the League itself".[20]

In this re-direction of Welsh politics, away from the Empire and towards contemporary Europe, Lewis set the tone for a long-standing debate within nationalism, the strains of which echoed until his death in 1985. It concerned his drawing upon Catholic Europe for inspiration and his personal advocacy of social and political policy, for Lewis had converted to Catholicism and been received into the Roman Catholic Church on 16 February 1932. Ostensibly radical, dissenting and Nonconformist, the Welsh populace did not approve of his political convictions and personal style. The Nationalist Party was criticised for being elitist, intellectual, and unpatriotic because some members appeared to support quasi-Fascist movements in Europe.[21]

In the post-war period a large number of capital intensive projects initiated by English local government so as to provide water, hydro-electric power, etc. resulted in some Welsh communities being expunged and several Welsh valleys being drowned to provide water for English cities.[22] When Gwynfor Evans became President of Plaid Cymru in 1945 he reflected a more typical strata of Welsh nationalism.[23] His Christian commitment to pacifism marked him out as a principled leader of his party[24] who refused to advocate the use of violence citing the Irish experience where the trappings of an independent state, had singularly failed to institute an indigenous national culture which is both popular and geographically widespread.[25]

How the national movement, especially Plaid Cymru, developed these principles has been the subject of much debate and analysis.[26] Since the early seventies Plaid Cymru's justification for advancing the cause of independence has widened considerably from the over-dominant language issue of the inter-war years to a more balanced and holistic view of Welsh problems in a broader British and European context (Williams, 1982, 1991b). It currently returns three Members to the Westminster Parliament, all representing

Table 8.1 2005 UK general election results in Wales

Party	Seats	Gain	Loss	Net	Votes	%	+/−%
Labour	29	0	5	−5	594,821	42.7	−5.9
Lib Dem	4	2	0	+2	256,249	18.4	+4.6
Conservative	3	3	0	+3	297,830	21.4	+0.4
Plaid Cymru	3	0	1	−1	174,838	12.6	−1.7

Heartland constituencies, and currently claims the political affiliation of about twelve per cent of the Welsh electorate (Table 8.1).[27]

At the beginning of 2007 Plaid Cymru was the second largest party within the National Assembly for Wales with twelve out of the sixty members whose party strength is as follows: The Labour Party 29 members, Plaid Cymru, 12 members, The Conservative Party, 11 members, The Liberal Democratic Party, 6 members while there was one member representing the Forward Wales and one independent member of the NAfW.

The most significant popular manifestation of the language struggle was the formation of *Cymdeithas yr Iaith Gymraeg* (The Welsh Language Society) in 1963 following Saunders Lewis' radio lecture, "Tynged yr Iaith" (The Fate of the Language). Initially concerned with single-issue campaigning in favour of reforms such as the production of official bilingual forms, tax and television licences, a separate Welsh-medium television channel and greater equality between Welsh and English in judicial affairs, *Cymdeithas yr Iaith Gymraeg* has developed into an influential direct-action pressure group; raising language awareness in conjunction with a number of other committed individuals and organisations (Williams, 1986; Philips, 1998).

Today the majority accepts that bilingualism is a distinct feature of society, of which a significant proportion see it as advancing their children's education, social and employment prospects. A minority of parents agitated for Welsh-medium education, which the Labour Party developed through its pioneering bilingual educational policies in anglicised Wales, especially Flint and Glamorgan.[28]

Paradoxically, perhaps the greatest opposition to the development of Welsh-medium education and of language issues also comes from within Labour-affiliated ranks are compounded by the language issue. The Labour Party is rooted in a British sense of identity which was predicated upon social class divisions not ethnic competition, and some still see any increase in the development of Welsh-medium education as necessarily weakening this British base in favour of a more focused Welsh national (if not necessarily nationalist) identification. Class, ethnicity and multicultural pluralism.

The first language census in Wales was conducted in 1891 and it recorded that 898,914 people spoke Welsh (54.4 per cent). Ten years later in 1901, 929,824 (49.9 per cent) were so recorded. At its census peak in 1911, the Welsh-speaking population numbered 977,366 (43.5 per cent), of whom 190,300 were monoglot Welsh. Continuous decline throughout the century resulted in a 1981 population of 503,549 speakers, of whom 21,283 recorded themselves as monoglot.[29] By 1991 the Welsh-speaking population had declined to 496,530, a fall of some 1.4 per cent (Aitchison and Carter, 1993).[30] The long trend of decline had finally slowed, compared with the acute fall of 17.3 per cent between 1961 and 1971, and the fall of 6.3 per cent for the period 1971–1981.

At the beginning of the twenty first century the Welsh-speaking population is predominantly aged; is concentrated in proportional terms in the north and west; is showing encouraging signs of growth amongst the younger age groups, particularly in the industrial south and east; this growth can be largely attributed to the development of Welsh-medium education in such areas, in combination with the wider scale revival of interest in the language and its institutionalisation in many aspects of public life. Welsh has become increasingly identified with government support and targeted for an increase in use within the economy. However, many find it difficult to secure adequate employment within predominantly Welsh-speaking regions, which atrophy because of the out-migration of the young, fecund and well educated and the in-migration of non-Welsh-speaking residents, who are attracted by a variety of factors. Thus a central issue is whether or not a viable Welsh culture can survive without its own heartland communities serving as a resource-base for language transmission.

A second trend revealed in the 2001 census is the substantial increase in the numbers of Welsh speakers aged between 3 and 15. Encouraging though these figures are, especially for Anglicised regions, one should not forget that many factors could reduce their impact on Welsh language reproduction. The development of mass tourism, seasonal employment patterns, out-migration, economic change and language of marriage partner will still influence rates of language loss and gain, but as each decennial census records higher and higher proportions in the younger age categories then the demographic future for Welsh seems brighter than at any other time since 1911. In raw statistical terms the trends of the past two decades allow us to say that the imminent death of Welsh was wildly exaggerated if we restrict ourselves only to the capacity to speak the language.

However, the geolinguistic pattern is not entirely promising. Figure 8.1 shows the proportion of Welsh speakers for electoral divisions. At the time of the 1961 Census, there were 279 out of 993 communities in Wales where at least 80 per cent of the population could speak Welsh; by the 1991 census only 32 of these communities remained (National Assembly for Wales Culture and Education Committee, 2002). This has led commentators such as Williams (1989a, p. 44) to argue that "instead of talking of a 'Welsh-speaking community', it is more appropriate to talk of 'Welsh speakers in the community', even within many parts of the heartland areas".[31]

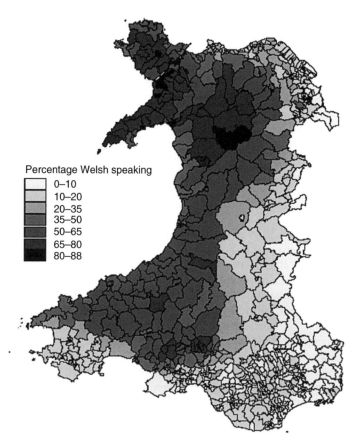

Figure 8.1   Percentage of Welsh speakers for electoral divisions (2001)
Source: Office for National Statistics (2003). Reproduced with permission from Higgs, Williams and Dorling, (2004), p. 194.

The number of wards where 60–70 per cent of the population speak Welsh has declined from 82 in 1991 to 54 in 2001; and from 55 to 41 where 70–80 per cent spoke Welsh and from 32 to 17 where over 80 per cent spoke Welsh (all, in 2001, within Gwynedd and Anglesey) leading to media concerns "that the Welsh Language Act of 1993 and the policies of the National Assembly have failed to halt the decline of Welsh as a living community language" (Western Mail, 2003b). At the other end of the scale, there was a significant increase in those wards where 10 per cent to 20 per cent of the population could speak Welsh (up from 156 in 1991 to 367 in 2001). These trends therefore represent a continuation of those found by Aitchison and Carter (1994) and have been variously attributed to the out-migration of Welsh-speaking populations as a result of poor employment or housing opportunities, the in-migration of predominantly monoglot English speakers and a decline in traditional industries which employed a dis-proportionate percentage of Welsh speakers (Aitchison and Carter, 1994; WAG, 2003a).

The changes in the percentages of Welsh speakers by Unitary Authorities are shown in Table 8.2. Cardiff recorded the largest absolute increase in numbers (up over 14,000), while Torfaen had the largest percentage increase (over 8 per cent).[32] Although the trends are not consistent at an aggregate level, there is weak evidence of a link with population change between 1991 and 2001. More analysis is needed to identify those communities that have experienced increases/declines in non-Welsh speakers/Welsh speakers and further research is needed to compare such trends with population change in order to examine the causes of such changes. At this scale, the unitary authorities that have experienced a decline in the percentage of people speaking Welsh are also those that have experienced significant in-migration since the last census. At the time of the 2001 census 11 per cent of the total population able to speak Welsh were born outside Wales (but whereas 24.7 per cent of the population born in Wales could speak Welsh only 9.0 per cent of those born outside Wales could speak Welsh). An extension of this research would be to identify where such population groups live and to examine their age structure (Higgs *et al.*, 2004, p. 196). Clearly questions of national origin, self-identification, language affiliation and group tensions are complex. The larger question to be examined requires an assessment of the strident claims that beneath the simplistic interpretation of census results what is really occurring is the demise of an indigenous ethnic identity. It is a slow death caused by a new and far more effective form of internal colonialism, a re-settlement of the heartland communities by the in-migration of relatively wealthy, generally conservative and unreceptive, English retirement and "new-age" settlers. Although "new-age" in England is not traditionally linked with concepts of conservatism and intolerance, it is enlightening to see that what can appear radical and anti-establishment one side of a national border can appear as colonialism the other! Emyr Llywelyn, leader of Adfer, phrased it thus in 1971, "Our territory is being plundered in our presence: we are being disinherited before our very eyes" (Williams, 1994, p. 130). Such concerns have also been echoed by Cymuned in the following manner:

"If the traditional Bröydd Cymraeg and Welsh-speaking communities cease to be the 'domains' of the language, Cymraeg will cease to be a living language because individuals and families cannot maintain a language in a vacuum, without an adequate broader social context. Cymry Cymraeg (Welsh-speakers) as a people and ethnic group will cease to exist" (Cymuned, 2003, p. 5). This has lead to a lively debate as to whether or not large parts of north and west Wales should be designated as an official Welsh-speaking heartland where discrete polices and planning measures could be applied, so

Table 8.2 Results from 2001 census (by unitary authority)

Unitary authority	2001 Population	Population change (1991–2001) – %	Percentage born in wales	Number and proportion of people aged 3 and over who can speak Welsh	1 or more skills in Welsh language (Numbers /percentages)	Percentage of people aged 3 and over with no knowledge of Welsh	Identified self as Welsh (Numbers /percentages)
Anglesey	66829	-2.9	67.6	39000 (59.8)	45534 (70.4)	29.6	12975 (19.4)
Blaenau Gwent	70064	-1.8	92.1	6000 (9.1)	9026 (13.3)	86.7	8417 (12)
Bridgend	128645	0.7	84.7	13000 (10.6)	24763 (19.9)	80.1	20275 (15.8)
Caerphilly	169519	1.5	89.9	18000 (10.9)	27228 (16.7)	83.3	26276 (15.5)
Cardiff	305353	8.0	74.9	32000 (10.9)	47998 (16.3)	83.7	40220 (13.2)
Carmarthen	172842	2.9	80.1	84000 (50.1)	106440 (63.6)	36.4	40471 (23.4)
Ceredigion	74941	19.8	58.6	38000 (51.8)	44635 (61.2)	38.8	16307 (21.8)
Conwy	109596	3.7	53.9	31000 (29.2)	42174 (39.7)	60.3	13289 (12.1)
Denbighshire	93065	5.1	57.9	24000 (26.1)	32469 (36.0)	63.9	9829 (10.6)
Flintshire	148594	5.5	51.1	20000 (14.1)	30660 (21.4)	78.6	8662 (5.8)
Gwynedd	116843	3.5	69.8	77000 (68.7)	85847 (76.1)	23.9	31356 (26.8)
Merthyr Tydfil	55981	-4.2	91.9	5000 (10.0)	9602 (17.7)	82.3	9065 (16.2)
Monmouthshire	84885	5.3	61.3	7000 (9.0)	10590 (12.9)	87.1	5871 (6.9)
Neath Port Talbot	134468	-0.8	89.5	23000 (17.8)	37551 (28.8)	71.2	22872 (17)

Table 8.2 (Continued)

Unitary authority	2001 Population	Population change (1991–2001) – %	Percentage born in wales	Percentage Number and proportion of people aged 3 and over who can speak Welsh	1 or more skills in Welsh language (Numbers /percentages)	Percentage of people aged 3 and over with no knowledge of Welsh	Identified self as Welsh (Numbers /percentages)
Newport	137011	3.2	81.1	13000 (9.6)	17622 (13.4)	86.6	12326 (9)
Pembrokeshire	114131	2.4	68.7	24000 (21.5)	32340 (29.4)	70.6	14912 (13.1)
Powys	126354	6.5	55.6	26000 (20.8)	36847 (30.1)	69.9	15927 (12.6)
Rhondda Cynon Taff	231946	0.5	89.9	28000 (12.3)	47213 (21.1)	78.9	38384 (16.5)
Swansea	223301	0.1	82.1	29000 (13.2)	48582 (22.5)	77.5	34135 (15.3)
Torfaen	90949	1.6	85.5	9000 (10.7)	12742 (14.5)	85.5	8934 (9.8)
Vale of Glamorgan	119292	2.1	75.7	13000 (11.1)	19453 (16.9)	83.1	15252 (12.8)
Wrexham	128476	5.6	71.9	18000 (14.4)	28401 (22.9)	77.1	12065 (9.4)
Total	2903085		75.4	576000 (20.5)	661526 (23.6)	71.6	(14.39)

Sources: ONS (2003); Higgs et al. (2004, p. 193).

Table 8.3 Change in Welsh language speakers (1981–2001) – using most comparable census data for 1991 and 1981 (*Source*: Office for National Statistics)

Unitary authority	2001 (%)	1991 (%)	1981 (%)	Change 1991–2001 (percentage points)	Change 1981–2001 (percentage points)
Anglesey	59.8	61.9	61.6	−2.1	−1.8
Blaenau Gwent	9.1	2.2	2.2	6.8	6.8
Bridgend	10.6	8.3	8.2	2.3	2.3
Caerphilly	10.9	6.0	5.2	4.9	5.7
Cardiff	10.9	6.7	5.8	4.2	5.1
Carmarthen	50.1	54.8	59.2	−4.7	−9.2
Ceredigion	51.8	59.2	65.1	−7.4	−13.2
Conwy	29.2	30.7	32.7	−1.5	−3.5
Denbighshire	26.1	26.8	28.5	−0.7	−2.3
Flintshire	14.1	13.6	12.7	0.5	1.4
Gwynedd	68.7	72.1	76.2	−3.4	−7.5
Merthyr Tydfil	10.0	7.4	8.3	2.6	1.7
Monmouthshire	9.0	2.2	2.7	6.8	6.3
Neath Port Talbot	17.8	17.5	19.1	0.3	−1.3
Newport	9.6	2.3	2.3	7.3	7.3
Pembrokeshire	21.5	18.3	18.4	3.2	3.1
Powys	20.8	20.6	21.0	0.2	−0.2
Rhondda Cynon Taff	12.3	9.0	9.1	3.3	3.2
Swansea	13.2	13.6	14.7	−0.4	−1.5
Torfaen	10.7	2.5	2.5	8.2	8.2
Vale of Glamorgan	11.1	6.8	5.9	4.3	5.2
Wrexham	14.4	13.8	14.6	0.6	−0.2
Total	21	19		2	

Source: Higgs *et al.* (2004) p. 195.

as to sustain and protect the threatened Welsh-speaking communities and networks which many consider to be a reservoir of indigenous culture, beliefs, values and life styles. Whether "Y Fro Gymraeg Mewnol" and/or "Y Fro Gymraeg Allanol" will be established is a moot point.[33] However, public policy is far more conscious of the need to target heartland localities and was explicitly mentioned as one of the aims of *Iaith Pawb* (Table 8.3).

Current language census figures reveal a welcome arrest of the sharp pattern of decline and may be interpreted as the first sign of reversing language shift. The acute difficulty, of course, is to determine to what extent such dynamics are the result of specific policies or mainly the cumulative effect of broader structural changes on society. What is not in doubt is the influence of the bilingual education sector and increasingly the whole school system which following the 1988 Education Act identified Welsh as a core subject in the National Curriculum. It is now possible to teach a wider range of subjects including Maths and Science, Design and Computing through the medium of Welsh in many English dominant schools. After 1994 all save a few opt out schools in the secondary sector were obliged to teach Welsh to their pupils in the lower forms. This, in turn, has exposed a far greater number of Welsh youth to the language and culture of their homeland but will require a continuous significant investment in teachers and resources if it is to be successful. Table 8.4 charts the proportions within each of the various combinations of language instruction over the period 1980–1990, that is, before and after the introduction of the National Curriculum which identified Welsh as a core subject. Three trends are evident, first that there has been a growth in the number of schools where Welsh is the first language of instruction; second, that there has been a growth in schools where Welsh is taught as a second language, up from 116 schools (48.7 per cent) in 1980 to 158 schools (69 per cent) by 1999; third, that whereas at the beginning of the period 35 schools (14.7 per cent) did not teach Welsh at all, this category had disappeared by 1999.

Table 8.4   Maintained secondary schools teaching Welsh[a]

Number of schools	1980/81	1990/91	1994/95	1995/96	1996/97	1997/98	1998/99
Schools where Welsh is taught as both a first and second language	82	68	48	50	50	54	51
Percentage of schools	34.5	29.6	21.1	21.9	21.8	23.7	22.3
Schools where Welsh is taught as a first language only	5	11	18	17	18	20	20
Percentage of schools	2.1	4.8	7.9	7.5	7.9	8.8	8.7
Schools where Welsh is taught as a second language only	116	129	158	159	161	154	158
Percentage of schools	48.7	56.1	69.6	69.7	70.3	67.5	69.0
Schools where no Welsh is taught	35	22	3	2	–	–	–
Percentage of schools	14.7	9.5	1.3	0.9	–	–	–
Total	238	230	227	228	229	228	229

[a] At January each year. Prior to 1993/94 at September each year. Includes grant maintained schools.

However, despite the fact that all students are now exposed to instruction in Welsh, a major concern is the inability of the bilingual sector to retain its numbers and proportions at each successive stage in the educational system. Thus there is an acute discontinuity between primary and secondary level. About 19 per cent of children leave primary schooling as first language (or fluent) Welsh speakers, but less than 14 per cent of Year 7 secondary pupils are taught Welsh as a first language. By year 11 about 12 per cent of pupils are taught Welsh as a first language.[34]

In Higher Education there is only a modest range of vocational and non-vocational courses available to full and part-time students. In all such developments the numbers involved within any particular course are small. Even so the trend and direction of change is significant for it extends both the domain use and practical utility of bilingualism in society.

The development of a lively and innovative publishing sector has also contributed greatly to the enjoyment of written and read Welsh. By comparison with English the range and overall quality leaves much to be desired; although given the constraints, which face any lesser-used language, the output is remarkable. A third of all books are school texts or children's books, initially dealing with Welsh themes by Welsh authors, but increasingly translating the more popular English-medium stories, reference books and visually stunning discovery and factual/documentary guide books. Adult books are dominated by literary conventions which prize verse, prose, eisteddfodic competition winners and the like, reflecting the niche market of Welsh-medium publishing.

The greatest boost to the popular and technical use of Welsh was the inauguration of Sianel Pedwar Cymru (S4C, a Welsh language television channel) on the 1st of November 1982. For thirty years there had been a gradually expanding television output in Welsh with far reaching consequences for language reproduction, bilingual employment possibilities and status reversal of Welsh.

At a voluntary level there is an active network of *Eisteddfodau* (competitive cultural festivals) which nurture school and community performances of Welsh plays, or plays in translation, of musical items, poetry, craft work, art and design and scientific projects. More recently, the Urdd (The Welsh League of Youth) has re-interpreted conventional Welsh mass culture by adding go-carting, tenpin bowling, discos, and surfing "in Welsh". An additional voluntaristic element is the adult learning of Welsh through Wlpan and related schemes which are geographically widespread and well attended. These in turn often feed Welsh clubs and social centres, which may have sport, folk dancing or music as their focus, but offer a wider entry into the indigenous culture. Capping all this is the healthy and vibrant Welsh popular music scene, which has emerged since the 1970s. It reflects a fusion of three trends: indigenous Welsh music, a revitalised Celtic music industry, and the international popularity of Welsh bands, such as Catatonia, the Manic Street Preachers and Gorki Zygotic Monkeys who perform in both Welsh and English.

Most of the financing for this burgeoning cultural revival has come from community support and Welsh Office/WAG funding for Welsh language education, together with many social activities, for example, Mudiad Ysgolion Meithrin (the Welsh Nursery Schools Movement, founded in 1971), Eisteddfod Genedlaethol Cymru (the National Eisteddfod of Wales), Cyngor Llyfrau Cymraeg (The Welsh Books Council) and some economic activities such as Menter a Busnes (Business and Enterprise), which promotes enterprise in Welsh-speaking networks and communities. However, there remain several crucial sociolinguistic questions. If provision is increasing apace in most domains, what of the actual usage, status and application of bilingual skills in the market place? What is the relationship between providing an opportunity to use Welsh and changing behaviour so as to take advantage of such opportunities? Can top down planning and legislation change the context within which English and Welsh compete?

A statutory framework for the Welsh Language

Legislation has been critical both in abrogating and in authorising linguistic rights, and in influencing the infrastructure wherein such rights can be exercised without let or hindrance.[35] Welsh social reform has been progressed in education, language rights and governance, by the *Education Act* of 1988, the *Welsh Language Act* of 1993 and the *Government of Wales Act* of 1998, which authorised the establishment of a National Assembly for Wales following elections in May 1999.

The *Welsh Language Act* 1993 has inaugurated a new era in language policy and planning, principally through the strengthening of the Welsh Language Board by placing it on a statutory basis. Although the Act is currently the subject of much criticism in that it has proved too restrictive in guaranteeing a wider range of opportunities to use Welsh in more situations, nevertheless it has triggered an improvement in the formal position of the language within Welsh public life. The Act's key provisions are that it places a duty on the public sector providing services to the public in Wales to treat Welsh and English on an equal basis. Currently the Act may be interpreted in terms of three relationships, namely that between the NAfW and Welsh public institutions, the NAfW and UK central government, and central government in relation to Wales. The functions for each set of relationship are identified in Wales Legislation Online as follows:[36]

1. Those Ministerial functions under the 1993 Act which are exercisable solely by the Assembly in relation to Wales, namely:

   - section 2 and Schedule 1: Appointment of members of the Welsh Language Board.
   - section 3: Power to approve the making by the Board of grants, loans, guarantees or the acquisition or disposal of land.

- section 4 and Schedule 2: Power to give directions to the Board as to the exercise of its functions; approval of number of and conditions of service of Board's staff; power to pay Board's expenses.
- section 6: Power to specify a person or a description of persons as a "public body" for the purposes of the Act.
- section 8: Power to determine objections to time limits placed on a public body by the Board to submit Welsh language schemes.
- sections 9 and 10: Approval of draft and final guidelines prepared by the Board and approval of revision of guidelines.
- section 14: Power to request a public body and the Board to reach agreement as to the contents of a scheme; power to decide the contents of a scheme if no scheme is submitted by a public body to the Board.
- section 15: Similar powers, as above, with regard to periodic revision of schemes.
- section 16: Powers similar to section 14 in respect of failure between a public body and the Board to agree amendments to a scheme.
- section 20: Power to issue directions to a public body which has failed to take action recommended in a report prepared by the Board under section 19 of the Act.

2. Secondly there are those functions exercisable by the National Assembly for Wales together with Central Government or other bodies. The following Ministerial functions are exercisable by the Assembly concurrently with any Minister of the Crown by whom they are exercisable

- section 25: powers to give Welsh names to statutory bodies, offices or places.
- section 26: powers to prescribe Welsh forms to any document or form of words.

Other provisions:

The Treasury approval requirement under paragraph 12(2) of Schedule 1 shall continue in effect. Schedule 1 paragraph 12(2): The statement of accounts shall contain such information and shall be in such form as the Secretary of State may, with the approval of the Treasury, direct.

The functions of the Comptroller and Auditor General in paragraph 12(3) and (4) of Schedule 1 are transferred to the Auditor General of Wales in relation to accounting years beginning in and after 1999 and in relation thereto paragraph 12(4) shall have effect so that for the requirement to lay before each House of Parliament the documents referred to therein, there shall be substituted a requirement for the Auditor General of Wales to lay those documents before the Assembly.

- Schedule 1 paragraph 12(3): The Board shall send copies of the statement of accounts to the Secretary of State and the Comptroller and Auditor General no later than the 31st August following the end of the accounting year to which the statement relates.
- Schedule 1 paragraph 12(4): The Comptroller and Auditor General shall examine, certify and report on the statement of accounts and shall lay copies of the statement and of his report before each House of Parliament

paragraph 6(3) of Schedule 1 shall have effect only to allow attendance at meetings of the Board of a person appointed by the Assembly.
Schedule 1 paragraph 6(3): The Secretary of State or a person appointed by him may attend meetings of the Board.

3. Thirdly there are those functions exercisable solely by Central Government in relation to Wales. The following Ministerial functions under this Act have not been devolved to the Assembly in relation to Wales

   "any function of the Treasury:

   - section 3(4): The Welsh Language Board shall not make a grant or loan, give a guarantee, or acquire or dispose of any interest in land, except with the approval of the Secretary of State given with the consent of the Treasury.
   - section 17(3): The Board may pay to any person who attends or provides information for the purposes of an investigation sums in respect of the expenses properly incurred by him, and allowances by way of compensation for the loss of his time, in accordance with such scales and subject to such conditions as may be determined by the Secretary of State with the approval of the Treasury.
   - section 24(3): The Lord Chancellor's powers to provide, employ and remunerate interpreters before courts in Wales shall be exercised with the consent of the Treasury.
   - Schedule 1 paragraph 3: The Secretary of State may determine such remuneration and allowances, the provision of pensions to or in respect of the members of the Board, whether there are special circumstances offering compensation to a person ceasing to hold office as a member of the Board, and it may determine the amount the person would receive from the Board, with the approval of the Treasury.
   - Schedule 1 paragraph 8: In determining the number of the Board's staff, the remuneration, allowances and gratuities to be paid to or in respect of the staff, and the other terms and conditions of the service of the staff, the Board shall act only with the approval of the Secretary of State given with the consent of the Treasury.

- Schedule 1 paragraph 1(9): The Board shall pay the treasury, at such times as the Treasury might direct, such sums as the Treasury may determine in respect of the increase attributable to sub-paragraph (1) above in the sums payable out of money provided by Parliament under that Act.

- Schedule 11: The expenses of the Board, up to such amount as may be approved by the Secretary of State with the consent of the Treasury, may be defrayed by the Secretary of State" (Source: Wales Legislation Online: The Welsh Language Act, 1993).

The 1993 Welsh Language Act's chief policy instrument is the Welsh Language Board, established on 21 December 1993, as a non-departmental statutory organisation. Initially funded by a grant from the Welsh Office, it is now funded mainly by the National Assembly Executive, which in the year ending 31 March 2008 is scheduled to total £13, 454,000. It has three main duties:

1) Advising organisations which are preparing language schemes on the mechanism of operating the central principle of the Act, that the Welsh and English languages should be treated on a basis of equality.
2) Advising those who provide services to the public in Wales on issues relevant to the Welsh language.
3) Advising central government on issues relating to the Welsh language.

The Board is an Assembly Sponsored Public Body whose funds are voted by the Assembly and whose eleven members are appointed by the Assembly Secretary through open competition.[37] Their responsibility is to provide direction to the Board and to guide and oversee its work. Although separate from the Civil Service, Board officials are public servants whose duty is to implement legislation. Despite its wide-ranging remit, the Board was for a long time a relatively small organisation, numbering 32 staff at 31 March 2003 which by 31 January 2007 had grown to 83 staff located in Cardiff together with regional offices in Carmarthen and Bangor.

The Board has five core functions, namely: (i) promoting and facilitating the use of the Welsh language; (ii) advising on and influencing matters relating to the Welsh language; (iii) initiating and overseeing the process of preparing and implementing language schemes; (iv) distributing grants to promote and facilitate the use of Welsh; (v) maintaining a strategic overview of Welsh-medium education. Though the Board's remit extends to cover anything to do with the Welsh language, direct responsibility for policy formulation and service delivery for the vast majority of Welsh language matters does not lie with the Board, but with other organisations. The Board acts as facilitator and advisor, working in co-operation and partnership with organisations and as the planning agency seeking to share its vision and mission with its partners.

At the outset the Board set itself four priorities:

1) to increase the numbers of Welsh-speakers.
2) to provide more opportunities to use the language.
3) to change the habits of language use and encourage people to take advantage of the opportunities provided.
4) to strengthen Welsh as a community language.

In order to increase the numbers speaking Welsh it has focused its efforts on normalising the use of Welsh, especially among young people, by seeking to:

- ensure that the provision of Welsh-language and Welsh-medium education and training is planned in conjunction with the key players, to ensure an appropriate level of provision for young people to obtain Welsh language education services;
- discuss and formulate policies and effective initiatives for promoting the use of Welsh among young people, in conjunction with relevant organisations;
- ensure the proper provision of public and voluntary services for young people through the medium of Welsh (in conjunction with public and voluntary bodies);
- provide grants for initiatives which promote the use of Welsh among young people.

The Board's second objective is

to agree measures which provide opportunities for the public to use the Welsh language with organisations which deal with the public in Wales, giving priority to those organisations which have contact with a significant number of Welsh-speakers, provide services which are likely to be in greatest demand through the medium of Welsh or have a high public profile in Wales, or are influential by virtue of their status or responsibilities.

In order to increase such opportunities the Board has:

- agreed Welsh language schemes with organisation in accordance with the stated objective;
- encouraged providers of public services to regard the provision of high quality Welsh-medium services on a basis of equality with English as a natural part of providing services in Wales;
- encouraged Welsh-speakers through marketing initiatives to make greater use of the services available through the medium of Welsh;

- worked closely with the voluntary sector in formulating and implementing Welsh language policies, particularly in relation to the delivery of child- or youth-related services and special needs;
- promoted and facilitated the use of the language in every aspect of education and training and ensured that appropriate provision is made for persons who wish to learn Welsh;
- maintained an overview of the strategic educational plans and schemes of all education authorities and establishments, and has created partnership with the agencies concerned to improve provision where appropriate;
- ensured that planning of provision for vocational education and training takes account of potential increases in demand from employers for Welsh-speakers;
- promoted the authorisation and standardisation of Welsh-language terminology, in conjunction with relevant academic and professional bodies;
- encouraged professional training and recognised standards for translators working with Welsh;
- ensured that appropriate Welsh-language software continues to be developed to meet the needs of users;
- encouraged the increased provision of Welsh in the private sector.

A third objective is to change the habits of language use and encourage people to take advantage of the opportunities provided. This is done through a series of innovative marketing campaigns, including attractive bilingual public display signs, the development of a Welsh spellchecker and on-line dictionary, a direct Welsh Link Line for queries regarding the Welsh language and language-related services, a language in the workplace portfolio/file, a Plain Welsh campaign with excellent guidelines for writing Welsh, a Welsh version of Microsoft computer functions and constant improvements to the IT infra-structure so necessary if a worthwhile language choice is to be made by the general public.

The WLB's fourth objective is "that Welsh-speaking communities be given the facilities, opportunities and the encouragement needed to maintain and extend the use of Welsh in those communities". The Board has committed itself to,

- undertake research into the linguistic make-up of Welsh-speaking communities and the social and economic factors which affect them;
- identify the main threats to the Welsh language within Welsh-speaking communities, and formulate effective action plans for addressing potential problems in conjunction with key players across all sectors;
- discuss and develop with unitary authorities, especially those in the traditional strongholds, their role in terms of administering language initiatives and co-ordinating language policies;

- promote co-operation between communities to foster mutual support, encouragement and understanding;
- assess the effectiveness of existing community-based initiatives (such as "Mentrau Iaith") as a means of promoting the use of Welsh and their usefulness as a model for facilitating the creation of new locally-run initiatives;
- facilitate the establishment of local language fora to promote Welsh language initiatives, to create opportunities for using Welsh and to motivate and encourage people to do so;
- promote the learning of Welsh by adults (including the provision of worthwhile opportunities to use Welsh outside the classroom and other ancillary support);
- provide grants to support activities to strengthen Welsh within the community. After five year's work the Board made the following observation on how it saw things developing.

The *Welsh Language Act* of 1993, the *mentrau iaith*, the spread of bilingual education at primary and secondary level, Welsh as a compulsory subject in the National Curriculum, the vitality of movements such as *Mudiad Ysgolion Meithrin, Urdd Gobaith Cymru,* local and national *eisteddfodau*, Welsh language schemes, increasing use of bilingualism and business and the economy are just a few of the many examples where language planning has successful bucked the trend of downward shift.

(WLB, Strategy for the Welsh Language 1999)

During 1999–2000 a revised strategy was formulated as "The Welsh Language: A Vision and Mission for 2000–2005" in which four areas of language planning were given priority.

1) Acquisition planning-producing new speakers of the language, through the school system and by teaching the language to adults.
2) Usage planning-increasing the opportunities to use the language through language schemes, running marketing campaigns to encourage people to take advantage of the opportunities.
3) Status planning – increasing the use of the language in domains such as information technology and the National Assembly for Wales.
4) Corpus planning-ensuring that standardised terms continue to be developed for new areas and ensuring that clear Welsh and user-friendly forms of the language are used by public sector bodies.

Operating on four fronts simultaneously is a huge challenge for any language promotional body, but the most concrete development to date is that since 1995 a total of 350 language schemes have been approved, including all twenty-two local authorities.[38] This has provided a series of contexts wherein Welsh can be used as a working language in accessing a range of services. Thus in a very real sense, despite all the attendant difficulties, the foundation for developing a bilingual public sector has been laid down. The next challenge is to maximise the use which citizens make of such provision.

Constitutional devolution and the bilingual operation of the National Assembly for Wales

A turning point in the struggle for recognition of Welsh as a national language was the establishment of the National Assembly for Wales in May 1999. The Government of Wales Act 1998 created the Assembly and it makes several references to the Welsh language.[39] The most significant and potentially most far-reaching is in section 32, which states that "The Assembly may do anything it considers appropriate . . . to support the Welsh language". The Act also established Welsh and English as the working languages of the Assembly which has operated from the beginning as a bilingual chamber, for it must treat both languages equally (as far as is both appropriate in the circumstances and reasonably practicable) in the conduct of its business; that is *all* its business, whether public or not. This is a more far-reaching norm that that previously encouraged under the 1993 Welsh Language Act.[40]

The Labour Government's unambiguous commitment to give equal status to both languages was transferred from its White Paper "A Voice for Wales" to the Government of Wales Act, and was warmly welcomed by many agencies and political parties.[41] The Assembly's standing orders have been devised so as to translate the principle of equal treatment into practice.[42] Accordingly the National Assembly is a body for the purposes of section 5 of the Welsh Language Act 1993 and has published Welsh language schemes in accordance with that section setting out how in its conduct of its business, including its business with the public, it proposes to give effect to the principle of equality.[43]

The Assembly's first term (May 1999–April 2003) was characterised by a number of initiatives and reforms, the most pertinent being the establishment of a powerful economic committee, the internal merging of key agencies to produce a more powerful and integrated Welsh Development Agency; the establishment of the National Assembly's bilingual structure and methods of operation, the development of vigorous education, training and language policies together with additional resources for a range of agencies, including the Welsh Language Board so it could implement its medium-term language planning and community development programmes.

A central issue facing the Assembly was to what extent Welsh was to become a cross-cutting medium of governance and administration and not limited to its own Culture Committee, that is, not become commodified and separated out as a "problem area". A second issue was the degree to which establishing a bilingual Assembly would influence the language-choice behaviour of the public. The Assembly recognised that it could directly influence related organisations by the manner in which it exercises its fundamental commitment to operating as a bilingual institution. This would involve the development of specialist bilingual translation and interpretation facilities, initiatives in terminology and corpus planning, the creation of bilingual and multilingual software, templates and computer programmes, all of which could be shared with other levels of government and improve the conduct of public administration. It would also influence the general public by scheduling a comprehensive televising of key debates, selected committee meetings and the adoption of sophisticated tele-communication systems to disseminate information.

Operational bilingualism, it should be remembered, is thus very new, quite novel in a UK parliamentary context and certainly not a prominent feature of the former Welsh Office system. Under the requirements of the Welsh Language Act 1993, the Welsh Office prepared a Welsh Language Scheme to be approved by the Welsh Language Board. However, subsequent developments have demonstrated that this formulation was essentially a patina of bilingualism, rather than an attempt to institutionalise Welsh as a language of work. This is significant because the Welsh Office was very much rooted in a monolithic English medium culture. Therefore, on devolution, the increasing expectations and pressure to work bilingually within the NAfW came as a jolt to the established working patterns of some and continues to be an issue of concern in the absence of a clearly defined and resourced internal bilingual structure. Many civil servants have yet to adjust to the legitimacy of effective working through the medium of Welsh, even if they have adjusted to the increased levels of responsibility they exercise.

Lest I seem too critical let me defer to Hazell who has commented that in terms of the devolution settlement "it is a tribute to the capacity of the Civil Service for muddling through that it works at all. But, as Rawling explains, that very capacity masks the need for fundamental change. To operate effectively the National Assembly is completely dependent on the political goodwill of Whitehall and Westminster, and with a change of government in London or Cardiff that goodwill could vanish in a trice" (Hazell, 2004, p. 247). One long-term implication within the devolution settlement is the possibility of establishing a distinct Civil Service for Wales, with all the attendant training requirements, including of course, the option for the successful acquisition of Welsh as a second language.[44] Currently, such provision is partial, fragmented and additional to statutory hours of work.[45]

A central determinant of the operation of a bilingual chamber and committee structure is the behaviour of the Assembly Members. One consideration for many AMs who use Welsh consistently is the perception that their contributions are under-reported by the media. Understandably this leads many to switch to English for selected parts of their contribution to debates or policy formulation. The Welsh language policy itself was initially entrusted to the Post 16 Education Committee, but after the creation of a coalition Cabinet it became the responsibility of a new Culture Committee. However, several of the AMs, together with the Welsh Language Board and independent commentators have questioned why Welsh (or bilingualism) was not made a crosscutting issue like Europe or Environment from the very beginning of the Assembly's life?

A more positive indicator is the willingness of AMs to either learn Welsh or to improve on their existing Welsh language skills. This is a major consideration if the Assembly wishes to be a more functional bilingual organisation and contribute effectively to social change.[46] Operating a bilingual public administration system in Wales poses a real challenge to the HE sector for there is an acute skills gap in the mediocre bilingual training on offer, especially in relation to legal affairs, IT and public administration.

The NAfW is responsible for developing its own internal language scheme and for devising a range of language policies to realise its aim of "creating a bilingual Wales". Interviews which I conducted during the first term of the operation of the National Assembly suggested that AMs welcomed the positive and instructive relationship between the NAfW and a strengthened Welsh Language Board. AMs recognised that there were pressing issues that only a stronger legislative framework could countenance, for example, the role of language in the workplace, in economic development and regional planning, in revitalising Welsh-speaking communities, in the judicial system, in health provision, and in retail and consumer affairs. The consensus was that this would be best achieved via amendments to existing legislation, although some expressed strong support for a new Welsh Language Act. Members welcomed the preparation of a new Assembly Welsh language scheme, within which bilingual conventions and practices could evolve. AMs use of Welsh in sessions was tempered by concerns over the cost implications of "un-prioritised" translation work, and the time lag in the receipt of Welsh versions of official documentation (up to five days later than English for committee papers) was said to disadvantage members who choose to work in Welsh.

A key division of the NAfW is the Translation Unit, which is performing exceptionally well even though for a long period it was understaffed. As at September 2000, it had a staff establishment of fifty-one. By April 2005 this staff complement had been divided into two services, fourteen worked exclusively for the Government while the remaining thirty seven worked for the National Assembly. However, recruiting high quality professional translators when offering only modest salaries remains a continuing problem.[47] The TU faces a number of other issues chief of which lies in convincing other elements of the NAfW that the role of the TU is to provide a translation service and not to be a one-stop shop for all matters linguistic. A second difficulty they face is overwork, for as the Assembly takes over the audit function of many agencies not previously subject to Welsh Office control, the translation needs of these agencies have been redirected to the Translation Unit. Currently the strategy that has been devised to prioritise and influence this exponential growth of demand for translation is still in its infancy.

A third difficulty is the perception that Welsh language planning need constitute nothing more than an efficient translation service. For some heads of section, there is little understanding of the skill and time requirements involved in providing a statutory bilingual service, and thus there is a tendency to underestimate the degree of professionalism and in-service training required in the discharge of this function.

A fourth consideration is the development of a bilingual Document Management System as a way of providing greater efficiencies. The *Cofnod* is both organic and adapted from *Hansard* and thus suited to British parliamentary procedures. The *Cofnod* offers a complete transcription service of all full meetings. It aims to provide an accurate bilingual record within twenty-four hours. The record of plenary sessions takes two forms: a) a working version for the Assembly Intranet within twenty-four hours; and b) an official bilingual version for archive use within five working days. Having translated contributions in Welsh into English, the remainder of the twenty-four hour *Cofnod* is sent to external professionals who translate it from English into Welsh. According to a six-month study of the *Cofnod*, this produces an average of 19,211 words in English per meeting. The resultant proceedings are saved in HTML and PDF format, and are mounted on a web server.

An abiding tension, as yet unresolved, is that the Presiding Officer's responsibility is to serve all AMs equally. Members of the Executive express increasing frustration that their urgent needs and special interests are not served preferentially by OPO personnel.

Future deliberations in national language policy will have to articulate how language opportunities and rights are to be implemented in relation to bilingual education and public administration, equal rights and the socialisation of citizens within civil society. This also involves *inter alia,* extra-Wales issues such as interaction with the British State and its unwritten constitution, the manner in which powerful UK departments, such as the Home Office and the Department of Works and Pensions, implement their Welsh language schemes, the European Union's language policies and the various international treaty obligations, such as the European Convention on Human Rights and the European Charter for Regional or Minority Languages. But the pressing concerns are the development of a bilingual society especially in terms of education, bilingual service provision in local government, health and social services and the legal system.[48] There is also an acute need for robust economic policies and regional development initiatives which seek to stabilise predominantly Welsh-speaking communities, to create employment, and to promote bilingual working opportunities. Doubtless there will be increased consideration given to the interests of the Welsh language and culture as they are impacted upon by town and country/structure planning and improvements to the transport system (James and Williams, 1997), even though it is difficult to determine exactly how the planning system can offset the most deleterious effects of house price inflation, property control and poor rural services. These are the stock-in-trade issues of those pressure groups such as *Jigso, Cymuned* and *Cymdeithas yr Iaith* which combine a concern with language survival with the quality of life issues of rural and small-town Wales.

A key difficulty which inhibits progress is the paucity of data available to inform evidence-based policy. There is an urgent need to supplement official language data by initiating a series of proposals which would include

a) regular statistical monitoring which focuses on real language *use* in addition to competence;
b) strengthening the relationship between the Welsh Language Board and the Assembly's Statistical Directorate, in order to provide appropriate data for language policy and planning;
c) collecting a wider range of socio-economic data which incorporates sociolinguistic indices;
d) together with the integration of the deliberations and the policies of stakeholder departments and the WLB, so that they have a mutually beneficial impact in the field of community development and economic regeneration (Williams, 2001).[49]

One professional field of great import identified by Rawlings is that "the provisions of the devolution statute ... signalled a new beginning, official commitment to the idea of Welsh as a living language of the law" (Rawlings, 2003, p. 258). There are several unique elements which pertain to the devolved administration such as its bilingual standing orders, bilingual debates, the bilingual daily record and the bilingual co-drafting of most of its legislation, comprising practically all of its general legislation as applied to the whole of Wales.[50] The consequence of this co-equal drafting will be an increased demand within the legal profession for bilingual lawyers, both within the National Assembly and within society.[51] Although the latter element is a departure within the UK's practice, it is commonplace within many EU jurisdictions and, of course, has become an integral feature of Canadian constitutional law. In 2000 and 2001, the Office of the Council General undertook a study visit to Canada and to New Brunswick (as the only bilingual province), so as to observe its constitution, system of government, law-making and justice that treat two official languages on a basis of equality. The resultant influential report resulted in changes to the Assembly's bilingual practice and policy and have recommended significant changes to the training and education of the judiciary in the use of the Welsh language and the use of the Welsh language throughout the whole criminal justice process (OCG, 2001). But it remains to be seen if these changes are fully implemented following the departure of their champion (Roddick, 2007).

Such lessons and subsequent changes are useful; however, the constitutional differences between the UK and Canada should not be glossed over.

> On the one hand, Canada is not only a bilingual but a bijural system (consisting of both civil law and common law jurisdictions). On the other hand, in contrast to a province like New Brunswick which also enjoys primary legislative powers, in the case of Wales it is only a kind of text – Assembly Orders – that has to be in two languages. At one and the same time, the scale of the task is much reduced, and a particular problem of fit with the other (English) legal sources is induced, most obviously in the form of a statute ... A further twist to the scheme of Welsh executive devolution is identified. Ideally, the minority language would be considered at the point of construction of any enabling power that is to be exercised bilingually. In a context of particular provisions in England and Wales legislation promoted by and negotiated with different central government departments, this is "pie in the sky". Turning the argument around, one point in favour of broad framework legislation on behalf of the Assembly is that this takes into account the necessary requirements of bilingualism by reducing the problem of language fit. A generous scheme of legislative devolution would effectively sidestep the problem.
>
> (Rawlings, 2003, p. 259)

This is precisely what the current arrangements seek to achieve, but it is far too early to gauge to what extent it is working.

Devolution has instigated other changes in the use of the Welsh language in the governance of Wales in fields of responsibilities not devolved to the Assembly, particularly in relation to the administration of justice in Wales. Since 1998, Cardiff's role as a regional centre for justice has been enhanced by the establishment of the Mercantile Court followed shortly thereafter by the Administrative Court of Wales. The Court of Appeal, Civil and Criminal Divisions, sit occasionally in Cardiff, the Employment Appeals Tribunal now sits in Wales in all cases arising from Wales and the Lord Chancellor has appointed to the High Court a judge whose fluency in Welsh enables him to hear and determine cases bilingually or entirely in Welsh, according to the wishes of the parties, without translation.

Contemporary Welsh language policy formulation

In June 2002 the National Assembly declared its aim of creating a bilingual Wales. This followed a comprehensive review of the language by the Culture and Education Committees, summarised in its final report *Our Language: It's Future*.

The Welsh Language Board, along with other participants, had pressed the National Assembly:

- To take ownership itself of the principles of holistic language planning;
- To treat bilingualism as part of its equal opportunities agenda, across all policy fields;
- To encourage every body which the NAfW sponsors to do likewise; and
- To investigate the true potential of existing legislation – both specific and non-specific to language.

The Government's response was its policy statement, *Dyfodol Dwyieithog: Bilingual Future* which asserted that the Assembly Government was *"wholly committed to revitalising the Welsh language and creating a bilingual Wales"*. It sought to support the language in a number of positive ways, by:

- Providing strategic leadership to sustain and encourage the growth of the Welsh language *"within a tolerant, welcoming and open Wales"*.
- Mainstreaming the Welsh language into the work of the Assembly Government and its agencies.
- Providing support for communities, including primarily Welsh-speaking communities, by pursuing policies which seek to create economically and socially sustainable communities.
- Ensuring that effective structures are in place to enable people to acquire or learn Welsh.

In 2003 the Assembly Government published its revised language policy, *Iaith Pawb: a National Action Plan for a Bilingual Wales.*[52] Its five aims are to:

1. By 2011 increase the proportion of Welsh speakers by 5 percentage points from the 2001 Census baseline.
2. Arrest the decline in heartland communities, especially those with close to 70 per cent + Welsh speakers.
3. Increase the proportion of children in pre-school Welsh education.
4. Increase the proportion of families where Welsh is the principal language.
5. Increase the provision of Welsh-medium services in the public, private and voluntary sector.

The measures set out in the Action Plan are to be assessed against a number of key targets while its principal policy options for achieving these aims are:

1. The WAG's newly established Welsh Language Unit.
2. Mainstreaming Welsh language considerations into all policy development.

3. Developing national language planning through the Welsh Language Board/Bwrdd yr Iaith which has been strengthened, in both human and fiscal resource terms (now 65 staff members and budget of c£12 million per annum), and given a central role in implementing the goals.
4. Developing the Welsh Language Board's research and analysis capacity.[53]
5. Creating evidence-based policies in the field of language revitalisation.

I have argued that *Iaith Pawb* is a genuine, historical commitment by government to put in place many of the recommendations highlighted by the Assembly's Education and Culture review, the most notable of which are:

- The operation of the principle of language equality.
- Devising an effective in-house bilingual culture.
- Deciding how Welsh will be a crosscutting issue in all aspects of policy.
- Producing bilingual legislation.
- Developing a professional bilingual legislative drafting team of jurilin-guists as in Canada.
- Developing innovative IT translation procedures.
- Prioritising the NAfW's translation needs.
- Finessing WAG's relationship with Welsh Language Board and its many partners.
- Relating its bilingual practices to other levels of government, institutions and to civil society.

Both statutory education and language transmission have been identified as the key arenas of action to achieve these targets. Successive campaigns have been launched to boost language acquisition, principally through the statutory 5–16 age education provision, life long learning, and latecomer centres. In an increasingly mixed language of marriage context the successful pilot project on Twf – the Family Language Transfer programme has been extended to other sites in Wales. There is also a commitment to boosting the bilingual services of NHS Wales, of *Iaith Gwaith,* the Welsh in the workplace programme. The government has also recognised that in order to access increased choice, there is a constant need to invest in language tools, resource development and the socio-cultural infra-structure.

But I have also argued that while *Iaith Pawb* contains fine rhetoric which legitimises policy, it is also replete with ill-defined mechanisms and says next to nothing on monitoring the effects of policies (Williams, 2004b). The discussion on education is a major weakness, and this lacuna is likely to be made good in a mid-term seasonal review. There is insufficient detail on developing Welsh within the statutory sector, on L2 learners, and no atten-tion at all to the rates of language attrition between primary, secondary, and tertiary level. Compounding this is that insufficient resources are available to deliver even what is promised in the strategy. Other main criticisms of *Iaith Pawb* that can be addressed towards this bold policy include:

- The lacklustre political will to implement the total strategy as a coherent package.
- Community regeneration is promised, but partial or deficient remedies are offered.
- Measures to safeguard the "heartland" are marginalised within the proposals.
- No focussed priority, thus the policy lacks political conviction.
- No proposed consideration of a stronger Welsh Language Act.
- Treatment of private sector is minimal and cursory at best.
- Far more professional attention to policy is necessary to make it convincing to economic interest groups.
- National planning policy needs specific guidance on how to treat the Welsh language as a material issue.
- Technical Advice Note 20 provides an outline of Welsh language considerations but is rarely invoked and in need of complete reform.
- No housing development guidance is provided.
- Linguistic impact assessments are needed.[54]
- Integration with Wales Spatial Plan is lacking (Williams, 2004b; 2006a).

In many ways the principal strengths of the *Iaith Pawb* strategy reflect the considerable input by the Welsh Language Board to the consultative process and to the formal and informal dialogue which is constantly undertaken between the Minister, the NAfW Language Unit and the WLB.[55] Recall that the WLB has both an advisory and monitoring role in terms of the NAfW's own Language Plan.

Even if government were to attend to the above, there would remain significant structural weaknesses in terms of the implementation of language planning in Wales. Thus even the agreed National Assembly Language Schemes can remain symbols of good intent rather than genuine services at the point of local demand. This not only bespeaks of an inefficient delivery of service but also suggests an absence of genuine participatory democracy. Secondly there is a critical need to monitor the aims and impact of all the language schemes, whether at national or local government level and within the public institutions, for many such schemes have been renegotiated and others have entered their third phase. The crunch question is just how much value has been added to public administration and bilingual service delivery by the adoption of such schemes? Has language-related behaviour changed? Finally and more philosophically the devolution processes promise of empowerment, ownership, participation and partnership needs to be rooted in a national infra-structure and not conceived as "add-ons" to an already over-worked if not overwhelmed public service.

Beyond the realms of public administration there remains the pressing need to promote Welsh within the private sector. This would include, greater political and legal encouragement, with sanctions where necessary, the adoption of holistic perspectives rather than a fragmented and sectoral mind-set; the development of appropriate terminology and sharing of best practice; a Language Standardization Centre; the highlighting of the economic benefits of bilingualism; encouraging a professional discussion regarding the role of Welsh in the economy; developing role models among the SMEs and larger companies; influencing key decision-makers who are often based outside Wales. Some of these issues are now being addressed for in the Autumn of 2006 the WLB established a Private Sector Division to add to its existing Marketing and Commercial Enterprise Division.

I have previously argued that if a revised strategy is to succeed it must tackle the following issues:

- Creation of a National Data Centre for the analysis, evaluation and monitoring of all types of statistics reflecting socio-economic trends.
- Establishment of a National Language Planning and Resource Centre centred on the Language Board.
- A review of the way in which Welsh is taught and used as a medium for other subjects within the Statutory Education sector.
- A comprehensive review of teacher training for Welsh medium and bilingual schools.
- Priority action in the designated "Fro Gymraeg" districts.[56]
- Action on the Concordats related to integrated planning and policy already entered into by the WDA, WLB, WTB, and ELWa.
- Urgent consideration to the need to expand the bilingual education and training opportunities afforded by the Welsh University and Further education sector.[57]
- Extension of the Welsh Language Act, to take account of the rights of consumers and workers within designated parts of the private sector (Williams, 2007).

Despite all the advances in the execution of language-related policy, both the political process and Welsh civil society has yet to determine the answer to several key questions which will influence our expectations as to what is appropriate action in the construction of a bilingual society. Thus we may ask in whom are basic language rights vested. Are they to be predominantly individual or institutional in character? Do individual citizens, regardless of where they live in Wales, have rights – or are we satisfied with restricting our statutory obligations to the public institutions charged with implementing an equal opportunities policy. How will the various European Conventions impact on this settlement and who deals with issue of monitoring. Very few opportunities had existed to debate such issues prior to devolution.[58] Since 1999 we have seen the development of think tanks, such as the Institute of Welsh Affairs, and many of the professions now have a stronger focus on Welsh affairs. Nevertheless the real danger in this scenario remains the inability of Welsh civil society to channel its limited energies into effective action. The absence of a mature civil society, which is underpinned by a number of national institutions, limits the full extent of citizen empowerment and engagement and thus reduces the practical import of deliberative democracy in policy formulation and the construction of an acceptable role for the Welsh language within the totality of civic and economic life.

A second set of issues is whether we maintain a public sector or plural domain approach to language policy? The initial language schemes were targeted at the public sector, education and the legal domains. But to be truly effective, language policy should seek to influence behaviour in most or all socio-economic contexts. Despite the tension between idealists and pragmatists which such an extension of social intervention occasions, there is an increased determination by language planning agencies and national government to promote bilingual work practices and champion Welsh language skills within the economy. Clearly there is the danger that such initiatives are driven from above only and that the heralded "partnership" conception of sociolinguistic intervention can appear hollow. Thus a critical question is how can the various partnerships between central and local agencies, community initiatives, the voluntary sector and the world of work, continue to mobilise society's energy to reinforce the central thrust of language promotion and implementation of language rights?

Vacillation and uncertainty: The pale shadow of "Y Dyfarnydd"

Language revitalisation measures and the devolution process have opened up new spaces and created new resources with which to construct a bilingual society. In that respect the characteristics of deliberative democracy enunciated earlier, namely reasonableness and partnership, have entered the debate over the role of Welsh in public life. However, elements of an erosion of this mutual trust and open, participative governance may be traced by reference to a number of significant changes. The first was the Assembly Government's decision in the summer of 2004 to abolish the Welsh Language Board and to integrate its functions within the Department of Culture, Sport and Leisure by April 2007. The second was the defeat of the government's proposed timetable whereby such integration would be achieved. A successful Opposition motion (NDM2613 on 11th October 2005) stalled the process. Plaid Cymru AM Jocelyn Davies (South Wales East) proposed that:

> The National Assembly instructs the Welsh Assembly Government to postpone the merger of the Welsh Language Board with the Assembly until the Assembly approves a motion which satisfactorily deals with the operation of the regulatory functions of the Board and the powers of monitoring the plans of local education authorities for the promotion of the language.

The motion was carried by a single vote as follows: For 29; Abstain 0; Against 28; Total 57. This development signalled two important changes in the discourse surrounding language. It demonstrated the Opposition's capacity to frustrate Assembly Government plans, in this case through a fairly acrimonious attack on the Government's record regarding the promotion of the Welsh language. Secondly the setback created a great deal of uncertainty, not only about the future direction and structure of the Welsh Language Board, but also in terms of how the Government was to handle the "integration" process.

In the event in July 2006, Alun Pugh the Culture Minister to whom the Welsh Language Board is answerable, announced that moves towards the integration of the Board would be suspended until several of the outstanding issues had been resolved. Four reasons may be given for this decision. First, a general unpreparedness on behalf of the Culture Department and of the Assembly to facilitate a smooth integration within the anticipated timescale. Secondly, a reaction to the specialist advice offered by the Welsh Language Board to the Assembly in relation to a number of key features regarding the consequences of its abolition and the need for further legislative reform. Thirdly the general drift of over 240 responses received as a result of the Assembly's Spring 2006 consultation process on the abolition of the Language Board. Fourthly the political ramification of Labour's failure to win the Blaenau Gwent National Assembly and Westminster seats on June 29th 2006.[59]

The Language Board continues to operate as if its status and role will remain relatively unchanged for the foreseeable future.[60] However, the recent debate concerning the need for additional legislation and regulatory clarity will intensify. In seeking to integrate the WLB the government announced that several regulatory and compliance aspects which the Board fulfils in accordance with the Welsh Language Act of 1993 would be discharged by establishing the post of *Y Dyfarnydd*.[61] On integration the government would assume responsibility for the preparation and revision of Language Schemes Guidelines and for the preparation of circulars on the implementation of Welsh Language Schemes. Government would also undertake the role of agreeing, monitoring and revising Language Schemes.[62] If however, the *Dyfarnydd* undertook these responsibilities that would necessitate direct involvement in policy development. The Welsh Language Board has argued that there is a need for keeping together the functions of agreeing and monitoring the implementation of schemes.

It is possible to argue that the *Dyfarnydd* could handle complaints regarding the operation of Language Schemes as part of the "regulatory cycle", as happens currently in some bilingual jurisdictions within the Commonwealth. This arrangement would also reveal how well bodies were implementing their language schemes. Language Board officials recognise that if these functions were separated, performance would be considered separately from the agreement on the content, and thus the *Dyfarnydd* would only consider the content of a language scheme and the complaint in question.

It is possible to strengthen the *Dyfarnydd's* remit by adding powers to conduct investigations where appropriate. Alongside this, consideration would need to be given as to whether the Government could also have the power to conduct investigations; since the Government's developmental work might draw attention to examples of non-compliance. An extension of this is the nature of the *Dyfarnydd's* adjudicative role in relation to a dispute between the Board and a public body, both in terms of the preparation of language schemes and in terms of their enforcement. A major weakness of the current system is that the Welsh Language Board has little real direct power to enforce compliance. Clearly it has recourse to normal procedures but when non-compliance is an obstacle to the implementation of the Act the only indirect avenue for the Board is to ask the political authorities, particularly its sponsoring Minister, to intervene.

In my opinion the following additional issues need to be addressed before government decides on the *Dyfarnydd* option. Should the appointment of a *Dyfarnydd* be a Ministerial appointment, or rather an appointment that is confirmed by the Assembly? Should the *Dyfarnydd* be an administrator or a public figure? Would a *Dyfarnydd,* or a Language Commissioner better serve the interests of the Welsh language? As it stands Government thinking about the role of the *Dyfarnydd* begs a number of questions. For example, there is little specification as to how members of the public might be able to complain directly to a *Dyfarnydd,* who may or may not be a publicly recognisable figure with a well understood remit. Neither is it clear how the *Dyfarnydd* would enforce the implementation of language schemes. Current arrangements do not require public bodies to provide information on request during an investigation, neither is there much evidence that individual bodies share their experience with other public bodies in dealing with such complaints. A stronger interventionist role for the *Dyfarnydd* could lead to a more consistent handling and resolution of complaints.

A further imponderable is what would happen if the *Dyfarnydd* were given the responsibility of adjudicating in any dispute between the Assembly Government itself and a public body regarding the content of a body's language scheme? Is this an essential function for the *Dyfarnydd?* Would there need to be reference to a further completely impartial body to determine the contours of language scheme enforcement? If not, how would the Assembly Government seek to handle cases where it itself was a plaintiff, an adjudicator and an ultimate arbiter for action?

Another issue is whether the *Dyfarnydd* should also be given a general advocacy role in relation to the language. This would be critical in relation to the implementation of the Assembly Government's Language Scheme and the Assembly Government's leadership of this particular policy area. Without this advocacy role, the Welsh language would be the only equality area lacking an advocate independent from Government. There are obvious dangers for the language in this respect. Section 3 of the current Act would enable the *Dyfarnydd* to undertake this role, but the boundary between the *Dyfarnydd's* functions and those of the Government would not be clear. New legislation could provide more clarity on this matter, conferring on the *Dyfarnydd* the right, and duty, to operate independently within a defined mandate.

Presumably the *Dyfarnydd* would have the right to ask a Court of Law for an order to enforce the recommendations. This would be the opportunity to appeal against the *Dyfarnydd's* judgements. This power would essentially mirror what is already included in the 1993 Act. A second issue would be whether or not bodies could be fined for language scheme non-compliance, and this would be related to the implementation of recommendations made by the *Dyfarnydd*. As a minimum it seems logical to revise current legislation so that the *Dyfarnydd* could consider the use of Welsh within public bodies, and within Crown bodies. It would also be possible to give specific powers to the Government to change the administrative language of its own offices, and those of other public bodies. A similar power has been established in Ireland under the Official Languages Act 2003. Current legislation does not give the Board a statutory remit in relation to Crown bodies. The Government will inherit this problem if it assumes responsibility for agreeing and monitoring language schemes. Placing the Language Schemes of Crown Bodies on a statutory basis would strengthen and simplify the regulatory system.

There is a risk that the *Dyfarnydd* would concentrate on the essential matters under the current legislation, namely the implementation of Language Schemes, and that other parts of the work of actuating and promoting Welsh would be lost within the office of the Assembly's Administrative Ombudsman. But as the Assembly Government has established independent commissioners for children and the elderly, the same independence, strategic overview and same status should be secured for the proposed regulator for the Welsh language.

Therefore it is vital that the proposed regulator be an independent voice for the implementation of the Act. This appointment should be for a fixed term, and should be made by the National Assembly rather than the Assembly Government. This would follow the pattern mooted in *Better Government for Wales*, for the Public Services Ombudsman and the Auditor General.

The proposed regulator should have the appropriate powers and resources to undertake his/her duties in a timely and effective fashion and have the defined role of supervising and implementing the linguistic legislation, in the exact same way as the other responsibilities provided, such as race and disability. In time one could envisage a network of Language Commissioners from Canada, Ireland, Wales, Northern Ireland, Finland and other parts of the world sharing their experience with Commissioners in cognate areas, such as Administration, Children, the Elderly, Health and Welfare.

While the proposed merging of the WLB and the establishment of *Y Dyfarnydd* has created a period of uncertainty, it has also exposed several structural weaknesses in the operation of language legislation and language policy. Some of these were contained in the WLB's response to the Government's consultation paper (WAG, 2006) concerning the integration of the Language Board and were expressed as follows:

- It is difficult to predict what effect the change will have on the position of the Welsh language. It could strengthen the position of the Welsh language, but it is quite possible that it will weaken it.
- The independent regulator suggested is not strong enough in terms of practical functions or arrangements. The independent regulator should be responsible for agreeing and monitoring the implementation of language schemes, and should be accountable to the National Assembly.
- The proposed regulatory structure has been complicated rather than simplified, with a risk that public services will decline and resources will be duplicated.
- There is a lack of clarity with regard to the arrangements for the interim period and when the *Dyfarnydd* will be established. Given this, would it not be more appropriate to establish the *Dyfarnydd* on a statutory basis before any powers are transferred? In making this proposal, it is not our intention to introduce any unnecessary delay into the process, but to ensure that the process and regulatory framework are both cogent and consistent, and build on the 1993 Act.
- The statutory function of promoting the Welsh language should be transferred to the Government or become the responsibility of the Government and the independent regulator.
- It will be necessary to maintain the flexible working methods and regional structure of the Board.
- The staff's right to work through the medium of Welsh must be protected and the staff must be maintained as a single entity.
- Success and progress should be measured on the basis of *Iaith Pawb* targets, the implementation of the Government's Welsh language Scheme and a strong statistical foundation (Welsh Language Board, 2006b).

A language commissioner for Wales

Establishing the role of *Dyfarnydd* would be a marginal improvement upon current arrangements, but I have cautioned that as it stands it is no more than an administrative tidying up exercise which falls far short of what is required (Williams, 2007).[63] For over thirty years I have been championing the case for a Language Commissioner who would undertake the following tasks:

- Conduct periodic and systematic investigations into the operation of Welsh Language Schemes.
- Investigate complaints and initiate investigations into breach of compliance.
- Supplement the Commissioner's traditional role as an ombudsman by expanding this protective role and serve as an educator, to better inform the Welsh people of their rights, and to consolidate the place of linguistic duality at the heart of Welsh identity.[64]

I believe that there are two overwhelming reasons why a Language Commissioner would be preferable to *Y Dyfarnydd*. The first is that the language struggle is far greater than an issue of administrative convenience and routine. The second is that by creating the office of a Language Commissioner greater attention will have to be paid to the issue of establishing language-related rights in Wales. In comparative terms, citizens in Ireland, Canada and Catalonia have a working understanding of what rights they enjoy in respect of official language provision and services. In Wales, it is difficult to be precise as to what exactly citizens may expect from government in respect of access to, for example, Welsh medium education or bilingual services. The 1993 Language Act places a duty on public bodies to treat both languages on a basis of equality in the provision of services to the public. This is done through the agreed language scheme which in practice can be unevenly and partially implemented. Consequently it is hard to generalise or predict the exact nature of the service being offered. Extending the range of language rights would fit into a pattern of explicating the nature of fundamental human rights.

While the Welsh language is an acknowledged part of the equalities agenda it does not figure prominently in comparison with discussions concerning discrimination on the basis of race, gender, sexual orientation or disability. The absence of such measures slows the growth of the use of the Welsh language in public bodies and inhibits the development and provision of Welsh language public services.[65]

I also believe that it is essential that the Office of Language Commissioner be established as an independent office charged with holding an overview of Welsh language legislation, dealing with complaints and undertaking investigations into the implementation of Language Schemes. But I own that currently it may or may not be advisable to ask such an Ombudsman to also act as a legal champion for the language, investigating issues regardless of whether or not an official complaint has been entertained.

A systematic examination of language rights reveals that it is in dealing with services to the public where the greatest discrimination appears. Both *Cymdeithas yr Iaith Gymraeg* (2005) and the Welsh Language Board have acknowledged that the origin of a service, whether it be offered by the public, private or voluntary sectors, is no longer as pertinent as is the nature of the service under discussion.[66] Clearly since the Welsh Language Act was passed in 1993, many parts of what was the public sector, such as the utilities, are now in private ownership. Sectoral boundaries are more fluid and it is increasingly common to see private or voluntary bodies providing services on behalf of the public sector. Thus bodies charged with providing a service to the public should be able to do so through the medium of either Welsh or English or both depending on the customer preference.

By specifying a range of conventional rights, the high level of uncertainty which currently obtains among the public would be reduced. A quick check list of some "rights" which have emerged as priorities would include:

- The right of children to receive Welsh-medium education.
- The right to learn Welsh as an adult.
- The right to correspond in Welsh with public bodies which come within the scope of the 1993 Act.
- The right to receive correspondence or information through the medium of Welsh from public bodies and designated private service providers.
- The right to use Welsh in a number of cases in dealing with the Health System, or in a public workplace.
- The right to contribute to a public meeting or inquiry through the medium of Welsh.
- The right to insist on a professional bilingual service from bodies whose Language Scheme has been approved by the Welsh Language Board.[67]

The National Assembly is the obvious forum for the enactment of legislation which would focus on the Welsh language to ensure that it can execute its policy responsibilities appropriately and fully.

New opportunities for "Better Government for Wales"

The White Paper on Devolution *Better Government for Wales*, published in mid-June 2005, presented proposals for amending the Government of Wales Act and is the Government's response to the Richard Commission. The Paper sets out how the Assembly's powers could be increased, giving it more freedom from Westminster legislation, how its structure could be reformed, separating the legislative aspect from the Welsh Assembly Government, and how its electoral arrangements could be changed. The White Paper's proposals offered the opportunity to transfer further responsibilities to the Assembly in future to legislate in specific areas.

An obvious and unique area where these new powers would be an advantage is in the formulation of language and education policy in Wales. Of course everything depends upon how the London and Cardiff governments would interpret their new relationship. But in theory, should the negotiations nominate bilingualism as a special policy area under the Welsh Government, this could give a significant boost to unique legislation in the area of bilingualism.

How would this transfer of function and responsibility be arranged? The "Orders in Council" are the key to this. They are Assembly Measures and not acts as such (although equivalent in their contents to Acts of Parliament) and it is wholly possible to identify the specific issues for which the Assembly would have statutory responsibility in ruling, say on linguistic matters, or education. Only those elements reserved either to Parliament or to the Secretary of State would be exempted from Assembly control. I have argued that the Assembly Government should make the transfer of powers pertaining to the Welsh language a priority in this respect. The creation of a bilingual Wales is a long term project and it will be necessary to amend the relevant legislation on a regular basis. Bearing in mind that the Assembly has executive functions pertaining to the Welsh language, it makes sense for the Assembly to have the power to change the legislation rather than having to compete for legislative time in Westminster. Any transfer of legislative powers should be broad enough to deal with a range of situations and policy areas pertaining to the Welsh language. What are the necessary steps in the proposed legislative devolution?

1. The Assembly Government and the Assembly submit an "Order" to the Secretary of State.
2. The Secretary of State lays the Order before Parliament.
3. House of Commons and House of Lords committees investigate the evidence and justification.
4. Debates of up to 90 minutes in both Chambers.
5. Approval from the Queen and Privy Council.
6. The Orders are subject to affirmative resolution but not to Assembly legislation.
7. The Orders include enablement conditions to allow the Assembly to prepare legislation.

In practice, this means that the Assembly can act as an informal Parliament, developing its powers in appropriate areas without having to go back and forth to Westminster. It is possible for the Assembly to claim that it has the responsibility and expertise to act on behalf of the language and therefore under this interpretation of the White Paper, the Assembly could request a near monopoly of power on developing its policies on bilingualism.

In furthering the legislative support for the Welsh language, the relevant clause for such an Order in Council could be as broad as "to protect and promote the Welsh language". This would accord with clause 32 of the Government of Wales Act, 1998. But in order for the Assembly to convince the Secretary of State, the Assembly is required to rely on Welsh civil society, prior to, during and following such legislation. In this respect, we would have a more comprehensive and constructive democracy than a number of other European countries, as henceforth the Assembly would be completely reliant on the public. A further implication would be to increase the legislative work load of Assembly Members. They would move from scrutinising subordinate legislation introduced by the Assembly Government to being legislatures of Measures all of which would have to be bilingual.

Here we must add a note of caution both in terms of the Assembly's lack of legislative experience and its tolerance for bilingual working practices. Rawlings has reminded us that "the scope for mismatch between the enabling statutes and subordinate legislation is bound to be increased by the disaggregation of the traditional central government model of doing business, and so call for even more careful policing in Wales ... As one would expect, the situations for 'adverse reporting' set out in standing orders closely echo the Westminster ones, for instance:

- doubt whether the legislation is within the Assembly's powers
- the legislation appears to make unusual or unexpected use of the powers
- the form or meaning needs further explanation
- the drafting appears to be defective.

The chief addition, naturally, is the bilingual element. The (Legislation) committee thus reports 'if there appear to be inconsistencies between the English and Welsh texts' which translates as seeking to ensure there are not" (Rawlings, 2003, p. 250). Speaking generally of legislative matters he warns of the need for vigilance against boredom and complacency for

> while there is an occasional nugget, so much of the committee's business is tedious in the extreme: an ambiguity here, a mis-translation there, and so on. It is worthy and necessary work, but from the view point of the political animal it represents the short straw. Against the backdrop, not only of subordinate legislation, but also of laws often driven from elsewhere, this is part of the grim realities of the life of the Assembly as a legislature (p. 250).

Nevertheless, following the May 2007 constitutional changes the Assembly Commission is the new legal body which holds the Assembly's property, appoints and lays down the conditions of service of its officials (who will no longer be civil servants) and controls its budget. My colleagues Lambert and Navarro argue that

> In losing its legal personality the Assembly will loose most of its executive powers. Instead of making subordinate legislation, the Assembly will have the power to approve or annul certain subordinate legislation made by the Assembly Government. .... Within the boundaries of the Orders in Council granted to it by Parliament, the Assembly will have the power to make laws which can contain provisions similar to those in Acts of Parliament. It can amend, repeal or add to existing or new Acts or make entirely new provisions in their place.
>
> (Lambert and Navarro, 2007, p. 17)

Naturally, all this raises fundamental questions regarding devolution. The implications of the full devolution of powers to legislate on the Welsh language for United Kingdom bodies which provide services in Wales would have to be considered. The Assembly should be responsible for setting the direction and determining the content of policies pertaining to the Welsh language. Given the appropriate powers so to do, legislative devolution of this kind would exemplify Rawlings' "deepening" and "widening" of Assembly responsibilities. For as he has observed

> items such as "culture, recreation and the Welsh language" speak for themselves. Fingered in an earlier age by the Kilbrandon Commission, it is inconceivable that a scheme of legislative devolution for Wales would not include them. If the Assembly cannot be trusted with full legislative responsibilities for such matters, which bear so directly on the "particularity" or national identity of Wales, what sensibly can it do?
>
> (Rawlings, 2003, p. 521)

The logic of legislative devolution would require a restructuring of the campaign for new Welsh language legislation through the "Orders in Council" which would require Westminster's seal of approval, but which would in turn transform the development and implementation of language policy made in Wales.[68] Seven steps are needed to turn promise into reality.

1) New language legislation enacted through the mechanism of "Order in Council";
2) Mainstreaming the Welsh language as a consideration and as a constitutional language in the preparation of the Assembly's legislative remit and as part of Westminster's general legislative programme;

3) Establishing the office of Welsh Language Commissioner;
4) Strengthening the Assembly's powers as a legislature;
5) Democratising the contribution of civil society by providing a truly valuable Language Forum or Welsh Language Council;
6) Integrating the work of the Welsh Language Board into the heart of Government as and when robust arrangements are completed;
7) Seek to convince the public and providers to change their behaviour in response to a combination of legislation, political ideology and the effect of the education system in creating greater linguistic awareness.

Much of this argument has won the day for following the establishment of a Coalition Government after the May 2007 elections, all political parties in Wales are committed to the establishment of a Language Commissioner. The precise duties and timing of such an innovative move are unclear, as is the future of the Welsh Language Board. Much depends, not only on how the Assembly Government wishes to handle the transfer of responsibilities, but also the interpretation which Prime Minister Gordon Brown's Cabinet and advisors places on the status of the Welsh language within the UK. However, what is not in doubt is the recognition that the Welsh language is now an integral element within the equalities agenda writ large. This recognition is a direct outcome of the devolution process.

Devolution and constitutional reform

Better governance has been ushered in by devolution, but it has come up against the stark logic of the exercise of power. That there was no clear long-term vision for the devolved territories is now very evident. But what has been achieved in a short space of time is truly remarkable.

> Between them, devolution for Scotland and Wales, subtle and far-reaching changes in the always distinctive governance of Northern Ireland, abolition of voting rights of most (though not all) hereditary peers, an Act promoting human rights, proportional representation for European Parliamentary elections and the devolved assemblies created by the devolution statutes, and a directly elected mayor of London have transformed the British Constitution, in a way that would have been unthinkable under the Thatcher and Major governments.
>
> (Marquand, 2004, p. 117)

This devolved constitutional pattern came about through successive stealth measures, none of which form part of a grand design and all of which appear to be pragmatic adjustment to a fast changing reality. The steps on the way include a *White Paper, A Voice for Wales, Llais dros Gymru,* (Cm. 3718 of July 1997), then a referendum held in September 1997, the *Government of Wales Act* of 1998 consisting of 159 sections and 18 schedules, the *National Assembly for Wales (Transfer of Functions) Order* (S.I. 1999/672), the *Memorandum of Understanding* and supplementary agreements between the United Kingdom Government, Scottish Ministers and the Cabinet of the National Assembly for Wales (Cm.4444 of October 1999), the *National Assembly for Wales (Transfer of Functions) Order* (S.I. 2000/253) which corrects a number of omissions and deficiencies in the first order of 1999 (see HL, Vol. 609, c488, 7 February 2000) and a variety of other related measures (Williams, D., 2000).

Despite such incremental pragmatism much concerning the devolution arrangement for Wales was novel within a British context. Sherlock (2000) underscores the fact by describing decentralisation, proportional representation, a bilingual Assembly and an obligation to develop bilingual legislation together with the obligation to comply with the rights set out in the *European Convention on Human Rights*, as truly radical departures from UK norms. She argues that

> The fact that an issue of such constitutional significance as the transfer of the bulk of the Assembly's powers could be achieved by subordinate legislation is also noteworthy. Likewise the regulation of intergovernmental relations within the United Kingdom not by legally binding instrument but by "concordats" described as a form of "pseudo-contract" by one academic is of interest.
>
> (Sherlock, 2000, p. 59)

Devolution has also changed the character of the British Constitution in requiring a greater degree of categorisation and definition in both the implementation of policy and the exercise of governance. Rawlings reminds us that previously internal processes of government are now external consequent to the establishment of formal inter-relationships between devolved administrations, and the subsequent awareness of the need for public accountability and scrutiny of these activities. The Assembly's procedures and structures are detailed in the *Standing Orders* that in turn reflect the *Government of Wales Act* 1998. In its attempt to ensure a form of inclusive politics the Act contains requirements which avoid the excessive dominance of any one group or the arbitrary exclusion of another. The Act also makes certain requirements of the standing orders of the Assembly together with the demands of a "full scrutiny" process.

Current arrangements are being revised to remedy two flaws, namely the fact that the NAfW has no legislative powers or powers of taxation. For unlike Scotland, Wales does not have direct revenue-raising powers, and unlike Scotland and Northern Ireland, the power to make primary legislation was not initially transferred. Equally significant, unlike Scotland and Northern Ireland, where all power is transferred except that which is expressly reserved, the NAfW may exercise only those powers expressly allocated to it under *section 21* of the Act. The Act is in essence an enabling mechanism under which the Orders in Council may be made to transfer specific powers to the Assembly. Some sections of the *Government of Wales Act* confer powers directly on the Assembly; e.g. sections 27 and 28. Orders in Council may not remove powers from the NAfW without the latter's approval. (See Jones, J., 2001, pp. 40–53 and Jones, T., 2001, pp. 6–12.)

Williams argues that the legislative devolution which has characterised the early life of the NAfW is federalism without the courage of its convictions, keeping Wales dependent upon Westminster and Whitehall. With regard to subordinate legislation and administrative action, the courts are equipped with the normal powers of administrative law, important in many instances, but removed from authority to strike down primary or quasi-primary legislation.

At first sight the eighteen subject areas in which the Assembly exercised competence up to May 2007 suggest an impressive array of domains in which all executive and subordinate lawmaking powers reside. However, rather than transferring powers to the Assembly by general area or subject heading, the preferred option has been to list powers section by section, sub-section by sub-section and to transfer the vast bulk of functions by an *Order in Council* of 1999 (S.I. 1999/672) (NafW, 1999).

Thus the initial division of powers within the Assembly was rather different from Scottish and Northern Irish arrangements in that the latter two legislative bodies had an Executive, which Wales did not. Thus while legislative and executive responsibilities were institutionally inscribed in Edinburgh and Belfast, the NAfW in Cardiff operated for much of its early life as a unitary "body corporate". In effect the Assembly had a unitary status but operated quite clearly with a Cabinet system. The growth of concordats between various UK governments and departments and the Assembly Cabinet, rather than the whole Assembly, turns on there being such a separation. Thus, critically when sharing information, the UK Government treated the Assembly Cabinet as a separate and distinct entity from the body corporate of which it is a part. This "body corporate" status had important implications, not only for "opposition" parties, but also for the position of the civil service within the Assembly. In contradistinction to Scotland and Northern Ireland where the legislative bodies have their own staff, which are quite distinct from the general civil service, in Wales no separate administration was established. Structural tensions were occasioned by such arrangements, as for example regarding the availability of legal advice for AMs, which is independent of the advice given to the Assembly Cabinet (Lambert, 2000, pp. 60–70). Clearly these lacunae have been addressed in the successive readings of the White Paper, *Better Governance for Wales,* and the consequent structural reforms that have made the National Assembly a more recognisable "parliamentary" institution.

Commenting on the first end of year report Sherlock concludes that despite all the constraints the NAfW has achieved a great deal.

> With limited extra staffing resources, the staff of the Welsh Office, largely concerned with the implementation of policy, have become the servants of a new legislative body which aims to innovate and develop, rather than merely follow, policy. Almost overnight there is a legislative body within the United Kingdom which drafts and makes its legislation bilingually and which sets its budget with input from "backbenchers". In terms of many of its procedures, it must be the envy of the most "modernising" Westminster parliamentarian, and its "family-friendly hours" approach leaves House of Commons all-night sittings looking rather archaic. The percentage of women both in the Assembly and in the Cabinet give a very favourable picture of intention to break new ground in the area of equal opportunities and it has remained well ahead of central Government in terms of freedom of information.
>
> (Sherlock, 2000)

A second issue revolves around parity with other nations within the UK. The membership of the British-Irish Council provided for in the Northern Ireland Act 1998 comprises in the words of the Good Friday Belfast Agreement "representatives of the British and Irish Governments, devolved institutions in Northern Ireland, Scotland and Wales, when established, and, if appropriate elsewhere in the United Kingdom, together with representatives of the Isle of Man and the Channel Islands". Remarkably the NAfW was the only body identified in this statement that does not have primary or quasi-primary legislative power.

There remains the West Lothian question. Currently Wales and Scotland are yoked together in most post-devolution discussions. However, whereas the Scottish White Paper of 1997 expressly envisaged that statutory provision for a minimum number of Scottish seats at Westminster would come to an end (4.5), and at the April 2005 General Election that number was reduced from 71 MPs to 59 MPs, the Welsh White Paper of 1997 expressly stated (3.37) that setting up the Assembly "will not reduce Wales's representation in Parliament". Williams (2000a, p. 55) avers that "if Wales is indeed to lose its admittedly preferential position at Westminster after all, then the scheme of 1997 will have delivered a double whammy to the Principality in the form of no primary legislative power in Cardiff and reduced representation in London".

A fourth issue is the doubt surrounding the future role of the Secretary of State for Wales, who should remain accountable and answerable in the House of Commons on major issues related to Wales. The consensus is that the Secretary, as representative of Wales in the Cabinet, should field questions related to Wales, even if there is a division of view between the

NAfW and Whitehall. A fifth issue is the contrast between the functionally clear and unambiguous Scottish scheme and the overly complicated and nuanced Welsh scheme. Williams argues that by nature the Welsh scheme of executive devolution involved not only a complex process of subordinate legislation, but also the inevitable particularity of the Orders transferring functions of the Welsh Office and other departments to the NAfW.

Clearly the constitutional settlement will continue to evolve; this has been recognised explicitly by a number of agencies and bodies, most notably the Royal Commission on the House of Lords in 2000 (Westminster, 2000) and the Richard Commission (2004). It was also the subject of the White Paper "Better Government for Wales" (2005). Devolution to Wales has brought many challenges as well as opportunities, for the development of distinct law and policy. Not the least of the challenges is that of establishing appropriate legal frameworks through Westminster legislation and Assembly subordinate legislation which would contribute to a body of Welsh law. I repeat that an appropriate issue for such unique legislation would be the fortunes of the Welsh language and the promotion of bilingual education (Williams, 2005b).

Finally both C.H. Williams and W. Roddick emphasise that devolution has not only made the Welsh dimension of generic UK policy more salient, but also that changes in the administration of the justice system have helped stimulate a greater sense of national identity in the practice of law, and by extension to other professional and public spheres. New institutional developments include, regular sittings of the Court of Appeal Civil Division and Criminal Division in Cardiff, the facility of issuing proceedings and having them heard in the Administrative Court in Wales, local sittings of the Employment Appeal Tribunal, the establishment of a Mercantile Court in Cardiff, the establishment of the Administrative Court of Wales, hearings in Wales rather than in London as was the normal practice of judicial review cases involving the National Assembly and all other public bodies in Wales. The appointment of a High Court Judge whose fluency in Welsh facilitates the conduct of trials bilingually or entirely in Welsh, according to the wishes of the parties, without translation is also significant.

Legislative empowerment

In May 2007 the Assembly became a legislature. The most novel feature of the Government of Wales Act 2006 is the way it creates scope to increase the powers of the National Assembly, by increasing its legislative functions in three stages (Trench, 2006, p. 689). Stage one in the transfer of legislative functions depends on the widespread use of framework legislation, an idea mooted by the Richard Commission as a transitional way of extending the Assembly's power. Trench argues that this convention rests on a slim foundation for such a significant constitutional development. He further argues that as permissive drafting needs application in each particular instance, it means that legislation will vary from Bill to Bill and function to function. More worrying there is no overall vision as to what the Assembly's functions are and how they are to be implemented.

Stage two involves the passing of Assembly Measures, by which the Assembly "may make any provision that could be made by an Act of Parliament" which are then approved by Her Majesty in Council, rather than receiving Royal Assent. Trench suggests that this is "clearly a considerable power to confer-especially on a body whose powers have hitherto been limited" (Trench, 2006, p. 691). He also charts the logic by which Orders in Council will determine which powers are to be transferred from Westminster. Inherent in this is the critical role of the back-bench Welsh M. P.s and the Welsh Affairs Committee in the Commons, whose debates will determine not just the principle of conferring legislative powers on the Assembly, but also the use the Assembly proposes to make of such powers. There is a clear implication that the scrutiny process could result in a confusion of the constitutional issues and the political ones resulting from the Assembly Government's proposed policy. In effect this "amounts to holding the Assembly directly accountable to Parliament rather than its own electorate" (Trench, 2006, p. 691). A further difficulty is that the scope of deciding what powers within the Act's framework are to be acquired and when it is an entirely political consideration. Currently a Labour administration governs both at Westminster in coalition partnership with Plaid Cymru in Cardiff Bay, but successive elections could give rise to an alternative scenario, whereby confusion and prevarication reign. Rather mischievously, Trench raises the possibility of a third option, namely that "the Bill creates a framework for the exercise of legislative powers that will be seldom used, at least while Labour is able to dominate governments in both Cardiff and London and framework powers in Westminster can be used instead"[69] (Trench, 2006, p. 692).

Stage three involves the holding of a referendum to enable Pt 4 of the Act to be implemented. Trench comments that it is the most notable area where the Act postpones key decision, and where decisions are kept from the Assembly and given to the Secretary of State instead. This is because a referendum will be determined by the Secretary of State following a request form the National Assembly.[70] The Assembly powers will be substantial but not "full" ones comparable to the Scottish Parliament. A great deal of legislation would still be made at Westminster, using a version of the Sewel convention provided the Assembly consents. In many cases it would be prudent for the Assembly to follow the UK government lead, but Trench concludes that by such an arrangement what "stage three heralds, then, is not so much autonomy for Wales in devolved fields or matters, as an increased degree of autonomy coupled with increased strength in intergovernmental matters. However, that increased strength will be limited by the powerful role that the Secretary of State will continue to play" (Trench, 2006, pp. 693–4). If the Assembly should gather increased powers unto itself, as seems inevitable, then the role of the Secretary of State at stage three will become increasingly anomalous, and rather than being seen as a conduit between Cardiff and London will be seen more as a barrier to greater autonomy in Wales.

For the immediate future, governments at London and Cardiff will come and go. Let me conclude by stating that in the meantime Welsh language policy will continue to evolve and be shaped as much by the contours of political life as by the needs of Welsh speakers, for as Alistair Cooke observed those many years ago

> since there is-thank God-no thumping majority for a single ideology, the incoming government liquidates its rhetoric and the outgoing government promises a livelier fireworks show next time. In the meantime everybody enters what a modern poet calls those "spaces between the stars" which say "what common sense has seen". We settle down to the long, gray pull of mending and making do, the day-to-day duties and favors and shenanigans and small kindnesses, and the grumbles and chores of life. In a democracy, anyway, most government-and most of life, I shouldn't wonder-is conducted In the Meantime.
>
> (Cooke, 1979, p. 273)

Notes

1. I make no claim here that the language struggle is coterminous with the national struggle, but that historically it is the most expressive element of national distinctiveness.
2. The First Statute of Westminster (1284), also known as the Statute of Rhuddlan, was designed "to put the country of Wales and her inhabitants under feudal authority ... and ... to annex and unify the said country with the crown of the Kingdom (of England) ... in one political body". The Statute was repealed by the Statute Law Revision Act of 1997. Such facts are constantly referred to in daily newspapers, in this instance by a letter to the Western Mail written by G.Hopkins of Llangennech, and published on December 7th 2006.
3. The Glyndŵr Rebellion (1400–1415) would be an obvious example of local opposition. I do not accept that it was a national uprising as many nationalist historians have sought to portray it. But I do accept that the plea for Welsh independence and the autonomy of a Welsh Church contained in the "Pennal programme" of 1406 became deeply engrained ambitions within popular consciousness well into the twentieth century. Significantly the rebellion also left a trail of national destruction, most especially the Welsh monasteries. See Williams, G. (1997, pp. 72–104).
4. This is best represented in the literary work of Dylan Thomas, Gwyn Thomas and R.S. Thomas. For an overview of the field see Thomas (2006).
5. More prosaically, it was a mass movement within which ordinary people could achieve some degree of upward social mobility. Its strength lay in its ability to represent marginalised people and places, particularly those drawn from the

Celtic periphery and from the burgeoning urban settlements that were under-represented in the Tory-dominated shire counties and long-established market towns.

6. Despite the ravages of secularisation the church and chapel system has long been a pillar of support for Welsh cultural maintenance and its impact even today should not be underestimated.

7. The nationalist movement sought to differentiate itself from political movements based upon imperialist or social class appeals, by advocating policy initiatives related to the restitution of Welsh as the national language and Wales as a self-governing nation. It is no exaggeration to claim that much of the language-related activity since the 1920s have been a playing-out of the agenda set by early Plaid Cymru leaders. For details and discussion, see McAllister (1995) and Gwilym (2000).

8. Nationalism is not an autonomous force, and we should be careful not to inter-pret individual nationalist activists as agents of a transcendent ideology, but rather as part of practical politics, providing a context within which one could measure the success of the national programme for the survival of a distinct Welsh identity.

9. See Goldring (1993), Brown (1985) and Ó Riagáin (1997). Individual groups, which subsequently merged with Plaid Cymru, were more heavily influenced by the Irish direct action methods, the best known of which were the Arfon slate quarry workers.

10. The very same religious press and élite had earlier condemned the use of violence against fledgling Afrikaner nationalism in the Boer Wars.

11. Again the exception would be the calculated symbolic use of destruction of state property in the burning of the bombing school in Penyberth, for details see Davies (1983), pp. 154–66.

12. At the 1938 Plaid Cymru conference held in Swansea, delegates adopted, by an overwhelming majority, Gwynfor Evans' motion that "as a party we completely reject war as a means of achieving self-government". In contrast Lewis had been disappointed by the performance of the Party since the Bombing School incident and took consolation from the pacifist supporters' recognition of the tactical utility of adopting civil disobedience on the Gandhian pattern. In arguing that sacrifice and suffering should characterise the struggle ahead, Lewis anticipated the actions of the language movement some thirty years hence when he asserted that "One path alone leads to the gateway of the Welsh Parliament. That path runs directly through the prisons of England". *Y Ddraig Goch*, September 1938 quoted in the detailed discussion of the conference in Davies (1983), pp. 167–8.

13. The three aims of *Plaid Genedlaethol Cymru* in 1925 were all related to the pro-motion of Welsh. The main aim of *Plaid Genedlaethol Cymru* was "to keep Wales Welsh-speaking. That is, to include (a) making the Welsh language the only official language of Wales and thus a language required for all local authority transactions and mandatory for every official and servant of every local author-ity in Wales; (b) making the Welsh language a medium of education in Wales from the elementary school through to the University". Quoted in Philip (1975), p. 14; see also Davies (1983).

14. Although preoccupied with questions of language defence, the nationalist intelligentsia did not adopt a narrow conception of their predicament.

15. Namely Liberalism with its insistence on individual freedom and mutual tol-erance as a means of overcoming the lack of social justice and Socialism with its materialistic explanation of inequality. Particularly significant in this respect

was the work of Davies (1931) whose admiration for Scandinavian social credit policies, economic co-operation and decentralisation of power were rehearsed also by Noëlle Davies (1939). For a critique of the class versus nationalist appeals see Davies (1980).

16. Control of the state apparatus so as to make it more accountable and more reformist was the principal goal.

17. There are many parallels to be explored between idealists such as Saunders Lewis and Sabino de Arana, Valenti Almirall, Yann Foueré, E.MacNeill and Éamon de Valera.

18. "The Principles of Nationalism", delivered at Plaid Cymru's first Summer School in 1926. For development of his ideas see the collections in Lewis (1985) and (1986). Lewis believed that medieval Europe possessed a unity of spirit and of law, which protected and nurtured small nations because diversity could only be accommodated within a universal European civilisation.

19. See Lewis, 1975, p. 7. For a variant on the same theme see also Jones (1994).

20. Quoted in Jones (1973), p. 33.

21. These conflicting interpretations are summarised in the exchange, which took place in the pages of *Y Llenor* in 1927. In responding to criticism of the rise of a "Neo-Catholic Movement in Wales", Lewis distanced himself from other nationalists, such as Ambrose Bebb, who were charged with admiring the ideas of Barres and Maurras and with advocating the adoption in Wales of the ideas trumpeted by *L'Action Française*. W.J. Gruffydd's reply has been described as "an eloquent statement of that radical liberal individualism which had been Wales's main political tradition in the second half of the nineteenth century". (D.H. Davies, op. cit. pp. 109–16). Whereas Lewis's ideas are based on a pristine conception of what Wales could and should be, Gruffydd and those he represented portrayed Wales as it was, and wanted to advance Wales into a co-equal, fully recognised partnership within the British state, wherein Welsh distinctiveness might be secured (Williams, 2000a). For a re-examination of the relationship between Fascism, anti-Semitism and the views of Lewis and his colleagues, see Jones (1998), pp. 324–35.

22. Of course, several valleys in the Peak District and in the Pennines were also converted into reservoirs, but that did not figure prominently in Welsh discourse.

23. His father, Daniel Evans, was a department store owner and a deacon at *Tabernacl* Independent Chapel, Barry, Glamorgan, then one of the most anglicised, thriving towns in Wales. Never fully conscious of his nationality until he went up to Oxford, and re-learned Welsh, he was always something of an enigma, simultaneously embodying and standing apart from mainstream Welsh culture. In protest at the jingoistic justification of the Second World War, he preached pacifism in his home-town main square among other places and shunned the armed forces for a life as a market gardener in Llangadog, then steeped in Welsh rural culture. For details see Evans (1986).

24. Evans acknowledged that "if I thought violence could ever be justified in the pursuit of any social objective it would be to secure freedom and full nationhood for Wales, the cause in which most of my life has been spent. But even this noble cause, on which the survival of the Welsh nation depends, does not in my view justify the use of violence" (1986), p. 16.

25. See Fennell's (1977) and Hindley's (1990) accounts of the slow death of Irish, which confirms this fact. Today many argue that Hindley's analysis is far too pessimistic and based on an insufficient understanding of current influences.

26. See J. Davies (1981); (1985) and Williams (1982); (1994). See also McAllister (1995).
27. The three seats held were Caernarfon, Carmarthen East and Dinefwr and Meirionnydd Nant Conwy, the one seat lost since 2001 was Ceredigion.
28. In part this was a response to Nationalist pressure and also to Labour's commitment to satisfying the desires of parental pressure groups, and the increased self-esteem of Welsh speakers.
29. This figure should be regarded with caution for it is highly unlikely that many individuals aged five and over are unable to speak English in Wales (Williams, 1982).
30. Care has to be taken in the decennial comparison 1981–1991 because the definition and treatment of absent households changed in the intervening period. Thus if the population base used in the 1991 census is adopted, the Welsh-speaking population of Wales would be 508,549, some 18.7 per cent of the total population aged three and over of 2,723,623. In crude terms this suggests a proportional loss of 25 per cent, down from 44 per cent in 1911.
31. More recently Osmond (2002, p. 2) suggested that the "notion of a Welsh-speaking Wales, in the sense of a geographical domain where Welsh is the dominant mode of discourse for a large majority of the population, no longer exists. Instead, we have a pattern of diverse bilingual societies within what used to be known as the Welsh speaking heartlands. At the same time, southern and eastern Wales can no longer simply be described as 'anglicised' but are also becoming bilingual, though again according to widely varying patterns".
32. For details of how census data can be compared over time see Martin *et al.*, 2002 (and Dorling 1995a,b). For a fuller discussion of the 2001 census results in Wales see Higgs *et al.* (2004).
33. Translated as The Inner Core Heartland and the Outer Core Heartland. Note how the discourse, if not the socio-economic reality, is similar to that which obtains in Ireland in respect of the Fhior-Ghaltacht and the Breac-Ghaeltacht.
34. Overcoming this dysfunction has been a central theme of the Welsh Language Board's educational initiatives. For an analysis see Baker and Jones (2000) and the papers produced by the WLB available at their website.
35. Since the *Acts of Union* of England and Wales, 1536 and 1542, Welsh had been proscribed as a language of officialdom and thus did not benefit from being institutionalised in the affairs of the state. These were in turn repealed by the Welsh Language Act 1993, section 35, Schedule 2. On legislation before the *Welsh Language Act* of 1967, see Walters (1978), pp. 305–26.
36. Wales Legislation Online is a service provided by the School of Law, Cardiff University to inform legal developments that pertain to the operation of the National Assembly for Wales. *http://www.waleslegislation.org.uk/*.
37. I recognise that the Welsh Language Board might be incorporated into the Wales Assembly Government sometime in the future. For the present its status and remit remain unchanged.
38. In 1998 notices had been issued to a further fifty-nine bodies to prepare schemes and, during 2000–2001, a further twenty-three language schemes were approved. By August 2006 a total of 350 language schemes had been approved (Welsh Language Board, 2006a).
39. A parallel attempt to strengthen Irish was occasioned when the Irish Government revised the Quality Customer Service principles and added three new principles, one being a new Official Languages Equality Principle. (Ó Ceithearnaigh, 2005, Personal Correspondence, Comdhail na Gaeilge, 23 November.)

40. Basic guidelines were specified in the *Government of Wales Bill* (1997), clause 46. While the *Welsh Language Act* (1993) speaks of treating Welsh and English on a basis of equality in the conduct of public business, the Bill, in Clause 46, is less limited in its scope.
41. See H.M.S.O. (1997).
42. The National Assembly Advisory Group (NAAG, 1998) outlined three principles regarding bilingual practice, namely that the Assembly should adopt and extend the Welsh Office's existing Welsh language scheme; that Members should be able to use English and Welsh in Assembly debates and committee meetings; and that members of the public should be able to use English and Welsh when communicating with the Assembly.
43. For a detailed elaboration of the legal implications of this requirement see Roddick (2007).
44. The Assembly's recruiting policy and training programme could also impact on the public sector and especially local government. Currently there is an acknowledged shortage of competent accredited translators, experienced language tutors, and skilled bilingual administrators and technical specialists. The training infrastructure for a bilingual workforce is woefully inadequate. Consequently special attention should be paid to how the Government's training agencies, are resourcing or failing to resource the required training programmes for an increasingly sophisticated, bilingual economy. The skills gap in the workplace needs to be addressed urgently if the relationship between the Assembly and the rest of the public sector is to operate harmoniously.
45. Several of the insights reported here relate to the findings of a study undertaken by Williams and Evas on "The Bilingual Character of the National Assembly of Wales" between May 1999–2001, and supported by the ESRC (Award Number R000222936).
46. When interviewed AMs and advisers noted significant difference in the linguistic working culture of the NAfW Cardiff Bay and the dominant monolingual operation of its Cathays Park site. Williams and Evas (1997, 2001) had earlier recommended that selected civil servants be released for extended periods of time in order to attend intensive Welsh language and language awareness courses.
47. The payment of translators was reviewed in the EU leading Ó Ceithearnaigh (2005) to argue that new recruits are now on a lower salary scale thus lessening the chances of recruiting top class staff.
48. Witness the recent establishment of three specialist legal associations, the Wales Public Law and Human Rights Association, the Welsh Personal Injuries Lawyers Association and the Wales Commercial Law Association. Cumulatively is estimated that legal services in Wales generate around £250 million of GDP that is around 1 per cent of the total and set to grow as the NAfW enacts more bilingual legislation.
49. As argued in Williams (2001), the WLB, the WDA, the WTB and their successor agencies needed to integrate their deliberations and policies so that they have a mutually beneficial impact in the field of community development and economic regeneration.
50. The necessity to produce bilingual legislation will also have a direct impact on the development of a Welsh-language legal community to match that of the media community, as co-equality of language use becomes a situational norm in many domains. It is imperative therefore that both the university system and professional training of legal specialist take due regard of this trend and attend to the very real employment and training needs of the profession forthwith.

51. David Lambert, at interview on 6th June 2005, advised that very good lawyers would need to be able to understand and interpret both Welsh and English versions of such legislation if they are to use the most favourable text for their clients.

52. Literally "Everyone's Language". It may be viewed on Welsh Assembly Government website www.wales.gov.uk.

53. The Assembly Government affirmed the WLB's role as the national language planning body which was central to delivering the Plan, and increased the Board's total grant by £16 million between 2003 and 2006.

54. Commissioned research on linguistic impact assessments involving 13 local authorities, two National Parks, the WLB and academic planners was sent for public consultation in 2004, but no significant decisions on revising the planning process have yet been taken.

55. The Welsh Language Board has been designated as the principal instrument by which this policy is to be realised and has been given significant additional resources so as to recruit more specialist staff, extend its remit and open new offices in Carmarthen and Bangor.

56. Of course this is dependent upon an official designation of the Welsh heartland districts and a consideration as to who will co-ordinate proposed remedial action.

58. I do not ignore the contribution of the National Eisteddfod and many pressure groups, as well as political parties, to the debate. However, in contrast to the more mature Scottish civil society, Wales lacks a set of authoritative and relatively independent conduits by which civil society can be informed and mobilised.

59. The vacancy in the Blaenau Gwent constituency was occasioned by the death of Peter Law on April 25th 2006 who held the seat at both the Westminster and Assembly elections. His Westminster seat was won on June 29th by Dai Davies and his Assembly seat by Trish Law the widow of the former incumbent. Both representatives sat as Independents.

60. At the time of writing a Labour-Plaid Cymru coalition government had been formed, following the May 2007 elections. It is too early to speculate on the possible permutations, but it is important to note that all political parties now support the establishment of a Language Commissioner. Should the Welsh Labour Administration be returned with a stronger mandate in future elections it could speed up the integration of the WLB. Alternatively should other political parties gain victory and establish a concordat between coalition partners then it is possible that we shall see the establishment of a Welsh Language Authority directly answerable to the First Minister, as is in currently the case in Catalonia.

61. Literally a referee or regulator. For details on this debate and the issues it brings forth see Williams 2007.

62. Legal specialists have suggested that there are two ways in which the Assembly Government, using powers which it currently holds, could establish a regulatory framework which would reflect the principles of the 1993 Act. The Board could retain its existing regulatory functions and the Assembly retain its existing appellate functions under the 1993 Act, even if all the other functions of the Board are transferred to the Assembly. Alternatively the Assembly could transfer all the Board's functions to itself, including its regulatory functions and its current appellate functions could be discharged by a Committee of AMs which would consider representations made under section 8(8) or 14(2) of the 1993 Act. There is a precedent for this in the Standing Orders of the Assembly in relation

to independent planning appeal Committees comprising AMs whose decisions bind the Assembly

63. The changing face of public-sector service delivery is reflected in the establishment of a Welsh Administration Ombudsman, with the promise of a revamped Wales Public Services Ombudsman, the Office of a Local Commissioner for Wales and Health Service Commissioner in Wales (HSCW) while the Children's Commissioner is to be supplemented by a Commissioner for Older People. None of the established posts have been over burdened with complaints from the public, partly, according to Rawlings, as a result of the lack of interface between public administration and civil society. Nevertheless for the period 2001–2002 the WAO "received fifty-six complaints, concluded fifty-nine cases without investigation (chiefly for lack of jurisdiction or no prima facie evidence of maladministration); and moved to a full investigation in only five cases. Although much higher (155 new complaints), the case load of the Health Service Ombudsman also appears unexceptional from the comparative viewpoint, both in terms of the rate of complaints and the subject matter" (Rawlings, 2003, p. 379).

64. Much of my thinking on this has been informed by a systematic analysis of the Canadian model since 1973 (see Williams, 1981, 1984 and 1996b) and more recently by my involvement with the "From Act to Action project".

65. Such considerations appear to favour *Y Dyfarnydd* rather than a Language Commissioner. The ombudsman model for local government would be read across to the language arena so that adverse publicity and political embarrassment would act as the principal instruments for compensation and restitution. Soft law, speedy internal processes of dealing with complaints, accurate feedback into policy and performance would all give the impression of responsive, open government. By integrating *Y Dyfarnydd* into an enlarged office comprising the WAO, the HSCW and others, systematic, routine procedures for dealing with complaints could be finessed with the minimum of disruption to the machinery of administration and good government.

66. This thinking has also influenced the position of Plaid, in respect of the report of their Welsh Language Policy Commission; see Plaid Cymru (2006).

67. In consideration of such rights there should be no legislative differentiation on a geographical basis, because it weakens the concept of equality within the nation, and because in comparable cases (Ireland, Belgium, Finland, South Africa), the pressure to alter the boundaries (that is to shrink them, not to extend them) about every ten years, tends to weaken the linguistic community.

68. I present this agenda for action conscious that political innovation, especially when it involves reshaping the British Constitution, hardly ever follows purely logical lines.

69. This would suit the political ambition of many Labour M.P.s who are either sceptical or hostile to the ambition of the Assembly to gain greater legislative competence in key areas of policy.

70. The Secretary of State, Peter Hain, has commented that he does not envisage such a referendum before 2011 and only then if the circumstances warrant. Who determines the "circumstances of the time" and who interprets how prescient are the recommendations of the Assembly and the Electoral Commission?

9
Recognition and National Justice for Québec: A Canadian Conundrum Revisited

This chapter examines the tension between the exclusive claims of Canadian statehood and national consciousness and the competing, not to say, resounding Québécois claim to national status as a distinct society. How the Canadian federal and provincial systems deal with Quebec's struggle for national survival and recognition exemplifies the modern state's difficulties in handling the existence of separate "peoples" within the boundaries of a single political construct. Thus the fundamental question to consider is whether Canada is one nation or two? A second is whether Canada should be governed as a multinational as well as a multicultural polity?[1]

What started as a constitutional federal partnership between equals in 1867 has transmuted into a "fading Canadian duality" (Castonguay, 1997) wherein the pivotal role of Quebec is increasingly questioned and challenged both from within and without.

Colonial rivalry between Britain and France from the seventeenth century onwards has shaped the question of nationality and statehood in Canada. Following the defeat of the French colonists in 1760 and the cessation of New France in 1763, Great Britain sought to govern the territory as an integral element of its North American realm. The principal instrument of British control during this time was the Quebec Act of 1774 which extended British control via Quebec west to the Mississippi and Ohio rivers. British settlement was augmented by the northward flow of displaced Loyalists following the American War of Independence in 1776; and as a result in 1791 the territory was divided into English-speaking Upper Canada, and predominantly French-speaking Lower Canada. Persistent pressures for self-government culminated in the 1837–1838 Rebellion. In his famous report Lord Durham's response was to recommend the political fusion of both Canadas, which was initiated under the Union Act in 1841. As the provinces of Ontario and Québec they formed the federal Dominion of Canada in

1867, together with Nova Scotia and New Brunswick. After Confederation, rapid expansion westward across the continent resulted in British Columbia joining the Dominion in 1871. By 1905 four more provinces were added and in 1949 Newfoundland voted to become the tenth province. There are also two established territories, the Yukon Territory and the Northwest Territories administered by the federal government (Williams, 1990), and a third, Nunavat, which is beginning its existence as a self-governing territory for Inuit.

This chapter focuses on how ethnic mobilisation and language-related issues have shaped the construction of Quebec's identity. As we have seen earlier in the volume, objectivist conceptions of ethnicity need to be tempered by critical analyses of more subjectivist and politically construed bases of identity. In many ways Quebec is the classic minority nationalist case which seeks to operate as if it were a sovereign territory, very akin to the Catalan ambition and national political programme. It is a dynamic context, for the cultural markers of ethnicity and civil nationalism are constantly being created, neglected, shaped and reshaped as the exigencies of political mobilisation demand. It is relatively rare for the contours of ethnicity and group identity to be either congruent or firmly demarcated within the political landscape (Williams, 1989b). Thus the struggle for hegemonic control and autarchy is a near-permanent feature of the relationship not only between Canada and Quebec, but also between proponents and opponents of increased autonomy within Quebec itself. Consequently Quebec may be viewed as a supreme example where government policy has influenced the power relationships between constituent groups at a variety of levels and contexts. The axiomatic consideration is whether Canada and Quebec should be conjoined indefinitely within one liberal democratic structure.

What distinguishes a separate but non-independent Quebec within a plural Canadian state? Is it the legal organisation of civil society, the Québec Civil Code which is different from that of other provinces; being the successor to the old seigneurial laws, as it draws upon the Code Napoleon? Is it a set of distinctive secular and provincial institutions built up largely over the last two generations to displace all those nurtured by the soil of pre-conquest New France? Is it a language and a culture associated with a particular territorial realm? Is it a new invention of an inclusive, modernised Québec giving a basis to all non-francophones who wish to be regarded as Québécois? How widespread is the genuine commitment to social inclusion discussed in Chapter Three, given that a powerful strand of Québécois thought insists on the primacy of ethno-linguistic distinctiveness as the defining characteristic of its distinct society? Recent evidence suggests that Quebecois leaders are conscious of the dangers of overplaying the nationalist card. They are aware of the damage created in the past by charges that non-francophone or non-Québécois born residents are inherently less central to the well being of civic society.

In the larger North American context there is no doubting that Québec is the francophone heartland of a dwindling cultural realm. Its attachment to collective identity has firm roots in a traditional society founded before the Aufklärung influences of later European migrants and is often counterpoised against American individualism. In his insightful and imaginatively argued essay "Impossible Nation", Conlogue (1996, p. 16) encapsulates the differences thus,

> Québec's struggle for cultural survival has depended on keeping the older collectivist idea alive, and it continues to do so. Today, this occasions much intolerance and misunderstandings on the part of English Canadians who find it "ethnic" or "racist". What is truest about it, however, is that it saved Québec's language and culture, and will continue to be a force so long as Québec feels that it is not "recognised" by English Canada.

Successive British governments since the Durham Report of 1839 have sought to anglicise Canada. Political agreement and guarantees given for the preservation of Québec's language, its religion and civil code, were brought in the 1850s, under an Anglo Attorney General, Drummond.[2] Nevertheless, generation after generation of francophone Canadians have protested that the "two nations" theory of state-building since 1867 has been grievously neglected by the dominant political élite. Evidence of neglect can be found in the erosion of the salience of dual-nation guarantees which were established as policy by a Royal Proclamation in 1763 and legislated as early as the Québec Act of 1774 (in respect of religious, judicial and seigneurial structures). Despite early institutionalisation, such as the recognition of French in 1792 as an official language of the assembly, the autonomous French character of the territory has been under threat, and frequently characterised as precipitating a national (Canadian) crisis.

This chapter seeks to analyse the current generation's response to the crisis of identity, political destiny and social choices confronting Québec as it strives to recover and re-create its nationhood in full. Since Confederation, Québec has consistently maintained its provincial autonomy within which the ethnically segmented character of society has been preserved. Nationalism has long been a dominant feature of Québécois life, expressing itself in a diversity of issues and agencies for the protection of institutional distinctiveness within the Canadian state. What disturbed this arrangement and mobilised separatist support in the post-war period was provincial modernisation, its chief characteristic being an attack on the domination of the Church in education, health and welfare services and in Québec society more generally.

This was the triggering factor, but behind it lay the more general phenomena of gradual disintegration of the French-Canadian identity largely forged and entertained by the Church after the crushing of the rebellion of 1837–1838. This rebellion was not approved by the hierarchy. Of course, the British exercised control over the appointment of Roman Catholic bishops; they expressly forbade any of proper French origin, although some were Savoyard. With the discrediting of *indépendantist*, lay ideals following that defeat, the Church emerged as the supreme articulator and instrument of French–Canadian culture, *en masse*. There was much expansion of settlement within Québec territory, and even – under the 1841 Constitution – into Upper Canada and New Brunswick. But the implosion of the Church-run French Canada which held sway for a century or so, *c.*1850–1960, produced ultimately a crisis of faith, of direction and of authority. The partial displacement of the old-guard, Conservative nationalist élite by a new, thrusting, technocratic, rational-bureaucratic élite tied to a provincial state apparatus as its source of legitimacy and power, created a new political context within which the earlier long-dormant seeds of the *indépendantist* ideal could emerge.

The new nationalism of the 1960–1970s was rooted in a radically different conception of politics which favoured rapid social and economic development as the key to Québécois prosperity and influence. Whereas the old nationalism had accepted Québec's role within Confederation (by and large), the new nationalism questioned the very basis of Confederation and pushed for recognition of French Canada's uniqueness as a co-founding nation and heartland of a distinctive francophone cultural system. It argued that Québec should not be considered as merely one of ten co-equal provinces, but rather as a nation which affirmed its identity through development and participation and was recognised by others as a "distinct society".

In consequence of the "Quiet Revolution", the old guard nationalists' suspicion and disdain of the state as an instrument of reform was displaced by an ideological commitment to state intervention and planning, so that control of the provincial state apparatus became central in the struggle for national survival and modernisation. Beyond this traditional-modern élite conflict was a much more pervasive and effervescent social reform. The old order collapsed under the unremitting pressure of North American materialism, which was born in Europe, its faith shattered by the experience of two world wars and its ideology scorned for having inhibited social and economic development. The "Quiet Revolution" promised reform, success, modernisation and democratic accountability. It captured the mood of young Québécois, eager to heed the call to liberty both of their nation and of their own selves where individual fulfilment had been smothered for far too long by the patronage of the Church and the Union Nationale party.

Public recognition of the worth of constituent cultures, as *permanent* entities in society, is what is at stake in liberal democracies. Indeed for many engaged in the politics of their group's survival this is precisely what democracy should guarantee in praxis as well as in principle. This, for example, is the nub of the Québécois argument to be treated as a "distinct society", and not one among many provinces within Canada. In various ways it is the preoccupation of all struggling minorities within North America. Recognition of the right to be permanently different and possibly separate is normally anathema to democratic practice based upon majoritarian rule. We recognise, with Amy Gutman, that "liberal democracy is suspicious of the demand to enlist politics in the preservation of separate group identities or the survival of subcultures that otherwise would not flourish through the free association of citizens" (Gutmann, 1995, p. 10). When it refuses to engage in the politics of recognition, liberal democracy appears arrogant and denies the life-enhancing spirit upon which all forms of democracy are based. It accentuates fragmentation and anomie within society, encouraging various forms of disengagement from public life and community responsibility and ultimately leading to demands for separatism (Williams, 1982).

Consistency and security are the watchwords of the responsive democratic state. For "democratic citizenship develops its force of social integration, that is to say it generates solidarity between strangers, if it can be recognised and appreciated as the very mechanism by which the legal and material infrastructure of actually preferred forms of life is secured" (Habermas, p. 290).

Canada's sheer size, location and ethno-linguistic history makes it a fascinating counter example to the dominant American method of state formation and nation-building. Yet despite their quite fundamental differences as regards the promotion of official languages, the inexorable Anglicisation of Canada's population and its incorporation within a North American Free Trade Area, renders Canada less and less distinctive within an American dominated global economy. Canada's absorption into the American narrative of the twenty-first century is, like Britain's, profound and unnerving. For some, the U.S.A's peculiar burden has displaced its unique mission destiny, as the guiding motive of contemporary politics.[3] Both loyalty and ambiguity towards America fuel the Canadian position on so many issues. Yet in terms of language policy and multiculturalism, Canada has offered a striking alternative to the American behemoth.

Standing fast on the rampart of liberty

A central pre-occupation of post-Conquest French Canada has been the defence of the right to hold to its own norms and traditions in an overwhelmingly Anglo-American continent. As one of the cultural hearths of Francophone North America (the others are the Maritimes and Cajun Louisiana), Québec has a significant role over and above that of being the home province of Québécois inhabitants.

Four key factors have threatened the reproduction of French identity and culture. First, Québec's industrial and economic structure has been dominated by an Anglicised élite of British and American-Loyalist origin, a division which harkens back to the Conquest. By the mid-nineteenth century this élite had established a cultural division of labour in the industrial centres of Montreal, Trois-Rivières Sherbrooke and Hull. Today the distribution of anglophones within Québec is overwhelmingly urban and concentrated within greater Montreal, providing a contrast to the more uniform distribution of anglophones elsewhere in Canada. West of Quebec francophones are largely found in the big cities: Ottawa, Toronto, Sudbury, Hamilton, London, St Catherines-Niagra, Oshawa, Winnipeg, Calgary, Edmonton and Vancouver. East of Quebec their geography is the opposite being distributed in largely rural areas, small towns and one nodal centre, namely Moncton.

Historically, the anglophone elite dominated activities such as the construction of transcontinental railways, state-wide companies, resource development, media control and capital accumulation. This led to sectors of the Québécois economy being integrated into the world system through the financial centres of London and New York. Economic success was unduly identified as the preserve of the anglophone community, and, despite internal social class polarities, English became the language of upward social mobility in all areas save religion, law, medicine and provincial politics.

Anglicisation and the heavy penetration of capitalism and industrialisation in the nineteenth century secured the primacy of English as the working language for many sectors of the Québécois economy. Diglossia in the workplace, with many of the dominant commercial élites using English, ensured the perpetuation of a cultural division of labour which had obvious ramifications for the power–relationship between the two language groups. It also had linguistic repercussions with heavy borrowing from English, particularly of newer technical, fiscal and organisational terms. The struggle to recapture nodal points in the Québécois economy, such as Montreal, through provincial language legislation and its impact on education, employment, public administration and urban governance is the major feature of post-war political life (Levine, 1990).

Second, differences between the élite and masses could be accommodated so long as Québec's birth-rate remained high. However, the sharp decline in the provincial birth-rate during the 1960s and 1970s exposed the underlying trends which had characterised Québécois society. The dilution of the influence of the Catholic Church, and the related dropping of the messianic French-Canadian world view, '*la revanche des berceaux*', as the solution to the conquest, had reinforced awareness of the high rates of outmigration of francophones to other parts of Canada and neighbouring New England, coupled with high rates of post-war immigration to Canada. The Church was well aware of the effect of the New England movement in the mid nineteenth century. What was startling about such migration trends was the pattern of immigrant assimilation into Québec's anglophone society. For instrumental, economic and social-esteem reasons, the immigrants, and especially their children, were drawn into the English school system rather than the French alternative. Even more markedly, as Castonguay (1992b, Personal communication May.) observes, the Catholic–run French school system refused to open its doors to, for example, Greek Orthodox children, so concerned was it with preserving a homogenous Catholic, French hegemony.

After reaching its zenith in 1941 the proportion of Canadian citizens with French as their mother tongue fell steadily from 29.2 per cent to 26.9 per cent by 1971 and 22.9 per cent by 2001 (Table 9.1). For Québec this has represented a decline in demographic and political weight as identified by demographers who in the early 1970s were predicting a fall in the proportion of francophones in the Province itself. Their forecasts were sharpened by a realisation that the non-French population was disproportionately represented in the Montreal metropolitan area. Within this area (containing 45.5 per cent of the Province's population), the French versus others proportion was five to three. Demographers had argued that if the current trends continued unabated, the metropolis would lose its French majority within two decades and the commercial heart of the Québec nation would be lost, whilst rural small-town Québec would provide only a partial defence for francophone interests in an increasingly technological and urban age (Hamilton and Pinard, 1982, p. 206).

Table 9.1 Total population and population of French mother tongue, Canada, censuses of 1931–1991

		French MT	
Census	Total population	Number	% of total
1931[a]	10,376,786	2,832,298	27.3
1941[a]	11,506,655	3,354,753	29.2
1951	14,009,429	4,068,850	29.0
1961	18,238,247	5,123,151	28.1
1971	21,568,315	5,793,650	26.9
1976	22,992,605	5,966,707	25.9
1981	24,343,180	6,249,095	25.7
1986	25,309,340	6,354,840[b]	25.1
1991	26,994,010	6,562,065	24.3

Sources: 1971 and earlier are from the census of Canada; 1976 figures are as calculated by Linda Demers and John Kralt in *On the Comparability of Mother Tongue Data, 1976–1981* (Ottawa: Statistics Canada, 1983); and 1981 and 1986 figures are from *Adjusted Language Data* (Joy, *1991,120*); *1991 data from Castonguay (1997)*.
[a] Data for Newfoundland are not included in 1931 and 1941. In 1931, the census question was different from that asked at subsequent censuses, but the data are probably reasonably comparable.
[b] In 1986, after imputations, the single response "French" was reported for only 6,159,740 persons (24.3 per cent of the total population); the additional 195,100 in this table represents allocation of multiple responses.

A third factor was the increased penetration of English, Canadian, and US media pressure in all its complex forms. Sociolinguists declared that though French continued to be the primary language of the community, many younger people were switching languages and/or adopting English idioms and style in their spoken French. This caused the Office de la Langue Française to emphasise corpus language planning and to introduce a wider technical vocabulary in speech domains previously dominated by the English language and now opened to francophones in business, commerce and public administration (Bourhis, 1984).

A fourth factor which underpinned the *survivance* complex was the conviction that the Canadian federal government was not carrying out its responsibility to honour the rights of francophones wherever they lived in Canada, especially the sizeable minorities in Acadia (New Brunswick) (Daigle, 1982), Ontario (Cartwright and Williams, 1982), and on the prairies. Despite the increased attention paid to the linguistic rights of minorities as a consequence of the Bilingualism and Biculturalism Report (RCBB, 1967), many in Québec still feared the inexorable trend of assimilation into a unilingual English–Canadian appendage of the United States of America. Indeed some opposed the whole thrust of bilingual policy, endorsed by the federal government. They argued that it was a Trojan horse conspiracy, first to isolate Québec still more, and, second, to guarantee federally-backed language rights to the large anglophone community within Québec, thereby institutionalising their position as the representatives of the majority culture within Canada. Geographically they occupied a key position, straddling the culture divide of the "bilingual belt" between English and French Canada together with significant "other" minorities (Joy, 1972, 1992).

Politically Québec had kept faith with the Federal Liberal Party and had sought, through federal legislation to further its "distinct society" position. In each of the general elections during the 1970s the province had returned a greater number of Liberal members of parliament than in previous elections, contributing on an average about half of all Liberal MPs throughout Canada – for example 56 out of 109 in 1972, rising to 67 out of 114 federal Liberal MPs by 1979. However, during this time the Québécois electorate was also characterised by increasing francophone support for the nationalist Parti Québécois at the provincial level, whilst simultaneously supporting Trudeau's Liberals at the federal level.

Québécois distinctiveness was part of a larger regional division within Canada which was characterised by many east–west splits on major issues. Resolutely opposed to Québécois autonomy, western conservatives were rehearsing modern variants of Lord Durham's thesis that Canada was essentially Anglo-Canadian with a significant francophone minority. Meanwhile, Federal Liberals, sympathetic to the notion of francophone cultural maintenance, sought to augment Québec's historical and socio– political role within federation and to give the whole of Canada a flavour of bilingualism through the development of the B. and B. Report Recommendations. Such reforms, however, did not assuage the rising tide of Québécois nationalism which breached the sea-wall defences of Québec Liberals in 1976.

The democratic basis of Québécois identity: Ethnic or territorial?

When the Parti Québécois (PQ) won the provincial election of November 1976, the rest of Canada was faced with a progressive government avowing separatism, promising the creation of a new state in North America, where French culture would be secured, and where state planning and social democratic principles would be influential in bringing about a more equitable distribution of resources within society. The active supporters of the PQ included the young, well educated, urban and upwardly mobile francophones (Hamilton and Pinard, 1982; McRoberts and Posgate, 1980). The PQ provincial government sought to extend its conception of national identity beyond the traditional core identity of the province's majority francophone population, aiming to create an extensive constituency in support of the independence ideal.

The first PQ period in office offers a fascinating illustration of how a nationalist intelligentsia sought to construct a social space within which its vision of political community could be legitimised. The government was committed to the establishment of a new language regime, and heralded its policy by the introduction of the French Language Charter in 1977, which superseded former language legislation (QCLF, 1978). Five months after the election, the Minister of State for Cultural Affairs in Québec, Camille Laurin (1977) dismissed the federal commitment to bilingualism, arguing that retroactive institutional bilingualism did not mitigate the fact that Canada was to all intents and purposes an English–speaking state. In contrast, the new provincial programme which he sponsored was designed to give Québec a thoroughgoing French character in as many linguistic domains as the government could influence.

> The Québec we wish to build will be essentially French. The fact that the majority of its population is French will be clearly visible – at work, in communications and in the countryside. It will also be a country in which the traditional balance of power will be altered, especially in regard to the economy; the use of French will not merely be universalised to hide the predominance of foreign powers from the French speaking population; this will accompany, symbolize and support a reconquest by the French-speaking majority in Québec of that control over the economy which it ought to have. To sum up, the Québec whose features are sketched in the Charter (of the French Language) is a French-language society.
>
> (Laurin, 1977)

Closer examination of the implications of such declarations reveal much ambiguity in the justification of majoritarian independence, and this is one of the prime pitfalls in using a cultural diacritical marker, such as language, for separatist mobilisation (Williams, 1982). Indeed this tension between the justification of a minority's rise to power and fresh interpretations of democratic accountability is a major feature of this volume's attempt to interpret the one among the many.

Knopff (1980) is especially sensitive to these implications, which produce in his terms a national conundrum. The stance of the Parti Québécois in claiming that French culture needs to be preserved in its own separate and distinct space is a classic nationalist position. It is reminiscent of nineteenth century Ireland, Hungary, and the Czech Republic together with more recent nationalist ideology in Catalonia, Euskadi, Estonia and Wales. What inhibited this claim being realised was that many PQ candidates, who had secured a majority of the francophone vote, had been kept out of office by a non-French block vote. In 1973, René Levesque "warned of the potentially explosive situation if the Anglophone minority [once again] kept in power a party not supported by a majority of Francophones" (quoted in Knopff, 1980, p. 639). Lévesque was appealing to the democratic principle of majority rule which he conceived had been distorted by the reaction and control of an unrepresentative minority.

Despite a clear victory in the 1976 election, the PQ opted for a referendum to endorse their mandate for Sovereignty–Association. Opponents of separatism argued that, given the importance of the issue to Québec and to Canada, a 55 per cent vote to separate was an inadequate endorsement. From the PQ perspective a 55 per cent positive vote would suggest acceptance of the principle by a "huge majority" of francophones, somewhere around 65 per cent of the French-speaking citizenry. The implication was that a genuine victory of the majority of francophones would then be assured for it is not the absolute majority which ought to rule but the majority of the dominant culture. The PQ were especially sensitive to this sort of assertion and have repeatedly stated that only if a majority of all Québec citizens, regardless of linguistic affiliation, endorse a Sovereignty–Association referendum would they be authorised to seek a revision of their relationship with Canada. In the event the results of the first referendum in May 1980 were clear–cut and decisive – 59.5 per cent voted no and 40.5 per cent voted yes. 80 per cent of Québec's 4.4 million voters had participated.

This tension between the "authentic" Québécois and the "others" was revived during the 1994–95 debate when the then PQ leader, Jacques Parizeau, claimed that Québec would be declared independent in 1995, if necessary, without the support of the province's (minority) ethnic groups. He asserted that

old-stock French-speaking Québécois can bring about Québec independence without support from the province's non-francophone minority
(*The Gazette*, 4th February, 1993)

Extracts from a meeting held on 3 February 1993 between six representatives of the PQ and six spokespersons for the coalition of ten ethnic organisations illustrate this tension. Parizeau and other PQ leaders accused the ethnic leaders of double standards when they urged their groups to vote yes *en bloc in* the Autumn 1992 Canada-wide constitutional referendum and then criticised the PQ for mobilising francophones to rally behind its drive for independence (*The Gazette*, 1993). He argued that

'he was merely recognizing reality when he said that old–stock Québécois cannot expect ethnic communities to support the PQ independence bid. "It's something everyone recognizes and which is regularly underlined in public–opinion polls".
(*The Gazette*, 1993)

Such controversy over citizenship and authenticity was intensified after the failed 1995 independence bid when Parizeau accused the non-francophone citizens of Québec of duplicity for not supporting his programme. This tension demonstrates the double bind of majority–minority relations at different levels in the scale hierarchy from federal, through provincial to local issues. Clearly majority-minority rights are determined by specific political contexts. Analytically they are quite distinct from the collective claims to independence as a right per se. This emphasis on the appropriate political context provides further evidence of the tensions inherent in the separatist ideal. Many within the PQ leadership have pressed the claim of the Francophone nation to independence because it is the dominant nation in Québec, arguing that other ethnic groups have a responsibility to participate and to co-operate to develop the national culture of Québec (Knopf, 1980).

However, Camille Laurin and others have used the term nation in a way which is synonymous with the state, and not the (francophone) *ethnie*. Separatist rhetoric refers to Québec as a nation (read state) struggling for independence. In order to do so this argument must maintain that the Québec state represents not only the embodiment of the French nation in North America (as used to be argued) but of all the people within it. The "national culture" of Québec, though decidedly French, is the common inheritance of all its citizens. Consequently the Quebec government has the responsibility to ensure that every citizen learns the single official language, French. The original version of the Language Charter declared that "the French language has always been the language of the Québec people, that it is, indeed, the very instrument by which they have articulated their identity". The French language was to be used as the instrument of French cultural promotion. Québec's non-francophone population saw in this for-mulation the establishment of an official state culture, with the implication that they would become disadvantaged citizens within their own province. Recognising this fear, the preamble to the new bill (Bill, 101) was modi-fied, referring to French as "the distinctive language of a people that is in the majority French-speaking . . . the instrument by which that people has articulated its identity".

This awkward reformulation does not remove the inherent ambiguity which gave rise to the legal enforcement of French culture in Québec. The philosophy and quest for national identity which this quotation exemplifies is not without its difficulties, and is a common predicament for many nation-alist movements who find themselves in power. The separatist cause is based upon the premise that ethnic majorities within a multi–ethnic polity have the right to constitute national governments in their own sovereign states. This is the essence of the right of national self–determination. Within our Western ideological framework such claims appear to be couched in major-itarian language and hence in reasonable terms, because they are inherently democratic.

Knopff (1980) recognises the conundrum in that the minority and major-ity are not defined in terms of collections of individuals, but by cultural (ethno-linguistic) groupings.

> What this implies is not that the numerical majority ought to rule, but that the majority *of the majority culture,* should rule; which is as much to claim a right to rule on behalf of a certain group within society, not simply by virtue of its being a majority, but, rather, by virtue of its cultural characteristics, or its substantive way of life. Thus, the important thing in an election is not to count votes, but to count French votes (p. 639).

This acid test of who really counts in a "national society" is an ever present conundrum when issues of tradition, representative values, religion or language are in the balance. It is even more pressing when the voice of the people is heard through national referenda on such critical issues as separation from a sovereign state and the formation of one's own independent polity.

Knopf (1980) avers that this forces the nationalist to embrace a majorit-arianism which negates a fundamental premise of nationalism, namely that nations and states should be coextensive. He draws attention to the diffi-culty facing any *Parti Québécois* government. Their rise to power had been based in part on appeals to ethnic nationalism (as well as a social democratic platform, anti-corruption, etc.), but rather than redefine Québec's bound-aries so that they now coincided with the francophone nation, they refer to the *Québecois* nation's right to self-determination, thereby converting an ethnic nationalism into a broader territorial nationalism. The party hoped to persuade non-francophones that its conception of nationalism was territorial and state-based, one in which they could partake if they would choose to exercise their newly acquired right to integrate into the "national culture" and become *Québécois* citizens rather than hyphenated Canadians. Whebell (1998, Personal Communication, 29 September.) has cautioned that according to the differentials of voting in the 1995 referendum, the majority "yes" areas coincide with neither the state territory (Québec province) nor with the majority Francophone population. Thus he asks rhetorically "Is the 'political nation' not necessarily a majority of the 'cultural nation' it proposes to speak for?"

The PQ government also officially recognised the Indian and Inuit peoples as distinct nations in a 1983 Assemblée Nationale resolution. This was strengthened in March 1985 through a "Motion portant sur la reconnaissance des droits de autochtlones" passed by the Assemblée Nationale which guaranteed their rights to culture, language, customs and traditions. However, they voted very strongly with a "no" in subsequent referenda on Quebec's future.

Language planning agencies and educational policies were central to the *Parti Québécois's* attempt at national congruence. In relation to non-francophone minorities it was assumed that the instrumental enforcement of French in the early days would give way to a genuine desire to identify with the francophone majority, because it was rational and normal so to do. Provincial legislation and formal education were to be the twin agencies of French cultural reproduction and the market place would reward French language skills in the form of increased remuneration and greater occupational choice and mobility.

Federal and provincial language strategy

The Canadian government's Official Languages Act (OLA, 1969) declared that English and French were the official languages of Canada "for all purposes of the Parliament and Government of Canada"; it recognised the "equality of status and equal rights and privileges" of both languages "as to their use in all the institutions of the Parliament and Government of Canada". It also declared that federal agencies were to accommodate the linguistic preferences of individuals whose mother tongue was either French or English (the two official languages), thereby introducing the "personality" principle into language planning. The Act also established the Office of the Commissioner of Official Languages, which is currently held by Graham Fraser.

According to the Act, a mother tongue official minority of over 10 per cent could be recommended by the Bilingual Districts Advisory Board for federal services within a specified area, provided that the provincial and municipal authorities would likewise cooperate (Mackey, 1992; Nelde *et al.*, 1992). Despite extensive efforts, the challenge of changing linguistic preferences and habits from coast to coast has proved too difficult for the policy instruments created by the Official Languages Act (Cartwright and Williams, 1982; Cartwright, 1991). The whole notion of bilingual districts has been discredited by the failure to adopt systematic and consistent guidelines (Reid, 1993). Territorial unilingualism, not individual choice, has won popular assent, even though this may anger and disappoint francophones elsewhere in Canada, together with sympathetic anglophones within Québec.

The federal policy of balanced bilingualism, symbolising a linguistic partnership from coast to coast and suggesting a more equitable basis for "national unity", did not appeal to the majority within Québec. Despite Trudeau's enthusiasm it was never likely to, for one of the most notable features of Quebecois society in the late 1960s and early 1970s was the growth of a new middle class, overwhelmingly concentrated in the burgeoning public sector, which recruited francophone social scientists, engineers, planners, business graduates, lawyers, and public administrators. It was clearly in the material interest of members of this new class to support moves toward French-language dominance in those spheres they could influence, for their social position was dependent, in part, on the establishment of a francophone provincial and local public-service sector. However, once the provincial sector began to be adequately manned, language proficiency and requirement became an important political issue of group conflict as the aspiring middle class, blocked in its expectation to swell the state bureaucracy, looked to the anglophone-dominated private sector for employment. Disadvantaged linguistically, and experiencing blocked mobility in both sectors, the thwarted aspirants backed those within the intelligentsia who saw in separatism a collective political solution to Québécois problems.

In his analysis of Anglo-Québecers' reactions to this shift towards unilingualism, Stein (1982) discusses the impact of the passage of Bill 22 by the Liberal Government in July of 1974. Law 22, the Official Language Act of 1974 (QOLA, 1974), made French the official language of the Province, thereby buttressing French interests against the very real threats identified above. There was a virulent debate as to whether the adjective "sole" should be added to the wording of section I of Bill 22 and the government refused to add it. Consequently under Bill 22 English remained official in the National Assembly and before the Courts as stipulated in the Canadian Constitution. Had the word "sole" been incorporated it would have created an immediate conflict of jurisdiction (Maurais, 1991, Personal Communication. 2 April.).

Stein (1982, p. 112) claims that these measures "were perceived by a substantial majority of both the anglophone and non-francophone immigrant communities as the first direct attack by the Québec authorities on their status and even as a threat to their survival". The position of Québec's anglophones is an interesting measure of the quite different political conceptions of the PQ, in contrast to the *Parti Liberal du Québec* (PLQ), although a comparison undertaken by Coleman (1981) of their legislative programmes suggests that the PQ "have simply extended . . . the legislative path of the PLQ . . . in order to penetrate further into society" (p. 459). Whereas the PLQ saw Québec as a constituent part of Canada, and English Québecers as part of the majority group "nation-wide", the *pequistes* (supporters of the PQ) viewed Québec as an "embryonic nation-state" and "tended to downplay the ties between Québec's anglophone community and the rest of Canada and preferred to treat that community as a 'national' minority. Accordingly the *péquistes* were predisposed to defining a unilingual policy for the new pluralist structures. The party were also less reluctant to push pluralism and dissolution of dual structures right to the local level" (Coleman, 1981, pp. 462–3).

The PLQ's preference for persuasion politics rather than for the PQ's coercive politics is attributed to their respective support bases and to the social backgrounds of their activists. The PLQ tended to draw more support from the business community and from private–sector professionals than did the PQ, whose support was largely rooted within the francophone urban mass, " . . . especially from the young, and well educated, the new middle class of journalists, teachers, academics and *fonctionnaires,* and from workers desirous of change" (Coleman, 1981, p. 463).

This difference in language and social philosophy of the *indépendantistes* from previous governments is evident in the first major piece of legislation introduced by the PQ after its election in November 1976, the "Québec Charter of the French Language" (QCLF, 1978) – Bill 101, sanctioned as law on 26 August 1977 after a number of important changes from its predecessor, Bill 1. Bill 101 declared French to be the official language of Québec, because as discussed earlier, it was deemed to be "the distinctive language of a people that is in the majority French—speaking" and was viewed as "the [principal] instrument by which that people had articulated its identity". It was resolved to make "French the language of Government and Law, as well as the normal and everyday language of work, instruction, communication, commerce and business" (QCLF, 1978, p. 103).

The PQ government insisted that Québec should be as French as Ontario is English. The *francisation* programme was to provide the legislative and political impetus to give a thoroughly French face to *Québécois* society. Passed only a few months after the election of the PQ, *La Charte de la langue française* (Bill 101) stated that there was only one official language, namely French, in Québec. The bill consists in provisions defining the rules which should determine the relations between French and English. The consequences of determining one official language were profound. Only French would be used as the official version of Québec's laws (nevertheless an English version would continue to be provided); only French would be used on public commercial signs (with due respect paid to freedom of expression as it was conceived of at that time). This entailed the provision that French was not compulsory for public messages dealing with religious, ideological and political matters (Maurais, 1991). The Bill also limited entry to English schools in the province to children with at least one parent who had attended an English school in Québec, but as Fournier (1991, p. 89) observed it included "traditional measures to avoid dividing the children in a family, as well as special dispensations for persons living in Québec temporarily".

Within the workplace Bill 101 obliged all companies with 50 or more employees to comply with a francisation programme. Contrary to Bill 22, where the practice was optional, the goals of francisation had to be implemented by firms in their internal workings, their hiring and promotional policy, their catalogues, instructions manuals and in their public face to the outside world. Clear sanctions against offenders were also established. Adopting a more comprehensive interpretation, Jacques Maurais (1991) of the *Conseil de la langue française* argues that it was

> deemed unrealistic to impose French as the only language in the workplace, the use of French should be generalised at all levels but, as part of its francisation programme, a firm may negotiate with the Office de la Langue Française the list of positions that require knowledge of another language with a view of ensuring communication among departments of the firm or with other companies outside Québec.

Instead, provisions were formulated whereby specific domain-related language use were required. For example, French is not mandatory in the communication of a firm with its partners outside Québec. Ten years after the passage of Bill 101, the Office de la Langue Française revealed that 40 per cent of Québec firms affected by the Bill still did not have a francisation certificate. A further 54 per cent of francisation committees were considered to be inactive and these were present in firms which represented less than half the workers in Québec affected by the programme (Fournier, 1991, p. 92).

The constitutionality of Bill 101 was also queried. The whole of Chapter Three of the French Language Charter, dealing with the language of the Assemblée Nationale and appearances before the courts (which was based on a similar bill adopted in Manitoba in 1890) was declared unconstitutional in 1979 by the Canadian Supreme Court. In maintaining the logic of its decision the Supreme Court also declared as unconstitutional Manitoba's law, almost a century after its adoption! In these domains, only French-English bilingualism in Québec is official, despite the wording of Bill 101, since its Chapter Three was rejected by the Supreme Court (Maurais, 1991, 1987, pp. 368–9). Bilingualism is also permitted in all the domains where Bill 101 does not require the exclusive use of French "where this act does not require use of the official language exclusively, the official language and another language may be used together" (QCLF, 1978, Section 89).

The francisation programme devoted to institutionalising French in the education system, the workplace, the service and retail sector and cultural landscape of the province did not play well with many parts of Canadian society. Federalists felt betrayed by this move, for it threatened to undermine the political principle of balanced coast-to-coast bilingualism (Cartwright and Williams, 1982), even though this principle would clearly never be realised as the social goal of bilingualism was restricted to the federal parliament, its departments and agencies and was compulsory nowhere else (Maurais, 1987, p. 363).

Besides, the division in authority and responsibility between federal and provincial governments perpetuated conflict as a structural feature of the Canadian state. Waddell (1986, p. 106) argued that

> the national government policies constantly threaten the provincial government in its actions and the provincial government provokes the national, generating misunderstanding, frustration and confrontation. Recent developments only confirm this historic pattern, as yet another legal judgement disqualifies yet another section of Québec's *Charte de la langue française,* the whole occurring in the context of processes initiated by Québec's anglophone minority and financed by federal funds.

Proulx (1985) has itemised four ways in which this structural impasse is articulated. First by proposing a "symmetrical bilingual model" and championing the rights of the official language minorities, the federal government was seen as defending the interest of Québec's anglophone minority rather than securing the cohesion of the francophone majority. Second, Waddell (1986, 107) notes that

> both provincial and federal charters of rights and freedoms seek to protect individuals and minorities from potential abuses by the majority. However, Québec society constitutes a Canadian and continental minority, and if the *Charte de la langue française* sought to give it the necessary protection as a simple law it is inefficient, because subordinate to both federal and provincial charters.

Third, it was argued that the federal Liberal government was electorally committed to the defence of the anglophone minority, making it difficult to realise a buttress for majority francophone interests by reference to pan-Canadian political parties. Fourth, Proulx argues that francophone militancy had disappeared because the Québec government has championed French rights and has itself become a prime instrument for linguistic affirmation.

Nonetheless, the passage of Bill 101 reversed several trends which caused anxiety to (French) language activists. In the first year of operation, 1977–1978, the number of children with neither French nor English as a mother tongue who enrolled in French-language schools increased by 6.4 per cent (Coleman, 1981, p. 470). The majority of parents whose mother tongue was neither French nor English enrolled their children in French-language kindergartens, whilst enrolment in the English-language equivalent dropped by 15.6 per cent (1981, p. 471). Critics of unilingualism argued that the erosion of a high-quality English-language school system would disadvantage Québec in producing skilled participants in a Canadian context. But it is in the economic domain that the most damning charges have been made by opponents who have detailed the outmigration of key firms from Montreal to Toronto or Calgary, ostensibly because they wished to avoid working in French, as well as of Québec's high personal and corporate income taxes and the ultimate threat of secession (Esman, 1982, p. 248). There is a strand of truth in these charges, but they also coincided with the shift of economic activity westward, which was largely due to economic forces and not cultural ones, independent of language changes emanating from the National Assembly in Québec City. The economic stagnation and partial deindustrialisation of the Province must also play a role in the departure of Anglo-Québec institutions and families.

Census results (Table 9.2) on mother tongues in Québec, for the crucial decade of 1971–1981, reveal a decline of the English mother-tongue

Table 9.2   Mother tongues in Quebec, 1971, 1976, 1981, 1986

Province/city	Mother tongue			
	French	English	Other	Not stated[a]
1971				
Province of Quebec	4,867,250(80.7)	789,185(13.1)	371,330(6.2)	–
Montreal	1,819,640(66.3)	595,395(21.7)	328,180(12.0)	–
Quebec City	458,435(95.4)	18,035(3.8)	4,030(0.8)	–
1976				
Province of Quebec	4,989,245(80.0)	800,680(12.8)	334,050(5.4)	110,470(1.8)
Montreal	1,831,110(65.3)	607,505(21.7)	295,770(10.6)	68,100(2.4)
Quebec City	513,895(94.8)	15,745(2.9)	3,595(0.7)	8,925(1.6)
1981				
Province of Quebec	5,286,228(82.1)	711,287(11.1)	386,225(6.0)	54,660(0.8)
Montreal	1,932,678(68.3)	527,532(18.7)	337,160(11.9)	30,975(1.1)
Quebec City	551,176(95.7)	15,354(2.7)	5,050(0.9)	4,500(0.7)
1986				
Province of Quebec	5,316,925	580,030	393,725	–
Montreal	1,974,115	433,095	344,965	–
Quebec City	575,395	10,750	5,425	–

Source: Statistics Canada, 1983, 21; Statistics Canada, 1987, 93–102, Table 1; 95–129, Table 1.
Figures are numbers of people speaking a particular tongue: those in parentheses represent numbers as percentages.
[a] Because of the unavailability of information on the impact of processing on the 1971 data, it is not possible to apply either the 1976 or the 1981 algorithms to the 1971 data. Consequently, the "not stated" population for 1971 cannot be separated from the French, English, and other populations.

population from 13.1 per cent in 1971 to 11.1 per cent in 1981 for the Province as a whole. But as the vast majority of people are concentrated in Montreal, the 1981 data revealed that the city's English community had declined below the historically stable level of 20 per cent. During the decade 1976–1986 the numbers of English mother tongue residents had dropped from 607,505 to only 433,095 (Table 9.2). Caldwell (1982, 4) suggested that this contraction would shape a new group consciousness amongst Anglo-Québecers, tempered by the erosion of the communal character of anglophone social-service institutions and traditional educational patterns. "That at least one-seventh of English-speaking families now send their youngest children to French schools is both a factor in and an indication of the potentially catastrophic nature of the enrolment issue" (Caldwell, 1982, p. 5). Anglo-Québec is reacting against the new-found dependency situation of being a minority within a majority in many ways. One is to partake in Camille Laurin's characterisation of Québec moving from a monolithic society to a pluralistic state within which minorities may be protected, so long as they adhere to the current conventions.

In general the secularisation of education and health care have been the most significant consequences of the Quiet Revolution causing Castonguay (1992, Personal communication. May.) to argue that the rise of French as the ethnic marker rather than Catholicism was "a consequence of this deeper mutation". McWhinney (1982, p. 37) observes that Bill 22 and Bill 101 were the most significant legal heritage of the Quiet Revolution. Outside Quebec there has been a tendency to interpret such measures as essentially linguistic issues rather than as an expression of a changing balance of forces. It is more pertinent to argue that legislation in the 1970s had enabled a social and economic revolution to be effected in Québec in the guise of linguistic reform (McWhinney, 1982). By today this has reversed the status of French in the work place enabling it to be both the functional and legitimate language of commerce and industry, whilst facilitating the emergence of a francophone decision-making élite. (The principal examples of which appear to be capitalists rather than intellectuals.) The local state has guaranteed the cultural reproduction of the francophone majority in Québec in the name of the people, but it is also a powerful agent in the economic transformation of society.

During the first referendum campaign in particular it was argued that the *péquiste* attack was directed towards the federal government's favouritism towards Ontario in its economic policy, rather than toward socio-linguistic issues. The *péquiste* campaign for independence was framed as much in rational economic terms as it was an appeal to a nationalist vision of a sovereign state. External constraints, such as Federal pressure, the need to impress foreign capital markets that any sovereign government of Québec would be "responsible and reliable" were well understood by René Lévesue and the PQ strategists (McRoberts and Posgate, 1980, p. 214).

The defeat of Sovereignty-Association referendum in the spring of 1980 was a severe blow to the *indépendantistes* with a resulting vote of 59 per cent to 41 per cent. But the subsequent re-election of the PQ on 15th April 1981 confirmed the PQ's hold with 49 per cent of the vote (the best result achieved until then by the PQ). Support for the PQ was not necessarily a vote for independence as Hamilton and Pinard (1982, pp. 208–23) made clear. Indeed successive Québecois governments since the early 1960s onwards have attempted to uphold the "dualism" inherent within Canadian federalism and have sought to maximise their own autonomy via five broad claims (see Gagnon's 1989, p. 153)

1. Recognition of Québec as a distinct society;
2. Reform of the federal constitution that guarantees Québec a veto power, and maximises the scope of Québec's jurisdiction in most policy fields;
3. Re-apportionment of federal-provincial fiscal resources to reflect Québec's needs;
4. A reduced federal role in the development, implementation and financing of provincial policies/programmes;
5. An increased role for Québec both in determining the composition and operation of federal institutions, and also in decisions regarding the development, implementation and financing of federal policies and programmes.

Ironically in the light of these autonomist principles, other provinces, especially Ontario, have made similar demands as part of normal provincial-federal relations.

Constitutional repatriation

The key question arising from these demands was whether recognition of Québec as a "distinct society" could be achieved within a re-formulated constitution or whether Québec was necessarily driven towards an increasingly "independentist" position.

Early evidence of the difficulty of accommodating Québec's renewed demands came in the critical period between October 1980 and November 1981 when Trudeau's "re-patriation" reform of the Canadian Constitution and the Charter of Rights and Freedoms was agreed by nine out of the ten provincial governments. The Charter[4] formally recognises the constitutional principle of equality of the two official languages of Canada.[5] This principle, according to the Supreme Court, has meaning: "It provides in particular that language rights that are institutionally based require government action for their implementation and therefore create obligations for the State".[6] The Charter also elevates the public's right to services in either official language to the constitutional level, while maintaining the proportionality of its application.[7] Tremblay (2006) judges that the single greatest development in the recognition of language rights in Canada occurred with the enactment of minority language educational rights.[8] He argues that Canadian courts have concluded that the provision of education in the minority language, in schools that belong to and are managed by the minority, is vital to the preservation of linguistic and cultural vitality: "It thus represents a linchpin in this nation's [Canada's] commitment to the values of bilingualism and biculturalism."[9] The Constitutional Drafters imposed limits on the scope of this fundamental right, allowing for the exercise of the right to minority language education "wherever ... the number of children. warrant[s]", thereby, implicitly allowing, according to Tremblay (2006), for pedagogical as well as economic considerations to come into the equation.

Trudeau's "renewed federalism" was decided upon in the absence of Québec in what has become known as the night of the "*longs couteaux*". René Levesque, then First Minister of Québec did not sign the agreement, for the question of the "Québec Nation" had not been resolved by the repatriation episode. The Canada Act 1982 may have marked a new era in Canadian nation-building, by cutting its constitutional umbilical cord with Britain, but it soured relations between Québec and the rest of Canada, which necessitated a second round of constitutional negotiations to bring Québec back into federation.

The nub of the problem was the extent to which there was a genuine desire to establish the promise of a "renewed federalism" which Trudeau had made to opponents of Québécois sovereignty as their reward for having voted "No" to the referendum on the 20th of May 1980. Fournier (1991) suggests that the patriation issue was a time-bomb and a crushing blow for Québec. It had lost its right of veto, which although not inscribed in the British North America Act had been normalised by constitutional custom. It had also lost its claim to being recognised as a constituent nation, or even as the only province with a francophone majority. Fournier further suggests that this "rejection was justified in the name of the equality of provinces, and the priority of individual rights" (1991, p. 12). The issue of collective-versus-individual rights is a classic problem for all states, particularly federal states, as we saw in the earlier discussion on Québec language laws. However, Trudeau's attitude to Québec's collective claims has been described as contradictory, for whilst denying the national group rights of his follow Québécois he affirmed the collective rights of other groups, such as Aboriginal peoples, women, the young and the disabled. Fournier is particularly scathing on this double standard,

> The trouble starts with "national affiliation". The Trudeauites maintain that the rights of a geographically based ethnic group should not be given the same recognition as the rights of natives or linguistic minorities. It is high time to denounce this double standard, this contradiction

that is at the heart of the elaborations of the former prime minister and his disciples. Ultimately, by denying the collective rights of the *Québécois,* Trudeau simply gave precedence to the collective rights of the Anglo-Canadian majority, thereby inevitably sanctioning its domination (1991, 12).

Patriation was perceived by many in Québec as a missed opportunity at best and a deliberate attempt by Canadian centralists to curb its historical rights as a co-equal, co-founding nation. Fournier argues that everyone, except Québec, gained from a renewed federalism that was, ironically, designed initially to meet Québec aspirations.

> The federal government obtained "its" Charter of Rights, the west won additional powers in the field of natural resources and "its" amending formula, the Maritime provinces obtained a firm commitment to equal-isation and to the principle of equal opportunities between provinces, and Ontario managed to avoid the imposition of bilingualism in Parliament and the courts, something which had existed in Québec since the early days of confederation (1991, p. 13).

For the next three years a series of events combined to presage a change in Québec-Ottawa relations. The economic crisis of 1982–83, the public sector cuts, the election of the Conservative Brian Mulroney (a bilingual Quebecois) as Federal Prime Minister and the defeat of the Parti Québécois in December 1985 at the hands of a resurgent Québec Liberal Party led by Robert Bourassa, all contributed to a climate in which fresh constitutional proposals would be put to the people and the provinces. This mood was given fresh urgency by the slump of 1989–1993 which quickened the demands to reform the economy and re-open negotiations on the Constitution.

Meech Lake and the 1992 referendum

Essentially the Meech Lake Accord was a pragmatic counter to the hiatus in constitutional affairs bequeathed by Trudeau's ideological excursions of 1980–1982. Whereas Trudeau had a firm vision of Canadian state development, Mulroney had a negotiator's eye on the process of reconciliation rather than the principled defence of the Canada Act 1982 which Québec had rejected. Consequently on 30 April 1987 the federal government and all ten provincial premiers agreed on a constitutional revision which would bring Québec back into the fold – *'dans l'honneur et l'enthousiasme'* to use Mulroney's words. This agreement was ratified in the constitutional accord of 3 June 1987.

Following Burgess (1988, 1990) and Fournier (1991) one may ask what did Québec want and what price was Mulroney prepared to pay for Québec's

signature on the Canada Act, 1982. In May 1986, at Mount Gabriel, the Quebec Liberal Party premier, Bourassa, presented six conditions for recognising
the legitimacy of the 1982 amendments to the Constitution and participat-
ing fully in constitutional reform. Five of these conditions were met at the
Meech Lake Accord and are presented below:

1. The recognition that Québec constitutes within Canada "a distinct
   society".
2. A formal voice in Supreme Court appointments: three of the nine judges
   will be nominated by the Québec Government.
3. Immigration policy: recognition that Québec has a particular interest in
   this and that it will negotiate an agreement with the Federal Government
   which will be constitutionally entrenched.
4. Limits to federal spending powers in areas of provincial jurisdiction:
   the federal spending power to remain an area of exclusive federal jurisdiction but provincial bargaining rights strengthened by stipulating
   that they should be compensated if they chose not to participate in
   national shared-cost programmes and decided instead to establish similar
   provincial programmes. This will not apply to existing national social
   programmes, such as Medicare, but only to new programmes established
   after the new provision comes into effect.
5. The provisional veto on constitutional amendments affecting the
   province: the principle of unanimity is operative for changes to federal
   institutions – the Senate, House of Commons, Supreme Court – and for
   the establishment of new provinces or their extension into the territories
   (see Burgess, 1988, p. 18).

The sixth condition set out by Gil Remillard at Mont Gabriel aimed
at improving the situation of francophones outside Québec. As Fournier
observes: "This proposal was rejected by some of the western premiers. The
francophones outside Québec weren't mistaken, then, when they accused
Robert Bourassa of abandoning them" (1991, p. 54).

Even so, for the first time since 1867, Quebec's distinct nature had been
formally recognised within the Canadian Constitution. Intended as a recom-
pense for the "*nuit des longs couteaux*", the Meech Lake Accord engendered
very different reactions and interpretations in English Canada and Québec.
This was because the Québec government agreed to the modification of
a number of the conditions but had to present a case that it had gained
everything it wanted when it defended the accord to its own constituents.
By contrast opponents of Meech Lake within English Canada argued that
Québec had been given concessions which were intolerable to most Canadians and had weakened the dualistic nature of federalism. For the first time
since 1867 Québec's distinct nature had been formally recognised within the
Constitution. Critics, such as Fournier, argued that "by creating the illusion

that it could lead to increased powers for Québec, the distinct society pro-vision concealed the main shortcoming of the accord, which was precisely that it established no new division of powers" (1991, p. 22). Furthermore, there remain inherent ambiguities as to what precisely the Accord meant in real terms in relation to such sensitive issues as immigration, federal spend-ing power, the right of veto, the distinct society and the whole question as to whether Canada itself constituted a "national" society in need of strong central (that is, federal) government and direction.

The Accord did not give additional powers to the provinces nor did it facil-itate Québec's desire to be the principal homeland for francophone interests in Canada in any particular manner. Indeed the eventual breakdown of the agreement, as we shall see, was taken by Québecers to imply that the rest of Canada was rejecting both Québec and its French distinctiveness. How-ever, this was not how the framers of the accord assumed their political machinations would be received. Clouded in secrecy, but confident of public acceptance, the provincial premiers assumed that their collective delibera-tions would be endorsed in each of the ten provincial legislatures long before the official deadline of the 23rd of June 1990. In the event three of the ten provinces balked at the accord. In Manitoba the Provincial Legislature on the 23 October 1989 refused to endorse Meech Lake unless significant changes were made. A day later, the New Brunswick Provincial Legislature also refused to endorse it and on the 21 March 1990 announced the intro-duction of a companion resolution. In Newfoundland on 6 April 1990 the Liberal government of Clyde Wells rescinded the earlier agreement carried by 28–10 on 7 July 1988 (for details see Burgess, 1990, pp. 288–9). A crisis First Ministers' meeting was held in Ottawa from 3 to 9 June 1990, but the Meech Lake Accord failed when on 22 June 1990 the Manitoba and Newfoundland legislatures adjourned without endorsing the constitutional amendment (all provinces had to endorse the Accord for it to pass into constitutional law). In the Manitoba case all the MPPs were in favour of debating it except Elijah Harper, a Cree. Technically, his repeated "no" vote was against changing the order paper in parliament; but his doing so ensured that Manitoba could not ratify in time (Whebell, 1998). On 9th March 1991 the ruling Liberal Party delegates in Québec accepted almost all of the Allaire report, a Party committee report on the future of Québec–Canada relations, which in effect recommended a dramatic take over of federal powers by Québec (Kallen, 1995). It proposed both the transfer of exclusive authority over 22 jurisdic-tions from Ottawa to an autonomous Québécois state and a referendum on sovereignty should post-Meech Lake negotiations with the rest of Canada fail. On 20 June 1991 the Québec legislature passed Bill 150, a law that paved the way for a referendum on sovereignty in 1992.

The failure of the Meech Lake Accord gave a new edge to the independence versus renewed federalism debate. Economic difficulties, the repercussions of the Free Trade Agreement between the USA and Canada in 1989, a revived separatist cause after ten years or so of beleaguered nationalism and a provincial government which had denounced the federalist option, have combined to create the conditions for a constitutional impasse.

The federal government response, "Shaping Canada's Future Together" was tabled in the House of Commons on 24 September 1991, led to a national referendum based upon the principles enshrined in the Charlottetown Accord, convened on 28 August 1992, namely regional equality across Canada, and the special status of Quebec as a co-founding nation in Canada. It was designed to incorporate two fundamental, yet contradictory, principles underlying the national unity debate. The result of the national referendum which was held on the date initially set by Québec for a provincial referendum on sovereignty – 26 October 1992 – was a resounding vote of "NO", not only by Québec voters, but also by all other Canadians. The federal government's strategy of making cultural concessions, but of not increasing decentralised power-sharing, backfired to the profound annoyance of almost all parties concerned.

At the turn of the decade even the business community was arguing that sovereignty or even independence would be beneficial to Québec's economy. Clearly the spectre of sovereignty no longer sent shudders through the chambers of Québec's banks and finance houses, or through the fax and internet facilities of its service industries. In academia, many experienced "language watchers", such as Bill Mackey of the *Centre International de Recherche en Aménagement Linguistique (Univeristé Laval)*, were concluding that "in the final analysis only two things are clear. First, the status quo is out of the question. Second, the bottom line is not whether Québec will separate. The question is when, how and how much" (Mackey, 1992, p. 14).

Irreconcilable nationalisms?

Prescient observers have argued that English-speaking Canadians can only act on their national identity through the federal government (Kymlicka, 1998). In consequence, they are compelled to reject any measure of decentralisation which inhibits the federal government's ability to forge national development policy and strengthen Pan-Canadian identity, hence the rejection in English Canada of the Charlottetown Accord. Conversely, the Québécois can only act on their national identity through the provincial government and thus would reject any constitutional reforms which do not reverse federal intervention in areas of social policy and strategic planning.

The PQ's response to this constitutional impasse was to demand a radically fresh Québec-Canadian relationship. The complexity of this impasse in terms of ethnolinguistic issues may be illustrated by trends throughout the 1980s and 1990s. The federal solution to language rights, expressed in the Official Languages Act of 1969 and resting on the "personality" language principle, as discussed earlier, emphasised individual citizen rights. It seemed to be irreconcilable with Québec's group rights approach which effectively "territorialised" the French fact throughout the Province. It might have been anticipated that the federal attempt to pacify Québecois *grievances* through institutional bilingualism would accelerate the shift toward provincial unilingualism. However, McWhinney (1982) argues that executive pragmatism had averted a potential crisis on language policy through the 1970s. Both the federal government, in resisting a direct attack on Québec unilingualism and Québec's own self-restraint in the application of its language-of-work stipulations, had demonstrated a political acumen in so much as "pragmatic adjustments and compromises . . . have facilitated coexistence of federal and Québec language policies, with distinct and separate, but not conflicting, zones of application for each" (McWhinney, 1982, p. 38). Given more recent trends (see below) one cannot afford to be so sanguine!

Throughout the 1980s federal backed interest groups sought to resist this trend toward linguistic territorialisation. For example, the first chapter of Law 101 (1977) to be struck down was the one making French the only official language. Many other sections were challenged in court by Alliance Québec, an anglophone interest group largely subsidised from federal coffers. Maurais (1987, p. 395) notes that of a total budget of $1,369,000 some $1,127,000 was granted by the federal government. In the Miriam case, brought in March 1984, the Court of Appeal ruled that French is compulsory only when an employer communicates with all his/her staff, but this does not prohibit the use of any other language provided that French is also used. The ruling also said that an employee may demand a communication in French from his/her employer.

In July 1984 the Supreme Court rendered Chapter Eight of Bill 101, on the language of instruction, inadmissible because it was incompatible with Article 33 of the 1982 Constitution Act. This judgement substituted the "Canada clause" for the "Québec clause" in Bill 101, enabling children to enter English schools if one of their parents had received their primary education in English anywhere in Canada (Fournier, 1991, pp. 93–4). This was a major challenge to the unilingual conception of Québec and a source of much confusion in the school system. Earlier trends had evidenced the impact of Bill 101, in that in 1976 16.6 per cent of all pupils in Québec were studying in English. By 1986 this had dropped to 10.4 per cent (Fournier, 1991, p. 90). Similarly in the same period the percentage of allophones attending English schools had dropped from 85 per cent to only 36 per cent. Later data suggested that in the early nineties (June 1990) 81 per cent of allophones who had attended French schools continued studying in French at the CEGEP (provincial further and higher education colleges) level.

Further evidence of the federal impress on Québécois language laws is provided by the Supreme Court judgement of 15 December 1988 which established that articles 58 and 69 of Bill 101, which prohibited the use of languages other than French in commercial signs, advertising or corporate names, restrict "commercial" freedom of expression (Fournier, 1991, p. 94). The emphasis on commercial signs is crucial here because, as Maurais (1991) advises, before the decision of the Supreme Court many interpreters assumed that commercial discourse was not included in the concept of freedom of expression. Such pertinent notions of freedom of expression – that is, political, ideological and religious messages – were not submitted to the requirement to use French only or even to have a French translation; they could be in a foreign language only without any translation into French. In Maurais' judgement this is a significant feature because "the provision on the language to be used on public signs is very often used to make Québec appear like a territory where fundamental rights are not respected".

Emphasis on the appropriate sociocultural context for the nurturing of French and/or bilingualism is an important reminder that questions of territorial control, the maintenance of contiguous regions wherein social communication networks can flourish in the threatened language, and relative geographic isolation from the anglicising tendencies of a metropolitan core, are often critical to the reproduction of a minority culture at the regional scale. But for how long? To what extent may these tendencies be accelerated by structural changes in a post-modern society which take less account of the friction of distance? Modern communication facilities shape new geographic realities and groups are not always so well equipped to adapt to changing climates. After all, a common (and ongoing) complaint of Francophones throughout Canada, despite all the Federal legislation, immersion education and public sector reforms, is the refusal of many federal and local agencies to recognise their claim to being a permanent national community, and not an ethnic minority, one amongst many. Multiculturalism policies and the trends in recent constitutional reforms suggest that Canada is moving inexorably toward a linguistic regime which legally favours the individual to the detriment of the group (cf. Kymlicka, 1998; Newman, 2007).

If one chose the group-rights approach as favoured by Québécois politicians one admits that the needs of the minority community are so great that they cannot be met on the basis of individual rights. This also institutes the legal separation of one group from another, which in turn will lead to the strengthening of group distinctiveness and group boundaries, hence the whole thrust of Québécois language, educational and employment legislation from the mid-1970s to the mid-1980s. Elsewhere, both New Brunswick and Manitoba have recognised the need to provide bilingual services for francophones. And, of late, Franco-Ontarians have come closer than ever before to receiving more equitable treatment within their own province. Cartwright (1988) has demonstrated that were the cultural zone of transition between Ontario and Québec to be adopted as a functional bilingual territory then a geographically limited but more socially effective delivery of public services such as French day care centres, recreational facilities and social and health services could be implemented (see Figure 9.1). This representation underlies the significance again of having a territorial domain, within which both languages are respected, but where the minority language can be nurtured without the ever present threat of displacement by the majority tongue. Obviously such a cultural zone would not be impervious to the overwhelming presence of English via the media and commerce, but it would allow scarce resources to be channelled more effectively so as to construct and reinforce a French-medium infra-structure.

More recently Cartwright (1991; 1998) has elaborated his earlier ideas with a model of cultural contact in geographical transition zones and empirical observations on its applicability to the Québec-Ontario border as described in Figure 9.2. On the basis of survey evidence related to inter-cultural accommodation in that zone he concludes that there is greater possibility for interaction and mutual respect among the younger generations either side of the political border. Speaking of programmes designed to encourage active interaction he urges that:

> These traits must be preserved. This geographical region is the one location in the nation where these activities can develop, flourish and contribute to the demise of ethnic, social and cognitive distances that have become endemic in Belgium and in Northern Ireland. An example is provided for the rest of the nation that two solitudes need not be a legacy for Canada, linguistic territorialisation, with its negative connotations, need not be inevitable and empathy between French and English Canada can be attained in time.
>
> (Cartwright, 1991, p. 243)

Symmetrical federalism under strain

The federal government's principle of symmetry would be greatly advanced by the adoption of Cartwright's regionalisation process. But it would not be universally welcomed. The Conseil de la langue française, for example, has officially declared itself opposed to the whole concept of symmetry. In its 1988 statement *'Le projet de loi federal C-72 relatif au statut et a l'usage des langues officielles au Canada'*, it argued *'l'egalité de statut et d'usage ne saurait être atteinte par l'application du mesures identiques 'a des situation différentes mais bien plutôt par des mesures adaptées dont l'effet est de donner 'a chacune des langues une méme sécurité de statut au 'anada'.*

Were balanced bilingualism and symmetry to be given a geographic context by having parts of Québec officially declared bilingual it is probable that such a proposal would be turned down by a majority of francophones. It would be further evidence of the federal government's "Trojan Horse"

330

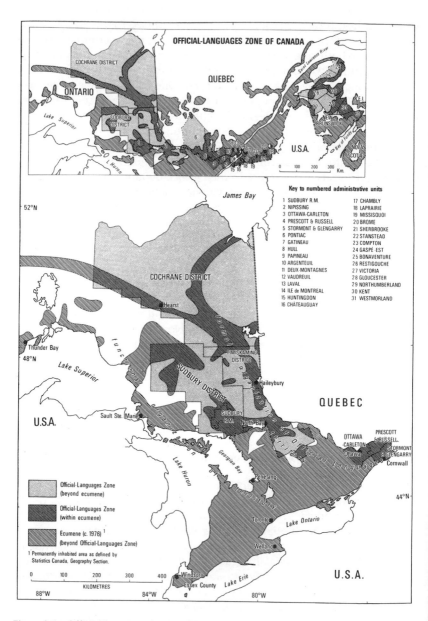

Figure 9.1 Official language zones of Ontario
Source: Cartwright 1988, redrawn and modified with permission.

approach to societal bilingualism. In effect, some parts of Québec are already functionally bilingual in that services may be obtained in both languages even in commercial outlets such as shops and other enterprises. However, many problems would arise if such bilingual districts were made official (Maurais, 1991). Some provision for social and health services in English has been made by Bill 142 (1986), and, as such, there may not be any need for further legislative action, especially in the current political climate which does not favour the extension of an out-moded federal conception of bilingual symmetry.

Cartwright's articulation of a cultural zone of transition leading to increased empathy appeals to nation-builders because it offers the possibility of reduced conflict, but cynics would argue that such cross-border accommodation has not reduced rates of anglicisation by one jot. Neither has symmetrical federalism guaranteed the survival of French outside the Quebecois heartland, for there has been a consistent decline in the proportion of the population who habitually use French as their home language (Cartwright, 1988; Joy, 1992). But as Table 9.3 makes clear the actual numbers increased from 5,546,025 in 1971 to 6,015,680. Even so, rates of anglicisation continue to worry francophone activists and demolinguistic commentators alike. Richard Joy (1992, pp. 51–2) reports that in the seven provinces and two territories west of Ontario and east of New Brunswick, the 1986 census recorded only 84,935 persons who spoke French most often at home, and a further 53,655 who reported that they spoke both French and English. He advises that these figures should be compared with 192,175 who gave French as their reply to the "mother tongue" question and the 49,535 who claimed that their mother tongue was "English and French". "Regardless of the way in which the multiple responses are treated, it appears clear

Table 9.3 Total population and population of French home language, Canada, censuses of 1971–1991

Census year	Total population	French HL	
		Number	% of total
1961	21,568,310	5,546,025	25.7
1971	24,083,505	5,919,855	24.6
1986	25,022,005	6,015,680[a]	24.0
1991	26,994,040	6,288,430	23.3

Sources: 1971, census of Canada; 1981 and 1986, *Adjusted Language Data, Joy*, 1992, 122.
Statistics Canada, 1994, Table A.2.
The "home language" question was asked if only a sample of the population, which excluded "inmates of institutions", in 1981 and 1986.
[a] In 1986, after imputations, the single response "French" was reported for only 5,798,470 persons (23.2% of the total population); the additional 217,210 in this table represents allocation of multiple responses.

that, as francophones move away from the Québec border, they can have little hope of hearing the French language spoken by their grandchildren" (Joy, 1992, p. 52).

A more promising context is afforded by northern New Brunswick and the east and north of Ontario where the geographic concentration of francophones facilitate language maintenance (Waddell, 1988; Williams, 1981; Cartwright, 1988). The initial enquiries of the Royal Commission on Bilingualism and Biculturalism (1967) and the two Bilingual Districts Advisory Boards (1971 and 1975) had established the geolinguistic patterns within New Brunswick and Ontario which formed the basis for many of the detailed recommendations of federal language planning policy.

Québec apart, Gauthier (1982, 8) reports that 75 per cent of those outside Québec claiming French as their mother tongue and 82 per cent of those in 1971 claiming to use it at home, live in New Brunswick and Ontario.

Table 9.4   Official bilingualism in each of several areas of Canada, censuses of 1961–1986

Census year	Area	Total population[a]	Bilinguals'	
			Number	% of total
1961	CANADA	1,82,382,231	12.2	–
	Quebec	52,591,339	25.5	
	NB	598	113	19.0
	Ontario	6,236	493	7.9
	Elsewhere	6,145	286	4.6
1971	CANADA	21,568	2,900	13.4
	Quebec	6,028	1,664	27.6
	NB	635	136	21.5
	Ontario	7,703	716	9.3
	Elsewhere	7,203	384	5.3
1981	CANADA	24,083	3,682	15.3
	Quebec	6,369	2,065	32.4
	NB	689	183	26.5
	Ontario	8,534	924	10.8
	Elsewhere	8,491	510	6.0
1986	CANADA	25,022	4,056	16.2
	Quebec	6,454	2,227	34.5
	NB	702	204	29.1
	Ontario	9,001	1,058	11.7
	Elsewhere	8,864	568	6.4

Source: Joy, 1992, 121, 122.
[a] "Bilinguals" are those who claim to be able to carry on a conversation in English and French. All numbers are in thousands.

This reinforces the long held view that the speed of assimilation is inversely proportional to the concentration of francophones in a region. It also reminds us that the only true areas with a significant bilingual presence outside Québec are New Brunswick and Ontario, highlighting the real difficulty of describing Canada in *toto* as a bilingual country. Table 9.4 charts the fortunes of bilingualism at the federal level and in these three specific provinces demonstrating the gradual rise in the proportion of bilinguals at each successive census count. However, as with all census data caution must be exercised in comparing trends over time. Castonguay (1990) has warned that a tighter formulation of the census question on self-declared ability to speak French

> would reduce by one third the number of non-Francophone Canadians declaring themselves able to speak French, but by only one-ninth the number of non-Anglophones able to speak English. In Québec the number of Francophones able to speak English would drop by one-sixth, while in the rest of Canada the number of Anglophones able to speak French would be practically halved.

He concludes that the looser formulation will have no doubt been adopted for the 1991 census and thus interpretations of that census have to be judicious in the extent one can extrapolate accurate trends about bilingualism.

Anglicisation and Language Shift

Fear of continuing anglicisation is a very powerful mobilising factor within Québécois politics as is the extent to which demographic trends are undermining even Québec's chances of seeing its French-language population remain at a stable level, let alone increase as Statistics Canada interpreters are wont to suggest. Lachapelle and Grenier (1988) and Joy (1992) document how up until the early 1960s, the birth-rates of French-speaking families throughout the country were sufficiently high enough to outweigh the effects of both immigration and anglicisation (Table 9.5). However, in the past four decades differences in fertility rates between francophones and anglophones declined then reversed, with anglophones registering higher fertility rates beginning in the mid-1960s. Thus the reason for the relative decline in the size of the francophone population lies in the phenomenal growth rate of the rest of Canada's population (Table 9.6). In consequence, Joy (1992, p. 34) observes that the proportion of French-speakers has dropped from its long-standing 30 per cent level to only 24 per cent by 1986. Yet the decline in the proportion of francophones does not necessarily tell the whole picture on language use. Lachapelle and Grenier (1988, p. 18) provides three definitions of the francophone population which must condition our

Table 9.5 Total fertility rate (children per 1,000 women) by mother tongue and differential fertility coefficient, Canada, 1956–61 to 1981–86

	Total	English	French	Other
		Total rate		
1956–61	3,865	3,796	4,314	3,479
1961–66	3,514	3,482	3,659	3,396
1966–71	2,490	2,460	2,359	2,849
1971–76	1,979	1,950	1,846	2,322
1976–81	1,746	1,681	1,718	2,110
1981–86	1,657	1,671	1,490	1,937
		Coefficient		
1956–61	100	98	ill	90
1961–66	100	99	104	97
1966–71	100	99	95	114
1971–76	100	99	93	117
1976–81	100	96	98	121
1981–86	W0	101	90	117

Source: Statistics Canada, Census of Canada, 1971, 1981 and 1986; more specifically: Lachapelle and Grenier, 1988, 33.
Note: The differential fertility coefficient is the ratio of a linguistic group's total fertility rate to the total rate of the entire population.

Table 9.6 Annual rate of increase by mother tongue, Canada, 1931–86 (in %)

Period	Total	English	French	Other
1931–41a	1.0	0.9	1.7	0.2
1941–51a	1.7	2.0	1.9	0.0
1951–61	2.7	2.6	2.3	4.0
1961–71	1.7	2.0	1.2	1.3
1971–76	1.3	1.8	0.6	0.5
1976–81	1.1	1.1	0.9	2.0
1981–86	0.8	1.0	0.3	0.4

Source: Statistics Canada, Census of Canada, Lachapelle and Grenier, 1988, 14.
Note: Newfoundland is excluded when the period is followed by the letter "a".

reading of the Canadian situation. They are: 1) all those who speak French; 2) the French mother-tongue group; and 3) francophones (home language). He reports that the first can be a useful indicator in measuring a television network's potential audience, the second could be considered for determining the demand for a school service and the third for estimating the demand for health or social service provision in French.

Table 9.7 Population by ability to speak French and English, Canada, 1931–86 (in %)

Year	Total	English only	French only	English & French	English nor French	English speakers	French speakers
					Neither		
1931a	100	67.5	17.1	12.7	2.7	80.2	29.9
1941a	100	67.2	19.0	12.8	1.0	80.0	31.8
1951a	100	66.2	20.1	12.6	1.1	78.8	32.7
1951	100	67.0	19.6	12.3	1.1	79.3	31.9
1961	100	67.4	19.1	12.2	1.3	79.6	31.4
1971	100	67.1	18.0	13.4	1.5	80.5	31.4
1981b	100	66.8	16.5	15.5	1.2	82.3	32.0
1981	100	66.9	16.6	15.3	1.2	82.2	31.8
1986	100	66.8	15.8	16.2	1.2	83.0	32.0

Source: Statistics Canada, Census of Canada, Lachapelle and Grenier, 1988, 15.
Note: Newfoundland is excluded when the year is followed by the letter "a". In the last two censuses, replies were accepted from individuals who claimed they could not carry on a conversation in their mother tongue. On the other hand, until 1971 it was assumed that those whose mother tongue was English or French could still use their language. For comparison purposes, this hypothesis was applied to the 1981 census results (figures for the year followed by the letter W).

Thus although the rates of monolingual French-speakers have declined from 19.6 per cent in 1951 to 15.8 per cent in 1986 the total proportion of all Canadians claiming to be French-speakers has remained remarkably stable at around 32 per cent (see Table 9.7). Lachapelle and Grenier (1988, p. 16) reasons that this is due to a decrease in the proportion of young children in the population which favours greater bilingualism and the enhanced status of French in society. Pressure on educational agencies and other public bodies to adopt French in non-francophone dominated areas has increased the incidence of bilingualism which counters to some extent the demolinguistic decline of francophones. Joy (1992, p. 35) would confirm this trend by noting that the actual number of children with French as their mother tongue was 25 per cent lower in 1986 than it had been in 1951, adding that the number of children (aged 0–4) with English as their mother tongue had risen by 25 per cent over the same period. If we turn our attention to cohort analysis in Canada we can see further evidence of the erosion of French. Castonguay (1992) has compared the number of francophones aged 0–9 with those roughly a generation older aged 25–34. Table 9.8 reports on his results which show how limited the renewal rates for francophones were in 1986, especially outside of Québec and New Brunswick. He reminds us poignantly that the current situation is now completely different from that which obtained when the Canadian official languages policy was being formulated for then francophone renewal rates of well over 100 per cent were recorded almost

Table 9.8   Renewal of French mother tongue populations, 1986 census

	Adults aged 25 to 34	Children aged 0 to 9	Approximate renewal rate
Newfoundland	600	300	50 %
Prince Edward Island	1,000	500	50 %
Nova Scotia	6,300	2,800	45 %
New Brunswick	44,100	34,900	79 %
Quebec	1,017,300	776,700	76 %
Ontario	89,600	52,600	59 %
Manitoba	9,100	5,100	56 %
Saskatchewan	4,000	1,500	38 %
Alberta	13,300	4,700	35 %
British Columbia	9,200	2,300	25 %
Yukonand Northwest Territories	600	200	30 %

Source: Castonguay, 1992.

everywhere for 1961. Both Joy (1992, p. 36) and Castonguay (1992, p. 3) aver that the francophone presence in Canada will diminish over the foreseeable decades. Only Québec and New Brunswick are in a position to delay this demise and only then if a combination of measures designed to increase assimilation to French, to attract a higher proportion of "francophonisable" immigrants and an unexpected return to high birth rates obtain.

Within Québec a quickened awareness of this threat of being submerged by immigration and the difficulties of advocating natalist policies has brought a new urgency to the support of French unilingualism. Loss of population through selective out-migration (particularly anglophones) has weakened Québec's demographic profile. Data from the *Bureau de la Statistique de Québec* indicates that some 323,000 persons left the province between 1976–81 and a further 234,000 moved out between 1981–1986. Joy (1992, p. 80) estimates that this outward movement affected chiefly the English speaking minority of Québec as revealed by Table 9.9. Of these, it was the young who were differentially encouraged to move with the consequent long term impact on the province's overall demographic vitality and on English language islands which could constitute any future cultural zone in transition.

The twin difficulties of a drop in birth rates and the selective outmigration of a youthful English-speaking population (Joy, 1992, p. 82) aggravate the politics of demolinguistics. In part it helps explain why Bourassa adopted Law 178 against his earlier, 1985 and 1986, promises to bilingualise signs. It also presents government planners with several dilemmas. Joy (1992,

Table 9.9 Province of Quebec, total population and "English" population, censuses of 1871 to 1986 (adjusted data)

Census	Total population	"English" population	"English" total (%)
1871 BO[a]	1,192[d]	243	20.4
1901 BO	1,649	290	17.6
1931 BO	2,874	433	15.1
1951 BO	4,056	492	12.1
EMT[b]	4,056	558	13.8
1971 BO	6,028	640	10.6
EMT	6,028	789	13.1
EHL[c]	6,028	888	14.7
1986 EMT	6,532[e]	679	10.4
EM	6,454	797	12.3

Source: Joy, 1992, 81.
a. BO = "of British origins".
b. EMT = "of English mother tongue".
c. EHL = "of English home language".
d. All numbers are in thousands.
Me 1986 total population used for home language was only 6,454,495; this figure excludes inmates of institutions as well as an estimated 7,815 persons living on certain Indian reserves.
e. The "English" population in 1986 included 676,050 persons who gave the single response "English" to the census question on home language, the figure of 796,695 is as published by Statistics Canada after allocation of all multiple responses.

p. 82) warns that there are "political dangers in any measure intended to openly encourage anglos to remain in Québec, since the departure of persons who prefer to speak English has been the most effective way of reducing the size of the linguistic minority in the province". Alternatively encouraging francophones from outside Québec or even from outside Canada to migrate to Québec has severe implications for the survival of minorities in other provinces and Québec's legitimate involvement in immigration policies. Notwithstanding these difficulties there remains French-Québec's pre-occupation with keeping the population growing, and at the same time keeping up the proportion of francophones in the province. It is no coincidence that the relative decline of Québec's political importance within Federation mirrors its fall in the proportion of citizens it contributes to the state, from a high 29 per cent in 1951 (the first census to include Newfoundland as part of modern Canada) to 25.4 per cent in 1991.

Both Canadian specialists and non-Canadian experts such as Fishman (1991) who have argued that the French language networks have been strengthened by the apparent shift from English to French in Québec have been guilty of misrepresenting the success of the process known as "reversing language shift". In successive contributions Castonguay has demonstrated how compared with the 1971–1986 series, the 1991 data overestimates the assimilating power of the majority languages, French in Québec and English elsewhere, on the provincial language minorities. Consequently, the number of Francised Anglophones in Québec increased suddenly in 1991, and the number of Anglicised Francophones declined abruptly. The raw numbers reveal the imbalance: 58,000 Anglicised Francophones in Québec in 1991, versus 54,000 Francised Anglophones. Multiple answers add to this 26,000 Francophones who claimed to speak English and French equally often at home, whereas only 12,000 Anglophones reported similar bilingual home language behaviour (Statistics Canada, 1993). Anomalies abound. Statistics Canada demonstrates that shift from English to French in Québec is more frequently of the deepest sort, involving loss of the ability to converse in one's mother tongue, than shift from French to English outside Québec. Castonguay avers that this seems absurd, arguing that the power of assimilation of English in the rest of Canada is notoriously greater than that of French in Québec. Three quarters of all shifts from French to English in Québec involves persons of French ethnic origin, and so appears of real significance, while half of claimed shifts from English to French also involved respondents of French origin, thus appearing of lesser significance. He also demonstrates that the position of French among Québec-born Allophones has not improved throughout the 80s.

While language shift is the best indicator of the relative strength of competing languages, it plays a minor role in Québec's demography as fertility and in- and out-migration are far more decisive. Table 9.10 reveals that since 1971 Quebec's anglophone minority has experienced two decades of extremely low fertility. Together with out-migration this has offset language shift.

Both French and English group's reproduction rate–the ratio of children aged 0–9 with a given mother tongue divided by the number of adults aged

Table 9.10 Total fertility rate by mother tongue, Quebec, 1956–1991

Period	English	French	Other
1956–1961	3.26	4.22	2.79
1961–1966	3.04	3.54	2.93
1966–1971	2.09	2.27	2.58
1971–1976	1.62	1.81	2.26
1976–1981	1.46	1.71	2.04
1981–1986	1.46	1.47	1.79
1986–1991	1.54	1.49	1.78

Source: Statistics Canada, 1994, Table 5.1. Castonguay, 1997.

25 to 34 with the same mother tongue–were in 1991 well below the 1.00 replacement level:

English Reproduction Rate: 0.78
French Reproduction Rate: 0.72

Both rates remain inadequate for insufficient birth rates wipe out any gains obtained by either group via language shift. Predictions of a decline in the absolute numbers of Quebec's Francophone population increase the perception of being an endangered people, even if outside specialists and most English Canadians choose not to share this perception. Neither can Quebec presume that the assimilation of Allophones will make a major difference to the numbers game. In Table 9.11 Quebec-born Allophones have been grouped with those who immigrated before 1966, since the relative Francisation of both categories remains around 25 per cent for all censuses. Similarly the three cohorts of Allophones who arrived since 1975 have been grouped, as their relative Francisation rates in 1991 were *c*. 70 per cent. The data show that language maintenance is the norm for all categories of Allophones. Second, that Allophone shift to French is in the thousands or tens of thousands. Castonguay (1994b) comments that to make up for inadequate Francophone fertility, whether in Quebec or in the whole of Canada, would require language shift gains for French of over one hundred thousand, every 5 years. Clearly only English, at the Canadian level, attracts numbers of that magnitude. Table 9.11 also shows a total of 52,700 cases of Francisation among Allophones who immigrated to Quebec after 1965. Had

Table 9.11 Language shift among Allophones, by immigration status, Quebec, 1991 (to the nearest hundred)

Immigration status	Total	Total shift (1)	Shift to French (2)	Relative Francization (2)/(1)
Total	582,000	220,500	86,000	39%
Quebec-born/ Immigrated-1966	303,900	134,400	33,800	25%
Immigrated 1966–1970	41,700	16,200	6,800	42%
Immigrated 1971–1975	43,100	16,800	9,300	55%
Immigrated 1976–1991	193,300	53,100	36,600	69%

Source: 1991 Census, special tabulation. Cited in Castonguay (1994b).

the relative Francisation rate remained at 25 per cent the French share of total Allophones shift would have been about 21,500 (25 per cent of 86,100). The additional 30,000 recorded is the total gain due to increased Francisation of Allophones who immigrated to Quebec over the past 25 years.

On the basis of his detailed analysis Castonguay (1994a) concludes that,

> the demographic impact of the reorientation of language shift in favour of French among Allophone immigrants to Quebec is slim, if not fragile. ... the greater part of the demographic gain for French is due not so much to measures intended to reverse – or reorient – language shift, like Bills 22 and 101, as to the change in linguistic make-up of Allophone immigration.

In 2001, 5.2 million Canadians (or 17.7 per cent of the population) considered themselves bilingual compared to 1.7 millions (or 12 per cent of the population) in 1951. More than 90 per cent of the population who declared themselves to be bilingual lived in the four provinces of Quebec, New Brunswick, Ontario and British Columbia. Sixty Seven per cent of the Anglophones living in Quebec were bilingual while 84.8 per cent of the Francophones living in provinces and territories other than Quebec were also bilingual. Table 9.12 reveals the distribution of English and French mother tongue population in 2001.

I have concentrated on the demographic trends because they reveal that the Canadian duality has been severely eroded and demonstrate that counter-measures to bolster the Francophone population are far from

Table 9.12   The distribution of English and French mother tongue population in 2001

Provinces/Territories	English	French
Newfoundland	500.1	2.3
Prince Edward Island	125.4	5.9
Nova Scotia	834.8	35.4
New Brunswick	468.1	239.4
Quebec	591.4	5,802.0
Ontario	8042.0	509.3
Manitoba	831.8	45.9
Saskatchewan	822.6	18.6
Alberta	2395.8	62.2
British Columbia	2849.2	58.9
Yukon	24.8	0.9
Northwest Territories	28.9	1.0
Nunavut	7.2	0.4

Source: Census of Canada 2001. Office of the Commissioner of Official Langauges.

predictable at either federal or provincial level. Much of the substance of popular politics deals with misconceptions as regards demo-linguistic competition and feeds on rather closed cosmologies vis à vis interpreting group identity and national claims and counter-claims. Nowhere is this more vital than in the contemporary discussions focused on the possibility of partitioning parts of Canada.

The issue of partition

We have seen that language legislation and planning in Québec has differed sharply from the Federal conception of language rights and language regimes. Whereas the latter sought to institute language parity from coast to coast, guaranteeing individual justice and access to public services, the *Québecois* provincial government sought through its language legislation a socio-political reform which would guarantee the primacy of group rights within the francophone heartland. The national construction of a particular version of social space is crucial to both sides of the argument.

The work of Cartwright and Williams (1982) and Bourhis (1984) should alert us to the fact that many language groups are not only internally differentiated, but also in some cases, do not endorse the wholesale application of language legislation and reform at the immediate point of local contact. Scale and sensitivity are important components of any successful language programme. Often standardised language planning rules are much less effective than anticipated in serving local needs, and this for a variety of reasons, not the least is the fact that many such services are designed without reference to the needs and interests of local residents. In consequence the gap between the potential and the actual use of government services often leave language activists embarrassingly silent.

In modern societies, control of the local state, as a limited expression of national autonomy, is vital for group survival. It is the local state which sets the conditions of possibility for cultural reproduction through the formal agencies of education, the law and public administration. However, there is a real danger that if language planning is embraced uncritically by the constituent group, it could lead to an even greater dependence upon the formal state apparatus. In effect, this is the Trojan horse argument used by *Québécois* opponents to the federal policy of equality, and of establishing bilingual districts within Québec which would increase the anglicised nature of federal bilingual services (Cartwright and Williams, 1982). But we must also recognise the irony that the local state is the only institution which can afford to mount the expensive services now deemed essential to minority cultural reproduction.

It has been claimed that if Quebec secedes then a further partition of its territory along ethno-linguistic lines should be instituted. Physical removal and separation of conflicting parties is a time-honoured expedient, but partition

is a complex multi-faceted process dictated as much by the external characteristics of the international system as it is by internal negotiation and
rapprochement (Williams and Kofman, 1989).

Many who have promoted partition have argued that any regions that
are to remain with Canada should be contiguous, thereby reinforcing a
geographic principle (The Ottawa Citizen, May 18, 1997; A14). Such advocates have fixed upon the situation of anglophones within Quebec with
little or no regard for the francophones who live between Montreal and
the Ontario border or for the neighbouring Franco-Ontarians, who, if we
are to consider democratic principles have a comparable right to have their
interests discussed. Speculating about these issues Cartwright and Williams
(1997b) have asked if the "rights" of Anglo-Quebeckers are brought forth,
can we ignore the plight of Franco-Ontarians who are contiguous with
Quebec and who live within the sphere of influence of that province:
that is, who are geographically similar in location and situation to the
Anglo-Quebeckers.

This is an important issue for three reasons. First as a matter of principle
any change to the constitutional status of Quebec will impact upon francophones living outside Quebec in other provinces. Second, many of the
Franco-Ontarians and Québécois, who voted "no" in 1997, who live in the
Ottawa Valley are deeply integrated into the federalist structure and serve as
a mirror for the rest of Canada as to how its bilingual citizenry operates in
and around the capital (Ottawa). Third, if the partition of Quebec becomes
a more pressing reality, there will be other voices questioning the right of
parts of Ontario to be seeded to Quebec. The implications are profound and
have been thoroughly analysed by Cartwright and Williams (1997a,b) whose
detailed argument we rehearse below.

About forty per cent of Ontario's 530,000 francophones live within or
near the Ottawa Valley, mainly in the Ottawa region and in the United
Counties of Russell and Prescott. Within the latter they are a majority, and
their counties abut the Quebec border. Most can trace their heritage to
the original settlers of the region who came from Quebec; and continuous
interaction with kin and kind across the provincial border has contributed
significantly to their cultural sustenance. A majority of Franco-Ontarians
have supported the federalist's cause, but in the event of separation their
cultural security in the rest of Canada would be called into question, as
would the constitutional recognition of Canada's two official languages.
This could bring an end to official bilingualism federally and for provin-
cially funded support for French-language services in education, the courts
and government services. In the face of the loss of cultural support systems that have been obtained gradually over several generations, it is not
fanciful to assume that many Franco-Ontarians who are adjacent to the
Quebec border may opt, as individuals, to relocate to Quebec or decide as
a group, to seek territorial inclusion within a contiguous sovereign Quebec.

This would be consistent with the partitionist's geographic principle, and could draw support from the data illustrated in Figure 9.2, which charts long-established settlement patterns. But even if never realised, such an expression of affinity would serve to entrench the situation of Montreal and the Ottawa Valley region (between Hull and Montreal) as federalist enclaves within Quebec.

A basic assumption of the partionists' argument is that the Anglophone regions of Quebec are contiguous to Ontario and thus constitute a natural extension of Anglo-Canada. Between the island of Montreal and the Ontario border, however, there are a large number of francophones in Sopulanges-Vaudreuil who voted "yes" in the last referendum. If those who voted "no" in this electoral district, and on the Island of Montreal, were revisited and told that partition was a definite federalist policy, one should not under-estimate the degree of solidarity that could arise in opposition to a threat against Quebec's territorial integrity. When we incorporate into this situation the possible wishes of the Franco-Ontarians, the distance of the Ontario border for Montreal and the Ottawa Valley has increased substantially.

Should partitionists recognise the enclave situation of Montreal and the Ottawa Valley, they must be prepared to address the problems of sustaining a demographically vital population, of attracting and holding investment capital and the inherent problems of travel to and fro from such enclaves that are surrounded by a country that is unsympathetic to their linkages with the rest of Canada. Inevitably such residents would be perceived by the rest of the world as second-class or diluted Canadians, with all the con-sequent negative implications for economic and social life. If the economy of Montreal has been weakened because of the recent uncertain political climate, it is doubtful that an enclave existence could improve on this.

The removal of even a portion of Montreal and the Ottawa Valley from the posited Republic of Quebec would be a serious blow to the economy of the nascent country and, consequently, may not be endorsed through international law. Similarly, the loss of the hinterlands in northwest Quebec, through demands by the indigenous people for partition, could constitute a further erosion of Quebec's economic viability. This is not to deny the right of the Aboriginal peoples to remain within Canada, nor that these lands do indeed adjoin the Rest of Canada, but such recognition must be balanced against the rights of Quebec to expect its northern territories to be used as a continued resource base. This area has received considerable capital development, and contains resources that are essential to Quebec's future economic well-being. Cartwright and Williams (1997a) have sug-gested that an accord could be reached for this frontier region similar to that for Northern Ireland (The Anglo-Irish Agreement, 1985) whereby Bri-tain and the Republic of Ireland consulted over the administration of that peripheral territory. Admittedly this is an uncomfortable precedent, but

344

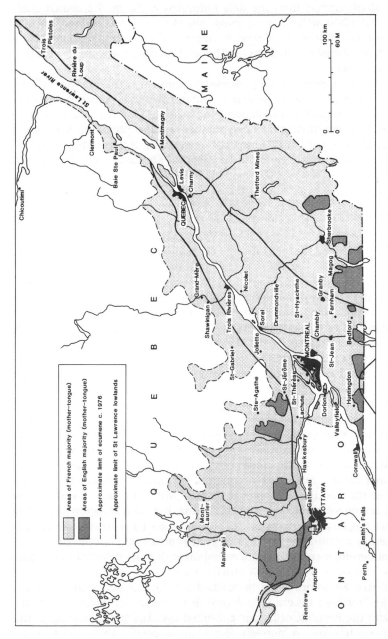

Figure 9.2 Areas of French and English settlement by mother tongue, Southern Quebec, 1976
Source: Cartwright (1980) reproduced in Williams (1994, p. 224) with permission.

joint administration would permit the Aboriginal peoples to retain Canadian citizenship, while Québec would have clear access to resources in the region.

Those who reject the Cartwright and Williams (1997a and b) position on the issue of partition will say that they have not fully addressed the wishes of federalists within Quebec who wish to remain a part of Canada. There are precedents in international law for their situation. While the Canadian government will not endorse the claim of sovereigntists that Quebeckers will automatically have a right to Canadian citizenship upon separation, individuals may apply for that right. Cartwright and Williams endorse such a provision as this would reduce the potential for conflict. In the future, if life in the Republic of Québec is not to their liking federalists may use that right to move to the Rest of Canada.

Such circumstances are anathema to those who envisage Canada as inviolable. They play down the fact that Canada has been subject to a number of different guiding ideologies and adopted radically different positions towards various groups. Kallen's (1995) analysis (see Figure 3.2 above) has summarised four policy strategies we may identify as the Melting Pot (Integration), a Mosaic approach (Cultural Pluralism), Dominant Conformity (Absorption) and Paternalism (Colonialism). Within these four models we have a differentiation between exclusive and inclusive definitions of civil rights. Kallen describes both the melting pot and mosaic models as North American myths. The myth of the mosaic model relegated cultural and structural pluralism for ethnic minorities to the private domains of life. Within the public sector, all individuals would be accorded equal opportunities without reference to ethnic classification. But with regard to collective rights, the public sector was regarded as an English or French Canadian cultural monolith. It is this conception which is enshrined in the world's first national Multiculturalism Act (1988) which recognises multiculturalism as a fundamental characteristic of the Canadian heritage.

By contrast many of those who are opposed both to an extension of multiculturalism and to Québecois "distinctiveness" are espousing modern variants of the Anglo-Canadian dominant conformity model of ethnic integration. In common with the rest of the western world, Canada is re-evaluating the structural transformations which have resulted in the weakening of its core ethnic nationalist base, an increase in social pluralism and a greater recognition being accorded to its own indigenous minorities. But just as many autochthonous minorities are finally being treated according to policies predicated on pluralism on the basis of equality, so non-indigenous minorities are still treated according to policies predicated on pluralism on the basis of non-equality. This is the basis of the paternalism model which has historically underlain the legal conditions of the Indian Acts (1896–1950). Despite improvements in recent decades the long term damage of paternalistic policies is profound and possibly irreversible in its consequences.

> While this paternalistic picture of dominant-Indian relations is slowly changing, the long-term outcome of paternalism was to create a stigmatised, dependent, welfare population, whose very existence at the margins of Canadian society, demonstrated unequivocally the dehumanising consequences of denial of human rights and the utter failure of policies predicated on the paternalistic ideology of the white man's burden.
>
> (Kallen, 1995, p. 184)

How do these two trends impact the one upon the other in matters of identity?

Respect for ethnonational identity in multicultural societies

The attempt to reconcile the differences both between Québec and English-speaking Canada, and between these dominant national groups and more recent immigrant cultures has had a chequered history. Dr Hedy Fry, Secretary of State for Multiculturalism, defined multiculturalism as the new framework for Canadian unity. "As a national policy of inclusiveness, multiculturalism's activities aim to bring all Canadians closer together, to enhance equal opportunities, to encourage mutual respect among citizens of diverse backgrounds, to assist in integrating first-generation Canadians, to promote more harmonious intergroup relations, and to foster social cohesion and a shared sense of Canadian identity" (Fry 1997; see also Canadian Heritage, 1998, 2007). The renewed multiculturalism programme has been charged with the responsibility of holding the country together. It has three objectives:

- **"social justice**: the program will seek to break down the barriers to equality, like racism and discrimination.
- **civic participation**: the program will encourage and enable individuals, groups, institutions and the private sector to ensure that all Canadians regardless of their origins, can participate fully in the social, economic, cultural and political life of the country.
- **identity**: the program will promote social equality and cultural diversity as fundamental Canadian values" (Fry, 1997).

This, of course, presumes that cultural diversity is a positive and growing feature of modern societies. It has value not only at the individual level of recognising human worth but also at a societal level as legitimising access to political power and free participation in the democratic process. It follows that the ways of managing cultural diversity will vary according to why we think it has value. Let us consider the difficulties of operating an ideology of Canadian multiculturalism within a model of liberal society which purports to recognise more than the mere survival of cultures by acknowledging their permanent worth.

In Charles Taylor's magisterial essay "Multiculturalism and 'The Politics of Recognition'" (Taylor, 1992) it is argued that the politics of equal respect embodied within the discourse of recognition, does not serve us well as we imagine. This is because there is "a form of the politics of equal respect, as enshrined in a liberalism of rights, that is inhospitable to difference, because (a) it insists on uniform application of the rules defining these rights, without exception, and (b) it is suspicious of collective goals". Taylor calls it inhospitable because:

> it can't accommodate what the members of distinct societies really aspire to, which is survival. This is (b) a collective goal, which (a) almost inevitably will call for some variations in the kinds of law we deem permissible from one cultural context to another, as the Quebec case clearly shows (p. 61).

The absence of due recognition can lead to a break-down of partnership, which Taylor (1994, p. 255) argues has characterised the Canadian experience of national identity. Let us illustrate the potential for partnership building by reference to the presumption that we owe equal respect to all cultures.

> If withholding the presumption is tantamount to a denial of equality, and if important consequences flow for people's identity from the absence of recognition, then a case can be made for insisting on the universalization of the presumption as a logical extension of the politics of dignity. Just as all must have equal civil rights, and equal voting rights, regardless of race or culture, so all should enjoy the presumption that that their traditional culture has value ... The claim seems to be that a proper respect for equality requires more than a presumption that further study will make us see things this way, but actual judgements of equal worth applied to the customs and creations of these different cultures.
>
> (Taylor, 1992, p. 68)

The dread hand of homogenisation can lie heavy on any attempt to maintain diversity through an appeal to universal considerations of human dignity and worth. But the filter process by which some decide the relative worth of others is far too imperfect. At its root there is an inherent paradox, between the demands for equality and the forces for efficiency.

The peremptory demand for favourable judgements of worth is paradox-ically – perhaps one should say tragically – homogenising. For it implies that we already have the standards to make such judgements. By impli-citly invoking our standards to judge all civilisation and cultures, the politics of difference can end up making everyone the same (p. 71).

Put in this form Taylor argues that the demand for equal recognition is unacceptable. Rather what we need is a more humble approach which does not imply the pejorativisation of all other cultures. Rather it requires "an admission that we are very far away from that ultimate horizon from which the relative worth of different cultures might be evident" (p. 73).

A great stumbling block in the recognition of equal worth is the operation of the market and bureaucratic state which as Taylor argues strengthens the "enframings that favour an atomist and instrumentalist stance to the world and others" (1991, p. 11). Community solidarity and public participation in the decision-making process are weakened and ethno-linguistic groupings, for example, are drawn closer into their own sub-cultures rather than form-ing a distinct part of the whole society. This fragmentation occurs partly through "a weakening of the bonds of sympathy, partly in a self-feeding way, through the failure of democratic initiative itself. Because the more fragmented a democratic electorate is in this sense, the more they transfer their political energies to promoting their partial groupings, and the less pos-sible it is to mobilise democratic majorities around commonly understood programme" (Taylor, 1991, p. 113).

Fragmentation and anomie seem to be winning the day for far too many previously committed citizens. And yet they all have, in principle, the right of free association, free speech and political representation, the hallmarks of a modern democracy.

A society in which this goes on is hardly a despotism. But the growth of these two facets is connected, part effect and part cause, with the atrophy of a third, which is the formation of democratic majorities around meaningful programs that can be carried to completion (p. 115).

One of the key determinants of majoritarian democracy in Quebec, no less than in Canada, is the degree to which immigrants feel sufficiently empowered both to trust the host majority and to align themselves with others to pursue common programmes of public good, whether that be in the field of conventional public services, such as education or more specialist interest-oriented projects, which do not necessarily have an ethnic overtone or implication of fragmentation (cf Williams, 1996b).

Clearly the Canadian state is deeply implicated in this process of change with regard to its multicultural policy, but the conventional focus on training in official languages to immigrant adults to integrate them in to the economy is now in straitened circumstances. In consequence the government is trying to find the means to withdraw from the financial implications of support and give back the matter to the provinces and the non-governmental organisations. The sharp end of this focus is immigration. Any disputes about the presence of immigrants are concentrated on issues such as employment and racism, the profile on language training is low and the language *per se* is not an issue, just access through to it via training. Such considerations appear to side-step the central obligation of the multicultural state to supply an adequate infra-structural support upon which may be grafted the aspirations and legitimate expectations of the constituent groups, so that they may flourish because of, not despite, state intervention and sustenance. This smacks of back-tracking from the central commitment of the seventies to promote universal bilingual education in both state languages, English and French, as the cement for nation-building. What of the demand for bilingual education outside Quebec? If Quebec becomes more detached from Canada will this demand decline for all save the social and economic elite?

What conclusions can be drawn from the immersion experience as to both the construction of a Pan-Canadian identity and as an appropriate methodology for language policy-making? Harley investigated graduates of French immersion programmes and found that few of them make substantial use of French. What does this mean in terms of identity formation and cultural empathy? She questioned whether this necessarily implied that they risked losing the second language skills they had acquired in school and offered four conclusions:

1) "Self-perceptions of language loss tend to be gloomier than objective tests reveal.
2) The higher one's initial proficiency, the better one's long-term proficiency is likely to remain.
3) Frequency of current use is related to language maintenance, particularly of speaking skills.
4) New exposure to the language can lead to rapid recovery of 'attrited' skills" (Harley, 1994, p. 240).

Rather than argue for more of the same, Harley commends a far greater emphasis on oral French both inside and outside immersion classrooms. This should incorporate what Stern has called " 'a general language education component' within immersion programmes, one that would focus on developing learning autonomy and a more pro-active approach to the use of French beyond the classroom context" (Harley, 1994, pp. 240–1).

These myriad policies have territorial considerations, but the linchpin of any development in Canada, is, the role that the people of Québec choose for themselves (Williams, 1996c).

Contemporary Québec

Identity construction through education and language entitlement through legislation are the twin hall-marks of Québec's strategy. The *Charter of the French Language* prescribes specific requirements with respect to the language of trade and commerce, the goal of these stipulations being to protect consumers and to confirm the French character of Québec. The *Charter of the French Language* thus makes general provisions for the mandatory predominant use of French in billboard advertising, a measure whose legitimacy has been recognised by the Supreme Court of Canada. The *Charter* also provides for the use of French labelling on products, their containers and packaging, as well as the documents and objects included with them. However, this general rule in no way prohibits the use of another language. This legislative measure has been adjusted to include various exceptions, formulated especially so that, under certain circumstances, documents can be drawn up, and posters, lettered, in a language other than French, without French being present (Dumas, 2007).

Québec's public administration plays a key part in enhancing the prestige of the French language, and it is entrusted to guarantee that the role of the language in society genuinely reflects its status as the official language of Québec. Thus, the public administration (including, most notably, the government as well as the various ministries, government organisations, municipalities, and educational and health care and social service institutions) has many obligations stemming from Québec's *Charter of the French Language* so that services must be delivered in French. However, the public administration can provide services in other languages considered opportune. Moreover, the *Charter of the French Language* makes provisions for the legal recognition of some municipal, educational, health care and social service institutions as "bilingual". That recognition gives them more leeway in some situations. Thus, they can use French and another language in their name, on signs and posters, in their internal communications and they can hire personnel who do not know French.

Dumas (2007) has described how the Charter is applied through three administrative bodies. First, the Office Québécois de la langue française (French language bureau) defines and implements Québec's linguistic research and terminology policy and ensures that French remains the language of communications, work, trade and commerce, public administration and company operations. It monitors the implementation of the *Charter* through responding to complaints or on its own initiative, carry out inspections and inquiries. Second the Commission de toponymie du Québec (Geographic names board) is responsible for officially approving and disseminating place names. Third the Conseil supérieur de la langue française (French language council) advises the minister on all matters related to the French language in Québec.

In all, these bodies have 260 employees and an annual budget of $22.5 million.

Dumas's analysis is sensitive to the false perception which outsiders have concerning Québec's language policy, for of course, this has a determining effect on issues such as investment, corporate relocations, immigration tendencies and the like.[10] Here are some of his examples of the general perceptions of participants:

- The public school system is French only, and Anglophones can only attend private or bilingual schools;
- As concerns the justice system, the defendant has the right to an English-speaking lawyer but not much else;
- English signs are prohibited, and offenders go to prison;
- Anglophones cannot live in English in Québec; and
- Québec's laws come from France, and a defendant is presumed guilty until proven innocent.[11]

Consequently there is a need to outline a few elements of the language policy which will help set the record straight by countering some of the more widespread negative perceptions:

- Québec's laws are published in both English and French and have exactly the same legal status;
- In Québec's courts, people can choose to use either French or English;
- With respect to education, the Anglophone minority has the right to its own publicly funded schools and school boards, and the same applies at the postsecondary level for colleges and universities;
- In the area of health care, the law also grants all English-speaking people the right to receive health care and social services in their own language;
- The Anglophone media network is very impressive indeed: it includes 17 radio stations, 3 television stations, 2 daily newspapers, 17 weeklies appearing exclusively in English, and 15 in both French and English. Among the magazines and periodicals sold in Québec, 27.5 per cent are in French (approximately 1,100), while the rest (in the neighbourhood of 3,000) are in English, representing about 70 per cent of the total Québec market; and
- Lastly, the Québec government funds and subsidises libraries, theatres, films, television and cinematic productions, as well as various English-language cultural institutions in the same manner and according to the same rules as those applied to their Francophone counterparts.

A second prominent feature of contemporary Québec is its changing relationship with both the ROC and the USA. This largely economic and strategic readjustment also has a language component which is related to the above discussion because in many cross-border situations linguistic externality comes into play, usually as a barrier and an extra cost for commercial interaction. Lisée (2000, 2007) has drawn attention to the language border effect and has queried why the linguistic border effect found elsewhere in the OECD by Helliwell is not an impediment to Québec's commercial surge as a region state. Lisée advises that if there was no language border effect before the seventies, it is simply because the people then in charge of the economic interface between Québec and the Anglo-American continent were Anglophones.[12] Today, although Anglophones still enjoy over-representation in management (26 per cent in 1988, given 10 per cent of the population), the French-speakers are for the first time in the majority (58 per cent, given 81 per cent of the population), Allophones accounting for the remaining 16 per cent. Francophones are now primarily in charge of the economic interface with Anglo-America. He argues that there should have been a concomitant surge of the language border effect, instead of a clearly unimpeded surge of the ratio of exports. But this has little to do with Canadian linguistic policy. In Canada outside Québec, decades of effort under the Official Languages Act brought bilingualism there from 9 per cent in 1951 and 9.4 per cent in 1971 to only 10.8 per cent in 1996. Surprisingly perhaps the rise in the level of bilingualism of Anglos in the ROC is also partly a (perverse) result of Québec policy. Lisée's calculations (2000, 134) based on Statistics Canada's sensitivity test of 1988 on what a real conversation is, show that at least 40 per cent of the new bilingual Anglos added in the ROC between 1971 and 1996 are in fact Québec bilingual Anglos having moved out of Québec, in part because they disagreed with linguistic and political developments in their home province. Overall, in the ROC, the proportion of Canadians that can carry a meaningful conversation in French has shrunk somewhat, from 8.2 per cent in 1951 to 7.6 per cent in 1996.

Thus he concludes that between 1971 and 1996 a threshold has been crossed that has prevented the advent of a linguistic border effect. For Lisée the bipartisan achievement of thirty years of linguistic experiment in Québec is the creation of a working population that retains, or in many cases gains, French as a real internal functional language; expanding the use of English as an indispensable interface tool; and doing this at a time when the linguistic makeup of the managerial class changes radically. Further when a majority of skilled Francophones and Anglophones are bilingual and when a majority of allophones speak three languages in a given region, there is a potent locational externality at play. Lisée avers that operational bilingualism enables Québec to provide a unique, real time connection to innovations in both French and English-speaking Europe and the Anglo-American continent. "It has effects in intra-industrial trade, in research and development, in post-secondary education, in public

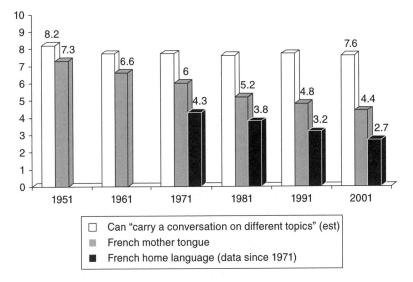

Figure 9.3 Fifty years of dwindling French minority outside Québec
Source: Lisée (2007).

policy experiments, in culture. Québec has the ability to import, blend and re-export concepts, no outside translation required" (Lisée, 2007).

Québec's new found economic strength will doubtless reinforce the territorialisation of official languages within Canada.[13] Lisée (2007), like Castonguay, comments that the rate of assimilation of French speakers has increased steadily from the outset of the Trudeau initiative when the rate of assimilation was of 27 per cent per generation to 36 per cent in 2001.[14] This means that, outside Québec and Acadia, each generation of French-speakers will be half the size of the previous one. English-Canada is thus in the process of successfully assimilating it's heretofore most important minority (Figure 9.3).

Asymmetrical federalism

Kymlicka (1998) argues that English Canadians perceive Canadian federalism in "territorial" terms, rather like the USA, while French Canadians have adopted a multinational vision of federalism whereby the constituent elements are people rather than geographical regions. Given the failure of the Meech Lake and Charlottetown Accords, along with previous attempts to save an essentially territorial conception of federation, "the only remaining question is whether English-speaking Canadians can be persuaded to accept the multination conception of federalism". By abandoning Pan-Canadian nationalism and adopting an asymmetrical federal structure, English Canada could engage with Quebec on a more realistic basis, always remembering that the right to secede by democratic means from this multinational federation would be guaranteed.

As society becomes more plural and social mobility increases, there is an increase in the tension between the functional provision of bilingual public services and the formal organisation of territorial-based authorities charged with such provision. This tension is exacerbated by steady immigration into fragile language areas, for it leads to language-related issues being publicly contested as each new domain is penetrated by the intrusive language group. This, not multiculturalism, is the pertinent linguistic reality of Canada. Some would argue that

> multiculturalism disguises the fact that Canada is divided into distinct linguistic and cultural zones, the anglophone and the francophone, each of which is separated from the other by a bilingual buffer zone, which, to the west of Quebec, runs down the Outaouais valley, and to the east cuts across northern New Brunswick. Apart from those zones, Canada is divided into two solidly monolingual areas, with a few marginal exceptions here and there. In a sense Wardaugh's (1983) "real" Canada is the most cogent single refutation of the multicultural model on its own terms, with a variety of other attempts to grasp the multicultural nettle becoming entangled in a web of regionalisms, interest groups, ethnic stereotyping and other factors. Various other non-Marxist analyses go beyond Wardaugh in linking the central dichotomy in Canada to the question of Quebec nationhood and traditional social inequalities between anglophone and francophone Canadians. . . . the real impetus in Quebec nationalism is not, surprisingly enough, considered to be primordial ethnic sentiment but rather 'class conflict in linguistic disguise.'
>
> (McAll, 1990, pp. 176–7)

In a number of detailed cameos Cartwright (1980, 1988, 1991, 1998) has illustrated this language contact situation with respect to Ontario, focusing on the implications of honouring the rights of francophone citizens in a predominantly anglophone society. An over-concern with linguistic categorisation and the charting of demo-linguistic trends can be dysfunctional and lead to a false impression of the abiding strength of ethnic identity as a social reality with meaning and purchase for every-day life. Critical in this obfuscation and myth-perpetuation is that central instrument of Canadian social engineering, the quinquennial census. Far from being a neutral instrument of record the Census interpretations are used by Government to signal key changes in the demo-linguistic balance, and it is to independent scrutinisers like Castonguay (1992, 1994a), that we have to look to find out what is really happening in linguistic matters.

In McAll's (1990) view "these various critiques suggest that the Canadian census has created the impression of continuing multiple ethnic distinctiveness in non-francophone Canada when, in reality, the mosaic has long been subject to a process of melting down". Traditionally 80 per cent of Canada's immigrants used to come from countries of European heritage; by 1991 almost 75 per cent came from Asia, Africa, Latin America and the Caribbean. Currently, Asian-born persons represent half of the immigrants who came to Canada between 1981 and 1991.

At the current rate of demographic change the population will start to decline by the 2020s. To avert this contraction – and the accompanying decrease in the size of the economy – it is estimated that Canada needs to increase its population by 1 per cent per annum, hence McDougall's proposed figure of an increase of 250,000 migrants per annum. However, during the first five years of nineties the actual immigration figure was approximately half the required total. The suspicion remains that this slow down is a calculated move on behalf of the federal government to appease a Canadian public that has become increasingly hostile toward certain "foreigners" as a result of structural economic difficulties occasioned by the recession/s of the 1990s and the perceived growth of terrorism and religiously inspired acts of violence. Coupled with this caution is a shift in emphasis within the Ministry of Multiculturalism towards combating racism and educating the public in being far more sensitive to the demands of a plural society.

Conventionally the concerns of "nonvisible minorities" in the past and visible minorities today are pragmatic and initially have to do with *freedoms from* such features as racism, exploitation, cultural marginalisation, and systematic exclusion from the full benefits of citizenship. The resources of multicultural agencies are utilised as a means of redressing past grievances, and serve as a buffer between the subordinate and the dominant organisations and value system. This is essentially the social justice view of multiculturalism we discussed earlier whereby it offers some means of protection from discrimination.

However, as they become better organised astute groups will press for a greater recognition of their cultural rights, over and above those already recognised, a drive we may call *freedoms to* such features as mutual respect, equitable employment, comprehensive education, individual choice and empowerment to decide their lifestyle and future prospects as participative citizens. Multiculturalism, from this perspective, is a set of institutional opportunities for individual and group advancement in a competitive environment. In other words it becomes a platform for social progress.

Yet such advances should not overshadow parallel attempts by the Federal Government to revitalise its commitment to offering both official minority communities robust public services. In summarising the Canadian approach to protecting and promoting English and French, Tremblay (2006) argues that Canada has adopted a progressive approach, which recognises the inherent value of linguistic diversity.[15] Such clarity of purpose in legislation has proven to be a key to its successful implementation, within which the Commissioner of Official Languages plays a vital role in a system wherein the Canadian courts have asserted their role in protecting minority language rights.

An improved *Official Languages Act* was enacted by Parliament in 1988.[16] Now federal officers and employees were expressly granted the right to work in either official language,[17] although this right is modulated: the right applies in delimited "bilingual regions", the right of the public to services in either official language prevails over those of federal employees to work in theirs, and the specific duties imposed on federal institutions, while reasonably generous, should not be equated with complete or absolute bilingualism in the workplace. As Newman (2004) has noted, "ensuring an effective environment for the use of the minority language within the internal activities of government, where the majority language tends to dominate" is one of the most difficult goals to achieve in practice".[18]

The November 2005 amended Part VII of the Official Languages Act is a case in point. All federal institutions are now legally required to adopt positive measures to ensure the equality of French and English, in fact and not just by convention. Such measures, according to the Office of the Commissioner of Official Languages, should be

> proactive, systematic, geared towards concrete and measurable results, and adapted to meet specific needs of communities. These measures should also help strengthen the social and community institutions at the heart of everyday life (i.e. schools, health care facilities, business development centres, arts and culture centres etc)
>
> (Bulletin Infoaction, 2007, p. 8)

The amendments also allow minority language communities to seek legal redress if their rights are not respected.[19] Thus from a top-down perspective there are ample opportunities to exercise language rights and to seek redress of grievances, but within the partnership communities, as Cardinal had demonstrated, not all is sweetness and light. Nevertheless Tremblay (2006) has concluded that the federal model is a "carefully modulated and adapted scheme, with built-in limits and carefully crafted equilibria too complex to be exposed summarily, all of which have played a role in ensuring that the minority rights could be advanced on a principled basis that responds to genuine needs in a feasible manner ... and builds on its own successes and is self generating.[20]

Yet Tremblay is also acutely conscious of some of the complexities of this arrangement, for he argues that

Ambiguity, perhaps deliberately built-in to our statutes, can come at a cost and undermine the very objectives of social inclusion and reconciliation that motivated the development of Canada's language scheme. Ultimately, where disagreements persisted, Canada's courts played a decisive role in defining and shaping the language provisions enacted by the Constitutional Drafters and by Parliament. The role of the courts as protectors of language minorities has engaged them in an ongoing dialogue with the Legislator, which in the main has assured a proper balance between the various branches of the State. More often than not, the executive and legislative branches have followed the teachings of the courts and gone on to the next step in the evolution of Canada's language rights regime, thus bringing us back to the starting point in the continuing cycle.

(Tremblay, 2006, p. 14)

Conclusion

We have seen that attempts by Québec to institute the widespread legitimisation of the French language have been largely successful within the public domain. Corresponding attempts by other provincial governments to serve their territorial minorities have been far less effective in Canada, though this is hardly surprising given the greater complexity of Canada's multiethnic society and the government's commitment to a policy of multiculturalism within a bilingual framework, initiated by Trudeau. The limitations of territorial language planning are evident in Canada and Quebec. The political power of Québecois nationalists has enabled the French language to be strengthened as the primary language of provincial government and also a language of commerce and private industry, thus rewarding language fluency in all aspects of socioeconomic life. To this extent the Québécois case would provide an important illustration of the centrality of capturing political control to legitimise a change in group relations and to provide the conditions of possibility whereby this change may be institutionalised within new patterns of labour. In consequence, I conclude that the issue of language promotion should be viewed not only in terms of cultural reproduction, but also in terms of a struggle for political and economic control which can increase access to resources and occupational mobility in a bicultural society. The trend toward establishing an autonomous public sector, separate from the governing state apparatus, will inevitably satisfy many of the legitimate demands of the French language community, but will also call into question its ability to influence the private sector in like manner.

The analysis has also demonstrated that the federal response has been to undermine the original French Canadian conception of confederation, because Ottawa, as Cardinal (1999) has argued, has attempted to transform the national question into one of an individuals' linguistic choice. In effect, speaking French in Canada is a reflection of an individual's characteristics, not a structuring element of a national community. Thus rather than fight for French as a common good of society, the state is functionally restricting its concerns to the rights of official language minority groups "where numbers warrant". It has sought to detach the question of language rights from the political context-that is, the recognition of Quebec as a nation (Cardinal, 1999, p. 85). This remains the abiding Canadian conundrum, for since 1867 elements within the federation have been grappling with the question of how to reconcile the claims of national justice in recognising Québec, while simultaneously recognising the evolving multinational character of Canadian society.

Notes

1. In 1988 Pelletier posed the dilemma thus, "Today, we are faced with two totally irreconcilable options on the Canadian political scene: on the one hand, the *status quo* option, which suggests that Canada can easily put up with the current situation, although it may require some new administrative arrangements which might bring about a small degree of decentralization; and, on the other hand, the sovereignty-partnership option which was vigorously relaunched by the *Parti québécois* during the October 1995 referendum, an option that was supported by 49.6 per cent of Quebecers" (Pelletier, 1998, p. 304).
2. By contrast the criminal code is British in origin and applies to all of Canada.
3. For critical comments on such relationships see Alterman and Green (2004) in terms of George Bush and Naughtie (2004) in terms of Tony Blair.
4. Part I of the *Constitution Act, 1982*, being Schedule B to the *Canada Act 1982* (U.K.), 1982, *c*.11.
5. Subsection 16(1) of the Charter provides: "English and French are the official languages of Canada and have equality of status and equal rights and privileges as to their use in all institutions of the Parliament and government of Canada."
6. *R. v. Beaulac*, [1999] 1 S.C.R. 768 at par. 22 and 24.
7. Subsection 20(1) of the Charter provides: "Any member of the public in Canada has the right to communicate with, and to receive services from, any head or central office of an institution of the Parliament or government of Canada in English or French, and has the same right with respect to any other office of any such institution where

   (a) there is significant demand for communications with and services from that office in such language; or
   (b) due to the nature of the office, it is reasonable that communications with and services from that office be available in both English and French."

8. Section 23 of the Charter provides: "Citizens of Canada

   (a) whose first language learned and still understood is that of the English or French linguistic minority population of the province in which they reside, or

(b) who have received their primary school instruction in Canada in English or French and reside in a province where the language in which they received that instruction is the language of the English or French linguistic minority population of the province,

have the right to have their children receive primary and secondary school instruction in that language in that province.

(2) Citizens of Canada of whom any child has received or is receiving primary or secondary school instruction in English or French in Canada, have the right to have all their children receive primary and secondary school instruction in the same language.

(3) The right of citizens of Canada under subsections (1) and (2) to have their children receive primary and secondary school instruction in the language of the English or French linguistic minority population of a province

(a) applies wherever in the province the number of children of citizens who have such a right is sufficient to warrant the provision to them out of public funds of minority language instruction; and

(b) includes, where the number of those children so warrants, the right to have them receive that instruction in minority language educational facilities provided out of public funds."

9. *Mahe v. Alberta*, [1990.] 1 S.C.R. 342 at p. 350.
10. Dumas (2007) advises that in 1999, Québec's *Secrétariat à la politique linguistique* (language policy secretariat) held focus group discussions in four American cities (New York, Boston, Atlanta and Chicago) involving seventy opinion leaders from the US in order to learn more about their perceptions and knowledge of Québec. In general, the participants knew very little about Québec, having heard next to nothing about the province except under special circumstances (referendum, flooding, ice storm, etc.). As a result, their perceptions and opinions concerning Québec were rarely based on reliable and objective information, reflecting instead impressions derived from rumours and hearsay.
11. Dumas adds that when focus group participants learned the true nature of Québec's language policy, a number of these false perceptions were dispelled, with participants affirming that Québec's *Charter of the French Language* seemed on the whole rather balanced.
12. He advises that in the sixties, an absolute majority of managers of Québec firms were members of the English-speaking minority (80 per cent of middle-managers, 60 per cent of senior managers) and, most of the time; they worked only in English (Office de langue française, 1988; Levine, 1990, 181–93).
13. Note that in 1971, 88 per cent of Canadians whose home language was French lived in Québec. In 1991, the ratio had grown to 89.9 per cent and to 90.6 per cent in 2001.
14. He adds that if one excludes the French region of Acadia in New Brunswick, a strong French-speaking community, the rate of assimilation is 46 per cent.
15. Marc Tremblay is General Counsel and Director of the Official Languages Law Group, Justice Canada. I am grateful for his permission in being able to quote from his notes used at the POBAL presentation and for interviews he gave me both in Ottawa and the UK.
16. S.C. 1988, *c.*38; R.S.C. 1985, c.31 (4th Supp.).

17. Part V of the Act deals with the language of work.
18. Newman adds that "the official languages policy on the language of work must be progressive, but its application must take into account the sociolinguistic, demographic and geographic realities of Canada." See Newman, "The *Official Languages Act* and the Constitutional and Legislative Recognition of Language Rights in Canada", unpublished, November 2003, at pp. 19–20. The extract has been published in French in Braën, Foucher and Le Bouthillier, eds, *Langues, constitutionnalisme et minorités* (Butterworths, Marham, 2006) 635 at 663 and 664; the English version is published in Colin H. Williams, ed. (2007) *Language and Governance*, Cardiff: The University of Wales Press, pp. 196–234.
19. This is to be done through section 77(1) of the Official Language Act which declares that "any person who has made a complaint to the Commissioner in respect of a right or duty under sections 4 to 7, sections 10 to 13 or Part IV, V or VII, or in respect of section 91, may apply to the Court for a remedy under this Part"
20. Tremblay (2006) adds that this was the view expressed by the Royal Commission on Bilingualism and Biculturalism in 1967, in advising that the level of services that are feasible vary according to the number of persons involved. "Thus, . . . the equality of which we speak is not absolute, but begins to be realized almost automatically as soon as it is feasible in a given area. . . . If the minimal conditions are present, the linguistic systems automatically assure that equality will be realized in concrete situations. To view equality in this way does not mean that we think the two main linguistic groups will enjoy the same services everywhere; this would be absurd in practice. It does mean that wherever similar conditions are found, similar services will be offered."

10
The Limits to Freedom

The argument advanced in this chapter is that steps are being taken to construct a political framework which acknowledges the positive virtue of cultural pluralism on the basis of equality as a necessary prerequisite for democracy and freedom of action in an increasingly multicultural world order. In Europe, this raises fresh issues concerned with the distribution of power in society and with the encouragement of democratic participation by previously beleaguered interest groups. This recognition demands both mutual respect and robust structures of freedom so as to guarantee the conditions for cultural reproduction.

However, the principal barrier which hinders this being realised is the configuration of the nation-state system as developed by national elites in the course of the nineteenth- and early twentieth-century. Its entrenchment results in a lack of congruence between multicultural citizenries and the sense of order prescribed by national conceptions of the modern state (Williams, 1989b). Even so, the global order is changing the structure and reach of the nation state. The evidence that transnational and international influences are having a fundamental impact upon the sovereignty of the state and on the conduct of domestic issues is now overwhelming. Sovereignty, as Held (2006, p. 303) demonstrates is already divided among a number of agencies – national, regional and international – and consequently is limited by the nature of this plurality. Democracy has to be re-conceptualised as a result.

Two questions lie at the heart of my investigation:

1) How do formerly marginalised language groups cope with the exercise of responsible governance which has been ushered in by recent political reforms in parts of Europe?
2) How have such reforms re-configured the nature of inclusive democracy, especially in relation to so-called "indigenous" and "immigrant" language groups?

We have argued that in some parts of Europe the neo-liberal conception of the unitary state, based upon representative democracy, is yielding to the logic of the enabling state, with its focus on participatory democracy. Much of this transformation has been driven by very practical considerations, even if the grounded theory and concepts used to discuss such considerations are often discipline specific and do not always command universal respect. At a personal level I am much taken with the potential of deliberative democracy as an explanatory framework, especially within several of the long-standing liberal democracies. Yet no matter how much attention is paid to the sophisticated logic of political theory or to the action-based imperatives of social justice and normative language legislation, little of lasting worth will be achieved in policy development until we take due cognisance of two key issues. The first is the need to conceive of RM and IM language groups in tandem as forming elements within a language continuum which is dominated by hegemonic languages. The clearest difference between RM and IM languages is their history, but the needs of the speakers to be recognised and treated with dignity is exactly the same. The second is the need to press continuously for high quality language-related data so as to inform public policy. My fear is that under other pressures neither of these concerns will figure very highly in the agendas of Europe-wide institutions and state statistical bureaus for reasons I discuss below.

The evidence from the case studies discussed in this volume points to fluctutions in the fortunes of some beleaguered groups. Such groups have long been the object of imperial absorption, religious and socio-legal discrimination and indeed periods of oppression during the nation-building era of the past four hundred years. This has ranged from land clearances, social persecution and dislocation, physical removal to frontier areas and to genocide. Today their situation and context has changed quite markedly. Yet ironically precisely at the moment that several of them, such as the Catalans and the Welsh, or further afield, the Québécois, are exercising a real degree of political autonomy, economic purchase and success in language policy terms, they are faced with an additional set of competitive claims which derive from the presence of a large and diverse immigrant populations in their midst. This has profound effects on their freedom of action to construct a new form of political community based largely upon indigenous cultural and political factors.

Three features influence their capacity to act and to sustain trajectories in keeping with the ideologies and values discussed in Chapter Two. First, international agencies such as the European Union and the Council of Europe, now seem willing, indeed eager, to honour the contribution of small European nationalities to the construction of a common European home. And this for obvious reasons to do with border security, diaspora populations, the bridging of major cultural divides. An excellent example is the pivotal role which Slovenia plays straddling Romance, Germanic and Slavic cultural and economic systems. It is recognised as a valuable small nation which strengthens common shared European values derived from religious precepts, the rule of law and the impress of the territorial-bureaucratic state. Its early adoption of the Euro and strong economic performance mark it out as an exemplar for other smaller nations in the region.

Yet there is a certain illogicality within the system, for at a superstructrual level great emphasis is placed on protecting diversity, of creating mantras such as "unity in diversity", while at lower levels in the political hierarchy diversity is being eradicated through nation-state policies.

Second there is the counter-trend of failing to tackle the issue of immigrant demands. Why, for example, do we face so many calls for immigrants to acquire the national language of their adopted country and simultaneously jettison their attachment to their "mother tongue" or "home language"? These constructs have become an increasingly puzzling matter for all concerned. But if this form of subtractive multilingualism is an issue for hegemonic language contexts, such as the predominance of English in the UK or of Spanish in Spain, how much more problematic is it for the National Assembly for Wales or the Basque Government to devise educational curricula which allow such immigrant children to gain fluency in Welsh and Basque as well as English and Spanish? Inherent in such programmes is a double identity complex, which is often construed by immigrant families as an additional barrier to their incorporation into the host society.

Third, there is a separate, if discernable, trend to view regional minority groups as the "obvious", "natural" role models for immigrant mobilisation and adjustment. Having achieved some degree of recognition without simultaneously threatening the survival of the sovereign state, it is argued that designated Irish or Welsh medium schools can offer interesting exemplars for those parents who wish to fight for the right of their children to be educated in faith schools or through the medium of Urdu or Arabic. Sufficiently distinct, but nevertheless part of the general fabric of society, such exemplars are a testimony to the resilience of determined parents and responsive local education authorities, or so the argument goes. In time immigrant communities could prosper and preserve their core values in similar separate, but equal, educational domains.

But so much of the activity which produces this discourse has to do with the legal recognition and the worth of communities as permanent entities within the European state system. Commentators, such as Extra and Gorter (2001) and Williams (2002) have asked rhetorically, why are autochthonous language communities now being singled out as role models and as "privileged" for legal protection and why are the European supra-national institutions, at long last, willing to support them?

Will Kymlicka has identified a number of the factors at work. The first relates to linguistic survival. He argues that in contrast to the Bengali immigrant community in Britain, if Scottish Gaelic disappears from Scotland, it will disappear entirely: for this is its homeland. So too with indigenous languages in Canada. Insofar as we wish to maintain linguistic diversity around the world, we have to give special protection to languages in their historic home-lands. Historically, as we saw in Chapter Two, this attention to the homeland is a central plank of nationalist doctrine and practice, now strengthened by environmental and ecological arguments concerned with the interpenetra-tion of bio-diversity and ethno-linguistic variety. While acknowledging the salience of this factor, Kymlicka asserts that many minorities are protected by emerging international norms regarding the language rights of national minorities.[1] The trend towards strengthening the linguistic rights of historic minorities applies whether or not their language is also securely protected in some other country.[2]

A second factor concerns consent. In contrast to those immigrants who choose to come to a new country, and acknowledge that this involves living and working in another language, historic minorities did not choose to leave their original community. In many cases they have been forcibly incorpor-ated into their current political state as a result of invasion, periodic warfare or such lands have been inherited as part of a dynastic marriage settlement. Kymlicka argues that processes of incorporation should not result in the diminishing of the right of a people to continue to use their language on their historic homeland. Yet even this cannot be the whole explanation for

> the idea that newcomers have understood and accepted that they are leaving one language community for another may apply to some immig-rants, but not to all. Refugees in particular did not 'choose' to leave their homeland: they were fleeing persecution. Indeed, in some cases, they were fleeing persecution precisely because they belonged to a linguistic minority (e.g., the Kurds in Turkey). In such cases, one could argue that refugees left precisely in order to be free to maintain their language, which was under attack in their country of origin.
>
> (Kymlicka, 2007, p. 281)

A third factor concerns the role of historic injustice. Historic linguistic minorities can plausibly claim that they have suffered injustice at the hands of the larger state, and that their language would be in a stronger position today were it not for that injustice (that is, there would be more speakers of the language, often over a wider territory, and more cultural products and publications in the language). The state arguably has some obligation to acknowledge that injustice, and perhaps to redress some of its effects. By contrast, most citizens of Western democracies do not feel they have any comparable historic debt regarding the language of newcomers.[3]

There are many other factors that can explain the variable treatment of immigrant and historic minorities in terms of language rights. But it is important to note that this differentiation is not limited to issues of language.

We see a similar differentiation regarding other forms of minority rights, including issues of self-government, legal pluralism, political representation, and (in the case of indigenous peoples) land claims. On all of these issues, we find systematic differences between immigrants and historic minorities, both at the level of domestic policies and international law. Thus within the broad category of historic minorities, there are important differences between "indigenous peoples" and "national minorities" (Kymlicka, 2001).

The core of Kymlicka's argument is that this systematic differentiation is linked to the way in which historic minorities have been able to draw upon ideas of "nationhood". He reminds us that national minorities and indigenous peoples have described themselves as "nations" or "peoples", even if their national homeland is now incorporated into a larger state, and have continued to demand various rights and powers in virtue of that status. While previous claims to nationhood were historically rejected by most Western states, current claims have become increasingly accepted, as have the more specific claims that are seen as flowing from nationhood, such as regional autonomy, the maintenance of distinct educational and legal systems, and the protection and use of national languages (Keating, 2001, Kymlicka, 2001).

Language policies, therefore, are one component of a much broader phenomenon of the revindication of ethnonational identities in the post-war era, and the rebirth of the "nations within" as self-consciously political actors and movements (Kymlicka, 2001). Despite predictions that they would disappear as a result of modernisation or globalisation, national identities and nationalist ideologies have remained powerful sources of political mobilisation in the contemporary world.

The role of language within such nationalist projects varies immensely. In some cases, as we saw in Quebec, language is the central marker of an individual's national identity, and ensuring the dominance of the language on the national territory is the prime goal of collective nationalist mobilisation. In other cases, such as Wales and Ireland, language is a widely accepted symbol of nationhood, and concern for the language is an acceptable goal of national political action. Proficiency in the language is not necessarily a marker of individual national identity (many people who identify themselves as Welsh or Irish do not speak Welsh or Irish). Moreover, while collective political action aims at the reproduction and promotion of the language, it does not aim to establish its dominance (that is Welsh and Irish are being promoted alongside, but not in place of, English, which will continue to be hegemonic).[4] In yet other cases, such as Scotland, language is controversial even as a symbol of nationhood (since Gaelic was historically used primarily by the highlanders, not all Scots), and it is disputed whether the language should be seen as a "national" issue, as opposed to, say, a more diffuse issue of "diversity" disconnected from the larger Scottish nationalist project (Williams, 2007).[5]

While the centrality of language issues to national projects varies, in all of the cases examined in this volume, there is an implicit or explicit assumption that it is up to the relevant national community to develop its own language policy. The Welsh, Irish, Scots and Québécois should be free to decide whether, or to what extent, they wish to adopt collective policies to promote their historic language. And in order to make such decisions, the national community requires some form of self-government. Indeed, one of the most widely accepted arguments for devolving power to "nations within" is that they need some degree of self-government precisely over issues of language, education and culture.

This in turn raises interesting questions about the complex linkages between language policy and national autonomy. Such appeals proved attractive in the nineteenth century when proto-nations insisted on the recognition of their unique language and history and encouraged the professional development of linguistics and archaeology to produce (or construct) the evidence to sustain such claims. But the causal relationship can also go the other way. According to Rainer Baubock (2000, p. 384) "rather than self-government being a means to preserve cultural difference, this difference is more often preserved as a means to justify the claim to self-government". This applies not only to linguistic differences, but also, for example, to distinct legal traditions (as in both Scotland and Quebec). Ethnonational groups are continually required to explain why they deserve self-governing powers, and having a distinct language or legal tradition provides one possible answer.[6]

This may help explain the otherwise puzzling fact that there is broad public support in Wales and Ireland for official bilingualism and linguistic revitalisation policies, even amongst people who have no serious desire or intention of increasing their competence or use of Welsh or Irish. Such policies help to reinforce a sense of national distinctiveness that provides legitimacy to claims of national autonomy. Even if the vast majority of the society remains English-speaking, and does not really wish to change this fact, the visible public commitment to Celtic languages helps to make clear that they occupy an identifiable homeland of a unique national group. This not only supports claims to distinctiveness, but also reminds newcomers that they have entered a separate national community, and are expected to identify with it.

Many language activists in Wales and Ireland complain that these revitalisation policies are half-hearted. Yet perhaps that is what one should expect if the public perceives these policies as primarily an instrument for symbolising and affirming nationhood. Many English-speaking citizens of Wales and Ireland want just enough linguistic revitalisation to secure their claim to nationhood, and to remind newcomers of that fact, but not so much revitalisation that they would actually have to change their language repertoire or language use.

In short, the trend towards greater recognition of non-dominant languages must be seen as part and parcel of a broader trend towards the resurgence of ethnonational identities and nationalist projects, although the connection between the two is complex. Language may be the substantive core of these nationalist projects, or merely symbolic of them (or both). Similarly, national self-government, now or in times past, may be demanded in order to adopt better language protection, or better language protection may be adopted in order to justify self-government claims (or both). Whatever the precise connection, in all of these cases, language policies have been carried along by broader nationalist political projects.

Of course this simply pushes the puzzle back a level. If increased support for non-dominant languages is tied to the growing strength of ethnonational projects, why have ethnonational projects become stronger? The chapters in this volume suggest a range of answers, including the delegitimisation of older ethnic/racial hierarchies, as well as neo-liberal restructuring of the state, which has (unexpectedly) created opportunities for non-dominant groups, particularly through promoting ideas of decentralisation and subsidiarity.[7] But the main change is the gradual recognition that these nationalist projects, including their linguistic aspects, are often wholly consistent with basic liberal-democratic values.[8] This is an important shift. In the past, it was widely assumed that ethnonational projects were inherently illiberal or undemocratic, grounded in reactionary (and ultimately futile) attempts to preserve community traditions from the inevitable changes brought about by modernisation, education and individual mobility. Today, however, it is increasingly recognised that such ethnonational projects can fully respect liberal-democratic constitutional principles, and can be open to the world (for example, in terms of support for free trade, or European integration), and indeed in some cases are actually leaders in terms of progressive social policy (for example, in areas of gay rights, immigration, women's rights, deliberative democracy or social justice).[9]

But the idea that the political projects of the "small nations" or "nations within" can not only embody, but even advance, liberal-democratic values remains contested. Many studies reveal the extent to which Quebec must continually struggle against misperceptions and double-standards regarding its nation-building projects, and the fear of being labelled illiberal is present in many of the analyses by Catalan, Basque and Welsh politicians and policy-makers. But while non-dominant groups must continually defend themselves against such charges, the reality is that these defences have been reasonably successful. There is in fact widespread public acceptance of the basic legitimacy of the Québécois national project within Canada, of Scottish and Welsh nationalism in Britain and of the right of Basques and Catalans to promote their identities beyond Spain to the rest of Europe.[10]

But here we reach an important difference between Canada and the European cases. In Canada, the legitimacy of the Québécois project stems in part from the fact that it relies on a fairly familiar model of a national political community, defined by a common language that is dominant over a particular territory. The Québécois simply insist that there are (at least) two such national communities within Canada, and that Canada must therefore be understood as a binational (or multi-national) state.[11] Official bilingualism at the federal level, on this model, is necessary to ensure that both language communities are equally represented in the central government, and equally able to access its services. But the assumption is that most individuals will continue to live their lives in relatively monolingual societies, each of which is institutionally complete. There is a francophone society in Quebec (and parts of Ontario and NB), and an anglophone society in the rest of the country, each with its own full set of economic, educational, media, legal and political institutions, and each with its own robust public debates. Keeping a country together with two parallel, institutionally complete and territorialised language communities is not easy, but part of what holds it together is precisely the fact that each community can see the other as forming a separate but "normal" liberal-democratic national political community built around a common language and territory.[12]

Speaking in 2005 at a round table on asymmetrical federalism hosted by the Qubec Government office, Ron Halford of the Canadian High Commissioner's office, observed that Canada has a vastly better developed official language regime than many other societies because such issues are central to the maintenance of Canadian statehood.[13] He emphasised statehood rather than nationhood, because the question as to whether Canada comprises one nation or two goes back to the different manner in which the Fathers of Confederation, having accepted a political compromise, sold the deal to their respective clientele. For English Canadians it was seen as an absorption of the French fact in Canada, for French Canadians it was interpreted as a recognition and an assertion of their distinct nationality. This sentiment echoes down the corridors of history for only recently the Canadian Prime Minister has repeated the recognition by announcing that Quebec could be seen as a distinct nation within the Canadian system.

In the Celtic cases, by contrast, the main goal of language policy is not to create two parallel and largely monolingual societies – a separate Welsh-speaking or Gaelic-speaking society alongside the English-speaking society.[14] Rather, the goal is to encourage greater bilingualism in everyday life, so that most citizens will feel comfortable operating in either language in a wide range of functions.

Viewed in this light, the Celtic cases offer the promise of a genuinely new model of a single bilingual national political community (in contrast to the sort of binational federation of two distinct monolingual political communities that we see in Canada or Belgium (Kymlicka, 2007)). This interpretation expresses the hope that this new model will not only be feasible and enduring but will also create forms of democratic inclusion provide new scope for a more deliberative politics, and create more empowered citizens. It seems too early to tell whether such hopes will come to fruition. We do not yet have either the practical policy experiences or the normative political theories that would identify the potential benefits and hazards that are likely to arise in the building of such new forms of bilingual democratic practices.

Methodological developments

I have argued throughout that we need evidence-based policy development. This requires the collection of sophisticated data and better techniques of analyses which shows the inter-relationship of state-wide, regional and immigrant languages as they act and react together to social forces.[15] Zelinsky and Williams (1988, p. 356) have commented that the territorial gaps in our knowledge of the geography of language functions were obvious enough. But what were more interesting and frustrating were the topical lacunae. Addressing these is critical if we wish to endorse evidence-based EU policy formulation. What we know about the geography of language via maps, words or statistics is confined almost entirely to what is spoken at home or to the census enumerator. Consistent time-series treatment of speech in the workplace, church/mosque and school and on the street would be extremely useful, if demanding in terms of fieldwork.[16]

Equally fascinating is that very few have tried to map functional literacy. Especially worthwhile would be time-series studies and maps of literacy and usage in non-official tongues, including circulation patterns for "ethnic" newspapers and magazines and listening/viewing areas and market penetration for foreign language radio and television programmes.[17]

Knowledge and consciousness of linguistically defined bounded spaces pervade most inhabitants' perception of ethno-linguistic urban neighbourhoods in the world's great multilingual cities.[18] We have adequate census-based identifications of ethno-linguistic neighbourhoods, but relatively little by way of detailed micro-level analysis of urban territoriality for language groups in such places as London, Paris, Rome, Brussels, Frankfurt, Budapest or Moscow. Mapping the subjective world of constituent language groups in relation to conflict over urban space and facilities, such as education, sports centres and the like would also be a fascinating cartographic and behavioural exercise. A related aspect of urban multilingualism would be to map the linguistic behaviour of non-official language groups in a wide range of social domains, including the workplace, places of worship and entertainment. However, because such data is often sensitive we should not be surprised that there is a paucity of mapped information (Zelinsky and Williams, 1988, p. 339).

The most sophisticated attempt to capture such dynamism is the European Science Foundation project on "Mapping Linguistic Diversity", led by Guus

Extra of Tilburg University and Monica Barni of Siena University.[19] The Project Team seeks to explore language spread, language's role as a marker, sociolinguistic dynamics and policy development; as a base for mapping diversity. Specifically the project aims to:

- Explore traditional and new methodologies for collecting linguistic data and their integration into a methodological framework addressing uses, needs and requirements previously identified;
- Compare the European state of knowledge with current initiatives being undertaken in other parts of the world.

The project has explicitly sought to integrate material on measuring both RM and IM languages within a single conceptual framework.

Identifying distinct groups within increasingly multilingual context is a difficult task, especially if the purpose is to measure degrees of vitality and solidarity over time. Two of the principal researchers of the ESF project, Extra and Yağmur (2004), had earlier tabulated the nationality, country of birth, language spoken at home and self-categorisation criteria for mapping diversity (Table 10.1).

Table 10.1 reveals that there is no simple solution to the identification problem. Different criteria may complement and strengthen each other. Complementary or alternative criteria have been suggested and used in various countries with a long immigration history, such as Australia, Canada, South Africa, and the USA.[20] To identify the multicultural composition of their populations, these four countries employ a variety of questions in their periodical censuses. In Table 10.2, an overview of this array of questions is provided; for each country the given census is taken as the norm.

The ESF Project notes "that both the type and number of questions are different per country. Canada leads with the highest number of questions. Only three questions have been asked in all countries, whereas two questions have been asked in only one country. But note that four different questions have been asked about language. The operationalisation of questions also shows interesting differences, both between and within countries across time."[21] Questions about ethnicity, ancestry and/or race have proven to be problematic in all of the countries under consideration, according to the ESF Project analysis. In some countries, ancestry and ethnicity have been conceived as equivalent with ethnicity relating to present self-categorisation of the respondent and ancestry to former generations. In what ways respondents themselves interpret both concepts, however, remains a problem that cannot be solved easily.

While an ethnicity question has been asked in recent censuses of two countries (see Table 10.2), four language-related questions have been asked in 1–4 countries. Only in Canada has the concept of "mother tongue" been included. It has been defined for respondents as the *language first learnt at*

Table 10.1 Criteria for the definition and identification of population groups in a multicultural society (P/F/M = person/father/mother)

Criterion	Advantages	Disadvantages
Nationality (NAT) (P/F/M)	• Objective • Relatively easy to establish	• Intergenerational erosion through naturalisation or double NAT • NAT not always indicative of ethnicity/identity • Some (e.g., ex-colonial) groups have NAT of immigration country
Birth country (BC) (P/F/M)	• Objective • Relatively easy to establish	• Intergenerational erosion through births in immigration country • BC not always indicative of ethnicity/identity • Invariable/deterministic: does not take account of dynamics in society (in contrast of all other criteria)
Self-categorisation (SC)	• Touches the heart of the matter • Emancipatory: SC takes account of person's own conception of ethnicity/identity	• Subjective by definition: also determined by language/ethnicity of interviewer and by spirit of times • Multiple SC possible • Historically charged, especially by World War II experiences
Home language (HL)	• HL is most significant criterion of ethnicity in communication processes • HL data are prerequisite for government policy in areas such as public information or education	• Complex criterion: who speaks what language to whom and when? • Language is not always core value of ethnicity/identity • Useless in one-person households

Source: Extra and Yağmur, 2004, 31.

Table 10.2   Overview of census questions in four multicultural contexts

Questions in the census	Australia 2001	Canada 2001	SA 2001	USA 2000	Coverage
1 Nationality of respondent	+	+	+	+	4
2 Birth country of respondent	+	+	+	+	4
3 Birth country of parents	+	+	−	−	2
4 Ethnicity	−	+	−	+	2
5 Ancestry	+	+	−	+	3
6 Race	−	+	+	+	3
7 Mother tongue	−	+	−	−	1
8 Language used at home	+	+	+	+	4
9 Language used at work	−	+	−	−	1
10 Proficiency in English	+	+	−	+	3
11 Religion	+	+	+	−	3
Total of dimensions	7	11	5	7	30

(*Source*: Extra and Yağmur, 2004: 67).

home in childhood and still understood, while questions 8 and 9 related to the language *most often* used at home/work. Table 10.2 shows the added value of language-related census questions on the definition and identification of multicultural populations, in particular the added value of the question on home language use compared to questions on the more opaque concepts of mother tongue and ethnicity. Although the language-related census questions in the four countries differ in their precise formulation and commentary, the outcomes of these questions are generally conceived as cornerstones for educational policies with respect to the teaching of English as a first or second language and the teaching of languages other than English.

Why is such data and evidence necessary and why be concerned about apparently slight semantic differences between forms of identification? Surely the important thing, according to sections of the popular press, is to count the number of those who belong and those who are "foreigners"? – The old issue of the "we" and the "they". How we count determines who we place in such categories and, throughout the EU, two criteria are used most widely. They are applied separately for two types of groups. Data on *indigenous minority groups* with a regional base (RM) are generally based on *(home) language;*[22] while data on *immigrant minority groups* (IM) are generally based on *nationality.*[23] Indeed, nationality-based data are the only ones available at a pan-European level from official data sources (e.g. Eurostat in Luxembourg). However, Table 10.1 shows that the *nationality* criterion has many limitations when it comes to identifying population groups.

Reflecting on this distinction the European Science Foundation (ESF) team suggests a number of qualifiers to the adoption of "nationality" as the key determinant of identity. 'Firstly, it very seldom reflects ethnicity and identity. African countries, whose borders were drawn artificially in the colonial age, are the extreme example. But the same is true also for supposedly 'homogenous' national states such as Italy, France or Germany. Secondly, even if we assume the nationality criterion as theoretically valid, we recognise that it is subject to statistical erosion due to naturalisation processes. This leads to a strong underestimation of minority groups in multicultural population statistics. Finally, some (e.g., ex-colonial) groups are given the nationality of their immigration country, again leading to a problem of underestimation. Similar criticisms would also apply to the country-of-birth criterion." (ESF, 2006).

Team members of the ESF Project argue that a convergence between the criteria used for IM and RM groups is needed and have chosen to focus on *home language* as a potential basis for mapping diversity in Europe for three reasons:

> First, questions about ethnicity (and similar concepts such as ancestry and/or race) have proven to be problematic in many countries.

> Second, mapping linguistic diversity offers valuable insights into the distribution and vitality of home languages across different population groups and thus raises the public and political awareness of multilingualism (which is a key feature of a multicultural society).

> Third, empirically collected data on home language use also play a crucial role in the context of education. Such data not only raise the awareness of multilingualism in multicultural schools; they are in fact indispensable tools for educational policies on the teaching of both the national majority languages as a first or second language and the teaching of minority languages.

> (ESF, 2006)

The short term goal is to build capacity by establishing an active network of specialist and stakeholders.[24] The ultimate objective is to provide the European research community with a blueprint for mapping linguistic diversity, identifying uses, needs, and methodological requirements for carrying out meaningful empirical research on diversity.[25]

Over and above these issues is the more fundamental challenge facing us as the EU contemplates another round of enlargement. Having welcomed Romania and Bulgaria in January 2007, the EU is now in negotiation with Croatia and Turkey, both of whom have quite different trajectories. The inclusion of Turkey has profound geo-strategic implications for the foreign policy of the West and also huge ramifications for migration patterns within existing EU member states and religious pluralism. The capacity of the EU to adjust to its entry, should it ever happen, has been quieried. We are faced with major challenges of how to deal with the sheer diversity of competing claims for recognition, rights and resources on behalf of those beleaguered groups who hitherto have not benefited from the institutional arrangements constructed by sovereign states in pursuit of cosmopolitan democracy. The art of political practice and policy formulation depends ultimately on interpreting sound evidence in context. We must find common ways of collecting, interpreting and using data on multilingualism. Nothing less will suffice if we seek to advance the principles of justice and equality in our nominally plural, deliberative democracies.

Language and governance in an enlarged European Union

A basic distinction can be made between the "institutional" and "non-institutional" aspects of EU language policy (Van Els, 2001). The statutory basis for the institutional use of languages is Article 217 of the Treaty of Rome, which charges the Council of Ministers to enframe all regulations. Theoretically, three broad principles govern institutional usage. First, all official documents are translated into all official EU languages and gain purchase in a member state when they are produced in the officially recognised language of that state. Secondly, all citizens communicating with central EU institutions are entitled to a response in the official language of their choosing. Thirdly, the EU's terminology database only gives full coverage in the languages designated as official EU languages (Labrie, 1996, p. 5. Quoted in Van Els, 2001, p. 320). Yet we know in effect that English, French and German dominate the EU's administrative workings.

What is not recognised so well is what Mamadouh (2002) has termed the dual influence of language diversity on national identities and on the ability of citizens to access supranational and transnational decision-making processes. Thus she argues that the most compelling question facing EU decision-makers today is "How should the mediation between speakers of different languages be organized?" Grid-group cultural theory provides one way forward for it can demonstrate how polices and practices are the result of competition between different rationalities and therefore depend on the influence, strategies and alliances of their adherents (Mamadouh, 2002). An equally promising rationality combines holistic thinking and ecological perspectives in order to justify linguistic diversity; although this approach is not without its detractors.[26] A third option is to focus on the interaction between citizens and various official agencies in influencing policy. Deliberation, discussion and disagreement are desirable, and are best advanced through the promotion of governance rather than direct government.

The success of "governance" as a guiding principle is due much to its potential in overcoming the classical division between the state and civil society in liberal democracies. New forms of interdependence, negotiation and co-ordination between power-brokers and multilevel arenas of action has occasioned a fresh interpretation of state–citizen relations. If the normative ambition of this refashioned relationship is to increase subsidiarity, whose objective is to bring the solution of problems as close to citizens as possible, then this poses the challenge of effective co-ordination and requires new forms of collective accountability. Stoker (1998, 20) argues that this new form of governance is characterised by the following five propositions:-

1. "governance involves the action of a set of institutions and players not all of whom belong to the sphere of government;
2. in a situation of governance, boundaries and responsibilities are less clear with respect to social and economic action;
3. governance shows interdependence between the powers of the institutions involved in collective action;
4. governance involves the action of networks of independent players;
5. governance starts from the principle that it is possible to act without surrendering to the power of authority of the State. The State's role is to use new techniques and tools to orient and guide collective action" (quoted in Cardinal and Hudon, 2001, 10).

The governance of European languages has never been subject to a grand design, but has evolved in an epiphenomenal way. While conventionally language policy has been the preserve of the individual state, there is increasing evidence of the effect of EU and Council of Europe policy statements impacting on the range and mix of languages honoured and used both within and between individual states. Up until the May 2004 enlargement, the EU had eleven official and working languages and a plethora of other languages spoken among the then 380 million citizens of EU states. After the 2004 enlargement there were 25 member states and 20 official languages. As of January 2007, Irish has been added to the official languages list. Also in January 2007 Bulgaria and Rumania joined. Thus official language policies now have to deal with a more complicated geometry of multilingualism with a possible combination of 253 languages to interpret and translate, all within a fresh impetus which champions linguistic diversity within the EU.

Phillipson (2003) argues that there are severe structural problems in achieving this political goal.

> For this to be achieved presupposes giving language policy a much higher profile, and an infrastructure in member states and in EU institutions that is well qualified to implement and monitor language policies. This is not the position at present. In fact there is a serious risk, at both the national and the supranational levels, of language policy remaining entrenched in linguistic nationalism, and obscured by a false faith in English serving all equally well. Language policy at the EU level is politically sensitive.
>
> (Philipson, 2003)

Within inter-governmental organisations the de facto trend may be moving toward the selection of a very limited number of trans-national working languages.[27] But do such institutional arrangements automatically translate into real world language switching within large parts of the EU?

The nature and pace of such change at the macro-level can best be measured by focussing on those historical language contact areas, such as the Baltic Region or the Julian Alps, where representatives of major language families such as the Slavic, Germanic and Latin come together. Language border areas can be used as a geo-strategic temperature gauge for the degree of inter-cultural co-operation and conflict which exists within cultural realms beyond the frontier. Borders, boundaries and frontiers are integral both to the geographer's trade and to the resolution of conflict within the European Union. In language border areas research has focused on simultaneous inter-lingual contact operating at a number of different scales ranging from the inter-state level, through intermediate trade, social and cultural organisations to the level of the individual. Much of this concern with borders and cultural transition zones has to do with respecting the minority linguistic rights of settled communities either side of the international or regional boundary (Cartwright, 1991, 1998). In consequence, the major challenge of such transition zones will be how to organise internal processes which will maximise the utility of all languages within the zones. Such zones can also act as bridges in the New World Order and thus symbolise a spirit of partnership and integration, wherein the free flow of goods and people may be encouraged. Bi- or tri-lingual inhabitants of such zones are set fair to act as critical elements in the integrative process. However, because such zones are also strategically significant and have a history of periodic violence, it is imperative that we fully understand the various socio-linguistic dynamics, which accompany such integrative measures.

A second impulse is the need is to measure the effect which globalisation and the transnational transmission of culture by electronic means has upon language. A new geography of language and communication is being fashioned, based upon networks and real time interaction, with enormous consequences for power relations, entertainment and sport together with commercial transactions across borders. All this encourages a shift from an over-dependence upon government and institutional behaviour and a more balanced view of governance in influencing state–civil relations.

The difficulties of language reproduction are well known, but the central justification for introducing greater holistic perspectives is that maintenance and revitalisation efforts rely on much more than language, education and culture. And yet too few official language planning agencies are really able to grapple with the multifaceted elements required, being limited primarily to social mobilisation programmes, educational initiatives and marketing campaigns. Too often they are bereft of any structural, and hence lasting, influence on issues of mainstream economic growth, regional development policy, labour migration, investment strategies and the like, all of which influence the vitality (or morbidity) of language networks and communities. Language planners conventionally cite the extra-linguistic impediments to effective policy implementation, but rarely engage such factors head on, presuming that they fall within the remit of other professional disciplines. Language planners within minority communities face the additional problem of having to resist a dominant rationality which places their efforts at revitalisation within an exceptionalist frame of reference.

Part of the answer as to why I believe that linguistic diversity is valuable, has to do with the unravelling of European history. The Basques, Catalans and Welsh, have long and rich histories which at various epochs since Roman times has made them more or less central to the whole course of European developments. The fact that none of their respective languages have official status at an all EU level does not detract from the inherent worth of their respective cultures and regional economies. Critics would ask why do lesser-used language agencies seek to create distinct networks to promote an alternative vision of European linguistic diversity to that which is advanced by the major states, economic actors and international organisations? The answer is that they are operating according to a different set of rationalities and political imperatives as opposed to hegemonic and immigrant language networks. Nevertheless a provocative challenge to the maintenance of such diversity is provided by Van Els who asserts that there are at least two myths which need to be deconstructed:-

"It is a myth that the great diversity of languages and cultures as such is a good thing and that, consequently, its present manifestation in the EU represents a great richness, a treasure that should be defended at all costs. It is one of the myths that co-determine current EU policy on institutional language use" (Van Els, 2001, p. 349).

"Another myth is that changes in language policy in one domain, in this case the EU institutions, should necessarily have consequences for other domains, in this case particularly for the language use in member states themselves" (Van Els, 2001, p. 350).

Such criticism reminds us that an over-generous and liberal interpretation of EU directed policies should not be entertained lightly. There remains a complex and unpredictable relationship between initiatives at various levels in the political hierarchy and we have hardly any robust models of harmonious linguistic pluralism for there are very few states in Europe which have a sophisticated approach to language planning. Even Spain, which has a quasi-federal apparatus to deal with language diversity, has a largely reactive state central policy and the real thrust of policy comes from the autonomous regions. Thus it is instructive to look at other examples of multilevel governance outside Europe.

Canada has a dynamic history of language planning which has involved a fundamental division of responsibility between federal and provincial agencies in a number of significant fields, notably education, public administration and justice. In the wake of the RCBB recommendations certain local administrative arrangements for the provision of bilingual services and opportunities were also set in place. Nevertheless, despite many decades of very public wrangling over the issue of French and English language rights in and outside of Quebec and many revisions to the operation of bilingual policy, there remains a constant need to overhaul the current system. Since the 1990s the federal government has put in place horizontal methods of coordinating action in the field of official language minority policy. It has created new committees comprising governmental and non-governmental actors, and has entered into new agreements, such as the Canada-community agreements, with the official language minorities. This new approach has demanded a far more systematic and planned approach to language services and draws on several strands of holistic thought and practice to realise the challenge.

Robust evidence of how effective such holistic analysis can be operationalised is provided by Cardinal and Hudon's (2001) study of the "Governance of Canada's Official Language Minorities". They identified four conditions for the effective governance of language minorities, namely:

1. "the method of accountability that will apply to the coordination of action;
2. a better understanding of the division of responsibilities between civil society and the State;
3. the possibility of ongoing interaction among the players, based upon collective learning resulting from the pooling of knowledge and expertise; and
4. the capacity of the State to serve as a catalyst to support the action of the networks of independent players" (Cardinal and Hudon, 2001, 11).

The authors comment that these conditions for the effective co-ordination of action depend on a series of factors that are difficult to control. The most important is that in Canada, the organisational culture of government is characterised by a system of vertical accountability, which is more conducive to centralisation and bureaucratisation than would be a system of horizontal governance. However, it is recognised that introducing holistic practices into a new form of governance is a major challenge and implies far more than merely a renewal of corporatism with a patina of new procedures. Such transitions require a new organisation of power and of collective action. All the players are required to accept a meta-principle or shared values based on openness to difference, communication and learning if they are to harness the diversity and dynamism that the new system will unleash. They are also required to entertain new rationalities and adopt a new discourse as to where linguistic minorities fit within the Canadian project.

While in Europe new forms of governance for language minorities can sometimes imply empowerment, for the most part the Canadian language minorities analysed by Cardinal and Hudon interpret governance as a loss of rights. This can lead to increased frustration and distrust of government initiatives, together with accusations that new forms of governance are no more than a thin patina for shifting responsibilities without the corresponding transference of necessary resources and power.

If experiments in governance can disappoint, so also can the grand rhetoric which declares that all languages are deserving of recognition within the common European home. It is difficult enough for lesser-used languages to press their case on a reluctant bureaucracy, but it seems to be more frustrating for those smaller, official EU languages, especially since the post 2004 enlargements. Some would argue it is spurious to insist that all languages are to be treated equally within both the market and the institutions of the EU, for as Van Els (2001) comments:

"The core problem is the fundamental equality of all EU languages as EU working languages. There is no linguistic insight that opposes the abandonment of this principle. Neither are the arguments for maintaining this principle tenable from a linguistic perspective" (Van Els, 2001, p. 349). Thus in relation to EU language policy, Van Els argues that the following basic principles need to be discussed:

1. "the principle of equality for all 'official' languages, also as 'working languages' of the EU, will be abandoned formally;
2. the basic principle will be, or remains, that none of the crucial interests of any member state or citizen of the EU may be harmed as a result of their language background;
3. another basic principle will be that individual pragmatic solutions will be sought for the language communication problems in each of the subdomains of the EU organisation" (Van Els, 2001, p. 350).

But in yielding responsibility for language policy there is always the second issue of weakened participative democracy and lack of empowerment, by which I mean the danger that citizens and communities will be relegated to the role of passive recipients of top-down political decisions and language planning, as happened in Canada. Thus as regards institutional language planning at various levels we should always seek to:

1. "involve the target speakers/users of services as much as possible in the language planning decision-making process;
2. engage the participation of inter-departmental agencies to realise language planning aims and programmes;

3. seek to introduce horizontal forms of governance where feasible, but expect only partial success given the tendency to centralise and bureaucratise language-related activity;
4. anticipate and resolve to overcome the barriers, vested interests, traditional thought and practice which arise from inter-departmental turf-wars and boundary disputes" (Williams, 2002).

Governance and Language: Opportunities and Challenges

Loughlin and Williams (2007) have argued that while the EU will have to come to a compromise arrangement for the relationship between the official and the working languages, the emerging governance paradigm also presents challenges and opportunities for less powerful, non-state languages. Among the opportunities may be listed:

1. The European Union provides a new context which *may* provide opportunities, including the gaining of political influence, new partnership organisations and networks together with additional financial resources to support their languages and cultures;
2. the weakening of the nation-state means also the weakening of the hegemony of *national* languages thereby giving minority languages a new legitimacy, if not necessarily an automatic boost to their actual use within civil society;
3. the emphasis on community, subsidiarity, regional devolution and local democracy provides a set of opportunities to develop distinctive political and institutional forms to give expression to their identities;
4. the possession of a minority language and culture *may* be an important asset in new models of regional economic development and it is encouraging that minority languages and cultures are now not dismissed as *obstacles* to such development.

Among the challenges:

1. The weakening of the nation-state is not an unmixed blessing as the nation-state is, in important respects, a bulwark against trends, such as cultural globalisation, that are even more harmful to minority languages and cultures;
2. the nation-state is also in possession of important resources, financial, administrative and policy in nature, that may be important for the preservation of minority languages whose populations and administrative structures will often lack these resources;
3. similarly, it is difficult for local and regional communities to possess all the resources necessary to transform their distinctive features from

obstacles to social and economic development to being assets in this development – if governance means less government, it also means less allocation of public policy resources to such communities;

4. "communitarism", like "multiculturalism" may be inward-looking, reactionary and stultifying and the mobilisation necessary to turn minority cultures into outward-looking, progressive and dynamic is difficult to achieve. What might be interesting is the notion of "interculturalism", as advanced by certain Quebecois scholars as a way of reconciling the assimilationist approach of traditional Jacobinism and the separatist or apartheid approaches typical of Anglo-Saxon or Germanic approaches.

5. partnership in terms of governance often introduces new actors into the policy-formation process. This is a positive move if additional resources are released which allow such partnerships to work. However, insufficient resources can often stifle the full impact of the transfer of responsibility from central control to local agencies resulting in a local culture of "blame" and "complaint" directed not at government itself but at the responsible partner.

6. a new emphasis on "capacity-building" within the lesser-used language communities has to overcome structural difficulties in realising the promise of service innovation, empowerment and institutional trust, the new leitmotifs of policies of social inclusion.

7. new technologies may provide different forms of networking and interaction which in turn may release additional energies and give rise to synergy and economies of scale in bi- or multi-lingual communication.

8. the skilling or commodification of language can provide new resources which appeal to the information-society and increase the economic purchase of bi- or multi-lingual employees.

9. community vitality and revitalisation can be achieved through a linguistic-led programme of socio-economic intervention.

In all these instances it is extremely difficult to isolate the patterns of cause and effect. Much of the dynamism behind these changes seems to originate in *economic* developments and in the avalanche of new technologies which have developed over the last forty years and which is now accelerating at an incredible rate. However, these economic changes are also dependent on other factors, such as new values and attitudes in society and new forms of state activity and design, with new roles, functions and types of relationships with other levels of government and with the private sector and society.

I also believe that it is important to isolate another contextual feature of the changes: the macro-context represented by globalisation and Europeanisation. In fact, Europeanisation is both a response to the threat of globalisation and an expression of globalisation. Take for example the earlier discussion which counter posed interculturalism and transnationalism as two alternative ways of locating minorioty cultures within the larger political framework. Transnationalism could be viewed as the positive aspect of glob-alisation, and thus considered, globalisation could lead to an enhancement of the minority's capacity to interact on a larger stage, because it breaks down the institutional barriers erected largely as a result of the nation-state project. Thus we might conclude that there is a need to rethink our political concepts and practices: nation and state and their combination into nation-state; democracy; representative government; institutions. To put it in a nut-shell, it might be said that we are starting the 21st century with political and administrative institutions inherited from the 19th century nation-state, which were built on the principles of the 18th century Enlightenment.

These transformations present RM and IM languages and cultures with a number of challenges and opportunities. Among the challenges is the very real danger that many cultures and languages will be engulfed by the vast economic and cultural forces at work in our globalised and hi-tech world. On the other hand, the loosening up of the nation-state and the possibilit-ies of new kinds of institutional design may also give these minorities the opportunity to adopt institutional and public policy models of social and economic development that will allow them, in collaboration with national and supranational levels of governance, to confront the changes and both protect and develop themselves. In short they may play a decisive role in developing cosmopolitan democracy.

Towards Cosmopolitan Democracy?

I have argued that language issues are directly related to questions of cit-izenship, identity, education, socialisation and participation in the public sphere. Both in political and organisational terms there is tremendous pres-sure on institutions within the EU to simplify and harmonise the range of services offered within a particular suite of languages. Countering such measures by formal language planning for smaller language communities, let alone disparate immigrant communities, becomes increasingly difficult. This is because the post-Enlightenment notions of inclusive citizenship are breaking down in the face of market segmentation and apparent con-sumer empowerment. This leads to a tension between commonality and fragmentation, between the basic needs of state socialisation, including com-municative competence in state-designated languages, and the reality of individual choices and the community-orientation of many interest groups. A major concern in this respect is access to public services by marginalised groups. As Marquand (2004) has observed "the barriers that once protected the public domain from the market and private domains grew up piecemeal, but it does not follow that they can be renewed in the same manner. In the twenty-first century, the inexplicit, half-conscious incrementalism of the late nineteenth century is unlikely to be enough" (p. 148). Even when relatively favourable conditions for sound governance in language policy matters are in place, there is no guarantee that empowerment and success will follow. It is even harder to envisage such empowerment taking place within polit-ical structures which are antipathetic to ethno-linguistic diversity let alone increasing communicative competence. But this is the common challenge we face as European citizens.

How are we to make sense of this in terms of democratic theory and practice? We started the volume with Held's concern with the articulation of the democratic good. His recent model of cosmopolitan democracy, which if adopted in the principal cases examined in this volume, would go a long way to resolving many of the unresolved issues above, because the principle of autonomy would be entrenched in diverse sites of power and across diverse spatial domains.

It is contended that the practice of democracy has conventionally been centred on the ideal of locality and place (e.g. the nation-state) but under the impresses of globalisation several powerful arguments assert that future democracy will be centred exclusively on the international global domain. Held (2006, p. 307) argues that this is a false conclusion and misrepresents the nature of contemporary globalisation. Drawing on Giddens, he reminds us that globalisation is a dialectical process whereby "local transformation is as much a part of globalization as the lateral extension of social connec-tions across time and space" (Giddens, 1990, p. 64). Rather than focus exclus-ively on the supra-state level and the operation of international agencies, Held returns to the central theme of this volume by emphasising that new demands for regional or local autonomy suggest a new possibility, namely "the recovery of an intensive participatory and deliberative democracy at local levels as a complement to the deliberative assemblies of the wide global order. That is, they portend a political order of democratic associations, cities and nations as well as regions and global networks" (Held 2006, p. 309).

Table 10.3 portrays the key features of Held's conception of democracy. I would argue that there are three reasons for advancing this approach. First it increases the practices of deliberation discussed earlier. Second, it should improve the quality of results obtained within the political decision-making system. The quality of legislation and the justice of laws should be enhanced if they have been subject, not only to institutional scrutiny, but also to public discussion and reflection. Third, by emphasising cosmopolitan democracy, the model set a premium on interconnectedness, and this surely draws attention to the role which various minorities may play within the democratic process.

The main attraction of this model is that it does not conceive of democracy as being applied only to governmental affairs and to issues of formal politics. Rather the model allows for democratic practices to be adopted also in terms of governance, the economy and civil society, which are so necessary if cosmopolitan democracy is to be realised. The argument advanced is that cosmopolitan democracy is better adapted and suited to our global age. In the

384

Table 10.3 Cosmopolitan democracy

In sum: model Xb
Cosmopolitan democracy
Principle(s) of justification
*In a world of intensifying regional and global relations, with marked overlapping
"communities of fate", the principle of autonomy requires enrichment in regional and global
networks as well as in national and local polities*
Key features
Short term   *Long term*

Polity/governance

Reform of leading UN governing
institutions such as the Security
Council (to give developing countries
a significant voice and effective
decision-making capacity

New charter of rights and obligations,
locked into different domains of
political, social and economic power

Creation of a UN second chamber
(following an international
constitutional convention)

Global parliament (with limited
revenue-raising capacity) Capacity
connected to regions, nations and
localities

Enhanced political regionalisation
(EU and beyond) and the use of
transnational referenda

Separation of political and economic
interests; public funding of
deliberative assemblies and electoral
proceses

Creation of a new, international Human
Rights Court; compulsory Jurisdiction
before the International Criminal Court

Interconnected global legal system,
embracing elements of criminal and
civil law

Establishment of an effective, accountable,
international, military force

Permanent shift of a growing
proportion of a nation-state's coercive
capability to regional and global
institutions

Economy/civil society

Enhancement of non-state, non-market
solutions in the organisation of civil
society

Creation of a diversity of
self-regulating associations and
groups in civil society

Experimentation with different
democratic organisational forms in the
economy

Multi-sectoral economy and
pluralisation of patterns of ownership
and possession

Provision of resources to those in the most
vulnerable social positions to defend
and articulate their interests

Public framework investment
priorities set through general
deliberation and government
decision, but extensive market
regulation of goods and labour

General conditions
Continuing development of regional, international and global flows of resources and
networks of interaction

Recognition by growing numbers of peoples on increasing interconnectedness of
political communities in diverse domains, including the social, cultural, economic
and environmental

Development of an understanding of overlapping "collective fortunes" which require democratic deliberation-locally, nationally, regionally and globally

Enhanced entrenchment of democratic rights and obligations in the making and enforcement of national, regional and international law

Transfer of increasing proportion of a nation's military coercive capability to transnational agencies and institutions with the ultimate aim of demilitarisation and the transcendence of the states' war system

---

Note: The institutional requirements of cosmopolitan democracy and the complexity of the major issues of reform as laid out here in a rudimentary manner. For further discussion see Archibugi and Held (1995), Held (1995), Held (2004).
Source: Held, D. Models of Democracy (2006) pp. 308–9.

face of the rise of racial and religious intolerance, nuclear proliferation, the so-called clash of world civilisations, ethnic chauvinism and the unilateralist policies of both hegemonic powers and "rogue states", it would be foolish indeed to abandon any framework which offers a modicum of additional participation and self-worth for so many peoples frozen out of formal politics by nineteenth century style representation and statecraft.

The Limits to Freedom

As with any policy agenda there are many barriers to the full implementation of agreed language policies within the local state. Here I want to address the most important limits to freedom.

Internal reticence within the bureaucracy

In many cases where lesser-used languages are incorporated into the machinery of government and administration, the biggest stumbling block to the implementation of worthwhile and comprehensive language schemes is the reticence and general attitude of civil servants not directly concerned with language planning schemes. Two temptations loom large. The first is to view all language-related issues as being the special responsibility of a Language Agency only (the ghetto approach); The second is to refuse to accept the legitimacy of cross-cutting language issues within key functions of the local state, for example, economic development, environment, health and social services (the head in the sand approach). Thus for example, within the Basque Government planners do coordinate their work to a modest degree. What weakens their effect is the tendency to assume that making Basque official is the unique responsibility of those planners alone and need not therefore have any effect on the practices of other government departments. This, according to Gardner *et al.* (2000), is because the maintenance and promotion of Basque is only one of the several object-ives pursued by governmental agencies and, for many of their members, a fairly minor one at that.[28]

Such cases demonstrate why holistic or systemic thinking is required. This is also the reason why the question "How should the mediation between speakers of different languages be organised?" is so vital, and should be extended to include the mediation between and within various responsible departments within the same system of governance.[29]

Developments in cognate areas, such as health planning and poverty reduction offer ways forward in terms of smarter territorialised governance and intervention around linguistic promotion. Smart reterritorialisation refers to the realigning of mandates, polices and resources to get the best out of them locally and to enable them to be responsive in terms of dealing with the multiple dimensions of language planning. Common accessibility arrangements for minority language schooling should reduce the amount of uncertainty and throughput from primary to secondary to tertiary levels of education, which characterises the system. Realistically any thing which can reduce the level of tension and anxiety between languages in contact must be a positive virtue within democracy. But so often partial and con-flictual reasoning damages the common wealth of society. What is needed then is a determined and co-ordinated representation of minority needs at both international and local level which advocates "joined up thinking" within and between government departments and their partner agencies in the community. "Holistic language planning" can so easily become "sectoral language planning"; and as a result it is far easier to lose heart and assume that no real social impact will ever be made to sustain the long-term prac-tice of language choice. Consequently holistic values and methods have to be deeply entrenched within the system. They cannot, and should not, be added on as mere appendages to mainstream issues as and when it suits the occasion.

Top-down or Bottom-up Planning?

How does the partnership between central and local agencies, vital com-munity initiatives, the voluntary sector and the world of work, mobilise and reflect society's language-related energy to reinforce the central thrust of language schemes? There is an understandable tendency to view cogent and professional language policy as originating solely or mainly from gov-ernmental agencies. This is regrettable for two reasons. First it tends to yield the future direction of language policy into the hands of the professional, technocratic elite. Second, it undervalues the very real, substantive and vital Language Planning activities that are undertaken at the micro-level, at the level of the community, and it reproduces the one size fits all language planning and language policy approach of the nation state system.

The real challenge is to harmonise both top down and bottom up schemes so that they become mutually reinforcing. Let us look again at the Basque example where most language planning from the fifties until Franco's death in 1975 can be considered bottom-up planning. By definition so much of early language promotion had been done by civil society and by private initiatives, but starting in 1981 the Basque Government focused on language promotion in education and in successive domains. Initial conflict between top-down and bottom-up planners, abated from about 1992 on, and led to the adoption of a *modus vivendi* (Gardner *et al.*, 2000).[30] The political cleavage between supporters of independence outside the Basque Government and moderate nationalist parties, usually in the Government, meant that the basic conflict about who should be doing what was often overlaid with mutual political suspicion. Conflict generating issues have included the creation of a Basque language newspaper, the organisation and financing of Basque language classes for adults and the financing of the *ikastola* school system and its integration in the state or private school system.[31]

In all cases of language revitalisation there is an acute tension in realising language schemes between advocates of front-line services and language teaching requirements, and those who, in addition, recognise that sound planning requires accurate trend and impact analysis. One of the chief dangers of putting plans into practice within difficult resource constraints is the temptation to neglect the audit and monitoring function of language planning. Consequently, little firm analysis of the effect of the language schemes, other than anecdotal or partisan information, is available to inform subsequent discussions and policy initiatives. This is a major weakness of most language planning programmes, as currently constituted, and could lead to ineffective use of time, money and ultimately political capital, if not addressed systematically.

Institutional or Individual Language Rights?

We may distinguish between the initial raft of human rights derived from the tumultuous consequences of the French Revolution in 1789 whose rallying call was *Liberty, Equality and Fraternity,* and the current concern with language and governance, whose cardinal principles are *Unity, Variety and Choice.* The former stressed statutory obligations in terms of individual citizen versus groups' collective rights, and framed language planning policy choices in terms of personality versus territorial rights. The latter places more emphasis on language as a symbol of group identity together with language variety as an expression of inter-cultural communication. Mamadouh's (2002) concern with mediation between speakers and the development of a range of language skills within which individuals may be empowered is entirely appropriate. The emergence of such rights may be traced to a series of declarations such as: 1. The UN International Covenant on Civil and Political Rights, 1966, especially Article 27. 2. The UN Declaration on the Rights of Persons Belonging to National or Ethnic, Religious and Linguistic Minorities, 1992. 3. The Organisation for Security and Co-operation in Europe (OSCE): especially the Hague Recommendations regarding the Education Rights of National Minorities, 1998. 4. OSCE: The Oslo Recommendations regarding the Linguistic Rights of National Minorities, 1998. 5. The Universal Declaration of Linguistic Rights, Barcelona, 1996. 6. The Council of Europe: Framework Convention for the Protection of National Minorities, 1998. 7. The European Charter for Regional or Minority Languages, 1998.

In the near future language rights issues are likely to feature in a reinvigorated campaign for a European Convention and thus the trend is to provide an increasingly binding international legal framework. We have come to realise that good will is not enough if a thoroughgoing choice of language service is the aim of the policy, whether at international or more local level. There is a critical need for statutory obligation and the testing of linguistic human rights. This is a major challenge to the EU and beyond and will certainly become a source of perpetual conflict in the coming years. In whom are basic rights vested? Should they be granted to individual citizens and/or to institutions responsible for implementing an equal opportunities policy? We recognise that establishing an institutional framework of collective language rights and services is one thing, guaranteeing individual human language rights is altogether more problematical. This is because those who advocate absolute language rights often do so in an idealistic manner without reference to the legal framework within which such rights are to be protected. International standards, such as those advanced by the OSCE, offer a minimum framework for individual minority members who seek equality both in law and practice. But all too often such standards do not offer sufficient immediate redress to calm the anxieties of hurting individuals. This is why some advocate the larger case for universal individual rights. Cynicism about the conditionality of interpretation of rights and the ad hoc manner in which such rights are applied, leads to more strident calls for the specification of individual language rights as a basic human right, a form of affirmative language action.[32] Champions of the latter course of action, such as Tove Skutnabb-Kangas (2000, 2002) or Robert Phillipson (1992) are to be encouraged for they often place the choices we face in stark power-relationship terms and bring out the hidden agendas of state-controlled vested interests. Liberal democrats may not approve of the rhetoric which talks of "state murder machines" or "linguistic genocide", but however one dresses up the process of language displacement and group violence, the end result is an acute diminution of linguistic diversity and a denial of the role of human creativity and communication within the wider global ecological system.

More cautious commentators would counter that in most cases, established linguistic rights are often no more than the special pleading of a beleaguered minority whose collective right to exist does not automatically transfer to any specific set of individually-ascribed language rights. In fact the whole notion of individual rights to language use within multilingual liberal democracies is fraught with difficulties. Even in successful cases of language revitalisation in Europe, rights are normally vested in broad spheres such as education or public administration. Accessing particular language-related services is often a question of socio-political pressure rather than reference to normative rights regimes. Consequently there is a yawning gap between the declared international rights conventions and the empowerment of individual citizens to exercise any substantive degree of real choice in matters of language use.

Symbolic or Practical Language Schemes?

A further difficulty is the practice within some states to rest content with symbolic language schemes which give the titular right to access to minority education or government services. Agreed language schemes, whether within National Parliaments/Assemblies or at the level of local authorities, can very often be symbols of good intent rather than genuine services for customers at the point of local demand/contact. There is a critical need to monitor the actual working of the schemes.

If they are merely symbolic then they are little more than a subterfuge by which minority groups are to be assimilated, using the hegemonic practices discussed earlier.

Hence there is an acute need to tackle the twin issues of adequate resourcing of language schemes and of target community implementation. Processes of empowerment, ownership, participation and partnership are far easier to assume as given rather than work on as part of infra-structural development of Language Planning. Thus special attention needs to be given to the auditing, monitoring and practical evaluation aspects of language schemes and of language legislation.

A contemporary example of such monitoring is the "From Act to Action" project which seeks to investigate and analyse the way in which instruments of language legislation are implemented within the public administrative system of Finland, Ireland and Wales.[33] The project was devoted to

1. comparing different systems (national level): legal and institutional framework.
2. comparing different mechanisms supporting the enactment of language legislation.
3. comparing individual public authorities and agencies within the three countries.

The research sought information on how well the language schemes were working from the practitioner's point of view, so as to provide information on what works, to identify good practices and to produce tools for diagnoses and performance measurement in a variety of European contexts (Table 10.4).

Table 10.4 A summary of the legislative and administrative systems

Rights Finland	Strong rights of individuals Relatively detailed statutory provisions by law Decentralised and non-standardised implementation of language act
Ireland	Weaker rights of individuals Less detailed statutory duties Centrally managed and standardised implementation of language act
Wales	Weaker rights of individuals Less detailed statutory duties Centrally managed and standardised implementation of language act
Public *Services* Finland	Central government authorities are bilingual Linguistic division of country into unilingual and bilingual authorities. Bilingual authorities have extended duty to provide services in two languages
Ireland	650 public authorities are listed in 2003 Official Languages Act Department of Community, Rural and Gaeltacht affairs requests authorities to prepare language schemes
Wales	Public bodies required to provide bilingual services are listed in section 6.1 of 1993 Welsh Language Act Minister can name additional bodies on the advice of the Welsh Language Board
Regulation/ *Monitoring* Finland	Decentralised implementation No statutory mechanism Passive role of central authority (Ministry of Justice) in implementation and monitoring of act
Ireland	Statutory language schemes Active role of central authority (Department of Community, Rural and Gaeltacht Affairs, Language) and of An Coimisinéir Teanga in the implementation and monitoring of act[34]
Wales	Statutory language schemes Active role of central authority (Welsh Language Board) in implementation and monitoring of act

Source: From Act to Action Project 2007.

The project compared the effects of different institutional arrangements and focussed on the relationship between the national authority in charge of the language act and the individual public authorities. Detailed case study material was gathered from four types of bilingual service context, namely a) central government (Ministries, departments, independent bodies) b) the health services, c) local/regional government and d) state authorities operating at the local/regional level (e.g. policing, taxation, social security, pensions, unemployment etc.). In addition evidence was gathered on the interface between the organisations and the citizens/customers so as to determine the contextual effects of the national administrative system, the local environment (in terms of number of minority language speakers, tradition, supply/demand), the institutional context (type of authority, command structure, decision making patterns etc.) and structural factors (such as staff, organisation, leadership).

The results demonstrate that each of the countries investigated had adopted very different institutional mechanisms – but experienced very similar challenges for individual authorities. Three generic determinants were operative, namely the level of supply and demand of bilingual services, the position/status of the target minority language within the organisations and the crucial role of staffing policies and of managerial attitudes towards both the implementation of legislation *per se* and to the increased demands placed on their organisation by having to operate bilingually.

Let me illustrate the broad findings with regards to Wales. It was concluded that the 350 or so Welsh Language Schemes agreed to date operate well at a procedural level. Complaints made by members of the public regarding the operation of a bilingual service or presumed language "rights" matters were received by the regulatory body, the Welsh Language Board, and handled professionally and with integrity. There is a relatively wide variation in terms of implementation of the language schemes within the organisations surveyed where internal arrangements also vary considerably. Stronger more pro-active organisations appreciate the interactive dialogue they have with the WLB in the preparation, implementation and revision of their language schemes. By contrast weaker, less committed organisations argue that the WLB should be more pro-active and involved, adopting a firmer regulatory approach to lack of compliance in language scheme implementation. Given that over 350 language schemes have now been agreed, many of them for their third five year cycle, there is a widespread experience within the system as to how to provide bilingual services. The evolving network of local government language officers allows for some degree of flexibility and relative independence from WLB initiatives and permits the services to be seen as part of the mainstream equalities agenda of public bodies rather than a language add on.

Civil society and many local government employees argue that there is a need to revisit the 1993 Welsh Language Act and have called for a fresh debate on aspects of language legislation, including introducing language clauses into subject-specific acts related to issues such as employment law, advertising, health service training and the like. Having embarked on granting institutions the responsibility to provide bilingual services, the Welsh case demonstrated the limits of this approach (as discussed in Chapter Eight) for the general public are often confused as to what are their "rights" and whose responsibility it was to regulate language schemes. The conclusion is that it is opportune to enact a series of measures which specify minimum individual language rights so as to reduce such confusion and promote the development of a bilingual society. But should such rights be confined to the public sector (broadly defined) or extended to all sectors of society?

Public Sector or Plural Sector Approach?

For very obvious reasons initial language policy schemes are targeted at public sector institutions and educational domains. However, to be truly useful, language policy schemes should have a medium term aim of influencing language rights behaviour in most socio-economic contexts. The private sector is notoriously difficult to penetrate and most often requires additional legislation to insist that it accommodates to the needs of bilingual or multilingual customers and employees. Evidence from Quebec and Catalonia demonstrates that such legislation is empowering when a majority of the intended beneficiaries have a command of the target language. Evidence from the Basque Autonomous Community and Wales reveals that it is far, far more difficult to advance an economic, let alone a legal, justification for encouraging bilingualism in the private sector. I agree that it's difficult to advance an economic justification in these circumstances. But advancing a legal justification is largely a normative matter – except in relation to things like consumer protection (i.e. making sure that labels are printed in a language consumers understand). But even that wouldn't apply in Catalonia since Catalan speakers can read Spanish (not so with the Quebecois and English, of course).

Nevertheless there are some elements of success, particularly in those SMEs located within the agricultural industry, tourism and Research and Development, whose rationale for increased bilingual working practices derive from added surplus value and quality of service arguments (Puigdevall and Williams, 2001). It is also increasingly the case that larger commercial and financial enterprises, such as supermarkets and insurance companies, banks and the like, are adopting a voluntary code of bilingual practice. The original domains where the Basque Government intervened and legislated in terms of language rights were related to education, mass media (and, increasingly IT), administration. However, Gardner *et al.* (2000) report that the advances in sub-domains with major impact in local communities such as health, the police and the courts, are very modest indeed. McCleod (2007, private correspondence) has questioned to what extent is this because of the inherent nature of such institutions and to what extent is the structure of Spanish federalism the issue? If courts in the Basque Country were under the control of the BAC government instead of Madrid (as is the case with the Scottish courts and the Scottish Executive) would things have been better?

Little attention has been paid to the private sector. The gains in terms of modern, urban, cultural service companies tend to hide the continuing losses in what might be termed "traditionally Basque firms", usually related to the primary sector, which have retained some degree of Basqueness to the present-day without conscious planning and which constitute an obvious area for intervention. On the whole the presence of Basque is extremely limited in industry and commerce, despite the obvious success achieved in the Mondragon initiative which is having some spill-over consequences in neighbouring locales.

The Basque case, in general, is of interest to many other language minority situations from which the following lessons may be drawn:

1. Some legal backing and access to governmental resources is essential for the minority language, as the very different fate of Basque north and south of the international border shows;
2. Language policies and their success or failure are conditioned by many factors: administrative organisation, political and sociological features of the society are all relevant;
3. The Basque case illustrates clearly the pros and cons of having one's language taken up by a political cause;
4. Basque language loyalists are not agreed on objectives: this has led to conflict on more than one occasion;
5. Excessive reliance has been placed on education: other domains have been largely ignored (family, health, police, justice, work, commerce);
6. The willingness of many in the administration to leave Basque language planning implementation to those specifically charged with carrying it out suggests a lack of ownership of the whole process on the part of government outside the language planning élite;
7. Some Basque language loyalists seem blissfully unaware of the need to attract good will and support from the monolingual majority: some proposals, not usually endorsed by the government, seem particularly provocative to the majority;[35]
8. The relative success of planning in the BAC has brought about an increasingly negative reaction from Spanish monolinguals: this is most evident in the educational sector;
9. Language planning has yet to be integrated with other forms of planning;
10. The university system has failed to provide intellectual backing: there are plenty of linguists and to some degree experts in the literature and

in educational sciences, but hardly any sociolinguists, historians of the language or economists with an RLS interest;
11. Insufficient evaluation work is being carried out (Gardner, Puigdevall i Serralvo and Williams, 2000 pp. 333–34).

Key Issues for International Agency Networking

In the early to mid-nineties I argued that the initial language planning bodies and sponsoring government departments were essentially a grant disbursement operation and very rarely operated as a genuine language planning and policy unit (Williams, 1993b, 1996c, 1997a). Too much of the budget of various Language Agencies/Boards were targeted to social partners and staffing costs, and insufficient resources were made available to sustain genuine language planning and language policy functions. This clearly seems to be the current dynamic with Bòrd na Gàidhlig, although a key issue is actually "under" staffing. As such bodies matured they recognised a critical need to construct an adequate budget to employ specialist "planners and forecasters" who could anticipate needs and save the Language Agencies from the trap of being essentially both a whipping boy and a post-box for the distribution of public monies to target audiences. Language agencies needed to direct change (policy) as well as service the existing needs of government and constituent citizens (practice). When truly effective they would be setting the agenda rather than reacting to the marginalia on language issues which generally ensue from governmental deliberations at whatever level in the political hierarchy. Such a transformation, I argued, required three conditions to be satisfied. The first was to change the rationale which framed the reasons why lesser-used languages should be promoted. The second was political engagement at the EU level to press home the common interests of these language policy agencies. The third was to garner evidence and time-series data which would support a robust analysis of such languages in context as a basis for sound language planning.

The increasing strength of languages of wider communication, such as English, French or German derive in part from their strategic role as contributors to a former colonial, imperial past and to current state hegemony. Their continued cumulative advantage, derived from the activities of the state and the international system, is not considered as a direct subsidy nor as an illogical intervention into the market place, but as normal policy and practice to execute daily socio-economic functions. Additional non-state support is offered by international commerce, science and technology for these languages as they function as purveyors of global knowledge, information and entertainment. The dominant rationality legitimises their position.

However, when it comes to support for historical language minorities exceptionalism rules, and the logic of such support is nearly always couched in moral, cultural and group identity terms, rather than in strict instrumental, functional terms. One need not necessarily subscribe to a materialist interpretation of the constitutive role of ideology to be convinced that alternative representations of reality are at work here.[36]

In such cases language, culture and economy are treated as autonomous spheres of influence and activity. They are not necessarily seen as mutually binding nor as constituting a sustainable alternative to the hegemonic language. And when any major case for structural reform is made it is nearly always advanced by language-related agencies rather than economic agencies. This makes it doubly difficult to mainstream language issues into political economic schemas, regional development programmes and the like. For so often language planning agencies can be accused of satisfying the interests of a small minority of citizens and of engaging in special pleading. This is an understandable, if regrettable state of affairs and a planned response to maximise the potential of such minority representation is thus needed.

The beginning of the twenty-first century heralded the fledgling organisation of such representation. Co-coordinated efforts to strengthen the voice of several language minorities have resulted in the creation of a network of official language boards/agencies. At a meeting in Brussels, November 2001, convened by the Basque Government, Foras na Gaeilge and the Welsh Language Board, seven European Regional/National Language Policy Bodies formed a network of responsible authorities charged with the twin task of bringing collective pressure to bear on European Institutions and disseminating good practice among the constituent language contexts represented. As one of the conveners, our ultimate aim was to have a permanent, direct influence on the formulation and application of EU policy as regards the so-called "lesser-used languages" and to increase cross-border and interregional co-operation. A more immediate aim was to formalise the already healthy exchange of ideas, programmes and personnel, which several of the official bodies had initiated, in terms of family language transmission, bilingual education, marketing minority languages and the like.

In diffusing our message in 2002, I argued that a major contribution could be made by this network if we decided to develop a robust series of economic, commercial and strategic arguments for our position as advocates of the smaller languages of Europe. Clearly this would also require pressure on appropriate governmental agencies and commercial interest to produce regular, consistent, comprehensive time-series data on language use to act as a statistical base for charting the development of our policies.[37]

The deliberations of that Finnish-hosted, and EU-sponsored conference, in Helsinki, October 2002, marked a further step in the process where key priorities were debated. Since then the active co-operation of Language Boards, representing autonomous or devolved governments within the EU, has encouraged a far stronger voice and responsibility for co-ordinated action among and between the member-states and the representative regions/nations. Multi-level and multi-function networking has also been enhanced by the clearer specification of the pioneering role of EBLUL, with its focus on the needs of newer members of the EU and its co-ordination of practical policy implementation through the Partnership in Diversity programme.

Early in 2006 the EU set forth its strategy for promoting linguistic diversity. In January 2007 Leonard Orban from Romania, was appointed as European Commissioner for Multilingualism and a strategic meeting was convened in Brussels for representatives of language minorities, such as the European Language Planning Boards, Mercator, EBLUL, the Federal Union of European Nationalities (FUEN) and the Youth of European Nationalities. After the meeting the Commission announced that it would provide financial support for five to seven language networks which could include a network for the regional- and minority languages. A second meeting in Amsterdam at the end of January formalised the shape and constitution of the European regional and minority language network and designated the Welsh Language Board as the secretariat to administer the network. The network is comprised of members and associate members[38] which currently includes the major players namely the European Language Planning Boards/Departments, Mercator, EBLUL, Adum, FUEN and NPLD. An annual General Assembly will set strategy and a Sterring Committee, meeting twice per annum will govern activities:[39]

The General Assembly has the overall control of the association with a view to accomplishing its goals. The General Assembly will:

a) adopt the annual report;
b) adopt the annual accounts and the budget;
c) appoint and dismiss the associate members of the Steering Committee;
d) ratify decisions concerning the acceptance or exclusion of members;
e) take decision whether members should become members or associate members;
f) take decisions with regard to amendments to the articles of the statutes;
g) take decisions concerning the voluntary dissolution of the association;
h) adopt and amend the standing rules.

The Steering Committee is responsible for:

a) convening the General Assembly;
b) preparatory work for the meetings of the General Assembly;
c) the preparation of the working programme;
d) the financial management;
e) engaging personnel;
f) drawing up standing rules;
g) the examination of application for membership;
h) other tasks which do not legally or statutorily fall under the responsibility of the General Assembly.

Agreed projects will be submitted to the Transversal Programmes of the European Commission drawn from the following fields: social opportunities for young people to speak the language outside the classroom; pre-school education; new media and film production; promotion of minority language within the private sector; issues in immigration; healthcare; new learners; and developing a common voice for minorities.

This network is likely to be the prime instrument for the promotion of such languages within an international frame. But it will have a limited effect only on the larger, often unresolved questions, which characterise the linguistic diversity of Europe.

Unresolved Questions

1. What are the core needs for language development in Europe? Who defines such needs and how are they translated into public policy?
2. Who is responsible for decisions to develop languages for education across the curriculum? How are these decisions made and directed? How are they assessed and audited? Are there reliable cross-national indicators of attainment?
3. How are compulsory forms of language education used to perpetuate discrimination and to create new forms of inequality in society?
4. Will multicultural cities such as Frankfurt, Paris, Brussels, Barcelona and London develop a specific range of multilingual policies that stress their comparative similarities, qua multi-ethnic nodes in a European metropolitan network, which will separate them further both from "national" curricula and training requirements and the considerations of historical linguistic minorities?
5. Will decision makers appreciate that such cities have additional sociolinguistic issues which can overburden language policy advisers? These relate to the sheer diversity of languages spoken in such locales, the tremendous additional resources required by public services, especially the health sector, and the dual effect which migrants can have on language primacy such as Catalan in Barcelona as the default language of integration, rather than Castilian.
6. How ready are the newer EU members be to enter into fresh dialogues and negotiations with the "Minority Language Community of Interests" as opposed to the "State/Majority Language Community of Interests"?
7. What is the role for "minority languages" in national curricula? Should "minorities" be treated as separate but equal, or separate and unequal constituents, within the educational system?
8. What are the perceptions held by consumers, agencies and educationalists as to what constitutes an appropriate place for proficiency in lesser used languages as opposed to languages of wider communication?

9. How are these perceptions/expectations shaped, monitored and reflected in planning discourse and policy implementation?
10. Will the strategies advanced by the European Language Boards Network garner sufficient support among their social partners and key actors within the economy to enable the specific initiatives proposed to be realised?
11. What sorts of structures are envisaged to promote dialogue and partnership and to secure credence for this new network and its initiatives?
12. What mechanisms need to be created to allow the regional minority languages (RM) and immigrant languages (IM) representative, both to speak to each other and to liaise with the majoritatian language interests which structure the limits of their freedom.
13. How can the diversity within regional or minority languages be respected?
14. Can recognition only be achieved at the cost of reducing internal variation and assimilation to a norm?
15. Must language planning and language policy for minorities necessarily parallel the old-style nation-building process, especially if conducted within a post-sovereign context?

Comparative Policy Implications

A pressing need is comparative work on bilingual/multilingual policy and language equality issues. Future policy could be directed toward instigating research-based investigations, which sought to:

1. Contribute holistically-derived theoretical and practical elements to Language Planning and Language Policy in Europe.
2. Assess the character, quality and success of the institutional language policies of the European Parliament, European Commission and related para-public agencies.
3. Investigate the complex nature of bilingual educational, language legislation and administrative systems in the constituent regions of the European Language Board Network.
4. Integrate the needs of linguistic minorities within the broader equality and rights agenda as it relates to bilingual education, civil rights and group equality issues.
5. Re-assess the role of cross-border arrangements for the increased recognition of lesser-used languages at the supra-national level.
6. Analyse the economic demand for a skilled bilingual/multilingual workforce in several sectors of the European economy.
7. Determine to what extent bilingual working practices, for example in Catalonia, offer exemplars for multilingual contexts within other

regions e.g. either in respect of several European languages or selected non-European languages such as Arabic, Urdu, Hindi or variants of Chinese.

8. Assess how policy reform within the newer states of the EU has impacted on the plurilingual character of their educational and public administrative services, together with the local government and legal system of neighbouring states. This is a particularly critical question in the Hungarian-Slovene-Italian, Polish-German, Czech-German-Austrian, Slovak-Austrian, Finnish-Latvian-Lithuanian-Estonian cross-border regions.

9. Analyse the extent to which European Union and Council of Europe language initiatives related to both the regional minority and immigrant minority languages are adopted and monitored in signatory states.

10. Strengthen the expertise of language planning agencies as they develop realistic co-operation in key areas, such as language transmission within the family, community language planning initiatives, adult language teaching methods, software developments, internet, mobile phone and telecommunications.

11. Adapt for local purposes the excellent work undertaken by Resource Centres for Standardisation and Terminological Development, such Termcat, Centre de Terminologica.

12. Investigate to what extent the dominance of English can be mediated to serve as a fulcrum for the closer integration of commerce and interchange in the evolving European political system.

Conclusion

The attainment of a degree of political autonomy and policy responsibility has led many of the institutional actors analysed in this volume to re-assess their relationship with local, regional, state and international bodies. This volume has traced the often torturous and idiosyncratic path of selected minorities in seeking, first, to gain recognition and representation, and then, to grapple with the new realities of inhabiting increasingly multilingual contexts which are characterised by diversity and differential responses to globalisation. The more politically mature polities, such as Catalonia and Quebec, have emerged as beacons of hope for the smaller, less well organised minorities. But they have also brought into sharp relief the newer challenges brought by political responsibility and identity construction efforts. Oakes and Warren (2007, p. 198) suggest that Quebec has much to offer other civil societies, principally "its continual reflection on the status and future of the French language within its borders puts it at the forefront of what it means to construct a modern, inclusive liberal democracy. For the question that Quebec constantly asks itself is how to create the conditions to generate a genuine sense of attachment to the collectivity amongst all its members, surely the fundamental question that all liberal democracies should be asking themselves in the present global conjuncture."

I would echo this judgement and add that increasingly the rehabilitation of long-beleaguered languages and their speakers is not a romantic project, doomed to failure, but rather a realistic response to the challenges of democratic marginalisation and globalisation. Political representation and largely autonomous policy making in the fields of bilingual education and language promotion, have transformed the conditions of possibility whereby the fate of languages we have been discussing can be improved. My concern with "the one and the many" will be a permanent dialectic, for despite some evidence of deliberative and cosmopolitan democracy being strengthened, the legal and political system does not provide sufficient guarantees for the protection of the interests of minorities. This is in large part because the representative system in most Western democracies fails to reflect the sheer diversity of its constituents. This is a doubly difficult issue within Catalonia, the Basque Autonomous Community and Wales, where recent attempts to promote the national language are interpreted by opponents as a weakening of the state-wide hegemonic culture and as an attempt to deprive the majority of their inalienable right to uniform service provision throughout the state. Others claim that the liberal democratic state is not sufficiently reflexive and that new forms of governance are needed so as to reinvigorate democracy and participation. I interpret the struggle in and over language in society as an example of the wider debate on equality. The substantive values of representation and equality are central to democratic deliberations. Certainly there will be opposition and conflict, reaching even to genocide at times, such is the fate of minorities in history. But "the very disagreements that are an ineliminable feature of a democratic community of free and equal citizens demand 'wide' liberties of conscience, religion and expression by denying the community or majority the legitimate power to enforce contingent consensus on moral matters" (Bohman and Rehg, 1997, p. xxvi).

To the extent that the political system allows for representative collective decision making it really does matter whether or not individuals participate equally. As Knight and Johnson (1997, p. 289) argue this conception "does not prejudge the exact nature of the relationship between deliberative democracy and representative institutions. It does not, in other words, presume that deliberation requires democracy." But it does demand engagement and the freedom to act in the name of the minority so as to enrich the public good. The difficulty, of course, is that not every one sees the promotional aspects of the Catalan or Welsh government in terms of language planning as enrichment. Indeed there are very deep concerns as to whether the mechanisms intended to promote substantive group equality may actually produce procedural inequalities within the political system itself and lead to a weakening of some aspects of inclusive democracy. A public philosophy incorporating the principles of equality, mutual respect and the honouring of diversity can only be judged useful in so far as it helps reconcile disagreements and resolve deep divisions in practical meaningful ways. Under some conditions this may entail an acceptance of inequalities in the treatment of citizens by the local state, such as the requirement that new residents be socialised in the language of the local majority in Quebec, Catalonia or parts of Wales. This is a difficult issue for both participants and liberal supporters alike and involves controversy, struggle and deep disagreement. But it is a necessary struggle if we are to honour the right of smaller nations and groups, not only to exist, but also to flourish within the conditions, which to the largest extent possible, are of their own making.

Notes

1. After all, even if French disappeared in Canada, it would continue to thrive in France. So too with many other historic linguistic minorities, such as the German minority in Denmark, the Hungarian minority in Romania and Slovakia, or the Turkish minority in Bulgaria (see Kymlicka, 2001, 2007).
2. Logically it also applies to immigrant groups e.g. the rights of Punjabi/Urdu speakers in the UK notwithstanding the strength of these languages in Pakistan.
3. Citizens in the West may feel some obligation to remedy the injustices of colonialism, particularly if they are former colonial powers, but this is unlikely to extend to assisting ex-colonial immigrants to maintain their native tongues.
4. This is meant in the Gramscian sense of hegemony.
5. As Williams (2007) notes, the promotion of Gaelic in Scotland is sometimes seen as a "minority" or "multicultural" issue, rather than a matter of Scottish national identity.
6. In the Canadian case, for example, the presence of the civil law tradition in Quebec not only provides an argument why Quebec should have autonomy, but also provides an argument why Quebec needs three of the nine seats on the Supreme Court (which sometimes has to rule on issues of civil law). If Quebecers gave up the civil law tradition, they would lose a central argument for autonomy and judicial representation.
7. One factor not mentioned previously is the "desecuritzation" of state-minority relations – i.e., the fact that national minorities in the West are no longer seen as potential fifth-columns for some neighbouring enemy. For a discussion of how such security fears have dissipated in the West with respect to national minorities (but not necessarily immigrants), and how it remains a powerful obstacle to greater accommodation of national minorities in much of the rest of the world, see Kymlicka (2004).
8. I recognise that those who claim that language demands are cultural not political would not accept this interpretation, yet the fact remains that much thought needs to be given to the positive actions by which such languages are to be honoured and promoted within the political system.
9. Catalonia is often pointed to in this context, as its policies on many of these issues are more liberal than that of the Castilian majority throughout Spain. The same is true of Quebec, at least on issues of women's equality, which are more progressive than those in the rest of Canada.
10. A stark contrast may be drawn between the lack of public debate in Spain and the UK regarding the signing of the Council of Europe Charter on Regional or

Minority Languages in contrast to the levels of engagement and opposition to this Charter witnessed in France.

11. Whether Canada is understood as binational or multinational depends, in part, on whether indigenous peoples are seen as "nations", or whether their self-governing communities are described in other terms.

12. The Official Languages Act can be seen as attempting to diminish the perceived territorialisation of Canada's two major language communities, by insisting that francophones and anglophones can receive federal services in their language "from sea to sea". But this (commendable) approach has not changed the widespread public perception that for most purposes, including political decision-making, French is the language of public life in Quebec (and parts of New Brunswick), and English is the language of public life in the rest of the country.

13. The principal speakers at the round table, held in Pall Mall, on the 26th of May 2005, were Rex Halford, Alan Trench, Stephen Driver, Alain Noel and Henry Milner.

14. Apart of course from the Gaeltecht and the few counties in Wales where native-speakers remain a local majority. Sustaining these linguistic enclaves is an important goal in both Wales and Ireland, but is not the main focus of the language revitalisation plans, which are precisely concerned with enhancing the status of Gaelic and Welsh in those parts of the country where it is no longer the language of daily life.

15. Problem-solving linguistics has tended to focus on various combinations of target state and "other" languages, most often separated out as modern languages, regional minority languages or immigrant languages. Despite our claims to be interested in the language continuum we tend to restrict our empirical investigations to one of these three broad areas. Clearly this will no longer do if we are to understand, and then interpret, the relationship between citizenship, migration and language.

16. Clearly there are numerous academic studies which tackle such issues, such as the pioneering Babylon Project at Tilburg University, and the current crop of case studies grouped under the title "Linguistic Landscaping". But relatively few of these studies are systematic government-sponsored investigations designed to inform policy development, and hardly any of them interrelate their GIS-acquired linguistic and socio-political data together with regional planning, urban form and function or economic profile data as gathered by municipalities.

17. In 1988, Zelinsky and Williams asked us to "imagine how rich the stimuli for scholars and government officials if we could consult detailed atlases of actual linguistic behaviour in such places as London, Toronto, New York City and San Francisco, with special reference to non-indigenous speech. In these and other geolinguistic endeavours, the findings obviously could be applied in socially constructive fashion by those legislators and planners who formulate public policy as well as by the scholar" (p. 356).

18. Thus van der Merve (1993) has mapped the geography of language shift in Cape Town and Williams and van der Merve (1996) have set forth a research agenda for Urban Geolinguistics which focuses on the linking of official census and specific social survey data, the vicissitudes of urban ecology, and the adoption of Geographic Information System methodologies. More recently van der Merwe and van der Merwe (2006) have produced a "Linguistic Atlas of South Africa".

19. The first ESF Workshop, held in Siena September 2006, brought together some fifteen specialists (of whom I was one) working on the linguistics of diversity in order to map the European linguistic space.

20. It follows that they have a longstanding history of collecting census data on multicultural population groups. For a splendid analysis of the immigration policies of the UK, USA and Germany in a comparative context see Joppke (1999).

21. For a discussion of methodological problems in comparing the answers to differently phrased questions in Australian censuses from a longitudinal perspective see Clyne (1991) and for Canada, see Marmen and Corbeil (2004).

22. RM languages tend to be the stateless languages who missed out in the processes of state formation. Centralising tendencies and the ideology of *one-language – one-state* threatened the survival of many RM languages. The greatest threat has been the lack of intergenerational transmission. Only in the last few decades have some RM languages become relatively well protected in legal terms, usually preceded by affirmative educational policies and programmes (at national or EU level). A map of RM languages compiled with a consistent methodology across Europe and supplying comparable data for comparative analyses is not available.

23. Although IM languages such as Arabic and Turkish, are often conceived of, and transmitted as, core values of culture by IM groups, they are much less protected than RM languages by affirmative actions and legal measures.

24. The new network will involve:-follow-up thematic workshops and joint publications; launching of joint research proposals for application to funding schemes at the European, national and local levels; networking with similar European and global initiatives, such as the Network of Excellence on Sustainable Development in a Diverse World, financed by FP6, Priority 7; the UNESCO programmes on Multiculturality – MOST ; and the Urban Audit initiative of DGREGIO in the European Commission for the joint organisation of events, publications and proposals; networking with national and European statistics institutes for the design of new survey and data collection initiatives.

25. National censuses in the EU generally ignore the presence of IM which makes the mapping of IM languages impossible. States, such as France, refuse to acknowledge that there is any territorial basis to their IM residents, although there are clear spatial concentrations. At a more micro-level, recent research has sought to map the language registers of pupils at schools or in neighbourhoods, using a mix of survey-based and visual inspection data, analysed with statistical techniques and Geographical Information Systems.

26. Edwards (2002) asserts that this is done because it is recognised that diversity is good in itself, because it involves a preference for heterogeneous landscapes and an aesthetic appreciation that values multidimensional perspectives. He also asserts that guilt is a powerful motivating factor at work when the champions of such diversity often emanate from outside the communities concerned! But is diversity in and of itself an inherently valuable thing?

27. I also recognise that there are other implications for an enlarged Europe which have more to do with direct citizen-to-citizen and company-to-company interaction. In this sphere central direction seems hardly likely to be more than a loose framework encouraging certain sorts of activity only.

28. "At worst, language legislation is skirted round and ignored. At best, that same legislation can serve to attain considerable advances in the promotion of the language, when, for example, in a small town, politicians favourable to the promotion of the language, officials competent to carry out the planning and grassroots organisations coincide in the pursuit of the same objectives." (Gardner, et al 2000).

29. It is difficult to imagine how language policies will relate to a reformed supra-national territorial system. But it is clear that the more strident and better

404 Linguistic Minorities in Democratic Context

organised sub-state nationalities, such as the Catalans, Basque and Welsh, have made significant, if insufficient, advances at the regional and international level in the promotion of their common cause. Will devolved regional/national administrations such as the Northern Ireland Assembly, the Welsh Assembly, the Basque Parliament and the Catalan Generalitat necessarily strengthen a new definition of various linguistic identities and with what consequence for the promotion of the principles of equal opportunity, pluralism and language of choice?

30. Government attempts to set up its own organisations fulfilling what often seemed to be identical objectives, thus threatening competition with the private sector, led to further conflict according to Gardner et al (2000).

31. Gardner et al report on another aspect of relationships between public and private sectors concerning the role of the coordinating bodies that the private sector has developed. *EKB*, set up in 1983, at times seemed to act as a shadow language planning body, often critical of the Basque Government, particularly of the failure to produce a thoroughgoing strategic plan for the language. This demand was not satisfied until 1999 when the Basque Government finally made its plan public. The new ambience is reflected in the recent increase of the number of members from NGO's on the Advisory Council for Basque.

32. It is recognised that this can lead to Utopianism, interpreted as extreme language as practice.

33. This is an EBLUL project (2005-07) financed by Foras na Gaeilge, Bwrdd yr Iaith and the Svenska Kulturfonden and the European Union. The team leaders are Siv Sandberg, Åbo Akademi, Peader Ó Flatharta, Dublin City University and Colin H Williams, Cardiff University.

34. Coimisinéir Teanga's role in implementation and monitoring is key, and probably much more important than the Department. One of the distinct features of the Irish model is the fact that the language board doesn't get involved in this. Indeed Foras na Gaeilge has no authority at all vis-à-vis the Gaeltacht, and one of the main thrusts of the Act is to offer better services to Gaeltacht residents. The third annual report was published on April 3rd 2007.

35. For example, the oft-repeated proposal to do away with the model A (Spanish medium, Basque as a subject) option in primary and secondary education.

36. I am thinking particularly of Althusser and materialism and the realisation that ideology embraces the whole of our existence, our material practice as much as our ideas and discourses.

37. I was honoured by being invited to present the key note address on "The Importance of Holistic Language Planning for the Promotion of Minority Languages", to the conference entitled Creating a Common Structure for Promoting Historical Linguistic Minorities within the European Union, Parliament of Finland, Helsinki, 12th October 2002.

38. Members would subscribe for €30,000, associate members would subscribe for €300. Membership is drawn from government departments, local and regional authorities, institutions, universities and research centres, newspapers and the media etc. Individuals may not join. Members form the Steering Committee while associate members may nominate two representatives to serve on the Steering Committee. As yet the three regional language agencies based within the Spanish state have chosen not to become full members, arguing that they would prefer to consolidate their own domestic position and make common cause within Spain.

39. The Commission will fund 7 language networks, to a maximum of €150k per year for three years. A minimum of 10 different countries will be required as partners, with projects to start in November 2007.

Bibliography

Abbey, R. (ed.) (2004) *Charles Taylor: Contemporary Philosophy in Focus*, Cambridge: Cambridge University Press.

Agirrebaltzategi, P. (1999) "Euskararen aldeko gizarte-mugimenduaren 25 urteok: EKBren ekarpena", *Bat soziolinguistika aldizkaria*, 31, 55–73, July.

Agnew, J.A. (1987) *Place and Politics: The Geographical Mediation of State and Society*, London: Allen & Unwin.

—— (1989) "Beyond Reason: Spatial and Temporal Sources of Intractability in Ethinic Conflicts", in L. Kriesberg (ed.), *Intractable Conflicts and their Transformation*, Syracuse, N.Y.: Syracuse University Press.

—— (2000a) "Global Political Geography Beyond Geopolitics", *International Studies Review*, 12, 91–99.

—— (2000b) "From the Political Economy of Regions to Regional Political Economy", *Progress in Human Geography*, 24 (1), 101–110.

—— (2000c) Classics in "Human Geography Revisited: Sack, R.D. Human Territoriality: Its Theory and History", *Progress in Human Geography*, 24 (1), 91–93.

Agnew, J.A. and Brusa, C. (1999) "New Rules for National Identity? The Northern League and Political Identity in Contemporary Northern Italy", *National Identities*, 1 (2), 117–33.

Agnew, J.A. and Corbridge, S. (1995) *Mastering Space*, London: Routledge.

Agnew, J., Mitchell, K. and Toal, G. (eds.) (2003) *A Companion to Political Geography*, Oxford: Blackwell.

Ahtisaari, M. (2002) Opening Statement, Conference on Creating a Common Structure for Promoting Historical Linguistic Minorities within the European Union, Finnish Parliament, Helsinki, Folktinget, 11–12 October 2002.

Aitchison, J. and Carter, H. (1993) " The Welsh Language in 1991 – A Broken Heartland and a New Beginning?", *Planet*, 97, 3–10.

—— (1994) *A Geography of the Welsh Language, 1961–1991*, Cardiff: University of Wales Press.

Akenson, D.H. (1988) *Small Differences: Irish Catholic and Irish Protestants 1815–1922*, Montreal and Kingston: McGill-Queen's University Press.

—— (1991) *Small Differences: Irish Catholics and Protestants*, Dublin: Gill and Macmillan.

Alexander, D. (2005) "EU needs to turn outward and think globally", *The Irish Times*, 21 October, p. 16.

Alter, P. (1994) *Nationalism*, 2nd edn, London: Edward Arnold.

Alterman, E. and Green, M. (2004) *The Book on Bush*, New York: Viking.

Amersfoort, H. van and Knippenberg, H. (eds.) (1991) *States and Nations: The rebirth of the "nationalities question" in Europe*, Amsterdam: Netherlands Geographical Studies.

Ammon, U. and Kleineidam, H. (eds.) (1992) "Language Spread Policy: Languages of Former Colonial Powers", *International Journal of the Sociology of Language*, 95, 1–148.

Amyot, M. (1980) *La situation demolinguistique au Québec et la charte de la langue française*, Québec: Conseil de la langue française.

An Chomhairle um Oideachas Gaeltachta agus Gaelscolaíochta (2005) *Staid reatha na Scoileanna Gaeltachta/A Study of Gaeltacht Schools, 2004*. Galway: An Chomhairle um Oideachas Gaeltachta agus Gaelscolaíochta.

An Comisinér Teanga (2005) *Tuarascáil Bhliantúil 2005/Annual Report 2005*, Glao Áitúil: An Comisinér Teanga.

—— (2006) *Ag cosaint cearta tanga/Protecting Language Rights*. Glao Áitúil: An Comisinér Teanga.

An Roinn Gnóthai Pobail and Tuaithe agus Gaeltachta (2004) *Treoirlínte/Guidelines. Section 12 of the Official Languages Act 2003*, Baile Átha Cliath: An Roinn Gnóthai Pobail, Tuaithe agus Gaeltachta.

Anderson, G. (2006) "Catalonia Votes for More Autonomy Within Spain", *Federations*, 5 (3), 15–20.

Anderson, M. (2000) *States and Nationalism in Europe since 1945*, London: Routledge.

Annamalai, E. and Rubin, J. (1980) "Planning for Language Code and Language USe", *Language Planning Newsletter* 4–7.

Archibugi, D. and Held, D. (1995) *Cosmopolitan Democracy*, Cambridge: Polity.

Arfé, G. (1981) "On a Community Charter of Regional Languages and Cultures and on a Charter of Rights of Ethnic Minorities", resolution adopted by the European Parliament, Strasbourg on 16 October 1981.

Azurmendi, M.-J. and de Luna, I.M. (eds.) (2006) *The Case of Basque: Past, Present and Future*, Soziolinguitika Klusterra.

Baker, C. (1996) *Foundations of Bilingual Education and Bilingualism*, 2nd edn, Clevedon, Avon: Multilingual Matters.

—— (2006) *Foundations of Bilingual Education and Bilingualism*, 4th edn, Clevedon, Avon: Multilingual Matters.

Bakert, C. and Jones, M.P. (2000) "Welsh Language Education: A Strategy for Revitalization", in Williams, C.H. (ed.) *Language Revitalization: Policy and Planning in Wales*, Cardiff: University of Wales Press, pp. 116–37.

Barni, M. (2006) Mapping Linguistic Diversity: Immigrant Languages in Italy. Paper presented at the ESL Mapping Linguistic Diversity Workshop, Siena, 16 September.

Basque Government, The Secretariat of Linguistic Policy (1986) *Basic Law of the Standardization of the Use of Basque*, Gasteiz: Basque Government, Central Publications Office.

Baubock, R. (2000) "Why Stay Together? A Pluralist Approach to Secession and Federation", in Kymlicka, W. and Norman, W. (eds.), *Citizenship in Diverse Societies*, Oxford: Oxford University Press, pp. 366–94.

Baudrillard, J. (1990) *The Transparency of Evil*, London: Verso.

Bauhn, P., Lindberg, C. and Lundberg, S. (eds.) (1995) *Multiculturalism and Nationhood in Canada*, Lund: Lund University Press.

Beck, U. (2000) *What is Globalization?* Malden, MA: Polity Press.

Behiels, M. (2004) *Canada's Francophone Minority Communities*, Montreal and Kingston: McGill-Queen's University Press.

Belfast Agreement (1998) *The Belfast Agreement-An Agreement Reached at the Multi-Party Talks on Northern Ireland, Cm. 3883, 1998*, Belfast: Northern Ireland Office.

Bentahila, A. and Davies, E. (1993) "Language Revival:restroration or transformation?", *Journal of Multilingual and Multicultural Development*, 14(4), 355–74.

Berriatua, X. (ed.) (1983) *Euskal Herriko Autonomia Estatutoa*, Vitoria-Gasteiz: Eusko Jaurlaritzaren Argitalpen Zerbitzu Nagusia.

Biancheri, F. (2004) "Languages and EU democratisation: The Need for an Efficient Strategy", *Newropeans Magazine*, 27 May.

Biteria, J.A., Errasti, M.P.S. and Perez, M.B. (2005) Basque Language Education in the Basque Country: From Quantitiy to Quality. Terra Report. Mondragon: Mondragon University.

Bjorklund, E. (1989) "Cultural federation or sub-cultural autonomy: Spatial aspects of Canadian separatism", in C.H. Williams and E. Kofman (eds.), *Community Conflict, Partition and Nationalism*, London: Routledge, pp. 86–116.

Blair, P. (2002) Promotion of Linguistic Diversity Through the European Charter for Regional and Minority Languages, Conference on Creating a Common Structure for Promoting Historical Linguistic Minorities within the European Union, Finnish Parliament, Helsinki, Folktinget, 11–12 October.

Blaut, J. (1987) *The National Question, Decolonising the Theory of Nationalism*, London: Zed Books.

Board na Gaeilge (1988) *The Irish Language in a Changing Society*, Dublin: Board na Gaeilge.

Bohman, J. and Rehg, W. (eds.) (1997) *Deliberative Democracy*, Cambridge, MA: MIT Press.

Bord na Gaeilge (1986) *Irish and the Education System: An Analysis of Examination Results*, Dublin: Bord na Gaeilge.

Bòrd na Gàidhlig (2005) *Annual Report 2005*, Inverness: Bòrd na Gàidhlig.

Bostock, W.W. (1988) "Assessing the Authenticity of a Supra-National Language Based Movement: La Francophonie", in C.H. Williams (ed.), *Language in Geographic Context*. Clevedon, Avon: Multilingual Matters, pp. 73–92.

Bourhis, R.H. (ed.) (1984) *Conflict and Language Planning in Québec*, Clevedon: Multilingual Matters.

Boyce, D.G. (1988) *The Irish Question and British Politics, 1868–1986*, Basingstoke: Macmillan.

—— (1995) *Nationalism in Ireland*, London: Routledge.

Bracken, J.A. (2001) *The One in the Many*, Grand Rapids: Eerdemans.

Braën, A., Foucher, P. and Le Bouthillier, Y. (eds.) (2006) *Languages, Constitutionalism and Minorities*, Markham: LexisNexisButterworths.

Brann, C.M.B. (1991) "Review of F. Coulmas, 'With Forked Tongues: What are National Languages For'?" *History of European Ideas*, 13, 131–35.

Breton, R. (1991) "The Handicaps of Language Planning in Africa", in D.R Marshall (ed.), *Language Planning: Focusschrift in honour of Joshua. A. Fishman*, Amsterdam: John Benjamins.

Breuilly, J. (1982) *Nationalism and the State*, Manchester: Manchester University Press.

Brewer, J.D. and Higgins, G.I. (1998) *Anti-Catholicism in Northern Ireland, 1600–1998*, Basingstoke: Macmillan.

British Council (1993/1994) *Annual Report*, London: British Council.

Broadcasting Commission for IrelandI/Foras na Gaeilge (2005) *Turning on and Tuning in to Irish Language Radio in the 21st Century*, Dublin: BCI.

Broughton, D. and Donovan, M. (eds.) (1999) *Changing Party Systems in Western Europe*, London: Pinter.

Brown, T. (1985) *Ireland: A Social and Cultural History, 1922–1985*, London: Fontana.

Brunn, S. and Leinbach, T.R. (eds.) (1991) *Collapsing Space and Time: Geographic Aspects of Communication and Information*. London: HarperCollins Academic.

Bryant, C.G.A. (2006) *The Nations of Britain*. Oxford: Oxford University Press.

Buchanan, K. (2005) "Lack of significant new powers for AMs 'a betrayal' ", *Western Mail*, 18 May.

Bufon, M. (1993) "Cultural and social dimensions of borderlands: the case of the Italo-Slovene transborder area", *GeoJournal*, 3, 235–40.

—— (1994) "Per una geografica delle aree di confine:il caso della regione transconfinaria Italo-Slovene nel Goriziano", *Rivista Geografica Italiana*, 101, 477–605.

—— (1996) *Caratteri e funzioni delle regioni transfrontaliere nel processo di unificazione europea, Regioni e reti nello spazio unificato europea*, Firenze.

—— (1997) "The Political and Ethnic Transformations in the Upper Adriatic Between Conflicts and Integration Perspectives", *Anali ze istrske in mediteranske studije*. 10, 295–306.

—— (2001) "Ćezmejne Prostorske Vezi Na Tromeji Med Italijo, Slovenijo in Hravśko", *Anali za istrske in mediteranske študije*, 11 (2), 283–300.

Bulletin Infoaction (2007) Commissioner of Official Languages Bulletin, Ottawa: Commissioner of Official Languages.

Burgess, M. (1988) "Meech Lake: Whirlpool of uncertainty or ripples on a millpond", *British Journal of Canadian Studies*, 3 (1), 15–29.

—— (1990) "Meech Lake: The process of constitutional reform in Canada, 1987–90", *British Journal of Canadian Studies*, 5 (2), 275–97.

Bwrdd yr Iaith Gymraeg (2001) *Adroddiad Blynyddol a Chyfrifon, 2000–01*, Caerdydd: Bwrdd yr Iaith Gymraeg.

—— (2005) *Dyfodol y Gymraeg-Cynllun Strategol/The Future of Welsh-A Strategic Plan*, Caerdydd: Bwrdd yr Iaith Gymraeg.

—— (2006) Data Sources, available at http://www.bwrdd-yr-iaith.org.uk/en/index.php.

C.L.F. (1988) *Le Projet de loi federal C-72 relatif au statut et a 1'usage des langues officielles au Canada*, Québec: Conseil de la langue francaise.

C.O.L. (1980) "Mother tongues in Canada and Québec", *Languages of the World*, Ottawa: Commissioner of Official Languages, p. 2.

Caimbeul, A. (2005) *Chief Executive's Report*, Bòrd na Gàidhlig Annual Report 2005, Inverness: Bòrd na Gàidhlig, pp. 10–12.

Caldwell, G. (1982) "Anglo-Québec on the verge of its history", *Language and Society*, 8, 3–6.

Caldwell, G. and Waddell, E. (eds.) (1982) *The English of Québec from Majority to Minority Status*, Québec City: Institut Québecois de Recherche sur la Culture.

Cameron, D. (ed.) (1999) *The Referendum Papers*, Toronto: The University of Toronto Press.

Campbell, A. (2006) *A National Plan for Gaelic*, Inverness: Bòrd na Gàidhlig.

Campbell, C. (2000) "Menter Cwm Gwendraeth: A Case-Study in Community Language Planning", in C.H. Williams (ed.), *Language Revitalization: Policy and Planning in Wales*, Cardiff: University of Wales Press, pp. 247–91.

Campbell, C. (2003) "Foreword. Dicey on Law and Opinion", in W.J. Morgan and S. Livingstone (eds.), *Law and Opinion in Twentieth-Century Britain and Ireland*, London: Palgrave, pp. xii–xiv.

Canadian Heritage (1998) *Multiculturalism: Respect. Equality, Diversity*, Ottawa: Department of Canadian Heritage.

—— (2007) *Official Languages. Annual Report 2005–6*, Ottawa: Canadian Heritage.

Cardinal, L. (1999) "Linguistic Rights, Minority Rights and National Rights: Some Clarifications", *Inroads*, 8, 77–86.

—— (2000) "Le pouvoir exécutif et la judiciarisation de la politique au Canada. Une etude du programme de contestation juriciaire", *Politique et Sociétés*, 9 (2–3), 43–64.

Cardinal, L. and Hudon, M.-E. (2001) *The Governance of Canada's Official Language Minorities: A Preliminary Study*, Ottawa: Office of the Commissioner of Official Languages.

Cardinal, L. et Hudon, M.-É. (2001) *La Gouvernance des Minorités de Langue Officielle au Canada*, Ottawa: Commissariat aux Langues Officielles.

Cartwright, D.G. (1980) "Language legislation and potential for redistribution of the anglophone population of Québec", *Ontario Geography*, 15, 65–81.

—— (1988) "Language policy and internal geopolitics: The Canadian situation", in C.H. Williams (ed.), *Language in Geographic Context*. Clevedon, Avon: Multilingual Matters, pp. 238–66.

Cartwright, D.G. (1991) "Bicultural Conflict in the Context of the Core-Periphery Model," in C.H. Williams (ed.), *Linguistic Minorities, Society and Territory*, Clevedon, Avon: Multilingual Matters, pp. 219–46.

—— (1998) "French-Language Services in Ontario: A Policy of 'Overly Prudent Gradualism'? " in T. Ricento and B. Burnaby (eds.), *Language and Politics in the United States and Canada*, Mahwah, New Jersey: Erlbaum, pp. 273–300.

Cartwright, D.G. and Williams, C.H. (1982) "Bilingual districts as an instrument in Canadian language policy", *Transactions of the Institute of British Geographers*, 7, 474–93.

Cartwright, D.G. and Williams, C.H. (1997a) "Les enclaves linguistiques ne régleraient rien", *Le Devoir*, 18 November, p. A9.

Cartwright, D.G. and Williams, C.H. (1997b) "If Quebec is divisible, so is Ontario", *The Gazette*, 22 November, p. B6.

Castells, M. (1997) *The Rise of the Network Society*, Oxford: Blackwell.

Castles, F. (1998) *Comparative public policy: patterns of post-war transformation*, Cheltenham: Elgar.

Castonguay, C. (1988) "Virage demographique et Québec francais", *Cahiers québécois de demographie*, 17 (1), 49–61.

—— (1990) "Census statistics and bilingualism", *Language and Society*, 31.

—— (1991) "Effondrement demographique des minorites francophones", *La Presse*, 27 September.

—— (1992) "The demographic collapse of Canada's French-speaking population" (mimeo), p. 3.

—— (1993) "Mesure de l'assimilation linguistique au moyen des recensements", *Recherches sociographiques*, XXXIV (1), 45–68.

—— (1994a) *"L'assmilation linguistique: measure et évolution, 1971–1986"*, Quebec: Conseil de la langue française.

—— (1994b) *Reversing Language Shift in Quebec – Fact and Fancy*. Mimeo University of Ottawa, November 16.

—— (1995) "Evolution recente de l'assimilation linguistique au Canada", *Acts of the Colloquium of Language, Space and Society*, Laval University.

—— (1996a) "Assimilation Trends Among Official language Minorities, 1971–1991. *Towards the XX1st Century: Emerging Socio-Demographic Trends and Policy Issues in Canada*", Ottawa: Proceedings of the Federation of Canadian Demographers Symposium. St Paul's University, Ottawa, 23–25 October, 1995, pp. 201–5.

—— (1996b) "L'intérêt particuler de la démographie pour le fait français au Canada", in J. Erfurt (ed.), *De la Polyphonie Á La Symphonie*, Leipzig: Leipziger Universitätsverlag, pp. 3–18.

—— (1996c) "Chrétien, Durham, même combat", *Le Devoir*, 22 August.

—— (1997) "The Fading Canadian Duality", in J. Edwards (ed.), *Language in Canada*, Cambridge: Cambridge University Press.

—— (1999a) Getting the facts straight on French. Reflections Following the 1996 Census, *Inroads*, 8, 57–76.

—— (1999b) French is on the ropes. Why won't Ottawa admit it? *Policy Options*, pp. 12–16.

—— (2002) "Nation-Building and Anglicization in Canada's Capital Region", *Inroads*, 11, 71–86.

—— (2005a) *Les inidcateurs généraux au Québec:comparabilité et tendances 1971–2001*, Québec City: Office québéois de la langue française.

—— (2005b) *Les caractéristiques linguistiques de la population du Québec:profil et tendances 1991–2001*, Québec City: Office québéois de la langue française.

—— (2005c) *Incidence du sous-dénombrement et des changements apporté aux questions de recensement sur l'évolution de la composition linguistique de la population du Québec entre 1991 et 2001*. Québec City Office québéois de la langue française.

Chaney, P., Hall, T. and Pithouse, A. (eds.) (2001) *New Governance, New democracy?* Cardiff: University of Wales Press.

Census of Ireland (2006) *Census Report on Irish Language*, volume 11. Dublin: Central Statistics Office Ireland.

Central Statistics Office (2004) *Census 2002. Volume 11: The Irish Language*. Cork: Central Statistics Office. Available at: http://www.cso.ie/census/pdfs/ vol11_entire.pdf.

Cerny, P. (1995) "Globalization and the Changing Logic of Collective Action", *International Organization*, 49 (4) 595–625.

—— (1999). "Globalization and the erosion of democracy", *European Journal of Political Research*, 36 (1), 1–26.

Chevrier, M. (1997) *Laws and Languages in Québec: The Principles and Means of Québec's Language Policy*, Quebec: Ministère des Relations internationals.

—— (2003) "A Language Policy for a Language in Exile", in P. Larrivée (ed.), *Linguistic Conflict and Language Laws*, Basingstoke: Palgrave, pp. 118–62.

Clark, M. (1996) *Modern Italy, 1871–1995*. Harlow: Pearson Education.

Clark, R.P. (1984) *The Basque Insurgents, ETA, 1952–1980*, Madison, Wisconsin: The University of Wisconsin Press.

Clark, T. (2002) *Martin Heidegger*, London: Routledge.

Cloke, P., Goodwin, M. and Milbourne, P. (1998) "Cultural change and conflict in rural Wales: Competing constructs of identity", *Environment and Planning A*, 30, 463–80.

Close, P. (1995) *Citizenship, Europe and Change*. Basingstoke: Macmillan.

Cobreros, E. (1989) *El regimen jurídico de la ofiialidad del euskera*. Oñati: Herri-ardiralaritzaren euskal erakundea.

Cohen, J. (1999) "Procedure and Substance in Deliberative Democracy", In: J. Bohman, and W. Rehg (eds.), *Deliberative Democracy*, Cambridge, MA: MIT Press. pp. 407–38.

Coimisiún na Gaeltachta (2002) Tuarascáil/*Report*, Dublin: Department of Arts, Heritage, Gaeltacht and the Islands.

Coleman, W.D. (1981) "From Bill 22 to Bill 101: The politics of language under the *Parti Québécois*", *Canadian Journal of Political Science*, 14, 459–85.

Colley, L. (1992) *Britons:Forging the Nation 1707–1837*, London: Pimlico.

Comhairle na Gaeilge (1971) *Institiúidí Rialtais Áitiúil agus Forbraíochta don Ghaeltacht*. Baile Átha Cliath: Oifig an tSoláthair.

Comhar na Múinteoirí Gaeilge (1981) *Tuarascáil ar an mBunoideachas sa Ghaeltacht*, Dublin: Comhar na Múinteoirí Gaeilge.

Comhdháil Náisiúnta na Gaeilge (1995) *Pleanáil don Ghaeilge 1995–2000/Planning for the Irish Language 1995–2000*, Baile Átha Cliath: Comhdháil Náisiúnta na Gaeilge.

—— (1998) *Towards a Language Act: A discussion document*, Dublin: Comhdháil Náisiúnta na Gaeilge.

Commissioner of Official Languages (1980) "Mother tongues in Canada and Québec", *Languages of the World*, Ottawa: Commissioner of Official Languages, p. 2.
—— (2005) "Annual Report 2004–5". Ottawa: Office of the Commissioner of Official Languages.
Conklin, N. and Lourie, M. (1983) *On a Host of Tongues*, New York: Free Press.
Conlogue, R. (1996) *Impossible Nation: The Longing for Homeland in Canada and Quebec*, Stratford: The Mercury Press.
Conversi, D. (1997) *The Basques, the Catalans and Spain*, Reno: University of Nevada Press.
Cooke, A. (1979) *The Americans: Fifty Talks On Our Life and Times*, New York: Knopf.
Cooper, R. (1989) *Language Planning and Social Change*, Cambridge: Cambridge University Press.
Coulmas, F. (ed.) (1988) With *Forked Tongues: What are National Languages Good For?* Ann Arbor: Karoma.
Council of Europe (1992) *European Charter for Regional or Minority Languages*, Strasbourg: Council of Europe.
—— (2005) *European Charter for Regional or Minority Languages: list of signatures and ratifications* [on-line], Strasbourg: Council of Europe. Available at: www.coe.int/T/E/Legal_Affairs/Local.
Cox, M., Guelke, A. and Stephen, F. (eds.) (2000) *A Farewell to Arms? From "long war" to long peace in Northern Ireland*, Manchester: Manchester University Press.
Cram, L. (1997) *Policy-Making in the European Union: Conceptual Lenses and the Integration Process*, London: Routledge.
Craig, D. and Porter, D. (2006) *Development Beyond Neoliberalism?* London: Routledge.
Crête, J. (1996) "The Quebec 1995 Constitutional Referendum", *Regional and Federal Studies*, 6 (3), 81–92.
Cronin, M. (2005) *An Ghaeilge san Aois Nia/Irish in the New Century*, Dublin: Cois Life.
Crowley, T. (2005) *Wars of Words*, Oxford: Oxford University Press.
Crozier, M. (1963) *Le phénomène bureaucratique: essai sur les tendances bureaucratiques des systèmes d'organisation modernes et sur leurs relations en France avec le système social et culturel*, Paris: Éditions du Seuil.
Crystal, D. (1987) *The Cambridge Encyclopaedia of Language*, Cambridge: Cambridge University Press.
Cymdeithas yr Iaith Gymraeg (2005) *Deddf Iaith Newydd-Dyma'r Cyfle*, Aberystwyth: Cymdeithas yr Iaith Gymraeg.
Cymuned (2002) "Equality and Justice, Cymuned's response to A Bilingual Future, A Welsh Assembly Government Policy Statement and Our Language: Its Future, The Policy Review of the Welsh Language by the Culture Committee", 5 August 2002, Aberystwyth, Cyhoeddiadau Cymuned.
—— (2003) "In-migration, yes; Colonisation, no!, Colonialism and Anti-colonialism in the Bröydd Cymraeg (Welsh-speaking areas of Wales)", Aberystwyth, Cyhoeddiadau Cymuned.
Daigle, J. (ed.) (1982) *The Acadians of the Maritimes*, Moncton: Centre Etudes Acadiennes.
Dalby, D. (1998) *The Linguasphere:Register of the World's Languages and Speech Communities*, Vol. 1. Hebron, Wales.
Davies, D.J. (1931) *The Economics of Welsh Self-Government*, Caernarfon: Plaid Cymru.
Davies, J. (1980) *The Green and the Red: Nationalism and Ideology in 20th Century Wales*, Aberystwyth: Plaid Cymru.
—— (1981) *Cymru'n Deffro*, Talybont: Y Lolfa.

—— (1985) "Plaid Cymru in Transition", in Osmond, J. (ed.) *The National Question Again*, Llandysul: Gomer Press.

—— (1993) *A History of Wales*, London: Penguin.

Davies, D.H. (1983) *The Welsh Nationalist Party 1925–1945*, Cardiff: University of Wales Press.

Davies, N. (1939) *Can Wales Afford Self-Government?* Caernarfon: Plaid Cymru.

Davies, N. (1996) *Europe: A History*, Oxford: Oxford University Press.

Davies, N. (2000) *The Isles: A History*, London: Macmillan.

Day, G. (2002) *Making Sense of Wales: A Sociological Perspective*, Cardiff: University of Wales Press.

De Grand, A. (2000) *Italian Facism*, Lincoln, NE: University of Nebraska Press.

Declaració de Barcelona (1996) *Declaració universal de drets linguistics*, Barcelona: International PEN and CIEMEN.

Department of Community, Rural and Gaeltacht Affairs (DCRGA) (2004a) "Conradh i ndáil le Staidéar Teangeolaíoch ar Úsáid na Gaeilge sa Ghaeltacht Fógraithe ag Ó Cuív." Press release from 31.01.2004. Available at: http://www.pobail.ie/ie/Preaseisiuinti/2004/Eanair/htmltext,4017,ie.html.

—— (2004b) "Chur (sic) Chuige Úrnua d'Fhorbairt na Gaeilge sa Ghaeltacht – Ceadaíonn Ó Cuív €1.36m faoin dTionscnamh Pleanála Teanga." Press release from 22.10.04. Available at: www.pobail.ie.

—— (2004c) *Tuarascáil Bhliantúil 2003/Annual Report 2003*, Dublin: DCRGA.

Department of Community, Rural and Gaeltacht Affairs (2005). "Athbhreithniú ar chumhachtaí agus fheidhmeanna Údarás na Gaeltachta – Cuireadh don Phobal."

Derderian, R.L. (2004) *North Africans in Contemporary France*, Basingstoke: Palgrave.

Devolution and Constitutional Change (2005) *Devolution in the United Kingdom: The Impact on Politics, Economy and Society*, Swindon: ESRC.

Dion, S. (1992) "Explaining Quebec Nationalism", in R. Weaver (ed.), *The Collapse of Canada*, Washington: The Brookings Institute.

Domenichelli, L. (1999) "Comparison entre les stratégies linguistiques de Belgique et du Canada", *Globe. Revue internationale d'études québécoises*, 2 (2), 125–46.

Donoghue, F. (2004) *Consistence and Persistence: Roles, Relationships and Resources of Irish Language Voluntary Organisations*, Dublin: Comhdáil Náisúnta na Gaeilge.

—— (2004) *Comhsheasmhacht agus Diansheasmhacht: Rólanna, Comhchaidrimh agus Acmhainní na nEagraíochtaí Deonacha Gaeilge/Consistence and Persistence: Roles, Relationships and Resources of Irish Language Voluntary Organisations*, Dublin: Comhdháil Náisiúnta na Gaeilge.

Dorling, D. (1995a) "The Visualization of Local Urban Change Across Britain", *Environment and Planning* B, 22, 269–90.

—— (1995b) "Visualizing Changing Social Structure from a Census", *Environment and Planning* A, 27, 353–78.

Driedger, L. (1996) *Multi-Ethnic Canada: Identities and Inequalities*, Toronto: Oxford University Press.

Drinan, R.F. (2001) *The Mobilization of Shame*, New Haven: Yale University Press.

Drinkwater, S.J. and O'Leary, C. (1997) "Unemployment in Wales: Does language matter?" *Regional Studies*, 31 (6), 583–91.

Dülffer, J. (1996) *Nazi Germany 1933–1945*, London: Arnold.

Dumas, G. (2007) "Quebec's Language Policies: Perceptions and Realities", in C.H. Williams (ed.), *Language and Governance*, Cardiff: University of Wales Press, pp. 250–62.

Dummett, A. (1973) *A Portrait of English Racism*, London: CARAF Publications.

Dunbar, R. (2001a) "Minority language rights regimes: An analytical framework, Scotland, and emerging European norms", in J.M. Kirk and P.Ó. Baoill (eds.), *Linguistic Politics*, Belfast: Queen's University, pp. 231–54.

—— (2001b) "Minority language rights under international law", *International and Comparative Law Quarterly*, 50 (1), 90–120.

—— (2003) *The Ratification by the United Kingdom of the European Charter for Regional or Minority Languages*, Mercator-Legislation Working Paper 10, Barcelona: Mercator-Legislation.

—— (2005a) "The Challenges of a Small Language: Gaelic in Scotland with a note on Gaelic in Canada", paper presented to a conference on "Debating Language Policies in Canada and Europe", University of Ottawa, 1 April.

—— (2005b) *The Gaelic Language (Scotland) Act 2005*, The Edinburgh Law Review, 9, 466–79.

—— (2006a) "Preserving and Promoting Language Diversity: Perspectives from International and European Law", *The Supreme Court Law Review*, 31, 65–81.

—— (2006b) "Implementing Language Legislation: A Comparison", paper presented at the Partnership for Diversity Forum, Skye, 29 June.

—— (2006c) "Is There a Duty to Legislate for Linguistic Minorities?" *Journal of Law and Society*, 33 (1), 181–98.

Dunnage, J. (2002) *Twentieth Century Italy*, Harlow: Pearson Education.

Dupuy, F. and Thoenig, J.-C. (1985) *L'Administration en miettes*, Paris: Presses Universitaires de France.

Eagleton, T. (1991) *Ideology*, London: Verso.

Eastman, C. (1991) "The Political and Sociolinguistic Status of Planning in Africa" in D.F. Marshall (ed.), *Language Planning: Focusschrift in Honor of Joshua. A. Fishman*. Amsterdam: John Benjamins, pp. 135–51.

Eastman, C.M. (1983) *Language Planning: An Introduction*, San Francisco: Chandler and Sharp.

Eckersley, R. (2004) *The Green State*, Cambridge, MA: MIT Press.

ESRC (2006) *Devolution in the UK: The Impact on Politics, Economy and Society*, Swindon: ESRC.

Edwards, J. (1994) *Multilingualism*, London: Longman.

—— (2002) *Linguistic Ecology and its Discontents*, Comments for a round-table discussion, Applied Linguistics Conference, Université de Moncton, August.

Eisenberg, A. (1998) "Individualism and Collectivism in the Politics of Canada's North", in J. Anderson, A. Eisenber, S. Grace and V. Strong-Boag (eds.), *Painting the Maple: Essays on Race, Gender and the Construction of Canada*, Vancouver: University of British Columbia Press.

Elliott, J.L. (ed.) (1979) *Two Nations: Many Cultures. Ethnic Groups in Canada*, Scarborough, Ont.: Prentice Hall.

Elliott, M. (2001) *The Catholics of Ulster: A History*, London: Penguin.

Elshtain, J.B. (1993) *Democracy on Trial*, Concord: Anansi.

—— (1994) "The Risks and Responsibilities of Affirming Ordinary Life", in J. Tully (ed.), *Philosophy in an Age of Pluralism*, Cambridge: Cambridge University Press, pp. 67–80.

Elster, J. (ed.) (1998) *Deliberative Democracy*, Cambridge: Cambridge University Press.

Equality Commission (2004) *Religious Belief and Political Opinion-Discrimination Law in Northern Ireland*, Belfast: The Equality Commission for Northern Ireland.

—— (2006) *Annual Report 2005–2006*, Belfast: The Equality Commission for Northern Ireland.

Erize, X. (1997) *Nafarroako Euskararen Historia Soziolinguistikoa (1863–1936)*. *Soziolinguistika Historikoa eta Hizkuntza Gutxituen Bizitza*, Iruñea: Nafarroako Gobernua.

ESF (2006) *Mapping Linguistic Diversity in European Societies*, Siena: Università per Stranieri di Siena.

Esman, M. (1982) "The politics of official bilingualism in Canada", *Political Science Quarterly*, 97, 233–53.

Eurolang (2005) *Eurolang Newsletter*, 25 November. Brussels: Eurolang.

Euromosaic (2004) *Euromosaic III. Presence of Regional and Minority Languages in the New Member States*, Strasbourg: European Commission.

European Cultural Foundation (2000) *Which Languages for Europe?* Amsterdam: European Cultural Foundation, vol. 1 (1999) vol. 2 (2000).

European Parliament (2001) "Lesser-used Languages in States Applying for EU membership", EDUC 106, EN Rev 1. Luxembourg: European Parliament.

—— (2002) "The Role of the EU in Supporting Minority or Lesser-used Languages", *EDUC 108, EN Rev 1*. Luxembourg, European Parliament.

European Science Project (2006) Mapping Linguistic Diversity in Europe (material prepared by G. Extra and M. Barni, workshop project co-ordinators), Siena University for Foreign Studies.

Eusko Jaurlaritza Kultura Saila (1995) *Euskararen Jarraipena*, Vitoria-Gasteiz: Eusko Jaurlaritzaren Argitalpen Zerbitzu Nagusia, [in Basque, Spanish and French].

—— (1997) *II. Soziolinguistikazko Mapa*, Vols 1–3, Vitoria-Gasteiz: Eusko Jaurlaritzaren Argitalpen Zerbitzu Nagusia.

—— (1999) *Euskara Biziberritzeko Plan Nagusia/Plan General de Promoción del Uso del Euskera*, Vitoria-Gasteiz: Eusko Jaurlaritzaren Argitalpen Zerbitzu Nagusia.

Eusko Jaurlaritza, Nafarroako Gobernua and Euskal Kultur Erakundea (1997) *Euskal Herriko Soziolinguistikazko Inkesta 1996/Euskararen Jarraipena II*, Vitoria-Gasteiz: Eusko Jaurlaritza, Nafarroako Gobernua and Euskal Kultur Erakundea, [also available in French and Spanish].

Evans, D. (2005) *Mussolini's Italy*, London: Hodder Education.

Evans, G. (1986) *For the Sake of Wales*, Bridgend: Academic Press.

Evas, J. (2000) "Declining density: a danger for language", in Williams, C.H. (eds.), *Language Revitalization: Policy and Planning in Wales*, Cardiff, University of Wales Press, pp. 292–310.

Extra, G. and Gorter, D. (eds.) (2001) *The Other Languages of Europe*, Clevedon: Multilingual Matters.

Extra, G. and Yagmur, K. (2004) *Urban Multilingualism in Europe: Immigrant Minority Languages at Home and School*, Clevedon, Avon: Multilingual Matters.

Extra, G. and Yagmur, K. (2005) *Multilingual Cities Project on Immigrant Minority Languages in Europe*, Tilburg University: Babylonia.

Farràs i Farràs, J., Torres i Pla, J. and Vila i Moreno, F.X. (2000) "El Coneixement del Català, 1996", Barcelona: Publicacions de l'Institut de Sociolingüítica Catalana.

Fasold, R. (1988) "What National Languages are Good For", in F. Coulmas (ed.) *With Forked Tongues*, Ann Arbor: Koroma, pp. 180–85.

Fennell, D. (1977) "Where it went wrong: The Irish language movement", *Planet*, 36, 3–13.

Ferguson, N. (2005) *Colossus: The Rise and Fall of the American Empire*, London: Penguin.

—— (2006) "The Next War of the World", *Foreign Affairs*, 85 (5), 61–74.

Fishman, J.A. (1969) "National Language and Languages of Wider Communication",. *Anthropological Linguistics*, 11, 111–75.

—— (1989) *Language and Ethnicity in Minority Sociolinguistic Perspective*, Clevedon, Avon: Multilingual Matters.

—— (1990) "Eskolaren mugak hizkuntzak biziberritzeko saioan", In *Euskal Eskola Publikoaren Lehen Kongresua*, 1, 181–188 [also in Spanish under the title "Limitaciones de la eficacia escolar para invertir el desplazamiento lingüístico", 1, 189–96], Vitoria-Gasteiz: Eusko Jaurlaritzaren Argitalpen Zerbitzu Nagusia.

—— (1991) *Reversing Language Shift: Theoretical and Empirical Foundations of Assistance to Threatened Languages*, Clevedon, Avon: Multilingual Matters.

Fishman, J. (ed.) (1999) *Handbook of Language and Ethnic Identity*, Oxford: Oxford University Press.

—— (ed.) (2001) *Can Threatened Languages Be Saved?* Clevedon: Multilingual Matters.

Fitzgerald, G. (1991) *All in a Life*, London: Macmillan.

Foras na Gaeilge (2001) *Ré nua don teanga/A new era for language*, Dublin: Foras na Gaeilge.

—— (2002) *Tá Gnó agat leis an nGaeilge/Irish does the business*, Dublin: Foras na Gaeilge.

—— (2005) *Corporate Plan 2005–2007*, Dublin: Foras na Gaeilge.

Fournier, P. (1991) A *Meech Lake Post-Mortem. Is Québec Sovereignty Inevitable?* Montreal and Kingston: McGill-Queen's University Press.

Francis, H. (1984) *Miners against fascism: Wales and the Spanish Civil War*, London: Lawrence & Wishart.

Fraser, G. (2006) *Sorry, I Don't Speak French*, Toronto: McClelland and Stewart.

Fry, H. (1997) "Multiculturalism – A Framework for Canadian Unity", *Profile, Newsletter of the Royal Society of Canada*, 5 (1), Spring 1–4.

Gagnon, A. (1989) "Canadian Federalism: A Working Balance", in M. Forsyth (ed.), *Federalism and Nationalism*, London: Leicester University Press.

Galtung, J. (1986) "The Green Movement: A Socio-Historical Exploration", *International Sociology*, 1 (1), 75–90.

Gaelic Language (Scotland) Act, (2005) Edinburgh: Parliament of Scotland.

García de Cortázar, F. and Lorenzo Espinosa, J.M. (1997) *Historia del País Vasco*, Editorial Txertoa, Donostia-San Sebastián.

Gardner, N. (2000) *Basque in Education in the Basque Autonomous Community*, Vitoria-Gasteiz: Eusko Jaurlaritzaren Argitalpen Zerbitzu Nagusia.

Gardner, N., Puigdevall i Serralvo, M. and Williams, C.H. (2000) "Language Revitalization in Comparative Context," in Williams, C.H. (ed.), *Language Revitalization: Policy and Planning in Wales*, Cardiff: University of Wales Press, pp. 311–61.

Garrett, G. and Lange, P. (1991) "Political responses to interdependence: what's 'left' for the left?" *International Organization*, 45 (4) 539–64.

Gauthier, D. (1982) "Justified Inequality", *Dialogue*, 21, 431–43.

The Gazette (1993) "PQ fails to clear air with ethnic groups", 4 February, Montreal: The Gazette, p. A1.

—— (1998a) "Split By Factions", 16 May, Montreal: The Gazette, p. A12.

—— (1998b) "Derision Greets Call For Boycott", 27 May, Montréal: The Gazette, p. A5.

—— (1998c) "Johnson Front-Runner: Poll", 29 May, Montreal: The Gazette, p. A10.

—— (1998d) "Alliance Leaders", 30 May, Montreal: The Gazette, p. A5.

—— (1998e) "Alliance Gets Tough", 31 May, Montreal: The Gazette, p. A5.

—— (1998f) "It's Time to Vote: A School-Board Primer", 6 June, Montreal: The Gazette, p. B2.

Generalitat de Catalunya (2000) *Catalunya-Quebec: Legislació i polítiques lingüístiques*, Barcelona: Publicacions de l'Institut de Sociolingüítica Catalana.

Gerholm, T. and Lithman, Y.G. (1990) *The New Islamic Presence in Western Europe*, London: Mansell.

Germain, A. (1997) *Case Studies of Research and Policy on Migrants in Cities – Montreal*, Utrecht: European Research Centre on Migration and Ethnic Relations.

Gibbins, R. and Laforest, G. (eds.) (1998) Beyond *the Impasse: Toward Reconciliation*, Montreal: The Institute for Research on Public Policy.

Gibney, M.J. (ed.) (2003) *Globalizing Rights*, Oxford: Oxford University Press.

Glazer, N. (1977) "Individual Rights Against Group Rights", in E. Kamenka (ed.), *Human Rights*, London: Edward Arnold, pp. 115–36.

Goldring, M. (1993) *Pleasant the Scholar's Life: Irish Intellectuals and the Construction of the Nation State*, London: Serif.

Gordon, D.G. (1978) *The French Language and National Identity*, The Hague: Mouton.

Gosar, A. and Klemencic, V. (1994) "Current problems of border regions along the Slovene-Croatian border", in W.A. Gallusser (ed.), *Political Boundaries and Co-existence*, Bern, pp. 30–42.

Gouvernment de Québec (2003) "About Quebec's Language Policy", Quebec City: Gouvernment de Québec.

Government of Ireland (1926) *Tuarascáil Choimisiún na Gaeltachta*, Dublin: Government of Ireland.

—— (1986) *Tuarascáil an Chomhchoiste um Oideachas sa Ghaeltacht*, Dublin: Government of Ireland.

—— (2002a) *Tuarascáil Chomhairle na nÓg*, Dublin: Government of Ireland.

—— (2002b) *Bille na dTeangacha Oifigiúla (Comhionannas), Official Languages (Equality) Bill*, Dublin: Government of Ireland, 24 April 2002.

Gregor, N. (ed.) (2000) *Nazism*, Oxford: Oxford University Press.

Gregory, D. (2004) *The Colonial Present*, Oxford: Blackwell.

Grin, F. (2003) *Language Policy Evaluation and the European Charter for Regional or Minority Languages*, Basingstoke: Palgrave.

Grin, F. and Vaillancourt, F. (1999) *The cost effectiveness evaluation of minority language policies: Case studies on Wales, Ireland and the Basque Country*, ECMI monograph 2, Flensburg: European Centre for Minority Issues.

Griffiths, D. (1992) "The political consequences of migration into Wales", *Contemporary Wales*, 5, 64–80.

Guibernau, M. (2001) *Nations Without States*, Oxford: Polity Press.

Guibernau, M. and Hutchinson, J. (2001) *Understanding Nationalism*, Cambridge: Polity Press.

Gunnermark, E. and Kenrick, D. (1985) A *Geolinguistic Handbook*, Gothenburg: Gunnermark.

Gunton, C.E. (1993) *The One, the Three and the Many: God, Creation and the Culture of Modernity*, Cambridge: Cambridge University Press.

Gutmann, A. (1995) "Justice Across the Spheres" in D. Miller and M. Walzer (eds.) *Pluralism, Justice and Equality*, Oxford: Oxford University Press, pp. 99–119.

—— (ed.) (2001) "Introduction" to M. Ignatieff, *Human Rights as Politics and Idolatry*, Princeton: Princeton University Press.

—— (2003) *Identity in Democracy*, Princeton: Princeton University Press.

H.M.S.O. (1997) *A Voice for Wales: The Government's Proposals for a Welsh Assembly*, Cardiff: HMSO.

Gwilym, N. (2000) *Lleoli Cenedlaetholdeb Cymreig*, Aberystwyth: University of Wales, unpublished PhD.

Haarman, H. (1990) "Language Planning in the light of a general theory of language: a methodological framework", *International Journal of the Sociology of Language*, 86, 103–26.

Habermas, J. (1996) "The European Nation-State – Its Achievements and Its Limits", in G. Balakrishnan and B. Anderson (eds.), *Mapping The Nation*, London: Verso, 281–94.

—— (2001) *The Post-national Constellation: Political Essays*, Cambridge, MA: MIT Press.

Halliday, F. (1999) *Revolution and World Politics*, Durham: Duke University Press.

Hamilton, R. and Pinard, M. (1982) "The Québec independence movement", in C.H. Williams (ed.) *National Separatism*, Cardiff: University of Wales Press, pp. 203–33.

Hardy, H. (ed.) (1990) *The Crooked Timber of History: Chapters in the History of Ideas*, by Isaiah Berlin, London: John Murray.

Harley, B. (1994) "After Immersion: Maintaining the Momentum", *Journal of Multilingual and Multicultural Development*, 15 (2 and 3), 229–44.

Harries, L. (1983) "The Nationalisation of Swahili in Kenya", in C. Kennedy (ed.), Language *Planning and Language Education*, London: George Allen & Unwin, pp. 118–28.

Harris, J. (1984) *Spoken Irish in Primary Schools*, Dublin: Institiúid Teangeolaíochta Eireann.

Harris, M. (2003) *The Catholic Church and the Foundation of the Northern Irish State*, Cork: Cork University Press.

Harris, R. (1993) *Modern Ireland*, London: Fontana.

Harris, R.C. and Warekentin, J. (1974) *Canada before Confederation*, New York: Oxford University Press.

Hartney, M. (1995) "Some Confusions Concerning Collective Rights", in W. Kymlicka (ed.), *The Rights of Minority Cultures*, Oxford: Oxford University Press, pp. 201–27.

Hastings, A. (2003) "The Clash of Nationalism and Universalism within Twentieth-Century Missionary Christianity", in B. Stanley (ed.), *Missions, Nationalism and the End of Empire*, Grand Rapids, Mich: W. Eerdmans, pp. 15–33.

Haugen, E. (1983) "The implementation of corpus planning: theory and practice", in J. Cobarrubias and J.A. Fishman (eds.), *Progress in Language Planning*, Berlin: Mouton, pp. 269–89.

Hável, V. (1990) *Disturbing the Peace*, London: Faber and Faber.

—— (1991) "A Freedom of a Prisoner" Opening Address to the Bratislava Symposium II, and reproduced in J. Plichtová (1992) (ed.), *Minorities in Politics: Cultural and Language Rights*, Bratislava: European Cultural Foundation.

Hazell, R. (2000) *The State and the Nations*, Exeter: Imprint academic.

—— (2004) "Review of Rawlings, R. (2003) Delineating Wales", Cardiff: University of Wales Press. *Contemporary Wales*, 17, 247–8.

—— (2005) "Westminster as a 'Three in One' Legislature", in R. Hazell and R. Rawlings (eds.), *Devolution, Law Making and the Constitution*, Exeter: Imprint academic.com, pp. 226–51.

Hazell, R. and Rawlings, R. (eds.) (2005) *Devolution, Law Making and the Constitution*, Exeter: Imprint academic.com.

Hechter, M. (1975) *Internal Colonialism: The Celtic Fringe in British National Development, 1536–1966*, Berkley, CA: University of California Press.

—— (2001) *Containing Nationalism*, Oxford: Oxford University Press.

Heine, B. (1992) "Language Policies in Africa", in R.K. Herbert (ed.), *Language and Society in Africa*, Johannesburg: Witwatersrand University Press, pp. 23–35.

Held, D. (1993) "Democracy: from city-states to a cosmopolitan order", in D. Held (ed.), *Prospects for Democracy*, Cambridge: Polity.

—— (1995) *Democracy and the Global Order*, Cambridge: Polity.

—— (1999) *Global Transformations: Politics, Economics and Culture*, Cambridge: Polity Press.

—— (2004) *Global Covenant: The Social Democratic Alternative to the Washington Consensus*, Cambridge: Polity.

418   *Bibliography*

—— (2006) *Models of Democracy*, 3rd edn, Cambridge: Polity.

Herbert, R.K. (ed.) (1992) *Language and Society in Africa*, Johannesburg: Witwatersrand University Press.

Hirst, P. and Thompson, G. (1996) *Globalization in Question: The International Economy and the Possibilities of Governance*, Cambridge: Polity Press.

H.M.S.O. (1997) *A Voice for Wales: The Government's Proposals for a Welsh Assembly*, Cardiff: HMSO.

Hettne, B. (1984) *Approaches to the Study of Peace and Development. A State of the Art Report*, EADI Working Papers: Tilburg.

Higgs, G., Williams, C.H. and Dorling, D. (2004) "Use of the Census of Population to Discern Trends in the Welsh Language: An Aggregate Analysis", *Area*, 36 (2), 187–201.

Hindley, R. (1990) *The Death of the Irish Language: A Qualified Obituary*, London: Routledge.

Hindley, R. (1991) "Defining the Gaeltacht: Dilemmas in Irish Language Planning", in C.H. Williams (ed.), *Linguistic Minorities, Society and Territory*, Clevedon, Avon: Multilingual Matters, pp. 66–95.

Hix, S. (1998) "Elections, Parties and Institutional Design: A Comparative Perspective on European Union Democracy", *West European Politics*, 21 (3), 19–52.

Hobsbawm, E. (1992) *Nations and Nationalism since 1780: Programme, Myth, Reality*, 2nd edn, Cambridge: Cambridge University Press.

Hogan-Brun, G. and Wolff, S. (eds.) (2003) *Minority Languages in Europe*, Basingstoke: Palgrave.

Hooghe, L. and Marks, G. (1996) " 'Europe with the Regions'. Channels of Interest Representation in the European Union", *Publius*, 26 (1), 73–91.

Horowitz, D.L. (1985) *Ethnic Groups in Conflict*, Berkeley: University of California Press.

Horowitz, D.L. (1991) *A Democratic South Africa?* Berkeley: University of California Press.

http://conventions.coe.int/Treaty/Commun/ChercheSig.asp?NT=148&CM=8&DF=3/17/05&CL=ENG.

http://www.pobail.ie/ie/Preaseisiuinti/2004/DeireadhFomhair/htmltext,4598,ie.html.

http://www.pobail.ie/ie/Preaseisiuinti/2005/Eanair/htmltext,4693,ie.html.

Hudson, R. and Williams, A.M. (eds.) (1999) *Divided Europe. Society and Territory*, London: Sage.

Human Rights Act (1998) *Human Rights Act, 1998*, Chapter 42, Westminster: HMSO.

Hutchinson, J. and Smith, A.D. (1994) (eds.) *Nationalism*, Oxford: Oxford University Press.

Ignatieff, M. (1998) *Isaiah Berlin: A Life*, New York: Henry Holt.

—— (2000) *The Rights Revolution*, Toronto: Anansi.

—— (2001) *Human Rights as Politics and Idolatry*, Princeton: Princeton University Press.

—— (2003) *Empire Lite*, London: Vintage.

Irish Primary Principals Network (2004) *The Future of Small Schools and Teaching Principalship*, Interim Report by T. Ó Slatara and M. Morgan, Dublin: Irish Primary Principals Network.

Irish State (1922) *The Constitution of the Irish Free State (Saorstát Eireann) Act, 1922 and the Public General Acts passed by Oireachtas of Saorstát Eireann during the year 1922*, Dublin: Stationery Office.

James, C. and Williams, C.H. (1997) "Language and Planning in Scotland and Wales", in H. Thomas and R. Macdonald (eds.), *Planning in Scotland and Wales*, Cardiff: University of Wales Press, pp. 264–303.

James, S. (1999) *The Atlantic Celts: Ancient People or Modern Invention?* London: British Museum.

Jeffery, C. (2006) *Devolution: Future Perspectives*, paper presented to ESRC Conference, Cardiff University.

Johnson, N. (1995) "Cast in stone: Monuments, Geography and Nationalism", *Environment and Planning D; Society and Space*, 13, 51–65.

Johnson, N. (2004) *Reshaping the British Constitution*, Basingstoke: Palgrave.

Johnson, R.J., Shelley, F.M. and Taylor. P.J. (eds.) (1990), *Developments in Electoral Geography*, London: Routledge.

Johnston, R.J. and Taylor, P.J. (eds.) (1989) *A World in Crisis?* Oxford: Blackwell.

Jones, D.G. (1973) "His Politics" in J.R. Jones and G. Thomas (eds.), *Presenting Saunders Lewis*, Cardiff: University of Wales Press.

Jones, E. (ed.) (2001) *The Welsh in London*, Cardiff, University of Wales Press.

Jones, J. (ed.) (2001) "Making Welsh law", *The Law Making Powers of the National Assembly: Conference report*, Cardiff: Wales Law Journal/The Law Society, pp. 40–53.

Jones, R.M. (1994) *Crist a Chenedlaetholdeb*, Pen-y-bont ar Ogwr: Gwasg Efengylaidd Cymru.

—— (1998) *Ysbryd y Cwlwm*, Caerdydd, Gwasg Prifysgol Cymru.

Jones, R.W. (2004) *Methiant Prifysgolion Cymru/The Failure of the Universities of Wales*. Cardiff: Institute of Welsh Affairs/Caerdydd: Sefydliad Materion Cymreig.

Jones, T. (ed.) (2001) "The subordinate law making powers of the National Assembly for Wales", *The Law Making Powers of the National Assembly: Conference report*, Cardiff: Wales Law Journal/The Law Society, pp. 6–12.

Jones, H. and Williams, C.H. (2000) "The statistical basis for Welsh language planning: Data, trends, patterns and processes", in C.H. Williams (ed.), *Language Revitalization: Policy and Planning in Wales*, Cardiff: University of Wales Press, pp. 48–82.

Jönsson, C., Tägil, S. and Törnqvist, G. (2000) *Organizing European Space*, London: Sage Publications.

Joppke, C. (1999) *Immigration and the Nation State*, Oxford: Oxford University Press.

Joy, R.J. (1972) *Languages in Conflict*, Toronto: McClelland and Stewart.

—— (1992) *Canada's Official Languages: The Progress of Bilingualism*, Toronto: The University of Toronto Press.

Judge, D., Stoker, G. and Wolman, H. (eds.) (1995) *Theories of Urban Politics*, London: Sage Publications.

Kagan, R. (2003) *Paradise and Power, America and Europe in the New World Order*, London: Atlantic Books.

Kaiser, R.J. (1994) *The Geography of Nationalism in Russia and the USSR*, Princeton: Princeton University Press.

—— (1999) "Geography and Nationalism", in A. Moytl (ed.), *Encyclopaedia of Nationalism*, San Diego: Academic Press.

Kallen, E. (1995) *Ethnicity and Human Rights in Canada*, Don Mills: Oxford University Press.

Kaplan, R.B. and Baldauf, R.B. (1997) *Language Planning From Practice to Theory*, Clevedon, Avon: Multilingual Matters.

Kay, G. (1970) *Rhodesia: A Human Geography*, New York: Africana Publishing Company.

Kay, G. (1993) "Ethnicity, the Cosmos and Plonomic Development, with Special Reference to Central Africa", Stoke on Trent, Staffordshire Polytechnic, mimeo.

Kearney, H. (1989) *The British Isles: A History of Four Nations*, Cambridge: Cambridge University Press.

Keating, M. (1988) *State and Regional Nationalism*, Brighton: Harvester.

—— (1992) "Regional Autonomy in the Changing State Order: A Framework of Analysis", *Regional Politics and Policy*, 2 (3), 45–61.

—— (1995) "Size, Efficiency and Democracy: Consolidation, Fragmentation and Public Choice", in Judge *et al.*, pp. 117–34.

—— (1998) *The New Regionalism in Western Europe: Territorial Restructuring and Political Change*, Cheltenham: Edward Elgar.

—— (2001) *Nations Against the State: The New Politics of Nationalism in Quebec, Catalonia and Scotland*, Basingstoke: Palgrave.

—— (2004) *Plurinational Democracy: Stateless Nations in a Post-Sovereignty Era*, Oxford: Oxford University Press.

Keating, M. and Loughlin, J. (eds.) (1997) *The Political Economy of Regionalism*, London: Frank Cass.

Kelly, A. (2002) *Compulsory Irish*, Dublin: Irish Academic Press.

Kennedy, C. (ed.) (1983) *Language Planning and Language Education*, London: George Allen & Unwin.

Kennedy, P., Messener, D. and Nuscheler, F. (eds.) (2002) *Global Trends and Global Governance*, London: Pluto Press.

Killilea, M. (1994) "On linguistic and cultural minorities in the European Community", resolution adopted by the European Parliament, Strasbourg.

Kingwell, M. (2000) *The World We Want*, Toronto: Penguin.

Kirby, P., Gibbons, L. and Cronin, M. (eds.) (2002) *Reinventing Ireland*, London: Pluto Press.

Klein, T. (1978) "Minorities in Central Europe", in A.C. Hepburn (ed.), *Minorities in History*, London: Edward Arnold, pp. 31–50.

Klemencic, M. and Klemencic, V. (1997) "The Role of the Border Region of the Northern Adriatic", *Anali za istrske in mediteranske studije*, 10, 285–94.

Klemencic, V. (1992) "Priseljevanje prebivalcev z obmoeja nekdanje Jugoslavije v Slovenijo", *Geografija v soli*, 2, 14–26.

—— (1994) "Uberlensemoeglichkeiten der nichtankerennted Minderheit der Slowenen in der Steiermark, Steirische Slowenen", Graz und Maribor: Zweispraech-igkeit zwischen, pp. 81–90.

Knight, K. (1997) "Students of Nationalism", *West European Politics*, 20 (2), 173–79.

Knight, J. and Johnson, J. (1997) "What Kind of Equality Does Democratic Deliberation Require?", in Bohman, J. and Rehg, W. (eds.), *Deliberative Democracy*. Cambridge, MA: MIT Press.

Knopff, R. (1980) "Democracy versus liberal democracy: The nationalist conundrum", *The Dalhousie Review*, 58 (4), 638–46.

Knox, P. and Agnew, J. (1989) *The Geography of the World Economy*, London: Arnold.

Kohler-Koch, B. (1996) "The Strength of Weakness: The Transformation of Governance in the EU", in S. Gustavsson and L. Lewin (eds.), *The Future of the Nation-State: Essays in Cultural Pluralism and Political Integration*, London: Routledge.

—— (1999) "The Evolution and Transformation of European Governance", in B. Kohler-Koch and R. Eising (eds.), *The Transformation of Governance in the European Union*, London and New York: Routledge, pp. 14–35.

Kuijpers, W. (1987) "On the languages and cultures of regional and ethnic minorities in the European Community", resolution adopted by the European Parliament, Strasbourg.

Kukathas, C. (1995) "Are There Any Cultural Rights?" in W. Kymlicka (ed.), *The Rights of Minority Cultures*, Oxford: Oxford University Press, 228–55.

Kuzio, T. (2000) "Nationalism in Ukraine: Towards a New Framework", *Politics*, 20 (2), 77–86.

—— (2001) "Nationalizing states, or nation-building? A critical review of the theoretical literature and empirical evidence", *Nations and Nationalism*, 7, 135–54.

Kymlicka, W. (1995) *Multicultural Citizenship: A Liberal Theory of Minority Rights*, Oxford: Oxford University Press.

—— (ed.) (1995) *The Rights of Minority Cultures*, Oxford: Oxford University Press.

—— (1998) "Multinational Federalism in Canada: Rethinking the Partnership", in R. Gibbins and G. Laforest (eds.), *Beyond the Impasse; Towards Reconciliation*, Montreal: The Institute for Research on Public Policy, pp. 15–50.

—— (2000) "Nation-building and Minority Rights: Comparing West and East", *Journal of Ethnic and Migration Studies*, 26 (1), 183–212.

—— (2001) *Politics in the Vernacular*, Oxford: Oxford University Press.

—— (2007) "Language Policies, National Identities and Liberal Democratic Norms", in C.H. Williams (ed.), *Language and Governance*, Cardiff: University of Wales Press, pp. 505–15.

Labrie, N. (1996) "The historical development of language policy in Europe", in P. Ó Riagáin and S. Harrington (eds.), *A Language Strategy for Europe, Retrospect and Prospect*, Dublin: Bord na Gaeilge, pp. 1–9.

Lachapelle, R. and Grenier, G. (1988) *Linguistic Aspects of the Demographic Evolution in Canada*, Ottawa: Statistics Canada.

Laitin, D.D. (1992) *Language Repertoires and State Construction in Africa*, Cambridge: Cambridge University Press.

Lambert, D. (2000) "The Government of Wales Act: An act for laws to be ministered in Wales in like form as in this realm?" *Cambrian Law Review*, 30, 60–70.

Lambert, D. and Navarro, M. (2007) "Holding the Reins", *Agenda*, Winter, pp. 16–18.

Landsbergis, V. (2000) *Lithuania Independent Again*, Cardiff: University of Wales Press.

Lapidoth, R. (1997) *Autonomy: Flexible Solutions to Ethnic Conflicts*, Washington DC: University of Washington Press.

Laponce, J. (1984) "The French Language in Canada: Tensions between Geography and Politics", *Political Geography Quarterly*, 3, 91–104.

Laponce, J.A. (1987) *Languages and Their Territories*, Toronto: University of Toronto Press.

Laurin, C. (1977) *Québec's Policy on the French language*, Québec: Ministry of State for Cultural Development.

Le Galès, P. (1999) *European Cities*, Oxford: Oxfrord University Press.

Le Galès, P. and Lequesne, C. (eds.) (1998) *Regions in Europe*, London: Routledge.

Letourneau, J. (1989) "The unthinkable history of Québec", *Oral History Review*, 17 (1), 89–115.

Levine, M. (1990) *The Reconquest of Montreal*, Philadelphia: Temple University Press.

Lewis, S. (1985) *Canlyn Arthur*, Llandysul: Gwasg Gomer.

—— (1986) *Ati, Wyr Ifainc*, Caerdydd: Gwasg Prifysgol Cymru.

Lijphart, A. (1995) "Self-Determination Versus Pre-Determination of Ethnic Minorities in Power Sharing Systems", in W. Kymlicka (ed.), *The Rights of Minority Cultures*, Oxford: Oxford University Press, 275–87.

Lisée, J.- F. (2000) *Why C-20 is a Democrat's Nightmare?* Ottawa: House of Commons, 22 February.

—— (2007) "How Quebec Became a North American States", in C.H. Williams (ed.), *Language and Governance*, Cardiff: University of Wales Press, pp. 460–500.

Llywelyn, D. (1999) *Sacred Places, Chosen People: Land and national identity in Welsh spirituality*, Cardiff: University of Wales Press.

Loughlin, J. (1996a) "Representing Regions in Europe: The Committee of the Regions", *Regional and Federal Studies*, 6 (2), 147–65.

—— (1996b) "Europe of the Regions and the Federalization of Europe", *Publius*, 26 (4), 141–62.

—— (1999) "Representing regions in Europe: The Committee of the Regions", *Regional and Federal Studies*, 6 (2), pp. 147–65.

—— (2000) "Regional Autonomy and State Paradigm Shifts", *Regional and Federal Studies: An International Journal*, 10 (2) Summer 2000: 10–34.

—— (2001) *Subnational Democracy in the European Union: Challenges and Opportunities*, Oxford: Oxford University Press.

Loughlin, J. and Letamendia, F. (2000) "Lessons for Northern Ireland: Peace in the Basque Country and Corsica? *Irish Studies in International Affairs*, 11, 147–58.

Loughlin, J. and Peters, B.G. (1997) "State Traditions, Administrative Reform and Regionalization", in M. Keating and J. Loughlin (eds.), *The Political Economy of Regionalism*, London: Frank Cass.

Loughlin, J. and Seiler, D. (1999) "Le Comité des Régions et la supranationalité en Europe", *Etudes Internationales*, décembre.

Loughlin, J. and Williams, C.H. (2007) "Governance and Language", in C.H. Williams, *Language and Governance*, Cardiff: University of Wales Press, pp. 57–103.

Loughlin, J., Aja, E., Bullmann, U., Hendriks, F., Lindström, A. and Seiler, D.-L. (1999) *Regional and Local Democracy in the European Union*, Committee of the Regions/Office of Official Publication of the European Union: Luxembourg.

Mac Donnacha, S. (2000) "An Integrated Language Planning Model", *Language Problems and Language Planning*, 24 (1), 11–35.

Mac Donnacha, S. Fiona Ní Chualáin, Aoife Ní Shéaghdha, Treasa Ní Mhainín (2005) *Staid Reatha na Scoileanna Gaeltachta/A Study of Gaeltacht Schools 2004*, Dublin: An Chomhairle um Oideachas Gaeltachta & Gaelscolaíochta.

Mac Donnagha, J. (1977) *Ireland: The Union and its Aftermath*, London: Allen & Unwin.

Mac Giolla Chriost, D. (2003) *Language, Identity and Conflict*, London: Routledge.

—— (2005) *The Irish Language in Ireland*, London: Routledge.

—— (2007) *Language and the City*, Basingstoke: Palgrave.

Mac Póilin, A. (1994) "Spiritual Beyond the Ways of Men'-Images of the Gael", *The Irish Review*, 16, 1–22.

—— (ed.) (1997) *The Irish Language in Northern Ireland*, Belfast: Ultach Trust.

MacCaluim, A. and McLeod, W. (2001) *Re-vitalising Gaelic? A Critical Analysis of the Report of the Taskforce on Public Funding of Gaelic*, Edinburgh: Department of Celtic and Scottish Studies.

MacIntyre, A. (1984) *After Virtue: A Study in Moral Theory*, 2nd edn, Indiana: University of Notre Dame.

Mackey, W.F. (1986) "The Polyglossic Spectrum", in J.A. Fishman (ed.), *The Fergusonian Impact*, Berlin: Mouton de Gruyter.

—— (1991) "Language Diversity, Language Policy and the Sovereign State", *History of European Ideas*, 13, 51–61.

—— (1992) *Assessing Canadian Language* Policy. Mimeo: Laval University.

Mackey, E. (2002). *The House of Difference: Cultural Politics and National Identity in Canada*, Toronto: University of Toronto Press.

MacKinnon, K. (2003) "Evidence from GROS Census Reports 1881–1991; Census 2001 Table UV12", Black Isle: SGRUD.

MacLaughlin, J. (1986) "The Political Geography of Nation-Building and Nationalism in the Social Sciences: Structural Versus Dialectical Accounts", *Political Geography Quarterly*, 3 (4), 299–329.

—— (1993) "Defending the Frontiers: The Political Geography of Race and Racism in the European Community", in C.H. Williams (ed.), *The Political Geography of the New World Order*, London: Belhaven/Wiley, pp. 20–46.

MacLeod, D.J. (2003) "An Historical Overview", in M. Nicolson and M. MacIver (eds.), *Gaelic Medium Education*, Edinburgh: Dunedin Press, pp. 1–14.

MacMillan, C.M. (1998) *The Practice of Language Rights in Canada*, Toronto: University of Toronto Press.

—— (2003) "Federal Language Policy in Canada and the Quebec Challenge", in P. Larrivée (ed.), *Linguistic Conflict and Language Laws*, Basingstoke: Palgrave.

McAll, C. (1990) *Class, ethnicity and social inequality*. Montreal and Kingston: McGill-Queens University Press.

McAllister, L. (1995) *"Community in Ideology: The Political Philosophy of Plaid Cymru"*, Ph.D. Thesis, University of Wales.

McCrone, D. (1998) *The Sociology of Nationalism*, London: Routledge.

McEwan-Fujita, E. (2005) "Neoliberalism and Minority-Language Planning in the Highlands and Islands of Scotland", *International Journal of the Sociology of Language*, 171, 155–71.

McGrew, A. (1997) *The Transformation of Democracy?* Cambridge: Polity.

McHarg, I.L. (1998) "Human Ecological Planning at Pennsylvania", in Novak, J. (ed.), *Regional Physical Planning-Practice and Challenge*, Bled: National Office for Physical Planning, pp. 43–53.

McLeod, W. (2001) "Language planning as regional development?" *Scottish Affairs*, 38, 51–72.

—— (2003) Gaelic Medium Education in the International Context, in M. Nicolson and M. MacIver (eds.), *Gaelic Medium Education*, Edinburgh: Dunedin Press, pp. 15–34.

McRae, K. (1997) "Language Policy and Language Contact: Reflections on Finland", in W. Wölck and A. de Houwer (eds.), *Recent Studies in Contact Linguistics, Plurilingua* XVII. Bonn, Dümmler, 218–26.

McRoberts, K. and Postgate, D. (1980) *Québec: Social Change and Political Crisis*. Toronto: McClelland and Stewart.

McWhinney, E. (1982) *Canada and the Constitution*, 1979–82, Toronto: University of Toronto Press.

MAGOG (2002) *A Fresh Start for Gaelic*, Edinburgh: Report of the Ministerial Advisory Group on Gaelic.

Magosci. P.R. (1993) *An Historical Atlas of East-Central Europe*, Toronto: University of Toronto Press.

Mamadouh, V. (2001) "The Territoriality of European Integration and the Territorial Features of the EU: The First 50 Years", T.E.S.G. 92, 4.

—— (2002) "Dealing with multilingualism in the European Union", *Journal of Comparative Policy Analysis*, June.

Mann, M. (2005) *The Dark Side of Democracy*, Cambridge: Cambridge University Press.

Marks, G., Scharpf, F. Schmitter, P. and Streek, W. (1996) *Governance in the European Union*, London: Sage.

Mar-Molinero, C. (1994) "Linguistic Nationalism and Minority Language Groups in the 'NEW' Europe", *Journal of Multilingual and Multicultural Development*, 15 (4), 139–28.

Mar-Molinero, C. and Smith, A. (eds.) (1996) *Nationalism and the Nation in the Iberian Peninsula*, Oxford: Berg.

Mar-Molinero, C. and Stevenson, P. (eds.) (2006) *Language Ideologies, Policies and Practices*, Basingstoke: Palgrave.

Marquand, D. (2004) *Decline of the Public*, Oxford: Polity.

Marshall, D. (ed.) (1991) *Language Planning: Focusschrift in honor of Joshua A. Fishman*. 3 vols. John Benjamin: Amsterdam.

Martin, D., Dorling, D. and Mitchell, R. (2002) *"Linking censuses through time: problems and solutions"*, *Area* 34(1), 82–91

Maurais, J. (1992) "Language status planning in Québec", in C. Lauren and M. Nordman (eds.), *Special Language*, Clevedon: Multilingual Matters, pp. 138–49.

—— (ed.) (1987) *Politique et Amenagement Linguistiques*, Québec: Conseil de la langue française.

—— (1988) Dossier sur l'Arnenagement Linguistique. Québec: Bulletin du Conseil de la langue française, 5, 1.

May, S. (2001) *Language and Minority Rights*, London: Longman.

Mazrui, A. and Zirimu, P. (1990) "The secularization of an Afro-Islamic language: Church, state and market-place in the spread of Kiswahili", *Journal of Islamic Studies*, 1, 24–53.

Mazrui, A.M. and Mazrui, A.A. (1992) "Language in a Multicultural Context: The African Experience", *Language and Education*, 6, 83–89.

Mead, W.R. (2006) "God's Country; Foreign Affairs", 85(5), 24–43.

Mendels, D. (1992) *The Rise and Fall of Jewish Nationalism*, New York: Doubldeday.

Mendras, H. (1997). *L'Europe des Européens*, Paris: Gallimard.

Menter a Busnes (1997) *Success Story: A Report on the work of Menter a Busnes, 1995–6.* Aberystwyth: Menter a Busnes.

Miles, R. (1993) *Racism After Race Relations*, London: Routledge.

Miller, D. (2000) *Citizenship and National Identity*, Oxford: Polity.

Milward, A. (2000) *The European Rescue of the Nation-State*, London: Routledge.

Minority Rights Group (1991) *Minorities and Autonomy in Western Europe*, London: Minority Rights Group.

Mlinar, Z. (ed.) (1992) *Globalization and Territorial Identity*, Aldershot: Avebury.

Monnier, D. (1986) *La perception de la situation linguistique par les Québecois*, Québec: Conseil de la langue française.

Moore, M. (2001) *The Ethics of Nationalism*, Oxford: Oxford University Press.

Moreno, L. (1995) "Multiple Ethnoterritorial Concurrence in Spain", *Nationalism and Ethnic Politics*, 1 (1), 11–32.

Morgan, K. (2004) "Bonfire of the Quangos: The Missing Debate", *Agenda*, Winter Cardiff: The Institute of Welsh Affairs.

Morgan, K. and Roberts, E. (1993) *The Democratic Deficit: A Guide to Quangoland*, Papers in Planning Research No 144, School of City and Regional Planning, Cardiff University.

Morgan, P. (2004) *Italian Fascism*, Basingstoke: Palgrave.

Morgan, W.J. and Livingstone, S. (eds.) (2003) *Law and Opinion in Twentieth-Century Britain and Ireland*, Basingstoke: Palgrave.

Morrissey, M. and Smyth, M. (2002) *Northern Ireland After the Good Friday Agreement*, London: Pluto Press.

Msanjila, Y.P. (1990) "Problems of Teaching Through the Medium of Kiswahili in Teacher Training Colleges in Tanzania", *Journal of Multilingual and Multicultural Development*, 11, 307–18.

NAAG (1998) *National Assembly Advisory Group Consultation Paper*, Cardiff: NAW.

Nahir, M. (1984) "Language Planning Goals: A Classification", *Language Problems and Language Planning*, 8(3), 294–327.

National Assembly for Wales (1999) *The National Assembly (Transfer of Function) Order 1999* (S.I. 1999/672), London: House of Commons.

National Assembly for Wales (2001) *Plan for Wales 2001*, Cardiff: NAW.

—— (2002) *Our Language: Its Future. The Policy Review of the Welsh Language*, Culture and Education Committee Cardiff: NAW.

—— (2002a) *Review of the Welsh Language Final Report*, Cardiff: NAW.

—— (2002b) *Review of Welsh Education Final Report*, Cardiff: NAW.

—— (2003) *Iaith Pawb: A National Action Plan for a Bilingual Wales*, Cardiff: Wales Assembly Government.

National Statistics (2003) *2001 Census of Population: First results on the Welsh language SB 22/2003*, Cardiff: Statistical Directorate, NAW.

Naughtie, J. (2004) *The Accidental American: Tony Blair and the Presidency*, New York: Public Affairs.

National Library of Wales (2004) *The Status of the National Library of Wales*, Aberystwyth: National Library of Wales.

Nelde, P. (1997) "On the Evaluation of Language Policy", in *Generalitat de Catalunya* (ed.), *Proceedings of the European conference on language planning*, Barcelona: Department de Cultura, 285–92.

Nelde, P.H., Labrie, N. and Williams, C.H. (1992) "The principles of territoriality and personality in the solution of linguistic conflicts", *Journal of Multilingual and Multicultural Development*, 13 (5), 387–406.

Nelde, P.H., Strubell, M. and Williams, G. (1995) *Euromosaic: the production and reproduction of the minority language groups of the EU*, Luxemburg: Official Publications Office of the European Communities.

Newman, W.J. (2004) "Understanding Language Rights, Equality and the Charter: Towards A Comprehensive Theory of Constitutional Interpretation", *National Journal of Constitutional Law*, 15, 357–63.

Newman, W. (2007) "The Official Languages Act and the Constitutional and Legislative Recognition of Language Rights in Canada", in C.H. Williams (ed.), *Language and Governance*, Cardiff: University of Wales Press, pp. 196–234.

Ní Chartúir, J. (2002) *The Irish Language*, New York: Avena Press.

Nic Craith, M. (1999) "Irish speakers in Northern Ireland, and the Good Friday Agreement", *Journal of Multilingual and Multicultural Development*, 20 (6), 494–507.

Nicolson, M. and MacIver, M. (eds.) (2003) *Gaelic Medium Education*, Edinburgh: Dunedin Press.

North/South Language Body (2005) *Annual Report and Accounts for Period Ended 31 December 2000*, Dublin and Belfast: North/South Language Body.

Ó Cinnéide, M., Mac Donnacha, S. and Ní Chonghaile, S. (2001) *Polasaithe agus Cleachtais Eagraíochtaí Éagsúla le Feidhm sa Ghaeltacht: Tuarascáil chríochnaitheach.* Gaillimh: Ionad Taighde sna hEolaíochtaí Sóisialta, Ollscoil na hÉireann, Gaillimh.

Ó Cuirreáin, S. (2006a) *Presentation to the POBAL Conference on a New Irish Language Act for Northern Ireland*, Belfast: Europa Hotel, 30th November.

Ó Cuirreáin, S. (2006b) *Presentation to the Culture, Welsh Language and Sport Committee*, Cardiff: National Assembly for Wales, 13th December.

Ó Cuirreáin, S. (2006c) *Presentation to the Welsh Language Board*, Cardiff: Welsh Language Board, 14th December.

Ó Flatharta, P. (1999) "On the delivery mechanism of social and economic development of the *Gaeltacht*", Paper presented at the ECNI International Seminar, Flensburg, ECMI, 18–20 June.

Ó Gadhra, N. (1999) "The Irish *Gaeltacht* communities on the eve of the third millennium", paper presented to the Nineteenth Annual Celtic Colloquium, Harvard University, 30 April.

Ó Gairbhí, S. (2004) "Foras 'i gcomórtas' le eagraíochtaí Gaeilge eile – tuarascáil", *Foinse*, 24 October.

Ó Laighin, P.B. (2004) *Towards the Recognition of Irish as an Official Working Language of the European Union*, Dublin: Clódhanna Teoranta.

Ó Laoire, M. (2006) "The Language Planning Situation in Ireland", *Current Issues in Language Planning,* 6 (3), 251–64.

Ó Loughlin, J. (1993) "Fact or fiction? The evidence for the thesis of US relative decline, 1966–1991", in C.H. Williams (ed.), *The Political Geography of the New World Order,* London: Belhaven/Wiley, pp. 148–80.

Ó Murchú, M. (2002) *Ag dul ó chion? Cás na Gaeilge 1952–2002,* Baile Átha Cliath: Coiscéim.

Ó Murchú, H. (2003) *Limistéar na Sibhialtachta: Dúshlán agus Treo d'Eagraíochtaí na Gaeilge,* Baile Átha Cliath: Coiscéim.

Ó Murchú, H. and Ó Murchú, M. (1999) An *Ghaeilge: a hAghaidh Roimpi/Irish: Facing the Future,* Dublin: EBLUL.

Ó Néill, D. (ed.) (2005) *Rebuilding the Celtic Languages,* Y Lolfa: Talybont.

Ó Riagáin, D. (1989) "The EBLUL: Its Role in Creating a Europe United in Diversity", in T.Veiter (ed.), *Federalisme, regionalisme et droit des groupes ethnique en Europe,* Vienna: Braümuller.

—— (ed.) (2003) *Language and Law in Northern Ireland,* Belfast: Queen's University.

Ó Riagáin, P. (1997) *Language Policy and Social Reproduction: Ireland 1893–1993,* Oxford: Oxford University Press.

Ó Tuathail, G. (1993) "Japan as threat: geo-economic discourses on the USA-Japan relationship in US civil society, 1987–1991", in C.H. Williams (ed.), *The Political Geography of the New World Order,* London: Belhaven/Wiley, pp. 181–209.

Oakes, L. and Warren, J. (2007) *Language, Citizenship and Identity in Quebec,* Basingstoke: Palgrave.

Oakeshott, M. (1962) *Rationalism in Politics and Other Essays,* London: Methuen.

Office of the Counsel General (2001) *Bilingual Lawmaking and Justice,* Cardiff: National Assembly for Wales.

Office for National Statistics (2002) *Annual Local Area Labour Force Survey Section 2: Wales Summary and Analysis.* London, TSO.

—— (2003) *Key Statistics for local authorities in Wales,* London, TSO.

O.L.A. (1969) *Official Languages Act. Elizabeth 11, chapter 54, session 1, 17–18,* Ottawa: Queen's Printer.

Official Languages of Canada (1988) *An Act respecting the status and use of the official languages of Canada,* 1988, c. 38 (Can.), Ottawa: Parliament of Canada.

Official Languages Act (2003). *Acht na dTeangacha Oifigiúla – Official Languages Act, 2003,* Dublin: Dáil Eireann.

Official Languages Act Regulations (2006) *Regulations Official Languages Act 2003 (section 9) Regulations 2006,* Dublin: Irish Parliament accepted 13 December.

Oliver, J. (2005) "Scottish Gaelic Identities: Contexts and Contingencies", *Scottish Affairs,* 51, pp. 1–17, see: http://www.scottishaffairs.org/onlinepub/sa/oliver_sa51_spr05.html.

Ó hÉallaithe, D. (2004) "Cé Mhéad a Labhrann Gaeilge? *Foinse,* 4 April 2004, 20–21.

Orridge, A.W. and Williams C.H. (1982) "Autonomist nationalism: A theoretical framework for spatial variations in its genesis and development", *Political Geography Quarterly,* 1, 19–39.

Osmond, J. (2002) "Upfront: Two tongues", *Agenda* (Winter 2002/3), Cardiff: Institute of Welsh Affairs, pp. 2–6.

Paddison, R. (1993) "New Nationalism in an Old State: Scotland and the UK", in C.H. Williams (ed.), *The Political Geography of the New World Order,* London: Belhaven Press.

Page, E. (1991) *Localism and Centralism in Europe,* Oxford: Oxford University Press.

Page, E. and Goldsmith, M. (eds.) (1987) *Central and Local Government Relations*, London: Sage Publications.

Patchett, K. (2005) "Principle or Pragmatism. Legislating for Wales by Westminster and Whitehall", in R. Hazell and R. Rawlings (eds.), *Devolution, Law Making and the Constitution*, Exeter: Imprint academic.com, pp. 112–51.

Paulson, C.B., Chen, C.P. and Connerty, M.C. (1993) "Language Regensis: A Conceptual Overview of Language Revival, Revitalisation and Reversal", *Journal of Multilingual and Multicultural Development*, 14(4), 275–86.

Pellatier, R. (1998) "Institutional Arrangements for a New Canadian Partnership", in R. Gibbins and G. Laforest (eds.), *Beyond the Impasse: Toward Reconciliation*, Montreal: Institute for Research on Public Policy, pp. 301–32.

Philip, A. B. (1975) *The Welsh Question: Nationalism in Welsh Politics, 1945–1970*, Cardiff: University of Wales Press.

Philips, D. (1988) *Trwy Ddulliau Chwyldro*, Llandysul: Gomer Press.

—— (1998) *Trwy Ddulliau Chwyldro*, Llandysul: Gwasg Gomer.

Phillipson, R. (1992) *Linguistic Imperialism*, Oxford: Oxford University Press.

Phillipson, R. (2003) "Union in Need of Language Equality", *The Guardian Weekly*, 30 January.

Pinder, J. (1995) *European Community: the Building of a Union*, 2nd edn, Oxford: Oxford University Press.

Plaid Cymru (2006) *Language Policy Commission*, Cardiff: Plaid Cymru.

POBAL (2006a) *Proposals for an Irish Language Act for Northern Ireland*, Belfast: POBAL.

—— (2006b) *The European Charter for Regional or Minority Languages*. Belfast: POBAL.

—— (2006c) *Briefing Paper on POBAL's Proposals for The Irish Language Act for Northern Ireland*. Belfast: POBAL.

Posner, R. (1991) "Society, civilisation, and mentality: prolegomena to a language policy for Europe", in F. Coulmas (ed.), *A language policy for the European Community*. Berlin: Mouton, pp. 121–37.

Proulx, J.P. (1985) "La Charte de la langue: Autopsie d'une bataille perdue", *Le Devoir 10* January.

Pryce, W.T.R. and Williams, C.H (1988) "Sources and methods in the study of language areas: A case study of Wales", in C.H. Williams (ed.), *Language in Geographic Context*, Clevedon, Avon: Multilingual Matters, pp. 167–237.

Puigdevall i Serralvo, M. (1997) *The Use of the Welsh Language in the Private Sector*, MA Thesis in Welsh Ethnological Studies, Cardiff University.

—— (2006) The Challenge of Language Planning in the Private Sector: Welsh and Catalan Perspectives. *PhD Thesis*. School of Welsh, Cardiff University.

Puigdevall i Serralvo, M. and Williams, C.H. (2001) *A Challenge Yet To Be Faced. SMEs and the planned use of Welsh*. Paper presented at the International Conference on Language Planning, Andorra, November.

Putnam, R., Leonardi, R. and Nanetti, R. (1993) *Making Democracy Work: Civic Traditions in Modern Italy*, Princeton, NJ: Princeton University Press.

Q.O.L.A. (1974) *Québec Official Language Act. Statutes of Québec, Chapter 6*. Québec City: Editeur Official du Québec.

Q.C.L.F. (1978) *Québec charter of the French Language. Statutes of Québec, Chapter 5*, Québec City: Editeur Officiel du Québec.

R.C.B.B. (1967) *Report of the Royal Commission on Bilingualism and Biculturalism*, Chairman: A. Laurendean-Dunton. Ottawa: Queen's Printer.

Rawlings, R. (2000) "Concordats of the Constitution", *Law Quarterly Review*, pp. 116. 250–57.

Rawlings, R. (2001) "Quasi-legislative devolution", in J. Jones (ed.), *The Law Making Powers of the National Assembly: Conference Report*, Cardiff: Wales Law Journal/The Law Society.

—— (2003) *Delineating Wales*, Cardiff: University of Wales Press.

—— (2005) "Law Making in a Virtual Parliament: The Welsh Experience", in R. Hazell and R. Rawlings (eds.), *Devolution, Law Making and the Constitution*, Exeter: Imprint academic.com, pp. 71–111.

Reid, S. (1993) *Lament for a Nation*, Vancouver: Arsenal Pulp Press.

Rhodes, R.A.W. (1997) *Understanding Governance: Policy Networks, Governance, Reflexivity and Accountability*, Buckingham: Open University Press.

Richard Commission (2004) *Report of the Commission on the Powers and Electoral Arrangements of the National Assembly for Wales*. Cardiff: National Assembly for Wales.

Richards, J. (1996) "Language Matters: Ensuring that the sugar not dissolve in the coffee", *Commentary: The Canadian Union Papers*. No. 84, October, Ottawa: C.D. Howe Institute.

Richardson, J. (ed.) (1996) *European Union: power and policy-making*, London: Routledge.

Richardson, J., Gustafsson, G. and Jordan, G. (eds.) (1982) *Policy Styles in Western Europe*, London: Allen & Unwin.

Robinson, C.L.D. (1992a) *Language Choice in Rural Development*, Dallas: Summer Institute of Linguistics.

—— (1992b) *Where Minorities are in the Majority*, paper presented at the International Conference on the Maintenance and Loss of Minority Languages, Noordwijkerhout, The Netherlands, 1–4 September.

Robinson, C.L.D. (1994) "Is Sauce for the Goose Sauce for the Gander? Some Comparative Reflections on Minority Language Planning in North and South", *Journal of Multilingual and Multicultural Development*, 15 (2 & 3), 129–45.

Robinson, P. (1997) *Ulster Scots: A Grammar of the Traditional and Written Language*, Belfast: The Ullans Press.

Roddick, W. (2002) "Creating legal Wales", *Agenda*, Spring, p. 38.

—— (2007) "One Nation – Two voices? The Welsh Language in the Governance of Wales", in C.H. Williams (ed.), *Language and Governance*, Cardiff: University of Wales Press, pp. 263–92.

Rorty, R. (1989) *Contingency, Irony, and Solidarity*, Cambridge: Cambridge University Press.

Ross, C.J. (2002) *Contemporary Spain*, London: Arnold.

Rowland, C. (1988) *Radical Christianity*, Oxford: Blackwell.

Rubagumya, C.M. (ed.) (1990) *Language in Education in Africa: A Tanzanian Perspective*, Clevedon, Avon: Multilingual Matters.

Russell, P.H. (1992) *Constitutional Odyssey: Can Canadians Be A Sovereign People?* Toronto: Toronto University Press.

Rystad, G. (1990) *The Uprooted: Forced Migrants as International Problem in the Post-war Era*, Lund: Lund University Press.

Sánchez Carrión, J.M. (1987) *Un futuro para nuestro pasado*, Donostia: Sánchez Carrión.

Saward, M. (2003) *Democracy*, Cambridge: Cambridge University Press.

SOAS (1993) *The Linguasphere Programme*, London: School of Oriental and African Studies.

Schmidt, R. (1998) "The Politics of Language in Canada and the United States: Explaining the Differences", in T. Ricento and B. Burnaby (eds.), *Language and Politics in the United States and Canada*, Mahwah, New Jersey: Lawrence Erlbaum Associates.

Scottish Executive (2004) http://www.scotland.gov.uk/News/Releases/2005/04/21162614.

Scottish Parliament (2004) http://www.scottish.parliament.uk/business/bills/bills InProgress/gaelicLanguage.htm.

Segrott, J. (2001) "Language, geography and identity: the case of the Welsh in London", *Social and Cultural Geography*, 2 (3) 281–96.

Sen, A. (2006) *Identity and Violence: The Illusion of Destiny*, London: Allen Lane.

Sherlock, A. (2000) "Born free, but everywhere in chains? A legal analysis of the first year of the National Assembly for Wales", *The Cambrian Law Review*, 31, 59–72.

Shklar, J.N. (1998) "The Work of Michael Walzer", in J.N. Shklar (ed.) *Political Thought and Thinkers*, Stanley Hoffman, Chicago: The University of Chicago Press, pp. 383–4.

Shortridge, J. (2004) *ASPB Reform: Circular Letter to Chief Executive Officers, Assembly Sponsored Public Bodies*, 2 August.

Skutnabb-Kangas, T. (1997) "Language Rights as Conflict Prevention", in W. Wölck and A. de Houwer (eds.), *Recent Studies in Contact Linguistics, Plurilingua* XVII. Bonn: Dümmler, pp. 312–24.

—— (1999) "Language, power and linguistic human rights-the role of the state", *Proceedings of the International Conference on Language Legislation*, Dublin: Comhdháil Náisiúnta na Gaeilge, February, pp. 50–68.

—— (2000) *Linguistic Genocide in Education*. New Jersey: Lawrence Erlbaum.

—— (2002) "Some Philosophical and Ethical Aspects of Ecologically Based Language Planning", in Boudreau, A. *et al.* (eds.), *L'Ecologie des Langues*, Paris: L'Harmattan, pp. 69–102.

Skutnabb-Kangaas, T. and Phillipson, R. (1996) *Linguistic Human Rights*, Berlin: de Gruyter.

Smith, A.D. (1981) *The Ethnic Revival*, Cambridge: Cambridge University Press.

—— (1982) "Nationalism, ethnic separatism and the intelligentsia", in C.H. Williams (ed.), *National Separatism*, Cardiff: The University of Wales Press, pp. 17–42.

—— (1991) *National Identity*, Harmondsworth: Penguin.

—— (1999) *Myths and Memories of the Nation*, Oxford: Oxford University Press.

—— (2000) *The Nation in History*, Cambridge: Polity Press.

Smith, D.M. (1997) *Modern Italy: A Political History*, New Haven: Yale University Press.

Smith, G. (1996a) (ed.) *The Baltic States*, Basingstoke: Macmillan.

—— (1996b) (ed.) *The Nationalities Question in the Post-Soviet States*, London: Longman.

Smith, G., Law, V., Wilson, A., Bohr, A. and Allworth, E. (1998) (eds.) *Nation-building in the Post-Soviet Borderlands*, Cambridge: Cambridge University Press.

Society for Threatened Peoples (2003) *Minority Languages in Europe*. Statement by Society for Threatened Peoples to the 59th Session of the Commission of Human Rights, Geneva: United Nations.

Stanley, B. (2003) "Christianity and the End of Empire", in B. Stanley (ed.), *Missions, Nationalism and the End of Empire*, Grand Rapids, Mich: W. Eerdmans, pp. 1–11.

Statistics Canada (1983) "Mother tongues in Canada and Québec", *Languages and Society*, 9, 20–1.

—— (1993) *Language Retention and Transfer, 1991*, Ottawa: Statistics Canada.

Stein, M. (1982) "Changing Anglo-Québecer self-consciousness", in G. Caldwell and E. Waddell (eds.), *The English of Québec from Majority to Minority Status*, Québec: Institut Québecois de Recherche sur la Culture, pp. 109–25.

Stewart, W.A. (1968) "A Sociolinguistic Typology for Describing National Multilingualism", in J.A. Fishman (ed.), *Language Problems of Developing Nations*, London: John Wiley, pp. 503–53.

Stoker, G. (1998) "Public-Private Oartnerships and Urban Governance", in Pierre, J. (ed.), *Partnerships in Urban Governance: European and American experience*. London: Macmillan, pp. 34–51.

Tägil, S. (ed.) (1999) *Regions in Central Europe*, London: Hurst.

Taylor, C. (1991) *The Malaise of Modernity*, Toronto: Anasi.

—— (1992) "Multiculturalism and 'the politics of recognition'", in C. Taylor and A. Guttman (eds.), *Multiculturalism and "the politics of recognition"*, Princeton, NJ: Princeton University Press, pp. 25–74.

—— (1994) "Reply and re-articulation", in J. Tully (ed.) *Philosophy in an Age of Pluralism*, Cambridge: Cambridge University Press, pp. 213–57.

—— (1999) "Nationalism and Modernity", in R. Beiner (ed.), *Theorizing Nationalism*, New York: State University of New York Press, pp. 219–45.

Taylor, P.J. (1985) *Political Geography: World-Economy, Nation-State and Locality*, Harlow: Longman.

—— (1993) *Political Geography*, London: Longman.

Termote, M. and Gauvreau, D. (1988) *La situation demolinguistique du Québec*, Québec: Conseil de la langue française.

The Anglo-Irish Agreement (1995) *The Anglo-Irish Agreement*, November 15, Belfast: HMSO.

The Times (2006) *How do you say wine lake, butter mountain and gravy train in Irish?* 23rd September.

Times Atlas of World History (1986) Times Books: London.

Thomas, B. (1959) "Wales and the Atlantic Economy", *Scottish Journal of Political Economy*, 6, 169–92.

Tishkov, V. (1997) *Ethnicity, Nationalism and Conflict In and After The Soviet Union: The Mind Aflame*, London: Sage Publications.

Tollefson, J.W. (2001) *Planning Language: Planning Inequality*, London: Longman.

Thomas, M.W. (1999) *Corresponding Cultures: The Two Literatures of Wales*, Cardiff: The University of Wales Press.

Touraine, Alain (1992) *Critique of Modernity*, Oxford: Blackwell.

Tremblay, M. (2006) "On getting Rights Right: The Canadian Experience With the Recognition, Protection and Promotion of Minority Languages", Presentation to a POBAL conference, Belfast November 30th.

Trench, A. (2005) "Whitehall and the Process of Legislation After Devolution", in R. Hazell and R. Rawlings (eds.), *Devolution, Law Making and the Constitution*, Exeter: Imprint academic.com, pp. 193–225.

—— (2006) "The Government of Wales Act 2006: the next steps in devolution for Wales", *Public Law*, 4, 687–96.

Trifunovska, S.N. (ed.) (2001) *Minority Rights in Europe*, The Hague: T M C Asser Press.

Trudgill, P. (1993) *The Ausbau Sociolinguistics of Minority Languages in Greece*, mimeo, Lausanne: Lausanne University.

Tuarascáil Choimisiún na Gaeltachta (2002) *Tuaithe agus Gaeltachta*, Baile Átha Cliath: An Roinn Gnóthaí Pobail.

—— (1926) *Gaeltacht Commission'*, Dublin: Government of Ireland.

Tully, J. (ed.) (1995) *Philosophy in an Age of Pluralism*, Cambridge: Cambridge University Press.

—— (1999) "Liberté et dévoilement dan les sociétés multinationals", *Globe:Revue internationale d'études québécoises*, 2 (2), 13–36.

Údarás na Gaeltachta (2004) *Tuarascáil Bhliantúil/Annual Report 2003*. Na Forbacha: Údarás na Gaeltachta.

Ulster-Scots Agency (2000a) *Annual Report 2000* [on-line]. Available at: http://www. ulsterscotsagency.com/aboutus-annualreport.asp.
—— (2000b) *Corporate Plan* [on-line]. Available at: http://www.ulsterscotsagency.com/ aboutus-corporateplan.asp.
UNESCO (1951) *The Use of Vernacular Languages in Education*, Paris: UNESCO.
Urwin, D. (1982). "Territorial Structures and Political Developments in the United Kingdom", in S. Rokkan and D. Urwin (eds.), *The Politics of Territorial Identity*, London: Sage Publications.
Vaillancourt, F. (ed.) (1985) *Economie et langue*, Québec: Conseil de la langue française.
—— (1992) "English and Anglophones in Quebec: An Economic Perspective", in *Survival: Official Language Rights in Canada*, Toronto: C.D. Howe Institute, pp. 129–33.
—— (1996) "Le Francais dans Un Context Économique", in J. Erfurt (ed.), *De la polyphonie a la symphonie*, Leipzig: Presses de l'Université, pp. 119–36.
—— (1998a) *"Langue et disparités de statut économique au Quebec: 1970 et 1980"*, Quebec, Conseil de la langue francaise, Collection Dossiers, p. 230.
—— (1998b) "The Economics of Constitutional Options for Quebec and Canada", *Canadian Business Economics*, Winter, pp. 3–14.
Van den Berghe, P.L. (1968) "Language and Nationalism in South Africa", in J.A. Fishman, C.A. Ferguson and J. Das Gupta (eds.), *Language Problems of Developing Nations*, New York: Wiley, pp. 215–24.
Van der Merwe, I. J. (1993) "The Urban Geolinguistics of Cape Town", *GeoJournal*, 31, 409–17.
Van der Merwe, I.J. and Van der Merwe, J.H. (2006) *Linguistic Atlas of South Africa*, Stellenbosch: Sun Press.
Van Els, T.J.M. (2001) "The European Union, its Institutions and its Languages: Some Language Political Observations", *Current Issues in Language Planning*, 2 (4), 311–60.
Vincent, A. (2002) *Nationalism and Particularity*, Cambridge: Cambridge University Press.
Waddell, E. (1986) "State, language and society", in A. Cairns and C. Williams (eds.) *The Politics of Gender, Ethnicity and Language in Canada*, Toronto: University of Toronto Press, pp. 67–110.
—— (1988) "The influence of external relations on the promotion of French in Canada", *Language Culture and Curriculum* 1 (3), 203–14.
Wagner, P. (1994) *A Sociology of Modernity: Liberty and Discipline*, London: Routledge.
Wales Office (2005) White Paper "Better Government for Wales" by the Wales Office, part of the United Kingdom Government, 15 June 2005. Cardiff and London: Wales Office. Can be viewed at http://www.walesoffice.gov.uk/2005/ better_government_for_wales_report.pdf.
Wallace, H. and Wallace, W. (eds.) (2000) *Policy-making in the European Union*, 4th edn, Oxford: Oxford University Press.
Wallerstein, I. (1974) *The Modern World System*, New York: Academic Press.
—— (1979) *The Capitalist World Economy*, New York: Academic Press.
Walsh, J. (2002) *Díchoimisiúnú Teanga: Coimisiún na Gaeltachta 1926*, Dublin: Cois Life.
—— (2005) "Language planning and socio-economic development in Ireland: towards an integrated framework? Paper presented to a conference on 'Debating Language Policies in Canada and Europe'," University of Ottawa, 1st April.
Walters, D.B. (1978) "The legal recognition and protection of pluralism", *Acta Juridica*, pp. 305–26.

Walzer, M. (1994) *Thick and Thin: Moral Argument at Home and Abroad*, Notre Dame: University of Notre Dame Press.

—— (1997) *On Toleration*, New Haven: Yale University Press.

Wang, J. (1994) "Pragmatic Nationalism: China Seeks a New Role in World Affairs", *Oxford International Review*, Winter 27–38.

Wardaugh, R. (1983) *Language and Nationalism: The Canadian Experience*, Vancouver: New Star Books.

Welsh Assembly Government (2003a) *Iaith Pawb: A National Action Plan for a Bilingual Wales*, Cardiff: Welsh Assembly Government.

—— (2003b) *People, Places, Futures: The Wales Spatial Plan*, Consultation Draft, Cardiff: Welsh Assembly Government.

—— (2006) *Iaith Pawb and the Welsh Language Scheme: Annual Report 2005–6*, Cardiff: Wales Assembly Government.

Welsh Language Act (1993) *The Welsh Language Act 1993*, Chapter 38, Westminster: HMSO.

WLB, Welsh Language Board (1999) *The Welsh Language: A Vision and Mission* for *2000–2005*, Cardiff: Welsh Language Board.

—— (2003) *Number of Welsh speakers increases for the first time for almost a century*, Cardiff: WLB, 13th February 2003.

—— (2006) *Response to Government Consultation on the Future of the Welsh Language Board*, Cardiff: Welsh Language Board.

Welsh Local Government Association (2004) *The Role of Local Authorities in a Post Quango Wales*, Cardiff: Welsh Local Government Association.

Welsh Office (1995) 1992 *Welsh Social Survey: Report on the Welsh Language*, Cardiff: Welsh Office.

—— (1997) *A Voice for Wales, Llais dros Gymru* (Cm. 3718 of July 1997), Cardiff and London: Welsh Office.

Western Mail (2003a) "Census shows Welsh language is marching on, Western Mail, Cardiff", Friday 14th February 2003.

—— (2003b) "Decline in number of areas where majority speak Welsh", July 1st 2003.

Westminster (2000) A *House for the Future (Westminster, 2000)* Cm.45334. Westminster: House of Lords.

Williams, C.H. (1977) "Non-violence and the Development of the Welsh Language Society, 1962–c.1974", *Welsh History Review*, 8 (4), 426–55.

—— (1981) "Official-language districts A gesture of faith in the future of Canada", *Ethnic and Racial Studies* 4, 334–47.

—— (ed.) (1982) *National Separatism*, Cardiff: University of Wales Press.

—— (1984) "More than tongue can tell", in J. Edwards (ed.) *Linguistic Minorities: Policies and Pluralism*, London: Academic Press, pp. 179–219.

—— (1986) "The Question of National Congruence", in R.J. Johnston and P.J. Taylor (eds.), *World in Crisis?* Oxford: Blackwell.

—— (1988a) "Language planning and regional development: Lessons from the Irish *Gaeltacht*", in C.H. Williams (ed.) *Language in Geographic Context*, Clevedon: Multilingual Matters, pp. 267–301.

—— (1988b) "Minority Nationalist Historiography", in R.J. Johnson. *et al.* (ed.), *Nationalism, self-determination and Political Geography*, London: Croom Helm, pp. 203–221

—— (1989a) "New Domains of the Welsh Language: Education, Planning and the Law", *Contemporary Wales*, 3, 41–76.

—— (1989b) "The Question of National Congruence", in R.J. Johnston. and P. Taylor (eds.), *A World in Crisis?* Oxford: Blackwell, 229–65.

—— (1990) "Canada and the Arctic: A stable democracy", in P. Taylor (ed.) *World Government*, New York: Oxford University Press, pp. 44–51.

—— (ed.) (1991) *Linguistic Minorities, Society and Territory*, Clevedon, Avon: Multilingual Matters.

—— (ed.) (1993a) *The Political Geography of the New World Order*, London: John Wiley.

—— (1993b) "Towards a New World Order: European and American Perspectives", in C.H. Williams (ed.), *The Political Geography of the New World Order*, London: Belhaven/Wiley, pp. 1–19.

—— (1993c) "Development, Dependency and the Democratic Deficit", Plenary Address to the Fifth International Conference on Minority Languages, July, Cardiff University and published in the *Journal of Multilingual and Multicultural Development*, 15 (2&3), (1994) 101–28.

—— (1993d) "The European Community's Lesser Used Languages", *Rivista Geografica Italiana*, 100, 531–64.

—— (1994) *Called Unto Liberty: On Language and Nationalism*, Clevedon, Avon: Multilingual Matters.

—— (1995a) "A Requiem for Canada?" in G. Smith (ed.), *Federalism: The Multiethnic Challenge*, London: Longman, pp. 31–72.

—— (1995b) "Global language divisions", in T. Unwin (ed.), *Atlas of World Development*, Chichester: John Wiley.

—— (1996a) "Ethnic Identity and Language Issues in Development", in D. Dwyer and D. Drakakis-Smith (eds.), *Ethnicity and Development*, Chichester: John Wiley, pp. 45–85.

—— (1996b) "A Requiem for Canada?" in G. Smith (ed.), *Federalism: The Multiethnic Challenge*, London: Longman, pp. 31–72.

—— (1996c) "Citizenship and Minority Cultures: Virile Participants or Dependent Supplicants", in A. Lapierre, P. Smart and Savard (eds.), *Language, Culture and Values in Canada at the Dawn of the 21st Century*, Ottawa: International Council for Canadian Studies, Carleton University Press, pp. 155–84.

—— (1996d) "Christian Witness and Non-Violent Principles of Nationalism", in K. Gerner *et al.* (eds.), *Stat, Nation, Konflikt*, Lund: Bra Böcker, pp. 343–93.

—— (1997a) "European regionalism and the search for new representational spaces", *Annales: Anali za istrske in mediteranske študje*, 14, 265–74.

—— (1997b) "Territory, Identity and Language", in M. Keating and J. Loughlin (eds.), *The Political Economy of Regionalism*, London: F. Cass, pp. 112–38.

—— (1997c) "Language Rights for All Citizens of Europe?" in W. Wölck and A. de Houwer (eds.), *Recent Studies in Contact Linguistics, Plurilingua* XVII. Bonn, Dümmler, 430–41.

—— (1998a) "Introduction: Respecting the Citizens – Reflections on Language Policy in Canada and the United States", in T. Ricento and B. Burnaby (eds.), *Language and Politics in the United States and Canada*. Mahwah, New Jersey: Lawrence Erlbaum Associates Publishers, pp. 1–33.

—— (1998b) "Legislation and Empowerment: A Welsh Drama in Three Acts", Proceedings of the International Conference on Language Legislation, 14–17 October, Dublin: Comhdháil Náisiúnta na Gaeilge.

—— (1998c) "Operating Through Two Languages", in J. Osmond (ed.), *The National Assembly Agenda*, Cardiff: Institute of Welsh Affairs, pp. 101–15.

—— (1999) "Nationalism and its derivatives in post 1989 Europe", in R. Hudson and A.M. Williams (eds.), *Divided Europe: Society and Territory*, London: Sage, pp. 78–106.

—— (2000a) "Adfer yr Iaith", yn G.H. Jenkins a M.A. Williams, (gol.), *Eu Hiaith a Gadwant: Y Gymraeg yn yr Ugeinfed Ganrif*, Caerdydd: Gwasg Prifysgol Cymru, 641–65.

—— (2000b) "Governance and the Language", *Contemporary Wales,* 12 130–54.

—— (2000c) "Development, dependency and the democratic deficit", in P. Thomas and J. Mathias (eds.) *Developing Minority Languages,* Llandysul: Gomer Press, pp. 14–38.

—— (ed.) (2000d) *Language Revitalization: Policy and Planning in Wales,* Cardiff: University of Wales Press.

—— (2001) "Current British-Irish Conventions on Identity, Diversity and Cross-Border Co-operation", *Annales-Anali za istrske in mediteranske študije,* 11, 2.

—— (2002) "The Importance of Holistic Language Planning for the Promotion of Minority Languages/L'importance de l'aménagement linguistique holistique pour la promotion des langues moins répandues." European Union, Creating Common Structures Conference, Parliament House, Helsinki, Finland, 11–12 October.

—— (2003) "Language, Law and Politics", in W.J. Morgan and S. Livingstone (eds.), *Law and Opinion in Twentieth-Century Britain and Ireland,* London: Palgrave, pp. 109–40.

—— (2004a) *"Iaith Pawb: Iaith Braidd Neb",* Public Lecture at the Welsh Institute for Social and Cultural Affairs, University of Wales, Bangor, 15 March. See institute's website for a copy of paper.

—— (2004b) "Iaith Pawb: The Doctrine of Plenary Inclusion", *Contemporary Wales,* 17, 1–27.

—— (2004c) "The Geography of Language/Geographie der Sprache", in U. Ammon, N. Dittmar, K.J. Mattheier and P. Trudgill (eds.), *Sociolinguistics-Soziolinguistik, Ein internationals Handbüch zur Wissenschaft von Sprache und Gesellschaft,* vol. 1, pp. 130–45, Berlin: Walter de Gruyter.

—— (2005a) *Deddf Iaith Newydd. Dyma'r Cyfle a'r Ymateb.* Address to Cymdeithas yr Iaith Meeting. Urdd Eisteddfod, Cardiff May 30th.

—— (2005b) *"Deddfwriaeth Newydd a'r Gymraeg/New Legislation and the Welsh Language",* Lecture delivered at the National Eisteddfod, August 4th. See http://www.cardiff.ac.uk/cymraeg/welsh/research/DarlithEryri2005.pdf.

—— (2006a) "The Role of Para-governmental Institutions in Language Planning", *Supreme Court Law Review,* 31, 61–83.

—— (2006b) "Deddfwriaeth Newydd a'r Gymraeg", *Contemporary Wales,* p. 19.

—— (ed.) (2007) Language and Governance: Cardiff: University of Wales Press.

Williams, C.H. and Evas, L. (1997) *Y Cynllun Ymchwil Cymunedol,* Caerdydd: Prifysgol Cymru, Caerdydd a Bwrdd yr Iaith Gymraeg.

Williams, C.H. and Evas, J. (2001) *The Community Research Project,* http://www.cymru.gov.uk/cynulliaddata/3AB9FCC30008CCBA00003DAF00000000.rt.

Williams, C.H. and Kofman, E. (1989) *Community Conflict, Partition and Nationalism,* London: Routledge.

Williams, C.H. and Smith, A.D. (1983) "The National Construction of Social Space", *Progress in Human Geography,* 7, 502–18.

Williams, C.H. and van der Merwe, I. (1996) "Mapping the Multilingual City: A Research Agenda for Urban Geolinguistics", *Journal of Multilingual and Multicultural Development,* 17 (1) 49–66.

Williams, G. (1971) "Language, literacy and nationality in Wales", *History,* 56, 1–16.

—— (1997) *Wales and the Reformation,* Cardiff: University of Wales Press.

Williams, G. (1992) *The State and the Ethnic Community,* Cardiff: University of Wales Press.

Williams, G. and Morris, D. (2000) *Language Planning and Language Use: Welsh in a Global Age,* Cardiff: University of Wales Press.

Williams, R. (1977) *Marxism and Literature,* Oxford: Polity Press.

Williams, R. (2000) *On Christian Theology*, Oxford: Blackwell.
Williams, D. (2000) "Wales, the law and the constitution", The *Cambrian Law Review*, 31, 48–58.
Withers, C.W.J. (1988b) *Gaelic Scotland: The Transformation of a Culture Region*, London: Routledge.
—— (1988a) "The Geographical History of Gaelic in Scotland", in C.H. Williams (ed.), *Language in Geographic Context*, Clevedon: Multilingual Matters, pp. 136–66.
Wolff, S. (2006) *Ethnic Conflict in Global Perspective*, Oxford: Oxford University Press.
Wright, S. (2004) *Language Policy and Language Planning. From Nationalism to Globalism*, Basingstoke: Palgrave Macmillan.
Zalbide, M. (1988) "Mende hasierako euskalgintza: urratsak eta hutsuneak", in *II. Euskal Mundu-biltzarra, Euskara Biltzarra/Congreso de la Lengua Vasca*, II, 389–412, Vitoria-Gasteiz: Eusko Jaurlaritzaren Argitalpen Zerbitzu Nagusia.
—— (1990) "Euskal Eskola, asmo zahar bide berri" in *Euskal Eskola Publikoaren Lehen Kongresua*, 1, 211–71, Vitoria-Gasteiz: Eusko Jaurlaritzaren Argitalpen Zerbitzu Nagusia.
—— (1999) "Normalización lingüística y escolaridad: un informe desde la sala de máquinas", in *RIEV* (*Revista Internacional de los Estudios Vascos*), 43 (2), pp. 355–424.
Zalbide, M., Gardner, N., Erize, X. and Azurmendi, M.-J. (2005) "The Future of Basque in RLS Perspective", in M.-J. Azurmendi and I. Martinez de Lunda (eds.), *The Case of Basque: Past, Present and Future*, Gipuzkoa: Soziolinguistika Klusteraa, pp. 117–39.
Zametica, J. (1992) *The Yugoslav Conflict*, London: Adelphi Papers of the International Institute of Strategic Studies, 270.
Zelinsky, W. (1988) *Nation Into State: The Shifting Symbolic Foundations of American Nationalism*, Chapel Hill: University of North Carolina Press.
Zelinsky, W. and Wiliams, C.H. (1988) "The Mapping of Language in North America and the British Isles", *Progress in Human Geography*, 12 (3) 337–368.
Zhao, S. (1997) "Chinese Intellectuals", Quest for National Greatness and Nationalistic Writing in the 1990s", *The China Quarterly*, 152, 725–45.
—— (2000) "Chinese Nationalism and its International Orientations", *Political Science Quarterly*, 115 (1), 1–33.
Zupancic, J. (1996) Slovenci v Avstriji:Sodobni Socialnogreografski Procesi in Ohranjanje Identitete, Unpublished Ph.D. University of Ljubljana.
Zupancic, L. (1998) "Identiteta Je Merljiva Prispevek K Metodologiji Proucevanja Etnicne Identitete", *Razprave in gradivo*, Ljubljana: Institute of Ethnic Studies, 33, 253–68.

Index